DIS-RUPT

Filipina Women: BEING

4.0

DIS-RUPT

Filipina Women: BEING

4.0

The Fourth Book
On Leadership
by the Foundation
for Filipina
Women's Network

Edited by
MARIA AFRICA BEEBE, PhD

Foundation for Filipina Women's Network
San Francisco, California

I AM, VILLANELLE

Aileen Cassinetto

San Mateo County Poet Laureate, 2019 – 2022

I am from balikbayan boxes, veiled markers of identity.
I am from sunken galleons, misspent fragment of empires.
I am from hand knotted piña fibers, a cultivar of possibilities.

I am from blue and white pottery, ghostly and full of stories.
I am from unglazed earthenware, seasoned with intent and fire.
I am from balikbayan boxes, movement of tenacity.

I am from the heartwood of wounded lign aloes, an unfortunate luxury.
I am from Glory of the Sea Cone, prized for its venom and spire.
I am from ocean crossings, an arbitrary and seaworthy possibility.

I am from repeated prayers and offerings, a Hail Mary pass and nine days to mercy.
I am from doomed love stories and ghosts with a grievance, manifesting ire and
    satire.
I am from a precarious bloodline, a balikbayan genealogy.

I am from the mother of all fiestas, sanguinary and exhibiting miraculously.
I am from broken rosaries, indulgence for blessed and blooded modifiers.
I am from possibilities in a family tree that doesn't end with me.

I am from buried treaties north of an archipelago, debris of synchronicity.
I am from a chronology of losses and one wedded and wilder soothsayer.
I am from balikbayan boxes, veiled markers of identity.
I am foreshadowed in good faith, a possibility, empire of sundries.

CONTENTS

FWN BEING

LIBERATION

TRANSFORMATION

CONTENTS

LEADING CHANGE: LEGACY

APPENDICES

Foreword

MARILY MONDEJAR

Founder and CEO, Foundation for Filipina Women's Network

The idea of collecting the leadership stories of FWN's "Most Influential Filipina Woman in the World" awardees in 2014 envisioned highlighting the accomplishments of Filipina women leaders in the global workplace. For so long, Filipina women leaders worked quietly behind the scenes, achieving excellence without fanfare and recognition. Many next-generation leaders lacked models and leadership paradigms to navigate the corporate hierarchies and overcome institutionalized barriers.

I have met all 143 authors of the four books we have published. Each has traveled her own path to BEING. One poignant story follows an eight-year-old's leadership journey from poverty and being sent to America so she can go to school and have a better life. She did not see her mother again for many years. However, her brilliant career in education opened avenues to advance from management roles to multiple terms as an elected school board trustee.

DISRUPT 4.0. Filipina Women: BEING. is the fourth book in the FWN DISRUPT Leadership Series. Thirty-six authors from nine countries—Austria, Canada, Italy, Japan, Philippines, Switzerland, United Arab Emirates, United Kingdom, and the United States.

The book is not abstract history. Instead, you will be reading first-person narratives on the three leadership themes of the 18th Filipina Leadership Global Summit convening in Lisbon, Portugal, on October 30 to November 4, 2022.

- Eleven LIBERATION stories about the right to live your life as you want.
- Five TRANSFORMATION stories about the internal shift that aligns us with our highest potential.
- Fourteen LEADING CHANGE stories about experiencing new and exciting things that affect how we see and relate to the world and understand our place in it.
- Five LEGACY stories about leaving footsteps for emerging leaders on a path to leadership.

As the COVID-19 pandemic gave rise to anti-Asian hate worldwide, this book's authors provide a deeper understanding of their struggles in bridging Filipino and global cultures in the workplace. Trailblazing leadership voices of Filipina women immigrants and Philippines-based leaders who have broken through glass ceilings and become founders of successful grassroots businesses. *DISRUPT 4.0* examines the leadership philosophies, styles, archetypes, and traits of Filipina women leaders in complex diaspora environments.

There are hundreds of articles on managing our professional careers successfully, but very few about how we derail ourselves. "Success" is the achievement of the highest level expected, and "derailment" is the involuntary stalling of a career through demotion, termination, or plateauing. The Center for Creative Leadership's derailment studies show there are many ways we derail our careers:

1. We ignore our flaws.
2. We over-rely on our strengths, often clinging to past successes.
3. We become "lazy learners," relying on trial-and-error learning instead of focusing on what we need to do differently in response to challenges.
4. We have a narrow leadership perspective. We pile up functional and technical knowledge but ignore interpersonal relationships and corporate politics in organizations.
5. We overmanage, become poor delegators, overcontrol and meddle.
6. We are unable to think strategically and unable to adapt to others with different philosophies and strategies. We focus excessively on ourselves, bruise people and become uncaring and insensitive to others.

Organizations have a hand in career derailment. Our achievement-oriented society equates success with moving "up" instead of moving "around" to confront new challenges. We perceive failure as "career-enders" instead of an opportunity to learn how to become calculated risk-takers.

The key to learning is to get "how you did it" feedback instead of "what you did" feedback. Studies indicate that many executives get their first "how you did it" feedback when they derail. Derailing is the beginning of learning.

Recovering from derailment narratives have implications for gender and intercultural leadership research practices and theories of women and how they lead. *DISRUPT 4.0. Filipina Women: BEING* answers the following:

1. What are the dominant leadership traits of Filipina women?
2. How does a Filipina woman leader lead and manage herself?
3. How does a Filipina woman leader lead and manage a team, a department, a division, or an organization?
4. What factors influence a Filipina woman's leadership philosophy?

This book and the three *DISRUPT* companion books are essential reading for corporate Employee Resource Groups (ERGs), and Human Resources Professionals, including Diversity, Equity, and Inclusion (DEI) consultants, Staffing, and HR Business Partners. Corporate talent managers will find much to learn from the Filipina women authors who have developed their leadership competencies while navigating the global workplace.

Marily Mondejar
Founder & CEO
Foundation for Filipina Women's Network
October 3, 2022

PREFACE

Power to Disrupt

SUSAN CELIA SWAN

Executive Director, V-DAY

You hold in your hands a user's guide to change. Stories told with the power to disrupt. Told in circles of sisterhood across the world. This volume of stories is a chorus of strong voices. They attest to what is possible when a Filipina woman's gifts, drive, dreams, and leadership are tested, tempered, and transformed in the crucible of cultural mores, traditions, and expectations. Like the Filipino diaspora, these stories extend beyond borders, pointing to the global impact such leadership is making and stands to make.

As one of the founding team of V-Day and now it's Executive Director, I have experienced the power of stories to galvanize communities, foment change, and inspire leadership. The stories at the center of *The Vagina Monologues*, the groundbreaking play written by our founder, V (formerly Eve Ensler), compelled and inspired women worldwide. Bringing the play to their own communities, these women helped to raise consciousness about how gender and violence connect. The success of these productions demonstrates how individual stories —and voices—can connect women around the world to each other.

As activists and organizers, these women fueled a movement that turns 25 in 2023. They have raised over $120 million for survivors and grassroots anti-violence groups. V-Day has grown to encompass the City of Joy, One Billion Rising, the Beyond Incarceration Project, Voices, and the Dismantle Patriarchy Project.

Filipina women have long been at the heart of this survivor-led and focused movement. They have pledged their time and talents to use the power of art and activism to change culture and systems and to foster global solidarity amongst those who seek to end violence against all women, girls, gender-expansive people, and the planet.

Marily Mondejar, founder, and CEO of the Filipina Women's Network, organized the first FWN production of *The Vagina Monologues* in San Francisco in 2003. I will never forget being struck by the dynamic energy and care Marily brought to every element—from the community engagement, media, business, and civil society outreach, the resource directory known as the *V-Diaries*, fundraising for the local centers supporting women survivors, to the artful stage direction and graphics campaign.

In 2013, to commemorate our 15th anniversary, V-Day created One Billion Rising. We invited activists everywhere to launch the campaign in their cities, regions, and countries. Marily and I joined forces in San Francisco, where thousands rose up at City Hall to demand an end to the violence that affects one in three women. After years of knowing her, it was a joy to work side by side and to witness how her inclusive leadership style and creativity directly supported the mission of ensuring that her community was free from violence.

Today, the Filipina Women's Network is a global force that has produced ten groundbreaking V-Day benefits, culminating most recently with a 2022 V-Day San Francisco performance to #StopAsianHate, performed by an all-women of color cast.

The Global Director of One Billion Rising is the extraordinary artist and activist Monique Wilson. After she brought *The Vagina Monologues* to Manila in 2000, Monique and the New Voice company, which she founded, went on to produce V-Day productions throughout the Philippines, Asia, and the world. Led by grassroots women, the Risings have changed laws and made a profound community impact through the Gabriela network and among women, indigenous, and youth leaders worldwide. Today, in her role as the global leader of OBR, she is at the center of a team of 50.

Like Marily and Monique, the women who lend their voices to *DISRUPT 4.0* exhibit a generous style of leadership: one rooted in the sense of service and caring and in a willingness to challenge the systems that, ultimately, serve no one. Their stories nourish and sustain, connect and inspire. In this way, they transcend community and promote solidarity. As the stories encased in these pages echo into a stunning crescendo, these women's voices, experiences, and efforts ripple outward into tangible change.

With gratitude to the Filipina women who have shared their stories and a vision for leadership that informs us all.

INTRODUCTION

MARIA BEEBE, Ph.D.

GLOBAL CONTEXT

In September 2018, the Filipina Women's Network (FWN) launched *DISRUPT 3.0 Filipina Women. Rising* at the House of Lords in the U.K. November 2022 is our launch date for *DISRUPT 4.0 Filipina Women. Being.* In between the most significant disruption, COVID-19 became a pandemic. Initially reported to the WHO on 31 December 2019, COVID-19 continues to spin off new variants. COVID-19 has had multidimensional domino effects. For example,

- In the 2020 report "Gendered Dimensions of COVID-19," the Philippines experienced the highest number of new confirmed cases per day, the second highest number of deaths, and the third highest infection rate.

- About four percent of registered nurses in the U.S. are Filipinos. Yet 26.4 percent have died of COVID-19 and complications. About 48.8 percent, just under half of the registered nurses of color who died during the first two years of the pandemic, were Filipinos.

Nevertheless, there was a bright side. During the COVID-19 crisis, women shone as excellent leaders. The discourse of Jacinda Ardern in New Zealand, Angela Merkel in Germany, Tsai Ing-wen in Taiwan, among others, focused on families, children, and vulnerable groups with messages of compassion and social cohesion. In contrast, men used war analogies and fear-based tactics more often (Orme 2021, Johnson 2021). In the 2020 Sergent & Stajkovic study, the question was: *Do states in the United States with women governors have fewer COVID-19 deaths than states with men governors, and why?* Their analysis revealed that states with women governors had fewer COVID-19 deaths than states with men governors. Furthermore, their findings underscore those states with women governors cultivated empathy and confidence more in their COVID-19 briefings than men governors.

The experiences of countries with female leaders managing the COVID-19 pandemic were explored on 25 November 2022 in a webinar, *"Ambassadors' Hour: On Women's Leadership vs. COVID-19,"* by the Asia Society Philippines and Manila House. Ambassador Delia Albert, a 2014 FWN awardee, indicated: *"When a woman becomes a leader, it's because she has been toughened and has been facing a lot of challenges. It's not easy. Sometimes, one has to feel that you have to work twice as hard—you take care of the office, you take care of the home, and you take care of children. The multitasking gives a woman that strength that is important in assuming a position of leadership."*

DEMOGRAPHICS: FILIPINA WOMEN AND MIGRATION

The Philippines Statistics Authority (PSA) estimates the current women population of the Philippines in 2022 as 55.3 million and the men population as 56.3 million. The Philippines ranks 19th out of 146 countries in the World Economic Forum (WEF) 2022 Global Gender Gap Index and records a gender gap of 21.7 percent, similar to last year. The report indicates that gender parity for legislative, senior officers and managers, and professional and technical workers remains constant. What is worrisome is that gender parity decreased at the level of enrolment in primary education, with a notably more significant share of boys than girls in growing enrolment numbers overall.

More Filipinas Migrate than Men

The Commission on Filipino Overseas summarizes the "2013 Philippine Migration at a Glance," stating there are 10.2 million overseas Filipinos. Of these, 4.8 million are permanent migrants, 4.2 million are temporary migrants (also known as overseas Filipino workers), and 1.2 million are irregular migrants in more than 200 destination countries and territories. The CIA World Factbook estimates a net migration rate of 0.13 migrants/1,000 population in 2022.

In 2015, the U.S. remained the primary destination for permanent migrants; emigrants are primarily female, the majority are single, young—ages 20-39 (41%), below 15 years (21%), a third completed tertiary education and up, and most were not employed before emigration (OECD/Scalabrini Migration Center 2017). Migration to the U.S. is linked to historical factors when the Philippines, a Spanish colony since the 16th century, was ceded to the U.S. in 1898 following the Spanish-American war. The introduction to DISRUPT 1.0. Filipina Women: Proud. Loud. Leading without a Doubt (2015) provides a succinct summary of the socio-historical and socio-cultural factors that shaped the leadership of Filipina women leaders in the global environment.

The PSA estimates the number of OFW (in thousands) in 2020 as 1,055 for women and 716 for men. However, Statista Research Department (2022) indicates that in 2019, the number of deployed overseas Filipino workers (OFWs) was 2,157,000. This number plummeted to 550 thousand in 2020 due to the COVID pandemic and increased to 745 thousand in 2021.

Economic and Social Impacts of Migration

Given the magnitude of Philippine migration, considerable research has been conducted. For example, the total remittances sent by overseas Filipino workers (OFWs) amounted to approximately 31.4 billion U.S. dollars in 2021. Moreover, personal remittances received in the Philippines accounted for 9.66 percent of the country's total gross domestic product (GDP) in 2020. Remittances have been used for housing renovation or construction, schooling of children and relatives, scholarships, and business startups that generate employment. However, the negative side is stories of children left behind (Asis, 2006, Graham, 2011, Dominguez, 2022).

The narrative has shifted from the Philippines' longstanding labor migration to incorporating migration into long-term development planning and strategizing the return and reintegration of overseas Filipinos (Asis, 2017). Mina Roces (2021) focuses on Filipino migrants as global agents of change, refusing to be marginal. The question is, should Filipino diasporic identities be viewed separately from Filipino identities (Aguila, 2015).

Undoubtedly, Filipina women rose to leadership positions not only in the Philippines but also in the diaspora. DISRUPT 4.0. Filipina Women: Being is the fourth book in a series on leadership by the Filipina Women's Network (FWN). As part of the strategy of FWN to recognize Filipina woman leaders in the global environment, FWN first established the US FWN100™ awards and, in 2013, the Global FWN100™ awards. About 143 awardees shared their leadership stories in the four DISRUPT books published by FWN. The books celebrate Filipina women leaders who have had an impact beyond the boundaries of the Philippines. The FWN books aim to make the stories of women leaders accessible to next-generation leaders while contributing to the scholarship on women and leadership.

DISRUPT 4.0. Filipina Women. Being

In January 2022, the Filipina Women's Network (FWN) called for abstracts on the theme of Filipina Women. Of those who responded to the call, thirty-six women shared their leadership stories of liberation, transformation, and change. Twenty women currently reside in the Philippines, seven in the United States, two in Canada, and two in Switzerland. Other countries of residence include Austria, Italy, Japan, UAE, and the U.K. Several maintain two homes, one in the Philippines and one elsewhere.

Of the thirty-six authors, thirty-four *DISRUPT 4.0* authors responded to a demographic profile questionnaire. Twenty-eight authors were born in the Philippines, five were born in the United States, and one was born in Canada. Of those born in the Philippines, fourteen immigrated to the U.S., and six identified as Overseas Filipina Workers. Others became U.S. citizens by marriage.

These Filipina women authors lived and worked all over the world. For example, Rhodora Fresnedi traveled and worked on seven continents, Gina Atienza was a Filipina scholar in the U.S. and the Netherlands, then lived and worked in Indonesia, Japan, and Brunei. Maria Beebe lived and worked as a U.S. expatriate in Sudan, the Philippines, Liberia, South Africa, and Afghanistan, with short consultancies in Botswana, Egypt, Ethiopia, Kenya, Malawi,

Namibia, Nigeria, Rwanda, Senegal, Tanzania, Zambia, Zimbabwe, and Uganda in Africa, India, Indonesia, Laos, Nepal in Asia, and Poland. Pamela Gotangco sums it up with Shakespeare, *"The world's mine oyster."*

Similar advocacy themes emerged, with education and digital literacy as the leading advocacy, followed by cultural diplomacy, women, and children. Other advocacies include healthcare, medical sciences, social work, labor and employment, seniors, and persons with disabilities. This group of authors represented advocacies in legal, philanthropy, and poverty alleviation. Most advocacies are consistent with their professions, with a few advocacies that tended to cross over to other areas of social influence.

We asked, *"What is your favorite quote?"* and *"If you could go back to the time when you struggled the most, what would be your message for yourself?"* Their responses give us an indication of their leadership, their being women, being Filipina women, and being Filipina women leaders. Here are a few of the responses from the authors:

"One person can make a difference, and everyone should try." – JOYCE JAVIER

"Plant your feet in every step and enjoy the walk ahead." – LAARNI SAN JUAN

"We have often heard how a journey of a thousand miles begins with a single step." – CORA DELA CRUZ-TORRES

"Opportunities don't happen, you create them." – ROSARIO CALIXTO CHAVEZ

"Drop by drop, it becomes an ocean." – MARIA AFRICA BEEBE

"Be strong. Be a warrior. Be your own [S]hero." – CYNTHIA MANALO RAPAIDO

"Nothing great comes easy, so keep going." – ILDEME "DEMEE" MAHINAY KOCH

"Bet on yourself. Don't be afraid of your own potential." – ALICIA MARIE DEL PRADO

"Be kind to yourself. We can't be perfect; we're human. Take time for self-care." – MARIETTA EVELYN PALACIO REVILLA

"God is not limited by your limitation. Focus on the goal. Let alone the nagging bystanders. Be resilient." – MARIVIC LUALHATI

"Struggles are like bumps in the road. Focus on what you are trying to accomplish and know the sacrifices you have to make. Reach out, put in the effort, and have faith." – MARIA FIDES BALITA

"Persevere, educate yourself as knowledge is power, connect with the community that empowers people like you, doing so with dignity, kindness, and integrity." – SONIA T. DELEN

"Determination under pressure, coolness under fire. Like a phoenix, I will rise from my ashes." – MILDRED CHRISTINE FLORES PIAD

"I did not lose track of where I came from but tried to remember who I was. No matter how difficult the struggle, I never lost sight of the idea that something better lies ahead." – CORA DELA CRUZ-TORRES

THE DISRUPT BOOK SERIES

DISRUPT 4.0. Filipina Women: Being is the fourth book in a series on leadership by the Filipina Women's Network (FWN). The purpose of this fourth FWN leadership book is to reflect on her trajectory to BEING who she is now—a global Filipina woman leader demonstrating leadership in her profession or industry in the global workplace and community. The chapters are first-person narratives reflecting on personal and professional lives as a Filipina woman leader in her home country, as an expatriate, or as a migrant; first, a second or third-generation immigrant who is exercising leadership in the diaspora. The themes that bind the chapters together are being a Filipina woman leader in the Philippines or her new home country overseas, her experience in migration, personal and professional development, and leadership challenges and successes. The narratives highlight liberation, transformation, and changes that lead to social and economic changes.

 DISRUPT 1.0. Filipina Women: Proud. Loud. Leading without a Doubt (2015) contributed significantly to redefining how Filipina women in the diaspora are perceived. The themes articulated by Filipina women in their leadership stories in *DISRUPT 1.0* concern the how and why of leadership that makes up their leadership repertoires (Beebe, 2017). The how of leadership consisted of actions that emphasized the centrality of relationships, the significance of values, and self-transcendence. The why of leadership for most women referenced finding purpose and meaning in life, achieving impact in their work, and giving back to their local communities. At the center of their leadership repertoires is the Philippine cultural value, *kapwa*. Translations for *kapwa* include "shared humanity," "unity of the self and the others," "shared inner self," and "together with the person." *Kapwa* is the core value that guides all forms of interpersonal relations and social interaction among Filipinos. Therefore, it stands to reason that *kapwa* would play a central role in their leadership, resulting from human interaction and negotiations.

DISRUPT 2.0. Filipina Women: Daring to Lead (2016) is an affirmation of the leadership competencies of Filipina women leaders (FWL) with a global mindset. The global FWL referenced competencies that were relevant in various global settings. Using the "Benchmarks by Design" (Center for Creative Leadership (CCL), 2015), the competencies can be organized into (1) **Leading yourself** – Filipina women leaders showed an awareness of their strengths and the capacity to adapt, learn, and cope in both the Philippines and in international environments; (2) **Leading others** – Filipina women leaders have shown that effectively leading others could be done as part of a team or as part of an organization; (3) **Leading the organization** – The Filipina women leaders have carried out their leadership roles for setting vision and direction, building commitment, and creating alignment.

DISRUPT 3.0. Filipina Women: Rising celebrates Filipina women who have emerged as global leaders despite varying levels of challenges. Some challenges were major setbacks while other challenges were minor. The same challenge was viewed as a failure by some and only an inconvenience by others. Filipina women discuss their responses to challenges and actions that led to success. They discuss the significance of their success and the implications of their leadership for their *kapwa* tao [fellow humans]. The readiness for the global leadership of Filipina Women Leaders consists of the dimensions of global competence identified by Hunter and Hunter (2018). These leaders are self-aware, open-minded, attentive to diversity, and risk takers; these leaders balance historical perspectives with global awareness, demonstrate intercultural capability, and collaborate across cultures. These leaders demonstrate their character strengths in virtues that are common across cultures (Patterson & Seligman, 2004). These are humanity, transcendence, wisdom, courage, temperance, and justice.

BOOK ORGANIZATION

DISRUPT 4.0. Filipina Women: BEING has thirty-six first-person narratives organized into three sections:

Liberation

The right to live our lives as we want

Liberation is the state of being free. Free to choose how we live. Free to choose how we lead. Liberation is when we refuse to accept our fate as an inevitable and often adverse outcome, condition, or end. Instead, we chose faith, a strong belief, and trust to triumph over it.

Transformation

An internal shift that brings us in alignment with our highest potential... (Cooks-Campbell)

Human transformation can happen instantly or through many transformative experiences to live up to our full potential to live with greater purpose, clarity, and passion. It means being intentional about developing our physical well-being, mental fitness, emotional health, and cognitive agility.

Change

Experiencing new and exciting things that affect how we see and relate to the world and understanding our place in it

Liberation and human transformation lead to changes within us which propel us to be a force for social and economic change. When stripped to its basics, leadership is a simple process of thinking well or thinking clearly about people and improving their conditions.

Finally, a **Synthesis** highlights the leadership themes of being Filipina, being Filipina women, and being Filipina women leaders punctuated by the time of COVID-19. Each influential Filipina shares her reservoir of psychological capital (optimism, resilience, hope, and self-efficacy), key life experiences, and perspective-taking that grows her authentic leadership. Self-development, enhanced performance, and the development of others are closely linked to her advocacies for social change and her arc to purposeful leadership within an intercultural milieu fostering diversity, equity, and inclusion.

The Filipina women leaders show us how to be more aligned with the Filipina woman leader we want to become!

FWN BEING

MARILY MONDEJAR

*Founder and CEO, Foundation for
Filipina Women's Network
President, Institute for Image Management*

Becoming Influential to be Influential

"*Did you know that your image influences the people you meet in the first five seconds?*" This statement was my opening pitch in 1984 when I started speaking about image and influence.

In his book, *Blink. The Power of Thinking Without Thinking* (2005), Malcolm Gladwell said snap judgments take two seconds. He tells the story about four art experts who felt "intuitive repulsion" in two seconds when they first saw the kouros (an ancient Greek sculpture of a standing youth) that the J. Paul Getty Museum purchased in 1986, which they believed was fake.

Since the Kennedy-Nixon debates in 1960, when television emerged as the primary staging ground for national elections, political success has become more a function of style than substance, appearance than issues. How the two presidential candidates packaged their appearances on TV influenced the viewers. Richard Nixon appeared sweating while Kennedy seemed calm during the debate. That first TV debate influenced the decision of millions of voters in America and decided whom to vote for in the first five seconds, perhaps two seconds, if you ask Gladwell.

"By the time the debate was over, America had elected a president," Don Hewitt, the executive producer of 60 Minutes, said. Americans decided, *"We like that young, handsome Catholic kid from Massachusetts better than the guy from California who looks like he needs a shave."* That "non-debate" was the beginning of "image influencing." Today, it is a multibillion-dollar industry.

Image-Influencing

The first turning point in my image-influencing career started in Bangkok in the late 70s. Bill Heinecke, the distributor for Time-Life Books Thailand, hired me to develop and train the all-women sales force and to prepare them for the launch of the Time-Life Books distributorship. I did not know what clothes to wear for the "big day." My Filipina colleague suggested that we wear Filipina *ternos* as Filipina women do at important events in the Philippines. Instinctively I knew this was wrong, but I did not know why (intuitive repulsion). She further said, *"I bet Queen Sirikit (our VIP guest for the ribbon-cutting ceremony to launch the book exhibit) will be wearing the Thai cultural outfit. We should be proud of our heritage and wear the terno."*

My Colleague was Wrong

The Queen and her ladies-in-waiting wore Chanel-style day suits. Joan D. Manley, the first woman in Time Inc.'s history to become a publisher in 1970, who flew in from the U.S. to attend this high-profile event, wore a dark suit. Joan was my first shero.

Bill later said he decided to hire me when he watched me present the *Wild Wild West* Books seminar. Bill was in the Philippines to observe Mondragon International's distributorship operations. He went on to talk to my boss about "borrowing" me away from her team.

Dressing for Success

Years later a Dress for Success seminar during our bank management training program in the U.S. was the second turning point in my image-influencing career. Two fashion consultants from Macy's were teaching us how to dress professionally in business. The emphasis was on the suits to wear at business meetings as bankers representing one of the largest banks in the U.S. We were appalled to learn that the clothes they were showing cost three times our salary! That notion that wearing expensive designer suits is your path to success provoked me to design my Dressing to Influence workshop series, which eventually became part of the leadership programs in two banks. I couldn't wait to launch my image-influencing practice.

Researching Impression Management

As I continued to develop my practice, I needed to ensure that my image concepts were grounded in research. I researched impression management, which inspired the development of two sets of tools that assess and manage a person's professional image: the Seven Aspects of Image for Influencing Results and the Image 360™ Degree Assessment Tool. These tools measured "Image Shown by the Manager vs. Image Required by the Job." The challenge was to influence business executives to act on two things. First is to acknowledge that their image is an asset. Second, they adopt image influencing as key to managing their careers and businesses, especially for those responsible for the organization's brand. I believe that image influencing is a competitive advantage.

The rise of image consulting flourished in the 80s. *Color Me Beautiful* became a best seller and made Carole Jackson famous. Beauty for All Seasons, Inc. became an influential leader in the burgeoning image industry. Career women finally found a way to organize their professional wardrobes on a budget. They went to department stores with their color palettes to choose clothes that complemented their skin coloring. John Molloy's book, Dress for Success, became the bible of professional women and men. Women were running around mimicking men's suits, wearing "Pussy Bow" blouses instead of the starched white shirt men work with a red tie. Clothing manufacturers capitalized on the rise of more women at work and came out with more reasonable options for business suits. Most consultants focused on color analysis, wardrobing, and personal shopping. I kept searching for my practice's unique value proposition, my differentiation, in a business with primarily women capitalizing on their fashion backgrounds. Department stores created Personal Shopping departments and hired many fashion and independent image consultants.

Finding My Niche

Then I found my niche.

My theory on Image Influencing promoted the awareness that a good public image makes it easier to make friends, build client loyalty, attract investors and motivate employees. Think of the many companies that lost market share because of mismanagement of their public image. Our image influences our reputation. Our reputation becomes our personal brand. A good image can almost always help us survive economic difficulties in meaningful ways. A weak image, however, will cost us opportunities to grow and sustain brand loyalty and, more often than not, drive us out of business.

Image is like the weather. People notice when it is extremely good or extremely bad. The two assessment tools I developed early on are about learning how to nurture our image so we can influence desired results.

The third turning point was when I met an attorney whose client was sued for medical malpractice. He was curious about my expertise and challenged me to apply my image influencing principles in affecting a positive outcome at trial based on refining the dentist's image. I worked with the dentist's image presentation to boost his confidence. I can claim that his strong personal appearance and improved delivery during the depositions weakened the plaintiff's quest to punish my client with multi-million-dollar punitive damages.

Flushed with success, I focused my image consulting practice on helping defendants, doctors, and corporate executives sued for malpractice prepare for depositions and court trials.

The fourth turning point in my image-influencing career was when I was featured in a cover story about risk management by *AGD Impact, The Newsmagazine of the Academy of General Dentistry* (Volume 16 Number 7). The media exposure propelled me to a broader national stage. Clients from around the US sought my services. The Dentists Insurance Company (TDIC) in California was my first big client. Gabor Nyary, the TDIC claims supervisor, sent four dentists with more than $100,000 in malpractice lawsuit, was quoted as saying, *"We want the doctor to present his best foot forward during a deposition or a trial. The investment we make in sending a dentist to an image consultant is relatively small but contributes greatly to significant positive outcomes."*

Becoming a National Consultant

I was on a roll.

To meet the challenges of sustaining my place on the national stage, I created a Competitor Wall, listing the Top Ten Image Consultants in the U.S. I examined their business differentiation. Gathering my competitor list inspired me to find my unique value and carve a larger, better place in the image business.

This list included Clint Reilly, a top political consultant. I was very interested in how he transformed political candidates to become influential city leaders and successful legislators. To promote the principles of my image-influencing theory, I published *The Image Report.* I covered leading stories and wrote about the implications of personal image on how the public believed or rebuked key players of Irangate (Iran-Contra) in 1988. The court wardrobes of Lt. Col. Oliver North, John Poindexter, Robert McFarlane, and especially Fawn Hall, Oliver North's secretary whose testimony was pivotal.

I was thrilled when Tracy Achor Hayes, fashion editor of the *Dallas Morning News,* consulted me on their special election feature "Dressing to Win" (September 28, 1988). She was interested in how I would "dress" the two presidential candidates' wives, Barbara Bush, and Kitty Dukakis. Notable local and national magazines and newspapers sought my theories on image influencing: the famous Joan Kron, the editor of Allure magazine, who wrote the lead article "The Image Police" (March 1991) for its premiere issue and Carol Jouzaitis, the business editor for the *Chicago Tribune,* who headlined the morning business section with her lead story, "Firms Help Clients Put Best Forward" (August 20, 1990).

Next, I organized leading fashion and image consultants by founding the Image Industry Council International (IICI) to support each other to be successful and more impactful consultants. The image industrys' pioneers: best-selling authors Carole Jackson, John Molloy and Mortimer Levitt, founder of The Custom Shop, and industry leaders Jinger L. Heath, CEO, and co-founder of BeautiControl Cosmetics, and Norma Virgin, president and founder of Beauty for All Seasons, Inc., at the time the largest direct sales company for color analysis and with over 10,000 consultants. BeautiControl legitimized the image industry when the company went public. The NASDAQ IPO price opened at $16.00 per share and went up to $24.75 in a few days with over $80 million in sales. Tupperware eventually bought the company.

Going Global

The fifth turning point in my image-influencing career propelled me to a global level. As I navigated growing IICI as a professional and trade association, I joined ASAE (American Society for Association Executives), who was then convening its annual conference in San Francisco's Moscone Convention Center. I met Bob Dahl, an independent marketing consultant, who was fascinated by my image concepts and wanted my help developing his marketing pitch to launch Cintermex, a new convention center in Mexico. I was happy to enter into another phase of image influencing. Our proposal was a finalist. They flew us to Monterrey, Mexico, to meet the Selection Team. Clara Dieck Assad, an economist, and the only high-ranking female executive at *Cintermex*, was on the Selection Team. She was preparing to launch the maiden issue of the *Cintermex Magazine.* Clara was on the Editorial Board and a senior staff editor. She was captivated with image influencing work and wanted to feature my theory and practice.

At the time, I had not actively thought about expanding my practice to Mexico or globally. While my niche in the U.S. was becoming larger, I had my hands full growing my business domestically and steering IICI to become an industry mainstay in the U.S. Nonetheless, I gave her my Image FAQs and authorized her to customize and translate my document into Spanish. When the magazine came out, my Seven Aspects for Influencing Results became the lead story. During Christmas week in 1995, I received an early morning call from the president of the largest cement company in Mexico.

That phone call was pivotal. The company became a client for many years. I was part of its globalization initiative, from opening its office in New York to buying the largest cement company in the Philippines, their first stop in Asia. Eventually, my client became the second-ranking executive in his company as the EVP for Strategic Planning which included Mergers and Acquisitions of many countries' cement companies. This opportunity opened global consulting gigs, allowing me to nurture the Filipina Women's Network into what it is today. Clara became my *femtor.* She influenced a lot of my thinking in image influencing. We're dear friends to this day.

So how do you become influential?

Without sharing confidential trade information, the Seven Aspects of Image for Influencing Results demonstrate that every aspect of a person's image is interrelated.

> *"Instead of hiring, corporations are casting, the way movie directors do." –* MARILY MONDEJAR

> *"The message must either disturb an established buying habit or take advantage of a disturbance caused by something else." –* WALTER LANDOR, Brand Consultant

THE SEVEN ASPECTS OF IMAGE FOR INFLUENCING RESULTS

1 COLOR ANALYSIS

We begin with color, which transmits specific and categorical meanings to the eye. Based on color research, this makes color that fastest and most immediate instrument in image influencing. The color industry is a multi-billion-dollar industry. The Color Association of the United States (CAUS), founded in 1914, is considered the "color arbiter" and is the first color forecasting organization in the U.S.. CAUS develops color standards and releases an annual color forecast that impacts the world's industries in four categories – Interiors, Women, Men, and Youth. These color forecasts aid designers, textile companies, and manufacturers in inspiring color trends. *"We live in a world being consumed by our eyes, and we ultimately end up with a physical impression that is an important part of making the right color decisions. Psychology and the economy are the two most important influences on the color trend palette,"* said Margaret Walch, CAUS color expert. Margaret Walch was one of my early *femtors,* and the CAUS has influenced my image consulting practice since 1986.

The Pantone Color Institute is another global source of color expertise. Pantone unites science and the emotion of color and guides companies in developing color strategies consistent with the company's brand vision. The Munsell Color Science Laboratory and the Program of Color Science united to form one of the world's foremost color science research and education organizations. They offer graduate color science degrees that explore all aspects of color, from lighting, to material properties, to human perception, at one of the world's top research facilities in the science of color.

Our color choices influence our message. Color communicates subconscious health, power, culture, and socio-economic position messages. I once assembled a court wardrobe for a doctor sued for malpractice. For his court depositions and an impending trial, I recommended a crisp, clean, white shirt with a burgundy red tie and a dark well-fitted suit. The white shirt evokes an attitude of professionalism, and white is associated with medicine. The color red travels very fast to the eyes. The use of red was to bring jurors' eyes directly to the client's face to make it easier to listen to what the client had to say. Visually, it was vital that my client looks appropriate and doesn't look offensive to the judge, opposing counsel, or jury members.

> *"Color preferences are regional. What people like in Phoenix is not the same as New York or Chicago."*
> – CARLTON WAGNER, Wagner Institute for Color Research.

Color is the heart of an image-influencing strategy—generally, the darker the colors, the more authoritative the message. Lighter colors are friendlier and more inviting.

Red: Can make time seem to slow down.

Orange: A declassifying color moves economic position downward and extends the appeal to a broader range of people.

Yellow: Conveys temporariness. Babies cry more in a yellow room.

Blue: Responsibility, knowledge, trustworthiness, caring, and mercy.

Brown: Not a color with authority in a business environment. Think of President Obama when he wore a light brown suit and the twitterstorm that his outfit evoked. Brown can also make you claustrophobic.

Green: Prestige, upper socio-economic state. A good color around food.

Grey: Sophisticated, excellent for business suits.

Black: Dignity, sophistication, refinement, authority. Great color for women's business suits. Men in tuxedos look elegant in black.

White: Delicacy, refinement, cleanliness, and precision

2 WARDROBE

Wardrobe strategies express our lifestyle and our profession. Clothing covers approximately 90 percent of the body and historically conveys information about an individual's status, background, occupation, and region. A company's dress code — or no dress code — reflects the corporate culture.

My first workshop has proven to be the most popular. "Dressing to Influence" has been a major component in the high-level leadership training programs of several banks over the yerars. Over 200 bankers attended my seminar.

> *"We use clothing as a tactical weapon."* – MICHAEL R.
> SOLOMON, author of *The Psychology of Fashion*

Alison Lurie, the author of *The Language of Clothes* (1983), said, *"The clothes we choose to wear say about us from four perspectives—historical, social-logical, psychological, anthropological—color, fabric, and cut are not mere whims of designers or manufacturers but constitute a vocabulary and grammar as precise and full of subconscious intent as any verbal language: how our clothes announce our sex, age and class often give important information (or misinformation) about our occupation, geographical origin, personality, opinions, tastes, sexual desires, and current mood."*

From *AGD Impact, The Newsmagazine of the Academy of General Dentistry,* Volume 16 Number 7, in its cover article about Risk Management:

One casually dressed dentist was sent to Ms. Mondejar. In extracting a tooth, the dentist had damaged a patient's nerve, which lends to numbness. The defense attorney's strategy was to demonstrate that the dentist was elegant and less likely to be rough and careless in treating a patient.

"The dentist was in his 50s and wore collegiate clothing, with the shirts frayed at the collar, the shoes scuffed, and the suit ill-fitting and worn out," said Mr. Berg, the dentist's attorney. *"He did not look like a good craftsman, intelligent, or capable as a practitioner."*

Marily Mondejar, the image consultant, changed the dentist's wardrobe, *"The goal is to make the client look credible to make it easy for the jurors to listen to the doctor's side of the story: I could have made a mistake; however, listen to my side before you judge me,"* said Mondejar.

"The case was settled on the morning of the trial," said Mr. Berg. *"He looked nice and smooth, that it would be fairly clear he couldn't have done something rough which might have crushed the mandibular canal. The case settled for substantially less than it could have been. The plaintiff didn't have an easy target."*

> *"Your clothing must be equal to the quality of your life. When you buy cheap, you get cheap."* – GAIL JACKSON,
> Crystal Brands for Evan Picone

3 GROOMING PRINCIPLES

Personal grooming habits describe how we take care of ourselves. It is about the fit of our clothes, crisp, clean, and not frayed. Shoes do not have to be expensive but do have to be clean and not scuffed. Invest in lavender-scented closet sachets, so your clothing and shoes are protected from moths and odor. Spend the extra money on clothing alterations when you lose or gain weight. Your iron or steamer is your best friend. Build your resources list to include a tailor, a good dry cleaner, and shoe shine services.

The grooming of a company is the visual expression of its environment, products, and services. How a company's office is interior designed, cleaned, and organized influences the clients who come in for comfort or advice. Creating a company's product packaging should match the benefits of its use. Many companies today utilize overseas banking, legal, accounting, and tech support companies. It is prudent to include culture training as one of the required specs when evaluating these off-shore companies.

Economist Clara Dieck Assad once asked me about my best grooming tip in that lead article on image influencing. My response is still the same today: Pay attention to your hair. Your hair reflects your leadership power. Since we communicate so much with our eyes and facial expressions, we don't want our hairstyle to interfere. When we're younger, we find a hairstyle that becomes our signature. However, we get stuck with it and do not stay current with the trends. Your hair should frame your face without overwhelming it. The style should not be distracting. Generally, for business, it's nice to see a bit of air between the bottom of the haircut and the shoulders. Color, fit, style, and personal grooming are critical to making an impression.

Lastly, fragrance or no fragrance is another critical step. Another significant *femtor* in my career is Annette Green, President Emeritus of the Fragrance Foundation. I met her early in my consulting practice at a Fashion Group meeting in New York. Annette was then the executive director of the Fragrance Foundation, founded in 1949. She turned this organization into a multi-billion industry under her leadership when she took over the fledgling organization in 1962. I remember distinctly at our first lunch meeting at the Metropolitan Club in the Waldorf Astoria how she turned the "Power of the Nose" research into the strategy for growing the fragrance industry. Her mantra was that anything that smells belongs to the Fragrance Foundation. Her advice to me was, *"Everything you see has a message, and that's what image influencing is about."*

Every aspect of a person's image is interrelated. When you lose weight, for instance, you buy new clothes because your old clothes don't fit anymore. You tend to upgrade to the latest fashion styles to reward yourself. You walk differently. Your posture is erect—your body language changes. You smile more often; your handshake is firmer.

Your habits change, and you pay more attention to your grooming. Hair, makeup, and exercise become part of your upkeep. You are more conscious about what you eat. You pay attention to getting enough rest. Your energy level is high.

Your house is neater. Your closet is more organized. Your new clothes are hung on the proper hangers, and your shoes are shined. You even consider upgrading your car. Your car is now regularly washed and detailed.

People start noticing these changes. You receive more compliments. Your self-confidence shoots up, and your work performance improves. You exude image messages of *"I'm a person worth knowing. I'm in control of my personal and professional life."*

*"Ugliness is a lack of care. Beauty is healthy. Your
kingdom is not so great that you don't have enough time
to groom." –* DANIEL LABERGE

4 COMMUNICATIONS

Communication is the delivery of our message through verbal and nonverbal messages. How we talk and react to certain situations influences our intended audience.

From *AGD Impact, The Newsmagazine of the Academy of General Dentistry,* Volume 16 Number 7, in its cover article about Risk Management:

"After showing the dentist how to dress, the next step is teaching the dentist to talk about himself in front of a camera. The videotape is used to evaluate verbal and nonverbal behaviors. Dentists are trained to avoid using technical terms, make eye contact, and humility, but still come across as confident professionals. But they should appear a little nervous," I advised – "because jurors don't like too much confidence."

I continued, *"When you start relating your side of the story, you may change judgments; you influence opinions. During a deposition, lawyers put a dollar value on the case based on many factors. Wheeling the plaintiff to court in a wheelchair is a dramatic play in getting visual sympathy from a jury. I could practice with a doctor who does not deny something went wrong with the medical procedure, but as a human being, he took all the precautions and disclosed that on the form the patient signs and approves."*

Lawyers concentrate on factual information on behalf of their client; image consultants can help clients relax and, most importantly, give the appearance of a competent practitioner.

*"You must gain the audience's attention and interest the
moment you walk on the stage. Without that attention,
you won't get your message across, you'll have trouble
sustaining whatever interest there is, and you won't have*

established your leadership and control—the keys to being a powerful speaker." – WESTSIDE TOASTMASTERS

5 PROTOCOL AND ETIQUETTE

In influencing results, protocol and etiquette are guidelines for how we treat people. It is a public statement of our values.

"Liquids on the right, solids on the left," my mother would teach us younger kids in table etiquette settings. Etiquette is a code of rules governing proper social behavior as established in any community for an occasion. It is also the unwritten code of honor of certain practices in some professions and learned through word-of-mouth or a mentor. Etiquette varies according to local customs or taboos. It can also refer to the rigid ceremonies of court, naval, and military circles and extend to the legal, medical, and other professions. Etiquette changes serve as a partial index to society's attitudes toward morals and conduct.

A protocol is a formalized code of conduct in business with procedural matters usually expressed in written instruments such as company mission statements, vision statements, statements of principle, preliminary agreements, or the formulary of etiquette to be observed by the Head of State in official ceremonies. Protocol describes the rules of etiquette and order. There are many events for which no protocol has been written, but good manners are always appropriate.

Manners refer to the customary way of doing things, as in the prevailing customs, modes of living of a people, or a class of people. Manners reflect a person's outward bearing or a person's way of treating others, a style of execution, a person's demeanor, or affectation. It is a well-known fact that J.C. Penney, a merchant who established one of the largest chains of department stores in the United States, would invite applicants for a management position to dine with him. He observes their table manners, what dish or beverage the applicant orders, and how they behave during meals. Did the manager talk while their mouth was full? Were their elbows on the table while eating? Did they slurp their food and/or beverage? *"Deals are closed during a meal. Dining behavior is the quickest way to assess how people behave,"* he said.

"The rougher the conflict, the more manners are needed. Only when insults, harassment, disrespect, and obscenity are banned can people engage in a truly substantive argument." – JUDITH MARTIN AND GUNTHER STEN

A U.S. businessman had an important meeting with a high-level executive of a global telecommunications company based in Mexico. After weeks of negotiations with intermediaries, they finally reached a critical phase in the projected partnership and agreed to meet. After checking in with the office building's security desk, he waited for about 20 minutes in a crowded reception room before he was led into a private elevator that opened into a plush executive suite. He cooled his heels for another 15 minutes perceiving the wait as a power maneuver. He was served coffee in fine China and given foreign magazines to occupy his time. When he was finally ushered into the executive's office, there were another 15–20 minutes of pleasantries, including a discussion of the artwork in the elegant suite. Curiously, one of the art pieces was an elaborately carved antique wooden funerary box that dramatically occupied the large office. What crossed his mind was, *"Why does this executive have a casket on display? What does this mean?"* The US businessman was confused with the images, symbols, and conflicting messages he was receiving. He was not sure how to proceed. He decided the safest alternative was to postpone any further business decisions because he was no longer in the mood to negotiate. The Mexican executive could not figure out why the US executive tabled the deal.

Culture mirrors leadership, and a company's culture is the real bottom line. The Mexican executive's personality and how he expressed it in his art and the situations the U. S. executive experienced influenced his behaviors and motivations that affected their cooperative endeavor. It created a dissonance that frustrated their project. The moral of this story is that *"Culture is neither right nor wrong. It simply is."* The challenge is to find common ground. Understanding local culture combined with the corporate protocol of a potential client encourages results and productive, cooperative behavior.

Multinational companies invest a lot of time and money doing business internationally. Much of it is spent on meeting governmental, legal, financial, environmental, and technological requirements and very little on understanding a country's unique business culture. The subtle differences in business perceptions, norms, and practices are based on unspoken rules and complicated codes unique to each Culture. It is difficult to measure the consequential impact on our behaviors. These differences alone can delay or derail many important business deals. So, how can we transcend these differences and transform them into opportunities?

6 IMAGE OBJECTS

These are the persons, places, or things that influence the perception of individuals, products, and companies. How we select and use image objects impacts our image-influencing activities. High-end or low-end image objects each carry a message.

Image objects—the car you drive, where you live, the brands of clothing and shoes you wear, the bags, totes, watches, jewelry, and other accessories you surround yourself—all convey an influencing image. These objects can either enhance or distract the messages you want to convey.

A fitness consultant, a career or executive coach, an image consultant, and a shopping concierge are image objects that say that you have reached a certain economic position level. Today memberships in high-priced private clubs are image objects and brands that send a powerful image of exclusivity. In the United States, by-invitation clubs like the Bohemian Club, The Metropolitan Club, The Battery, The Pacific-Union Club, Soho House, and CORE have high initiation and membership fees that ultimately provide access and opportunities to meet high net-worth individuals.

The most famous image object is the bag. A Louis Vuitton, Chanel, or Gucci bag says, *"I have arrived. I can afford this bag now."* Image Objects are global ways of understanding a customer and managing a business. Luxury brands are a multi-trillion industry spending millions on messaging. *"The concept of luxury is as old as humanity; a discriminating understanding of it makes it possible to define the rigorous rules for its effective management."* (The Luxury Strategy, 2009).

> *"Accessories are key ingredients in your look. Take away all the chrome, and all you have is a black car."* – PETER LANIAK, CEO, Escada

7 INNER IMAGE

Inner Image is your reputation and relationship with yourself: your values regarding security, self-image, belonging, purpose, and competence. Our inner image drives our public image. As your external image improves, your internal image is also affected. You start examining your values and how they impact your lifestyle. If the outer and inner images do not align, a "disconnect" happens.

"Disconnects" confuse and disappoint us. Intuitively, we sense a "disconnect" when something doesn't fit. For example, we expect someone who dines at fine restaurants not to drive a dirty car. People who wear fashionable, expensive clothes are expected not to decorate their homes with cheap furniture.

> *"The truth is nobody knows what's inside of you. Only you know what's inside of you. Only you know what you can accomplish. What you're capable of. Your dreams, your desires, your ability. Whatever you feel in your gut, follow that."* – JENNIFER LOPEZ

However, we feel about having to look the "right way" or to behave "a certain way" or to value the "right things" to become successful in life and career; these image aspects do exist. They were created and evolved by our family, our circles, our communities, our colleagues, our organizations, our professional fields, and our countries over decades and eras. And we follow them and pass them along.

But these ways of influencing also do change and transform over time. The power suits of the 80s corporate world have made way for the jeans and effortless cool of the 2000s tech industry. They were transformed by influential people in our companies, industries, and societies.

So how can you be *influential? By becoming influential.*

LIBERATION

ANNA ISABEL C. SOBREPEÑA

Writer
GLOBAL FWN100™ 2019

GRACE. In the Time of COVID-19

I am a writer by passion and inclination, but I answer to storyteller when asked about my designation. From this position, my narrative unfolds, both a chronicle and a reflection on a journey towards self-mastery. It begins with an obituary and negotiates through pages of mimeographed paper, broadsheets, a glossy magazine, and into the setting of a worldwide disruption brought about by a health crisis. Values and a faith life underlie the passage through time and space and are key to my story. I will refer to principles shared by experts in the science of mental characteristics and attitudes, but this will mostly be the development of a life view formed over the years.

An Unusual Beginning

My first published work was a notice of death for my grandfather. He was a beloved person in my life, and his sudden passing while on a trip abroad was a loss deeply felt. During the night, while waiting for his remains to be brought home, my uncle assigned me to prepare an announcement for the newspapers. Within the hours before dawn, I grappled with words, wanting to convey the exceptional person he was and how dearly he meant to us, his family. I felt he deserved more than the standard notice of death. My high school self drew from the words of a Scottish poet Thomas Campbell, words that I read in a Harold Robbins book. I also referenced Lebanese- American writer and poet Khalil Gibran. My literary tribute saw print on the first day of his wake, and I was told it was very nice.

An obituary has no bylines but having words I had crafted, which were published, was a trigger. I felt my writing was deemed good enough for the public to read. When the obituary was used a few weeks later for some person unknown to me, the indignation of being plagiarized gave way to an affirmation that I could actually write something worth reading and copying.

A couple of years later, we used the same obituary for my father. An editor in a broadsheet, who was dad's friend, read it and asked to see a sample of my works. Up until then, I was only scribbling verses for personal consumption. So when she enthused about my scribbles and published my attempt at poetry on a full page of a Sunday magazine, I knew I wanted to be a writer.

Clear Vision

Knowing what we want to be is an essential foundation for self-mastery. Self-mastery requires having a vision for our self. Business coach and writer Scott Jeffrey says it is more than just self-control or managing impulses. Instead, he says, "self-mastery is directing ourselves towards a future of our choosing. We learn to master ourselves by getting out of our own way, stripping away what we are not to realize who and what we really are, actualizing our potential in the process." For me, that meant becoming authentic, so I could live my best life.

Authenticity happens with self-knowledge, finding who we are, what we want to be, and our strengths and limitations. Becoming a writer took a circuitous path. I enjoyed other things besides writing. Art was one of them, and my father, an empowering example of the male species, encouraged all his four daughters to go to college, not with the aim to get a job, but to do something we enjoyed. Since I found pleasure in painting and sculpting, I enrolled in the University of the Philippines College of Fine Arts, but as early as my freshman year, I discovered these were not my greatest asset. I had ideas, but translation fell short in the visual execution. Worse, my ideas were being rendered by classmates who could draw and paint better than I. The one thing I did not want to be was mediocre.

Acceptance of our limitations is part of the elimination process. I was not a painter but an art lover. Consequently, I switched courses and became immersed in literature. Reading has always been a source of many delights and thought stimulation. After a range of books and additional units, I graduated as an English Major. There were a lot of writing requirements, and for one particular class, our final grade was determined by a magazine project. I was designated editor of our mimeographed edition. It earned a flat 1, the highest mark possible in the U.P. grading system. Indeed it was an affirmation of what I was good at, and I built on it.

Practice is Part of the Commitment

Becoming a good writer was my compelling vision. Compelling is the operative word. Scott Jeffrey says it is important to make the vision "something to move toward, something that inspires you and not just something you think you should move towards."

I pursued higher studies while working in a Christian publishing house, where I got to do more writing. Consistent practice is necessary to yield results. Somewhere on the way to my getting my M.A., I ended up with an MRS and became a full-time wife and mother. But I kept writing. I contributed to *Mabuhay* magazine, the in-flight magazine of Philippine Airlines, to *Design and Architecture* magazine, a few publications in Korea and the U.K., and occasionally for local broadsheets and a few other glossy magazines.

The support of my husband was invaluable. One of the hardest things about writing that I contend with from time to time is finding my opening line. On one occasion, when I was facing a blank page and an approaching deadline, he booked us into a hotel without the children, treated me to a fine dinner, then closed the door to the bedroom, leaving me in the anteroom to work on my opening line.

Being a contributor gave me leeway to be there for our family while indulging a passion for the written word. By the time the children were finishing college, I had been moved to the peripheries of their life and could pursue a career when others were thinking of retirement.

Moving Out of Familiar Zones

The path to growth and self-mastery will have difficulties because moving out of our familiar zones is uncomfortable. I recognized the privilege of having been able to prioritize what was important to me - building our home life, and being there for my husband and children. As I entered into another chapter of life, opportunities presented themselves that aligned with my compelling vision. Still, I hesitated. My life was on cruise control. Why disrupt? There was also an underlying concern that I could fail. After many considerations, I chose to rejoin the workforce. It was part of my compelling vision for a meaningful life, but it was not a walk in the park.

When I joined the publishing industry as editor-in-chief of the longest-running glossy magazine in the country, the reaction was to dismiss me as a housewife wannabe and a socialite looking to keep herself busy. While I had been an occasional contributor to different newspapers and magazines locally and abroad, I was primarily known as the wife of an accomplished professional.

During my first month, an editor asked, "Where did you come from?" Another media person told me I had lowered my status in the social strata by joining the working class. Industry people called me a housewife looking for something to occupy my time. After my second issue, another editor called my mobile and accused me of copying their magazine's font. (Not true, by the way)

Despite the less than positive reception from industry colleagues, I chose not to give energy to the naysayers. Instead, I focused on creating content, expanding the magazine's reach, and getting to know the stakeholders. I tapped my network of persons who were the target market of our publication, the A-listers who happened to be among the people with whom I circulated. I felt that our specialty would be those who were hard to get, the public figures people were curious about but had eschewed publicity. During the first quarter, our pages featured industrialists such as Jorge Araneta, who had declined all other requests but agreed to be on our cover as an accommodation to our friendship. It was a sold-out issue.

Before completing my first year, I put together a power issue with some of our country's foremost industrialists and national leaders, including then sitting president Gloria Macapagal Arroyo. The cover of the Power issue were media-shy persons, Metrobank taipan George S. K. Ty and his sons Arthur and Alfred. They had never headlined a lifestyle magazine or any other publication, much less allowed such access. It was the first and last time Dr. Ty agreed to be featured; an accommodation obliged because of our personal ties. That sold-out issue won a merit award from the International Association of Business Communicators, Philippine Quill, for the cover story I wrote.

That same awards body also recognized our September cover photo shot on location in Paris. I flew my team to Paris to shoot designer Monique Lhuillier and her sister Yvette Warnod, both in the fashion capital for Fashion Week. The cover was a statement that Philippine talent held its own among the leading names in fashion and where else was that more pronounced than in the fashion capital of the world. The photo received a merit award the same evening as the George Ty cover story. The recognition had effectively silenced my detractors.

I made it a point to get to know our advertisers, public relations managers, and potential collaborators. Personally, it was more about building relationships than transactional engagements. I have held that who we are precedes what we do. Applying this mindset made it easy to relate to people regardless of their position or affiliations. Friendly connections were made even with industry competitors, making it easy to be with them on media trips. Seeing persons rather than their titles did not differentiate principals of companies and agencies from their staff. Each was regarded and appreciated as the unique individual that they were. While it was not a conscious strategy, it became key to building ties at all levels and proved advantageous in getting support for our work. Airline and hotel sponsorship here and abroad, exclusive stories, invitations to international events, and one-off interviews contributed to the monthly edition offerings. We became the reference for our target market, based on anecdotal feedback given to us and market studies.

Before signing my contract, I had conveyed to management that I would do the work only if it were meaningful to me and if I were left a free hand to define the magazine's direction. Meaningful meant sharing personal values in the pages to define the magazine's tagline of living at its finest to mean more than just visible wealth. I shared this vision with my team and mentored them not just in skills building and proficiency but also in adhering to the values of integrity and professionalism.

For instance, during one editorial meeting, I had assigned a staff member to cover a wine tasting dinner. He, however, asked to be excused explaining that he did not drink alcohol. Being a valid reason, I designated someone else but was taken aback when he volunteered to accompany his colleague for the free dinner. It was a teaching moment on professionalism and probity. I explained to the team that we should never sell ourselves for a free meal, a free trip, a bag, or any privilege, and that our byline should be untainted and our name unsullied by personal gain. While it has become commonplace to give media practitioners gifts and accord special treatment in exchange for coverage, I hoped to ingrain in my young colleagues a sense of ethics, morals, and standards of behavior that will define our magazine above the norm of entitlement.

It was also important to me to pass the need for excellence in the workplace, to strive to exert their best whether they were layout artists, editorial assistants, writers, or photographers. Excellence was not about having all things perfect but about applying energies in whatever imperfect conditions to the best of abilities. I mentored our young writers to explore other sources beyond the primary interviews and read up, research, and go beyond google to improve their stories. They had to read and reread their works before submission and to aim for error-free write-ups. Skills-building was necessary to grow in competence and excellence.

It was a joy to work with a team eager to grow and open to learning. Their positive attitude and development energized me. They grew as professionals. They became adept at writing about various features beyond their initial interests. I believe it widened not just their abilities but their appreciation of things previously beyond their scope.

MEANINGFUL LIVES

The nature of the magazine was luxury and addressed a niche audience. Beyond the accouterments of refined and gracious living, I had put forward the definition of luxury to reflect values of the highest order. Philanthropy and generosity were increasingly becoming the buzzwords in the corporate world. My team and I brought the tenets of privilege and corporate social responsibility (CSR) together to highlight the good that advantaged men and women do. The magazine content expanded beyond being a purveyor of premium goods to highlight meaningful lives. I emphasized this in my first editor's message: "What is becoming more pronounced is an elegance of spirit emerging in a new breed. The definition of luxury extends beyond the latest cutting-edge gadget or jewel-encrusted stemware. Giving back has become the mantra, and it is the privilege of doing good that continues to raise the bar for what is truly the best of living... it is this nobility of spirit that separates the rich from the truly rich." (*Lifestyle Asia*, Dec 2007?)

Enterprise necessarily provided that we feature the products and services universally regarded as excellent for the interest and consumption of the target audience. Content, however, increased considerably to include stories about the good people were doing. These were crafted within a setting and circumstances that the target readership could identify with and still be enjoined to make their contributions to a better world.

Achieving this could arguably be measured by more awards received over the years as well as the distinction of making it to the monthly bestsellers list in leading bookstores. In addition, the target audience we addressed responded favorably by establishing our brand as the market leader in our sector. The independent U.K.–based research company Synovate and later the Paris-based IPSOS documented this over the years.

Facing Down Fear

Admittedly, it was challenging to steer the monthly editions towards what I deemed consequential. There was always the consideration of promoting premium consumer goods and services vis a vis what was purposeful and substantial. I needed the buy-in of my team to navigate a balance that would fulfill management's business goals without compromising the fundamental ideals. The most basic requirement was for them to believe with me in a meaningful life that did not discount the finer things but went beyond owning yachts, traveling first class, and a wardrobe of designer clothes. It was foundational to build credibility with my team. Working closely together was key to establishing the authenticity of what I was calling them to imbibe. We spent time in work situations and leisure activities to build trust and acceptance. I created activities that helped us to get to know each other and appreciate persons beyond their functions. I would say that spending time with each other outside the workplace was beneficial towards gaining their trust and confidence that we could apply our highest ideals in the work we were doing.

Such a belief necessitated a sense of honor, not pandering to requests accompanied by cash gifts for primarily self-promoting features. We also had to work with our advertising department that needed to generate the funds for the continued production of the glossy. Transparency protected the staff's integrity and guided conduct to professionalism. We were building our ethical identity by not promising what we could not deliver to persons and companies who wanted publicity stories in the magazine. Our storyboard meetings approved and vetted content based on merit, not personal entitlements offered to us.

I also impressed upon the team that while there were other magazines in our class, the focus of competition was ourselves. It dispelled negativity and an unhealthy practice in the marketplace to undermine the work of others. I encouraged them to go beyond their reach, aim high and write the stories they could proudly affix their names; in short, subscribe to the standard of excellence.

Our issues, while primarily lifestyle in content, were also used to make a statement. Being advertisement driven, we would not be outright advocates, but we could share a position through stories. One example was a Travel issue where we identified Turkey as the location for the cover shoot. Turkey was going through a time of political unrest and had to deal with terrorist activities, including a bombing at a popular tourist attraction.

The editorial team had been cautioned and discouraged by well-meaning persons from pursuing the trip to Istanbul. I had been in coordination with the Turkish embassy to support the project, weighed the risks, and decided to push through with the trip. I felt that aborting the trip and looking for another location would have given terrorists the victory.

After the assurance of the Turkish embassy about our safety, our team traveled to four different locations in five days to produce four stories. In my editor's note, I said, "... allowing fear to bear on the decision [to abort] would have been a triumph for forces that instigate violence to get what they want. We cast our lot with peace, respect for fellowmen, courage, and hope. It was the underlying reason for choosing to be there." (page 14, Editor's Note, *Lifestyle Asia*, May 2017)

Marriage of Enterprise, Marketing, and Good Works

Some of the magazine's efforts went beyond the pages of the magazine. Since the nature of the magazine catered to premium lifestyle patrons, it could be far removed from the realities facing a majority of our countrymen who were not interested in Baccarat and Bernardaud, Michelin star dining, Hermés, or Bentleys. Rather than be constrained by this limitation, I saw an opportunity to engage both our readership and our sponsors.

The February edition had always been earmarked as the Eligibles issue and featured the young people dominating the social scene. Maintaining the focus on the youth, I steered the focus towards the potentials and possibilities of the rising generation. We selected the roster of scions and girls from notable families based on their contributions to society. It held up youth efforts towards a better world. Then, instead of a party to mark the issue, I arranged for a tree planting activity in partnership with a land developer advertiser. Planting trees was a way of replacing those used to make magazine pages. It was an effort to reduce our carbon footprint, care for the planet, and engage people in meaningful activity. Subsequently, the magazine had several tree planting activities through the years with civic groups, a local government, and advertisers who shared a heartbeat for the environment.

The theme of the November issue had traditionally been Entertaining, a collection of gracious living experiences with accompanying accouterment. However, while preparing the magazine content on best restaurants, chef offerings, and fine dining options, the country was hit by one of the worst typhoons, international name Haiyan. The super typhoon brought widespread devastation, loss of lives and property, and displacing many communities. It was a very different situation from Veuve Clicquot and celebrity chef dinners, E-class rides, and the clubbing scene being laid out in the pages.

The urgency to respond to the great need due to the super typhoon inspired an idea. I thought of asking some five-star establishments to create a dish or a drink that would be co-branded with our magazine and offer it for a limited time on their menu. Every order would contribute to a fund for the relief and rehabilitation of the typhoon victims. I also enlisted the Metrobank Foundation to receive the donations and send the money to the relief efforts through their extensive network. Project Spreading the Table was born. Hotels and restaurants participated during the proposed duration of one month even without any formal memorandum of agreement. I also got The Metrobank Card company to promote the campaign in the statement of accounts they sent to their clients. At the end of 30 days, donations were turned over to the Foundation, documented on the front pages of the largest circulating national daily. It was a marriage of marketing and enterprise borne of a desire to do good.

When the magazine reached its quarter of a century anniversary, management prepared to have a ball to celebrate the milestone. Not particularly fond of extravagant events, I proposed that in keeping with the core values I had ingrained as the magazine's fundamental heartbeat, the evening affair should contribute to different philanthropic efforts and organizations. It was a bit bewildering for me that the company would spend so much for a one-night bash but be reticent about giving back for the success translated into favorable revenues. Management, however, gave me leeway to pursue my proposal, and I tapped different companies to contribute to several charities close to my heart. As a result, on the night of the 25th anniversary, I had checks for organizations, such as Operation Smile, Gifts and Graces, and The Joy of Urban Farming. Moreover, the charity component elevated the black-tie event by its bent to reach out to the marginalized and support the environment. Henceforth, the annual anniversary event integrated a giving back component and expanded the magazine's network to corporations that may not have been lifestyle in nature but were agreeable to the association for meaningful engagements.

I have held that true wealth is not an accumulation of material things or measured by bank accounts and net worth. So, solidifying the intent to define the magazine's tagline of living at its finest, I created a regular section in every issue entitled Giving Back. The stories captured people pursuing something bigger than themselves that contributed to the greater good. It featured people from the privileged class who would expend energy to build classrooms, plant trees, promote clean air and water, and source food directly from farmers to support agricultural livelihood. This page, which I initiated, ran every month for 11 years while I helmed the number one luxury magazine in the Philippines.

A Valediction Complete with Fireworks

I disengaged from the company in October 2018 when there was no longer an alignment of values with management. While preparing for my last issue, I received an unexpected recognition. The Asia Leaders Award conferred me the 2018 Editor of the Year for professional integrity and competence. Tributes poured in with congratulatory messages published in two leading national dailies. The Bank of the Philippine Island, Metrobank, and Bulgari extended their felicitations publicly in print media. My final magazine issue had several pages conveying well wishes from different advertisers.

It was overwhelming to receive messages from notable names in different sectors. Prominent citizen and philanthropist Bea Zobel Jr. said, "Anna turned that magazine around and made it what it is today. I never bought it until she took over." Prominent Entrepreneur Ben Chan said, "[Her] hard work and dedication have extended to make this lifestyle magazine relevant to the times." Civic leader Lizzie Zobel messaged, "Anna has done an outstanding job at Lifestyle Asia, bringing her extraordinary energy and commitment for the benefit of the reading public." My colleague in the industry, Raul Manzano, himself an editor of a glossy magazine, said, "She is not only the best editor of *Lifestyle Asia*; she is the best magazine editor in the Philippines, barring none."

Vice-President Leni Robredo was among those who sent a lengthy message. "Long before I personally got to know Anna Isabel Crisostomo Sobrepeña, I have been reading about her work and found myself moved by the depth of her commitment to creating a world unmarred by social divisions. Beyond her accomplishments in the publishing industry, I have come to know Ms. Sobrepeña as a woman of remarkable vision and generosity of spirit.

"Under her guidance, *Lifestyle Asia* became a platform for transformative collaboration, civic work, philanthropy, and nobility of spirit. This was a departure from what most people thought a glossy lifestyle magazine was supposed to be: full of glitz and glamor, power and prestige. In 2016, she steered the magazine towards a new direction by reaching out to marginalized and vulnerable sectors of society.

"What made me admire her, even more, was her firm belief that the cries of the poor and underprivileged are serious concerns we must all listen to, discuss, and address—with empathy, not just pity. With homegrown values of truth, accountability, honesty, and integrity. Indeed, her invaluable contribution to promoting good governance, ethical leadership, and uplifting the lives of fellow Filipinos gives us hope during these extraordinarily dark times. Through her struggles and successes, Anna inspires other women, both here and overseas, including myself, to conquer their own struggles with defiant hope and courage."

There were more heartwarming accolades on the night of the awards. I was particularly moved when a video presentation brought together people I highly esteemed. Then Archbishop of Manila, His Eminence Luis Antonio Cardinal Tagle said, "Anna shares her faith as a laywoman should. She sanctifies the workplace and "tastes" and "trends" by bringing the gospel to them as a leaven, hidden but powerfully alive." Weeks prior, he had already sent a message. "While other publications came out with special editions on Pope Francis, hers was the only secular magazine that came out with Pope Francis in a regular issue, showing foresight and courage to tell his story."

The Best Editor distinction, the generous remarks of people I respected, and six awards from the International Association of Business Communicators-Philippine Quill were icing on the cake. I found much satisfaction in what I did during my 11 years in publishing. That was more than enough. Summing up the accomplishments during the awards night, I said, "Not bad for a housewife."

The Filipina Women's Network awarded me as one of the 2019 Most Influential Filipina Thought Leader and Innovator the following year. I joined a roster of awardees who surmounted such odds to realize their potential and make a difference in their circle of influence. The recognition affirmed that I was on course to a future of my choosing.

Storytelling in Words, Pictures, Haikus, and Virtual Platforms

Following my departure from the magazine, I discovered another avenue for creative expression. The ambassador of Japan Koji Haneda had selected me to visit his country and write a story on Fukushima, that was published in one of the national dailies where I was a contributor. When he saw my photographs, the idea of exhibiting the pictures snapped from a phone camera took off. The Japanese embassy in Manila and former Philippine Ambassador to Japan Manuel Lopez sponsored the exhibit held at the Rockwell Powerplant. The caption for each enlarged photo was a haiku that I wrote.

None of the works were for sale, but if anyone wanted any of the framed photos, I said they were welcome to take it home and make a contribution towards the education assistance for children in war-devastated Marawi. The generous response was overwhelming, and a few months later, the collection of photographs made a gallery debut when a gallery owner offered to launch not just another physical show but also a virtual exhibit. Again, proceeds contributed to the Marawi children's education assistance.

The exhibit gained even more traction when CNN Philippines featured it and interviewed me about being an editor, writer, and now poet and visual artist. Expanding my storytelling to visuals and poetry was a happy development but writing was still my natural bent. I was invited to join two national broadsheets as a columnist, helm another magazine, and put together three coffee table books. I opted for the last as well as a project to do the biography of a prominent citizen of the republic. I also did consultancies to increase brand awareness for different clients.

Fifteen months after I left the magazine, COVID-19 happened and the world shut down. The health crisis turned life as we knew it on its head. A hard lockdown had Metro Manila urbanites and populations in other parts of the country confined to our residences. Staying home became the government prescription to address the pandemic that had hospitals swelling with infected persons. Health care providers were stretched and occupancy in the medical facilities was beyond capacity. While vaccines were being developed little was known about the deadly virus sweeping across continents. People were dying by the hundreds daily, and the layman could not determine what was happening.

Working from home became the norm, and staying connected through technology replaced physical interactions. There were many challenges for the digital immigrants forced to enhance their limited skills. I, for one, had been heavily dependent on assistants and a daughter to negotiate cyberspace but because we now cocooned in a bubble consisting of household staff and my husband, it was necessary to accelerate my digital fluency and adeptness with devices, technology, and the internet. I was apprehensive, so when invited to participate in a webinar as a reactor, I felt compelled to enhance my ability to communicate with an inanimate object. Speaking to a camera without a visible audience, I found it difficult to gauge whether I was reaching them or not. Even if another person popped up on the screen, it felt strange, and I blanked out a few times. Gratefully, it was not a live recording, and the technical staff edited my silent stare and fumbling when connectivity fluctuated.

I quietly decided that I would no longer accept online interactions because of fear. Fear I needed to overcome, a fear of technology that I had managed to push back because previously, people attended to it for me. I had sufficient know-how to get by, but if I wanted to keep up with the fast-moving world, I needed to educate myself even more. The isolation brought about by the coronavirus became an opportunity to develop skills necessary to live in a world of advanced computer technology.

The encouragement and support of my digital native daughter were a big factor. She patiently tutored me through the keyboard shortcuts and commands, setting up software on my phone; de-mystifying what I perceived were enigmas of a constantly evolving universe of apps and clouds. She was my troubleshooter when an article I was working on disappeared or when the screen suddenly went blank. She would walk me through by remote, calmly giving directions on the other end of the mobile line. I learned, however, belatedly, to address this electronic world, no longer dependent on staff, although within calling distance for assistance.

Virtually Yours

I was still more comfortable writing and continued to contribute to national dailies and online publications. Still, virtual interaction was becoming another platform to share my ideas and support for causes and actions toward a better world. When the invitation to speak before an international conference on the other side of the Pacific was extended, I knew it was time to set aside lurking apprehensions about connecting over digital space.

The NaFFAA Southern Leadership Conference, organized by the National Federation of Filipino American Associations Southern Region asked me to give an inspirational message. However, it was only after I accepted the invitation did I realize it was not only a time zone away but that there would be a live question and answer portion. It was numbing enough to deliver a prepared speech to an audience I could not see but a Q & A was potentially petrifying. I grappled with the mild terror of making a fool of myself at 2 o'clock in the morning, Manila time. This is when I fell back on the foundational truth upon which I had built my life.

Underlying this journey to self-mastery is a relationship that has given meaning and purpose to everything in my life, without exception. Knowing God and who He is formed who I want to become, essentially a good person, kind, compassionate, generous, and forgiving. Keeping close to Him will enable the ultimate transformation to reflect God Himself, the ultimate good.

Offering my anxieties together with the opportunity to share a message of hope in cyberspace provided some measure of confidence. I kept repeating to myself, *"This is for God."* Finally, on the day of the conference, bleary-eyed and praying all would go well, I delivered a short message that can be summed up in three statements:

1. Our meaningful lives are the healing stories we need to tell a wounded world.
2. This crisis we are in will end. We who will come out of

this pandemic alive have an extraordinary opportunity to redefine the world we want to live in, respecting our fellowmen, extending ourselves for the welfare of the marginalized, and taking responsibility for our planet.

3. Even while we live under a cloud of this disease, we can win the war by letting kindness fight our fears. Social distancing, yes, but solidarity too, even from our isolation places. Prayer is foremost because underlying any successful, sustainable effort is a faith life that gives meaning and purpose to everything.

I did not know if I made a fool of myself or if anyone paid attention but I stopped being afraid when my turn to speak came. I felt God accepted my effort and fears, which was all that mattered. What kept running through my head was *Ad Majorem Dei Gloriam*. For the greater glory of God. God can take our little-ness, including our fears, and bring good out from them. People sent positive feedback after the presentation, and the president of NaFFAA himself reached out to affirm the message had been well received.

This would be the first of other invitations to speak to a virtual audience. Association Internationale des Étudiants en Sciences Économiques et Commerciales-UPM had a video series to mark Women's Month, and I was among the panelists in their AISEC-UPM "Kakaibabe," where we spoke of women's concerns. The series, posted on Facebook, supported CRIBS New Beginnings Program for the healing of sexually abused minors.

Staying Positive in the Time of COVID-19

Birds of Happiness
colored paper cranes
each folded with a prayer
for good days to come

When the local chapter of Mary's Way Foundation sent an invitation to speak to their members on any subject of my choice, I recalled one of the questions posed to me during the NaFFAA conference. How does one stay positive amid the havoc brought about by the virus? Mental health was becoming a concern as people were confined to private spaces. The world changed overnight. Movements were restricted. People had to wear masks, stand far from each other, and instead of spending time with those we love, staying home and away became the loving thing to do. Medical experts projected life for those over 60 would never return to what it had been, even when a vaccine for the corona virus was found. It was looking bleak, and keeping a bright outlook was proving to be a challenge for many. I decided this was going to be my subject matter.

The title of my talk was "Love in the Time of COVID-19," recalling Gabriel Garcia Marquez' *El Amore en los Tiempos del Cólera* or "Love in the Time of Cholera." Cholera is a highly infectious disease that is potentially fatal. Literary analysts have said that Gabo, as Marquez was also called, equated cholera to love and ultimately to death. His excellent work of fiction was about love in the time of a pandemic. It was a springboard to share about love in the time of our current pandemic but not the kind Gabo wrote about.

I summarized into three statements how we could win the war against loneliness, fear of infection and fear of loss:

1. Love God.
2. Be Kind
3. Fall In Love Again and again

I chose to tell three stories that would convey a mindset to get an upper hand in negotiating the unusual times.

Love God

The first story was about loving God. I talked about a cabinet official at Malacañang Palace some years ago who became a casualty of an ambitious politician. The power-hungry person maneuvered to remove the cabinet secretary to another office in a downgraded capacity so he would be the closest to the sitting president from whom he hoped to secure an endorsement for his presidential bid.

The staff members of the downgraded officer went to their boss' office agitating to expose what they perceived was a power grab for personal gain. The young, idealistic, and angry men and women wanted to let the chief executive know about the lapses that had been happening since the new person joined the Office of the President. Their boss quietly listened to their indignation, and after they had spoken, he looked at them and calmly said, *"If Jesus Christ, whom I serve, stooped to wash the feet of his disciples, who am I to hold on to a title or a position?"* What had been a room full of angry voices had become very silent.

That one response conveyed so powerfully a love for God, a humility to turn the other cheek, and a decision to put the needs of others before his well-being. Infighting would not only create dissension within the office but be an added burden to the president, who had had to deal with grave matters of state. Moreover, it would disrupt the delivery of services necessary to address the country's needs. His decision not to contest was based on a firm belief that all was in God's hands.

It highlighted how loving God enables us to make sacrifices for the greater good. It nurtures a generosity of spirit knowing much has been received from God. The downgraded government official was a praying man. He began his meetings at the office with prayer. He allocated time daily reading scripture and quiet reflection. Prayer is key to knowing God's love and the only response to being loved by God is to love him more than a position of power, the prestige of a title or even the security of a job.

I concluded the story by relating it to their situations that were not as highly-charged or dramatic but which also confronted them with daily choices to love God in the ordinary circumstances of our everyday lives. 1 Corinthians 13 tells us that love is patient and kind, love is gentle, seeks not its own way, not proud, not haughty, not entitled.

Love is not merely something that God does, nor is it His attribute. Love is who God is. How do I love God? I wish I could enumerate an impressive list of good things I have done. The reality is the natural man within is in constant conflict with the spiritual self. The commandments are a good checklist, but more than following a set of rules is following a Person, the One who is Love. I keep trying to love Him when the cook burns the roast chicken, when the hubby eats in the room and scatters crumbs on the bed, when the things I need have been borrowed by the children who forget to return the items. I need grace to be patient, forgiving, and kind. Because loving God is not just a spiritual experience.

The president of the Catholic Bishops Conference of the Philippines, His Eminence Pablo Virgilio David, said that many Catholics today tend to reduce Christianity to piety. It resonates with the Apostolic Exhortation *Gaudete et Exsultate* of Pope Francis where he says, "Holiness...is about not swooning in mystic rapture. Living the gospel in an authentic way needs to hold together both a relationship with the Lord and actions of mercy and justice...." The spiritual should not be separated from practical action.

The protagonist in the story was applying actions of love, humility foremost, subjugating pride for the greater good. Because of the peaceful transition of power to the ambitious politician, there was no disruption in the delivery of services to marginalized communities, no scandal in Malacañang Palace, and no ill feelings. A few years after that episode, they ran into each other, and I witnessed the downgraded officer cordially greeting the person who had caused his demotion. I asked why he extended his hand to the person who undermined him, and he looked quizzical. There was no resentment or reproach in his heart. He had forgotten the infraction.

As a postscript to the story, a few months after our protagonist left his post, the president became aware of the lapses and irregularities that the new officer had been doing and was summarily dismissed. The person faded into political oblivion together with his ambition of becoming president of the country.

Be Kind

One of the descriptions of love is kindness. That was my second story. One summer many years ago, young boys who liked to play basketball formed a team that joined inter-village competitions. These were regular guys in their teens, students with parents who could afford to send them to reputable schools. They thought of doing something for another young basketball aficionado they learned about through the Make a Wish Foundation.

Jay R Mingao, an indigent patient in PGH, was a cage fan. He suffered from rheumatic heart disease and had been bed-ridden for several years. His condition was, in fact, terminal. The teener lived inside the Himlayang Palanyag, a Parañaque public cemetery. Because of his affliction, Jay-R had to give up playing the sport, but he dreamed of having a basketball court where the neighborhood kids could play instead of gambling or doing drugs.

Jay-R's wish impressed the boys. They said, "He could've asked for anything for himself, but he chose to wish something for others." His dream became the basketball team's dream, and they began to raise funds to build the basketball court. The boys organized an exhibition game between the Phone Pals and Ginebra San Miguel at the Adidas Sports Kamp, with players from both teams participating in full force. Eric Menk was on the injured list then, but he showed up just the same. Talk 'N' Text team owners Manny Pangilinan and Henry Cojuangco were also present. The game raised about P200,000 and got the construction of the court going.

When the boys learned that Jay-R was a fan of Talk N Text center Asi Taulava, they arranged for Taulava to visit him. It was one of the happiest days of Jay-R's short life to come face-to-face with his idol. Jay-R passed away before the court could be constructed, yet the boys pursued his dream. Under the guidelines of Make-A-Wish Foundation, a person's wish is forfeited once he dies. Yet even without the Foundation's support, the boys raised another P100,000 to finish the project. It took two years before the court was inaugurated at Tramo Dos in Parañaque, but Jay-R's neighbors are now using the cemented court and the roll-on, roll-off goals. Kindness is a generosity of spirit that everyone, bar none, can extend to our fellowmen. I related Jay-R's story to situations and instances not unfamiliar to my audience's realities, encouraging them to continue the good they had already been doing. Kindness can be tiring and inconvenient; however, it blesses not just others but ourselves. Someone said that the best remedy to feeling downcast was to do something kind for someone. Helping another person removes the focus away from our ills, our petty concerns, and sorrows.

I concluded the narrative by referring back to the basketball team who did not ask their parents for help but worked out the financials and logistics, and organized the games and fundraisers among themselves without adult supervision. Their actions came from their hearts. And get this: the name of their team was Faith. So they were known as the Faith Basketball Team.

Fall In Love

The last story was about loving, not romantic love but rather a metaphor to describe a mindset, an outlook, and a position of the heart. It is well articulated by Fr. Pedro Arupe, S.J., the 28th Superior General of the Society of Jesus.

He said, "What you are in love with, what seizes your imagination will affect everything. It will decide what will get you out of bed in the mornings, what you will do with your evenings, how you spend your weekends, what you read, who you know, what breaks your heart, and what amazes you with joy and gratitude. Fall in love, stay in love and it will decide everything."

I told them about a woman named Cecilia. She was married for 21 years before her husband passed away at the age of 48. Cecilia was attractive, smart, a mother of four daughters, and a widow at 43. She was feisty, strong-willed, and straightforward. While intimidating to most, her husband was drawn to her intelligence and free spirit. He was the traditional alpha male challenged by the girl who told him to maintain the palm distance while dancing the foxtrot.

Through the two decades of their married life, they had become very good friends who whistled Rachmaninoff together over the breakfast table. When it rained, they put on their raincoats and wellingtons and went to Binondo to eat at their favorite Chinese restaurant. They listened to symphonies full blast, played poker on weekends with a small group of friends, and went bowling together.

She was the complete wife of a successful professional who entertained his friends and colleagues at home. Cecilia was always more comfortable in casual clothes, preferring jeans and rubber shoes, but she would dress as the occasion merited and was a stunning companion by her husband's side. She did not withhold the support he needed and used her extensive creative skills to prepare unique corporate gifts, decorate his events, and create a comfortable home.

She painted, sewed, designed jewelry, did leather crafts, and made things with her hands. Her husband wanted a full-time homemaker, and she acquiesced. She was in love with her husband. Life changed when he passed away a mere five months after they accidentally discovered he had advanced-stage lung cancer. She prayed numerous rosaries and novenas for him to get well, but God had other plans. For a while, she seemed to have lost her bearings. When her husband was around, she could pursue her numerous creative interests. After he had gone, she had to learn how to withdraw money from the bank, arrange car tune-ups, and manage resources so their children could finish college. And they did. Two became medical doctors, another completed her doctoral degree, and the other became a successful professional. She now has 11 grandchildren and five great-grandchildren.

She jumpstarted her recovery from grief and loss by going back to school. Already a double degree holder, she returned to the university and enrolled in her then-current interest, which was archaeology. Her classes included field trips that had her climbing mountains to digging sites with students more than half her age. She also had more time to indulge in favorite past times like reading, doing Chinese brushwork, painting, and sewing. Cecilia made friends with her pain and learned to move on. She spent time with her preferred company, cooked food for her family when she felt like it, and asked them to treat her to her favorite restaurants when she had a craving.

She opened her heart to new possibilities. She fell in love again and again each new morning, happy to hear her grandchildren's laughter, have conversations with her daughters, and prepare her special corned beef. They went on holidays and played endless scrabble games. Her grandchildren adored her. She had a zest for life that made her feel younger than her years.

Like most of us, she has been in quarantine throughout the pandemic. Her family visit and have conversations behind screen doors; she inside the house, they in the driveway. Her days are filled with music, listening to concertos in full volume. She paints, reads and most of all, she prays. She prays for the country, the sick, for each and every one of her children and grandchildren and now her great grandchildren. She stays in love.

Being in love makes us get up each day grateful to be alive. There is an anticipation of good things to come. When we are in love, everything is new. We are excited to face the day. Fall in love again and again is a perspective. I encouraged the listeners to do more things that make them happy and then share that happiness with others.

Pantries for the Poor

Connecting through the digital world began to suit me, and I was becoming quite comfortable staying home. However, the situation for a majority of our countrymen was becoming increasingly difficult. Businesses, jobs, and livelihoods were severely affected. The economy was spiraling downwards. I was unsure how to reach out to marginalized sectors until I read about Patricia Non's community pantry table. She put foodstuff on a table along the street with a sign that said, "Take what you need. Give what you can." In a couple of days, the news of her initiative went viral.

I thought it was a really good idea, so I posted it in our village viber group, saying it was something we might consider doing. I rarely post and have no personality in our residential community, never having been active or visible throughout the 35 years we have lived here. So I was stunned when a few hours after my online suggestion, someone sent a viber message asking me to organize and lead the community pantry of our village.

I had no experience doing anything like this. I was wary of going out for fear of exposure. It was also intimidating to deal with neighbors I did not know. The group who organized themselves as the core had strong personalities and apparent leadership skills. I was willing to help, but my movements were restricted. I did not leave the house not just to avoid infection but also to protect my husband Chito who had serious comorbidities and our household from exposure. But they insisted I take charge.

I felt inadequate and anxious about dealing with people whose faces I did not know, but God was providing an opportunity to do something for those in need. So, in less than 48 hours, we launched our community pantry. I brought out two tables and set them up outside our village gate, with baskets and boxes where people could give what they could so others would get what they needed.

What happened after was clearly and undisputedly an act of God. Residents started bringing canned goods, vegetables, eggs, and noodles. Passers-by would take from the boxes which were constantly replenished. It was not long before people were queuing outside our village, and we counted as many as 300 to 500 people daily availing of the generosity of our neighbors. When the supplies ran low, one text message to the viber group brought fresh packs of rice and food. Children donated their savings, wrapping coins and putting them in a box for those who needed transport money to go home. People opened their homes as repacking centers and storage for donations.

Just as inspiring were the people who lined up. They not only heeded the call to take what they needed, which essentially would be food for one meal, but they shared. They divided loaves of bread so that there would be more for others.

Most of the time, I went to the site before the volunteers, and the beneficiaries arrived to check that things were in place. Sometimes, I passed by but stayed in the car just to see if anything else was needed. I was being cautious and kept distance, but one day, Chito, who accompanied me, went down and started helping. At that point, trusting in God's protection was the only course. Henceforth, we not only joined the pantry on certain days, we also went to other pantries that Chito's office, the Metrobank Foundation was also helping.

In the past, I felt that prayer and making donations were sufficient. Particularly during the pandemic, it was more prudent to stay home. But, this time, God wanted more from me. He wanted presence not just to help others but also to bless me. Being in close contact with His poor and disadvantaged expanded my heart. God loved them and He wanted me to love them more than I thought I could. Seeing them standing in line for hours, way before the pantry opened, under the sun's heat, sitting on the hot pavement stirred empathy and a desire to do more for them. And that is how I became involved in a political campaign.

LugawOne for the Hungry

The 2022 elections threw me into a crusade for good governance. While I have exercised my right to vote since I was 18 years old, politics was just too messy and contentious to get deeply involved. The need for leaders who would help, especially those on the fringes became part of the equation for loving the poor and loving our country. The last few years seemed like the reign of evil and darkness in our archipelago, but when Leni Robredo threw her hat into the presidential derby, I felt prompted by the spirit to take an active part in working for her victory, she who resonated Kingdom values in her life and actions.

The Irish statesman and philosopher Edmund Burke said that the only thing necessary for the triumph of evil is for good men to do nothing. Once again I had to face fear of infection by going out to campaign. The day of the nationwide motorcade was the day I went out after several months of quarantine, following the COVID infection of our household, Chito and myself included. But it was important to stand up and be counted. Seeing the many volunteers helped to strengthen a resolve to be part of the movement.

We also participated in a LugawOne in Chito's hometown in San Jose City, Nueva Ecija organized by his brother. We served the rice porridge and when the people sat down to eat, we talked to them about Leni, her track record, integrity, and competence. We went to three of the five LugawOnes in the vicinity organized by other groups and talked to people in the marketplace and the farms.

When the recent typhoon affected many of our countrymen, Leni called on the volunteers to suspend campaigning and help in the relief work. This was really pushing the envelope for me, to go out by myself and be with complete strangers. I had no idea if they were vaccinated or carriers, but putting a lid on my anxieties, I went to the Katipunan Center and worked with people from different walks of life, most simple folks wanting to help out.

It has been impressed upon us by Leni's campaign leaders that it was going to be an uphill fight but could still be won through a one-to-one engagement. First, we needed to meet the people, not just to tell them about Leni and the good she has done and can do, but to do truth-telling to dispel historical revisionism, lies, and falsehood that have been circulated over the last few years.

Once again, I was tasked to lead our residential community in the campaign efforts. We are part of District Three in Quezon City, and in coordination with other gated villages, we campaigned in barangays assigned to us. Wearing a mask and distributing comic books as information aides, I talked to wait staff, grab drivers, street cleaners, construction workers, basureros and dyario-bote guys, and people I asked God to lead me to. We supported house-to-house visits in marginalized communities especially where the survey frontrunner is strong. Sometimes people listened, and a few times I was dismissed but the experience of rejection was no longer daunting. When I could not go out, I gave money to Jun, the taho vendor who came to the neighborhood. I asked him to serve taho to people on the street and tell them about Leni.

The political exercise was way out of my comfort zone. Still, Leni showed that empowered women leaders step beyond boundaries in response to a sense of purpose, a mission benefitting the greater good. The outcome of the polls was heartbreaking, but it does not take an electoral victory to determine a true leader. Without skipping a beat, she rallied her discouraged and despondent supporters to pursue the radical love she had bannered throughout her campaign. She invited those who had organized community pantries, lugawans, and information drives countering falsehoods to continue the good they had begun throughout the seven months leading up to the elections. A foundation she was launching would provide a platform where people could channel their energies to help others in the spirit of volunteerism that had propelled what has now been called a movement, a crusade.

Night Ride

The train ride through pain
will slow down for a stop on
the platform of hope

Despite the grief over Leni's loss, and the missed opportunity for our country to be led by such a competent, honorable, and admirable leader, I am personally inspired to follow her lead. There was a lot of self-discovery brought about by the disruption of an election and the pandemic. The meaningful life I had aspired to live expanded to embrace new challenges that can be unsettling.

I still deal with different apprehensions of being inadequate, not doing enough, and, yes, of getting infected. Still, this inner prompting calls me to pursue more than my safety and comfort. It is not about being brave or fearless because I am neither of those on my own. Instead, my experience of overcoming challenges and fears has been a continuing lesson of self-mastery, guided by the hand of God. The story will continue to unfold, and hopefully, when the final sentence is dotted with a period, I will realize all my potential and achieve genuine authenticity.

ANNABELLE MANALO-MORGAN, PH.D.

Co-Founder, Masaya Medical, Inc.
Lead Scientific Advisor, Nasdaq company Flora Growth Corporation
GLOBAL FWN100™ 2021

Macario's Oil

In September of 2021, I received a 'Most Influential Filipina Woman in the World' award for my global innovator and thought leadership. I finally acknowledged my heritage's importance or genetic gift when I was selected. Before that, I never took the time to uplift myself based on ethnicity or appreciate the differentiating values of being a Filipina. Everything I have been eager to portray about myself results from my hard work, basketball skills, and science degrees. Up to this point, I never fully embraced the very thing I inherited, my heritage.

I grew up in Saskatchewan, Canada, to two first-generation Filipino parents with my big brother, Kuya, Russell. There were not many Filipinos in this part of Canada, so at a young age, we had to learn that people are sometimes treated differently based on the color of their skin. We were instant extended family to the few other Filipino families within the community and celebrated birthdays, weddings, etc., every week. It was a never-ending karaoke competition and lumpia party. I was definitely a tomboy that played almost every sport that could keep me busy. Eventually, I left Saskatchewan to seek the opportunity to play college basketball in the United States. Although I was a worthy college athlete, the unexpected turns of life led me to a Ph.D. candidacy in Neuroscience and then eventually Cell and Development Biology. Today, I am a mother of a daughter and four boys, and I travel globally, leading clinical trials and educating on a variety of diseased conditions. A google search would lead you to numerous articles on my work in the cannabis industry and the story on how that 'career choice' was also an unplanned necessity that embraces who I am today. And so, I would say that I have been incredibly obedient to adapting to change, and as a result, I am certainly shaping out to become who God has intended me to be.

Recently, I opened my eyes and realized that my upbringing, the foundation my parents had set, and the cultural experiences I had shaped the successes I have today. My athleticism and love for basketball, my God-gifted intelligence, and my unparalleled drive and motivation have been genetically instilled in me and are a product of my roots. In life, we move so quickly and are somewhat distracted by our motivations that we never pause to have gratitude for the simplest things we already possess. A sense of humility comes from growing up amongst extended family from the Philippines, who my mom had sponsored, and who sought a more stable life. For my mom, success is more than about herself; the satisfaction in uplifting others is a feeling that no money can provide. But at a young age, I ignored how my family and my Philippine culture have influenced my being who I am.

My journey to success has not come easy; there was no red carpet in front of me. I experienced tragedy, pain, and disappointment but always focused on the solutions. I chose to be positive. And when I wrote my first book, entitled *Mighty Flower*, the message that I was trying to portray was that miracles and the ability to overcome are genuine. I was lucky enough to have Filipino parents that indirectly embedded those traits and values in me. The following excerpt from my book is an introduction to me and a direct intention to motivate, empower, and influence those who read it.

Presenting the *Mighty Flower*: Power and Potential

The *Mighty Flower* book is for the student of life. One who shapes their dreams around a personal drive and a belief that they can make a positive impact and effect change. One wants to lead based on truth and a lack of fear in their mind. The *Mighty Flower* book is a story of how, if you are open to the dynamic shifts of life, you will learn vital lessons, discover the unimaginable, make an impact, and witness miracles. The *Mighty Flower* book is a story about all that is wrong with our medical industry—and all that is right. The *Mighty Flower* book summarizes where the cannabis industry was in 2020, how it came to be here, where it's headed, and how—along with modern medicine—we are in a novel place in time. Some may even call it a revolutionary place in time.

I have balanced multiple roles in life thus far—a basketball player, a mother, a wife, a scientist, an entrepreneur, a healer. At my core, however, I see myself as a revolutionary. That is not what I necessarily aspired to be as a young eleven-year-old girl growing up in Saskatchewan, Canada. Still, my experiences shaped me in ways I could never have expected—and instead of defining myself against them, I learned from them and grew strong from being able to hold all the disparate pieces of my own life's puzzle in my heart. As Walt Whitman once said, we are large—and we contain multitudes. As long as we believe in our own capabilities, we will find what life's guiding us toward. If we zoom out the lens, we can find a fluency in all the chapters of our lives—and we can begin to see the thread of purpose that binds those chapters together. Being a revolutionary simply requires recognizing that thread and putting it to good use in changing the world.

Mighty Flower defines me. It defines the life circumstances that have shaped me and helped me grow, and it defines my strength not just to overcome the challenges but to incorporate them into my very substance—and to bloom. At the same time, *Mighty Flower* defines the cannabis plant that this book is about—a plant with so much power and potential. It's time to let cannabis bloom into everything it could be.

Being a Mom. Scientist. Author.

Our bodies are amazing feats of nature. The way a single cell, or a cluster of cells, can impact other biological processes can seem random, but in fact, there's often a dynamic system at play. One element impacts another. Problems can be isolated, and yet that isolation occurs in a larger context. Processes play off one another. There's a method to the madness.

Studying problems at the microscopic level is crucial to my work as a cellular biologist and my field of disease research. And yet, so much of what we could discover about our biology—and our humanity—is only visible once we zoom out the lens.

Nothing exists in a vacuum. While uniformity and regularity may be determined by the laws of physics and biology, the fate of specific human bodies and minds are far from predictable. The reason is simple: those bodies are sentient. They can think and communicate. They can understand language. And they exist within time and space, within cultures, civilizations, and eras.

Humans have studied their inner bodily workings for millennia. The scientific revolution, the advent of the scientific method, and the invention of the microscope are all milestones that have taken place within the last five hundred years. The history of modern medicine began just two centuries ago. With each new era of discovery, our collective knowledge and understanding of how the world works shifts.

Old ideas are replaced and updated and in many cases, looked upon by new generations with a sense of embarrassment or with one eyebrow raised. Ancient Egyptians believed disease was caused by supernatural powers and that the heart played an outsize role in bodily ailments (Barr, 2014). Modern science proves much of Egyptian thought on diagnosis incorrect. And yet as early as 1500 BCE, this civilization had developed some healing remedies that were not based on magic but the natural composition of substances within their reach. They used honey as a natural antiseptic, they treated burns with aloe (Abuelsoud, 2010) and they were already using opioids as painkillers and cannabis as a narcotic. Ancient Egyptian physicians described depression and dementia as physical as well as mental illnesses born of the heart (Khalil and Richa, 2014). Entire generations of physicians passed before the scientific community acknowledged what the Egyptians clearly understood: that the mind-body connection is real and that mental afflictions nearly always have a biological component. That component is not the heart but the brain—and yet does this misidentification on the part of Egyptian physicians render their entire body of thought irrelevant? After all, we are internally interconnected. We don't always understand where the root of the problem comes from.

It's human nature to focus on what's in front of us. But just as a cell exists within a body that exists within a time and place, so, too, does our current scientific thought and approach.

Civilizations across the globe have relied on natural remedies to biological problems for thousands of years. And those remedies were so effective, entire schools of thought were built around them, from Chinese medicine to Ayurvedic medicine and many cultures of healing in between. The scientific community now has tools available to us that the earliest practitioners of those ancient traditions could have never dreamed of. I know firsthand what our labs are capable of creating. And yet our science practice has so far focused only on the new and has neglected to learn from those traditions, let alone integrate them into a holistic school of thought.

The prescription medication we can create in the lab has changed the world. But what are we missing? What's behind the curtain—and why aren't we collectively jumping at the chance to peek inside?

Macario: My Blessing

In 2016, I gave birth to a beautiful baby boy. My husband, Gramps Morgan, and I named him Macario. The name is the Filipino word for "blessing," and we knew that's what he would be to us. We loved him from the second we saw him. It's a special thing to be joined together by parenthood—and when I look back on the events that occurred after those first forty-eight hours, I feel blessed beyond belief that it was Gramps who was by my side the whole time. It was Gramps who first saw Macario, just two days old, foaming at the mouth, seizing, and twitching.

We rushed Macario to the hospital and were told our son had suffered from both a stroke and uncontrollable seizures. Over the next few weeks, those seizures would begin to occur up to two hundred times a day. These weeks were made up of moments that every parent dreads. Times like this are supposed to be relegated to the world of nightmares, but we couldn't wake ourselves up. Every drug regimen was attempted before we realized that the seizures would not stop and could soon take over the rest of his brain.

We were left with allowing the neurosurgery team to perform a significant brain surgery that resected 38 percent of Macario's brain. We understood that Macario would likely never speak normally, would have limited movement, and was looking at a future defined by challenges none of us could fully predict. He was on so many different prescriptions that he was nearly unresponsive. Strangers would tell me he behaved so well, like an angel. They didn't realize the reason he wasn't crying and fussing was because he was continually under the fog of medication.

After his surgery, I did what any mother would do—I desperately searched for any possible remedy or cure or aid that could help in Macario's recovery and give him a better chance at life. And because I am a scientist by trade, I translated my desperation into invention. So many innovations are born from a time of need, underpinned by similar desperation or life-or-death drive, and what I did in the lab for my son is no different.

In the summer of 2016, I developed the purest and most consistent form of cannabidiol, or CBD oil, that my scientific expertise would allow, with no other cannabinoids or fillers. I took my son off his heavy drug regimen and began administering my creation directly through the feeding tube protruding from his little belly.

Three years later, as I write this in 2019, Macario is now playing catch-up to his peers in preschool—and he's very nearly there. He can walk and run, he can giggle and play, and he can speak in the broken, fluttery English that defines toddlerhood. The *Mighty Flower* book, and my story, begins with the blessing of Macario. The book tells the story of what bridged the huge gap between what our current scientific moment would predict for my son and what I knew was possible.

Becoming Me

As a cellular biologist, my work is both systematic and spontaneous. Through my years of research and hours in the lab, I have come to understand that the road you take to reach a particular discovery or conclusion is long and winding. Certain inputs can completely change the outcome of an experiment. Being open to the multiplicity of possibilities is crucial to any good scientist's work. Life can work similarly—what seems like a straight path toward the future can easily twist, turn, and sometimes throw you completely off the trail. And like a good scientist, the best way to live with unpredictability is to embrace it simply.

I was born in Saskatchewan, Canada, a province where some of North America's first inhabitants settled and where many of those first peoples' descendants still live. Our family was small and close, just me and my big brother Russell. Russell beat me up and teased me for having two buck teeth. My nickname was Rabbit. Like most big brothers, he was a pain in my butt, but looking back, Russell taught me always to stand my ground and that being a crybaby would not get you very far. So we grew up in small-town Saskatchewan, but in many ways, the origin of my story began halfway across the globe.

My mother was born in one of the poorest regions of the Philippines. But she was born with a gift that would change her world. She had a beautiful singing voice, and as she grew older, she would go into town to compete in singing competitions, winning a little bit of money but making an even bigger impression. She did this for years until one day, her big break finally came: she was given the opportunity to leave the Philippines to sing for a band in Europe. After months of touring, she landed in Canada, where she met my father, a fellow Filipino who had already made his home there. They married soon after and had two children: my brother, five years older, and me.

My mom never took her good fortune for granted. She made it her mission to provide for others the same opportunities she was blessed with. Under her guidance, our family sponsored over forty relatives from the Philippines and helped them settle in Canada. Russell and I watched as my mother nurtured these relatives and their children, building up their confidence and helping the kids get a great education. She was like a warrior for them—but she was a pioneer to me. The time, effort, and energy it took to create a new path for so many of her loved ones must have been incredible. But instead of being weighed down by her responsibilities, she thrived. Watching what she could do when she put her mind to it—and how much she could do—was one of the greatest gifts of my childhood.

Even before my mother, my grandmother *Lola* Rose was another pioneer woman I admire. *Lola* had no limits. God rest her soul. She was jumping on the trampoline with me in her sixties. She was the only one on the dance floor at our family parties. As a young girl, that was normal to me. But as I grew up, I started to see how unique my *Lola* was. The memory of *Lola* remains dear to my heart, and I gave my first daughter, my only daughter, her name: Aaliyah Rose. I remember *Lola* telling stories about how poor my family in the Philippines was and how she raised thirteen children alone. My grandfather died young, but you would never know based on *Lola's* positive demeanor. My *Lola* never complained or spoke of her pain. She only said how she found a way forward with multiple jobs and no education. And I suppose as generations pass, I can be happy that my *Lola* would be proud of me. In the same way, she saw something special in my mom, the second oldest of all her children; she saw something special in me.

Before I was born, *Lola* came to Canada in a Saskatchewan snowstorm to be by my mom's side. My mom was the first of her family to leave the Philippines, not to be held down by circumstances but to achieve something great and provide a platform for the rest of the family. That platform has become a foundation for me, as I am the first in my family to receive a Ph.D. (Holding on to what inspires me—Aaliyah was a singer I aspired to be like. At a young age, I did not know if I wanted to sing, play sports, bake, or become an astronaut. My mind was free. And it seems as we grow older and move further in time generationally, we lose the ability to imagine and dream. I know my daughter, Aaliyah, will achieve something great, as my grandmother's heart lives in her as well. I am so grateful to be able to identify with it and guide her at such a young age.

My mother was not the only one who refused to limit herself based on what others thought was possible or impossible. My father, an engineer, taught me early on that every opportunity I could dream of was within my reach. Unlike so many parents of his generation, he did not have a prescriptive outlook on my future. He did not try to harness my potential or push it toward any premeditated path. Instead, like a mad scientist, he did everything he could to foster the potential itself, and as I matured, he watched it grow outward in every direction. I like to say that my dad is the reason I am who I am today. Between observing my mom and questioning my dad's love, I would rather not choose who impacted me more. Honestly, it was the perfect formula for Dr. Annabelle.

My dad was the type of parent who never gave me praise. He was at every sporting event, tutored me in every subject, forced me to play the piano, and drove me everywhere I needed to go. All while providing for our family. You see, my dad is a structural and civil engineer. He grew up believing in perfection. And it always seemed like he never demanded it from my brother, Russell. But he did from me. I remember getting praise from my peers for hitting the winning jump shot or being the only one to get over 90 percent on an exam. So often, I would feel like I was on top of the world! And Dad would come shut that down. Why did you throw the ball away on that play? Why did you miss a free throw? How could you get all those questions right on your math test but get that one wrong? He always brought me back down to earth—and quick! And on my wedding day, just shy of a year of the release of this book, I realized during my father-daughter dance that the way Dad loved me, in a way that needed no words, was exactly what I needed to become me. It made me pay attention to detail. It made me take my time. It made me realize that I could always be better despite what everybody else was saying or portraying me. Dad made me expect more from myself. And to this day, I always do.

A Basketball Dream, Come and Gone

Growth is not necessarily linear, and potential can be an unpredictable, dynamic force capable of bursting forth in unexpected ways. It seems my father knew something essential about who I was becoming: he knew that only by following my dreams and trusting my intuition would I understand my capacities and learn to thrive. He did not want me to strive for perfection. Instead, he encouraged me to trust in the power of my dreams and my intuition; he taught me to strive for innovation and invention, something even greater than what my imagination could dream up. He pushed me to think outside the box. And my first big dream was not just out of the box. It was out of the country.

I began my path with the singular dream of becoming a professional basketball player. As a kid in Saskatchewan, this was a big and somewhat unimaginable idea. Basketball scouts never came to our schools. It just was not something that happened. Thanks to the twists and turns, however, I ended up graduating early and getting recruited to play ball for Dillard University in New Orleans.

However, dreams and interests change. Sometimes, the change occurs simply as a by-product of growing up and being open and adaptive to the lessons life is trying to teach. Other times, the course is changed because of an occurrence so significant and immediate that all you thought was stable gets swept out from underneath you—and from that place, all you can do is rebuild. What's rebuilt never looks quite like what's being replaced. In 2005, Hurricane Katrina hit New Orleans and shook our world. I transferred to Eastern Kentucky University my senior year, but my dream of playing basketball got lost somewhere in the wreckage. I focused my energy on graduating, and when I was offered a chance to play basketball overseas, I turned down the opportunity to focus on a new potential that was growing in my life: a journey with my first boyfriend who had gotten drafted to the NFL. And soon, I was pregnant with my first child—Aaliyah.

Pursuing Science: Another Path Forward

In the months during my pregnancy, I thought of my own mother. Kids learn from what they see, and I grew up with a mother who could do everything. Her boundless energy and passion made me feel like anything was possible just as much as my father's belief in me did. Looking up to a strong, capable mother was a core part of my childhood experience, and I wanted to give that inspiration to my children. So, with a degree in biology and chemistry and an ongoing interest in science and medicine, I pursued an MD at Georgetown University.

Another unpredictable event changed the course of my dream of becoming a doctor—my father was diagnosed with stage IV cancer of the esophagus. As you'll read in the pages of my book, every doctor said my father would die. When he didn't, I wanted to know why—not necessarily why he, specifically, survived against all odds, but what was happening inside his body that ensured his survival, rather than his untimely death that every professional predicted.

This averted tragedy brought me closer to my higher calling. I didn't want to simply administer diagnoses to patients. I wanted to understand at a cellular level why these diagnoses occurred, what underlying mechanisms played a role, and what unexplored solutions there may be that target those mechanisms and change their expression. In my father's path to recovery, I saw the adaptive power of the body, the psychological power of belief, and the healing power of nature. My new dream was nothing short of understanding how all of these forces worked together.

Life imitates art—but it also imitates science, if we look close enough. My life led me to plenty of unpredictable outcomes. Yet when I reflect on my own story, it seems like every twist and turn was preparing me for Macario and what I was able to develop in the lab to save him, and many others since. In many ways, motherhood set my course—it showed me what was possible as a child, and I pursued higher education because I wanted to give that same inspiration to my daughter. And it was motherhood that revealed my life's true purpose. As a mother, I was willing to do anything to help my baby live and thrive. What I discovered in that desperation is what led me to write this book.

Cannabis: Looking Beyond the Limits of What's Possible

Despite an inundation of the substance in the market, most individuals still don't understand what cannabis, and in particular, cannabidiol or other molecules of the plant, can do for our health—and that includes individuals in the scientific community of which I'm a part. The industry is booming and there's money flowing in seemingly every direction outside of the lab itself. We understand the potency of cannabis as a recreational drug—but we are only on the cusp of truly understanding its medicinal powers. It's time to cast off the taboo of weed culture and approach this plant with the level of scientific rigor it deserves.

Through my work developing pure cannabidiol oil in the lab during my son's time of need in 2016, I saw the huge medical potential of cannabis firsthand. And in my work since, discussing my cannabis discoveries to dozens of in-need individuals and groups around the world, I've also seen firsthand that there are countless sick individuals who don't know what they should try. This book is an attempt to get this conversation started—to share my scientific understandings and to give individuals a clearer understanding of the limitations of our scientific moment, but also the bright future ahead.

In the book *Mighty Flower*, you will find Macario's story, and how his challenges brought me to develop the best possible cannabis solution for my son that could not be found on the market. You will learn how it helped him. But you will also find an in-depth exploration of cannabis, both as a drug and as a taboo, and a critical analysis of what the future holds for this powerful substance, both in our country and around the globe. Cannabis is just a small part of the bigger picture I hope that as the story unfolds in the *Mighty Flower*, you begin to see the untapped potential in the world of science, but also in our own bodies and minds. We are capable of great things: incredible growth, recovery, and innovation. Let the *Mighty Flower* book be a testament to what we have the power to achieve once we look beyond the limits of what's possible.

As I have indicated earlier, I hope to inspire that young Filipina reader specifically. Leadership comes from an embodiment of experiences that no journey is a straight line. I am always asked how I balance five kids, my traveling schedule, and my demanding career. My mindset and faith, which I now know come from my ancestral roots, are my focus and have carried me through some impossible times. A tragedy is simply a shift, a detour, and most importantly, a learning experience. As you shape your story, do not become embedded in that trauma but rise above it and be grateful for the lessons it teaches you. Add it to the list of what you have overcome and understand that within our society, being a woman and a Filipina woman at that, you have every reason to hold your head high because you are a product of a people that are courageous and who sacrifice for others. Our greatest gift is our mindset and the courage to do what is in our hearts to do. Becoming a leader is possible once you are not afraid to face challenges repeatedly. Ultimately, your ability to be an authentic leader will depend on diverse experiences that help you relate to people from different walks of life. I challenge you to have faith, live confidently about the foundation of being a woman of Filipina descent, and inspire others who will look up to you. Others will look up to you for inspiration. For the work, you have done to represent our being Filipina women. Being Filipina women leaders.

CORA DELA CRUZ-TORRES

President, Trade Alliances Canada Inc.
GLOBAL FWN100™ 2017

Leading My Life

"*A truly extraordinary individual who knows well how to embrace technology, share her knowledge and experience, focus her energy, manage her time and effort despite all the demands of life (as an individual, being a parent, a spouse and a caregiver, a friend, and a leader), she is a positive influence on the lives of many, as you will soon find out. With your unceasing interface with the people around you, you are doing an excellent job and providing great service and support to many. We salute you!*" (Mangahas, *Philippine Times Magazine* 2008)

Documenting one's life journey is a daunting task. I have to go back five decades to capture the moments that summarize the leadership skills I learned throughout those years. I think my leadership skills would benefit my family, children, and grandchildren, the Filipina worldwide who can recognize, relate to, and be inspired. Writing my leadership memoir by focusing on my personal to public life gave me self-revelation and understanding of the many things I have seen in my early life. Reflecting on these experiences gave me a strong desire to do and achieve something more significant, inspiring me to work harder with great determination.

HUMBLE BEGINNINGS

Early childhood memories of growing up in the Philippines come naturally to me. I was born in 1950, second to the eldest of 10 children in barrio Aguso, Tarlac. I am not ashamed to say I was born poor. Life was very hard. My parents tried to ensure we had food, shelter, and clothing. They worked extremely hard to support and sustain us. I remember when they barely made both ends meet. My mother was a vendor, engaged in a small-scale make-and-sell business, and involved all children in working. My mother's perfect *"burong isda"* [fermented rice with fish] was one example. As a young girl, I helped sell this in the barrio while my mother was trading in the market. To further supplement the daily sustenance, my mother made *"kakanin"* food [native delicacies] to sell.

Self-Reliance. Being Responsible

At the same time, while I helped look after my younger siblings, I felt responsible for ensuring they were safe while my parents were away. On a few occasions, while waiting for my parents to come home from work, I had to apportion the food for dinner because the limited food served was all that we could have. I was "empowered" and given the responsibility to ensure my siblings got supper on time early enough, as we did not have electricity yet in the barrio then. I remember I had to improvise with what I was to serve.

I thought a cup of rice would feed a few but a cup of rice, when cooked as *"lugaw"* [rice porridge or congee], goes a very long way. If these many children were vying for food during mealtime, you had to be quick; otherwise, you would not get the best part of the food or none at all. So no one arrives late at the dinner table. My parents instilled the value of work while we were children. At a young age, I took pride and felt blessed as I had the opportunity to help and support. I learned what empowerment could do. I learned to become self-reliant.

Shaping My Values

I grew up with parents who fostered a sense of worth and a strong work ethic. As I have gotten older, I have learned to trust my instincts, be more assertive, and stay true to myself. Self-worth comes from within.

I just turned 15 when I graduated high school. I learned typing from the old manual typewriter my father borrowed from his boss. He was a carpenter in the Bureau of Public Works. The routine was simple. He borrows the old manual typewriter from his boss' office, takes it home every Friday, and returns it Monday mornings.

Determined to help my parents and siblings, I lied about my age when I applied for a job. Thankfully, I got a full-time day job at a farmers' cooperative. This enabled me to help my parents, especially in sending my siblings to school. My brother studied at the National University in Manila, while my sister attended the University of Santo Tomas. I put myself, as well, into a local college for a night course in Secretarial Science, followed by a path leading to a Bachelor's degree in Business Administration.

When I was 16, while working at this farmers' cooperative, an old woman, a *"manghuhula"* [palm reader], came by the office and started doing palm readings. The girls, my office co-workers, lined up to have their readings done. To my surprise, she read my palm, and said I would be going abroad! I did not pursue the conversation, but remained skeptical and started giggling. I could not believe what she said. As young as I was then, I never left our small town. I have never taken a big bus to go to a bigger city. I never traveled to Manila, let alone go abroad. Four years later, I immigrated to Canada.

Meeting the Challenge

When I was 19, three work associates approached me to visit the Canadian Embassy in Manila. The Embassy was accepting applications from those willing to go to Canada. All three did not pass the initial qualifying exams required for secretarial positions. They asked me if I could do the test for them. In return, each would pay me one thousand pesos. That was a lot of money then, and I thought I could buy about five bags (about 25 kilos each bag) of rice for my family. So I asked permission from my father to go with my co-workers. My father did not allow me to do that. Instead, he encouraged me to go to the Embassy with my (late) brother and do the tests myself.

It was a four-hour trip by bus to go to Manila from Tarlac. As I gazed at the crisp, beautiful sunrise, I daydreamed. I began to entertain the idea of traveling and living abroad. I suddenly yearned to see foreign lands, work abroad, and earn lots of money so I could improve our way of life. I had dreamt big dreams and these dreams were my vision of the future. Although I had no concept of doing all these, I was determined to pass the test and whatever requirements. I knew things would follow.

Finding the Resources: a Door Closes, a Door Opens

Within a few months, my immigrant visa was approved. I left Canada on the day my visa would expire. I generally do not wait to do things until the last minute, but there was a compelling reason for this. No funds were available to pay for my passport, plane tickets, and incidentals. My parents did not have the resources to support my journey. They tried to apply for bank loans and sought the help of family members and friends but were all rejected. Then my father and I approached his boss, a loan shark, who asked my father why he was letting me go abroad. He further said, *"Ang ganda ganda ng anak mo, baka mag pok-pok lang siya duon"* [*"Your daughter is beautiful; who knows, she may become a 'prostitute' there"*]. I could not quell the unsettled feeling in my heart that day. I saw the sadness in my father's eyes. I knew then how poor my parents were.

I was challenged and determined to find the resources I needed. But how? I only know one thing for sure: I know God provides. He was watching. He was listening. An acquaintance of my father approached him and asked if I could be a godmother to their newborn girl. While I was talking with the family, they found out that I was going to Canada, but we were still looking for resources. This family then secured a loan from the bank, making their piece of farmland as collateral, and lent us the proceeds payable whenever I got settled in Canada.

OFF TO CANADA ALONE: FINDING MY STRENGTH

At this point, I was determined to go, primarily to seek greener pastures and help my family. I started to dream. I imagine doing something, going someplace, becoming someone, and making a difference. I had always envisioned myself as a successful career woman in a corporate setting, leading a team within a company. Without that aspiration, nothing can happen. Yet how far do I get? Do I allow setbacks to slow or stop me? Do I lose confidence? The fear of the unknown made me question my plan to go to Canada. I knew that more Filipinos were going to America than to Canada. My friends discouraged me. They told me that I would be living with the brutal, harsh winter cold weather with salmons and sardines to pack as my form of employment in Canada. But I knew the possibilities were endless, and opportunities were boundless. I knew then this was one way, or I thought the only way, to fulfill my dream.

The scene at the airport was confusing and a bit terrifying for me. I will never forget the scenery, the people, and my family. I knew it was tough for my parents to let me go, especially my mother, though she did not show it. My father was more emotional. He was crying. My boyfriend, who would later follow me after a year and eventually became my husband, was also there. Finally, it was time to say goodbye. My parents looked at me, hugged and kissed me, and my eyes swelled with tears. Before I turned and walked away, I remembered my father's words, *"don't be scared, you're special, don't be just ordinary when you can be extraordinary!"* These words later became, until today, my daily advocate for spiritual guidance and emotional inspiration.

I was petrified when I boarded the plane. I thought that was the end of my life while holding my knees trembling because the jumbo jet plane was accelerating. I thought of my entire family. Would I ever see them again? My flight had a stop-over in Tokyo. The plane was late for an hour, and we landed in Chicago too late to connect to my scheduled flight for Toronto. There were a few of us who missed that connecting flight. Little did I know my visa to enter Canada had already expired that night. I was issued a "transient" label to stick on my coat. An Immigration Officer escorted us into a hotel. I never slept. All I did was cry, and pray, my rosary with me. A shuttle picked us up in a few hours and put us on a plane first thing in the morning. Then I heard, *"Welcome to Toronto."*

Adapting to Canadian Standards

When I first arrived, I was excited about living in Canada and the adventures ahead. For the first two weeks, I was very excited. Everything was new. Then I found out that it was not easy to find a place to stay, let alone find a job while fighting my jetlag.

As I reflect on my life in the old country and what this new life in this new country meant to me, I cannot help but rewind to all the beautiful memories that bound us as a family. I remember the days when my brothers and sisters formed closer relationships over performance on assigned household chores. I bonded with my sisters over countless tasks, with me being the ring leader.

I began counting those amazing pieces of our lives, and at the end of the day, before we slept, we gathered around over songs with my Dad on the guitar and my Mom singing some Ilocano songs. Despite life's hardship, one word to describe these evenings was the spirit of joy, enthusiasm, high spirits, and happiness.

The education and skills I gained in my home country were not of the same value. They said I lack "Canadian experience." Speaking and hearing English all day made me feel tired. Even though I learned English, I must concentrate on understanding the Canadian accent. Concentrating can be tiring, as I have to repeat myself several times for others to understand my accent.

It took some time to become comfortable in a new culture. I quickly found out that life was still challenging, even if you were happy here. There was a conflict between the values of my original culture and the Canadian one. At times, I wondered where I belonged. I found out this was normal. Some people seem to adapt quickly, but others take a long time to settle into a new place. Culture shock may fade quickly, or return repeatedly, but it does not last forever.

One may assume that I know just about everything there is to know about Canada and Canadians. The opposite is true. I was trying to convince myself I knew everything. But it seemed the more I felt I knew, the less I knew. It was hard to explain. But so are a lot of things in life.

Rising as a Public Servant

I was shy, unassertive, and soft-spoken when I entered the Ontario Public Service in early 1972. After passing the required tests at the Civil Service Commission for the position I applied for, the Commission asked me what level I wanted to proceed with and what compensation rate I wanted to start. I thought those were odd questions, and I shyly responded that I would accept any position and start at the bottom with the lowest salary rate. At this point, the examiner told me I could start at the top level. I was too humble, too naïve. Worrying that my "English" was broken and having a strong accent, I insisted that I start from the bottom. All I wanted was for the Civil Service to take me in. I started working as a typist, progressively and quickly moving to the highest level of a secretary; to a Senior Team Leader in a secretarial pool of 25 staff; to a Senior Manager with a staff of 55; to Budget, Planning, and Resources Officer with an annual budget of $20 million; to Ministry Systems Coordinator and Technology Officer; to Provincial Regulator for The Real Estate and Business Brokers Act; to Project Director for the Transition Team of the Province's Travel Industry Act; to the Provincial Regulator for The Cemeteries Act.

Hard as it was, I welcomed the challenges that made me stronger. You gain more trust and confidence when you focus on fulfilling your tasks. I joined new projects, memberships in new committees and task forces, secondments, and assignments. For example, I became a member of the Ontario Securities Commission Review Task Force for the review of the administrative and legislative roles of the Commission; the drafting and introduction of the Ontario Freedom of Information and Privacy Act, the re-development of a major and significant commercial registration, inquiry, data and tracking system accommodating seven pieces of Ontario consumer protection legislation, among others. I believe the secret to success is to multi-task and compartmentalize. I took great pride as a public servant, working honorably in discharging my duties and responsibilities conscientiously with dedication and commitment.

During my early years in the service, I found that whatever education, training, or experience we had in the Philippines was a rude awakening. We still needed to undergo training starting at the beginner's level. So during those years, while working with the government and raising a family, I enrolled at York University as a mature student. I went to school at night and worked during the day to obtain a Bachelor's Degree in Administrative Studies.

As I moved along within those positions, I experienced subtle and overt discrimination, especially when I became the first colored woman and Asian to become the Registrar for the Province of Ontario Real Estate and Business Brokers Act. Attending a national conference in the Province of Alberta, I was introduced as a "Mr." as I was supposedly an older, Caucasian white male. Naturally, I was offended by the introduction; however, I did not show it. But I graciously responded quickly by saying, *"Thank you for the introduction, but fortunately, I am a woman, and my name is Ms. Cora dela Cruz. And I proudly represent the Province of Ontario."*

I also became the first colored woman and Asian to become the Regulator for The Cemeteries Act for the Province of Ontario, which includes aboriginal and native sites. When I represented Canada at the North American Cemeteries Regulators Association Convention in the U.S., I was nominated and won a seat on the Executive Committee of this North American Association, representing the Province of Ontario and Canada. It was a prestigious position with demanding responsibilities. When I returned from the Conference, some media critics questioned how I got into the role.

Being a Businesswoman and Entrepreneur

One of my significant influences as a young entrepreneur was my hardworking, inspiring, and incredible late mother. In my early years and while growing up, I saw the spirit of entrepreneurship and mindset in my mother, creating small and start-up businesses—primarily motivated by her desire to sustain our family.

In the early 1970s, I took advantage of Canada's family reunification and sponsorship programs and sponsored immediate and extended family members. Although these were great opportunities provided by the government, sponsors bear some responsibilities in making sure the sponsored relatives do not create a burden on the community. Inspired by my mother's entrepreneurial spirit, I decided to open a family business in the travel industry, to provide regular travel and tour services to the Filipino and Canadian communities.

Over time, the travel company's purpose became so empowering that it became a training ground for new and extended family members to give them first-hand "Canadian work experience." It gave them an opportunity to hone their English skills, introduce them to the community to reduce "culture shock," and gain confidence in speaking to customers and the general public over the phone. It ensured employment for my new immigrant families and extended family members.

I established the Delamar School of Business, a private and vocational school registered and approved by the Private Career Colleges Act of the Ontario Ministry of Education. Delamar School provided students with hands-on skills and knowledge that prepared them to enter the job market and get employed. I set up the school for everyone, specifically for the underserved and those that may have been left behind in our communities. I set it up essentially with the new *"kababayan"* [fellow Filipino] in mind, empowering them, upskilling, and increasing their confidence when they begin their careers.

I also set up the Phil-Can Remittance Center in Canada, an accredited tie-up partner of the government-owned Development Bank of the Philippines. I decided to partner with DBP mainly to offer the opportunity and make the community aware of the many financial assistance and livelihood programs offered by DBP for the Overseas Filipino Workers (OFW), their families, and beneficiaries.

Starting a business is by itself an accomplishment. My rewards of going into business or entrepreneurship were many. I never realized I was developing my business and community leadership skills. I never dreamed of owning my business. In doing all these, I employed workers and paid them income, improving their lives. As an entrepreneur who succeeds and grows, I also helped suppliers, sub-contractors, dealers, and other businesses connected to thrive and grow too.

Being a Community Leader and Volunteer

When asked to become a member of any association, I usually ask myself, *"What am I supposed to learn from being a member that will help me serve better? If I become a member, how do I get actively involved?"* These two questions rattle my being. The first thing I would like to know was a common purpose. Could it be just networking, could it be just a group of people with a cooperative spirit or an association with voluntary membership? I searched for a particular purpose that would enable me to contribute to the shared value and meaning of the association.

A quote from *Philippine Times Canada*, September 15, 2008, R. Mangahas wrote of Cora, *"...if she has touched you through her community volunteerism or services, you should be able to identify her instantly. And to certain individuals, groups, and in our community, including others, she is well respected and known for her dynamic leadership. She is a positive influence on the lives of many."*

I was mindful of Filipino migration into Canada, particularly from 1990 to 2000. Those years were when the Canadian government first launched the Foreign Live-In Caregiver Program. When Canadian and permanent residents are unavailable, Canadian families can hire a foreign caregiver to provide care in their own home, children, seniors, or persons with medical needs.

Many Filipino caregivers and nannies were hired directly from the Philippines by Canadian employers. Their stories humbled me that they came to work as nannies with the pain of leaving their families back home. Many came from different countries working there as foreign nannies and could transfer and move to Canada under the Live-In Caregiver Program. They were mainly nurses and teachers, and many others were college graduates. Once they have served their work contracts and meet the government requirements, they can apply for residency status.

I greatly respect our overseas workers, who work as domestic helpers. I knew I could provide some mentoring help and assistance to improve and build meaningful careers while applying for their residency status. For example, I rented a space and leased eight to ten computers to provide free tutorial lessons on learning computers, keyboarding, conversational English, interview and presentation skills, self-marketing techniques, confidence building, and tips on becoming assertive. I took a sense of pride in being able to mentor and develop some of my *"kababayans"* who needed help in transitioning from their roles as domestic helpers to their chosen careers.

The Philippine Chamber of Commerce-Toronto

I became President of the Philippine Chamber of Commerce Toronto (PCCT) from 2005 to 2007. PCCT is an association of business and professional people who share a common interest in developing linkages between the Philippines and Canada in local and international trade, business development, technology exchange, and networking. It is the voice of the Canadian-Filipino business community in the Greater Toronto Area.

The National Alliance of Philippine Business Trade and Tourism Canada

From 2009 to 2012, I was President of the National Alliance of Philippine Business Trade and Tourism (NAPBTT) in Canada. This organization is comprised of Filipino-Canadian business companies and professionals representing different business sectors in information technology, retail and distribution, travel and tourism, import-export, and food processing.

The Canadian Association of Philippine Travel Agents

As Filipino migration to Canada continued to rise, the demand for travel and tourism between the Philippines and Canada also increased. I co-founded and became the first President of the Canadian Association of Philippine Travel Agents (CAPTA). It was established in 2001 to promote travel and tourism to the Philippines. We rallied the Philippine government for the successful opening of a marketing and tourism office in Toronto.

The Canadian Chamber of Commerce of the Philippines

In September 2012, I accepted the appointment of National Executive Director for the Canadian Chamber of Commerce in the Philippines (CanCham) to execute the Chamber's mandate to represent, support, and promote Canada-Philippines business interests, including investment, trade, and business mobility between the two countries.

Reaching out is a valuable act of leadership in itself. I considered it essential to know who were the Canadian companies doing business with the Philippine community and who were the Philippine companies doing business in Canada. Therefore, I forged partnership agreements with Canada-Philippine business associations in Toronto, Vancouver, and Winnipeg and local Chambers in the Philippines in Baguio-Benguet, Cagayan Region, Cagayan de Oro City, Cebu Province, Cebu City, Davao City, and General Santos City, as well as with the national Philippine Chamber of Commerce and Industry (PCCI).

Gratitude for Recognition Awards

As a volunteer, I am always grateful for what I do. I have experienced joy repeatedly, the pleasure of giving—instead of receiving. As a volunteer, I discovered that many are inspired when time, talent, and treasure are shared generously and freely. I thank God for the recognitions I received:

DATE	RECOGNITION
October, 1998	One of the Most Outstanding Filipino-Canadians in Canada.
March, 1999	One of the Most Outstanding Presidents of Philippine Associations in Canada.
March, 2004	"In celebration of International Women's Day in March 2004, several hard-working women in Canada who have accomplished so much—specially in business and entrepreneurship. Dela Cruz honored woman entrepreneur." "Markham Small Business Enterprise Centre, in partnership with YMCA Business Centre and WINGS Canada, celebrated Women Entrepreneurs in recognition of International Women's Day on March 8, 2004." (Garcia, 2004, P.R.)
May, 2009	Under the Business/Public Service category – Asian of the Year 2009 during the Third Annual *Asia*

Network Magazine's Asian of the Year Awards, held at Parliament Hills, Ottawa, Canada. (Pinoy Eh News, 2009, Vol. 8(3).

October, 2017   One of the 100 Most Influential Filipina Women in the World at the Global FWN™ 100 Leadership Summit in 2017, held in Toronto, Canada.

Leading Oneself

Success in leading oneself comes to those who know themselves—their strengths, values, and how they best perform. The first person you need to learn to lead is yourself. And then go on the people you lead.

I did not lose track of where I came from but tried to remember who I was. No matter how difficult the struggle, I never lost sight of the idea that something better lies ahead. As infants, we crawled before we walked. We rose, wobbled, fell, rose again, and steadied ourselves on an object. The view changed once we stood in place, as did our perspective. This new goal was to stand without props. Once we achieved this, we started to ambulate. Then we fell. We struggled back to our feet and tried again. Finally, we had the confidence and hunger to set new goals, and thus we walked. Then we realized we could see more if we picked up the pace. We put a new plan, and therefore we began to run. Then it became a question of whether we would be held back by others' limits or test our limits of endurance and stamina. We should take responsibility for our insecurities, be brave enough to go deeper, and let God work inside us. It takes a lot of confidence to break through the pressure to prove and live one's purpose. (Dooley, 2019, p.47). You should overcome barriers as they are not the stopping point but simply another milestone along the way. Step over it, using it instead as a stepping stone to ultimate success. The ability to continue is the key to success.

As I look back at my life journey, doing my self-reflection, I smile distantly, thinking of my parents, for they made possible who I have become. One does not realize how much a sacrifice is until you have your children. Now that I am a parent and grandparent, I recognize the gift that my parents endured to give us a better life. I am truly indebted to my parents' sacrifice and love. I know you are watching over us. Thank you, *Inang* and *Tatang* [Mom and Dad]. I am forever grateful!

Goals and Milestones—Allow Yourself to Dream

Everybody is telling us *"go after your dreams"* or *"find your purpose."* But dreams are free. So you can dream big. They float around and land on people like spores and seeds. Sometimes they land on the sidewalk, where they cannot grow. So pick the right place and time. Make a Goal. Write it down. Commit. Try to do it. Fail. Retry until you reach a milestone. Then set another new goal. Retry. Now you have success. And so it goes; seemingly unreachable milestones are reached, thus becoming stepping stones to further achievements. (Harrison, 2002 pgs.12-13).

LEADERSHIP TIPS I LEARNED ALONG MY JOURNEY THAT I WOULD LIKE TO SHARE:

1. ***Set Your goals.*** Our goals help us become focused and give us purpose. Pursue each goal, and it becomes a milestone. Then it becomes a stepping stone to further accomplishment.

2. ***Get started.*** We have often heard how a journey of a thousand miles begins with a single step. Once we make that initial step, however far we must go, we are on our way. Do not stop. Keep moving. Remember that no one is going to do it for you except yourself.

3. ***Gain momentum.*** But how do we get the momentum going? Maintain your resolve. We must keep our goals in sight and endeavor to make progress every day, week, and month.

4. ***Persevere.*** How do we persevere? The secret comes from maintaining focus. We often write down our goals and post them in visible places to see, sense, and smell the finish line.

5. ***Success.*** With the finish line in sight, we plan our last triumphant steps. And yet, this success is not the final chapter. Success is just another weigh station. J.P. Morgan put it well: *"If you go as far as you can see, you will see enough to go even farther."*

6. ***A new perspective.*** Now the view is different. You see new mountaintops, new possibilities. With newfound confidence, what once seemed

unattainable is now accomplished. New challenges await. Seize the moment and put all of your energy and passion into it.

7. ***The more significant the challenge, the more satisfying the accomplishment.*** The greater the milestone, the more powerful it is as a stepping stone to ultimate success. Focus on your milestones, then move forward.

8. ***Learn to say no.*** Most of us know we need to get better at saying no. Work on being free to say no; your yes will be more focused, meaningful, and powerful than ever before.

9. ***Learn the wisdom of simplicity.*** Adopting the understanding of simplicity will lead to greater clarity about who you are and what matters most. Simplicity will lead you to make better decisions.

10. ***Be inspired.*** Inspiration brings the best out of us. Motivation plays a critical role in our lives. What motivates you? Whatever it is, find a way to build it into your daily routine. We are at our best when we are inspired! Inspiration triggers creativity, and creativity changes how we see everything and do anything. Life is what you make it.

11. ***Have a personal philosophy by which you choose to live.*** I believe Jesus' teachings are the best way to live. They apply to everyone, everywhere, in every situation. How about you? Do you have a process? Do you have guiding principles? Life can seem confusing and complex because every time you have a decision to make, you need to build a philosophy from scratch. In addition to helping you make better decisions, it empowers you to make decisions with speed, clarity, and confidence.

TO MY READERS

I wanted to do something real and share my experiences with others. I know I can play a pivotal role with a genuine appreciation of my life's blessings. The most rewarding was the privilege to help others and provide them the opportunities to improve their lives. Remember, finding yourself will not happen when you find your purpose; knowing who you are is the key to living it out. I hope you can draw some inspiration and insight as you pursue your journey to discovering yourselves and building your future with success and fulfillment.

TO MY INSPIRATION: CHILDREN BOBBY AND LIZA, GRANDCHILDREN LAILA AND NICA

I hope that my life story has inspired you. Your parents have worked hard to give you a good life and a great foundation. It is essential to stay connected and rooted to the family as the central source of values and inspiration. Laila and Nica, you can fly when you are ready to make your own decisions. I encourage you to explore, to open doors I did not even know existed. I also encourage you to try some things that bring you life and joy, even if they do not correlate with your career or obligations. Take in all the possibilities. Live your lives with purpose. Believe in yourselves, and believe in God.

ISABELITA T. MANALASTAS-WATANABE

Founder, President & Representative Director,
Speed Money Transfer Japan Kabushiski Kaisha (SMTJ)
Founder & President, Speed Japan Consulting Services, Inc.
GLOBAL FWN100™ 2013

Just Me, Lita's Mother

Hi, My Name is Let

My parents named me Isabelita, little Isabel, after my grandmother. My friends call me Lita or Lits, while my mother calls me "Let." There was only one person I felt comfortable confiding in the deepest secrets of my heart; only one person I leaned on, my pillar of strength, my mother, my *Ima*. I could not be this open with my father. I always respected him, was mindful of his needs, and loved him dearly until his death in 2019. Yet I could not confess that I lied to him. I could not reveal the truth about my marriage. He met our Lord Jesus Christ in heaven without knowing what I had done.

EXCELLENT START

I Had Dreams... Big, Big Dreams.

I was ten when I wrote my first business plan: Projections of where I will be, what I will be, and when, big dreams for a young girl of ten.

But dreams are dreams. They are free but also free to change at any time, at any point in one's life, depending on circumstances, challenges, and fate. So maybe God has plans for us even when we were just in the womb of our mothers.

At some point in my life, I thought I would be a good doctor. I wanted to go into medicine to help others in need of care, particularly the poor. If lawyers can be referred to as "pro bono lawyers," maybe there should also be a "pro bono doctor?" Indeed, some doctors volunteer their time and knowledge for free in the Philippines. Still, I have never seen nor heard the term "pro bono doctor" used to describe them in newspapers, television, or social media.

I was born in Pampanga and graduated as valedictorian from a public elementary school. I went to Jose Abad Santos High School (JASHS) for high school, which has now reverted to its original name, Pampanga High School. JASHS was arguably the best high school in Pampanga, private or public. To enter JASHS, one had to pass an entrance examination. If you passed, you would get sorted into the different class sections, from Section 1 to 24, with the crème de la crème assigned to Section 1.

In my first year at JASHS, most of my classmates were valedictorians, honor students, or in the top 5% percentile, where they finished Grade 6 in various elementary schools all over Pampanga.

During one of our recent reunions, a former high school classmate told us, "*Meka-pangisnawa kung maluwag, at milaku ing stress ku, when I was dropped to Section 2.*" ("*I was able to breathe easier, and my stress was gone, when I was dropped to Section 2.*")

I excelled in academics and was one of the top ten students in the school during my first year. I actively participated in school activities, was a Girl Scouts leader, and represented the school in various conferences.

One such conference was the CMLI held in Baguio. The one strong memory of my time in Baguio is the clean, minty scent of the pine trees and the beautiful flowers in bloom. I fell in love with the place.

My stay in Baguio formulated my dream of purchasing a vacation house there. I fulfilled this at 36 years old, but the sharp and refreshing smell of the pine trees is gone, and in its place is the sickening smell of vehicle exhaust from the cars and jeepneys that permeate the city. Thank God Baguio's spring-like weather is conducive to the wide variety of flowers that bloom all year round.

I was proud to be on the honor roll during my first year of high school, yet I did not graduate at the top of my class. Instead, my grades started slipping during my third year of high school.

I had no one else to blame for this but myself. The truth was, I fell in love. I made my boyfriend my number one priority, and my studies took the second stage.

Added to that, I suffered from a mysterious ailment that, to this day, remains undiagnosed. My body stiffened when an episode happened, and my fingers bent backward. There was no relief. All I could do was cry. I had an attack on graduation day and could not attend the ceremony. I was not even in the official class photograph.

Yet God always gave me something else for every dream I had that failed to materialize. During my senior year, I received the Most Outstanding Student of the Year award—one of two students in the whole graduating class of 1970.

Falling Apart?

When I was 12, against my wishes, my parents sent me to live with my Chinese grandmother, *Lola* Isabel.

Living with *Lola*, away from my parents and siblings, did not strengthen family bonds. At the start of my stay with *Lola*, I slept in the room reserved for household help. Later, I moved into my grandmother's bedroom and slept beside her. It was a slight improvement but restrictive. *Lola* had a lights-off policy early. Even if I were still working on my homework, she would turn off the lights at 8:30 p.m. I was forced to wake up early to complete my assignments.

Life with *Lola* was not easy. I had chores to complete (which I detested)— dusting the furniture and sweeping the floor. I also cooked with *Lola* Isabel directing me in the kitchen.

Furthermore, I had a strict and early curfew. I had to head home as soon as classes ended. There was no opportunity to socialize with friends.

I started to rebel. I snuck out of school when I could and would spend more time with my boyfriend. So, unsurprisingly, my grades started slipping, and that's how I lost my spot on the honor roll.

Falling in Love

My high school sweetheart and I were best friends with his classmate and my batch mate. Of the four of us, one graduated valedictorian of his class and, later, *summa cum laude* from a top university in New York. Their relationship is one that I hoped I would have because they ended up committing to each in front of God and man.

My relationship ended in a commitment done in secret. Only one of his high school friends and that friend's girlfriend then, knew we had gotten married as they were our witnesses to our civil wedding in the Philippines in 1976. My high-school sweetheart wanted us to get married before going for my research scholarship in Japan in 1977. Then, my husband disappeared while I was still a student. I searched for him for two decades and finally gave up and applied for an annulment. I tried to contact him through his family and friends, but all in vain. He disappeared without a trace. But, according to his mother, he hid from us because my brothers would kill him (false) for deserting me.

How did this happen? How could he have betrayed me like that?

I was in Japan, on a two (2) year research scholarship. Part of my Japan scholarship is a 6-month Japanese diploma course at Osaka University of Foreign Studies. Before my research scholarship ended, I decided to take the entrance exams for an M.A. in Economics at my assigned research university, and passed it. I finally earned an M.A. in Economics in 1980, also under a full scholarship from Japan's Ministry of Science and Education (Mombukagakusho).

While diligently pursuing my studies in Japan, my sweetheart was teaching at a University of Santo Tomas, in the Philippines while waiting for his immigration papers to the United States. Unbeknownst to me, he as also, busy paying regular visits to one of his students. She was in love with him, and he took advantage of the opportunity. She got pregnant, and he was "forced" to have a shotgun wedding. In the Philippines, divorce is not recognized, and he never filed for an annulment. How he was able to re-marry remains a mystery to me. I was shocked when I learned that when her water broke, our *"ninong sa kasal,"* brought her to the hospital. The sense of betrayal I felt was indescribable.

I had a chance to visit his second family in the Philippines, while I was still a student in Japan. Prior to going home, I went to the U.S. to visit his *Lola* and other relatives in Oklahoma who sent me gifts for him, his mom, and his siblings. I could not find him at his house, and his mom will not reveal his whereabouts. My persistence paid off, if only to find the apartment of the second wife. When I saw their pretty baby girl, I surprised myself. I did not get angry. I saw a little angel born into this world without her consent or fault. But, despite being part of why my marriage broke up, I held no hatred for her. For the sake of the baby, I decided to be amicable with his second family, although the pain of the betrayal remains to this day.

I advised the "second wife" to ensure that she went with her "husband" when he left for the U.S. so she could be assured that she and their child could have a better life. I felt this was a supreme sacrifice, but seeing that little, beautiful angel's face melted my heart.

Reconsidering life with *Lola*

I had always questioned the decision to send me to *Lola*. Years later, while working as a diplomat in Japan, heading the Investment Division of the ASEAN-Japan Centre in Tokyo, I understood why. I was sent to live with *Lola* to learn and understand the value of hard work and how to live, interact, and treat others as equals. Under *Lola*'s guidance and watchful eye, I learned the importance of discipline in my studies, the value of honesty, for example, I could have kept those diamonds I found, while doing my regular chores of cleaning her office—she was a jeweler—sold them, and bought my dream watch, but I didn't, and finally, being a good cook.

A MOTHER'S PAIN, A MOTHER'S GIFT

I returned to my mother's house to retrieve my old, dusty books and documents from her attic while she recuperated at my brother's house from Covid-19. What I found changed my life forever. I found a letter *Ima* wrote.

I will let her tell you, my story.

=====

Dear Vicky,

I thought I could keep all the hurt in my heart. I just can't, so I have to write to you to ease the burden of what I feel.

For the past 20 years, I kept alive the memories of a man, so gentle, so good, so thoughtful, and so caring. These are what I remember about your brother. I remembered him just like that —nothing more, nothing less.

In fact, when Lita told me that she and your brother got married, I was so happy for them. I thought it was the beginning of a happy life for both of them. Until the inevitable happened.

Your brother got married again, this time to Virna. My daughter was so brokenhearted. I felt sorry for her. I was the most affected because I love my daughter. In spite of what happened to her, she even went to Laguna to see Virna's father. Lita assured him that she won't resort to any action that might break up your brother's second marriage. I admired my daughter for that.

From then on, she devoted her time to her work. She remained true to her marriage vows. She didn't entertain any suitors—although there were several of them. To name a few: a minister from Malaysia, a doctor from India, a shipping magnate from the Philippines, a noted banker, a U.P. professor, and a businessman from the U.S.

Why do I tell you this? It's just to let you know that Lita remained true to your brother. She hasn't broken (sic) her marriage vows. If what happened to her happened to you, what would you have done?

Being alone, she saved for her future. Now she's financially secure. She may not be rich by your standards, but she's probably richer than your brother. Some of her assets are two houses and lots in Angeles, a townhouse in Baguio, a condo unit in Buendia, another condo in Pasig, a 24-hectare mango farm in Santa Ana, Pampanga, a gasoline station in Angeles, a two-door apartment in Seattle, Washington, and a sizeable bank account.

I don't brag about all these. I just want you to know that she can well afford everything without your brother or anyone else. She doesn't need sympathy. What she needs is understanding.

Remember, too, that she's not getting any younger. When she was nearing her 40s, she wanted to have a child of her own, but she wanted to [have] a child by your brother, because she's married to him. I can't blame her for that. She did all she could to find your brother but to no avail, because your mother, your sister E, and you, most especially, became instruments in making it impossible for her to meet your brother. You hid him from her. I don't know how and why you did that to Lita.

So, she decided to have a child by artificial insemination. The more I admired her for that. All the while, she's using your brother's surname on all her official documents. Her son is using Manalastas.

When they came home for the holidays last year and learned that your brother was also here, she told me of her plans to let her son be adopted (even on paper only) by your brother. She thought of going to Laguna to ask the help of Virna's father. Remember, she assured him before that she will not create trouble, so it was her turn to ask him to mediate between her and your brother. That did not materialize. We decided instead that it was better if she will tell your brother in your presence, in Virna's presence, and my presence, about her plan. She doesn't want to deceive anybody.

What happened in that meeting will never be erased from my mind. Virna didn't like the idea. I understand her. Lita was competition. What I didn't understand was why your brother was so reluctant about it. Maybe he's afraid of his wife, but is not Lita the rightful one? Your brother has no principle, and he has no backbone to stand up for himself.

You too. You did not even say a word in Lita's defense which led me to believe that you (maybe) connived with your lawyer to dash all of Lita's hopes of giving a decent name to her son.

All of you have treated my daughter like dirt. You have not tried to understand her even a bit. I was so hurt by your actions that I cried on our way home. I pitied my daughter. She has not wronged you, your family, or your brother, and yet you treated her so badly. She deserves better than that.

I could hate you for that, but I won't. I will not forget what you did to my daughter as long as I live, and may God grant me the will to forgive.

Did you know that one of your uncles tried to molest her? What did he think of my daughter? May God punish him for that.

Did you know too that Lita wanted to help your brother? She was planning to send him to college to pursue a medical degree. She also wanted to help him put up a business of his own.

Can't you see how good Lita is? All you did was paint a bad picture of her. You didn't try to understand her. All of you conspired to keep her apart from your brother. She didn't give you trouble. All she asked for was something for the good of her son.

Now that I have told you what I feel, I hope you'll understand that I'm only a mother who wants the best for my daughter and her son.

Just me,
Lita's mother

Let,
The letter I wrote to Fann is similar to the contents of this, only with a strong and threatening nature. I made sure he'll repent.

====

She wrote this letter on 23 January 1991 and addressed it to one called 'Vicky.' I cried when I read it. I realized that what happened to me was not my pain alone. My mother carried that pain with her for as long as she lived. I read and felt how my mother suffered silently. A mother's heart breaks when her child gets hurt. I never realized how she felt until I found that letter.

I regretted not having told her how much I appreciated her love for me during all those years I was in crisis. She was already frail and the family wanted her to be happy during her final days. But I had a sense of peace, that my Ima will continue to look over me, when she finally joins her creator.

The letter also reminded me how great my mom is. Leadership lessons from my mom can be gleaned from her letter. At least two are apparent.

Great moms, like great leaders, make sacrifices. They commit their time, energy, and devotion.

Great moms, like great leaders, see and celebrate the best in their children. They cheer us on with gusto, advocate persuasively for us, and support us without a doubt.

There is no limit to how deeply a mother loves her child. There is no predicting what a mother would do when her child suffers. And I realized how much my Ima was hurting for me. How much anger can a mother hold in her heart and keep for ages? What great suffering my dearest *Ima* went through, which she did for loving me.

Mothers are the most remarkable people on this earth. Let us all love and respect our mothers and thank them for their selflessness and their quiet sufferings unbeknownst to us. Finally, let us thank them for the influence they have in our lives.

PAYING IT FORWARD

Part of what I found in *Ima*'s attic were long-forgotten plaques of appreciation from my jobs at the ASEAN Promotion Center on Trade, Investment and Tourism (ASEAN Centre) in Tokyo and the Philippine National Bank (PNB). I needed the plaques and documents to support my nomination for the University of the Philippines (UP)'s Most Outstanding Alumna for Banking and Corporate Social Responsibility. The nomination was an unexpected gift. I got selected. The confirmation would be an incredible honor if I got selected. My father's encouragement to pursue Economics in college paid off. It led to excellent career advancement opportunities, leading up to my current position in 2022 as President and Representative Director of Speed Money Transfer Japan K.K., headquartered in Tokyo, which I established.

Planting The Seed

For the past 40 years, I have received many blessings, financially and professionally. I have received opportunities to work and live in Japan and Europe. And I have not forgotten to pay it forward.

I have sponsored many "personal scholars." One of them achieved his Ph.D. from Vanderbilt University. He sent me a beautiful note after his graduation, promising to repay my faith in him by continuing to pay it forward and sponsor deserving, financially challenged youth to pursue a college education. Another personal scholar landed in the top ten of the Engineering board examination, and another passed the 2022 Bar exam. I feel a deep sense of gratitude, fulfillment, and reward to help those who deserve the chance to achieve a productive future.

I also recognize our overseas Filipino workers (OFWs) and their contribution to our economy. They, in a sense, paid for my salary as a former banker and continue contributing to my success when they use the money transfer company I head in Japan. To return the generosity and support, we organized *Pangkabuhayan* (Livelihood) seminars to help our OFWs plan their return home.

I also speak at various forums for business, academia, media, community organizations, and international conferences.

"Dear Tita Lits" for Japan OFWs is an advice column published by *Jeepney Press*, considered the most widely read online newspaper for Filipinos in Japan. I have been writing this column for more than ten years, helping solve or alleviate our *kababayans'* problems. The positive reactions and comments from followers tell me that "Dear Tita Lits" is making a difference and positive impact.

I love writing this column and learned to set aside my emotions when I read tragic stories. I get too emotionally involved, and I need to minimize their situation's impact on this senior citizen. Writing the column is a rewarding social responsibility, I also learned a lot from my audience and followers.

A NEW CHALLENGE

Ima passed away at 4:40 p.m, April 30, 2022, at Angeles University Foundation Hospital. She suffered from complications stemming from infections affecting various internal organs. We are thankful she did not suffer. A priest came by to pray over her, and the next day, she joined her creator in heaven. No more heartache, no more pain. She must have had a very happy reunion with my father. *Ima* would have turned 89 on June 12, 2022.

And just when I thought that my trials would be over, I faced a new challenge. Four years ago, I started exhibiting behavior that concerned my friends, family, and colleagues. I was chattering non-stop; I had difficulty sleeping. My hands trembled. I had mood swings, was irritable one moment, happy the next, and suddenly would feel very sad. A consultation with my doctor at St. Luke's Hospital in Tokyo confirmed my suspicion. I was diagnosed with mild depression.

Mental illness has a negative connotation, especially in conservative Japan. The stigma of mental illness in Japan is so pervasive that treatment of the disease is so covert. You will not find a psychiatry department in hospitals, especially at St. Luke's. You will find a department called Liaison Department, where patients with mental illness receive treatment. I decided to speak out about my situation and share it in print to remove that stigma and encourage anyone to seek treatment and help. When I feel physically sick, I go to the doctor for treatment. My depression is no different. I need medical care and support, which I actively seek.

In the deepest corners of my heart, I carried a heavy burden. For the past few decades, the pain and suffering from what I felt was my greatest failure festered and grew in darkness. One of my biggest dreams of having a big family did not come true. Despite that, Ima gave me a letter, a gift to allow me to live my life in freedom and light. With her letter, I can face the past without fear or embarrassment. Now I can finally tell my story.

I read somewhere that life starts at 80. Wow, I still have 12 good years to enjoy the rest of my life on this earth. I am hopeful that I will find what I have been seeking, enjoy life to the fullest whatever surprises come my way, and continue to pay forward.

At the ripe age of 68, I finally had the courage to bare my soul, to tell the world who I was/am. *Ima*'s letter gave me the courage to bare-it-all. Hopefully, my life story imparts the lesson that, no matter the gravity of missteps, no matter how many times a person stumbles, you, my dear reader, can know that with determination, hard work, and focus, you can rise again.

I love you all!
Let

JOANNE DE GUZMAN RICO

*Head of Marketing, Salma Rehabilitation Hospital
(under Abu Dhabi Health Services Company)
GLOBAL FWN100™ 2021*

Gusto

Becoming A "Little Mother" at an Early Age in the Family

I started my leadership role early in life. In my father's absence, my mother, *Nanay* Elsie, took full responsibility for raising her children. I am the eldest of four children. We were not well off. We lived with my late grandfather, *Lolo* Ely, a hardworking barber; my grandmother, *Lola* Upeng, a loving housewife; and my late aunt, *Tita* May. They gave my mother invaluable support in raising us, her children. My siblings were still very young when my parents separated, so at an early age, I had to mature fast and become the little mother when my mother was not around. I often had to take charge of all the responsibilities at home and take care of my sister and two brothers. But more importantly, I had to teach them how to become responsible, independent, and united in the cause of supporting our family in every way possible—physically, financially, emotionally, and morally. I had to remind them that our family situation should not discourage them from dreaming big and soaring high, exploring their full potential, and becoming their best version. But I knew that the only way they would understand this wisdom was by showing them. Do not just talk about it; be about it (Marshall and Jones, 2007). I had to lead by example.

No matter how poor, our grandparents instilled in us the value of education. They said, *"Ang edukasyon ang tanging maipapamana namin sa inyo na hindi kailanman mananakaw ng ibang tao."* [*"Education is the only legacy which we can pass on to you, that no one can ever take away from you."*] *Lolo* Ely worked as a barber, standing from day to night, cutting hair and offering quick massages to customers as a value-added. *Lola* Upeng sold *lugaw* [porridge] at the side street while managing her gazillion house chores to send their four children to school. A generation after, *Nanay* Elsie worked hard as a single mother to send us to respectable schools. My mother's sacrifices and my siblings' future became my fuel. At an early age, I had to be a source of strength for my mother and a role model for my younger siblings. Because of our limited resources, I studied hard to earn a scholarship from primary and secondary schools to help finance my education. In addition to my heavy academic load, I took leadership positions in various student organizations. After years of determination and hard work, I graduated High School Valedictorian with seven other academic, extracurricular, and special awards.

As I planned for tertiary school, I aspired to join a university where I would get a quality education without our family spending so much. I passed and became a state scholar at the University of the Philippines, Diliman, where I took a Bachelor of Arts, Major in Philosophy at the College of Social Sciences and Philosophy. I rose to leadership posts in high-profile university organizations. I took with grit all academic and extracurricular mandates. I kept in mind: that grit is the "extra something" that separates the most successful people from the rest (Bradberry, 2015). Semester by semester, I became a college and a university scholar. In 2003, I graduated *magna cum laude* with a General Weighted Average of 1.34 – 0.09 points away from being a *summa cum laude*.

As I joined the workforce, my grit and resilience paved the way for more promising positions in large organizations in the Philippines and the Gulf. These career opportunities provided well for my family and relatives. After years of hard work and teamwork, our family paid for our house in full, purchased vehicles for operational use, invested in real estate properties for rent, and created other income streams through investments. We could now afford to travel as a family in the Philippines and around the world. But above all, the family heirloom called education is passed on: I was able to help send my siblings to school. My sister, Vyna, graduated Valedictorian with nine other academic, extracurricular, and special awards in high school. Vyna became a consistent college and university scholar, graduating *cum laude* from the University of the Philippines, Diliman. She completed her MBA at the University of the Philippines, Manila, and is now a Learning and Development Manager. My brother, Abraham, graduated Valedictorian with six other academic, extracurricular, and special awards in high school. He became a scholar at the Maritime Academy of Asia and the Pacific, where he finished his Bachelor's Degree in Marine Engineering. He then joined well-known maritime companies as a full-fledged seafarer and raised his rank on every boarding. My youngest brother, Rolando Jr., was finishing his Bachelor's Degree and opted to work simultaneously in a business process outsourcing organization. If my actions have inspired my siblings to dream more, learn more, do more, and become more, I am sincerely grateful knowing that I have done my part not only as their big sister, but also as one of their life mentors.

Assuming Leadership Role at a Very Young Age in the Corporate World

As I continued my journey, I pursued marketing instead of law. However, my career journey was not a walk in the park. Although I graduated with a strong academic profile, the new batch of graduates added to the oversupply of the workforce in the Philippine job market. Employers had the upper hand and preferred applicants with formal education and professional experience in marketing. My application got rejected several times by big brands. The closest offer to marketing was a Researcher-cum-Sales Administrative Associate in a manpower agency for Globe Telecom, one of the largest telecommunication companies in the Philippines. Since I was only a contractual worker, I applied for an open post to become a direct employee of Globe Telecom: Customer Service Associate. I planned to use customer service as my entry point to a big brand, then shift to Marketing a year later. Instead of merely killing time, I made my stay in customer service fruitful by training and sharpening my emotional intelligence (EQ)—the attribute I lacked most. It was not easy to handle irate subscribers and take complaints daily. When I was about to give up, I reminded myself of my purpose, so I went on, even if it was emotionally difficult at times. With focus and resolve, I received awards and special recognition from management. Working for a large, well-established company gave my family and me sound compensation and benefits. However, my career path at Globe Telecom did not open the door to marketing, so I had to look for other opportunities.

My first break in corporate marketing began when Ministop Philippines hired me as a Franchise Marketing Officer. Although I do not have a formal education in marketing or business management, the Head of Franchising and Business Development saw my gusto in learning marketing, so he took me into his team. Compared to my counterparts in our sister companies like Universal Robina Corporation (URC), Sun Cellular, Cebu Pacific, I began as the least experienced and the least educated in theoretical and conceptual marketing. But I took that as a challenge rather than an obstacle. Right from the first day, I studied the business model and landscape. If there were concepts I did not understand, I sought input from my immediate superior. I asked questions to my colleagues and our vendors. I attended trainings and seminars on marketing, retail, franchising, and entrepreneurship on weekends. I read books and articles on brand management. Alongside my manager, we identified touch points with potential investors and devised a plan to grow the number of leads for each touch point. In just three months, we nailed the process, captured the leads, and doubled the number of investor inquiries. As a result, we increased franchise sales from an average of 1 investor per month to an average of 5 investors per month, with each investor shelling out at least PHP1.5 Million to own a Ministop franchise in 2005. In my 6th month, I received the Rookie of the Year Award.

In my 7th month, I was hand-picked from a pool of 100+ employees and promoted to Advertising and Promotions Manager. I was only 23 years old then, so I became the youngest staff to become a manager in the franchise's history. As the Advertising and Promotions Manager, I headed a team of 7 marketers and power-moved an emerging brand with a chain of over 100 stores all over Luzon. It was a daunting task: the company's top and bottom lines depended on my team's performance, and the staff I led were either older or more senior by tenure than me. Since I was young and new in the retail industry, some managers and subordinates undermined my capacity. I took this as another challenge. I wasted no time learning about our retail business, consumer spending habits, and the retail industry. The ability to learn is a leader's most important quality (Sandberg, 2013). I studied and observed retail operations first-hand. I talked and listened to customers. We did not have the budget to syndicate our research, so I reached out to my counterparts in Robinsons Supermarket to get market insights and trends. I networked with trade suppliers from various categories to understand the product landscape. I polished my negotiation skills to increase our savings from non-trade vendors. I devised roadmaps on how we can save marketing spending while growing our market reach. Digital marketing was an emerging platform, so I created campaigns that leveraged free digital channels to raise awareness and engagement with our brand. As a leader, I knew I had to work with people. Real influence comes when others feel understood by you—that you have listened deeply and sincerely and that you are open (Covey, 2004). No matter how good the battle plan was, I could not win the war without soldiers. I exerted my best efforts to bond with my teammates, understand their capabilities, gauge their potential, and know them better professionally and personally. I shared with them our goal as a team and explained why and how each member played a key role in reaching our Key Performance Indicators (KPIs). I gave them roadmaps, then empowered and supported them in executing their functions.

In 2006, I was sent by the company to Ministop's Head Quarters in Tokyo, Japan, for franchise training in advertising and promotions, so I could learn, replicate, and implement the core brand strategy in the local business arena. The business model became a success, and we expanded quickly. We opened and operated 250 franchised and directly-owned stores in 3 years. As a result, Ministop overtook 7-Eleven, the convenience store retail and franchise leader, for over 18 years. In 6 years, we grew Ministop to become the fastest-growing convenience store in the Philippine market.

My love for marketing grew by the day. However, I wanted to reach greater heights, so I combined powerful tools: formal education and hands-on practice. In 2006, I took my Master in Business Management at the National Graduate Office for the Health Sciences, University of the Philippines, Manila. In 2008, I took Strategic Marketing and was awarded Best Real-Life Marketing Plan by the University of the Philippines Institute for Small Scale Industries (ISSI) and Small Enterprises Research and Development Foundation (SERDEF), University of the Philippines, Diliman. A year later, I trained for a Post-Graduate Diploma Program in Marketing at the Center for Continuing Education, Graduate School of Business, Ateneo de Manila University. The academic training provided a conceptual framework for my accelerated marketing practice in Ministop.

Being a Woman and Asian in International Waters

In 2009, I received an offer from Al-Ahli Hospital, the largest private premium hospital in Doha, Qatar. I was in a dilemma. On the one hand, I wanted to provide well for my family; the offer was very tempting. On the other hand, I was not ready to leave my growing Marketing roots in Ministop. In the end, my love for family won over my Ministop career. I accepted the offer and was posted as an Executive Assistant to the Managing Director and then as an Executive Assistant to the General Manager. I was confident I could quickly move to marketing later on, but I was wrong. The Middle East has a different context where being an Asian and a woman bore significant weight in winning or losing opportunities. In many circumstances, women were seen as the lesser gender, and Asians were stereotyped as blue-collar workers. These dynamics did not stop me from pursuing my marketing career. We cannot change what we are not aware of, and once we are aware, we cannot help but change (Sandberg, 2013). In addition to my regular work, I volunteered to help with marketing-related projects and assignments. I floated campaign concepts and ideas to the Managing Director and the General Manager. In a place where staff members often lacked the initiative to look at pain points and improve business processes, I ran the extra mile. I worked with cross-functional groups to understand the healthcare industry. After a year, I became the hospital's Marketing Executive. Officially, I was the first Filipina woman to breakthrough in the healthcare marketing space in Doha, Qatar. With the ever-changing marketing landscape, I advanced my *métier* by taking a Certification in Digital Marketing from the Ateneo de Manila University Internet and Mobile Marketing Association of the Philippines while overseas.

In 2012, I received an offer from Burjeel Hospital, a premium hospital in Abu Dhabi, UAE, and joined as a Marketing Executive in its inception stage. My main task was to introduce Burjeel in Abu Dhabi and grow its market share in the emirate, within the country, and within the region. As a result, I became the first Filipina woman who market-pioneered a large healthcare brand in the emirate. In the inception and growth stages of Burjeel, I single-handedly managed marketing campaigns of the brand across all platforms: thematic and tactical communications in print ads, radio ads, car ads, electronic ads, SMS promotions; media-related activities such as press releases, press conferences, media interviews, film shootings; online presence via website, social media, search engine optimization, online advertising, and mobile application; community events including wellness camps, screening campaigns, health lectures, health-related world celebrations, Corporate Social Responsibility (CSR) activities, and customer retention events; corporate events such as contract signing with new partners, unveiling/opening of new facilities, recognition gatherings for physicians, annual day celebrations for staff members; medical events including medical conferences and Continuing Medical Education (CME) lectures for Burjeel physicians and community-based doctors; educational materials and literatures for guests; and all relationship-building initiatives with internal and external stakeholders. Campaign by campaign, Burjeel gained recognition and became an essential player and a strong force in the market. In five years, Burjeel owned and operated 13 healthcare facilities across the region, all brand-managed by a central marketing team in Abu Dhabi, where I belonged. I was awarded Burjeel Star Employee in 2013 and recognized as Burjeel Star during Burjeel's 2nd Annual Day in 2014. In 2015, I was promoted to Senior Marketing Executive, and in 2016, I became the Assistant Marketing Manager of the brand. While we cannot always choose what happens to us, it is true that we can choose our responses (Covey, 2004). I chose to fail forward.

Widening Responsibilities in a Global Market

Bareen International Hospital began its operations in 2015 and had negative profitability during its first three years under the original owners. In January 2018, NMC Healthcare managed Bareen International Hospital, and I received an offer to join the team as Marketing and Sales Manager. Initially, the CEO preferred to hire a male Arab national, but my professional track record spoke volumes of my capacity as a marketer. The CEO took me in, albeit half-heartedly. As soon as I onboarded, the Director of Corporate Operations Strategy from NMC Healthcare gave a tall order to turn around the company in less than six months. I moved from neutral to third gear immediately. I identified business gaps: (1) ambiguity in the brand essence and the brand positioning; (2) absence of insightful, relevant, and competitive marketing and sales plans and strategies for the company; (3) lack of organizational structure in Marketing and Sales Department; (4) shortage of manpower bandwidth who will implement and execute 360-degree roadmaps and campaigns of the brand; (5) lack of clear and well-defined policies, processes, and procedures for campaigns and projects initiated by Marketing and Sales Department; (6) absence of marketing communications and collaterals that will strategically position the brand in the minds of the target audience.

After months of strategizing, planning, and implementing marketing campaigns, the hospital has seen steady growth in patient volume. After six months, Bareen has reached the highest number of patients and has finally achieved break-even. Most importantly, the company crossed over and started gaining profits. The continuous rise in patient numbers in outpatient and inpatient clinics prompted us to expand by adding more clinics and beds. The hospital became a significant feather on the hat of Bareen and NMC Healthcare. I am grateful to be the first Filipina woman in the mostly Arabic and Indian leadership team. Due to the record-breaking success, NMC Healthcare stepped up expansion plans, acquired more medical centers in the emirate, and winged each medical facility under our team. Bareen has grown from one to eight medical facilities in less than two years and is now considered a cluster. With Bareen International Hospital as its main hub, NMC Bareen Cluster has flourished to manage and operate various medical centers located in the emirate of Abu Dhabi, UAE –

- NMC ICAD
- NMC Oxford Medical Center
- NMC Medical Specialty Center
- NMC Royal Medical Centre – Karama Abu Dhabi
- NMC Royal Medical Centre – Shahama
- NMC Alpha Medical Centre
- NMC Golden Sands Medical Centre

At the same speed, I became the Head of Marketing and Sales of NMC Bareen Cluster in less than 1.5 years. In this role, I spearhead marketing and business development functions, from brand positioning to increasing brand awareness and growing brand loyalty to the facility, from increasing footfall to generating revenue and raising profitability for each medical facility. The biggest challenge is turning the business from negative at acquisition to positive profitability.

When I took the new role, I had a very limited budget, so I screened and hired team members from within the company. While technical knowledge in graphic design, photography, and videography was essential, the applicant's passion for marketing was more critical. IB, a female Jordanian, was a Patient Relations Executive at the hospital. I took her into the team and mentored her from ground zero to full implementation of marketing campaigns. After three months, she could already execute marketing campaigns with very minimal supervision. I then took and mentored AT, a female Macedonian, from being a Front Office Executive to being the Marketing Executive of NMC Royal Medical Centre – Karama Abu Dhabi. A few months later, I took and mentored RL, a Filipina, from being a Receptionist to being the Marketing Executive of NMC Golden Sands Medical Centre. After a few months, I took and mentored NH, a female Palestinian, from being a Front Office Executive to being the Marketing Executive of NMC Royal Medical Centre – Shahama. Shortly after, I took and mentored FK, a female Bangladeshi fresh out of school to handle the Business Development and Marketing campaigns of NMC ICAD.

In addition to Marketing and Sales, I was posted to look after the Call Center strategically. The COVID-19 pandemic prompted many calls from patients, so I monitored and analyzed the productivity of the Call Center individually and as a team and mapped out a strategic plan to streamline operations. I worked alongside, mentored, and coached RW, a Filipina in charge of Call Center. After a careful study, I aligned resources, launched, and implemented three critical changes in the department: (1) I revised the IVR system so answers are ready for frequently asked questions without speaking to a live agent; (2) I launched Bareen WhatsApp Business so that patients will have a new channel of communication with the hospital; (3) I increased the bandwidth of the call center while monitoring individual productivity. The new dynamics played a key role in converting the call center from a qualitative to a quantitative and result-oriented unit, producing clear and measurable performance evaluation and benchmarking outputs. We reviewed data and statistics regularly based on designed metrics in terms of increasing productivity per agent, lowering handling time, waiting time, missed calls, and abandoned calls; increasing appointments; and addressing no-shows. Since this is RW's first foray into a supervisorial position, I coached her on navigating workplace vertical and horizontal relationships on top of the work's operational and strategic aspects.

These women reminded me of my earlier years when I was still starting my career. I was eager to be a marketer, yet no brand would open doors because I had neither academic background nor professional experience to present. All I had was a desire to learn marketing and the grit to become one of the best in the field. I saw myself in each of these women: where no one else was ready to give them a break, I unlocked opportunities for them to learn and grow. I learned that leadership is about making others better due to your presence and ensuring that impact lasts in your absence (Sandberg, 2013).

Giving Back to the Community

My greatest dream is to serve, give back to the Filipino community who sent me to school and be an instrument of change. Having experienced it myself, I have a strong personal advocacy for the right of children to education, especially the underprivileged ones. I have been a resilient sponsor of World Vision Philippines for 15 years. I have supported several children with their families and communities in depressed areas in the Philippines. I began sponsoring my first World Vision child, despite earning a minimum wage when I landed my first job. My salary was not even enough to cover my family's and my needs, yet I shared what little I had because I knew how it felt to have nothing. As years passed, whenever I have a life milestone, a promotion, salary increment, overseas opportunity, I sponsor another child; it is my way of thanking the Lord for His blessings. After all, when you focus on being a blessing, God makes sure that you are always blessed in abundance (Osteen, 2016). A blessing is not a blessing unless shared.

For this cause to be more significant, I leveraged the power of influence. While working at Ministop Philippines, I spearheaded the World Vision Coin Bank campaign across 250 Ministop stores. Customers donated and dropped their coins in the bank. Franchisees returned the filled coin banks and exchanged them for new ones. The initiative raised PHP0.6 Million in just 12 months. I introduced World Vision's Child Sponsorship Program to JG Summit employees and Ministop franchisees. The campaign raised an additional 20 World Vision sponsors in just one month, with each sponsor taking approximately one to three children and donating PHP450 per child per month (2006) onwards. Affluent sponsors opted to add one child every sponsorship anniversary. In 2016, I supported two World Vision staff members from the Philippines to launch World Vision's Child Sponsorship Program in the UAE. I became one of the pro bono organizers of the event and hosted both programs held in Dubai and Abu Dhabi. All proceeds from the event were donated to the foundation, and the two events produced over 100 new World Vision sponsors for underprivileged Filipino children, their families, and their communities. In a longer term and a grander vision, I dream of starting and building a foundation that will support the right of underprivileged Filipino children to education.

I am a member of Singles for Christ, Light of Jesus, and Divine Mercy Family in Abu Dhabi, UAE. I have been engaged in programs that help Overseas Filipino Workers (OFWs) connect with the community, strengthen moral ties and support, and discover a family away from home. I have been frequently invited as a speaker in various conferences, seminars, and teachings so I can share and inspire with my life story fellow Filipinos who are undergoing the same struggles. In addition, I lead small groups to serve my fellow compatriots within various communities by sharing my time, talents, and treasure at every possible opportunity.

I do pro bono marketing, PR, events, and hostings for some Filipino community programs outside work. In addition, I teach and mentor OFWs on marketing, especially those who desire to become professional marketers or enhance their marketing skills. I do this due to my relentless desire to uplift the Filipino community across all fronts, back home and overseas. And what better way to do this than by doing the thing I am passionate about and sharing it with others, especially those in need.

My Message to the Next Generation of Filipina Women Leaders

First, undertake your life journey with deep faith in God. My journey was and will not be a walk in the park. I have faced many seasons in life: ups and downs, struggles and successes, failures and victories. Sometimes, after soaring high, I hit the ground running. There are times when, after a remarkable achievement, I hit a dead end, and it seems there is nowhere else to go. Sometimes, after a big break, I feel too burdened and tired and just want to give up. But I know my family, friends, and churchmates are with me every season. And more importantly, I know God is with me. When I am faced with the most significant problems, either in my professional or personal life, I begin to doubt and ask questions that perhaps no one will even be able to answer. During these times, I put on my shield of faith and remind myself that there is a reason for everything. God loves us so much and only wants the best for us. No matter how challenging, I continue to journey with my family in faith with a purpose to serve others. I do my best in every circumstance and let God be the pilot.

Second, live and lead with a strong sense of purpose (IQ) combined with passion (EQ). We need to develop the heart as much as we need to develop the head. In today's global society, everyone is focused on being better, smarter, faster, and one notch higher than the other. IQ (intelligence quotient) is our right to play, our means to compete. But when coupled with EQ (emotional quotient), this is what defines people who change the world. EQ is about doing what I love and loving what I do. EQ is courage and conviction: being able to question fundamental assumptions, speaking confidently about my beliefs without fear of being judged or criticized, and championing change that will positively impact the lives of those I serve. EQ is humility: accepting that I do not always know all the answers, knowing when to let others shine, and when to drive others to realize their best potential. EQ is compassion: having a genuine concern for and desire to help others, sincerely reaching out to know and provide for the community's needs. In all these years, my one authentic learning is that we must develop a balance of substance and soul. Lead with intellect and the head, but do not forget to lead with a heart. And I think the heart is what will make a difference in today's world.

Third, champion life with grit and resilience. Human beings falter and get hurt. How we deal with crises and choose to move forward defines our character. My life is not perfect. At a very early age, I already faced many problems and challenges. More than winning, I learned not to be afraid of failing. Failures make me wiser, bolder, and stronger. They make my breakthroughs more fulfilling and my achievements more rewarding. And if I do make mistakes, I push with tenacity, learn from my experience, bounce back, and move forward, knowing that I am one step closer to my victory.

LAARNI SAN JUAN

Public Health Nurse
GLOBAL FWN100™ 2007

The Beauty of Windows

I like windows open in my home. That is how my mom liked it when I was growing up. I looked up to her and emulated what she did for our family. The pungent odor from my father's cigars had the chance to flow out, although the strong stench rarely escaped. As an adult, I long for fresh, clean air to breeze in, even on the coldest days. An open window allows the smell of freshly cooked meals to seep out into the neighborhood. It also allows moisture to escape from hot steamy showers, so potential mold growth gets stopped in its tracks. The essence of being is seen through the window of the mind and spirit. An open window is an open mind, free spirit, and energetic flow. A closed window is shut where nothing escapes while conserving energies and protecting the space inside.

As I contemplate my life journey, I am grateful for all the windows that have opened and closed, whether by choice or circumstance. I believe each of the five foundational bricks of my being: family, education, community, career, and health possess unique windows to my soul. From within the bricks are stories that yield the dimensions of my livelihood, beliefs, and dreams.

I recognize that I have come a long way when I look at old photos of my younger self from the 1970s with crooked teeth, thick glasses, and an awkward frown. I figured out how to crack open windows so the fresh breeze could push me to where I wanted to go. The wind in the form of mentors and support systems helped me overcome being sad, stressed, overwhelmed, and burned out. I live and truly appreciate where I have come from, all that I am today, and where I want to be tomorrow.

FAMILY

Feeling Shy

I was painfully shy in my early childhood. I often imagined doing what the more assertive and brave kids did in and out of the classroom, like raising their hands, asking questions, and playing sports. I could not get myself to speak with certainty, nor did I have the opportunity to learn any sport-like activities because my parents were unaware of such things. I am uncertain if my childhood was fun because I seem only to recall memories of strict parents who only cared about a noiseless clean home. A spotless house was the norm. I do not remember getting praised or hearing *"I love you."* I did not have a lot of toys except Barbie dolls that I received on Christmas. I played with my brother's hot wheels and fanatically organized the two-inch small cars into the plastic case where they belonged. I often had my 64 Crayola crayons sharpened and neatly tucked in the box. I proudly pulled them out when I used them for the 25-cent coloring books my father bought at Woolworths. We did not go on vacations, nor did my parents ever volunteer at the public schools I attended in San Francisco. Our version of what seemed like a vacation was the yearly *kababayan* picnics held in Morgan Hill, a suburb south of San Jose, California. It was a gathering of provincial neighbors from Morong, Rizal, our hometown in the Philippines. Families brought a dish to share with the hundreds of attendees dressed in polyester bellbottoms and flowered-pattern swimsuits. My father in his fedora hat hauled in pre-cut watermelon slices from the back of our Plymouth Chrysler. We all sat on our personalized *banig*, the straw mats that proudly boasted our embroidered family name, San Juan, on it.

I realize today that neither my mother nor my father had any sort of playfulness in them. Their demeanor was a serious undertone in our household.

My maternal grandmother, who immigrated to Daly City, California, in 1977 once told me that she kept each of her 12 children indoors until six months of age because she *"did not want to expose them to the outside world."* That may explain my mother's early (non)attachment style to others and her inability to be physically affectionate, communicative, or playful. I never owned a bicycle as a child. It was only through my cousin, who lived around the corner, that I had any remote chance to experience a hard bicycle seat and wobble my way up and down the street. I do not know how to swim, and I am afraid of water. When I was eight years old, my free-spirited uncle promised to teach me how to swim, and I trusted him. His idea of teaching a terrified child was laughing while leaving me helpless in the middle of the pool. I remember vigorously flapping my arms and crying at the same time. I was sure that I was drowning and would never recover. The memories of that experience are still traumatic, and I have not fully overcome them in my adult life. While I have learned to love my uncle despite his version of humor, I continue to have a love-hate relationship with water.

My elementary school photos were pictures of a tanned brown girl with straight oily black hair and a grimace that looked like fear and discomfort. I often cried in class whenever the teacher asked me a question because I internalized any confrontation as punitive. I wet my pants after school at least once a month because I was too scared to ask the teacher to use the bathroom during the school day.

Feeling Loved

Despite the memories of what felt like lackluster joy, I still felt loved and safe. My mother, the breadwinner of our four-person family, immigrated to the United States in the late 1950s and steadily worked as a lab researcher at Kaiser Hospital and then at UCSF where she finally retired in 1990. Her Bachelor's degree in chemistry from Adamson University in the Philippines was an ante for her to secure a good-paying job in the big city life of San Francisco. She bought a modest home in the Mission District in 1967 for $19,000 and a Plymouth Chrysler to drive us around. My father, who was 26 years older than my mother, came to the U.S. in the 1920s and often shared stories of his manual jobs working in the fields of Alaska and California. He retired as a janitor while I was still in elementary school. My father walked me to and from school every day for many years. During our walks, he often spoke about the discrimination he experienced as a young single man and how his wage of ten cents a day as a day laborer picking lettuce was better than if he stayed in his island homeland. During our outings, I painfully endured weekly tauntings by young non-Filipino kids as we waited for the bus to our usual day trips to Chinatown. These memories of discrimination and violence imprinted social ills at an early age. While my father casually shrugged off the attacks, I felt helpless and did not have the quick instinct or courage to fight those kids back. These vivid childhood memories inspired me to address social justice issues and find solutions in my adult life.

My parents did not openly share their feelings about their daily hardships. Instead, they remained focused on providing for the family and our extended family the best they knew how with the resources they had. I witnessed their commitment to their American dream, for they never spoke of any return back to the Philippines. My mother and father spoke to us in *"taglish"* [Tagalog and English code-switching] and readily accepted our responses to them in English. They were not interested in my brother and me learning and speaking Tagalog. They were determined to sustain the life they started in the United States.

They followed the rules, obtained U.S. citizenship, paid taxes, and remained steadfast in providing for my brother and me to attain an education. That was their ultimate goal. My parents equated going to school with job security and an abundant future. I embrace that value and have proudly passed it on to my daughter.

EDUCATION

My parent's version of nurturing a family did not entail hugs or words of endearment but instead ensuring we always had food to eat before and after school. They also ensured we had pocket money to buy what we needed to be good students.

Being Teacher's Pet

I was not a leader type growing up, nor did I know how to express myself adequately with words. Even in my quiet and awkward state, I did well from a report card perspective. My parents were extremely proud of my straight A's and zero absences which I maintained for years. School felt easy when I did not have to deal with interpersonal conflicts with classmates or intimidating teachers. I often became the teacher's pet and felt obvious resentment from the rowdier classmates. I was reliable, I wrote legibly, and I never missed assignments. I listened to teachers and submitted homework on time. During recess, I played with a quiet group of girls. School life, however, became more challenging in high school, where assignments required me to articulate myself and provide rationales. That was not my forte. I struggled. In time, the difficulty ate away at my self-esteem, and I slowly gave up on my ambitions to do well.

Feeling Lost in High School

I attended an elite public high school in San Francisco. While I completed first year with some confidence, the next three years were tainted with low self-esteem, experimenting with risk-taking behaviors, and hanging out with friends I knew my parents would not approve. My reading comprehension was below average, and it was extremely difficult to read fiction books beyond a hundred pages. I knew my less than 3.0 GPA closed the windows on any remote chance of getting into my dream school, Stanford. My father refused to read my acceptance letter to a college in San Diego. We compromised, and I attended San Francisco State University with low ambitions, no focus, and no major. Life felt so-so and I felt lost.

Finding Joy in the Science of Nursing

It took me seven years to finish my undergraduate studies. I initially started with business classes, accounting courses, and eventually physical therapy. I did not enjoy any of the prerequisite courses for those majors. I enjoyed math and science but did not have a pathway to pursue. I felt clueless. My mother, working at UCSF then, came across a flyer to attend a nursing workshop. I did not know anything about the profession because no one in my immediate family pursued the field. I was open-minded, however, and attended the event. I do not recall exactly what inspired me, but I soon applied for the major, took courses, and my college life suddenly became interesting. I found joy in the science and art of nursing, especially in the clinical rotations where we spoke to actual patients and applied the pathophysiology principles learned in the classroom. I simultaneously developed a passion for exploring injustices in the healthcare system as I found myself asking more why questions.

As I immersed myself in my nursing classes, college life became more exploratory when I took my first ever Asian American class. It was inspiring that the course was taught by a Filipina-American professor. We had the same skin color. She was funny and intelligent, and she inspired me to strengthen my reading skills. My second course was taught by a Filipino-American who looked like my brother. Not only did I feel safe in his classroom, the course provided a unique space to explore who I was, learn more about the culture, and ask questions without doubting myself. I started to gain momentum in learning who I was and who I was becoming. For once in my life, I felt good about myself. I felt proud. I felt happy. I was 23 years old, and the themes from my father's repetitive storytelling all came together and gave me real-life a-ha moments. My mother's stories of her family's whereabouts during World War II in the Philippines were elaborated in class with the historical context that allowed me to understand her ways better. I started to love school, and I wanted to learn more! Professor Dan Gonzales referred me to speak with one of his colleagues, a distinguished Filipina woman who had a nursing degree and a Ph.D. I had no idea what a Ph.D. meant, but I felt a sense of pride in meeting her and eventually calling her my very first mentor. She held my hand as I navigated this phase of self-discovery. I was loving who I was becoming, and I felt my dreams and goals become more apparent as time passed. My life journey reached a new climax: I graduated from San Francisco State with *cum laude* honors with a major in nursing and a minor in Asian American Studies.

Feeling Nostalgia

During my collegiate experience, I often rummaged through the stacks of family photo albums my mother meticulously stored in the brown wooden cabinet in our living room. I asked many questions and felt nostalgic when I ran into photos of myself as a toddler in my *terno* outfits. The 3x3 inch photos of my mom and her siblings as immigrants to a new country with their serious facial expressions in neatly ironed dresses proved they were successfully part of the American fabric of immigrants.

COMMUNITY

Expanding My Circle

With my newfound identity as a nurse and eager learner of social justice issues, I got involved in various community groups in San Francisco. For example, I attended late-night meetings of the Pilipino Mental Health Resource Group. I observed genuine passion from each of the health professionals who committed themselves to improve the communities. I fell in love with their energy and witnessed the qualities of strong leaders.

In time I became a master networker expanding my circles and forming relationships with individuals and influencers. I was constantly refining my own art of meeting and communicating with people. I have come a long way from the painfully shy young girl I was in my youth. I eventually became more confident in myself and my ability to collaborate and lead groups. There were many awkward moments I fumbled through, and all while doing so, I learned the power of persistence and consistency even when life felt uncomfortable.

Understanding Mental Health

One of the most amazing women I met during this period was Dr. Ruth Hill, a Filipina psychologist. We worked on a grant together to help high-risk elementary school children in the South of Market Area of San Francisco. She was my first ever encounter in the world of mental health. I often caught her looking at me the way psychologists do: her head tilted with a pencil in hand, observing my behaviors, and giving feedback. It was the first time I got teary-eyed whenever I spoke about my family. I was vulnerable, yet I trusted her when I shared my innermost feelings. When she spoke, I was moved. I felt appreciated. She was empathetic and described my emotions and situations. I felt supported. No one ever spoke like she spoke with me and to me. From her guidance, I learned how to give myself permission to unfold, speak out and not apologize. I learned the power of understanding one's mental health.

Embracing My Self-Growth

I embraced the growth in myself and my community involvement so much that I decided to pursue a master's degree in public health. I applied to one school and was determined to be a graduate student. When I received the acceptance letter to UCLA, I cried tears of joy when I showed my mom. I proved that desires could be fulfilled when hard work and commitment are apparent. When I walked across the stage during commencement in 1997 in my heavy velvet graduation robe, I was proud of the two degrees I possessed at this junction of my life. I confidently knew that all I had learned would serve as my ante in creating the life I wanted with meaning and passion.

CAREER

Practicing Nursing

When I returned home to San Francisco from Los Angeles, I postponed all job prospects. Instead, I cared for my father, who had obvious signs of dementia. This window was closed because it was too emotionally tough to grasp his declining medical health and still manage my own job-hunting prospects. However, I eventually opened the window to the workforce after twelve months of caretaking and unfolding my new identity. I excitedly accepted the position as a Public Health Nurse in February 1998 for a local health department doing home visits with low-income pregnant mothers and children. The job took me to apartments, homeless shelters, jails, and anywhere at-risk families needed help. I recall my first business cards etched with my name and credentials that I proudly gave to patients and at community events.

Networking

In 1999, I received a letter in my work mailbox. The envelope had flowers on it, and my name was handwritten in blue ink. It certainly did not look like the usual correspondence letters I received from social services, medical reports, or nursing symposiums. It was an invitation to come to a Filipina women's group hosted by a UC Berkeley alumni. I attended and met other like-minded women who were equally excited and passionate about talking about community. Unfortunately, the young woman who facilitated the get-together announced she was officially leaving the group for personal reasons. I did not know the history of the group, but I instinctively did not want this group's demise. I felt unique energy with the attendees and I wanted to continue being part of the group.

I immediately consulted with a community icon leader, Alice Bulos, with whom I was already working on other projects. She assumed that I was referring to the FAWN group (Filipino American Women's Network, a group formed many years earlier comprised of older Filipina women involved in politics), but I quickly clarified that this was a different group made up of aspiring younger professionals. For the first time, I learned how members and groups in the same community are not necessarily bridged together.

Marily Mondejar, a friend I met at the initial women's event, also expressed interest in community building. She and I had a mutual passion for continuing the women's group, so we stayed in touch. We brainstormed at late-night dinners and decided to continue the group, naming it the Filipina Women's Network. We agreed that the target audience for the group was professional women or those who aspire to lead. Marily's expertise in teaching frameworks for personal development, professional growth, and high-level leadership attracted newcomers, and the network eventually grew internationally.

Starting My Family

While my career and community life stayed busy, my social life was also high speed. I was single, and I ventured out with my core girlfriends, new friends, and new acquaintances. I was open to new experiences to travel and visit places. This time was special as I learned about myself and what I did not like. Since I cared for my father into my mid-30s, my chances of dating and getting to know someone were low. My father passed away in 2002. As fate would have it, I soon met my future husband. I knew the man of my dreams would show up in my life only after I completed caring for my father. While one window closed, another opened. My husband and I had a daughter, and my journey to motherhood began. Although it was unplanned, I was excited and ready.

An extensive family support system surrounded us who wanted to help care for our daughter. I returned to work as a nurse, and because of the support, I felt confident and continued to immerse myself back into the community as a volunteer. At work, I gained momentum as a nurse leader and a union rep. I relentlessly advocated for those who experienced work condition issues or do not have the bravery to express themselves. I felt bolder and unapologetic at work meetings, even when my professional opinions fell on deaf ears. However, I quickly learned how systems really work. I witnessed unqualified personnel get promoted on premises that made no sense to me. When I was called a derogatory name, and I formally made a complaint following all policies and procedures, the outcome of the investigation did not favor me. Instead, individuals whom I thought would protect me turned against me. This experience was a huge turning point in my career and a rude awakening to who I was in the workforce. While many well-meaning colleagues quickly offered their support, I went inward and questioned how I could ever rise back up from the apparent blows.

The stress from the experience forced me to take a closer look at who I was and how I would deal with it. This particular moment felt like I had reached rock bottom, and my frustration was getting the best of me. The blows continued, and I was called on my eye rolling and what they subjectively judged as disrespectful. I felt numb, and my health suffered, yet the fighter in me knew I had to figure a way to bounce back.

HEALTH

Dealing with Health Issues

Getting the surprising news that I was in early menopause at 36 years of age spiraled me into a depression. I sobbed as soon as the uncaring physician broke the news of my low egg count. I immediately deciphered that to mean I have a slim chance of ever getting pregnant again. My first immediate thought was that I had let my husband down. Oscar is so full of life, loves children, and truly enjoys our one and only child, barely two years old. When I got the news about my sudden infertility, it saddened me, as I had envisioned us having a brood of children because we made such a great team.

I changed healthcare providers and switched out of that HMO after experiencing the uncaring and cold nature of the physician who read those lab results to me. Because of my new health condition of premature ovarian failure, I knew that I would experience a cascade of new health issues that would propel me into an older woman's body. I transferred my healthcare into a university setting where I was guaranteed unending care. I would first be seen by a provider, possibly including a medical student, a resident in training, and then maybe even a fellow knowledgeable of all the research on a particular diagnosis. I was right about the cascade to come. I was soon diagnosed with hypothyroidism, osteoporosis, lack of vitamin D, and high cholesterol. With all the hormone changes, it was no surprise that my mental health also suffered.

Appreciating My Heritage and Life

I had to figure out this health thing, or else I would only cause more harm to myself. So I decided to step away from the chaos and environments that triggered me. I decided to travel more, so I accompanied my mother on her trips to the Philippines. Traveling opened up my heart while also healing it. Visiting my mother's province and barrio taught me to see a different perspective on life and living. The unpaved roads lined with crowds of people in slippers, tank tops, and umbrellas contrasted with what I was familiar with in America. I got used to hearing roosters with their cock-a-doodle-doo.

After I visited the Philippines for the fifth time in 2019, my appreciation for life and what I have in America would no longer be taken for granted. I realized that I live in excess in the U.S. and that my health should not be ignored or pushed aside. So when I unexpectedly got shingles on my face in May 2021, that experience reminded me to rest more often and manage my stress.

The aging process has undoubtedly been an interesting aspect of my life journey. I have always looked younger than my age, but that comes with an inherent age bias from others. It can feel like a compliment on a superficial level, but the comments that follow in the conversation are an indirect form of micro-aggressions. Comments often assume the lack of skills based on how one looks. Since I was young, I felt I needed to work twice or even three times harder to prove my worth. Work promotions where older white unqualified women passed me up validated my hunches.

OUTLOOK

Caring. Learning.

As I reflect on all the shortcomings and downfalls I have experienced, I learned that the ability to bounce back only strengthens the mind in what is possible. Regardless of what situations have come before me, the truth of my being remains the same: I care for people, I value learning, I give without expecting in return, I help those who want support, I strive for independence yet recognize when I need help, and I communicate with clarity. Family is important, making money is important, I understand everyone is different, health is important, and tending to our mental health is key.

LESSONS LEARNED

1. There is no such thing as multitasking, especially regarding family.
2. Create order and organization before going to bed each night.
3. Have friends from all walks of life.
4. Know the human development spectrum and stay two steps ahead so you know what to expect.
5. Go to therapy and have a therapist you like.
6. Hang around people that you aspire to be. Get to know their habits and what differentiates them from average.
7. Show up each day. Get ready. Fix your hair and makeup.
8. Pick a life partner that aligns with your values and with whom you are genuinely compatible with.
9. Make yes or no decisions, and avoid the gray and wishy-washy.
10. Think so positively that you drown out the negative.
11. Stay unique.
12. Open windows. It's an opportunity to breathe fresh air.

LUCIA OLALIA REYES RN, MN

University of Calgary
GLOBAL FWN100™ 2021

Living the American Dream at the Heart of the Canadian Prairies

"The American dream subscribed to the belief that anyone, regardless of where they come from, can attain their own version of success in a society where upward mobility is possible for everyone." (Investopedia.com (2022).

I would love to share my career journey about living the American Dream by exploring life and career at the heart of the Canadian Prairies. My chapter will illuminate some of my early life vignettes that helped shape my journey while at the same time balancing it with family life. In each vignette, I will describe some of the leadership competencies and strategies that have resulted in my success

According to a 2020 CNN Life Philippines report by Portia Ladrido, the Philippines is the biggest supplier of nurses worldwide. For instance, there were 150,000 Filipino nurses in the U.S. in 2020. However, according to Catherine Choy, a professor of Ethnic Studies at UCLA, the migration of nurses is not new (Choy, 2003). In her book Empire of Care, Choy says that the demand for Filipino nurses in the U.S. originated from the Philippines being a U.S. colony, where the colonial regime established an Americanized education system, including nursing education. Unlike the U.S., migration of Filipino nurses started at a slower pace in Canada mainly because most of the Nursing Recruiters are from the U.S. and because of the differences in educational requirements. In Canada, the migration of Filipino-trained nurses has seen a progressive increase between 2011 to 2020.

The narrative that follows is the story of one Filipina nurse's leadership journey within the Canadian Public Healthcare.

Migration of Filipino-Trained Nurses, 2011–2020

2011	2012	2013	2014	2015	2016	2017	2018	2019	2020
7,887	8,095	8,807	9,415	9,858	10,397	10,903	11,220	11,072	11,638

Source: https://cihi.org

Growing Up in the Philippines: Giving your Best in Everything You Do
Growing up, and every day, my father would tell me to recite these short verses, *"Lord help me to give my very best today,"* and in the evening, before going to bed, he would ask me, *"what good did you do today?"* These reflective questioning exercises shaped the persona of who I am today. The commitment to doing good every day has laid a solid foundation in my healthcare career. My introduction to public health care started at a young age when I accompanied my father, a vet technician, on his trips to remote areas near our home in the Philippines to vaccinate the villagers for tuberculosis. Learning by watching, I began giving vaccinations when I was in Grade 5. These experiences created my passion for learning more about public health care, so it was no surprise that following high school, I enrolled in the nursing program at the Far Eastern University, where I graduated with a degree in Nursing. It was 1970 and a proud time for my family, but tragedy struck. I witnessed my father having a cardiac arrest, and the team could not save him. I felt so inept as a new nursing graduate. This experience motivated me to explore how I can be more helpful to others in need.

After my father's untimely death, I continued to work in one of our community hospitals. Although this experience gave me the needed skills as a novice nurse, I wanted to explore other opportunities that would help me grow and flourish in my chosen career. I researched the different nursing journals available and found an opportunity in one of the American Journal of Nursing publications, *"St. Michaels Medical Centre in New Jersey is looking for new graduate nurses. Please apply."* I updated my resume and obtained transcripts, and sent them to the Human Resources office directly. To my surprise, I received a reply advising me on how to proceed. While most applicants go to a travel agency, I decided to do this on my own to learn this process and save on paying travel consultants' fees. I was on my first plane leaving for New Jersey a year later. To my surprise, I was not the only health care worker on that flight. Other nurses and doctors were going to the same state. What was different was that most of them received assistance from one travel agent; hence they traveled together. I made friends aboard the flight. We landed just before midnight and were met by the hospital's Human Resources person. In our tiny voices, we all said, *"We are in America."* Deep in my heart, my father's word resonated, *"I want to give my best in everything I do."*

Living the American Dream: Developing Your Passions and Mastering Them

"The American Dream is the belief that anyone can attain their own version of success in a society where upward mobility is possible for everyone." The Exchange Visitor program was an excellent immersion for foreign-trained nurses wanting to advance their careers. The nurses received a minimum salary and stipend. Housing was provided free within the hospital compound. We would work during the day, supplemented by structured daily evening classes, totaling more than 12 hours of combined work and study. During that exchange program, I initially worked as a novice staff nurse, and upon completion of the program, I was promoted to a case manager for cardiac surgery patients. It was my first foray into the world of cardiac care, where cardiac arrests, similar to what took my father's life, occur daily. Initially, I could see my father's face when I was summoned to attend a Code Blue emergency, but this soon passed as I gained more knowledge and skills in cardiac care. I was offered other promotions in New Jersey, but in 1975, I married my high school classmate and immigrated to Calgary to join him.

Leadership at the Bedside: Capitalizing on Your Challenges to Yield Better Results

It was like a catch-22 when we landed in Alberta. Jobs for nurses were scarce, and even though I came as a registered nurse (R.N.) from the U.S. with cardiovascular experience, I could not get my credential licensure as I needed to have Canadian experience. Still, nobody was interested in hiring me in acute care. I went door to door to the continuing care centers to find my opportunity. When hired, I told them my reason for applying was to get my R.N. license approved and that acute care was really my passion; however, I would do my best while working for them. After a month of being employed at a continuing care center, I got my R.N. license to practice. I went back to the Calgary General Hospital to update them on my application. Unlike now, where job applicants apply online, I showed up in person, screened from head to toe, and then booked an interview. I got accepted into (ICU) Critical Care. All the ICU nurses on this unit were local graduates except for one other *Pinay*. I got comments, such as, *"So you came from the U.S., fancy ICU."* During my three-month probationary evaluation, my head nurse wrote, *"Lucy has adjusted very slowly in ICU but is now ready to take charge."* I challenged her comments telling her that her note was contradictory. *"How could my adjustment to Canadian nursing be termed as slow when at three months I was already taking charge?"* I asked her to reconsider her notation but to no avail. One month passed, and I watched my every move on the unit, always trying to give my very best, which my dad taught me during my youth. I could not have another negative evaluation, or I would lose my job, hope, and career. I prayed for new beginnings, and one Friday afternoon, my head nurse announced that she was moving out of the country. I felt like jumping with joy in anticipation of another new beginning, a new head nurse, a new opportunity to prove my best.

I met Marg, my new head nurse, as a stark contrast. She was a certified critical care nurse, and we often exchanged ideas on critical care nursing. There was restructuring in the department, and I was on maternity leave with my second child. Marg asked me if I was interested in applying for the new Nurse Clinician position, and if I was, I must stop short my maternity leave. I came back from my two months leave knowing that opportunities only knock once at your door, and I must grab it. It was a good choice as it laid the foundation and start of my journey as a leader at the bedside. While normally, there will be an orientation period for an existing position, I was fortunate, along with two other colleagues, to lay out what the position entails. It was another exciting opportunity to be able to map this role. Leadership at the bedside works best by Managing by Wandering Around (MBWA). I wanted to learn how care is delivered and what our care recipients say about our service. I wanted to see how each team member contributes to the common good of our unit. I also wanted to see what improvements our team needs to continue to excel in this area of public health care. We celebrated small successes, and eventually, we developed a cohesive team. More than a year later, I was invited to apply for a head nurse position in another department. I was successful—another positive step in my career journey. I was a frontline manager of a very busy Internal Medicine unit. I was the first visible minority to hold such a position and knew I must continue to give my best in everything I do. I demonstrated some long overdue improvements for this department, from boosting staff morale, improving staffing levels, and formalizing patient and family feedback regarding their care, to establishing certification processes for new programs. While these were all successes in a positive direction, I felt the need to equip myself with Canadian credentials to solidify my progressive career journey. I must think outside the box. I started part-time graduate studies at the local university while at the same time working full-time as a mother of two girls. Mission accomplished. I was the first internationally educated nurse (IEN) to graduate with a master's degree in nursing. Some of my learnings are as follows:

- Leaders can set the direction of where the organization will move by assessing how it functions and what improvements are needed to achieve its goals.
- Frontline leaders must constantly adapt to new realities and create new growth opportunities for themselves and their teams.
- Leaders are key enablers for change.

Leadership From the Bedside to the Boardroom: Learning is a Lifelong Journey

The mid-nineties were marked by massive restructuring in public healthcare throughout the province. Lower-paid employees were replacing professional nurses. As a frontline manager tasked with downsizing, I felt the need to collaborate with our professional association to share my views. I ran for one of the elected provincial councilor positions for the province to represent the almost 23,000 professional nurses. I was elected for a two-year term and re-elected for another term. Another Pinay trend-setting to bring what I am passionate about nursing to the association's boardroom. With this political exposure, several more opportunities surfaced. At the end of one political term, I was nominated recipient of the Vogel Award for Exemplary Service to Provincial Council. After this award, I received subsequent nominations for different professional governance committees, such as the Alberta Health Expert Panel Advisory Committee to Health Restructuring, and at the national level as an adjudicator for the Canadian Nurses Protective Society and the Canadian Nurses Ethics Expert Panel to review our Code of Ethics. The word is out: Lucy Reyes is becoming known within the health community, but one thing remains the same, I am still the person who always wanted to give her best. During this transition, I learned the following lessons as an elected provincial councilor of our professional association:

- Advocacy for the Nursing Profession amidst downsizing during management meetings
- Information sharing of what we need to have to continue to deliver quality care
- Process assessment of current practices, analyzing gaps, looking for opportunities for care transformation within a LEAN organization
- Engaging the people at the frontline to make it happen

Leadership Amidst Chaos: Integrating Change

Y2K preparation became a high priority for healthcare organizations. The degree of preparedness for all was a priority, and hospitals were worried about the viability of their computer systems. While carrying the responsibilities as a manager, I was also seconded as the Client Project Director. My task was to lead the planning and implementation of an existing computer system from another hospital to ours. Time was of the essence as our old computer system was nearing its end. There was no time to prepare the hospital staff for this change, nor prepare them with their new workflows with the activation of the newer system. I knew this was not ideal as the technology must align with the processes. Thinking outside the box, we put our efforts into putting the processes in place to proactively resolve any issues that might arise by creating a team of diverse providers and leaders. This thinking outside the box worked very well. How do you manage change amidst turbulent times? What are some of the lessons learned?

- For change to be successful, focus your efforts on the people who will be impacted the most. In this case, the frontline clinical providers.
- Change-oriented thinking is part of everyday practice. Seek out people who can become your change ambassadors.
- Technological advances are rapidly evolving. Keep yourself ahead of them.
- Learn from crisis to prevent them from happening again.

Leadership and Innovation: Balancing Priorities

Following the successful and smooth Y2K transition, I became the first Nursing Informatics Senior Specialist within the I.T. department. I was to establish and develop this role. Subsequently, this role expanded to at least four major acute care hospitals and other community health services. Working alongside my medical counterpart, we started developing a proposal for an 80-million-dollar start-up project to procure a fully integrated electronic system. Our proposal succeeded, we received funding from the government, and a new era of work was about to happen. My leadership role in this project was to be the Clinical Lead in Enabling this Change. Using my newly acquired skills in Health Informatics along with my advanced graduate preparation as a Clinical Nurse Specialist, my goal was to use this as an opportunity for practice transformation and use quality improvement methodologies to support change. It was a four-year project, and we did it. Here are some building blocks for our success.

- Engage people into collective action to build a sustained future
- Keep a balance between short-term goals and long-term innovation
- Communicate, communicate, and communicate

The Heart of the Matter: Creating a Culture of Innovation

Global restructuring continued with public healthcare for the province, integrated under one corporate structure; a very lean organizational structure.

Management Leaders were reduced by half. First, I was deployed to the cardiac sciences portfolio to manage the two acute cardiology units in one of the tertiary centers. Then a few months later, my role expanded to cover all six cardiac clinics at the same hospital; these positions were formerly administered by several managers.

Moreover, I was also appointed to coordinate the work of the Strategic Clinical Network Arrhythmia and Stroke working group. My interest in people gained acceptance in working with other clinical frontline leaders across the province to create the landscape for the care of the patient population with Cardiac Implantable Electrical Devices (CIED). CIED was a four-year project to connect this patient population remotely while living in either rural or urban areas. A very exciting project, but then tragedy struck. My husband's declining health necessitated me to reduce my workload and retire from my manager position. But subsequently, I was hired in a Research Administrator position as the overall project coordinator to continue the work of PERFORM (Performance Evaluation and Rhythm Follow-up Optimization through Remote Monitoring). At the same time, I was the Clinical Lead for the Remote Monitoring project that connected patients living with a CIED to their designated programs remotely across the province. My team completed the project at the end of 2018. CIED impacted approximately 5,000 people across the province, transformed all the different clinics caring for this population, and reduced practice variation to align everyone to the existing standards.

The COVID-19 epidemic arrived in Canada the following year, and the care of this patient population remained unaffected.

My team was the recipient of the 2020 Patient Experience Awards: Inspiring positive change by Quality Council of Alberta and the 2022 Canadian Council of Cardiovascular Nurses Health Promotion and Advocacy Award.

I always want to give my best in everything I do and strive to be the best Pinay leader I can be. My story is an example of one woman with a humble beginning whose determination, resilience, and lifelong learning made her the best. My key takeaways as I continue to be actively involved in another sphere of Public Health care: Patient Oriented Research

- Continue to build your professional presence, power, and positive relationships and networks ("Chief Nurse Blog: Nursing Matters" February 2022 | ICN ...")

- Adopt practices that spark positive emotions as well as hope and compassion
- Recharge your energy often to avoid intellectual fatigue and have a personal life.
- Emotional intelligence requires our mind and body connection, knowing our strengths and limitations, and sticking to our values and purpose.

Reflections From the Author

The COVID-19 pandemic and my family's losses in 2021 have tested my whole persona. My successful nomination to the FWN 100 Awards gave me some rays of hope for what is yet to come. My utmost gratitude goes to the FWN100 2021 selection committee and board for becoming part of my extended family. The award was titled Innovation and Thought Leader, and I would like to end my story with these two concepts combined. *"Thought leadership is something going beyond promoting yourself as a technical wizard in your particular profession."* (Prizeman 2015)

For me, thought leadership is about cultivating my ideas and assessing the fit with the organizational strategic priorities. Using a different set of colored glasses to look at the big picture of where the organization is going will help define the structures and processes to get there.

As I reflect on my leadership journey, although it was full of surprises and challenges, I vividly recall my first management meeting. One of the male managers asked me if I worked in housekeeping or the kitchen. I looked at myself; I was in a full business suit. I was not carrying a mop or kitchen tray. I took him aside without telling him who I was. I asked him why he thought so. He explained that these were the areas where Filipinos work. Upon realizing I was one of the new managers being introduced, this guy stood up and admitted how wrong he was to stereotype people who did not look like him. When introducing myself, I said, *"Good afternoon, everyone. My name is Lucy Reyes. I look different and sound different, but I have a special request to listen and use my different looks and sounds to remember the rest of my speech."* From then on, people in the organization remembered me as the first visible minority to hold a prominent position. My ten-word acceptance speech at the 2021 FWN gala, *"When Someone puts you down, Rise up. Prove them wrong."*

To the emerging leaders of tomorrow, we can be unique in our own little ways and still make a difference in the communities that we belong to and to the larger society. When people ask me what the secrets of my leadership strategies are, I sum them up in with these two acronyms: CREATE and RAVEN

CREATE

Celebrate small successes

Reflect on new ideas

Engage all levels of personnel

Accept risks and learn from others

Trial new ideas

Evaluate and continue to evaluate strategic directions

RAVEN

Recognizing

Appreciating

Valuing

Encouraging

Nurturing

MARIA SANTOS-GREAVES

Founder & Owner, Surrey Hearing Care, Inc.
GLOBAL FWN100™ 2015

Find Ability in Disability

When I was writing this piece, I was reminded of Facebook CEO Sheryl Sandberg, who, in her speech to the graduating class at UC Berkeley, spoke from her own life experience about overcoming hardships. To her, the difficult moments challenge and shape who we are: *"You will not be defined not just by what you achieve, but by how you survive it"* (Sandberg, 2022). I learned that to be true, there is beauty in embracing hardships. The hardships took me to heights I never once thought I could achieve.

Being an Entrepreneur

I recall that in my twenties, I experienced highs overshadowed by lows. Tumult and regret seemed to storm my life at different points. A self-starter, I took bold steps, such as launching my own business selling women's apparel. In my parent's home, I put together a wooden desk, a swivel chair, and my dad's old filing cabinets for what I proudly called Maria Nieves Santos' home office. It served as my sanctuary. There, I would spend long days—even some nights working on orders and ensuring that every customer was satisfied. I had a small team: a secretary who helped me stay on top of things and an assistant who worked on my day-to-day tasks. I experienced empowering moments that drove me to more inspiration. Every day, I poured my heart and soul into my business because I wanted it to succeed —and it did. Slowly but surely, I could see my investment paying off. More orders were coming in, my customer base was growing, and my small team was in perfect synergy. All the risks I took to follow my entrepreneurial gut signaled new heights.

Losing My First Business

But the success was not for long. As an entrepreneur, you deal with people from all walks of life. You must have a keen eye for discerning people. As I witnessed my business hit better margins, so did others around me. I trusted people— maybe one too many. There were those whom I thought would help me build my business further, but they blindsided me. I learned the hard way what it means to be embezzled. It was gut-wrenching. My blood, sweat, and tears went down the drain in one snap. Watching my business crumble felt like seeing the ocean consume a sandcastle I built. The more I tried to save it, the more it went to ruins. I was helpless, and I hit the wall hard. Worse, I was not the only one who lost. The people who depended on me lost their livelihood too. Inevitably, the fire in my belly extinguished.

Heartbroken, I spent days locked up in my room, with the darkest clouds looming over my head. I shut out the world and wanted to be alone. I didn't eat, do anything, or speak with anyone—including my family. It was a point in my life that I would not wish even upon my worst enemy.

Thankfully, I had a strong support system. Despite rejecting help from my parents, they did not give up. Soon, I sought medical attention. I was diagnosed with depression and received treatment. But recovery was not a walk in the park. For months, negative thoughts consumed me despite being surrounded by love and care. But little by little, it helped me get back on my feet.

Hearing Calls

One day, I was walking in a mall looking for a job. While scouring the stores to see if any of them was hiring, a small advertisement caught my attention. Without hesitation, I walked in and submitted my resumé. Believe it or not, I did not even know that it was a hearing clinic. I just wanted to land a job and find my purpose again. Although the type of business was unfamiliar to me, they called me back for an interest assessment. I remember receiving a book for me to study. Then I took an exam which, surprisingly, I passed. To this day, this accidental encounter is still beyond me. Little did I know that this would be a job upon which I would build my career for the next eight years.

I worked as an Audiometrist—the equivalent of a Hearing Instrument Practitioner here in Canada—and I fell in love with it. At work, I knew I was learning from the best people in the industry. There, I also met lifelong friends. I never imagined I would enjoy working at a hearing clinic, but it happened.

Fast forward to five years later, I was promoted, and I began doing marketing work. I learned more about the industry and widened my network. Coming to the clinic was something I looked forward to every day. Not many people enjoy their jobs, but I did—very much. But what I ultimately did not expect was that my depression would come back and haunt me. I relapsed.

Losing My Ability to Hear

Because I had not been taking my medications consistently, my recovering body had fallen off the healing track. I know that medication is merely thirty percent of the equation; the rest depends on my willingness to get better. To this day, I believe that. But at the time, I was also overwhelmed with everything that had happened—both the bad and the good. I woke up and got out of bed on what I thought would be a typical workday, but something did not feel right. It was as if I was floating on a hammock. I called for help, and when my mom came to check on me, I realized that I seemed to have lost hearing in one ear. I was rushed to the hospital. My hearing loss was validated. We were nervously waiting for what the doctor would say. I thought, *"Will I ever get my hearing back?"* Then, I was told it was a side effect of an antidepressant medication. Just when I thought I was getting my life together, my fears reemerged.

What had happened afterward was a series of admissions to the hospital. For months, I went in and out of Medical City as if it were my second home. Then, as if things could not get worse, I developed another serious condition. On one of the rare times, I was just at home, a longtime friend, Dr. Edwin Bernardo, dropped by our house to visit me. But what he saw was not what he had anticipated. I had blotches and blisters all over my body, beginning with my face. I was almost unrecognizable. He called an ambulance and had me taken to a hospital—again. I had developed Steven-Johnson Syndrome. A fatal allergy condition caused by medication that mainly affects the skin. But it could have been worse if not for Dr. Bernardo's quick thinking. My internal organs could have been affected as well. At this point, I had gotten used to being in the hospital. I was confined at the basement level because my condition was deemed very serious. Mirrors were even removed from my room because the doctors did not want me to get a glimpse of my reflection. They were afraid that it would trigger my depression once more. On top of this, I did not get my hearing back either. It felt like the world was against me. The same medication that helped me get by and recover brought me to an even lower point. I kept hitting rock bottom only to go deeper.

But deep in my heart, I knew that I was a fighter. I wanted to get better for myself, and the only way I could do so was if I would lead myself out of it—so I did. I had embraced my scars and accepted that life is never easy. What happened to me is a testament to how strong I had always been. It opened my eyes to God's plan for much better things in my life.

Canada Calls

In 1999, I received an invitation from my sister, who had already moved to Canada for work. Since my parents already had planned to travel to Canada, I decided to take a leave for two months. The night before my flight, I received a call from my boss asking for reassurance that I would return. I laughed it off and told her that I had no intentions of staying permanently and leaving the company. I simply wanted to take some time off and make memories with family.

Canada was my second overseas travel. I did not know much about the country except for the stories my sister told me. It was summer when we came. Back in the Philippines, the sun would be scorching hot, and people would flock to malls to escape the heat. But it was a novel experience to feel the cold breeze during this season when I came to the Great White North. In the next two months, I toured around Metro Vancouver, saw new places, and discovered as much as possible.

Love Calls

One day, I went to a mall in Surrey with my mom. It was supposed to be a quick stroll. We wanted to look around and pick up a few things we needed for the next few days. Unbeknownst to her, I was also meeting up with someone. His name was Sam, and I met him through a common friend. We met at the food court and grabbed coffee together. We chatted, talked about our families, and learned more about each other. Time flew by, and I had to bid him goodbye before my mom grew skeptical. Then came a second date, a third one, and so on. It had been a while since I saw someone. I had unpleasant experiences in the past that sowed fears in my heart about falling in love again. I remember thinking to myself back then that I would not marry anymore. Instead, I just wanted to take care of my parents. But God had a different plan.

Soon, I introduced Sam to my parents. At first, they were unsure of him—especially my dad. Coming from an utterly different background, Sam was unlike the men I had dated before. He was blunt and unpretentious, yet showed caring traits. I knew that he loved me. I was hoping my parents would see that too. With him, I felt freedom like no other. I was in a new country, made new friends, and met someone. My two-month vacation was more than I had anticipated. It was just the beginning. As Sam and I knew each other better, we started to think of starting a life together. We would imagine where we would live, our house, and how many kids we would have. I will never forget how I felt the moment he proposed to me. I did not think I would find love again, but there he was. I said yes, and we got married. Our love blossomed, and shortly after, we welcomed our child.

On the afternoon of September 17, 2000, Sebastian was born. It is true what they say about motherhood—it changes you. I had never felt happier the first time I held our son. Sebastian brought joy not only to us but also to my parents and in-laws. To this day, I crack a smile when I recall that moment.

Raising a child in a foreign country was not the easiest. Financially, we were surviving. Sam had seasonal jobs but was earning enough to support our family. What was challenging was the prejudice people had against me as a woman of color married to a Canadian. When we would go out and take our son to the park, I would get looks from people. Sometimes, people would even ask if I was his nanny. I eventually learned to laugh it off.

Time truly tests all relationships. In the next few years, cracks emerged in my marriage. Sam and I did not always see eye-to-eye. But we knew all couples fought, so we tried to work through our issues. We thought of Sebastian, too, of course. He was so young. But I learned that sometimes, holding on does more damage than letting go. It felt like I was losing myself. The freedom that I felt before slowly faded away. I did not know who I was becoming anymore. The last thing I wanted was for it to affect my relationship with my family, especially my son. Sam and I eventually split up.

Being a single mother is already difficult by itself. But to be one in a foreign country was a different struggle altogether. I was not employed during my marriage with Sam because he wanted me to focus on raising our son. So, when I left him, I felt like I had lost a limb. It was my first time being truly on my own in Canada. I did not even know how to go around the city without a car. I had to learn how to ride the bus, learn all the routes, and memorize the street numbers. Every day, I would call the operator to ask what buses I should take to get to my destination. Sometimes, I could not ask anyone to look after Sebastian, so I would take him with me. Then, I would be on the SkyTrain at 7 a.m. to look for a job downtown. I would go from building to building while pushing a stroller to drop off my resumé, hoping to get called for an interview.

Because of my background in the hearing industry and my degree in pharmacy, I thought about working as a pharmacist for my first job. But I quickly learned it was not the same in Canada as in the Philippines. I needed more training and education to qualify. After submitting a hundred applications, I finally got a job. I worked as a cashier at a dollar store. Working full-time as a mother was challenging to say the least. I am grateful for the people around me who looked after Sebastian while I was busy at work.

As my son grew up, I realized that motherhood is more than just doing things for your child. A lot of it was also about listening. My son witnessed my struggles as a person with hearing loss. Many times, he would think that I was not paying attention to him or that I was shouting at him. It was hard to explain to a six-year-old what hearing loss was and why it seemed like I was ignoring him. But it also inspired me to get back into the hearing industry.

Hearing Calls Again

Undeniably, my heart desired to work again at a hearing clinic. It had become my passion, and I genuinely wanted to help people hear better. As someone who had experienced its challenges first-hand, I knew how tough it could be. You miss out on some family moments, it presents challenges at work, and sometimes, you are misunderstood because one of your senses is not fully available. Rediscovering this part of me that I lost ignited my desire to look for a hearing clinic where I could work. That was when I found a local hearing clinic in my city. I did not have a lot of connections, but my experience spoke for itself. The owner saw my potential and hired me as a receptionist. Love felt sweeter the second time. I enjoyed the job because I learned more about the hearing industry here in Canada. Financially, it also helped my son and me. Everything was falling into place once again.

The hearing industry is small and tight-knit. Competitors know each other and the people who work within their clinics. Whether service is good or bad, word will get out. A competing clinic had heard about us and the work that I had done, presumably from clients. Because of that, I was pirated by another clinic. There, my responsibilities were more than I was expecting. Aside from assisting patients and making calls, I was also tasked to attend to their appointments.

Initially, I was happy because my boss trusted me. But I knew that it was not right. Owning a clinic may be business, but at the end of the day, people would understand if you were only after their money. So, after eight months, I left. I was determined to put up a clinic of my own.

Owning My Hearing Clinic

People doubted me, but it did not come as a shock. In an industry dominated by men, starting my own business would never be easy—especially for an Asian woman. My former boss even told me I would never succeed because I did not have a license. But, with confidence, I said to him that I would find one. Soon after, I did. The network I had grown working in the hearing business here in Canada paid off. I sought out people, asked for their advice, and ultimately received help. It was at this point that I met Jim and Vicky. Jim was not working in any clinic, but he saw that I desperately wanted to establish my own. On the other hand, Vicky was a licensed practitioner. Jim helped me look for a location and pointed me to the right people and lent me the equipment and a hearing booth.

But frankly speaking, I did not have anything to fund my business. However, Vicky believed in me and my passion, so she loaned me money. Together, we put up our own clinic. It was not a clinic with rooms and a receiving area, rather, a bare-bones clinic with only a booth and other necessities to test people and assist those interested in having their hearing checked. Life came full circle because, once again, I became a business owner. Like my first venture back in the Philippines, we were a lean team of three. But we made it work.

My clinic was running smoothly, and more patients started coming in. I can say that all my experiences in the clinics I worked at helped me tremendously. Not only did I learn the tricks of the trade, but I also developed genuine care for the hard of hearing. But unlike the people I had worked with in the past, I did not feel I was given control and trust. Although I was co-owning the business, my movement was limited. Learning from the past, I listened to myself this time. With nothing but guts, I bought out my partner. That way, I could call the shots and serve my community better. For several years, I paid my business partner every month. Luckily, she agreed to a small amount because she knew I did not have much.

What is yours will find its way to you. That is how I felt as help came my way as I managed the business alone. Soon, I had my own space—a full-fledged clinic with testing booths, a receiving area, and an office. My responsibilities were growing, but it only encouraged me to work better and harder. I became known as *"The Hearing Lady"* by my local community. Many older adults came to my clinic to seek my help and put their trust in me. Even though I had bills to pay, I still wanted to help them in any way I could. After all, that is why I started a hearing clinic. I contacted all the hearing aid brands and asked for deals, and they obliged. Like any other service-oriented business, trust is crucial, and it is built through the years. I gave clients affordable hearing services and slashed the prices as much as possible. At the same time, I needed to prove myself credible, so I ensured that all their hearing needs were addressed when they came to my clinic.

My business grew, and shortly after, I opened my second location. I would go back and forth between the two sites just to be present in their appointments because they all wanted to see me. Although it was challenging, I was glad I could serve more people because my clinic was now at two locations. Then came a third branch, and then a fourth. We joined different events, placed multiple ads in Filipino and other local newspapers, and sponsored various activities. We went all-out to market our name in Metro Vancouver. Because of that, more people, especially seniors, became familiar with Surrey Hearing Care, Inc.

The clinic had grown so much from a team of three and is now run by over 15 people at our now-five locations. I am extremely grateful because with me on this journey is my son.

Sebastian learned more about the practice and had grown fond of it. When he was in high school, I would already take Sebastian with me to work so he would be familiar with how the clinic is run. At first, he was not interested in it, but eventually, he listened and paid attention to what my colleagues and I were doing. He took up the hearing practitioner program in college and passed with flying colors. One of my proudest moments was when he got his license and became a registered practitioner. He has been of great help to me in running the business. Whenever he would tell me stories about his clients, I would be in awe of the professional he has become. Despite the difficulties that my "disability" presented in rearing my son, it helped him better understand our clients' struggles.

Managing five clinics and different teams can be tricky. At first, I was frustrated when expectations were not met. I used to treat my staff like I treated myself—and I can be my greatest critic. I want to get things right immediately. But I realized that working in hearing care is not a simple job. You must learn about hearing and sincerely care for the clients you serve to understand how important you are to the clinic. I always remind my staff that my success is theirs, too. The better the clinic performs, the better it is for everyone.

Gaining From Hearing Loss

Life does not stop with a loss or two. Through the many losses I experienced, I learned that we could power through them and lead ourselves to brighter days. For example, when I lost my hearing, I thought I would miss out on many opportunities and experiences. But my hearing loss led me to where I am today. I believe that I am more compassionate, more persevering, and more caring because of the struggles I have gone through. This is not to say that we should seek nor be excited about loss. Instead, we should face and embrace it. We are allowed to grieve and be sad about losing something. Doing so will make us accept our situations better and prosper despite the challenges. Without experiencing loss, I may not have experienced victories.

Fifteen thousand clients later, Surrey Hearing Care has reached heights I had never imagined. It is now one of the city's most awarded clinics with five service locations. Various care facilities have also partnered with us. But almost thirty years into it, I am still learning so much and have no plans of stopping soon. I firmly believe that when you take care of clients, they will keep coming back. I often visit them at their homes and assist them with things because I want them to know that we are here for them. As a result, some come back to us with multiple purchases even if years have passed. Had I not lost my hearing, perhaps I would not be this trusted. Clients believe in our mission to help more people hear the world because of its sincerity.

I let and led myself out of darkness because I saw hope in the people around me. But I also had to believe in myself to get out of it. American entrepreneur Scott Belsky calls it "self-leadership." It is difficult to lead others if you cannot lead yourself. But he said that a combination of awareness, tolerance, and belief in your capabilities could lead you to a better you. I knew my weaknesses through my losses. I also learned to be more forgiving of myself and care for my well-being. No matter how many times I fall, I can pick myself back up because I know that loss, in all its strange forms, is not defeat; but often the universe's way of redirecting our life's trajectory. In my disability, I found my leadership ability. Listen to yourself, and you will hear the fighter in you—I know this to be true.

MARIA ZELDA "MARIZEL" MAGISTRADO ROJAS

President, Bikol Society Austria (BSA)
Founder/Chairperson, European Network of Filipino Diaspora – Austria (ENFiD-Austria)
Founder/President, Philippine Austrian Cultural and Educational Society (PACES)
President, Vienna International Centre Club Filipino (VIC CF)
Board Member/Newsletter Editor, United Nations Women's Guild (UNWG)
Board Member, United Nations Correspondents Association Vienna (UNCAV)
Board Member, European Network of Filipino Diaspora (ENFiD)
Counsellor, European Police Association (EPA)
Treasurer, Comprehensive Nuclear-Test-Ban Treaty Organization Staff Council (CTBTO/SC)
Founder/Secretary, Vienna International Centre Group of Polynesian Friends (VIC GPF)
Founder/Secretary, Vienna International Centre Latin Dance Club (VIC LDC)
Member, Filipina Women's Network (FWN)
GLOBAL FWN100™ 2019

Predestined: #SerialOrganizer

A decade of leadership is a chapter of my life that is part of the stories of countless overseas Filipino migrants across the globe. It is a story that resonates with many, with all the similarities in the challenges, trials, and tribulations. And like any story, it has its twists, one of which is the metamorphosis into a serial organizer.

Coming from the small, picturesque town of Camaligan, Camarines Sur, in the region known for its active volcanoes, serene whale sharks, and spicy cuisine, Bicol, I did wish to go abroad. I did dream of touching snow. I did have a vision of myself traipsing around the world. But I did not want to go abroad forced by circumstances—illness in the family, worse, crime and death.

Disruptions in My First Home: Crime and Death

In 1986, I graduated with a Bachelor of Science in Physics for Teachers degree from the Philippine Normal College – De la Salle University consortium as part of the four-year scholarship program of the National Science Development Board (NSDB) – National Science and Technology Authority (NSTA) Project 8102. I was one of the 25 students chosen from different parts of the Philippines to be trained to teach Physics. As part of this scholarship grant, I was contractually bound to teach for at least four years in a public school of my choice.

I chose Camarines Sur National High School (CSNHS) in Naga City, where I was a happy-go-lucky teacher, content with the meager salary I earned because of the sense of fulfillment I derived from converting Physics haters into Physics lovers. This task was not easy for a fresh graduate like me, especially with the welcome I received on my first day. I had to run the gauntlet, with male students checking me out from head to foot, with catcalls and wolf whistles, on my way to the classroom, where fifty students were waiting for me.

The contentment I felt as an underpaid and overworked Physics teacher stemmed, too, from the fact that I belonged to a group of young, mostly fresh graduate teachers. We made sure that teaching had that element of fun, ensuring that the extracurricular activities complemented the learning process within the four walls of the classrooms. We were known as the SWAT: *"Samahan ng mga Walang Awang Teachers,"* mostly major subject teachers who were strict in the classroom but very approachable to students after classes. An enthusiastic, inspired, and inspiring group who made sure that life in CSNHS was anything but boring with all the activities we organized with our students: academic and talent competitions, cultural and contemporary shows, and many others.

I would have probably continued teaching until I retired, had not my father gotten seriously ill. The harsh realization that I could not pay for the hospital bills incurred made me decide to go abroad. But a few days before my flight, I received the sad news that my 18-year-old brother was murdered with thirty-two stab wounds and four knives on his way home. It became even more urgent for me then to leave the comfort of my home and go abroad to earn enough to pay for hospital bills and legal fees in our desperate fight for justice for my brother.

Helplessness is a feeling I do not ever want to feel again. This thought was foremost on the plane bound for Austria.

Disruptions in My Second Home

I arrived in Austria on 4 November 1991, on a cold, grey day, forever etched in my memory. I had left behind my family, friends, and the financial burden I knew not yet how I would resolve. I clearly remember the mixed feelings I had: gratitude to the relatives who helped me travel to Vienna, apprehension for the unknown, especially because of the language barrier, excitement for what might be, and optimism that the journey I had started would be the solution I was seeking.

I had a six-month tourist visa. I had no idea how this visa can be extended or converted. I did not know German. I had no job prospects. Instead, I had parents, five brothers, relatives, and friends waiting to hear about my success or failure. These were just some of the seemingly insurmountable challenges I had back then.

"Verlaengerung ausgeschlossen" visibly stamped on page six of my first Philippine passport, were the first words I learned in German. It meant extension excluded, which referred to my six-month tourist visa. If I did not have an employer who could sponsor my stay in Austria before my visa expired, I would be forced to go back home empty-handed. Therefore, finding a job, any job, or anyone who could help me with the visa was imperative!

I was almost raped. In my desperate quest for work, for anything that would allow me to make money, I was answering ads in a newspaper called *Bazaar* left and right. One was for a window cleaner, which I thought I could easily do. Yes, it was a man who answered my call, but surely, even men needed window cleaners, too. The voice on the phone sounded non-threatening, the conversation noncommittal, but the terms clear on the rates and the duration of the work. Later I found out, while I was already in his tiny apartment, that what he was looking for was women to pose nude for him. He explained this as he was showing me photographs of Asian women in varying poses and stages of undress and, at the same time, unbuckling his belt. I do not know what he intended to do, but I know I had never run as fast as I did that day. Out on the deserted street, there was a slight drizzle. I ran sobbing, the rain mingling with the tears on my cheeks. I do not deny that I felt vulnerable and defenseless at that time. But, wiping my tears, resolving not to tell anyone about the incident, I thought that vulnerable and defenseless would define me if I let myself be. And that I was not willing to do.

Fortunately, I found someone through an ad in the same newspaper who helped me with a visa through a Legitimation Card issued by the United Nations. I am beyond grateful to the Austrian lady who employed me as a nanny for her five-year-old daughter. My duties entailed picking her up from school every day, tutoring, and taking care of her until her mom arrived from work. They treated me like family. They allowed me to have a small flat next to theirs, which was my haven for five years. I was a nanny by day during the weekdays and a "Part-timer" on weekends and any other free time. What this meant was I took on any job paid by the hour: cleaner for offices & houses, babysitter, tutor, caregiver, cook, waitress, dog walker, name it, I did it. And I am proud of all those odd jobs that ensured I lived well and had enough money to send my family back home. Undeniably, my self-esteem suffered, but I did not wallow in this state. I firmly believe that life is neutral—it is up to me to make it positive or negative.

Learning German was one of my priorities. As early as the month I arrived, I found free German courses at the University of Vienna. Since they were offered at lunchtime, I could attend classes from Monday to Friday, unaware I was attending levels 1 and 2 simultaneously, German 1 on Monday, Wednesday, and Friday, and German 2 on Tuesday and Thursday. I remember wondering how I could hardly understand anything on some days and was pleasantly surprised to receive two passing certificates at the end of the courses. This started my love for language learning which I would pursue years later. To date, I have learned French and Russian, raising the number of languages I know to seven: Bicol, Filipino, English, Spanish, German, French and Russian. Someday, I hope to complete the six UN languages by learning Arabic and Chinese and continue learning more languages.

Though difficult, financially and time-wise, I enrolled in a one-year Secretarial Course at the European Business School (Europa Wirtschaft Schule). I had learned that the United Nations in Vienna usually hired staff from this institution. And therefore, it would be a good investment.

I applied for jobs wherever I could, collecting a scrapbook of rejection letters in all forms. Some letters saying that I am overqualified, others telling me I am underqualified or some simply informing that they have no vacancy. I could have given up then since I was anyway already earning enough. But I did not give up because I had someone who believed in me and encouraged me to continue applying despite all the rejections, my husband, Joel.

My patience and perseverance paid off. On 4 November 1998, I was offered temporary employment at the Comprehensive Nuclear-Test-Ban Treaty Organization (CTBTO) in the United Nations headquarters in Vienna. Twenty-four years later, I am still working in the same organization as an Administrative Assistant, enjoying my work that ensures a world free of nuclear testing.

My blessings multiplied when, after a couple of miscarriages, I had my daughter, Sarah Jozelle, in 2002. I never really wanted to have a child. Back then, I considered a child a hindrance to my planned career and the carefree life I wanted to live. However, I am glad I let my husband and my parents' prodding and pleading convince me to have one. For in my daughter, my life is complete.

In 2013, I thought I had everything: a simple life, a loving and devoted husband, an adorable daughter, and a wonderful job. However, it took the most powerful tropical cyclone, known in the Philippines as Typhoon Yolanda, to catapult me into action. It was then I realized that there are so many people in need of help, especially during natural and man-made calamities, and that I was in the position to help. Abundant blessings I had received. It was time to pay forward. With that as my mantra, my involvement as a leader in the Filipino community began—first, as the President of the Vienna International Centre Club Filipino (VIC CF), then as the Vice President of the Council of Filipino Associations in Austria (CFAA), President of Bikol Society Austria (BSA), President of Philippine Austrian Cultural and Educational Society (PACES), Chairperson of the European Network of Filipino Diaspora in Austria (ENFiD-Austria), Board Member of the United Nations Women's Guild (UNWG), Counsellor of the European Police Association (EPA), Board Member and Newsletter Editor of the United Nations Correspondents in Vienna (UNCAV). Simultaneously at the helm of these organizations, with the support of the officers and members, I spearheaded activities, events, and projects to raise funds for beneficiaries and promote Filipino culture, traditions, and talents.

COMPULSION & CONVICTION

What happened in a decade, between 2012 and 2022, with my active involvement in the community, is a story worth sharing in the hope that an ongoing journey that started from tragedy will inspire others to get actively involved in the communities where they are, whether at home in the Philippines or their second homes abroad. Because trite as it is, *"together, we are stronger!"*

After witnessing, albeit virtually, the destruction caused by Haiyan, something compelled me to do something, anything! I remember coming to the office in a daze, wondering how I would organize fundraisers for the typhoon victims, who I should contact, where I should get the paraphernalia, and so on and so forth—more questions than answers. But then the *"Bayanihan"* spirit kicked in. Numerous volunteers responded to the request I sent out for help collecting money in the public spaces on the UN premises. I collaborated with different organizations to put up shows and events as fundraisers. And with the members of the VIC Cub Filipino, I was able to raise money which we sent to the typhoon victims through Red Cross, Medecins sans Frontieres, and other groups and beneficiaries. To me, that was a turning point. That was when I realized how much we could do as a community when we put heads together, and work together. But critical to this was having people who could lead. And I realized I was one of them. Sadly, it took a calamity to trigger my involvement with the community organizing and awaken the dormant leader. But at least it gave me a clear vision about what else I wanted to do and could.

Serial organizer is what my daughter coined to describe me and what I do. The different organizations I currently lead simultaneously, provide me with great opportunities to organize activities and events of varying genre, the core of which is helping others.

Bikol Society Austria

"Sararo maski harayo" is the motto of one of the most dynamic organizations in the Filipino community in Austria, Bikol Society Austria (BSA). Established

in 1993 primarily to promote the devotion to the Patroness of Bicolandia, Our Lady of Peñafrancia, fondly known to most as *"Ina,"* BSA is also a platform for promoting camaraderie among Bicolanos and for promoting Filipino talent, culture, and traditions.

My involvement in BSA started when I became the *"Hermana Mayor"* in 2012, working closely with BSA Officers in organizing the ten-day festivities in honor of *Ina*. The ten-day activity consisted of nine-day Novena Masses and Agape, a fluvial procession on the Danube River with almost 600 pilgrims on board the largest ship in Vienna, and a concelebrated Mass on the last day. This meant organizing logistics, sponsors and donors, and the full program. It was not an easy role but something I gladly did. I felt at that time that with all the blessings I had received, it was time to give back. What better way than propagating my devotion to *Ina* through BSA?

"Un pueblo amante de Maria," a people devoted to Mary. Unapologetically, I am one fervent devotee, forever a child turning to its mother for everything. Every achievement, every milestone in my life was through the intersession of *Ina*. So many difficult school examinations I took, job applications I submitted, health concerns I was going through, and special wishes were accompanied by prayers and Novenas to my *Ina*. So, therefore, I thought, why not take on the BSA presidency when the time came that no one wanted to take it on back in 2016. Again, I saw it as a way to give back.

It has been six years, and yet it seems just like yesterday. Organizing BSA activities and events have been challenging, especially in 2020-2021 with the raging COVID-19 pandemic. Still, challenges were overcome by God's grace, with our Lady of Peñafrancia's intercession and the valuable assistance of its officers and members.

Vienna International Centre Club Filipino (VIC CF)

The face of the Filipinos with respect to the international community, VIC CF is an organization of Filipinos working at the different organizations in the United Nations headquarters in Vienna, established in 1997 in preparation for the visit of President Fidel Ramos. It is providential that I work in CTBTO. Therefore I had the possibility of joining the VIC CF.

Typhoon Haiyan/Yolanda catapulted me into a frenzy of actions in 2013 as VIC CF President, and this frenzy has not waned. However, looking back at all the activities and events I spearheaded, I tend to wonder how it was possible to do all of what we did. Through the years, since 2013, we have organized different activities and events to promote Filipino talents, culture, and tradition. For example, we organized the annual Independence Day Celebration *"Almusal para sa Kalayaan,"* the traditional annual charity dinner "A Spring to Remember," the Philippine-Austrian event "Octoberfest," Painting and Photo Exhibitions (Agenda Humanity 1 & 2, *#pinoygaling, Lakbay Sining*), Philippine Food Stall at the annual United Nations Women's Guild (UNWG) Bazaar, special events such as the Symposium for Miss Earth, Requiem for Honourable Domingo Lim Siazon Jr and many more.

"We" is what made it possible. We did everything as a team, an indefatigable one at that. My dream team.

Leading the VIC CF provides ample opportunities to conduct fundraisers for beneficiaries in the Philippines and Austria. What a blessing it is for us and those whose lives we touch!

Scholar Paying Forward

When I was recruited to be among the founding members of the Philippine Austrian Cultural and Educational Society in 2016 by then Philippine Ambassador to Austria, Maria Zeneida Angara Collinson, I had to think twice about accepting. At that time, I already had two organizations, both very active vis a vis the Filipino and International communities. But having the first-hand experience of being a scholar, grateful for the subsidy I received to finish my degree, and keeping my promise to pay it forward, made me decide to join PACES and subsequently be its President. It was also an honor to be among Ambassador Collinson's hand-picked like-minded members of the Philippine-Austrian community. They believed in promoting the study of science and technology as a vehicle for development and progress when she established PACES. From its Secretary, I am currently the President of this organization, whose mission is to support needy but outstanding Filipino university students in the form of scholarships in the fields of Science, Technology, Engineering, and Mathematics (STEM). It is very fulfilling to work with an Executive Board that continues to work towards the achievement of PACES' vision for a sustainable scholarship program in STEM (Science, Technology, Engineering, Math), leading toward a solid scientific and technical base in the Philippines.

PACES' core activity is a scholarship program—STEMS70—which provides full scholarships to four deserving students in the Philippines pursuing college degrees in the scientific fields who graduated in 2020-2021. We currently have four scholars under STEMS75.

Signature activities of PACES include lectures, in person and online, organized at the Philippine Embassy, at the United Nations in Vienna, and at Vienna's University of Business and Economics.

We also organize the annual commemoration of the proclamation of Philippine Independence, in collaboration with the Philippine Embassy and the Vienna Mayor's Office, in the form of Floral Offerings at the Catalpa Trees in front of the City Hall every 12 June. The Filipino community leaders planted these trees during the Centennial Anniversary of the Proclamation of Philippine Independence in 1998.

European Network of Filipino Diaspora – Austria (ENFiD – Austria)

Galvanized into action—was how I felt after attending an Annual General Assembly of the European Network of Filipino Diaspora in Essen, Germany, in September 2017. There I met leaders from different European countries who inspired me to aspire to be like them. I established ENFiD – Austria on 15 October 2017.

ENFiD – Austria is among the 17 countries members of the European Network of Filipino Diaspora (ENFiD) Europe, which is a non-political, non-sectarian and not-for-profit network. ENFID envisions a community of Euro-Filipinos whose talents, contribution, and potential as social and economic remitters are recognized *glocally* (global and local) and fully integrated in Europe, keeping their cultural values and traditions while enriching the diversity in Europe and being cognizant of the future generation.

Though recently established and with only eight members, ENFiD – Austria has spearheaded different activities, events, and projects under the four programs, 4Es, on Education & Learning, Empowering the Euro-Pinoy Youth, Elevating the Arts & Culture, Embracing the Environment. Most important among these took place in 2020–2022, during the COVID-19 pandemic. For example, the Philippine Folkloric Festivals, *"Pamana II and III"* Philippine Austrian Festivals Parade to commemorate 75 Years of Diplomatic Relations between the two countries, and a lockdown project in the form of a cook book, *Recipes for Keeps.*

"Joining Hands to Help Children"

The *raison d'etre*, the purpose of the establishment and existence of the United Nations Women's Guild (UNWG), is to assist children in need or mother–childcare programs throughout the world. For this reason, I accepted the nomination to be a Board Member and Newsletter editor of UNWG in November 2020, even though I was already leading many organizations at that time. It is a decision I have not regretted. Although it is time intensive with the production of weekly updates to members and monthly Newsletters as well as the monthly meetings and all the activities and events we organize, the sense of fulfillment is more than a reward. I regret not having more than 24 hours each day so I can do more for every organization I lead.

UNWG, founded in 1967, is a charity organization with members from over 100 countries. It is open to staff members or spouses of staff members of United Nations or Permanent Missions in Vienna, with members enjoying social, cultural, and educational programmes. Each year, the UNWG organizes a day-long Internal Festival Bazaar, which supports children's charities in Austria and developing countries.

Pink Wave

With nostalgia, I look back at the 80s in the Philippines. I vividly recall the palpable idealism of the youth, the contagious activism. I am proud to say that I was among those idealistic activists during the peaceful People Power Revolution in February 1986. I bravely marched on the streets of Manila. I shouted chants until I was hoarse and blue in the face. I dodged water cannons shot from fire trucks during the rallies. I gagged and choked from the tear gas in canisters thrown at rallyists. I fled from policemen chasing us through narrow streets in Mendiola. I joined the siege of Malacañang Palace. I saw the ouster of a dictator. I witnessed the ascension of a woman to the Philippine presidency. I rejoiced at the dawn of a new era for the Philippines, free of authoritarian rule.

Living in Austria, comfortable in the life I have made, gave me a feeling of living in a protective bubble. Everything works in Austria. It was easy to ignore the state of the Philippines that I saw on the news and social media and heard about from my relatives. I did my part in supporting my family back home, which was the extent of the involvement I chose to have with my country.

Then came 7 October 2021, when Leni Robredo filed her candidacy for the 2022 Philippine presidential election. Leni Robredo was the vice president of the Philippines from 30 June 2016 until 30 June 2022 and was a former representative of Camarines Sur's third congressional district from 2013 to 2016. But, more importantly for me, she was a classmate, a friend, from my elementary and high school days in Colegio de Sta Isabel. I know her as someone in the best position to lead the country as its President. I know because ten years at the same school during our formative years is more than enough time to get to know someone, to know who they are. It provides ample opportunity to understand someone's virtues and values. Growing up in a small city like Naga is enough time to see a person's character and credibility.

So, I decided to ride the pink wave across Austria, across Europe. With some friends, I initiated a movement, *"Kakampink* Austria," a crusade for the election of Leni. We started with a Holy Mass at the St. Stephens Cathedral in Vienna on 9 October 2021, thanking God for the emergence of a Presidential candidate in the person of Leni.

Sitting huddled in a small restaurant, we mapped the way forward in a two-pronged approach: campaigning and fundraising.

As part of the campaign, we organized a series of brainstormings and devised our calendar of activities. We had round table discussions on vote delivery and vote protection. We had strategic meetings with other groups of supporters in Austria. We had weekly prayer brigades. We joined online meetings with different groups and movements in the Philippines and Europe to learn from each other. Most importantly, we organized rallies.

I printed and distributed copies of the voters' list in Austria. Then, painstakingly, we went through each name, identifying those we know, classifying them of pro, con, and neutral vis a vis our candidates, and then mounting a one and one campaign over the phone, by email, on social media, and in meetups.

Organizing the biggest rally with speakers and attendees from Austria and Belgium, Czech Republic, Germany, Hungary, Italy, and Switzerland meant many sleepless nights. It was not easy to get a permit, but we managed. Choosing the optimal venue was critical, and we were lucky to get the permit to have the rally right in the heart of Vienna, at the Plaza next to St. Stephen's Cathedral. Most importantly, we managed to get our candidates' messages and projected them on screens for all to hear.

We also went to join rallies in Paris, France, Munich, Germany, and Reykavik, Iceland. We were so inspired to meet leaders in these countries who were so engaged and generous, so full of conviction and fearlessness.

Nowadays, fearlessness is a much-needed characteristic one has to have in speaking up and espousing one's political choices. Because the attacks on social media can be more detrimental than the effect of the tear gas I experienced during the rallies back in the eighties.

Using different social medial platforms such as Facebook, Twitter, Instagram, TikTok, we expressed our views, connected with like-minded Filipinos, and campaigned for our candidates. I have never posted as much as I have posted during the campaign.

Witnessing the counting of votes as a Pollwatcher at the Philippine Embassy was heart-breaking. It started in the afternoon, and as the day progressed into the night and the night into day, that unexplainable feeling of hopelessness just kept getting stronger and stronger.

My candidate lost. I have come to terms with the election results. It is not what I wanted, not what I fervently prayed for. The end of corruption, incompetence, and culture of violence is not yet in sight. But I take comfort in the Bible verse, Romans 8:28–30 *"And we know that all things work together for good to them that love God, to them who are called according to his purpose."*

Being

The organizations I am currently leading are different in their missions and visions, in their *raison d'etre*. BSA is religious, propagating devotion. VIC CF is the face of the Filipinos vis a vis the international community. PACES supports scholars in the Philippines, believing that STEMS is the key to a country's development. Finally, ENFiD-Austria is a forum for diaspora interaction among Filipino organizations in Austria and across Europe.

Different they may be, but there are similarities as well. The organizations:

1. Promote Filipino culture and traditions, showcasing them to the residents in our second home and the international community. This ensures our Filipino identity is passed on as a legacy to the second, third, and subsequent Filipino or Austro-Filipino generations.

2. Provide assistance to beneficiaries such as victims of natural and man-made catastrophes, deserving scholars who will hopefully pay forward someday, and charitable institutions in the Philippines and Austria.

3. Support and promote Filipino talent, #pinoygaling, in creative, performing, and visual arts, in Austria and other countries in Europe.

4. Provide a forum for connecting with our country and with our second home.

Perfect Imperfection

My life as it is now may not be perfect. But I could say it is a life where some of my dreams come true. As a child, whenever I was asked what I wanted to be when I grew up, quick as a bullet, I would reply, *"stewardess or witch."* Adding *"because I want to travel, and I want to see snow."* Travel is a part of my life now, whether for pleasure or work. Updating my profile on a social media platform, I counted 32 countries I have visited. Snow, yes, yearly, I see snow. Dreams do come true.

But, after more than half a century in this world, as of this writing, for reasons I cannot fathom, I still feel that I have not done much in my life for myself, my family, my community, and my country. I see before me endless possibilities. There is much to do, many places to explore, many projects to undertake, many challenges to face, and many people to help. Have I done enough? Am I on the right track? Should I continue? I usually use a wise young lady I teasingly call my clone as my sounding board. Allow me to share my daughter, Sarah Jozelle's point of view.

#UNICAHIJA'S POV

A force to be reckoned with. A phrase that pops up every time I witness any new escapade you dare to take on and any grandiose plans for the future you come up with. I have racked my brain to come up with an adjective to describe you, but I could, for the life of me, not minimize your essence to a single word. A single word could never encapsulate who Maria Zelda Rojas truly is.

Maria Zelda, Zelda, Marizel, and to me, Madre. A mother, wife, and a woman. Ever since I can remember, I have been in awe of you. Constantly wondering how you could juggle your job at the United Nations, raise a child and simultaneously lead several of your numerous organizations. You are someone I'd like to call a serial organizer. Although you were busy 24/7, I never felt neglected or unloved. Quite the opposite, I am glad you have finally focused more on yourself.

When I was younger, you always put my needs before yours. Made sure you were present for every significant event. Pushed me out of my comfort zone. Stood by me even when I did something wrong and constantly and continuously show me how you love and cherish me endlessly. I wholeheartedly believe that without you, I wouldn't be the person I am today. You nurtured me and made me the woman that I am now and instilled morals into me, which I live by. You never failed to give me all of the things that you longed for in your childhood. Growing up in a middle-class family of six and being the oldest and only girl must have come with a lot of sacrifice and compromise. Therefore, I appreciate all the hard work you put in to give me a life like mine. A life where my opportunities are endless, where I never have to worry about the next meal or where I can afford to study what I want. Truly a life that every child deserves and dreams of.

Now that I'm older and more independent, I sincerely hope and believe that you should refocus on yourself and your goals. You deserve it. Not only did you pour all your effort, love, and time into me, but also your countless organizations. Having witnessed everything from the beginning only confirms my belief that you deserve more me-time. All the sleepless nights, and thankless donkey work you did by yourself without ever breathing a word about it, made me question your sanity at times. But then I realized that this was once again one of the things that make you so amazing. Validation and Recognition. Two things most people in this world search for and want from others. You, on the other hand, don't crave these externally. Quite the opposite, it's intrinsic. Whenever I would ask you why? Why do you break your back for people that don't even appreciate, much less notice, what you're doing? You replied: *"Because I can and want to."* That's when I realized that your goal in whatever you were doing was never to satisfy your ego, raise your status, or boost your self-confidence. Instead, all you truly wanted to do was to make a positive impact on people's lives by coming up with new ideas to preserve our culture, continuing projects dedicated to appreciating our heritage, and integrating and educating the youth. You have truly made a difference on this planet.

So mother, *mudra*, mom have no doubts. Although the future is uncertain, I know you are on the right path. Continue being who you are, for you are a force to be reckoned with.

QUO VADIS?

In 1991, unwilling, and unprepared, I journeyed to Austria. With the experiences I gained through the years, I have evolved into the person I am today, a leader in my own right. And with the decade of experience I have, these I know:

To be an effective leader, I have to be passionate, persevere, patient, and forgiving.

I choose to lead, lead by example, and lead as a servant leader. Passion is the key to everything that I do. When I do anything with passion, I give my all. I focus on the goal. I accept the result as the best possible result.

In pursuing a goal, setbacks are inevitable. I have organized numerous events, and if I had let the setbacks stop me, I would end up not organizing. Instead, I have to persevere, every time, all the time.

Patience does not come easy to me. Yet, I am aware that it is critical in everything that I do. I learned it by practicing mindfulness: being in the moment, accepting the situation, being tolerant, slowing down as needed, and communicating better.

Forgiving myself is just as tricky as forgiving others when things don't go how I expect them to. I have organized numerous events in the past ten years with varying degrees of success. One thing I know for sure is none had been perfect. I had to learn not to flagellate myself and not to lash out at others. No blame game for this brings nothing good.

What do I still want to do in my life? To achieve even the seemingly unachievable. To go on to greater heights. To take on more challenges. To overcome more trials and tribulations. But, above all, to be God's instrument in choosing to continue to do good for others.

"What lies in our power to do, lies in our power not to do."
— ARISTOTLE.

PAMELA GOTANGCO

Founder/President, PamPinay
Pamana ng Pilipino, Presidential Awardee 2021
GLOBAL FWN100™ 2018

Heart Full of Passion

Falafel

In 1993, two years after the Gulf War, a small white shuttle bus ferried me from the airport to my new home. I was twenty years old and fresh out of college from the Philippines. The drive seemed forever, and my heart was beating so fast as we drove through the barren desert, occasionally passing through small towns showing evident remnants of the war. Everything looked beige, gray, and dreary. From afar, I could see dark clouds gathering on the horizon, enveloping the entire city. Our driver explained that this was called a sandstorm. We stopped at a small cafeteria by the road where our group host, Madam Fatima, got off the bus to buy snacks for everyone. Processing our paperwork to start our legal residence and employment in Kuwait took a long time. Already, it was past lunchtime, and everyone was tired and famished. When she got back on the bus and offered us sandwiches, she proudly announced that these were called *"Falafel"* and it was a vegetarian dish. I had no idea of the concept of vegetarianism at the time. The sandwich looked dry, unappealing, and just different from what I was accustomed to. But as we went through the thick sandstorm entering Kuwait City, I took a bite of my *"Falafel,"* and I instantly fell in love with it. I have applied this approach to life ever since that day. But, just like my *"Falafel"* and the sandstorm, I would never know how good it tastes or what is behind it until I try.

Kuwait: Becoming a Global Filipina

I regard my first experience as a migrant in Kuwait as having shaped the foundation of my being a global Filipina. I was an Overseas Filipino Worker (OFW) in Kuwait at the age of twenty. I was part of a group of brave, young Filipinas chasing the dream of becoming a Flight Attendant, receiving an international wage, and seeing the world for free. I finally embarked on a journey I saw in my father's *Life World Library* books collection. I remembered it was the most read collection from his bookshelf in our home. Canada was my favorite, with its cover showing the golden yellow color of autumn, while my sister Gemma loved the Balkan.

I welcomed the change with open arms. I have met many beautiful, kind, and accommodating people in Kuwait. I learned to graciously integrate into my new environment and adapt to the new culture without losing my identity as a Filipino. We were training alongside different nationalities —Greeks, Moroccans, and Singaporean women, some of whom I keep in touch with till today. I learned to be adventurous with food and curated favorite dishes from other countries. Working with more than thirty nationalities, I quickly picked up words in different languages to enjoy a basic conversation. I learned how to respect and enjoy other cultures and let others appreciate and enjoy mine. My first week in Kuwait made me realize that I was no longer in my small town surrounded by rice fields. The world is big, and I must learn how to live in it peacefully with others to enjoy what life has to offer fully.

The metaphor 'The world's mine oyster,' from Shakespeare's comedy, *The Merry Wives of Windsor*, became my reality. Logging about 800 flying hours per year and longer lay-overs in destinations during early 1990, I managed to visit the same places several times almost every week. I frequented museums, art cafes, galleries, and funky streets and alleys all over the world. Pretended to be a princess while walking the corridors of Taj Mahal in Agra, India, Neuschwanstein Castle in Bavaria, Germany, or Windsor Castle in England. Celebrated *Diwali* with my Indian colleagues, got wet during *Songkran* festival in Thailand, practiced fasting during Ramadan, and experienced Venice by gondola a few times. The Islamic Proverb *"A lot of different flowers make a bouquet"* is absolutely right. I have collected many beautiful bouquets of memories by being open to diversity and inclusion.

Louise, My Beautiful Driving Force

"Polly Flies High" is a collection of early world learning books about a scarecrow and its adventure with its flying friends. It was written by Felicia Law and released by Worldbook International. I became a Worldbook International sales agent at the age of twenty. I recently graduated from Miriam College with a degree in Bachelor of Arts in Communication but have already signed a contract to work overseas. Selling books did not particularly pay high, but the offer of receiving a free set of *Polly Flies High* convinced me. It was my first part-time job, and I was working towards getting my daughter a farewell gift. Luckily, my cousin, Mirella purchased an entire set from me. I left my daughter a complete set of the books and my whole heart. It was my most difficult goodbye: no words but tears. Part of my being artistic comes with an abundance of blind and burning emotions. I was in a hurry to feel romance, to be in a love story and to be in my ever after. But as we all know, not every story has a happy ending. I was a teenage mom living in the custody and care of my eldest sister, Giselle. My daughter and I were at the mercy of my family when I became a single mother at the age of 19. Though I am fortunate to have the loving and financial support of my family, I wanted to be able to provide for my daughter. I wanted not just to be able to provide but rather give her the best.

I named her Louise after a famous Ketchup brand TV advertisement in the nineties, "Ketchup please, Louise." I initially wanted to call her Lindsey Feliz, but when I presented the name to my sisters, I was immediately encouraged to say the name out loud over and over again. After a few rounds of laughter, Lindsey Feliz was immediately off the table. From then on, I learned to review, reassess and rethink most ideas I have before presenting them to an audience for both my personal and professional life.

Louise was the most beautiful person I had laid my eyes on. I felt real love the first time I held her tiny body in my equally fragile and young arms. There were times when I asked myself how I deserved to have this beautiful person as my child when I had nothing to offer. I was young, working my way to finish college, and with no money. Louise became my driving force to strive for better. So intense that I was almost impatient to be successful. The sudden need to adult up became imminent. My dream of becoming a creative writer for an international advertising company based in Manila did not materialize. Instead, the ten-fold salary lured me if I worked as a flight attendant in Kuwait.

Family with Empowered Women and an Empowered Man

I am lucky to have four empowered, kind-hearted, accomplished and beautiful sisters. Most of the time, I see myself in all of them. Giselle is our eldest and is the family compass that gives us all the proper perspectives. After a long career with Philippine Airlines, she now dedicates herself to her family and God. She serves her parish in Parañaque dutifully and constantly prays for her siblings' well-being. Maybe, more for me during my younger years as a free-spirited *probinsyana* who moved to the capital of Manila. Gemma is the multiple degree holder scholar in the family who now runs a successful business in beauty and wellness called "Bathgems" specializing in artisan soaps. My sister Grace paid for my college tuition fee and spent most of her life living in Hong Kong as a purser for Cathay Pacific. Grace has now retired to her sanctuary resort in Baler, focusing on her crafty, artistic side. Gwen is an accountant who advocates for a healthy lifestyle. They inspired me in many ways, and I am always grateful to be part of this family. All of them are instrumental in what I have accomplished through the years. All of them will always be instrumental in achieving my dreams and aspirations.

We lost our father to an illness when he was only fifty-four years old. But our parents had undoubtedly set us up for life early enough to be socially responsible and empowered women. I remember when we used to gather in our living room after dinner in front of our black and white TV set. One of our favorite shows was *"Wonder Woman,"* starring Lynda Carter. We were also fans of the Olympic gold medalist gymnast Nadia Comaneci from Romania. My dad was never fond of watching Filipino *teleserye* or reading Filipino *komiks*. He would carefully inspect our fingers when we arrived home. Black ink on our fingers means we rented and read *komiks* on our walk from school to home. I must admit that I had rented *"Aliwan"* or *"Hiwaga "* *komiks* a few times. Instead, he encouraged us to read *Time Magazine*, *Reader's Digest*, and *Manila Bulletin*, to which he had subscriptions. He often told us stories of amazing women like Queen Elizabeth, Amelia Earhart, Joan of Arc, and even Lady Godiva.

On weekends, he would take us to our fish pond to feed or collect the fishes. As a social event, he took us to the cockfighting arena. And on good days we came home happy with our rooster and had delicious *"arroz caldo"* for dinner. And on bad days, we had delicious *"arroz caldo"* for dinner but with tears in our eyes. He also built us toy trucks made from wood with wheels made from tin cans. Sometimes in late evenings, we would sit by the front terrace and watch the satellite go by in a dark starry sky. Sometimes with the promise that I can be an astronaut someday. My father never limited our imagination; rather he presented us with choices that we could freely choose regardless of our gender.

So from early on, I have never understood why girls had to wear pink and boys blue.

Why would girls play with dolls and boys with cars?

Why in child play, the women were sales girls and men were policemen.

Why were all the mayors in my town, when I was growing up, all men and their secretaries all women?

Why would boys pretend to be soldiers and women nurses?

Why would boys pretend to drive the car and girls pretend to be the passengers?

It already did not all make sense back then, but I never asked. I thought maybe that is just how society works.

However, it became inevitable not to question while growing up. My father's stories and the constant reminder that we could be whatever we wanted to be regardless of our gender were engraved in my mind. Seeing my mother take a more prominent role in the family when my father fell ill, and my sister's nurturing guidance when my parents passed away, led me to advocate for the empowerment of all women and girls.

As a visual artist, I have created several art pieces as either tributes, protests or responses to cases where women became a subject of abuse or unfair treatment.

As an entrepreneur, I give income opportunities to women while practicing their crafts and at the same time raising their children.

I am active in using my influence to inspire and be a catalyst that would create gender parity across all fields.

I advocate for channeling collaboration over competition. I insist that women must support other women.

Living Away From Home at Eleven Years Old

"Aim high and hit the target, good luck," wrote Sir Baroman in our graduation book in University Science High School at the Central Luzon State University. I was not the brightest in class. I actually did poorly compared to the other scholars that year. Yet, that message testified to Sir Baroman's faith in what I could accomplish if I put my heart into it. And so I did, and am still trying my best to aim high and hit the target.

My mother would neatly segregate and fold my weekly outfit every Sunday when I was due to travel back to my school. In pursuit of an excellent high school education, my father encouraged me to take a comprehensive exam given by Central Luzon State University every year. I was among the top eighty qualifiers with an annual average of 400 applicants. My parents arranged for my board and lodging inside the campus in my first year. Our town of Rizal is a bit more than thirty kilometers from the campus, the roads were not paved, and the rivers overflowed during monsoon season. In some cases, the only viable way of crossing the rivers would be via what we called then *"Wipon"*: a military weapon-carrying truck that was turned into a passenger vehicle. So coming home every day would not have been possible. I had to wean myself off my parents at age eleven. This time of my life became a training ground that prepared me on how to be partly independent.

Learn It 'Til You Make It

Most of us are familiar with the English aphorism *"Fake it till you make it."* And while it could be helpful, it is often not enough. Having confidence and an optimistic mindset surely helps, but nothing compares to hard work. So I prefer the mantra *"learn it 'til you make it."*

In late 1997, I ended my career as a flight attendant for Kuwait Airways in New York City. I was ready to terminate my OFW employment and settle back in the Philippines. I came home grandly as an expatriate in my homeland as the only woman and the only Filipino in a team that brought ZakNet, a pioneering internet-via-satellite service, to the Philippines. It was no easy task; I had to learn and adapt to my new professional environment. The internet was new to everyone's lives. I had to understand the concept and learn jargon that may be part of our lives nowadays but very new then—PSTN, www, html, 64kbps, Cisco routers, US Robotics Modems, network, and firewall became my everyday words.

Every day I lugged my back, breaking three-inch-thick Compaq Presario with mandatory notebook paraphernalia in the nineties, including diskette and CD-ROM drives, in various hotel lobbies in Makati for my meetings. Netscape became part of my day, and McAfee seemed so necessary then. I read, listened, and patiently watched our engineers' presentations during our meetings. I attended conferences and seminars and actively engaged my colleagues in conversations to learn more. Finally, after a few months, I understood and designed a basic network architecture incorporating ZakNet internet via satellite services. With high heels on and a mini skirt matching suit, I could install a ZakNet MCPC adapter card in a computer's motherboard and connect to the LNB (Low Noise Block) on a 1.3-meter satellite dish located on the roof of buildings in the Makati central business district.

I am extremely proud of this event in my professional life. The arrival of ZakNet in the Philippines was recorded as part of the timeline of significant events in the Philippines cyber age. It was indeed an exciting time for the Philippines Internet age. The same year, Urban Bank introduced its Home Virtual Banking (HVB) system to corporate and individual clients, becoming the first to offer true Internet banking services. Philnet launched SARNET (Science, Academe, and Research Network) to bring more than 2,000 schools online. PLDT launched PhIX (Philippine Internet Exchange), which would interconnect local ISPs. It allowed local Internet Service Providers, with a main connection to the global internet, to access and exchange local Internet transactions without accessing the Global Internet. My role as ZakNet Product Manager for the Asia Pacific was to launch our services initially in the Philippines, then to other countries in Asia Pacific. I launched ZakNet the following year at the Rigodon Ballroom of the Peninsula hotel Makati after forging a partnership with BayanTel, International Micro Village, and PhilWorld Online. The same year, President Fidel Ramos signed Congressman Leandro Verceles Jr.'s RPWeb initiative that would connect more than 12,000 government offices and schools. He also proposed the formation of a Department of Information Technology and Communications (DITC).

Most national internet service providers, schools, and private and government offices quickly became subscribers to ZakNet services. For some time, we were the only internet service provider who offered 192kbps download speed as opposed to 56kbs using dial-up on PSTN. However, that same year, cable TV operator Destiny Cable launched cable internet services. Though the physical laying of cable takes time, it has proven to be a cheaper alternative in the long run compared to internet via satellite services. The internet delivery platform via cable progressed to more advanced and higher capacity services. A few years later, ZakNet ceased operations in the Asia Pacific.

However, I stayed behind and happily focused on the arrival of my second child, a son I named Matthew, my mini-me, and my gift from God. A year and a half later, I assumed a new role as Product Manager for NetSource Asia, an internet security company. Later, it was absorbed by the US partner Siegeworks LLC, an Internet Security Company based in San Francisco, USA.

Being Superlucky and Superman

The day after our wedding reception in Boracay, my husband and I lounged on the beach with the family while my brother-in-law took random family photos. My husband and I were in our swimwear and he looked pretty good in his while I was trying to fit in mine. Friends say he looked like Chris Evans in the 2011 *Captain America, The First Avenger* movie. On the other hand, I was more like the *Ate Guy*, the Nora Aunor version of *Darna*. In my mind, though, I'd like to think that we were more like John Smith and Pocahontas but allow me the freedom of imagination. As we posed between two coconut trees getting ready for that post-wedding snap, I overheard a group of giggling passersby. *"Look, it's Superman and super lucky,"* pointing at us.

I took no offense as it was and still is the truth. I am indeed super lucky to be married to this Superman who put my life in order, my heart at peace, and my personal and professional progress on course. After marrying him, I gained a new faith in myself after the painful havoc life had been previously thrown at me. I had been cheated on, belittled, and left hurting by my previous relationships. As a result, I raised two children independently with no financial or emotional support from their biological fathers. I learned how to be both a mother and father to my kids while ensuring I could raise them financially. At the same time, I learned to console myself and forget the emotional trauma I endured. I consider myself a strong woman, but the philandering activities of my previous partners always derailed me. It disabled my progress, led me to pitfalls after pitfalls of mistakes, and nearly destroyed me. My life was chaotic. I felt lifeless. I was twenty-six years old and broken.

One beautiful December night, when Manila's Christmas spirit was in full swing, I attended a party in Forbes Park. I was not particularly keen on going as I was enjoying the company of my best friend Ting for dinner. However, the host had introduced me to many people who attended and contributed to my yearly "helping hand" charity program. That year's project had been a Christmas party organized by my sister Giselle for the orphans in the care of the House of Bethlehem in Bulacan, headed by Father Boyet. Many locals and expatriate friends who were based in Manila joined us. Young interns from several European embassies and consulates, employees of the United Nations and Asian Development Bank and some from private international IT firms based in Manila. It was my good friend Greg Kittelson who mobilized the volunteers to support the event. It was also him who hosted a thank you party in his beautiful home at the time in Forbes Park. It was at this event that I met many people that up to now are still part of, and are playing roles in, my current life.

I arrived late, and the party had already started. It was the usual Makati party atmosphere, vibrant and upbeat. The setting was beautiful in a lush tropical garden with a swimming pool and elegantly decorated with Christmas lights in a very Forbes park manner. A perfect venue for the 30-degree centigrade humid weather. Back then, I was no social butterfly but a Norma no-mate as I had lived outside the Philippines for many years. So I searched for the people I had recently met at the orphanage party and found them in one corner, with my future husband. He was due to move back to Germany after his term as a foreign exchange student at the Asian Institute of Management. However, after meeting me that night, he stayed for a year. Eventually, he stayed in my life. Since then, my beautiful fairy tale life began, and the universe has been continuously orchestrating my life events grandly. So yes, I am indeed super lucky to have this loving, generous and gentle superman as my better half. While it may look like there is some sort of witchery involved for an average *Darna* like me, trust me, there is none. Only mixed potions of honest love, respect, and putting God at the center of our family.

Turning Passion Into Business

Superman was excited as he entered our then home in Zollikon, Switzerland. *"Come, honey, help me unload stuff in the car,"* he asked. A bit strange as he usually would only have one suitcase after a trip to Bavaria to see his client. I happily obliged and followed him to the car park. From afar, I could already see that the car seemed packed full. But because it was particularly cold and grey that winter of 2009, and I had my heavy parka on as it was snowing, I could not see better what was going on. He opened the car trunk and happily announced *"surprise!"* with a big smile on his face. There were more than a dozen canvases of different sizes, paint brushes of all types, complete sets of acrylic paint, and an easel loaded up in his car. Everything is for my perusal. My sweet surprise. It was a sleepless night for me. I was on a mission when I woke up the day after. I took my husband's act of kindness as a sure sign to focus on my art. Approximately six months after that winter night in April of 2010, I had my first exhibit in a small cafe in Zurich called the ApArt GrünKultur Cafe. I had eleven guests and sold one painting to a sweet lady named Tanaka Ruhukwa. Since then, I have participated in fifty-four group, solo, and digital exhibitions and art fairs in major cities worldwide. Art Takes Time Square in 2012. Contemporary Art International Zurich in 2014. Manila Art in 2016 and 2019. SCOPE Basel during Art Basel in 2016. Art Shopping in Carrousel du Louvre in 2016, to name a few art fairs. Currently, I am being represented by Art 333 in Zurich and FrontofBicycle Art Agency in Basel. I had my homecoming exhibition in the Philippines with Galerie Y in 2016, Manila House in 2019, and a special homecoming exhibition in my province Nueva Ecija organized by Armando Giron of Gallery A in 2019. And recently, I received the 2021 *Pamana ng Pilipino* Presidential Award for exemplifying the talent of Filipinos by bringing honor and recognition to the Philippines through my work as a visual artist.

We got married in March of 2008 in Boracay, Philippines, witnessed by both our families and friends in an intimate ceremony in Friday's Resort. As hopeless romantics, we had previously eloped the same month and got married in Haderslev, Denmark, with just the two of us. Then, we moved to Switzerland in 2009 with my children so we could start living as a family in one country. After we had moved to Switzerland, my husband encouraged me to revisit my passion for creating art. He probably noticed my frustrations and impatience of being unable to get employment because of the language barrier. We settled in the German speaking town of Zurich. Back then, my *"Deutsche Sprache"* was too *"schlecht"* [bad] to land a career in sales or marketing. He knew I loved to create art, but previously I had other priorities in life, such as providing for my children. Until then, my art had just been an avenue for self-expression. As a constant recipient of those artworks, he enabled me to pursue my long-time dream of becoming a visual artist.

Freedom in My Art

"Pamela Gotangco—Bold and not for the faint-hearted," was written on one of the exhibition posters of Front of Bicycle Art Agency in Basel. During the Art Basel month in June of 2017, art collectors, enthusiasts, artists, and galleries flocked to Basel to witness what's on offer at the mother of all art fairs. I exhibited my series on "Tinder Prince," which was later renamed "Prince Char" for Manila Art in 2019. The series shows differently dressed frogs mounted on a canvas frame that mimics a dating app's interface. On each canvas, I mounted my subject, a painted dried frog complete with a brief profile explained in less than 150 characters. Each frog explores a different persona that embodies an air of the "Prince Charming Syndrome." I aim to attempt to mirror stereotypes of male users on Tinder, one of the most popular online dating apps to date and question the success of marriages born out of swiping left and right. At the same time, it was to take a humorous jab at warning men not to act like toads and women to guard their hearts when looking for love online. In this particular series, my aim is for my art to question and create discussion among the viewers.

I am an autodidact, and my medium of choice is acrylic on canvas, but I also work using found objects for installations. Conventional techniques do not bind me. I create my own balance, unity, and harmony based on feelings and instinct. I am obsessed with the use of repetitive patterns due to their therapeutic effect on me. I enjoy my freedom when working on my canvas, and through that, I am able to achieve a style and stroke that is distinctly mine.

I anchor my art to all my advocacies. The primary one is to empower women and girls. I create art that highlights women. My art exudes positivity, peace, and unity. I chose subjects that are, in general, representative of women and transcend the female form. I aim to highlight the role of women in present society, our hopes, dreams, struggles, and triumphs in my artwork.

My choice of palette is a result of my being a global Filipina. The bold colors I used on my subjects represent my roots and my intense love for Filipino culture and heritage. It is influenced by *Fiesta, Santacruzan*, the *Ati-Atihan* of the South, and *Panagbenga* of the North. Meanwhile, the subtle colors I employ in the background imitate the hazy shades of winter or the fresh, vibrant undertones of spring in countries with four seasons that I have called home.

At the beginning of my career as a visual artist, I experienced a confusing loss of identity. Being a Filipina visual artist outside the Philippines, I tried fitting in by constantly worrying if my work was on par with European taste in art. And when I was in the Philippines, I worried that my European-influenced color palette was not enjoyable to the Filipino audience. It brought me nowhere. When I stopped worrying and started focusing mainly on my instinct, I could use my inherent cultural and acquired environmental influences as an opportunity instead of a setback. Now I am at peace with my art. I do believe that I have achieved harmony by incorporating both aspects of my life into a frame. To me, it somehow tells the story of my life as an artist.

Pinakbet of *PamPinay*

Spring of 2021 was gorgeous, especially in picturesque Switzerland. The sky appeared bluer, the budding trees seemed happier, and the air smelled minty but sweet. It was like the Earth went on a holiday for a year and returned vibrant and rejuvenated. On the contrary, I was not at my best. It had been a year since the COVID-19 pandemic paralyzed the world. The lockdown and negative news were taking a toll on me. I had to wear many hats at home, all my art exhibits were canceled, and I missed my family back in the Philippines. One night, after I put my youngest to bed, I went down to my atelier and started painting. With no theme in mind, I picked several colorful acrylic paints from the shelf and just went for it. It was a very unlikely approach for me as a figurative artist. I usually plan what I want to manifest in my canvas. This time I had the urge to be careless, to be free, and to be playful. A self-portrait in pop art form, crying and shouting *"I want Pinakbet!"* appeared on my canvas a few minutes before midnight. It was an honest visual expression. I love *pinakbet*, but that phrase in my art is not limited to my love for the dish but rather a visual rant. Perhaps my *"Pinakbet"* symbolizes everything that I miss. My canceled reunion with my sisters and friends back in the Philippines. The occasional Filipino events in Switzerland. The *apero* on an opening night in an art gallery. Random get-together with friends. Or a day alone at home without anyone else.

I was pleased with the painting and decided to share it on my social media. The engagement was overwhelming. Family and friends were able to identify with the piece. Perhaps because they have their own version of *"Pinakbet"* that they were missing

Meanwhile, my long-time friend and now entrepreneur partner in PamPinay, Christian Belaro, had been encouraging me to print my painting on clothing since 2016. But back then, it did not feel right. At that time, there was no need for it.

But in 2020, the COVID-19 pandemic happened, and the world stopped. As a leader, I was thinking of innovative ways on how my art could create a positive impact on others. I have donated artworks that benefited some organizations helping the needy. However, this approach will never be a sustainable practice.

PamPinay was born at the height of the global pandemic as a social project with a mission to provide income opportunities for women while staying at home. Today, PamPinay has three main missions: To empower women by providing income opportunities for women while staying at home, to promote Filipino weaving handwoven by the master artisans of the indigenous communities in the Philippines, and to follow and advocate for a slow fashion approach by being considerate on our entire supply chain.

Three brands were born out of PamPinay: the PamPinay Collection, the PamPinay Curated Treasures, and the PamPinay Collaboration Couture. The pieces are all unique, meaningful, beautiful, stylish, and versatile. It encourages thoughtful buying and establishing a personal style based on culture and meaningful stories rather than a style based on mainstream logos. So I say it's not so bad for being honest about wanting *"Pinakbet."*

"Nelia: Hi Ma'am, good morning. Nelia Tesoro Ardaniel loom weaving Abra po..." read a random message on my Facebook messenger last July 15, 2020 at 5:16 a.m. Attached were several photos of *Binakol* and *Kantarines* handwoven fabrics. *"Beautiful!"* was my reply on the same day at 9:40 a.m. I get constant random messages from weavers in the Filipino indigenous communities because I am an avid fan of Filipino handwoven fabric. I support Filipino designers and wear indigenous textiles in my *vernissages* and formal events. I showed my sister Grace the photos of the fabrics sent to me by *Manang* Nelia, and we ordered them for our personal use. *Manang* Nelia continued sending photos of her products, the last one before we started our business relationship was December 27, 2020 and it read, *"Ma'am order na, pabagong taon nyo po sa amin."* It had been almost a year since the COVID-19 global pandemic had

disrupted lives and paralyzed economies. It was a rallying cry to action for my business partner Christian and me. We decided to heed the call of *Manang* Nelia and many others like her. We started to shape the guiding principles on how we could be part of the solution to the challenges the pandemic posed to the women weavers and seamstresses in the Philippines. I placed my first order of *Binakol* handwoven fabrics with *Manang* Nelia last June 2, 2021. One thousand one hundred twelve yards of fabric, four major fashion shows in major cities worldwide, and twenty-eight product lines later, we celebrated our first anniversary last March 23, 2022.

The future is looking bright for our small brand. It was not easy, and we faced many challenges. However, we will continue to strive harder as the past year has proven to change lives in the communities that we support. Now we support three co operative weavers in Abra, one in Lake Sebu, and five seamstresses in Manila. To me, PamPinay is more than just a business. It is the hug that *Ate* Bibeth, our head seamstress, gave me when I first met her on my trip to Manila after the lockdown last April. It was the honest gratitude in the voices of the weavers and our seamstresses in the 2021 Christmas video greeting we created for our collectors. It was the pure joy Christian and I both felt when we celebrated our first anniversary with the PamPinay team in Manila last April 4. It is the hope and the *"Bayanihan"* spirit. But, this is just the beginning.

Inspiring the Future Generation

In March of 2020, a particularly challenging time due to the COVID-19 global pandemic, I was invited by my alma mater as a guest speaker to address the 2020 Miriam College graduates in the Baccalaureate ceremony. On most days, this is an exciting task. But in a world where the younger generation will start their professional lives in a society ridden with adversities, it was somehow a daunting task. How do I promise a bright future to this generation of future leaders? How do you congratulate young men and women when global leaders are uncertain of the future? For weeks I thought hard, long, and searched my heart until I came up with the speech below. I am honored to share part of my speech.

"Welcome to a brave new world, my fellow *Maria Katipuneras*!
Know that there is no bigger honor than to address you in

these difficult times due to a global pandemic COVID-19, to make sure you are all reminded of what you've achieved today. Well done!

To celebrate today is not futile or wasted—in fact, today, we should all claim our accomplishments. I understand your mixed emotions, frustrations, and perhaps even anger. Classes were cut short, friendships and camaraderie were put on hold, suddenly memorable goodbyes are no longer possible.

You have the right to be upset. I am. But as humans, we have proven to be exceptionally creative, resilient, and persistent. This pandemic shouldn't put us down, this should provide an opportunity to establish and create new ways to live more profoundly. I'm quite sure most of you have done zoom happy hours, have called people more, and have expressed love passionately. This is who we are as humans. We just need to remember this every single day.

Class of 2020, you are more than special, you are historical! From here on out, Class of 2020 from all over the world will have a special sense of camaraderie for a lifetime. I'm not trying to downplay this pandemic, quite the opposite. I want you to celebrate amidst this devastation and be that change you want to see in this world. We can achieve this by internalizing the importance of the following:

- Egoistic displays of power, political or military, will not save us.

- The poor are the most affected by this.

- And Leadership is key. Understanding this—be that leader, and be that change. And know that as you navigate this selflessly, Miriam College will be right there with you.

- Power only works where there is empathy. The use of power for the good of others is what should resonate in our efforts, to reflect what we learned within the walls of Miriam College.

- The poor need us more than ever today—our brothers and sisters who are the most affected should have us as their allies, their champions, their advocates.

- More importantly, Miriam College taught us to be thoughtful leaders and so we should be. Leadership with action, leadership with empathy, leadership with heart.

- And as we do this, know that no man is an island—we need partnerships and collaborations, remembering that more brains work better than a handful, and connections are what makes us better citizens of the world.

Now, I have come to the part of this speech where I'm supposed to share with you my mantra: *Success is not just measured by the two metrics of money and power. It is also determined by the positive impact you've made in people's lives.*

With these, I want to share four guiding principles that I follow:

- Set achievable goals. In a world where everything is rushed, we should be able to focus and filter false goals. Instant success and overnight sensations only happen on social media. If you set a goal that is unrealistic, you might end up compromising your values. That is not the Miriam College way. Our values should ground us as well as set our goals in motion. Nothing beats hard work.

- Let your heart be your inner compass that will help you navigate through life. This has helped me through my professional and personal life. On Palm Sunday, I live-streamed Pope Francis' service. It was when Italy's despair was in full swing, where we started to see thousands of infections and casualties worldwide. Global economies were also starting to hurt. During the homily, Pope Francis shared, *"always say yes to love without if and buts."* I find comfort in these words because it sparks resemblance to my second personal guiding principle of using my heart as my inner compass. If we all live by saying yes to love—without question or compromise—it is testimony to God's strong and pure presence in our lives. With these, making decisions for both professional and personal lives, we instill truth, justice, peace and integrity in our existence. This again, is the Miriam College way.

- Find an advocacy and anchor your work and life to it. There is no greater pleasure than knowing that what you do directly creates a positive impact on other people's lives. The Miriam College outreach programs have already paved that way for all of us. We were all introduced early and molded to be agents for positive change. Now it is just up to each one of you to choose an advocacy that you strongly believe in and follow through.

- And more importantly, embrace failure and learn from it. Humans are flawed by nature. That's what makes us special, unique and extraordinary. If we were all molded to perfection, there is no point to strive and so failure is an expectation, and failure can be a sweet experience for without it there is no opportunity for growth. Failure without giving up

means moving forward, conquering it means coming
out of it better and better and more solid than when
you started. You shouldn't think failure as a blemish
on your character—it's a battle scar, so wear it with
honor, because that is when success is the sweetest.

Aspirations

Recently my friend Jeno asked me, *"What's next for Pamela Gotangco?"* I always find this question rather difficult to answer accurately especially when the COVID-19 global pandemic is not entirely over and in the middle of the Russian invasion of Ukraine.

However, as a leader, I will be that positive change who will be the future of humanity. I choose to focus on what I can influence and impact in this time of adversity.

For my art to continuously provide a voice to the voiceless and to be a medium to find ways to solve contemporary issues that will create positive change in people's lives.

For PamPinay to innovate new ways to empower women and promote Filipino culture and artisans. We have built retail partnerships in the USA, and this will be followed by UAE, Canada, France, and Australia.

And for me as a person, I will remain to be my own version of *Darna!*

ATTY. ROSARIO CALIXTO CHAVEZ

Former Bank Executive
Lawyer
Financial and Investment Consultant
Civic Leader
GLOBAL FWN100™ 2019

Creating Destiny

"Leaders aren't born, they are made. And they are made just like anything else, through hard work. And that's the price we'll have to pay to achieve that goal, or any goal."

— Vince Lombardi

So goes my leadership story! I was born and raised in modest places in Paco and Malate, with a father's income barely enough to sustain the needs of a family of seven and a mother giving up an affluent life to focus on building a model family. That fueled my extreme desire to succeed in life at an early age. After graduating valedictorian in kindergarten, I continuously challenged myself to excel in academics and extra-curricular activities, as I knew this was my only road to a better life.

I studied in Paco Catholic School, a parochial school run by the same Belgian sisters of St Theresa's College, a school for well-to-do families, where my mother attended elementary and high school.

The nuns were happy to extend financial assistance to the children of an exceptional alumna and math genius, as her batchmates called her. The help came initially through a part-time job in the school bookstore, where two of my sisters worked while studying.

I was always different from my siblings! While we were all achievers in school, I knew there was more to just being on top of the class, an editor, or a declaimer. I was neither proud of attaining high grades nor being just a champion declaimer because I was good at memorizing. Instead, I wanted to become more adept at extemporaneous speech, hold solo guitar concerts, or join the volleyball or soccer varsity teams. Since my mother was a good pianist and my father was a champion tennis player who finished his engineering course through a sports scholarship, I knew I had the talent!

So, despite being granted a full scholarship in high school due to my academic achievements in elementary, I gave it up in my second year to transfer to the Philippine Women's University (PWU). Its core values that focused on a holistic approach to character development, the preservation of cultural and national heritage, family solidarity, ethical professionalism, and service to the community were what I felt I needed!

Back then, it was a total disappointment to the priests and nuns who lobbied to grant me the scholarship. And the bold move somehow did not appear to be fair to my parents, who were sending seven children to school and who could hardly make both ends meet.

Later, however, I could prove that it was not an impulsive move. And it was not long before I could take another scholarship in PWU high school—the Parent Teacher Association scholarship.

BREAKING BARRIERS

*"Great leaders do not fear challenges, because challenges
do not break leaders but sharpen them."*
— GIFT GUGU MONA

I thought I was prepared for a drastic change. The paradigm shift from a traditional learning environment to a progressive education system that values the student's self-esteem by advancing a pedagogic philosophy anchored on discovery and learning by doing, dedicated to peace and environmentalism, cooperation rather than competition, cultivating freedom of spirit, exploration and expression with the ultimate goal of attaining balanced development and growth, put me to the test!

Adjusting to the new structure was not easy. First, I had to deal with blending with students whose first language was English, both written and spoken. In addition, these students were multi-talented as their parents enrolled them in sports clinics, and schools for art or music during summer, and they had the luxury of time for their studies as they had chauffeurs and maids at their beck and call!

PREPARING FOR SUCCESS

"Humble words and increased preparations are signs that the enemy is about to advance." — SUN TZU

There was No Turning Back!

For a head start, I did a SWOT analysis. Then, after identifying my strengths, weaknesses, and threats, I drew a game plan that would mold me into the person I wanted to be. And I specifically chose the recognized leader of our batch as my benchmark. Aside from excelling academically, she won in almost all student competitions, from essay writing, oratorical, declamation, interpretative reading to extemporaneous speaking contest. And a distinct advantage was her coming from an affluent political family, with no less than a bar topnotcher and a legal luminary for a father.

It was a tough road to navigate as it entailed a great deal of self-discipline. As English was my perceived weakness then, I set aside time to read a book and write each word I learned every day, participated in interpretative reading and extemporaneous speaking contests, and joined as many clubs as possible which carried responsible roles and major tasks. Eventually, I found myself gaining self-confidence.

PASSING THE TEST OF LEADERSHIP

"No tyranny of circumstances can permanently imprison a determined will." — SYDNEY M. BRENNER

Finally, the day of reckoning arrived! The overall atmosphere in the Senior Class Organization high school polling place was overwhelming as I won the election. The euphoric feeling of emerging as a winner for the position of President against a strong candidate was beyond words!

But since I won only by one vote, my opponent demanded a recount. She won in the second tally for the same margin. And as students were preparing to cast their votes again, I told everyone that it was no longer necessary. I conceded!

As far as I was concerned, I was already a WINNER! For me, earning my classmates' trust and confidence was the true test of LEADERSHIP. Winning against a lone opponent who was a strong candidate was just a bonus. And I knew that for my opponent, winning was important to her as she had an image to uphold.

Later on, this person would turn out to be my best friend for life as she never forgot my conceding in the bid for Presidency. The full support I gave her during her incumbency paved the way for the "Seniors making History" for garnering the top award in the Annual Acquaintance Party, something that all high school students aimed for at the start of the school year. And the rest was history.

LAYING THE GROUNDWORK

"Victory is always possible for the person who refuses to stop fighting." — NAPOLEON HILL

I always dreamt of spending my college at the University of the Philippines. That was where my mom went and got straight A's in the College of Medicine. She could have been a very successful doctor if not for the breakout of war and her early marriage.

It was heartbreaking, however, when my mom did not support my decision for the first time. And my father reinforced it!

For my parents, finishing college was of utmost priority. And maybe they were right. Being a free-spirited, extrovert, and independent person, I would have ended up in the mountains if they had allowed me to pursue my college education there.

Why not? Growing up, I did not always conform to my mom's rules. Against her will, I played with street children who wore tattered clothes. It was easy to spot me whenever I was with them, as I always wore shoes and socks in a white dress with the usual ribbon tied at my back. My mom assumed these children were going to be a bad influence. But at that age, we were just happy playing with each other. So, my mom did her best to make me stay at home just like my other siblings. She taught us Scrabble and other card games that made us busy when not in school or on vacation.

So, I spent my college years at PWU. Graduating with honors and receiving the top Service Award in high school was a definite advantage! So, I no longer had to prove my worth as a leader to be elected President of the Freshman Class Organization, considered the most influential group with a 2,000-strong voting population in the university.

But easy as it may have seemed, it turned out more arduous as I assumed multifaceted leadership roles amidst the most tumultuous period of Philippine history that was Martial Law.

Martial Law led to so much student unrest. But, while I believed in what the students were fighting for, I did not support the boycott of classes. There were other ways of expressing our discontent about the government. Cutting classes was not doing justice to our parents, who worked hard to send us to school. It was our loss, more than anything else.

This position caused the ire of the incumbent student council officers. They resorted to dirty tactics to prevent me from taking on an elected position in the student council. Barring all these antipathies, I still managed to win by a landslide.

Belonging to the minority did not discourage me from aiming for a higher position the following year. I ran for Internal Vice President and won again. It was really just a matter of time before my dream of becoming the Student Council President in college would turn into fruition.

However, fate did not allow it! Martial Law resulted in the suspension of student council operations, which marred my dream of assuming the Presidency. But I was not the person who would give up easily. Instead, I redirected my efforts toward campus journalism. I accepted the position of Editor-in-Chief of the *Philwomenian*, the official student paper of PWU. In addition, I assumed other significant positions as Chairman of the College of Business Administration and Captain Ball of the Varsity Volleyball Team, bringing the first WNCAA championship title to PWU.

By the time I earned my Bachelor of Science in Business Administration, major in Accounting, I had landed top ten of the 1974 graduating class as First Honorable Mention. In addition, I was conferred the top University Leadership Award.

MOVING TO GREATER HEIGHTS

This academic excellence and leadership qualities paved the way for my being adjudged Most Outstanding Coed in Metro Manila by the Department of Education and Culture. And later on, becoming PWU's pride, I was chosen as one of the nominees after attending a week-long leadership seminar sponsored by the U.S. Embassy. Ultimately I earned the highest honor of representing the Philippines as the lone delegate to the Asia Pacific Leadership Project, held in the United States of America, besting all student leaders from the various universities in the Philippines. This three-month exchange program, which the U.S. Department of State sponsored, was participated in by student leaders from Tonga, Papua New Guinea, Singapore, Thailand, Japan, Korea, and Malaysia.

I was met at the airport in Honolulu, Hawaii by a U.S. Department of State representative and brought to the hotel where I stayed. Starting officially at the East-West Centre of Hilo, Hawaii, the program then brought us to the home for the aged and black school in San Francisco, California, for observation. And to experience the American way of life, we spent a week in a black community in Atlanta, Georgia, and lived with families in San Diego, California, and Spokane, Washington. I was fortunate to have as foster parents, husband and wife lawyers, and a dentist father doing volunteer work on an American Indian reservation.

To have a feel of student life, we slept in dormitories at Harvard (where I became green with envy as students enjoyed 24-hour library operations). We were also able to experience an essential milestone in U.S. history as we witnessed the proceedings involving the Watergate scandal in the White House, Washington DC.

But amidst all these successes, nothing could be as rewarding as bestowing upon my father the distinct privilege of going up the stage to receive all my awards during the PWU Commencement Exercises, as I had to leave for the U.S. before graduation.

Unknown to many, PWU provided me with a full scholarship in my first year, two tuition privileges for three years starting in my second year, as University Scholar and as a student assistant in the Office of the Dean of the College of Business Administration and in my fourth year, an additional tuition privilege as Editor-in-Chief of the *Philwomenian*, a total of three. As I only needed one to pay for my tuition, I was able to convert the other privileges to cash, which I gave immediately to my mom.

I consider the Top University Leadership Award my best of all these accolades. It was an affirmation that, indeed, my giving up the scholarship in my second year in high school in the parochial school and transferring to PWU was the best decision I ever made in my life

WORKING ON THE FULFILLMENT OF MY DREAM

"Determine that the thing can and shall be done and then we shall find the way." — ABRAHAM LINCOLN

While I was given the opportunity to attend an international law school in San Diego, California, and potentially work in Price Waterhouse, which my foster parents arranged for me in the U.S., I opted to return to the Philippines to fulfill my goal of building the dream house for my mother, not to mention a comfortable life to bring her back to where she came from.

Immediately after I arrived, I started accepting job interviews to the many job offers waiting for me after graduation. I ended up in the Hong Kong and Shanghai Banking Corporation (HSBC), a British corporation where I would serve for thirty-five years. It was also where I would eventually realize my dream.

It did not take long for HSBC management to recognize my potential. So, when they decided to set up its Electronic Data Processing Department (EDP), they asked me to join the team. The flexible working schedule and a better salary package lured me to accept it. After all, I had already taken on the sole responsibility of caring for my parents. And it was an opportune time to carry on my plan to pursue a law degree as a working student.

A sudden turn of events, however prompted me to leave the EDP Department. The registration of the union was cancelled, and the union members sought my help. Being a confidential employee would not allow me to help them, so I returned to rank and file status.

Soon after registering a new union, I took on the leadership as President, whose primary responsibility was negotiating for a new Collective Bargaining Agreement (CBA). This complex role coincided with my preparation for the bar examinations. And yet, I continued working in the bank, which made it possible for me to take bar review classes at Ateneo Law School from 1:00 to 5:00 p.m. as I reported in the bank for four hours (8:00 to 12:00 p.m.) in the morning and the remaining hours from 6:00 to 10:00 p.m.

THE BAR EXAMINATION MONTH

"You cannot keep a determined man from success. Place stumbling blocks in his way and he takes them for stepping stones." — ORISON S. MARDEN

When I applied for a one-month leave to take the bar examination, the bank disapproved it. As Union President and an ongoing CBA negotiation, I knew I had a strong case against the bank. The disapproval of my application for leave constituted UNFAIR LABOR PRACTICE. It did not take long for them to reconsider their decision after I wrote them my first letter, and they approved my "LEAVE WITHOUT PAY."

After learning that I was going on leave without pay, the union members immediately passed a resolution setting aside the total union collections for the month for my allowance during the bar examination month. From the money turned over to me. I kept enough for my transportation and food allowance and gave the rest to my mom for her and dad's monthly sustenance.

In contrast to other bar takers who stayed in various hotels for pre-week review, I, together with five other classmates, slept in the school where we were taking the pre-week review classes. The janitors allowed us to use two dressing areas in the school auditorium. Our room was tiny, but we managed to fit in three foldable beds and one electric fan. The lack of comfort balanced the time we saved from shuttling as we only had to go down to the bar review room in the morning.

The janitors took care of food, with each of us contributing Php 5.00 per meal. Saturday nights were spent with my married sister's family in the big ancestral house of her husband in P. Guevarra Street, San Juan. She provided us decent dinner and sleeping quarters to ensure we were well rested before taking the exams on all four Sundays of the bar examination month.

I passed the 1981 bar with one take—truly a remarkable accomplishment with only one-month leave for the bar and the simultaneous preparation for the CBA negotiations as Union President.

A RECORD-BREAKING CBA!

"Success comes to those who dare and act. It seldom goes to the timid who are afraid of the consequences." — NEHRU

Becoming a female union leader in the banking industry in the 1980s was already a remarkable feat, but getting a record-breaking salary increase for the HSBC employees under my leadership, with 50 percent for the first year, five percent for the second year, and five percent for the third year was phenomenal!

All these were products of thorough planning and responsible leadership. Our CBA negotiations could have failed if things had gotten out of control.

Our union's "bizarre" protest actions made newspaper headlines as:

1. Male front-liners came in "skinhead" haircuts;
2. Female tellers donned dusters/rollers;
3. Employees resorted to noise barrage;
4. Union officers hinted at an impending strike.

The attempt of management to file a case against us did not prosper. We did not violate any provision in the Labor Code nor violated company policies. We continued reporting for work and delivered the service expected of a world-class bank. Yet, even my pronouncement of our employees going on strike during an interview with Reuters was not enough for the Department of Labor to assume jurisdiction. Why? Because we did not file our notice of strike!

Our unprecedented CBA success paved the way for my becoming the Legal Counsel of the Bank Employees Labor Alliance, Chairperson of the Labor Division of the Integrated Bar of the Philippines, and representing the banking industry in the drafting of the rules and regulations of the National Labor Relations Committee (NLRC). I was also given a scholarship to attend a course in the Labor Institute at the University of the Philippines, where I became President of the class.

My leadership ability was again put to test when in a meeting of all Union Presidents of the foreign banks (HSBC, Bank of America, Citibank, and Standard Chartered Bank) in the Philippines, we all decided to do industry-wide CBA negotiation. As a result, the industry-wide CBA yielded an all-time high of 90 percent salary increase for all rank employees in the first year.

The 1980s propelled me into high profile leadership roles for the community. I became the Charter President of the first ever all-woman club in the world of Kiwanis International, a male organization. In those days, wives were just expected to provide support to their husbands in their projects. And I am proud to say that our club even earned the much-coveted International Honor Club, a multiple service award from Kiwanis International, during the International conference held in St Louis, Missouri, USA.

THE BLESSING OF A SON

"A new baby is like the beginning of all things- wonder, hope, a dream of possibilities." — EDA J LeShan

After all these accomplishments, I felt that nothing could beat my having been bestowed by God the most important award in my life—being a mother to my first son, Chuckie. So far, everything has gone as planned! I finished Law as a working student, built my own house where my parents would stay with me for the rest of their lives, and had a family of my own.

Taking over the care of my parents was a daunting task, but this turned out to be a blessing. Aside from helping with my son's assignments, my mom instilled in him the same values she taught us while growing up, while my dad provided the security when my husband succumbed to the allure of the American dream.

LET ME HEAR YOUR VOICE

"A mother understands what a child does not say."
— JEWISH PROVERB

February 1990 saw a turning point in my life with the birth of my second son, Anton. In his first few months, Anton neither exhibited eye contact nor signs of early speech. I knew something was wrong, but my mom thought otherwise. She said that I was only comparing him to my first son, who could already write and recite nursery rhymes at the age of two.

The world almost crumbled when a developmental doctor finally delivered the findings. Anton had "Autism Spectrum Disorder." This diagnosis meant that he would be non-verbal for life and not capable of emotions.

And I thought I planned my life very well! I turned down an offer for an international assignment, a first in fact for a female officer in the Philippines.

I was not definitely giving up on my son! For me, the family was everything! I could never consider myself a success if I was a failure at home. Therefore, at this stage in my life, I decided to lay low and focus on my special son's therapy.

A decade of hard work, dedication, and close coordination with developmental doctors, special education teachers, and therapists of Anton finally paid off! Aside from becoming self-reliant, Anton could talk and, most importantly, able to express his basic needs.

OVERCOMING MY FEARS

"There is no limit to what one can attain in my life regardless of age. With sheer determination and proper preparation, I overcame my fears, endured the challenges in the most difficult situations, and survived."
— Rosario Chavez

It was time to move on! My first shot at returning to public service was taking on the Presidency of the Tahanan Village Homeowner's Association of the subdivision where I reside.

As President, I initiated a Solid Waste Management System, a waste segregation scheme for 900 homeowners that became a model for the neighboring villages and Parañaque's pride. The implementation of the project was not easy! It required political will to get homeowners to segregate waste as a way of life.

The success of this Solid Waste Management System ushered in new opportunities for my love for the environment. For example, the paper I wrote relative to the Corporate Social Responsibility (CSR) project of HSBC attributed to my selection by HSBC London to join a project in Tasmania, Australia, a world heritage area.

You can imagine how I, at age 50, managed to survive the physical demands and hazards of the project involving spotted skinks on the high-altitude sites of the Central Plateau of Tasmania, Australia, like: (1) snake bites. Three species of venomous snakes were found in the sites; (2) mosquitoes and huge march flies, and (3) rocky terrain.

The study carried out by Earthwatch Institute and supervised by Dr. Joan Whittler of the Department of Anatomy and Developmental Biology at the University of Queensland, provided information on how these reptiles coped and adapted to environmental change and extreme habitat. The findings helped formulate recommendations for the future conservation management of the endemic lizard fauna of Tasmania.

MY OWN VERSION OF SUCCESS

*"Success is not just about receiving awards but how many
people's lives one has touched."* — ROSARIO CHAVEZ

The first civic organization I joined after a brief hiatus was the Rotary Club of Makati Jose P. Rizal, an all-woman club in District 3830, Rotary International. Being a part of a group of empowered women put to the test everything I learned through the years.

As President, I earned for the club the Five Star Mark of Excellence Award for achieving the hallmarks of a Total Quality Rotary Club for impactful projects. These projects included: *the Model United Assembly (MUNA)* which enhanced understanding of international affairs with students assuming roles of diplomatic representatives and stimulating the proceedings of the United Nations; the *Bahile Project,* a socialized housing venture in a 13.7-hectare in Palawan, which provided a roof above the head for families of fishermen; *Search for Most Gender (GAD) Responsive Barangay,* which recognized the exemplary performance of the *barangay* which promoted mutual respect and equal opportunities for empowered citizenry through multi-sectoral participation in the formulation and implementation of gender-responsive and non-disciplinary policies, structures, system processes, programs and projects; *Karunungan para sa Kaunlaran,* a project which improved the English reading and comprehension competency of our student beneficiaries (out-of-school youth) in the Don Bosco Technical Institute in Makati, through a software program that was developed by award-winning Canadian neurologists who arrived at a unique approach to diagnose learners' needs and addressing individual learning deficiencies, for training and eventual overseas job placement.

The awards would then pave the way for my assuming responsible roles at the district level of Rotary, like twice as Editor of the *Governor's Monthly Letter,* Assistant Governor, Governor's Representative to the *Philippine Rotary Magazine,* Chair, Leadership Institute, and twice as District Coordinating Chair for Service Projects covering Community, International, Vocational, Youth and Areas of Focus.

It later opened the doors for my chartering of the Zonta Club of Parañaque, which focuses on an advocacy closest to my heart—women empowerment.

Espousing the organization's tenets became easy. Immediately after my club was chartered, the incumbent Governor Georgitta Puyat invited me to join her team of Area Directors and District Officers in Bangkok, Thailand, for an immersion.

Our landmark project was the annual Milk Letting Activity where we tapped lactating mothers from the different *"barangays"* of Parañaque to donate breast milk to premature and sick infants at the National Intensive Care Unit Philippine General Hospital while explaining its health benefits to the mother and child. The project is based on study that infants fed with breast milk enjoyed increased intelligence, low risk of sudden infant death syndrome, contracting childhood onset diabetes, asthma, eczema, obesity in later life, psychological disorders, middle ear infection and providing flu and cold resistance.

THE MANAGER AND THE LEADER

"Management is efficiency in climbing the ladder of success; leadership determines whether the ladder is leaning against the right wall." — STEPHEN COVEY

"Leadership is unlocking people's potential to become better. Management is about arranging and telling."

— BILL BRADLEY

As I continued to receive awards for my humanitarian services, I maintained my dedication to the company that provided my family with our bread and butter. After turning down three promotions and two successful CBA negotiations, I finally joined the management.

My greatest accomplishment was being appointed as Overall Project Coordinator involving the conversion of the computer system of sixteen branches of the PCIB Savings Bank, which HSBC acquired in 2001, and getting the much-deserved commendation from the Group Head Office. And to quote, *"the Project Team's dedication and hard work were exemplary, and the team spirit and enthusiasm which prevailed throughout the project were commendable. Without this level of planning and commitment, a conversion of this size and complexity could not have been achieved successfully within the prescribed short frame (barely two months)."*

Another feather to my cap was when I achieved an all-time high in collections for HSBC Manila, considered the largest agency credit card portfolio in Asia. The significant initiatives and incentive systems I put in place like (1) adapting the account management approach to collection agency management; (2) introducing a mapping strategy that showed a more equitable distribution of accounts-based consistency of performance and capacity, and (3) the holding of a monthly fellowship social among accredited collection agencies, which became a venue for awarding outstanding performance and sharing of best practices, accounted for my success.

COPING WITH CHANGE: TRANSITIONING TO ONLINE LEARNING AS THE "NEW NORMAL"

As the new decade beckoned, I was called to serve the academe. In late 2019, I accepted a post as a law professor at Centro Escolar University Las Piñas. Just when I thought it was time to slow down, the COVID-19 pandemic set in. Colleges and universities worldwide had to transition to online learning quickly. Teachers were faced with the challenge of learning to become effective communicators by designing modules using digital tools. Students had to be equipped with computers and given access to the internet.

These made me re-think Zonta Club of Parañaque's priorities and instead focus on areas of concern where we could best serve our communities. Then, by leap of faith, I found an answer from a project that *Kaisipan* just launched, with Dr. Maria Beebe, a fellow awardee of FWN's Most Influential Woman in the World in 2019.

The iLearn, iCreate, iShare, a digital capabilities framework for Philippine educators, provided the scaffolding for *Kaisipan's* learning and teaching approach. Thus the partnership with Kaisipan, Inc was formed with *"Tuklas Karunungan sa Kaisipan"* as Zonta Club of Paranaque's flagship project for Biennium 2020–2022. The webinars that *Kaisipan* organized will likely benefit 44 public schools with 110,000 students in Parañaque.

IT'S MY TURN TO HELP MY ALMA MATER

In 2020, my PWU high school 1970 batch was supposed to celebrate our golden anniversary with a big bang. It was for this reason that I accepted the nomination to run for the Board of the PWU Alumni Association to become its President eventually and assume concurrently the post as member of the PWU Board of Trustees in an ex-officio capacity.

The COVID-19 pandemic, however, changed all my plans for a grand celebration. Students stopped going to school as their parents lost their jobs. My desire to help the students and our Alma Mater, experiencing a decline in enrolment, prompted me to make scholarships our main thrust. It was my way of expressing my gratitude to the university, which molded me into the person I am today.

VALIDATION OF MY SUCCESS AS A LEADER

Lives of great men all remind us
We can make our lives sublime
And, departing, leave behind us
Footprints on the sands of time

— LONGFELLOW

As PWU Alumni Association 2019–2022 was nearing the end of its term, I initiated the first ever-virtual musical event at PWU. The purpose was two-fold: firstly, as a musical tribute to my role model, Senator Helena Benitez, fondly called Tita Helen by us, and secondly, to augment the funds we have earlier raised for our scholarship project, hoping to encourage other organizations, groups, and friends of PWU to follow suit.

Dubbed *"TITA HELEN: Musicale on her Life, Philosophies, and Aspirations,"* it touched on the crucial stages in Tita Helen's life as a youth, educator, legislator, environmentalist, and diplomat, as interpreted through a compilation of different songs and genres and dance performed by PWU alumni.

As an Educator, Tita Helen believed that it was not enough to equip the students with skills and knowledge in school. Developing a sense of belonging is essential. Self-awareness and understanding heritage, culture, and environment are important to succeed. And all these can only be achieved through shared responsibilities. Tita Helen became one of the notable Filipina women leaders in her generation. Her successful advocacy of women's rights and potential to service made her an ideal exponent for other global concerns, especially on youth, the environment, and human settlements.

This event gave rise to two articles released in *Manila Times*, a major newspaper with wide circulation, both written by Leah C. Salterio. The first article was about the Musicale.

The second, entitled "Tireless Achiever," featured my life journey...

"Successful is perhaps one word that best describes the corporate journey of Lawyer Rosario Calixto Chavez. She had all the reasons to fail because of daunting life experiences, but she persevered and rose above all those challenges."

"This feisty community leader apparently has a lot on her agenda even in these daunting times. Yet she is not complaining. In fact, she wakes up each day driven and passionate about starting anew."

That feature then paved the way for my being invited in August 2022 to the Leader's Edge talk show by no less than Dina H. Loomis, the President and CEO of Talent Management Director of the South East Asia Speakers and Trainers Bureau, Inc . (SEASTBI), the first female Philippine District Governor of Toastmaster Inc and a sought after platform speaker and trainer on a wide range of topics.

Entitled the "The Making of a Leader," Dino Hermosisima Santos, who acted as Host of the show, had this to say:

"Rosario Calixto Chavez or Chito to her friends is an ebullient and interesting study in contrasts. She is both accessible and steadfast in how she looks at the qualities of leadership. In our time together as the guest of the video log or YouTube channel called "The Leader's Edge by SEASTBI," she was filled with eagerness to express the key points that shaped her life. And yet resolute in her desire to serve as a servant leader. The closest analog I can think of is how she and Miriam Defensor Santiago would have likely found kindred spirits in each other. Thus, I believe that Chito is a force of nature who can drive her goals and those around her to action. She is a leader made and meant to succeed."

They may seem like belated testaments, but for me, those features are added validation of what I have attained, as my leadership story continues!

TRANSFORMATION

ALICIA DEL PRADO, PH.D.

Psychologist, Author
del Prado Counseling & Consulting
GLOBAL FWN100™ 2021

Follow Your Heart: Leadership Lessons

I was two years old when my parents separated. My Filipino American father, Norman, and Italian American mother, Judy, proved too different and too young to make a long haul of their marriage. Nonetheless, I was surrounded by love and felt nurtured by the cultural traditions of extended family cohesion and gatherings around food. I remember fondly traveling to the iconic Mitchell's ice cream shop in San Francisco in my parents' green 1973 Plymouth Duster, where some of our favorite flavors included mango and *ube* [purple yam]. At the time, my biracial identity was not at the forefront of my mind. However, it was undoubtedly a pivotal part of how the world saw me and how I would eventually come to see myself. Growing up as a biracial girl in the 1980s in the Bay Area, I struggled to become comfortable in my own skin. However, I eventually embraced self-acceptance and learned the importance of an inclusive, diverse community. Through introspection and wisdom from family and mentors, I grew into the woman, psychologist, author, leader, wife, and mother I am today.

My parents' divorce has impacted my life, weaving its way into my weaknesses and strengths. For many years, I felt incomplete and insecure. I was a people pleaser and frequently worried about everything. I worried if I would do well on my tests, if I hurt someone's feelings, and if I would give a good performance in dance class. I worried about my appearance: Is my brown hair too curly? Am I too tall? Is my skin tone the "right" color? I tried to be "perfect," and when I received approval from others, my anxiety temporarily lessened. I remember when my aunt jovially called me a *"worry wart."* Her comment showed me that what I was thinking and feeling was not actually what most other children experienced. When my dad's girlfriend gave me "worry dolls" from Guatemala, I remember welcoming them as a way to let go of my worrisome thoughts. I spoke to each tiny one with a worry I was ready to let go of and placed them under my pillow, eager to embrace a good night's sleep. I did not know until later in life when I was studying psychology, that I likely suffered from generalized anxiety.

My worries were also functional and moved me forward. My appetite for perfection and approval motivated me to excel in school and do my best in all tasks I endeavored. I did well in school, earned scholarships to private high schools and universities, and felt driven to excel. I was also kind, relatable, and inspired to be of service. When I realized that my professional passion was to help people through the discipline of psychology, I chose to pursue my Ph.D. in counseling psychology with an emphasis on cross-cultural and multicultural psychology. My personal history with fractured family relationships, mental health, and ethnic identity were important pieces leading up to this career path. As a psychologist, I now help others with their anxiety and other psychological and health concerns. I have co-authored books, chaired committees and conferences, co-founded a psychological division, taught and mentored university students, and started my own small business.

When reflecting on the words of wisdom that have been the essence of my leadership style, they come down to the following ten guiding principles. Each quote originated from pivotal life experiences and wisdom gained from important influencers in my life, ranging from my loving and fierce *lola* [grandma] to the terminally ill cancer patient Javier whom I met at a hospital. My approach to leadership is grounded, relational, pragmatic, and culturally attuned. Perhaps not surprisingly, as a psychologist who practices from a cognitive-behavioral and interpersonal framework, I believe in the power and impact of the thoughts you tell yourself and others. I hope that these leadership tips will guide your day, especially in decision-making and doubtful moments. I hope these phrases will serve as milestones on a map to discover more about yourself and support your journey to develop into a secure, genuine, confident leader.

LEADERSHIP LESSON 1:
FOLLOW YOUR HEART

Like many 1st year Filipina American college students, I started pre-med studies. During the late 1990s, the professions of medicine, computer science, and engineering were seen as the gold standard toward a future of job security and financial rewards. At Santa Clara University, I passed but struggled through many of the prerequisite chemistry, biology, and calculus courses. My friends questioned why I could not spend more time hanging out with them as I poured myself into my books. I interned at the University of California San Francisco's hospital to learn more about being a medical doctor. I would get some hands-on experience while building my resume for medical school applications. My uncle, a faculty member at UCSF's dentistry department, helped me feel like I belonged in this prestigious academic and clinical setting.

I volunteered on the oncology floor, although my job was to push the book cart up and down the hospital hallways. Cancer is a disease with an especially dark presence in my family. Cancer had already killed my *Nonna*, my maternal grandmother, in 1980. She was only 55 years old, and I had not even reached my 1st birthday. Cancer started in her breasts and ultimately spread throughout her body, into her hip, and finally occupied her brain. Pancreatic cancer came for my *Nonno*, my paternal grandfather, in 1996. These loving grandparents, this beautiful couple Marion and Johnny, these heads of our family, left this earth too quickly. The word cancer was whispered in my home like an unwanted guest you could not figure out how to get rid of. Yet there I was walking the halls where all the patients had cancer. I felt simultaneously scared and brave, pushing my cart, hoping to be helpful, and trying to make even an ounce of a positive difference.

The book cart was full of magazines and novels, providing mental escapes in hard copy form during a time that preceded the popularity of the Internet, the smartphone, and social media. While some patients found interest in selecting something to read, others seemed to appreciate the opportunity to chat. One patient, Javier, spoke to me the longest. Javier's energy was inviting and warm. He had a sparkle in his eye, which detracted from his bald head. He told me about his time at UCSF and how his wife would sleep at the hospital to keep him company. Javier also asked me about myself. I opened up about my career indecision, interest in becoming a doctor, and desire to make a positive difference in others' lives. Next, Javier shared about his social worker and how her role in his treatment was truly healing. The social worker listened to him, supported his fears and feelings, and helped his wife find housing and other resources since the top-rated hospital was hours away from their home. I saw the relief in Javier's face when he spoke endearingly about the social worker. I felt something stir inside me. My angst about which college major to pick began to lessen, the dread of powering through the pre-med curriculum melted, and in their place, I felt light and excitement. And then Javier gave me captivating advice. He shared, *"Follow your heart."* The phrase shattered any remaining self-doubt and uncertainty about which path to take. Javier's legacy in my life had been planted. When we wrapped up our conversation, I practically ran down the hallway with clarity and the freedom of a young woman who knew which direction she was going.

Like I do with many great moments, I called important women in my life. This time it was my mom and my godmother Nancy. They listened as I told them I experienced a "sign," and I no longer wanted to be pre-med. The reputable doctors I observed at UCSF saved lives and needed to act swiftly to get the work done. The services I wanted to provide aligned much more with what Javier described the social worker offered. An intentional space allowed for active listening, attunement to a person's emotional, behavioral, cognitive, social and physical needs, and the facilitation of solutions and resources to meet these needs.

I have been following my heart ever since. My heart helped me tell my dad and my *lola* that I wanted to pursue psychology even when they had healthy skepticism if it would help pay the bills. My heart led me to take risks by applying to graduate programs all over the United States because I needed to cast a wide net to increase the chances of getting into a program that would train me in cross-cultural psychology. When I co-founded the Asian American

Psychology Association's (AAPA) Division on Multiracial and Adopted Asian Americans and served in the first female chair duo for AAPA's Division on Filipinx Psychology, my heart guided me to invest my time building the infrastructure for these amazing communities. And when I accepted the FWN 100 Most Influential Women in the World award in 2021, my 10-word speech was, *"Follow your heart, and use your brain to get there."*

LEADERSHIP LESSON 2:
KEEP YOUR WORD

Being reliable is fundamental to being an effective and trusted leader. Consistency, however, is no easy task. It can be tiring and even boring always to follow through. Yet, it is imperative to being a leader whom people will listen to for the long term. If you say something, do it. If you promise something, deliver. And if for some reason you can not, explain and give context for why you fell short.

Words matter. As a psychologist, I see this front and center with my clients. Mean words linger in recipients' brains long after the words have been uttered. Kind words continue to give comfort even if the people who first shared them are no longer in our lives. However, even before I learned through clinical observation how the word can cause pleasure and pain, my paternal grandmother Maria Mercedes cautioned me early on to mean what you say and keep your word. When as a child, I would tell my grandmother I would call her back and then did not, I received a stern reminder from my *lola* that this was not right.

I had not realized that my promise mattered to the family's matriarch. Her scolding stuck with me when I chose my words in other conversations. Years later, I would remind this same grandmother that she promised to take me to the Philippines. She often replied, *"when you get older."* When I became a teenager and asked her yet again; she laughed and said, *"you didn't forget that promise, huh!? Well I better keep my word."* I turned 16 years old in the Philippines, a monumental coming of age birthday in North American culture. I experienced different communication styles, gender norms, and prayer time with extended family. I ate mango daily, rode a carabao, met an abundance of cousins, *titas* [aunts], and *titos* [uncles], and adjusted to artificial Christmas trees. I needed to visit the land where my grandparents emigrated from and the archipelago that gave the context for my tanned skin. I wanted a tangible connection to my paternal roots. This trip helped me return home to the United States, being more grounded in my identity and familial history.

When leading a group, whether it is with a committee, a board, a classroom, or a family, I aim to keep my word. I know that I do not necessarily "look like" a typical American leader. I am a woman and a woman of color. I do not have credibility by default. My Ph.D. helps sometimes, but often it is after people experience my work ethic that they then see my leadership potential. Someone once referred to me as a "doer." I attribute this in part, because to keep your word, it takes action. It takes doing what is hard to get the job done and follow through on a promise.

LEADERSHIP LESSON 3:
DELAY GRATIFICATION

One of my favorite psychological experiments is the "marshmallow study" by Walter Mischel in 1972. Small children were given one marshmallow and told if they could wait for some time, they would receive two marshmallows instead of just one. The experiment assessed the ability to delay gratification as well as impulsivity. The sweet treat is hard to resist. Longitudinal data suggested that the children who could wait longer and delay the reward tended to have more positive life outcomes.

Patience while waiting for my marshmallow is my core strength. I sacrificed immediate fun and pleasure after college graduation for what I envisioned to be longer-term rewards and success. I moved from my home in urban California to go to graduate school in rural Washington at Washington State University. While no doubt this was an opportunity, it also meant leaving my boyfriend of 7 years and moving on my own to a new place when I was 21 years old. Endurance and perseverance were qualities I leaned into to survive the endless studying and occasional loneliness. While my boyfriend and friends at home seemed to be partying on weekends, I tried to ace the exams, comprehend psychological theory, connect with new clients, and write a dissertation. I learned how to be the best therapist I could to a range of clients whose needs and stories varied: a man questioning his sexuality while also feeling guilty about his attraction to younger boys; a woman trying to forget the flashbacks of being raped; a college student unable to afford glasses trying to decide whether to stay in college or work on her family's farm. My family visited and kept my stamina up. My dad and I went to local coffee shops so I could study. My mom reminded me that she knew I was born to do this work, describing me as a natural listener with a helpful way of talking to people.

During college, I accumulated some debt through student loans but knew it was the path to my dreams. I completed the Ph.D. program in 6 years. During that time, I drove a gray Buick with a red interior, a gift from my dad. At one point, something went wrong with the battery, and I had to disconnect the battery with a wrench each time I parked it so that it would not drain. My sister Vanessa and I laughed as we connected and disconnected the battery. She supported the process with a "check check," confirming it was loosened or tightened enough. I went home to California for the summers, longing for the familiarity of family and my old stomping grounds. I would leave the Buick in the parking lot of my apartment complex. When I returned one fall, wasps had built a home in the door and side mirror. An exterminator helped me get rid of the pests. I was ready to set the Buick free when I left to start my predoctoral internship at UC Berkeley.

I lived with my grandparents in Daly City during my internship. Papa, my paternal grandfather, would ask, *"Is it harvest time yet?"* My Papa would frequently ask me the "harvest" question, usually when walking through the kitchen and always with a smile. I did not have much money in my bank account and felt I was still working the fields and not yet enjoying the harvest. So my response was, *"not yet, Papa, but soon."*

The first time Papa asked me, it took me a while to understand the meaning of his question. Papa planted the first seeds of the harvest when he survived the trauma of World War II, having witnessed Japanese soldiers kill Filipino civilians on the streets. Then a teenager, Papa planted produce in a vacant lot near a building destroyed by war. He pushed around a cart of food and other commodities to sell to the American soldiers. Papa eventually joined the U.S. navy when the Philippines was a commonwealth of the United States. There were tough entrance exams and a tight quota. Admission was an opportunity and accomplishment, but Papa faced discriminatory practices. The sacrifices Papa made had a larger purpose so that we, his family, could enjoy the harvest in the United States of America. For Papa, harvest meant security, success, and financial comfort.

No doubt, being able to delay experiencing immediate fun paved the way for a fruitful career and formal education no one can take away from me. The ability to postpone pleasure for longer-term rewards began with earlier generations in my family and is also a lesson I want to pass down to my children. Whether I am fundraising for a non-profit or mentoring graduate students with their doctoral research, I know an approach incorporating long-term planning tends to lead to the most gains. You can enjoy the moment while postponing instant gratification for more marshmallows in the future!

LEADERSHIP LESSON 4:
YOU ARE LOVED. I AM LOVEABLE.

No matter how much you accomplish, it is pivotal to embrace unconditional positive self-regard. Carl Rogers spoke this truth when formulating person-centered, humanistic psychology. Most clients I work with have an extremely hard time internalizing that they have worth merely because they are human. Their self-esteem is usually closely tied to how well they assess they are doing in their career, their relationships, and their physical appearance. Cultivating self-worth, no matter what is typically a radical concept. From a religious perspective, unconditional self-love ties into the concept that we all have worth because we are children of God. From a spiritual framework, we are all inherently good because we are part of the larger universe and mother earth.

In my youth, my *lola* Mercedes frequently told me, *"you are loved…you are so lucky because you have so many people who love you."* Then she would list the relatives who loved and cared about me. She wanted to drill this into me so that I felt special. Despite coming from divorced parents, not being a planned pregnancy, and my dad living separately from me, I am loved. My godmother Nancy also offered what therapists call a corrective emotional experience. Perhaps due to the circumstances I was born into, I sobbed and shared feeling unwanted. My Aunt Nancy reassured me, *"oh honey, you were very much wanted."* I trusted my grandmother and godmother, and so I accepted their assurances. I believed, and I felt loved.

Embrace Positive Core Schemas.

You are enough. You are strong. You are loved. Internalizing these core beliefs will help you when leading others. Believing in yourself is needed when others doubt.

LEADERSHIP LESSON 5: TAKE CALCULATED RISKS

I am not naturally a risk taker. When I took a college career test, I scored low on my willingness to take risks. This finding confirmed that I like predictability and making choices that lead to things I expect. I do not want to fail. However, some of the best outcomes in my career have come from some thinking, some analyzing, and then leaping after weighing the pros and cons.

While on maternity leave with my son Mason I saw that the AAPA's Division on Filipinx Americans (DoFA) needed board members, specifically a treasurer and co-chair position. Excited to get involved, I expressed interest in the treasurer position, not because I like accounting, budgeting, or finances but because I thought it might be a way to lean into leadership slowly. This was an example of my calculated risk approach. However, the person in charge of the search, Dr. E.J. David, suggested I try for the co-chair position instead. I thought, *"well, if this person believes in me, sure, I'll throw my name in the ring."* To my surprise, I saw my bio and write-up sent to the entire DoFA membership for a vote. For some reason, I naively thought select eyes would review my nomination behind closed doors. I internally panicked when realizing I would be judged and elected this way. My calculated risk had turned into what felt like a big risk. Yet, what an amazing outcome it turned out to be. I was elected, along with my colleague Dr. Richelle Concepcion as the first women co-chairs of the organization. This position also contributed to me chairing the first Filipino American Psychology Conference in 2016 at the Wright Institute in Berkeley, California. Our board and DoFA leadership had no idea if there would be interest in this conference. Yet the conference sold out. We also ended up streaming it live to accommodate interest during a time when this technology was still very new. The bi-yearly conference continues to this day. My decision to run for co-chair also led to other amazing experiences. I received a DoFA Service award, co-edited the first ever peer-reviewed Filipino American Psychology journal, and made lasting friendships with people I admire and respect.

LEADERSHIP LESSON 6:
THERE'S A SOLUTION TO EVERY PROBLEM

When things seem bleak, do not give up. During childhood, I experienced some periods of depression. My sixth-grade teacher commented on my report card that she was concerned about me being melancholic. I saw a helpful school counselor. Prayer and faith that things could improve helped me get through these difficult times. During this time, I also decided to run for student government. I won student body Publicity Officer in seventh grade and Vice President of the school in eighth. I put myself out there even when I was unsure what would happen. In retrospect, these elections were pivotal moments that built confidence, especially during a time of self-doubt. These leadership roles taught me that taking chances can lead to positive outcomes, hopeful ideas could become a reality, and others trusted me to make decisions. I was a girl in a Catholic school uniform at Holy Angels School in Colma, and the foundation was forming for the woman leader I would become.

When in graduate school in Washington, I learned that my long-term boyfriend of 8 years was cheating on me. He confessed after learning that he impregnated the woman he had been seeing while we were long distance. I was devastated. I lost weight and had trouble sleeping. I felt like there was a big hole inside me that spanned my chest and stomach. I tried to hide my pain, but the loss I felt was visceral. At the time, I was unsure how I would adjust to life without him. However, I kept going despite the uncertainty that lay ahead. I eventually accepted that he was not the man I thought he was and let go of the future I envisioned with him.

Fast forward 20 years later, my husband Joel often reassures our sons that *"there's a solution to every problem."* Even when you do not believe it, there is a way to get through the obstacles that arise. This family motto came decades after my break-up and childhood depression. In my 20s, I was not sure how I could trust again. I did not know if I could feel happy again, partner again, or envision a new future for myself. Yet, I learned to be more independent and found a way to keep going. So I say with confidence that there is hope after hopelessness.

LEADERSHIP LESSON 7:
CULTURE IS COMPLICATED. EMBRACE IT.

My racial and ethnic heritage strongly influences how the world sees me and, in turn, how I see myself. These forces were at play before I even had names for them. When I was five years old, I decided to take a walk on the beach by myself. I probably walked for almost an hour until finally, my cousin Steven found me. I did not know I was lost until my frantic mother hugged and scolded me simultaneously, and then recounted with laughter how she approached the lifeguard about my disappearance. The lifeguard inquired, *"What does your daughter look like?"* My mom quickly replied, *"she's a mixed kid,"* to which the lifeguard responded with a perplexed look. I recall having positive feelings about the story but did not initially understand the racial aspect of what happened.

I was drawn to cross-cultural and multicultural psychology because they seemed like paths for answers. In graduate school, I learned about concepts like ethnic identity, acculturation, enculturation, and white privilege. I connected with a very diverse group of colleagues and friends. Together, we explored and embraced our complex cultural identities. At times, it bothered me when people would try to figure out my physical appearance; the grocery store clerk asking me where I was from and trying to pinpoint my ethnic heritage; the pharmacy assistant questioning the racial background of my family. While I have every right to feel annoyed by being asked about my ethnicity at inopportune times, I am leaning into accepting my ethnic ambiguity and complexity, and at times even see it as a strength. When Kamala Harris won the vice presidency, my husband surprised me with the shirt, *"My VP looks like me."*

For years I tried to simplify how I self-identified racially and ethnically. I gave answers I thought would be more straightforward for others to understand because I found it exhausting to explain and wanted to minimize differences. I now embrace that my multiracial identity can be fluid, contextual, and non-fractional. In 2015, the Pew Research Center reported on being "Multiracial in America" and interviewed Roo, a gay Catwaba Indian and White man. Roo described the complexity and uniqueness of identity: *"it's not like a Lego set where you can just put the pieces of identity on top of each other, but it's much more fluid and complicated like if you put some dye into a river or something. It becomes something entirely different than just... building block pieces."* This beautiful imagery of a colorful river is the complexity of culture worth embracing.

In 2010, Dr. A. Timothy Church and I published the first enculturation scale for Filipino Americans (ESFA) designed to capture an individual's values, attitudes, and behavioral traditions associated with Filipino culture. I chose to create a quantitative measure because it paves the way for more research on and for the Filipinx community. The measure has helped elucidate findings on help-seeking approaches, colonial mentality, parenting practices, as well as emotional and cognitive well-being. The ESFA assesses a Filipino American's cultural affiliation at one point in time and can be an introspective result. It is crucial to remember though that cultural identity is more complex than a score. If you do not fit the cultural boxes given to you by society, make your own boxes and build your own table to sit at. With this mentality in mind, in 2017, I co-founded the Division on Multiracial and Adopted Asian American Americans (DMAA), one of eight divisions in the Asian American Psychology Association. DMAA aims to shine a light on the experiences of adopted and multiracial Asian Americans often overlooked within mainstream conversations around Asia America.

When leading a team, embrace the uniqueness of each person's cultural identity. Through intentional inclusivity, the person will know you want to accept them for who they are. Research shows that having a positive racial and ethnic identity can buffer stress and is overall connected to good health outcomes. Pride in one's cultural roots can be a tool for resiliency. When you need to challenge a team member, they will also be more likely to receive such challenges.

LEADERSHIP LESSON 8:
BE PROUD OF WHO YOU ARE

Self-acceptance is an important ideal and is a core ingredient for high self-esteem and self-confidence. As a young girl, I played and always beat my *lola* in Chinese Checkers. But when we played when I was in college, she defeated me. I realized then she had been letting me win all those years. Through her wisdom and humility, she built up my self–confidence that I ultimately generalized to other situations.

In 2020, my best friend Shebani Patel and I co-authored a storybook, *Proud of my Mommy*. Shebani is a partner at a prestigious global firm, manages large teams, serves clients across industries, and has been very successful in her career. With her intense work days and travel schedule, Shebani also wanted to relay to her two daughters the meaning and relevance of her career. Shebani is passionate about children feeling a solid bond with their mom even when not physically together and was excited to have the opportunity to reinforce this in *Proud of my Mommy.* As the first woman in her family to attend college, Shebani believes in encouraging and supporting women who want to have a career. A mom of two sons myself, I related to her goals. We felt proud of the professionals we had become and wanted women who also work outside the home to be able to experience more harmony and synchrony between their careers and caretaking roles. A fan of storytelling and children's literature, I thought a storybook was a perfect intervention point, especially when seeing the absence of such a children's book. *Proud of my Mommy* features culturally diverse characters and highlights a range of professions, including the medical field, business, military, teaching, first responders, and the service industry.

Embracing what makes you different and being proud of your uniqueness can set you up for success. People often experience shame around what makes them stand out, especially if that the difference is not societally valued. Some conformity can be very helpful for group cohesion and team building. However, uniqueness contributes to innovative and creative leadership.

Radical self-acceptance and pride in oneself, while also not being condescending and dismissive of others is worth practicing.

LEADERSHIP LESSON 9:
CONNECT THROUGH CONVERSATION

Words are powerful tools that can either bring us together or distance us. In 2019, my friend and colleague Dr. Anatasia Kim and I wrote *It's Time to Talk (and Listen): How to have Constructive Conversations about Race, Class, Sexuality, Ability, and Gender in a Polarized World.* In this book, we identify steps and exercises for practicing genuine interpersonal exchanges. When in roles of leadership, such an approach can be especially difficult to embrace and yet a pivotal one for building and maintaining an inclusive, diverse, and healthy team. I extracted a few key principles from the book that can help get you started with connecting through conversation.

Identify the internal and external barriers that get in the way of you having open conversations. List out the fears that prevent you from leaning in. Having an honest understanding of what is holding you back will allow you to break those barriers. Common internal barriers are fear of: conflict, losing one's temper, and losing credibility. Common external barriers are social norms and lack of time.

Anchor yourself in your values to guide the conversation and navigate the barriers. Core values can act as a flashlight when you can not find the right words. These values might be ones you have embraced since childhood or ones you have sought to integrate into your life as an adult. Still not sure what to pick? How about courage, integrity, honesty, gratitude, hope, or humility?

Open up conversations with your values. Integrate the values into your opening statement, such as, *"I'm hopeful we can have an open conversation even though this is a tough topic to broach."* Let the person know why you are engaging in dialogue. *"I value you and so want to speak more about something that has been on my mind. I trust that we can get through this and discuss this together."* Combining "I statements" and "we statements" can help you speak from your own experience while inviting collaboration.

Listen attentively. Once you've shared your thoughts, now it's your turn to be all ears. Dr. Miguel Gallardo said in his Cultural Humility podcast, *"We were given two ears and one mouth for a reason."* Use appropriate eye contact to let them know you are listening. Keep your body language open to show your interest. Pay attention to their words and body language. No matter how tempting it is, don't focus on planning what you'll say next. Instead, really listen to the other person's ideas, even if you disagree.

A conversation that incorporates genuine self-disclosure and authentic listening can be healing, generate growth, and bridge deeper connections. What is lost during the silence when cultural norms make such conversations taboo? Take an intentional, calculated, interpersonal risk to dialogue with each other about things that matter.

**LEADERSHIP LESSON 10:
HAVE FAITH**

Becoming a psychologist is truly my vocation. I remember when a priest visited my third-grade class and wrote the word "vocation" on the blackboard. When asked the meaning of this new word, my classmate gave an adorable answer: "a trip." Perhaps because of the mistaken definition, this learning moment stands out in my memory. We were encouraged by the priest not to find a job but to follow God's calling. In my younger years, I considered becoming a nun, a hairdresser, and an aerobic instructor. Ultimately, my service to society was not to give good hair, facilitate fitness, or live at the convent. Instead, it was to serve through the profession of psychology.

All the signs, including my conversation with Javier, pointed me in the direction of the field of psychology. My favorite psychology professor, who often told exciting stories to demonstrate the meaning of a psychological concept, resembled my beloved, deceased paternal grandfather *Nonno*. His silver hair, lean stature, and wrinkled hands signaled that my career path was going in the right direction. My professor's stories about traveling and other anecdotes inspired me. Long before the days of laptops in class, I wrote them down frantically in my notebook. I told my mom that this sign was a further nudge to declare my major in psychology.

While my passion for psychology became apparent, the path to pursue it was not easy. Faith was fundamental to my journey. Prayer and patience gave me endurance when I was lonely, tired, and felt like giving up. I also had faith in myself—a biracial Filipina Italian woman from California—that my hard work would pay off and lead to a fulfilling future. While intangible, faith is a helpful outlook that can ground you through uncertainty. In the wise words of Dr. Joe White, the godfather of black psychology, I also invite you to *"keep the faith"* on your personal and professional journeys.

ALICIA DEL PRADO, PH.D

ANGELICA URRA BERRIE

Philanthropist
GLOBAL FWN100™ 2014

Becoming Ruth:
A Transformational Journey

"The ability to tell your own story, in words or images, is already a victory; already a revolt." — REBECCA SOLNIT

The Philanthropic Journey

Growing up in Catholic convent schools in the Philippines, the word "philanthropy" was not a part of my vocabulary. I entered a whole different world when I married New Jersey sales entrepreneur Russ Berrie, whose success with teddy bears and trolls fueled our philanthropy.

I came of age during the Marcos regime, in the season of protest between the assassination of Ninoy Aquino and the triumph of the People Power Revolution. Standing with nuns in front of military tanks, clutching a Bible and rosary, was a defining moment in my life. I was among a sea of people who surrendered our sense of safety, armed only with our Catholic faith. I never imagined that the convent girl I was then would later convert to Judaism, take Ruth as my Hebrew name, and embrace Israel as my spiritual home. Russ introduced me to the world of philanthropy. As a newlywed, I had to endure solicitations by organizations seeking funding from my husband. Making decisions about who to give to and how much was overwhelming. It would have been much easier to let him make these decisions for us, but he taught me to ask tough questions, set conditions before making a gift, and "inspect what you expect." He always said that writing a check was easy, but the hard part was making sure what you give actually makes a difference.

He encouraged me to pursue my own passions, yet when my friends enlisted me to found a Gilda's Club in New Jersey, a free social and emotional cancer support community named after Gilda Radner of Saturday Night Live, he told us: *"I will pay you NOT to do this!"*

He knew it would be challenging to fundraise for a start-up nonprofit, but we proved him wrong by raising three years of operating capital before we opened our doors. Writing my first significant check for the mortgage of Gilda's Club Northern New Jersey Clubhouse led to my next step as Board Chair of Gilda's Club Worldwide, a network with over fifty clubhouses around the world.

Working with other women to make something good happen was a valuable growth experience. I learned I could be more than "Russ Berrie's wife" by harnessing my own connections and creativity to give fully of myself. Since then, I have chosen organizations where I could really add value beyond writing a check. Discovering the satisfaction of giving, connecting the dots among people, ideas, and issues I was passionate about was the beginning of my philanthropic journey.

Becoming Ruth

My marriage was an interfaith adventure. As an intermarried couple, we celebrated our holidays in harmony. I learned to recite Shabbat prayers; he joined me for midnight Mass on Christmas Eve. We went to shul on Rosh Hashanah and Yom Kippur. Our mingled faiths led to the founding of The Center for Inter-Religious Understanding, where I understood that to be religious is to be inter-religious.

After ten years of living and giving in a Jewish community, I chose to convert. After a childhood shaped by nuns whose influence left an imprint on my subconscious, coming to Judaism was a leap into the unknown. Integrating my Jewish Catholic Filipina *"halo-halo"* identity became easier after Pope

John Paul II walked into the synagogue in Rome, called the Jews "our elder brothers;" acknowledged Judaism as the root from which the Catholic faith sprung; negated the accusation of deicide by Jews which was the basis for anti-Semitism; and officially sanctioned diplomatic relations between the Holy See and Israel.

During my conversion process, Rabbi David Hartman imparted a life lesson I have carried in my heart. When I asked if conversion meant discarding my Catholic identity, he said: *"You bring all of who you are, all of who you are becoming, to where you are going."*

My journey has taken me from the Philippines to America, from my Catholic faith to the Jewish tradition, to a global world of inter-religious dialogue. These encounters shaped my work as President of the Russell Berrie Foundation, providing valuable insights on philanthropy as a force for good, bringing people together by connecting core values to the task of repairing the world.

Like the Biblical Ruth, I had a mother-in-law named Naomi, became a widow, and embraced my husband's people. When my husband died of a stroke on Christmas Day of 2002, my philanthropic journey took a lonely turn.

Awakening

One morning, I woke up and knew nothing in my life would ever be the same again Overnight, I was a widow, CEO and Vice-Chair of a public company on the New York Stock Exchange, and President of The Russell Berrie Foundation. It was a bolt of lightning that put me at the helm of a public company in the process of being sold while stepping into my husband's philanthropic shoes in our community. Leading in this time of loss allowed no time to grieve. I did not have a choice.

Every morning, I had to be my bravest and most authentic self. The day after he died, I was appointed CEO. At my first board meeting, I hid in the bathroom and cried. Then, when I had to move into Russ' office, I cried. On my first trip to China without him, I cried. Operating on automatic pilot, I went on with all my company obligations. Just days after the shiva, I hosted dinners for retailers at our home, met with customers at the office, and attended Gift Shows in Atlanta and Chicago, where long lines formed outside our showrooms as people in the gift industry came to pay their respects.

I visited distribution centers in the U.K., Australia, Canada, and traveled to China on buying trips. Carrying on philanthropic commitments barely a week after Russ' death, I sat numbly in the theater where we held his funeral service for a gala I organized. The headliner was Paul Anka, who came down from the stage and danced with me. It was surreal! Just weeks after being widowed, I hosted a political fundraiser for Presidential candidate Senator Joe Lieberman at our home. I flew to Israel on a 24-hour mission to persuade the Economic Minister, Ehud Olmert, to match our Foundation's $24,000,000 grant for nanotechnology. It was a transformational gift that aspired to put Israel among the Top 15 countries in the world in nanotechnology.

On my way back to the airport at 4 a.m., Russ' favorite song, "My Way," came on over the radio, and I wept at the thought that he was not here to experience this significant achievement.

At the time of my loss, I was making my way through the dark. I sought counsel from widows leading foundations, whose friendship and support inspired me to develop my philanthropic voice and carve my own path.

As a widow, I had to struggle to be seen as my own person and not a shadow of my late husband. I was expected to do what people thought he would have done if he were alive. I was seen as someone who carried his legacy but had to struggle to make my voice heard. It still astounds me to recall how people I had known and trusted would say: *"If Russ were here, he would have done this..."* I only wish that Russ was here and did whatever he wanted, but sadly, I was standing in his enormous shoes and realized that it would never fit. I simply had to learn to walk in my own size five shoes.

As the face of the Russell Berrie Foundation, I often had to deliver speeches. Like most people, I was terrified of public speaking. So, in writing my own speeches, I would tell my story; first, from a safe distance, without revealing too much vulnerability. With time, my ability to relate my story evolved as I connected with women in the audience who resonated with the narrative of my journey. Expressing who I am in my own words, from my personal experiences, helped me overcome my fear of getting naked emotionally. Finding my voice as a woman in philanthropy, discovering other women who shared the wisdom of their experience with me, and learning how philanthropy expresses who you are in how you give, taught me leadership lessons no guru could ever impart.

Transformation

Death is a powerful growth catalyst. Even in the depths of our brokenness, we can see our life clearly. Becoming human, we find the touchstones of our values and purpose, our calling. Awareness comes even in a fog of grief. Our response to the painful invitation to grow becomes a spiritual adventure. In my dark night of the soul, I sought a jolt of awareness to propel me toward my growth challenge. I received an invitation to a Vision Quest for philanthropists that was my call to adventure.

Fasting 36 hours alone in a tent in the woods, armed only with a pen, flashlight, and bear spray, we had a question to answer: *"What is the promise to myself it would kill me to break?"* In the morning, hearing thunder outside, I knew what I had to do. Scrambling out of my tent, I climbed to the top of the mountain. My heart beating wildly, I started to undress, tying my pants to a tree branch to keep them from blowing away. I was half naked when a Park Ranger appeared on horseback. He took one look at me and said, *"Lady, if I were you, I would remove your watch and any metal objects in case lightning strikes!"* and galloped away. I lay on the ground like a sacrificial victim, needles of rain and blades of grass pricking my skin. Eyes shut and limbs trembling, headlines flashed through my head: *"Naked philanthropist struck by lightning!"*

The departure from ingrained convent-bred bonds of modesty was the awakening I needed to recognize the fears that kept me small. Encountering myself in the wild revealed the "inner nun" who guarded my hidden desires, and Reader, it was Me! My naked adventure on the mountaintop remains a fierce reminder of the promise to free myself from the bonds of safety. As women, we bear the unspoken expectation to keep ourselves small, stay safe, and be seen and not heard. As a result, we readily give up our power, so we don't attract lightning.

In ancient wisdom, immortality is not about conquering death but transcending our fear of change. Fear holds us back from leading our best life. In her book, *Fear of Flying*, Erica Jong said, *"I have accepted fear as a part of life.... specifically the fear of change.... I have gone ahead despite the pounding in the heart that says, 'turn back.'"*

In our lives, we dare not name our desire, for once it has a face and a voice, it might claim us, requiring a commitment we may not be prepared to make. A decision to veer off the path of safety, leave our jobs or our husbands to change our life, would be a death-defying act. Yet the moment we decide we want something more than we are afraid of it, we are free to pursue that with all our might.

When I find myself at a fork in the road between safety and fear of the unknown, the voice of the Persian poet, Rumi, rings in my soul. *"Forget safety,"* it thunders, *"Live where you fear to live."*

On Rosh Hashanah, the Jewish New Year, my rabbi reminds the congregation how most of us are afraid to live in touch with our souls. We put off doing brave and important things for fear of altering the course of our lives. Grasping the tiger's tail to live the life we always imagined is terrifying. In our hearts, we yearn to feel truly alive, to heed Joseph Campbell's "call to adventure," to pursue the thing we think we cannot do. This *"inner journey to the edge of what is known,"* as Campbell describes it, is the *"liminal in-between zone where transformational magic occurs."*

As widows, we find ourselves in this zone of becoming, a place where we have never been before, the blank space in which we are transformed into something we could never have imagined. Widowhood was the soul-making passage of my becoming. Sometimes, it takes a catastrophe to awaken us into who we really are. It is the bolt of lightning that jolts us into fearlessness, forces us to surrender to a state of "not knowing," and sets us unwillingly on the path of self-transformation. To be a vessel for change to happen, we must find ourselves in the gap between our becoming and our unbecoming, the crack where we can let go of who we think we are and discover who we are meant to be. Navigating that distance between is the essence of our transformational journey. Leonard Cohen sang: *"There is a crack in everything. That's how the light gets in."*

Life as a Sacred Pilgrimage

The journey of becoming is a pilgrimage toward our better self. Somewhere along the way, we encounter ourselves on the road of life. My loss was a catalyst for change. I found the courage to embark on a spiritual quest that I had always longed to undertake, a walking meditation to Santiago de Compostela, a UNESCO World Heritage pilgrimage site. We are all pilgrims on a quest for meaning. Joseph Bedier, a medieval historian, wrote: *"In the beginning was the road..."* The Way of St. James, known as the Camino, is an invitation to unwind, to let go of who we were, and to surrender to the sacred, one footstep at a time.

Walking the Camino is to leave all things behind, shedding the skin of our old self along the way. Free of distractions, the mind slows down, releasing the busy-ness that passes for substance in our daily life. With no appointments to rush to, every day unfolds as the world presents itself in small doses. Emptied of our past, we find the interior space from which we can see ourselves and our life more clearly. Walking intentionally for hours, day after day, suspends time. Time is the first and most challenging obstacle in our pursuit of the sacred. The President of Friends of St. Jacques de Compostelle, Bertrand Saint Macary, explained the resurgence of the Camino: *"People today have an overdose of modernity. Our main enemy is time, and, on the pilgrimage, the pilgrim can live outside time. To walk to Santiago is to find our true nature."* Finding our true selves is the journey of our lives. Channeling the gift of our life and connecting it to purpose is the pilgrimage of our life on earth.

Widowhood as a Master Class in Leadership

Becoming a widow forced me into a leadership role I never wanted. Struggling to be human in the throes of acute pain was a growth lesson that allowed me to witness *"who am I being while I'm doing what I'm doing."* The path of a widow is paved with leadership touchstones. Like many leaders, widows are forged in an epic crisis. Personal catastrophe triggers a radical change that opens us up to sense the world from a unique perspective. At the end of the tunnel, we emerge with greater empathy and compassion as we rise in courage to meet the moment every single day. The path of leadership requires personal transformation. Rising to the call of leadership, we encounter our own source of power as we are transformed.

Every woman has the power to express who we want to be in this world. Nobel Laureate Leymah Gbowee tells us to *"do one thing everyday that everyone else is scared to do"* as only when we believe in ourselves can we realize that *"everything is within our power, and our power is within us."* Transmuting this gift of power to create a better world is our sacred task as transformational leaders.

The world needs more transformational leaders, leaders who can transcend the curve balls of life. Widows forged in crisis can become the leaders we never imagined. Realizing the full leadership potential of widows is the life's work of Carolyn Moor, founder of the Modern Widows Club. Carolyn leads a revolutionary movement to create a million widow leaders whose influence could transform the world. She taught me how empowering widows to be leaders changes lives globally. Her movement has 37 chapters across the United States, with over 3,000 members, providing services to over 15,000 widows. Unlocking this leadership potential would yield economic returns by lifting "powerless" women who have historically been the most underserved members of our society. Developing the power of resilience in the most marginalized women is an opportunity the Filipina Women's Network cannot afford to miss in our mission of female empowerment.

As a widow, I bear witness to countless "Ruths." Becoming a statistic in a world inhabited by 260,000,000 widows put me in a club where no one wants to belong. Yet, at some point in our lifetime, we will be among the countless uncounted who make up seventy percent of women who are widows. Unseen, unsupported, and unmeasured, widows have no voice, but not all widows are powerless. Widows have led empires, revolutions, and countries as change agents in society, bridging leaders in communities and transformational figures in history.

In the Philippines, widows who emerged as leaders include President Corazon Aquino, who led the peaceful People Power Revolution that toppled a dictator. Becoming President of the country while in mourning after her husband, Ninoy Aquino, was assassinated is a story that inspired people around the world. Filipina Women's Network awardee Vice-President Leni Robredo ignited a Pink Revolution that awakened millions of Filipinos. She speaks of her late husband as crediting her with more power than she knew she had, long before anyone realized she would step into his political shoes.

Both women did not seek power, but like the humble Biblical widow, Ruth, they played a transformational role in Philippine history.

The Gift of Who You Are
"All you have is what you are, and what you give."
— URSULA LE GUIN

As a Filipina, a woman, a widow, and a Jew — I bring all of who I am to where I am going. Speaking from my bravest and most authentic self to tell the story of who I am and what I stand for has been a journey of becoming. In the stories we tell about ourselves, we are taking back our voices, reclaiming our power as women, and leaving a trail for others who follow. Putting our leadership journey into words shapes our life story into a heroic tale of healing, wisdom, and courage. Leadership matters. It matters across cultures. It matters across time. It matters across generations. It matters greatly because it is the gift we leave behind. Transmitting our stories, in our own voice, we transcend our fears to become immortal.

> "The meaning of life is to find your gift. The purpose of life is to give it away." — WILLIAM SHAKESPEARE

> "The promise it would kill me to break."
> — DAVID WHYTE FROM "ALL TRUE VOWS"

KRISTINE CUSTODIO SUERO

Commissioner, City of San Diego
Citizens' Equal Opportunity Commission
Senior Paralegal/Business Development Director,
Butterfield Schechter LLP
GLOBAL FWN100™ 2012

Designing Sisterhood:
From Fears to Fierce

Our lives sometimes may not feel like our own, especially as women, depending on the current role or roles that we are playing and the season of life that we are traversing. As a daughter of immigrants navigating the complexities of the immigrant experience in the United States, my life sometimes does not feel like my own. I carried a certain sense of obligation to fulfill my parents' dreams of migrating to the "land of plenty." My father, once a career Navy service member, and my mother, a teacher turned entrepreneur, stand at the center of that backdrop. On the surface, yes, certainly familial and generational success surfaced. Yet the stories of struggle to self-actualization and everything in-between lurk beneath that veil of perceived success. Those stories await being told.

Our stories, the ones of the Filipina experience across the globe, must be told authentically and meaningfully. Sharing our most vulnerable moments opens the dialogue to deep connections with others. Particularly in a community where *hiya* [shame] is so deeply embedded, our forlorn and emotionally drained selves desperately seek outlets for release, inner peace, and comfort. If we do not hold space for one another to love our whole selves, then what of us, our community, and humanity? The facets and nuances of living out one's personal purpose, indeed, in a sense, is an individual journey, but the true joy of life is in fellowship. We must know that we are not alone in this world. Moreover, the power in sisterhood can and does propel us into being the women and leaders we are destined to be and whom the world desperately needs during this transformational time in human history.

My story of how I went from fears to fierce tells of my family's history and opportunities that would ultimately lead to generational wealth and legacy beyond our bloodlines. How did I shift from the heavy burden of paralyzing fear and grief in losing both of my parents within a year and a half of one another to finding myself—the fearless, fierce me? This chapter will share just that and serves as my loving tribute to my beloved and selfless parents, Roland and Zena Custodio. And to Francine Maigue, the Filipina Women's Network Face of Global of Pinay Power who uplifted Filipinas in their leadership journeys by her example, generosity, and kindness and who tragically lost her courageous battle against cancer. Your influence, my dearest, and most precious FWN sister, inspired and shaped my path to finding me, the unapologetic, fierce me. May you rest in power. *Mahal kita.*

> *"The circle of women around us weave invisible nets of love that carry us when we are weak and sing with us when we are strong."* — SARK

If ever a person who embodied and lived daily the sage words of wisdom, never give up, Francine Maigue did just that to the very end. Her tremendous impact on the many lives she touched during her short four decades on this planet encouraged, uplifted, and empowered many. That impact is undoubtedly her legacy.

Our texts and calls always started with, *"Hey, Sis!"* I first met Francine at the Hancock Park home of Edwin and Lani Raquel in December of 2014. Her effervescent demeanor radiated as we spoke after the book reading from the maiden *DISRUPT: Loud. Proud. Leading Without A Doubt.* Francine's sister, Theresa Maigue Bendorf, was also in attendance that evening. The evident unbreakable bond between the two struck me as our conversation continued.

Upon learning that we all hailed from San Diego County, we exchanged information and thus began my life-changing friendship with this incredible, one-of-a-kind, unforgettable human being.

Similar in age, Francine and I learned that we were on similar professional paths with our blossoming careers and passion for advocating for the advancement of women and girls. Francine, at the time, was the President of the Filipino American Chamber of Commerce of San Diego and the District Director for the former Assemblywoman Lorena Gonzalez Fletcher. Before long, Francine asked me to join the chamber as its secretary. I happily obliged as I knew that my goals aligned with Francine's vision for the chamber and uplifting Filipino-owned businesses.

Over the two years of Francine's tenure as President, we curated and produced several events for our business community and collaborated on projects to amplify the voice of Filipinas. Watching Francine in action was magic. Her demeanor, grace, tact, laser focus, and organizational skills left me awestruck. As a legal professional, the all too familiar knowledge, skills, and abilities required to manage complex legal matters were not lost on me.

Proudly, Francine was my nominee for the 2015 Filipina Women's Network Global 100 award. Francine embodied everything that FWN represented. She would later become the first face of Global Pinay Power, lead a *DISRUPT* book reading in San Diego, and co-emcee the FWN awards program with Rowena Romulo in London. Francine always dreamed big and encouraged others to do the same.

In May of 2019, a week before my wedding, I received a phone call from Francine. Throughout the years, long after our FilAm Chamber days, I had kept her updated with the life events happening to me, including losing my mother in June of 2018 and eventually my father in November of 2019 due to lung cancer. I will never forget that phone call. It was the day that Francine told me of her own diagnosis of Stage 4 lung cancer. We wept but remained optimistic. Despite her own health challenges, Francine remained positive, upbeat, and true to her character, serving others by educating everyone about healthcare advocacy and self-care.

Francine continued to write her column, *The Pampered Pinay*, for a local Filipino community newspaper sharing scrumptious recipes and stories of her experiences. She appeared on local news stations sharing updates on her battle with cancer. She continued to work in government in her role as District Director. We continued to communicate. Her support and encouragement to me were unfailing, as was her honesty and directness.

On February 22, 2022, Francine took her last breath at 7:58 p.m. surrounded by her family, whom she loved fiercely. I, along with our whole community, was shattered at her loss. The only comfort I have is knowing that Francine will live on forever. We carry her in our hearts and continue her legacy in our work. We always said to each other, love and miss you, Sis. Though Francine's physical presence is no longer here, the extraordinary power of sisterhood still propels our hearts and minds into action.

On my 45th birthday in October 2020, I decided that, as a gift to myself, I would give a SUE Talk for the Connected Women on Influence professional organization. SUE stands for Successful, Unstoppable, and Empowered. These talks serve as "story-sharing" as a vehicle to inspire other women in their respective personal and professional leadership journeys. It is, however, more of a performance, almost a monologue, rather than an educational speech.

I chose to give a SUE Talk because I had just been through the most challenging part of my life, losing both of my parents within a year and a half of each other. As a result, I landed on the other side a little older, a bit worn from punch after punch, yet determined to help other women going through similar times in their lives.

To this day, I still feel like an orphan. My mom died in 2018, and my dad died in 2019. It was the first time in my whole life that I felt like my support system, the safety net, got pulled from under me. I suddenly felt like a "real bona fide adult."

I sat at the edge of the bed, holding my precious mother's hand. Her barely audible voice, trembling to eke the words out: *"whenever you need me, I'll always be there. Just look to the brightest star in the sky, and that'll be me looking down on you."* Cascades of black-stained mascara rivers dripped down my face as I stared at her. My heart shattered, and the lump in my throat choked me, but the words still came: *"please don't leave me, mama. What am I supposed to do without you? How am I supposed to do all of this without you?"*

Our daily intense how-to note-taking sessions of CEO and teacher extraordinaire passing on a lifetime of wisdom stopped on June 6, 2018. She would not meet my future husband. She would not plan my wedding with me. Her huge presence in our daily lives forever gone.

I am the daughter of Zena, yes, like the Warrior Princess, who was an immigrant beginning her journey in America with a college degree, $200 in her pocket, and a dream. Zena was a teacher by training and a "Tiger Mom," active in every aspect of my educational career and pursuits.

I was a shy and angst-ridden 16-year-old when I boldly told Zena I wanted to be a civil rights attorney. We were in the car idled at a stoplight with the sun blazing on my face when I declared to Zena: *"Mama, I want to be a civil rights attorney."* My immigrant mother reacted something like this: *"Uh, no. You are going to be poor your whole life. You are going into a stable job. You are going into the medical field."*

Imagine, at the tender age of 16, in a valiant attempt to exercise my independence and my agency, proclaiming my dreams, then squashed in a millisecond! Yet, with that prescriptive voice, my safe path was now my reality as I made my way through college to become a physical therapist.

Fast forward. It was during my summer break before my last semester of college, the chilly breeze of the air conditioning blasting on my face as I steadied myself in the Mercedes Sprinter van zipping around the curvy roads of the lush hills of the Baguio mountains in the Philippines. My cell phone rang. It was my dad: *"I'm sorry to tell you this but your mom had a stroke. She's in the hospital. You need to come home."* After a week and a half into my college trip to my parents' homeland, I was back on a plane to face a new reality.

That 14-hour flight back home was the Indy 500 for the circling worries and anxieties of the unknown. Is my mom going to die? What's going to happen to our business? Am I going to be able to finish school?

I moved home for the summer to help with Zena's rehabilitation and to run our business. I helped until there was some sense of normalcy and returned to school in the Fall to finish my last semester. No graduation ceremony. No pomp and circumstance. I quickly moved back home to San Diego to run our family's business as soon as the semester ended. At the age of 21, I became the matriarch of our family.

Doubt. Insecurity. FEAR. How am I supposed to handle all of this? I have no idea what I was doing. But as with any challenge in life, we rise. I slogged through the heavy burden of fear and fought analysis paralysis. I put one foot in front of the other as I made hard decisions that would determine my family's livelihood.

On the other side of fear, I found faith in myself—knowing, believing, and trusting my instincts. When fight or flight kicked in, I flew higher. Some days, I didn't think I could even get myself out of bed, let alone run a business and have others depending on me, my choices, decisions, and leadership. And still, I flew, blindly, boldly, fiercely.

I found myself with no present options to pursue my graduate degree in physical therapy. But while sifting through the mail one day, as if guided by the universe, I happened upon a University of California, San Diego Extension course catalog and flipped through the pages until I landed on the paralegal program. The dreams of 16-year-old Kristine reignited. I never stopped listening to the voice within, telling me that my gifts of education and encouragement called for something greater even beyond taking the helm of the family business and keeping on going.

You know, those knock-you-to-your-knees moments in life? They have a way of bringing perspective and clarity once the clouds of despair lift. Our inner voices are set free by our power and strength to drown out the noise of dreams, hopes and timelines that others dictate for us.

Never satisfied with the status quo, I set upon my parallel journey alongside running my family's business. I dove headfirst into my new career as a legal professional. I got my first taste of the nonprofit world by running a professional trade association, eventually ascending to the role of President. During that time, I learned that the power of one could be the spark for the power of many. Being brave and vulnerable paved the path to opportunities for all of us.

Enveloped and embraced by my people, they who cared so deeply about the world around them, I thrived. The helper in me thrived, especially when I engaged with eager students hungry to start their journeys into the law. I went on a speaking tour across the country, sharing my story, encouragement, and message that it only takes one person, one voice, to make a difference in this world. In helping others find themselves, I found me, the fearless, fierce me.

It's an interesting thing. I did not come into this world with a golden microphone. I hated public speaking. Even detested it. Remember that quote from Jerry Seinfeld? I'd rather be IN the casket than giving the eulogy. That was me. But I pushed myself to get into the arena. The antidote to despair is action. Do something that scares you every single day. That's where real growth happens when we are UNcomfortable. Be brave. Take risks. Be fierce.

I'm still learning, but this I know. The true gift in helping others: I came alive by speaking life into other people. Alo-ha. Aloha. Aloha. This literally translated means the breath of life exchanged. The joy in life is fellowship. We need others to enjoy a whole and joyful life.

Change Agent. Disrupter. Educator. Legal Sherpa. Career Architect. I am all these things and more. I learned a great lesson in life. The heart always wins when it comes to matters of the head and heart. And, I know, even if and when I have to ugly cry, I always get back up when it gets hard.

Never give up. It's still the best advice I have ever received and what pushed me from FEARS to FIERCE.

> *"There is a special place in hell for women who don't help other women."* — MADELINE ALBRIGHT

Reflecting on my earlier years of life during childhood and adolescence, it became abundantly clear that what set the stage for my tenacity and resiliency began with watching my first and earliest mentor, my mother, in how she navigated through life as a woman of color. I watched how she developed and fostered important connections with other women who would help, shape, mold, and push her beyond her comfort zone.

Full disclosure, my mother and I had a complicated relationship. She was a fierce tiger mother. In her mind, she was a CEO raising a future CEO. That was her approach to raising me. I knew I was in a different world from a young age.

I was obsessed with reading and learning. My curiosity often led my mother to design intellectually stimulating and challenging tasks such as balancing her checkbook from age seven. I still vividly remember lying on the floor with my nose buried in my parents' treasured leather-bound Encyclopedia Britannica books. My mind soared to the far-off places like India that I read about on all those magical pages. My imagination ran wild on many adventures.

Exposed to arts, culture, and music during my formative years, I began learning to play the violin when I was eight years old until high school with my mother shuttling me to my private music lessons. As an adult, I can now see how my mother lived her own dreams through my opportunities as a child born and bred in the United States of America. Like many other immigrants from the Philippines, my mother grew up with modest means. She dreamed of playing a musical instrument, but there was no access to such luxuries during her childhood.

"I lived with your Auntie Nena when I was going to school. They did so much for me. Auntie Nena's dad gave me $200 when I immigrated to America. That was a lot of money back then! My dad was a tailor, and my mom only had a fourth-grade education and stayed home to raise her children. They did not have a lot of money to send me to school. I only had a little bit of money for my lunch every day. I remember that I had holes on the soles of my shoes."

My mother rarely cried. She was tough as they made them. But at this moment, I witnessed a single tear stream down her right cheek. She quickly brushed it away.

"You have no idea how lucky you and your sister are. I am so grateful to your Auntie Nena because she was always kind and generous. Her family helped me so much when I was going to school."

My mother would earn her bachelor's degree and begin her career as a schoolteacher before moving to the United States, where she met my father and started their family adventure.

It was around my age now when my mother decided to become an entrepreneur. I wish I had had more discussions with her when she was alive about how she felt during this time in her life. Frankly, I wish I had interviewed and preserved the history of both of my parents about their lives and experiences of what they were like as children and what they felt as they decided to leave their homeland for a foreign country. I would love to know what their stories of trailblazing and risk-taking were all about.

Capturing our stories is important. Creating content to relate to while navigating through struggles and challenges must be prioritized for our community. We are quick to report to friends and family about all the successes. But what about all the hard times that ultimately shaped and molded us? Yes, we talk about the grace, but what about the grit? Our culture already stigmatizes discussions revolving around mental health with *hiya*. We are told not to "air our dirty laundry." We often hear about the "crab mentality," the literal pulling down of others during times of success, of other Filipinos not celebrating the success of their fellow *kababayan* [fellow Filipino]. Imagine live crabs in a pot of boiling water, pulling each other down to save themselves. Consider how the unchecked colonial mentality of subjugation and oppression still live in our present-day behaviors when communing with one another.

Where are the resources, books, podcasts, movies, and counselors readily accessible to youth of Filipino descent from which to seek guidance? We still hear of these tragic statistics of young Filipina girls ranking the highest in suicide ideation before the COVID-19 pandemic. Where are these young women to go? Who will swoop these budding women and future leaders up in loving arms to tell them everything will work out as it should and hang in there? Where can these young women go to seek refuge and to be seen and heard? It is in the sisterhood of Filipina women who have found success and joy in their professions and want to pay it forward to the next generation. This sisterhood is precisely why the FWN is so critical in the development of young Filipina leaders. We, sisters, cast the vision far and wide so that beyond our lifetimes our next generation can and will, enjoy the journey with grit and grace.

Of course, my fearless mother served as my first role model and mentor, but it would not be until high school that I would hear about another Filipina teacher. Imagine, from grade school through eighth grade; all my teachers were Caucasians. It was not until ninth grade that my English teacher, and most influential, would be a Black woman. Interestingly, I am now a teacher myself, just like my mother. I teach post-graduate students Introduction to Law at the University of San Diego School of Law Paralegal Program. Many of my students tell me that it is the first time that they have someone, a person of color, as their teacher. I, therefore, find it compelling to make it a point to structure my class with opportunities for self-reflection. I empower and encourage my students to dream big and to cast an expansive vision for their chosen professions. I am not interested in teaching my students to get a job. I am interested in teaching my students to become career architects to design the career of their desire, whatever and however that may look. I tell them from day one that success is defined differently by each of us, and that is precisely how it should be.

My experience in choosing my career did not mirror what I asked of my students. I was guided by my "tiger" mother, who had dashed dreams of pursuing a career in the medical field and projected those dreams onto my life. I like to say that I was appointed and anointed to seek a career that used my head and heart to help others. Curiously, my mother encouraged me my whole life to partake in social justice activities and introduced me in early childhood to matters of equity and fairness. I was taught early on about the Southern

Poverty Law Center, the Anti-Defamation League, and other civil rights organizations. As I entered high school, I was expected to volunteer my spare time helping vulnerable populations, including unhoused and under-resourced people. It is no coincidence that I ultimately made my way to the law and social justice endeavors.

Though circuitous as it was, each experience in my life and career shaped and prepared me for the opportunities that ensued. I reflect on the early part of my career journey and see how my connections and relationships were instrumental in facilitating these opportunities to manifest themselves. To this day, my network and, even more specifically, my close relationships always lead to the next life changing options.

When I speak in the community on professional and leadership development, I am often asked if I would have changed anything or if I have any regrets. Upon reflecting on this question, I realized that my only regret is that I did not do things sooner. Now, in my mid-forties and after the passing of my parents, I know that time is my most precious commodity. However, the richness of wisdom certainly comes with time and experience, with the successes and the failures alike. The most meaningful growth happened when I was most uncomfortable, like when I finally found my authentic voice and overcame the fear of public speaking. That was a hard lesson to learn—to get comfortable with being uncomfortable.

As a young child, sometimes I wanted to shrink myself when my fearless mother would make a scene. As Shakespeare said, *"Though she be but little she is fierce."* My mother was my greatest advocate. I was a painfully shy child and did not find my voice, and did not use it often until after college.

I had to be around seven or eight when my mother got into a screaming match with a racist man. This memory is burned forever in my mind. We were then at Sea World with our family enjoying ourselves. Seated on the bleachers in our tank tops, shorts, and tube socks pulled up to our knees with our golden-brown skin soaking up the San Diego sun when we heard a man nearby bellow so that all ten of us could hear, *"why don't you speak English or go back to where you came from?"*

My tiny, five-feet tall mother jumped to her feet, screaming at this man, questioning his intellect, and hurling many other insults at him. I wanted to die. I wanted to crawl under the bleachers. My mother would not be bullied. She would not allow anyone to demean her, no matter who they were. My mother knew her worth. Bearing witness to that scene at such a young age shaped my character because I, like my mother, am justice-centered. Where does my directness come from? My mother. How would that benefit me as I came into my own skin and embraced my whole self, flaws and all? Entering a profession where diversity is lacking requires someone with tough skin.

My mother prepared me for the challenging world that she endured as a woman of color and immigrant. She knew that I would also face these same situations and circumstances decades later when I came into adulthood. She showed me how to use my voice to stand up and be heard because I matter. As I charted my career path, several other women would mentor me, provide wise counsel, and often serve as a sounding board when I found myself in tumultuous situations that seemed unfair, stifling, and sometimes oppressing given the culture and environment of the law. According to the Institute for Inclusion in the Legal Profession's 2019–2020 report of The State of Diversity and Inclusion in the Legal Profession, advancements of women and people of color in leadership are slow to change despite their increasing numbers in law school and entering the legal profession. Many times, I still find myself as one of the few Filipinas in leadership in the legal profession.

Sometimes I wonder how on earth I made it this far in my life and career, despite all the barriers and obstacles, not only in my chosen profession of the law but also in academia and higher education. I still recall when I first began teaching legal classes in 2010. A Black woman hired me. She was magnificent and the Chairperson of the Criminal Justice Program, where I was invited to teach. Dr. Tammy Hodo became my role model of fearlessness and confidence in owning my power in this space. I recall bouncing into our first faculty in-service in my gray slacks and white blouse cloaked by a cheerful yellow cardigan. I was one of two women, the only woman of color, the youngest instructor in the room, and the most colorful. Walking into that room, fear could have paralyzed me to stay in my lane, not to set goals beyond my comfort zone, yet I persevered. Spaces such as these became commonplace as I continued to access leadership roles. I kept and keep on going. Why? Because I know that though I may be the first, I will not be the last. And I surely tell all my students just that. I am planting seeds.

It still sometimes causes me to pause to realize that my passion for teaching and encouraging my students sets them on their life paths where we change the world together. We are all collectively giving each other a hand up. I learn as much from my students as they learn from me. I hope to impart to them the importance of building their networks early and intentionally. I develop close relationships with others aligned with my core values and goals of shifting the moral arc of the universe toward justice, equity, and fairness. These values and goals set me on the path to teaching, coaching, and consulting. Teaching has given me a platform of influence in the workforce and in career development, ultimately revealing my purpose in life.

My mother died during my first semester of teaching. When I think back to this time, though as physically and emotionally leveling as it was, I see how my mother was handing the baton to me, from one teacher to another. I have never enjoyed another job as much as I enjoy teaching. And I never aspired to teach. These are the types of life experiences and stories that, when shared, can inspire others who are also going through difficult times. When someone can lend a compassionate ear to truly and actively listen, this can make a world of difference for someone who feels overwhelmed, alone or isolated. My office hours involve listening to students bare their insecurities and fears. Together, we work through these thoughts and fears to a place of hope and focus. To feel supported, seen, heard, and valued shifts minds and hearts to a place of innovation. And that is the magic of teaching.

I never genuinely shared with anyone the extraordinary amount of pain and the weight that I carried and experienced in becoming the caregivers for my parents. It was the most challenging part of life that I have ever experienced. But candid and candor-filled conversations with my support network saved me. The painful conversations and questions about my choices for my parents' well-being racked my soul with guilt and doubt. All of this, amidst my ascending legal career weighed heavy on my burdened heart and soul. My daily prayer at the time of extreme caregiving for both of my parents became: *"Please, Lord, don't let me die now. Who will take care of my parents?"* The constant adrenaline buzz during those four and a half years as my parents' primary caregiver and designated agent carried me through without a doubt.

Surviving this experience set a fire within me that I did not know existed. Women going through these situations should not feel alone or lost. Finding your support group and network of family, friends, and confidantes is crucial. Associations like FWN, church groups, and other women's organizations are essential during this season in life. Sisterhood heals, celebrates, uplifts and grieves together.

But where are the books and resources dedicated to helping women during this time of life? According to the website www.caregiver.org, "upwards of 75% of all caregivers are female, and may spend as much as 50% more time providing care than males." And we wonder why pay equity and parity exist to this day? Did the pandemic not lay bare the unpaid labor of women in this country who suddenly became online teachers in addition to their paid careers? How can we, as Filipina women, support one another? Check-in on each other. Create check-in systems with one another. Yes, we are all exhausted. This pandemic has skyrocketed mental health issues across the board. But we as women know how to mobilize and make things happen. We must take care of each other.

More than ever is a need for self-care for our survival and well-being. Self-advocacy and advocacy for others are desperately needed. Attending to our whole selves is needed. But, how can we care for others when our proverbial cup is empty and does not runneth over?

My husband, a U.S. Navy veteran, told me this is a military mantra known to the SEALS and the elite forces of our military—*"Embrace the Suck!"* Such is life, the beauty, and the betrayal. The finiteness of life is now top of mind for many of us. How we invest our time, energy, and precious resources has become of utmost importance. Prioritizing life with a lens of brevity and boldness is ever more pressing. I am on it.

THE SPEED OF LIFE

Dear Kristine at 45,

You survived. You are on the other side of grief. Your parents, rest their souls, have departed for three years. You are okay. Need not spend another moment in incessant worry and anxiety. Your health is your wealth. Self-care is selfless, not selfish. Carrying the weight of the world on your shoulders and your constant need to fix everything does not serve you. Set. It. Down. Prioritize yourself. Your beloved. Soften to him and his need to protect and shield you from yourself. Impostor syndrome, negative self-talk, and doubt—these things will attempt to pervade and invade your space. Just stop the noise. Honor yourself exactly as you are. Perfectly imperfect. Keep your eyes on the speed of life, over before you know it. But, dear one, what is your legacy? Have you changed the world, set it on fire, the way you encourage others to do? Do as you say. Do as you do.

In love and solidarity,
Kristine at 55

MARIETTA EVELYN P. REVILLA

Corporate Relations Consultant,
Italtrans Racing team Moto2 Grand Prix
Founder and President, Sodalis Association in Milan
GLOBAL FWN100™ 2018

Reflection on My Leadership

"**M**s. Marietta Evelyn Revilla is a golden-hearted person with a clear vision that motivates, inspires, and leads people to achieve a common goal within the Sodalis & friends community. A leader who is visionary and drives the organization in turning that vision into a reality. Being a woman leader, she exemplifies the common traits or nature of a woman in leading the organization like team approach, clear vision, believing oneself or self-confidence, and willingness to ask for help or guidance from other trusted persons. The chapter about her life is an account of remembering, reminiscing, and reflecting on experiences from her personal life. It is a story of her life exemplifying qualities of being a Filipina woman leader." Stated Maritess Malco, a former country manager & legal representative of DMCI Europe.

MY FILIPINA HERITAGE

I was born in the Visayas region, in the Philippines to two wonderful parents, Leon Villacastin Revilla and Esmeralda Palacio Revilla. Together, they had five children, the eldest girl, Carmencita, followed by Evangeline, Leonardito, the only boy, me, and Emily.

Education was very important for my father. He would always say, *"The best inheritance I can leave you all is to give you a good education that would lead and provide you with a better future."* And he and my mother worked hard to make that happen.

My father worked at Escano Shipping Lines, from janitor to supervisor to operations manager. He was hardworking, diligent, honest, and patient; qualities I must have inherited from him. When he received the promotion to operations manager, he was offered the opportunity to move to Manila. My aunt, Flores Nack, his sister, suggested that we relocate to Manila so that he could provide a brighter future for us. I was six years old when I left my beloved Cebu.

Learning Family Values

Back in Cebu, our modest house was the place of refuge for our friends and family, where they stayed for some time. As a result, we were all squished together. Girls would bunk in one room; guys would scatter in the living room, and my parents, of course, had their space. When we settled in Manila, the same thing happened. Our house became the temporary residence for relatives visiting or studying in the city.

I learned the family values of being hospitable, sharing, helping the less fortunate, flexibility, and learning how to cope during tricky situations. No matter how difficult the situation could be, my parents never turned away a relative needing a place to live temporarily or food to eat. Our doors were always open.

Family support has been a crucial factor in my life. Although my father was earning more, we continued to struggle financially. To help my father, my mother opened a small convenience store. My mother was entrepreneurial, a quality I learned from her. In addition, my older sister, Carmencita, paid for my college tuition fees as my father's income could not send five children to private schools/universities. My sister, Evangeline, was in nursing school, my brother, Leonardito was at an engineering university, and my sister, Emily, was still in a private Catholic high school.

Yet even during these financially stressed times, our parents continued to strengthen our family bond. Like Pope Francis would say, *"The family remains the basic unit of society and the first school in which children learn human, spiritual and moral values which will enable them to be the beacon of goodness, integrity, and justice in our communities."*

Learning to Work for a Living

During college, one of the requirements for my business program was completing a college internship. Therefore, I took my "on-the-job training" (OJT) at Nippondenso Phils. Corporation. After completion, before graduating, I interviewed for a position as secretary to the marketing consultant, Mr. Masaaki Adachi, and got it.

This job opened a new door for me. Nippondenso became my training ground. As secretary to Mr. Adachi, I learned various tasks in sales and marketing, aside from the regular duties of answering phones, dealing with customers, maintaining filing systems, and appointment scheduling. I learned how to be well-organized and meticulous. However, my job was insufficient as I wanted to expand my knowledge for much better opportunities. I always aimed to go higher. I decided to continue my studies at the Philippine College of Commerce.

I was a working student and was burning the candles at both ends. At 4:00 p.m. after work, I would catch a train from my office in Makati to Sta. Mesa, where the school was located. Travel time was approximately 30 minutes. My schedule was difficult to keep up with, but I was happy, inspired, motivated, and looked forward to a brighter future. I tried to make the best of my situation and enjoy my work, studies, family, and friends. I met people from diverse backgrounds, young executives, salespeople, office clerks, engineers, and higher levels of education.

Dancing to Learn, Enjoy and Earn

Dancing has always been a passion since childhood. So my feet were itching to move, and I auditioned and got accepted by The Pacifica Cultural Dance Company, formerly known as The Polynesian Dance Company. Ma. Rita Mateu Ocampo known as Chiqui Ocampo was our dance instructor, choreographer, and director. The group performed at the Cultural Center of the Philippines, The Plaza Restaurant, and other venues like resorts and hotels. We performed modern and traditional dances like Rigodon, Filipino folk dances, hulas of Hawaii, aparima, and Maori.

We also appeared on TV and in media advertisements for General Motors and Coca-Cola. We were also called to model and participate in fashion shows. Being part of this dance group brought me to a unique experience level and raised my self-worth. The lesson I learned from these experiences is that whatever type of work, if you work hard and do an excellent job, passion and success will come your way. What was important to me at that moment was to learn, enjoy, and at the same time, earn.

I will always have *utang na loob* [debt of gratitude] for Tita Chiqui. The Pacifica Cultural exhibition gave me a chance to travel through Europe. I will never forget this and will always be thankful for the opportunity Tita Chiqui gave me. I also see this as a blessing God granted me, and I trusted Him to keep me safe.

STEPPING TOWARDS A NEW FUTURE

I was struggling to keep two jobs simultaneously, and I ultimately had to choose. Since I was so passionate about dance, I opted to leave Nippondenso, which saddened my Japanese boss. However, my income at the dance company was not much. So, when my cousin and B.F.F. (best friend forever), Marissa Montfort, asked me to collaborate with her at Blue Horizon Travel, I took the offer and kept on dancing.

My cousin Marissa is one of the most influential people in my life. Aside from being cousins, we were also good friends and partners. She knows everything about me. She knows my secrets and vice versa. We lost touch for a while when I left for Europe and reconnected when I visited my sisters in New York. I reached out to Marissa, who lived in New Jersey. From then on, we never lost contact again. So many things bind us, family, countless memories, hours just spent talking about our craziest and silly teenage experiences, and trips together. True friendships require loyalty, respect, agreeing to disagree, and tolerance, among other things. Marissa and I have that, and to this day, we continue to travel together and create memories.

Blue Horizon Travel meant a new job, new experiences, new people, and brand-new challenges. I visited various places, assisted tourists during cruises, conducted hotel ocular inspections, and met tourists of different nationalities. All these were remarkably interesting and exciting for a young person during that time. Very educational, too, as this new undertaking was quite rewarding as well as challenging and fulfilling because I was part of making someone happy during their travels.

Leaping to Opportunity in Europe

I have always been a big dreamer and a go-getter. So, when we got the contract in Europe, I was excited, amazed, and nervous. That was the start of a new beginning.

I thought of my parents, especially my father. He told me once that I could not be a dancer for the rest of my life. But that was not my main objective. Dancing was my passion, but I saw it as an opportunity for a bigger, brighter future.

The dance group was composed of nine women. We represented the Philippines by performing in Philippine cultural shows. Our first destination was Cairo and Alexandria, Egypt, where we stayed for four months. The Philippine embassy personnel in Cairo welcomed us. Our first show was in one of the theaters in the city center of the capital. I was overwhelmed by the heartwarming welcome and appreciation by the locals and foreigners. I met the son of the Egyptian ambassador to Switzerland, Mounir, and we became good friends.

After Egypt, we left for Milan, Italy. When we first arrived in Italy, there were less than 15,000 Filipino migrant workers. In 2022, there are roughly 120,000 documented Filipinos. Undocumented Filipinos in Italy range from 20,000 to 80,000, with most women and the majority working as domestic helpers.

During the 1980s, there were only a few Filipinos in Milan. Italians were curious about us, and luckily, we barely encountered racism. I remember walking along the streets of Milan, and people would look at us. They would ask where we came from and would request a photo. They were curious but never impolite.

We were fortunate to be protected by our agent and well cared for by the owners of the hotels or apartments where we stayed. However, we did experience a few "scary" instances. One example is when we were in Valdobbiadene. We were being forced to do "extra jobs." We immediately called our agent and were able to escape right after the show.

Italians trust Filipinos and rarely get in the news for being rowdy or troublemakers. Like Filipinos, Italians are family-oriented, and we have similarities in culture and religion. They love to talk with a lot of hand gestures.

We stayed in Italy for nearly two years, moving from city to city, one town to the next. We traveled extensively, recognizing that our aspirations were turning into reality and our dreams were coming true.

After our contract in Europe expired, my friend Rosemarie and I were offered a job in Milan. Silvano, Rosemarie's boyfriend, and now husband, helped us get our *"permesso di soggiorno"* or permit to stay in Italy.

At first, seven of the nine girls stayed. Eventually, two of them returned to the Philippines; some traveled throughout Europe. One girl, who shall remain nameless, stayed, and married Vincenzo Reggiani, the stepbrother of Patrizia Reggiani, the ex-wife who ordered the murder of Maurizio Gucci, the onetime head of Gucci fashion house.

Rosario, Zenaida, Victoria, and I, stayed and eventually married our Italian boyfriends.

Starting Over

Once again, to survive, we had to work hard. Our first job was at an import/export company, Sirio Srl, located at Viale Tunisia, Milan, where we stayed and worked for six months. Our office space was huge, it was our work area during the day and our living place after work hours. I decided to study Italian to communicate better with the locals. That helped me develop my speaking, listening, and writing skills and grammar awareness. The Italian language, written and verbal, is complicated and confusing, different from English or my native language, Tagalog.

After several months, I met my husband, Germano Bellina, in Milan. We were in our twenties when we met; for me, it was "love at first sight." I knew that he was going to be my husband.

It was not an easy relationship, but I was deeply in love with him and ready to commit and compromise. We faced challenges in our relationship, such as difficulties in communication, different personalities, different priorities, and financial pressure. Despite that, we seldom argued. Instead, we worked hard on our relationship.

Creating a Family

I continued to work and reside in Milan, while Germano lived in Bergamo, 45-minutes away. At that time, he drove a truck for a living. Sometimes I would not hear from him for 48 hours since there were no cell phones then. He could only call me when he had to stop for fuel. On his days off, he spent and stayed with me in Milan. He has always been a hard-working person, reserved, diligent, patient, caring in his way, helpful, and a perfectionist.

We had been together for three years before we decided to get married. I was happily living in Milan, seeing Germano, and working. After three years of being together, we decided to get married. I had never met Germano's family before, and I was apprehensive when we traveled to Bergamo. Germano wanted to introduce his new wife and the mother of his child. Yes, I was pregnant with my eldest, Stephanie, when I first met my in-laws.

Pregnancy was more complicated than I thought, primarily due to morning sickness, which lasted the entire day. Then, during the sixth month, I got ill, and there was a danger of losing my child. My Italian friend rushed me to Ospedale Macedonia Melloni, for that time Germano was out of the city working. Lucky for me, I made it to a complete term.

 Unluckily for me, Germano was working when I did go into labor. I was alone in the hospital. Finally, after two nights of labor, I gave birth to my beautiful daughter, Stephanie. I heard that labor normally lasts from eight to twelve hours. Mine lasted for more than 18 hours. After delivery, I had mixed emotions – exhaustion from labor pains, overwhelmed by the miracle of childbirth, and in awe of my beautiful baby. When Germano arrived the next night, he held me closed and kissed me. He was speechless, confused, and tearful. He gently caressed the hand of our newborn. I was emotionally overwhelmed. We decided to name the baby "Stephanie Lucia."

I had developed deep friendships in Italy. My Italian language classes paid off. If you want to meet Italians, learn the language. That is what I did. Living in Milan has given me many opportunities to meet amazing people. My Italian friends were there for me, Micaela, Yolanda and Antonio. Several workmates helped me. They became my foster Italian family who looked out for me, especially when Germano was away.

When Stephanie was three months old, she needed to be confined to the hospital for bronchopneumonia. I received a surprise visit from Germano's mom, his two brothers and wives, and his only sister, Rosalba. I had never met his siblings before, and I was apprehensive about their unannounced visit. But there was nothing to be worried about. Their visit was enjoyable, and there was a feeling of contentment and happiness on both sides. They were willing to engage in friendly conversation despite my difficulty speaking Italian.

As a newlywed and a new mother, taking care of my husband, new baby, and home was a struggle. I had no support from my husband, who was often out of the house for days as he worked his trucking job. It fell on me to tackle all the obstacles, balance my time, manage our money, and look after Stephanie's needs. I worried about how to evolve my duties as a wife and mother simultaneously. I missed my family back home. I felt insecure, lost, and confused about which path to take in my life.

That Christmas, Germano, 5-month-old Stephanie, and I spent the holiday with his family. We were welcomed warmly with so much joy from the Bellina family. My father-in-law called that visit a very special occasion and mentioned that Stephanie was their *"bambino Jesu"* [baby Jesus.]

Adapting to Change

My journey from Milan to Bergamo was a turning point in my life. Relocating to a new place, leaving old friends, meeting new people, and adapting to a new situation were nerve-wracking. Dealing with change was stressful and caused anxiety.

I knew I needed to adapt and integrate with the family and community to survive and make it in Bergamo. I learned to cook, care for the house, and look after my family. The first thing I did was to apply for a driver's license. After that, I needed to look for a job.

At that time, my sisters-in-law worked on the family farm, harvesting crops for salads. I asked my father-in-law if I could work with them. He was hesitant as he looked at my manicured nails. He knew I had not done any field work. In the end, he said *"bene,"* [fine,] and allowed me to join the team. I was ready to start at 6 a.m. the next day and worked side-by-side with my sisters-in-law, Franca S., and Adriana B.

That first day, I was excited as I picked up my gloves and hat. I prepared and took care of the house before I left. Before leaving for the farm, I cooked lunch, did laundry, cleaned the house, and saw that everything was in order.

My first day working with my in-laws was fun. I learned to harvest *"radicchio verde."* With a serrated knife, I would take a few leaves with my palm and cut the stems just above the ground and bound them with a rubber band. I would place the bundles in a wooden crate box which I would fill up with around twenty bundles of the radicchio.

I started earning money, and I was happy. I challenged myself to this kind of job, something different, but I found it fun. It became my livelihood. Some days I would bring Stephanie with me, and she would sleep calmly and quietly in her stroller while we were harvesting vegetables at the family's greenhouse. When returning from the fields, we would have lunch, or dinner, meals my mother-in-law prepared for everybody. As in the tradition of an Italian family, we all ate together. To this day, we keep this tradition alive.

I kept working in the fields as I aimed to buy a house for my parents in Cebu. My husband supported my goal, and after a few years, I was able to buy them a house. It was one of the most significant accomplishments in my life.

Growing the Business

Germano and three of his brothers owned a small business that grew into Italtrans and Ortobell. After a few years, the brothers had different visions for the business. Tino wanted to invest in agriculture land whereas, Claudio wanted to invest more in transport. Laura Bertulessi, who managed the companies' finances, suggested that they split the business into two companies; Italtrans would focus on logistics, and Ortobell would focus on farm productivity.

By then, I graduated from working in the fields and became an employee of Ortobell, and I took a short course in accounting to help with the books, while Laura stayed on with Italtrans.

Embracing Entrepreneurial Spirit

I enjoyed being part of Ortobell, but I was offered an opportunity I found hard to turn down. I was thrilled and excited when Daniela Bertulessi, sister of Laura, offered me the chance to open a clothing shop in Bergamo.

I discussed the offer with Germano, and he agreed it was too good to pass up. We decided to sign up as a franchisee for *"Appunti dì Viaggio."* So, we opened our store in Bergamo. We designed the store to look like a pirate ship made of natural solid wood. Beautiful! The fashion collection's theme was travel outfits. The clothes were meticulously chosen, especially the materials. Our collection was offered as a travel capsule wardrobe where pieces were interchangeable with other versatile and comfortable pieces.

We decided to sign up as a franchisee because we needed the expertise of an established business to help us. Franchisors usually had an established business model and provided the training required in operations, accounting, hiring, and all the other aspects we needed to learn to run a business. As a result, franchises have a higher rate of return than start-up businesses.

Failing the First Venture

However, luck was not on our side. The company started to have problems with product distribution. Apart from that, we also experienced losses due to a natural calamity. Right after the completion of the spring collection, we were hit by a strong storm. Water leaked everywhere, and the store got flooded. The humidity and the rain damaged both spring and summer collections. It was terrible. We reported the leak to the property owner and the damage to our product. We were in legal negotiations for ten years before we settled.

We had to give up the store but continued looking for another franchise. We found Prenatal *"per mamma e bambino,"* a business that caters to expecting mothers.

Prenatal was one of the first stores in *"Centro Commerciale Curno"* also known as the Curno Shopping Mall. The location was perfect for us as it was only six kilometers from the outskirts of Bergamo.

Being a retail store business owner means I had to work long hours. I was lucky to have found a partner, Daniela, who was as dedicated and worked as hard as I. We had a staff of eight sales ladies and two store managers who worked in shifts. Once they left, Daniela and I stayed until closing. Daniela and I stayed in the shop for 9–12 hours during our first few years, especially Friday and Saturday. We both had young children, and we would bring them to the store, where they would stay until we finished for the day. Working in a mall was crucial, as we relied a lot on foot traffic, which was challenging. However, I always tended to see the positive side of things, and I was thankful for a business I could call my own. At the end of our first year, we received the best and highest-selling shop award in Lombardy. Receiving the award was an incredible experience! And we could take an all-expenses paid trip to Mexico for a week as our prize.

I learned a lot while managing a retail business. Being part of a franchise, I took part in training programs. As a result, I learned how to plan, strategize, and manage the store's finances. I also was able to gain skills in marketing and, most importantly, in how to sell.

We put up certain events at the store to market our products and services. One of them was the Layette Program. We targeted expecting parents who were around 34 weeks pregnant. I shared tips on how to prepare for the baby's arrival, what items they would need in their hospital bag, and what to prepare for the baby's first three months. Other topics discussed were feeding, how to swaddle a baby, the correct way of changing a diaper, what clothing to prepare for the baby, blankets, bath time, skin care products, cribs, and travel systems, including strollers and backpacks.

Public speaking or being in front of an audience was not comfortable for me. I had to speak to our customers in Italian and English. Speaking in front of strangers gave me the self-confidence and pride to share what I knew.

Italtrans S.P.A. Succeeds

While I was busy looking after Prenatal and building my business, my husband and his brothers were becoming more successful with their business.

To date, Italtrans S.P.A. has about 1000 units of specialized cargo trucks and a logistics capacity of 877,000 square meters throughout Italy, including Calcio (Bergamo) with an automatic warehouse and Covo with a planned surface area of 85,000 square meters.

I enjoyed working at the store, yet the long hours and demand of running a business took their toll. In addition, after many years, Stephanie and my second daughter Sheela had grown to be teenagers. So, I decided to give up my shares in the store and opened a travel agency in Milan in 2003.

Through this all, I continued to nurture my passion for dance. I taught Filipino-Italians, born and raised in Italy, Philippine cultural dance when I had the time. I am so enthusiastic about our culture that I made it a mission to teach the second generation. Teaching Filipinos in Italy our culture through dance.

Fast-forward to the present as the Bellina family business expanded. Stephanie and Sheela now have their own families and are likewise involved in their chosen careers. Stephanie ventured into fashion. She managed a retail shop named Touchdown based in Bergamo. She decided to close down the shop after COVID pandemic. At present she's the Managing Director of Lodauto S.p.A. in Bergamo. An authorized dealer and workshop of the prestigious brands of Mercedes Benz, Amg and Smart.

As a typical Italian family, my daughters learned to work the hard way. When Sheela was 16 years old she would work during summer as a dishwasher and Stephanie as waitress for a restaurant owned by a family friend. Sheela started her work training in Italtrans after college. After which she handled several positions in order to understand the operations of the company. After years of training, Sheela has been given the responsibility of being the Sales and Marketing Director of Italtrans S.p.A. Managing and controlling all the flow of goods throughout the supply chain and ensuring that products are delivered within the timeframe requested. She learned to build career from scratch and is now a successful corporate career person.

I am involved with the Italtrans Moto2 Racing team, as Corporate Relations Consultant, together with my sister-in-law, Laura Bertulessi, wife of Claudio, who is now the C.E.O. of Italtrans. We travel extensively to keep track of the Grand Prix for motorbikes. It was formed through Germano's passion for the engine.

Aside from being my sister-in-law, Laura is a dear friend to me. I remember meeting her first at Germano's house that fateful Christmas day. She was the only one who spoke a little English, and we got along fast.

Laura welcomed me and made me feel part of the family. I remember when Laura asked me to accompany her to the office, and it was snowing. I did not prepare for the bad weather and wore a pair of black loafers. Laura took me to a shoe shop. She chose two pairs of shoes and asked me to try them on. She thoughtfully bought me a couple of boots. I was shocked but grateful. Laura is a person with a generous heart. We often go out on Saturdays, which we call women's night out, and we sometimes include our friends from Moto2. I want to cherish these fantastic moments when reflecting on my life experiences.

ITALTRANS AND THE FILIPINO COMMUNITY

Italtrans sponsored two Filipino brothers, Troy and TJ Alberto, for a European racing competition. In addition, Italtrans' partner has employed 350 Filipinos, La Coopital, and the closely-knit Bellina household management and business properties.

When Italtrans needed at least 200 truck drivers, I contacted my friend Denissa Venturanza from Manila, Managing Director of Globaldev Consultant Services, to assist and explore the possibilities of opening these services for the workers in the Philippines. We would be able to offer opportunities to hundreds of our *kapwa* [fellow humans] for a better and financially stable future.

One of my strongest desires is to uplift the lives of the Filipino people. 2018 was my last visit to the Philippines. The COVID pandemic kept me away for almost four years.

Last May 2022, I was able to travel back home to accompany my 88 years old auntie, Flores Nack. Arriving at the airport, I felt a mixture of anticipation, melancholy, and excitement. Ninoy Aquino International Airport is now huge. Porters lined up, angling to offer their services for a small amount of pesos. Leaving the premises, I felt the hot weather that came at me like waves of stormy weather. When I saw my brother Boy and received a hug from my sister-in-law Nini, I knew I was home.

Much had changed since the last time I was home. The roads were wider, there was less traffic, maybe because people still fear going out. I could see the lives of the people in the streets. Mall children, 3–4 years of age, were with their *nanay* [mother] in the middle of the street, begging for alms or food. When we stopped at a gasoline station, the kids would come up to the car, trying to sell something, and if you didn't buy, they would ask for a small donation. I feel their pain. There are lots of these scenarios. How can I help? How can we uplift or change the life of every Filipino?

If I can be successful and push through with our project, hire people to work for Italtrans, in a small way, I could help give my *kapwa* a better life.

Coping with COVID-19

In December 2019, a coronavirus was identified in a cluster of patients with unexplained pneumonia in Wuhan, China.

Following the outbreak in Wuhan, Italy was the first European country to experience the COVID-19 pandemic. First reported in Feb. 2020 in Lombardy, a 38-year-old Italian who was already infected but did not know it visited his relatives, infecting them, and it quickly spread to the surrounding community. Unfortunately, this was at the early onset of the pandemic, so we were unaware of the precautions we should have taken then.

The infection spread swiftly through other areas in Lombardy, including Bergamo. The first cases were reported on 23 February 2020 in two small villages, Nembro and Alzano Lombardo, in the upper city of Bergamo (Citta

Alta.) Bergamo locked down two weeks later. Thousands of people had fallen ill by then, including my friends and family. I was terrified. Hospitals were congested. The often-interminable sirens of the ambulance became the defining sound of COVID emergency.

On 8 March 2020, I got infected with corona virus. It started with fever and fatigue, and then the next day, I lost my sense of taste and smell. I was seriously sick for five days and stayed in isolation for almost fourteen days as I wanted to make sure I was not infecting anyone. I was lucky. I did not have to go to the hospital. My brother-in-law was brought to the hospital. My husband got infected as well. Scared of hospitals, he opted to stay home. During the outbreak, I lost so many friends who were brought to the hospitals.

The news headlines were about military trucks transporting coffins from Italy's worst-hit city (Bergamo) to remote cremation sites because morgues could not cope with the surging Coronavirus death toll. Bergamo's mayor, Giorgio Gori, called for aid. At least ten military truck convoys passed through the city to the cremation sites in 12 Italian towns. My beloved town was under siege from the virus.

Italtrans played a crucial role during Coronavirus. It never faltered in protecting the food supply chain. The company continued operating, delivering the needed supply, mainly to supermarkets. With its 1,000 vehicles, Italtrans guaranteed food supply through its large-scale distribution system throughout Italy with thousands of daily home deliveries.

The company also generously committed to supporting the fight against the virus. Italtrans allocated two hundred thousand euros for purchasing medical equipment, and protective devices for health personnel, in addition to covering expenses for doctors and nurses in Bergamo and beyond.

With my Filipina household assistant, Maria, we prepared and contributed 500 boxes of groceries to the Filipino community in Milan and more or less 300 boxes in Bergamo. We did not forget the homeless community and prepared boxes for them.

The COVID-19 pandemic changed our lives individually, from our daily routines to our dreams and priorities. I became more devoted, and my faith and trust in God strengthened. Prayer's work.

During the pandemic, we celebrated the third birthday of my first granddaughter, Andrea, the first daughter of Stephanie and Marco. We were socially distant, yet we made the most of what we could do. It was difficult not celebrating her birthday with her grandparents and her cousin, Asia, the first child of Sheela and Cristiano. During the lockdown, Cristiano relocated his family to a secluded, peaceful country farm and ranch far from the city owned by the parents of Cristiano.

As grandparents, we take immense pride in the energy, youthfulness, creativity, and love we offer our grandchildren. COVID-19 may temporarily alter the format of our relationships with them. I continued connecting with my children and grandchildren through Facetime or WhatsApp. Despite the distance, there are many meaningful and joyful ways to communicate with our grandchildren.

To Ukraine with Love

It was dawn on 24 February 2022 when we faced another global crisis. Russia launched an unprecedented assault on Ukraine. Everyone hoped that this war would end quickly. But, instead, as of this writing, the war continues. Millions of refugees fled Ukraine to neighboring countries, and many countries have rallied in support of Ukraine.

Always a leader on the front lines, Italtrans supported the initiative of the humanitarian emergency. Hyena Ismaele La Vardera, of *Le Iene TV* program, contacted the Bellina family through Laura Bertulessi. He indicated that a convoy of seven trucks brought humanitarian aid. Three of the trucks were supplied by Esselunga Supermercato, a client of Italtrans. Appeals for assistance started to appear on social media networks, and in a matter of hours, help arrived from different places. Trucks left from the Calcinate warehouse to the Ukraine border, driven by volunteers from Ukraine, Romania, and Italy. The trucks delivered two hundred pallets of necessities like food, pasta, rice, medicine, hygiene products, clothing, toys, water, and many other products, all donated by clients, families, and employees of Italtrans and other local businesses.

I was so proud of my family and my fellow citizens. We all rallied to assist the people of Ukraine. The caravan, which included two buses, measured close to one hundred meters long and crossed Slovenia, Hungary, and Romania to arrive in Ukraine. They were escorted by soldiers who arrived in Chernivtsi, a town 40 kilometers from Kyiv.

On the return trip, the two buses were loaded with women and children, heartbroken and anxious at having to leave their husbands, fathers, brothers, relatives, and friends behind to fight the war. There was no guarantee that they would meet again. My heart broke for them.

The refugees are currently guests of the community of Santa Fede in Cavagnolo (Turin). Volunteers from social media continued to recruit actively and organize additional relief efforts for Ukraine. In March 2022, Laura B. and Ismaele alerted me of another humanitarian action. This time, the plan was to organize a caravan of cars and vans to drive to the border and pick up Ukraine refugees in Przemysil at the Polish border.

At first, I was hesitant to join. Our daughters did not favor the idea. I wanted to go. I wanted to help the refugees and see for myself the real situation. My sister-in-law and I were blocked by the constant "No's" of the kids.

However, the day before the meetup, Laura and I decided we would do it. I feared our decision, but on the other hand, I was glad I did. Three of us went on this journey, Laura Bertulessi, Laura Locatelli, a friend and myself. When I called Laura L. and told her our decision, there was no hesitation on her part in joining us. She wanted to support this caravan, considering the situation of women and children leaving their husbands in the battle.

The next day was full of emotions. We left at nine am to reach Udine in three hours. When we arrived at Udine, some buses were already there. We waited for almost an hour for the other volunteers to arrive. It's a caravan of hope and courage.

We spent one night in a hotel in Kraków. However, we had not planned to stay when we learned that there was a bombing twenty-five kilometers away from Pryemysl. We had no choice. We could not get close to the border that night.

Everyone was exhausted, and we only thought of getting a warm bath and sleep.

When we got up the next day, I felt sore. When we got to the hall for breakfast, other volunteers were already there and shared information about the situation at the border. Finally, we all got ready for the seventy-two-hour journey to the Polish border. Poland had opened its doors to over two million people from the start of the war between Ukraine and Russia. At the Humanitarian Aid Center, Ismaele from *Le Iene TV*, coordinated with the authorities to identify the refugees traveling with us to Italy.

At the camp, we downloaded the boxes of goods we brought and announced to the guards that we had five vans to help transport some refugees. We took in forty-five refugees. We could see that they were frightened and did not trust us. You could feel the tension in the air.

I remember Katryna, a mother of a four-year-old girl. She spoke English, so it was easy for us to communicate. She opened up and shared her stories about the war. The first part of the trip, however, was tense.

Most of the refugees had relatives in Italy and would join their families after registering and completing a swab test. The Welcome Center for Refugees assisted those who had no firm destination in Turin.

The trip from Poland was tough. Approximately 1450 kilometers, it took us fourteen hours and 45 minutes to Palazzolo sull'Oglio, province of Brescia. It was almost six a.m. when we reached the reception center. The volunteers welcomed us with balloons in the hall and breakfast with juices, bread, and croissants. The warmth of the welcome immediately made our Ukrainian guests feel at home.

Our Journey was celebrated by Brigg Brijuega, our Sodalis Vice President, who said, *"At the invasion of Ukraine by Russia, Evy's family was one of the first who, with only 24 hours of preparation, managed to bring seven caravans of humanitarian aid into war-torn Ukraine. And finally, a few days later, Evy, with two other Italian friends, volunteered and defied the Polish-Ukrainian border for over 14 hours to pick up Ukrainian refugee women and children and take them to their new, safer, and warmer Italian homes. When I think of Evy, I cannot help but imagine the image of a large lake receiving large volumes of water only to distribute them generously through its many rivers and streams and smaller tributaries so that the green watershed can feed its lush, and the vast irrigated lands of fruits, vegetables, and grains could continue to feed the hungry mouth of the world. This is Evy. Someone who has received so many blessings but probably shared more than she had. Someone who has been a constant source of inspiration for us Pinoys here in Milan. Someone who continues to be a source of joy for all of us. This is Evy. A real woman for others."*

Community Engagement Sodalis Association

My professional life is centered around Italtran's MotoGP Racing team. However, my community life belongs to the Sodalis Association, of whom I am currently the president. Our main objective is to promote social integration, including solidarity, social assistance, protection of civil rights, and social-cultural promotion among Filipinos.

During the Coronavirus pandemic that significantly affected Bergamo, as president, I organized the distribution of food packages to Filipino families with the help of the Sodalis group and L.B.C. I likewise started collecting stuff and donations for the homeless in my town in Cebu during the typhoon Odette. Furthermore, I continuously exert efforts to do fund drives for Filipino friends and relatives every time calamities hit the Philippines.

Former president of Sodalis, Giorgio Casadio, had this to share. *"Evy was the first enthusiastic member of the Sodalis Association. She is a natural leader that involves, without weighing, a great desire to do not only for herself but above all for others. In summary: her slight leadership that does not order you, but convinces you, is a mysterious equation that only a person like Evelyn has the solution."*

Other Civic Activities

Recently, through my request, Italtrans has generously pledged funds to commission a bust of Dr. Jose Rizal, to be created by Philippine sculptor Toym Imao. The statue is approximately thirty-six inches high and 24 inches wide, with a depth of 14 inches. The projected weight is around 130 kilos. The Knights of Rizal (KOR) Milan chapter, consulting with the Philippine Consulate General in Milan, proposed the installation of the bust of Dr. Jose Rizal, the Philippine national hero, in an area in one of the parks where Filipinos converge, especially on Sundays. The City Council of Milan will designate this area.

The proposed project would be of great importance for the Filipinos to see as a reminder of our courageous and rich heritage. Milan has become the home to approximately 40,000 Filipinos in the last 20 years.

As a religious person and a Cebuana, I am one of the Execom members who volunteer our time for the Sinulog Fiesta of Sto. Niño in Europe, with my friends Ritchie, Sis Leonor and Luz. In 2023, we will be celebrating the festival in Milan, and our work has already started. Arranged by Filipino community organizations on the occasion of Senior Santo Nino in Northern Italy, our Senior Santo Niño, the festival is highlighted by the Sinulog Street dancing performed by Cebuanos and devotees of Santo Niño from all over Europe.

I recognize my role as an entrepreneur, community leader, a wife, mother, and grandma. I look back at what I have accomplished, I know I also need to pay it forward, and I do so by mentoring young people. I share my life story, struggles, lessons learned in being a woman in business, and the need to engage in civic and cultural activities. With the mentorship projects I have been doing,

I am proud to have established strong relationships with others. Take the Rauto sisters, Marga and Gianna, for example, I have always treated them as my daughters. Marga and Gianna were one of the teenagers that formed part of the cultural dance troupe that I organized and sponsored in Milan. They initiated and became active in projects concerning the young generation of the Filipino community by collaborating with the local institutions and Philippine Consulate in Milan. Marga is now the Manager of the famous Asian skincare brand, New World Europa Srl, which has been managing for four years that has extensively grown in Italy and other parts of Europe. Gianna on the other hand used to be an intern at my travel agency, Italpoint during the early years of 2000. After graduating in Political Science, she worked in the editorial offices of Marie Claire and Elle, an international monthly magazine. Gianna is now the manager of the customer relations for Launch-Metric, a leading performance I cloud brand for fashion, beauty and luxury. She analyzes and studies the world market of client brands to offer the best marketing and business strategies.

I have always been proud of the Rauto sisters. I appreciate the time spent and the nice words from Gianna to quote "Tita Evelyn is a strong, tenacious, courageous, sunny, ambitious, brilliant, full of strength, determination, love for neighbor, love for her work great tireless worker, sincere, true, and super generous person." Marga and Gianna would also join me as I organized community events and shows for the Filipino and Italian communities. I am glad that our relationship forged a love of our customs and traditions.

My heart swells with gratitude when I hear Marga say, *"Tita Evelyn is a role model for people, a mentor, and an example to follow if you want to succeed. And she does it with great humility. My greatest wish is that one day I can become like her, an extraordinary person inside and out. There are no words to express our deep gratitude and admiration for all she has done. When it comes to helping someone, she doesn't hold back. She's always in the front line. How can you not admire such a woman."*

Upon reflection, I remember this quote from Ralph Emerson, *"The greatest gift is a portion of thyself."* I have been so blessed throughout my life, and I now focus on giving back and returning those gifts I have received. The energy of sharing becomes a routine, a habit. I believe in goodness, and I hope I exemplify generosity in action. Please remember that your deeds will return to you a hundredfold in parting.

DENISE J. LOPEZ, PH.D.

Alliant International University
GLOBAL FWN100™ 2021

Sugarcane Princess, Steely Sampaguita: From Privilege to Purpose and Authenticity

As I write this chapter, a video feature on me has just come out on social media for International Women's Month (March, 2022). The popular Filipino lifestyle store Kultura selected me as one of ten diverse women in their "Celebrate Every Filipina" campaign. This campaign highlights the Filipina's "quintessential spirit and grace." Among the Filipinas to be featured are Ces Drilon (Filipino broadcast journalist), Margarita Fores (2016 Asia's Best Female Chef), Berna Puyat (Philippine Department of Tourism Secretary), Agatha Wong (international gold medalist wushu athlete), and myself.

Kultura's March 2022 #CelebrateEveryFilipina feature on me reads:

"Leadership coach, professor, and consultant Dr. Denise Lopez has not only been mentoring business leaders around the world for 25 years—she has co-authored an Amazon bestselling book about it (Lead, Motivate, Engage: How to INSPIRE Your teams to Win at Work with Dr. Pearl Hilliard). Recognized as one of

*the 100 Most Influential Global Filipinas by the Filipina Women's
Network, Lopez actively supports causes in the realm of education
and professional development, social justice, and discrimination in
the workplace."*

Being in the limelight is something I am not comfortable with. It's quite ironic, given that I am a highly experienced professor and consultant who often gives presentations domestically and internationally. I have no problem performing on stage as a former ballet and jazz dancer and singer. My sisters and closest friends laugh because they know I am always game to burst into song or dance. But on all these occasions, the focus of the audience's attention is the song, the dance, the intellectual topic, the message, or the medium—not necessarily me.

People say that to be successful, you must promote yourself. This advice does not sit well with me because I am inherently introverted and value humility and service to others. At times there remains a little voice inside me asking whether I am a leader or if I am good enough to be one of the most influential Filipinas in the world. I, too, suffer from impostor syndrome, which can cripple people, particularly minority women. But despite these doubts, I persist because I know in my heart that I have worked hard. Thus, I am up for the challenge if I can inspire one more Filipina girl to reach out for more in her life by reading my story.

The Beginning: A Sugarcane Princess

A black-and-white photograph of my third birthday party evokes memories. Dressed in a polka-dotted Spanish flamenco outfit, I am in the arms of my *Yaya* [caregiver], with my younger brother also carried by his *Yaya*. He is in an adorable matador costume, complete with a cape. The Spanish costumes were a gift from my godfather, Tito Jorge, who had just arrived from his regular European trip. Around us are several young children in costume, all carried or flanked by their white-uniformed *Yayas*. According to my mother, this party was at the Seabreeze hotel, the fanciest hotel in Bacolod City, Negros Occidental, at the time. As the celebrant, I stared into the camera with my huge dark and serious eyes. My mom was very proud of that party and of me, her eldest child. She would always recount how everyone cooed over me since I was a baby, marveling at how fair and pretty I was. *Ay, ka-guwapa! Ay kaputi!* [Oh, how pretty! How white she is!]

I grew up in a sugarcane hacienda. My father, Isidro de la Rama Lopez, was the eldest son of a large and affluent family. My father and his brother stayed at the hacienda. They managed the family's agrarian affairs in Negros Occidental while my paternal grandmother, her daughters, their husbands, and children remained in Manila. My mother, Estela Reyes Justiniani, was an extroverted and popular beauty from a prominent family in Manila. Like many Filipina socialites at the time, she went to Assumption Convent, where she met my father through his sister. They married just after she turned 21. Before her marriage, my mom had been twice around the world and to Europe and the United States. Interestingly she decided to marry my father without even visiting Negros. She probably had visions of Tara, the fancy white estate with vast fields in the movie *"Gone with the Wind."*

Reality set in for my mother when she went to Silay City, Negros Occidental, and realized that her home would be a large but simple house in the middle of sugarcane fields. No more big parties and photo ops published in the society pages. But soon, she had me, then my brother and two sisters in later years. I believe she devoted a lot of her frustrated energies to her children. My various academic and extra-curricular accomplishments in piano, ballet, jazz, painting, singing, sports, valedictorian of grade school and high school, and summa cum laude in college were primarily the result of her efforts. She firmly believed that we should have the best training and opportunities even though we were in the province. She was my biggest cheerleader and remained throughout her entire life. As for myself, I had started to rebel against the early labels of being a pretty face. I did not like to be compared with others in terms of beauty. From an early age, I worked harder than most to prove myself through my accomplishments. And because I never thought of myself as the smartest person in the class, I spent years honing my reading, writing, and mathematics skills. In a way, I made myself smarter.

Developing a Growth Mindset

Emerging research in psychology and neuroscience supports my naïve theory of developing intelligence. For example, Carol Dweck (2007) talks about the benefits of having a learning orientation instead of a performance mindset.

In her research, students taught to view their intelligence as fluid rather than fixed were more likely to develop a learning orientation. Students with this orientation are motivated to expand their learning rather than just meet a performance standard. They are more likely to adopt good study habits and succumb less to the negativities of failure because they are open to learning from their mistakes. As a result, students with learning orientations develop their mental, emotional, and physical capacities significantly higher than those with fixed or performance orientations. Dweck's research has spawned programs that promote the growth mindset. I have gone in-depth on this research not just because I am a professor but because I genuinely believe that this was how my mother encouraged my motivation to learn and grow. This theory has also inspired some of my research and philosophy in teaching students and coaching leaders.

Because I grew up on a farm, I was not a princess who sat on silk pillows, ate strawberries or mangoes, and embroidered the whole day. Many of my earliest memories were climbing trees, swimming in our pool and in the river, visiting the chickens in the poultry, biking around the sugarcane fields, and eating freshly cut sugarcane. Until I was seven or eight years old, my two ladies-in-waiting were Suzette and Jemima, the children of my father's farm workers. Together we played with my dolls and expensive imported dollhouses that my mother ordered from the Sears Roebuck catalog. But we also explored the countryside extensively. I distinctly remember visiting their houses and realizing how much smaller and primitive their homes were. I shared whatever I had with them, not wanting to be seen or treated as superior to them. I was starting to realize how much more I had and how privileged I was. My early friendship with Suzette and Jemima profoundly influenced my values for equal treatment and inclusion, simplicity, generosity, and humility.

Countering Prejudice

My parents would take us to Manila and Hongkong during Christmas and summer. I distinctly remember our first family trip to the United States, where we visited Hawaii, San Francisco, and Los Angeles for a month. I was 13 years old. Having just graduated valedictorian in 7th grade, I felt carefree and on top of the world. But during that trip, something happened that remains in my memory. It was not a big thing—certainly not that we were physically attacked or got into an accident. My cousins and I were hanging out in a square near Market Street in San Francisco. We had just gone shopping in Macy's and contemplated going to Woolworth, the large famous dime store, to spend more of our allowance. The square had a lot of people, including some who looked poor and maybe homeless. As I was getting up to leave, a white-bearded man who looked quite unkempt came up to us and stood in front of me. *"Yucch!"* he said disgustingly, *"You're ugly."* Then he left.

I was shocked, then outraged. Who was this dirty white trash who had the gall to think I was ugly? In retrospect, this experience stood out because it was a startling contrast to my privileged life in the Philippines. I realized that although I was a big fish in my small pond, there were bigger and different ponds. Maybe this man felt superior because he was born in the United States while I was from a lesser country. Like most Filipinos, I had a bit of a colonial mentality. Or maybe this grubby white man was lashing out at foreigners invading his space, taking away what he thought was his privilege. Whatever the explanation, this early experience helped me identify topics I was passionate about, such as discrimination, equity, and inclusion. It would inspire me to write and speak about the effects of bias and exclusion on self-esteem, motivation, and well-being and the critical importance of feeling included and accepted at work and in the community.

Resilience

My idyllic life as a probinsiyana princess came to a halt when my dad suddenly passed away in January 1981. I was sixteen, and my youngest sister was only five. While I was very close to my mother, I felt a special bond with my father. We were similar in temperament, being more reserved, thoughtful, and artistic. My dad did not have any high society aspirations. He enjoyed the simple beauty of nature, particularly the sea. He was the intellectual soul of the family, while my mom was its passionate heart. My father's early passing profoundly affected my siblings and me regarding how we viewed the world. We bonded together. Through it all, my mother stood proud and indomitable. Though she was only 37 at the time and had never worked formally, she brought us back to Manila and provided for us well. My mother's example taught me several lessons, but the most important one was resilience. When life throws you a hard ball, pick yourself up and move on. Moreover, you never know when God will call you home, so lead a full life and use all your gifts. Finally, cherish every moment you have with loved ones as you will never have this precious time back. This last lesson always brings tears to my eyes, as my mother too died unexpectedly in 2019, the morning after we had a family dinner in Manila before my scheduled flight back to the States.

HACIENDA GIRL MOVES TO BIG CITY

Social and developmental psychologists talk about the different stages in a person's life during which a person matures as a function of their biological and sociocultural experiences. For example, according to Erik Erikson's model of psychosocial development (Mcleod, 2018), people pass through eight life stages, from infancy to late adulthood. During each stage, they experience a psychosocial crisis which they need to navigate as they grow in psychosocial maturity.

Facing Crisis: Identity. Confidence. Impact.

My personal journey leads me to propose that from teenage to adulthood years, we will face at least three crises that may repeatedly occur in our lives and not necessarily in sequential order as Erikson suggests. These are: (a) crisis of identity, where we will struggle to determine who we are, what our purpose in life is, and where we are going; (b) crisis of confidence, where the challenge is owning our strengths, managing our doubts, and pushing forward with self-assurance; and (c) crisis of impact, where we wonder about our legacy and overall contributions. When all is said and done, what is the lasting impact we have made on this world?

After my father passed away and I started college in Manila, the identity question started weighing more in my mind. I graduated valedictorian in high school but did not really know where I was going. Like many Asians, I was told to pursue medicine or law because these would ensure great careers. My mother wanted me to be a doctor, so off I went to the University of the Philippines in Diliman, Quezon City, where I decided to stay in the dorm.

I was utterly miserable in the dorm. I felt homesick and cried when I visited my family every weekend. Being in the dorm put me in contact with hundreds of young men and women from different places and walks of life. Many of these people I am now dear friends with, including my husband, who I met there but only developed a relationship until much later. During that time at UP, I struggled with unexpected attention. Apparently, the word in the dorm had gotten around that there was this very pretty and smart girl from Bacolod. I was followed by boys, some of whom shouted *"I love you Denise Lopez"* in the middle of the night. The stress, poorly nutritious dorm food, and lack of sleep quickly made me anemic. I retreated into my shell. Looking back, it was a case of culture shock. The sheltered Sleeping Beauty was not ready for the real world.

When faced with a challenging environment, leaders need to make courageous leaps. I decided to leave UP, not because I could not hack it but because it was not the right place for me at the time. Like Goldilocks, I was looking for a bed that fit best for me. I recall meeting with Father Kreutz, the Ateneo admissions director, who had previously accepted me to Ateneo before I decided to go to UP. I remember making him a promise: *"Father if you accept me to Ateneo, I will make sure you never regret it."* I made sure to keep this promise.

Ateneo proved to be a nurturing environment that helped me explore my identity and extend my wings. The most critical decision I made there was choosing my major—psychology. It was different from what other people had advised, but it was the choice of my heart. And because it was compatible with my values and aspirations, it formed the basis of my entire career. More than thirty years later, I am teaching industrial-organizational psychology at an American university and using the knowledge and skills derived from this field to help leaders make their work environments more inclusive, engaging, and productive.

Like my college experience, my early work experiences involved an exploration of identity. I landed my first job in marketing at Unilever, a prestigious multinational company. I learned a lot about business and made lifelong friends. But it was also not quite the best fit. After the initial glamor of marketing personal products had worn off, the work did not feel very meaningful. Instead, I found myself more interested in the process of helping leaders and professionals grow in their careers. So, I left this lucrative job and went for further studies in the United States.

But first, a personal detour: Around the time I was thinking of going to the U.S., my friendship with my co-worker Gilbert Santa Maria had become romantic. We both dreamed of furthering our careers abroad. An electrical engineer by training, he sought to earn an MBA from a prestigious school, while I sought a Ph.D. Unfortunately, Gilbert was not my mother's choice of a life partner for me because he was not, in her eyes, *"de buena familia."* Though Gilbert was an extremely smart, promising professional from a respectable family with parents from Leyte and Butuan, my mother had hoped for someone more suitable, with premier social status, wealthy, and handsome. Suffice it to say, this situation created much drama within my family, to the point that I left my house for several weeks because my mother and I were severely at odds.

I share this deeply personal story with you because we need to make difficult choices in life. And choices require firm conviction because they involve giving up some things and taking risks. At that point in my life, I needed to seek broader pastures, pursue a degree and a future career that was unavailable in the Philippines, and follow my heart. Was I entirely sure of what I was doing? My confidence level was probably 70%. I believed in my abilities and my relationship with Gilbert, yet there were so many unknowns. Nevertheless, I approached this as if there was no going back. I wanted to prove to my mother and to myself that my values and my choices were right. This gave me courage.

THE BIG APPLE: *EL CAPITAL DEL MUNDO*

It is funny that several years after my unfortunate experience in the UP Kalayaan dorm, I was back in another dorm at Teachers College, Columbia University, in an even bigger city—New York City. But this time, I was mentally and emotionally prepared, and I decided to treat this as an adventure. My graduate studies in New York proved to be highly instructive, not just about what I was studying but about life itself. I took the bus, subway, and train everywhere; I got groped a few times in packed subway trains and, pickpocketed in Times Square and Penn Station. I was no longer a sheltered sugarcane princess. I was becoming more like a steel Sampaguita, pretty and delicate on the outside but with a core strength that does not easily waver. After I chose the title for this chapter, I looked up Sampaguita. Not only is it the national flower of the Philippines, but the Sampaguita is also a symbol of purity, simplicity, dedication, humility, and strength—all things important to me.

Nurturing Mentors

The professors I worked with at Columbia University, especially my female mentors, significantly impacted me. As an international student in an Ivy-League Ph.D. program, I experienced many crises of confidence speaking out in class and debating with scholars. But my education and training were, in fact, more than good enough, and I ended up as a teaching assistant in multiple courses. I was also fortunate to start doing executive education and consulting with Dr. Anna Duran, a trailblazer in her own right. She conducted diversity and inclusion (D&I) research and workshops with large corporations in the nineties before these concepts became mainstream. Her mentorship helped build my confidence to work at a world-class level.

FINDING MY VOICE

One thing that leaders have in common is the ability to communicate effectively. To do this, they must find their voice. Having a voice means expressing one's ideas and opinions clearly and persuasively, but also in a manner that is true to one's values. Having a voice is critical in my chosen career as a professor, consultant, and coach. It is our currency—how we demonstrate competence, build reputation, and develop followers. That voice must also be ethical because when all is said and done, the trust of our students, colleagues, clients, and the academic and business communities determines our continued credibility and effectiveness.

I would like to say I found my voice at a young age, but in truth, I did not blossom career-wise until my 30s and 40s. Even now, my voice is still evolving. It took years of experience to find what truly matters to me and what I am great at. I still face crises of confidence. We will never be rid of these crises, but the test is how we face them head-on.

Becoming Self-aware

One such crisis of confidence occurred when my husband Gilbert and I decided to return to the Philippines in 1996, shortly after I had finished my Ph.D. and had given birth to our eldest son. Gilbert had completed a few years at a top consulting firm and wanted to return to the Philippines to give back to the country. He ended up as the youngest General Manager at Pepsi-Cola. I ended up at the Asian Institute of Management (AIM) as one of the youngest faculty members. Teaching in a large amphitheater-like classroom to a class of about 70 students was terrifying. I had never used the case method, which was more of a facilitated discussion rather than a lecture. I felt inadequate with all my book learning since it was impressed on me that all MBA students care about is practical learning. A lot of people commented about how young I looked. I struggled for a year or so to find a voice that combined my years of academic training with a practical, engaging style. I remember a senior professor, Bobby Lim, sitting at the back of the class with a videographer filming my class. Afterward, we viewed the tape at my office, and he critiqued my teaching. It was a humbling but enlightening experience.

After my first year of teaching, my boss Horacio "Junbo" Borromeo, promoted me to program director of the largest batch of MBA (Master of Business Administration) students at AIM. It was another trial by fire. My job involved working with approximately 30–40 core and adjunct professors to ensure the quality and effective delivery of the MBA program. Most of these professors were old enough to be my parents. They were highly experienced and very opinionated. Initially terrified to lead faculty meetings and committees, I figured out over time what mattered to them in key policies and decisions. I leveraged my strengths in relationship-building and demonstrated how my training in Organizational Psychology complemented their skill sets in Strategy, Finance, Accounting, Marketing, Operations, and Data Analytics.

Experiences like these taught me several lessons about finding one's voice. It starts with the fundamental belief that you have many things to offer. Regardless of where you are or who you are dealing with, remind yourself of what you offer, especially what makes you different and unique. Trust yourself and your preparation and training. Understand your audience or stakeholders and be flexible enough to adjust your content, style, emphasis, and voice to what they are most predisposed to receive. Finally, cultivate relationships with mentors and sponsors who will open doors.

BECOMING A GLOBAL CITIZEN AND CULTIVATING IMPACT

Around 1998, a financial crisis in Asia and a shift in Philippine politics triggered my husband's and my decision to return to the United States. I promptly found a consulting job in the San Francisco Bay Area and relocated there with my two boys. Meanwhile, my husband had decided to try his luck at a dot.com in Singapore. It was a challenge for us to navigate a long-distance relationship between the U.S. and Asia for approximately two years.

Working at the consulting company exposed me to the challenge of managing large global surveys for various for-profit, government, and nonprofit clients such as Toyota, Sony, Schering-Plough Pharmaceuticals, Lawrence Livermore National Lab, and the California Department of Transportation. I learned to work with demanding clients and lead cross-cultural teams based in multiple locations, including Europe and Asia. In addition, I learned how to sell projects and influence clients.

Balancing Work-life

As a working mother and full-time consultant, I experienced many work-life balance issues, such as leaving my house at 4:30 a.m. for a meeting in another state, then returning home before 6:00 p.m. to pick up my kids at daycare. The work ultimately got to the point where I asked myself: *"How fulfilled am I? Is this what I want to do with the rest of my life?"* Do not get me wrong. I was grateful for my research consulting job, which brought me back to the U.S. I was doing important work, but it was getting repetitive. There were many other ways I felt we could help our clients, such as through training, performance management, coaching, etc., but the company preferred to stay within its niche. Additionally, the stress and travel were getting in the way of my personal and family responsibilities. The answer to my existential questions about impact and identity became clearer. This life was not for me.

In 2004, my husband found a job with a business outsourcing company in southern California. Thus we decided to move the family to Los Angeles. I joined the core faculty of the Organizational Psychology program at Alliant International University, where I have worked for nearly 17 years. Finding Alliant was like finding a Goldilocks bed that fit just right with my values and interests. I was doing what I enjoyed best—teaching and mentoring students in a program that coupled high-level academic preparation with real-life practical training and a multicultural/international emphasis. Working in academia also gave me the flexibility to build an independent coaching and consulting practice with diverse clients in the U.S. and the Philippines.

Creating Impact

Today I feel like I am at the point of my career where I know what makes me feel most alive, and I can confidently present myself. So now the third challenge about impact poses these questions to my mind:

- Who do I want to impact? Do I focus primarily on developing students into influential leaders and practitioners, or do I wish to spend more time working directly with leaders and organizations?
- How can I make the most impact? What topics or issues should I be talking about? In what ways can I make my voice heard?
- Where else can I create an impact? Which communities and causes bring me passion, and how do I help?

I have started using my voice to create an impact by writing a practical leadership book with my consultant friend Dr. Pearl Hilliard. Though it took us a few years to complete our book, the result was an Amazon bestselling book entitled *Lead, Motivate, Engage: How to INSPIRE your team to win at work* (Hilliard & Lopez, 2019). Our book presents an academically sound but practical model that leaders can utilize to engage their people. Our INSPIRE framework stands for:

I: Ignite people through meaningful work and positive communication
N: Nurture people's growth and development
S: Identify and leverage strengths
P: Manage performance through coaching and feedback
I: Be inclusive. Respect and utilize the power of diversity.
R: Relate to people with authenticity and emotional intelligence
E: Empower people to make choices and take charge

Looking at the INSPIRE model, it becomes clear that these pillars of engagement represent not only what the empirical and business literature identifies as the best practices to motivate people; they also represent many of the principles which have helped me succeed as a professional.

Speaking of creating more impact, let me share a recent experience that has inspired me anew to speak out with purpose and authenticity. If you recall, one of my early critical experiences was a hate incident in San Francisco. In the years I have lived in the United States, I have invested significant time writing and speaking out against bias, hate, and systemic discrimination in organizations and communities. I have become more active in the Asian-American community, joining the board of Leadership Education for Asia-Pacifics (LEAP) and the Ateneans for Social Justice. Increasingly I think about writing a book on inclusive and authentic leadership, particularly for Asian women leaders. But with my various responsibilities, this idea has often fallen on the back burner. However, something significant happened to me before Christmas last year, which I shared on Facebook:

> *"So...someone just called me a "fucking monkey!" On December 22, 2022, I was having a pleasant morning walking my dog Shugo on the sidewalk in my city of Arcadia, CA. We were almost home when a tall white-bearded fit-looking man came jogging fast in the opposite direction. He decided to turn left suddenly in front of us and yelled, "Breach." It took a couple of seconds for Shugo and me to stop, but by then, he had crossed and turned back, shouting, "What are you, a fucking monkey?" It was too late for me to shout back.*

After this happened, it took quite a while for me to process the disbelief, paralysis, and painful emotions of what happened. Now I am a big proponent of kindness, but sometimes, it feels like we women and we Asians need to defend our status. So, thank you, white man, you have inspired me to write my second book on leadership, and it will be dedicated to the people who have called me, and people like me, a fucking monkey!

I pray I will have the courage, energy, and drive to complete my next book and create a lasting impact on Asian and Filipina women and our communities overall.

Living a Life of Purpose and Authenticity

Let me outline some ideas about becoming an authentic and influential leader. I am particularly drawn to the concept of authenticity because other leadership frameworks tend to be prescriptive regarding what leaders should do. For example, many consultants advise Asian women to be more assertive. Interestingly, FWN's first book on Filipina leaders was entitled *DISRUPT Filipina Women: Proud, Loud, Leading Without a Doubt* (Beebe & Escudero, 2015). It's a powerful and catchy title. Assertiveness is important, but it isn't easy to sustain without a clear understanding of one's deeper values and purpose. While it is important to show up with pride, one does not have to be the loudest in the room to be heard. There is a way to present oneself with calmness, competence, confidence, and dignity that is consistent with our sociocultural roots. Otherwise, our attempt to show up as leaders will be awkward and shallow.

Finding the Authentic You

The academic literature defines authentic leadership as a pattern of leadership behavior that reflects positive psychological traits and moral reasoning. Authentic leaders are highly self-aware, utilize balanced reasoning in making decisions, act from a strong internalized ethical core, and display transparent behavior (Walumbwa et al., 2008). In layperson's terms:

- Authentic leaders lead from the heart. They inspire people because they care about the greater good rather than their own interests.
- Authentic leaders are honest and transparent. They don't pretend to be people they are not. They are not afraid to laugh at their foibles or learn from their mistakes. Because they show they are human, others can identify with and trust them more.
- Third, authentic leaders leverage their strengths and encourage those around them to leverage theirs. They appreciate diversity because they realize greater success comes from bringing out the best in everyone.

As you think about how you can become a more authentic leader, consider these questions and suggestions:

- **What is important to you?**
  - » Review the choices you have made. What were the underlying values that drove your decisions?
  - » What do you hope to have accomplished if you happen to pass away tomorrow?
  - » What would people say about the impact you have made on their lives?

- **What are you passionate about? What are your strengths, and how can you leverage them?**
  - » Remember that your voice is most powerful when you talk about what you are most passionate about.
  - » Own your strengths, and do not be afraid to step into the light.

- **Stay true to your personality and style, but do not be afraid to stretch.**
  - » I do not like the question "what's your brand" because it seems rather contrived. Instead, I would ask how you want others to experience you genuinely. In my case, I have gradually defined how I wish to be viewed by others as someone who combines high achievement standards with kindness; perseverance with optimism; and curiosity with collaboration and humor. But, most importantly, I wish to be someone who supports and uplifts others.
  - » Do not be afraid to challenge boundaries. When people ask *"why,"* answer, *"why not?"* For example, when people ask me why I am in the U.S. while my husband works in the Philippines, I respond, *"Because I have my own career and a husband who fully supports me. He gives me the freedom to pursue my goals, and I do the same for him."*

- **Remember where you came from. Be proud and grateful for the privileges you've received.**
  - » When I introduce myself, I always mention that I am originally from the Philippines. It is a way to honor my heritage.
  - » Turn your cultural heritage into an advantage. I have learned to be fine with my Filipino/Ilonggo accent. My accent reminds me that I am unique and that I speak more than one language.

- **The impostor syndrome is mainly in your mind.**
  - » Remind yourself of your accomplishments. Most likely, you are underestimating yourself.
  - » Know that other people will feel like impostors in different settings. White males can feel like impostors amidst an all-Filipino team.

- **Be grateful.**
  - » When people pay you compliments like how pretty and accomplished you are, say "thank you" gracefully. The older you get, the more grateful you will be.
  - » Then turn the conversation around and find something to appreciate in them. Use this as a springboard to build or strengthen your relationship.

- **Build relationships and help others.**
  - » Expand your world. Get to know different types of people, not just Filipinos.
  - » Pay it forward, as Marshall Goldsmith says (Cohn, 2017). When someone does something for you, go and help another person. Make a goal of spreading love and kindness every day, even in a small way. These blessings have a powerful boomerang effect.

As global Filipina leaders, we shine brightest when we are clear about our values and goals. We consciously leverage our unique styles and strengths while being open to new learning. We show up best when we are authentic.

LEADING CHANGE:
EDUCATION

ARLENE FERROLINO

Owner, Piano Studio-Arlene Ferrolino
Pianist, organist, accompanist, MTAC, MGPT, AGO
Former President, Filipino American Symphony Orchestra
GLOBAL FWN100™ 2021

The Joy of Sharing Music: How It Determined the Course of My Life

My heart was ablaze with pride. Chills ran up and down my spine. I felt tears welling up in my eyes. As we rose to the majestic strains of *Lupang Hinirang*, the Philippine national anthem played by the orchestra, I scanned the concert hall. People were proudly singing at the top of their lungs. In our maiden performance at the renowned Walt Disney Concert Hall, we, the Filipino American Symphony Orchestra (FASO), the first and only Filipino symphony orchestra outside the Philippines, filled this iconic venue.

Bringing the music of our country to this, one of the most highly desired concert halls in the world, was a feat all in itself.

As I looked out into the audience, I reflected on the journey that my life had taken. How it is that I found myself here in this glorious moment. During one of the highlights of that memorable evening, I would have the opportunity to stride purposefully to center stage in front of a crowd of more than 2,000 people. Together with Maestro Robert Shroder, FASO's conductor and musical director, and Dr. Louie Ramos, FASO's Vice-President and arranger-in-residence, it would be my great honor and privilege as the President of this illustrious organization to present a medallion of service and volunteerism to Andy Tecson, one of our outstanding members and co-founder of the orchestra.

Words cannot even begin to describe it. The time, energy, effort, and dreams of so many that collaborated to get our organization to this moment, the joy of sharing our music at this most revered concert space, brought forth a flood of emotion. How did I, the once shy, nervous, and anxious little girl get from meager and unassuming beginnings to this renowned concert stage?

Musical Beginnings

I used to be shy—an incredulous statement to many who did not know me as a youngster. Indeed I was a shy child, painfully shy. Probably because my father's career moved us from one corner of the country to another every few years, I would not readily talk to people outside my family circle.

As the second of three children born into a military household, some of my earliest recollections are of a massive stereo cabinet in our living room. My father would play LPs of Burl Ives, Englebert Humperdinck, Andy Williams, and Frank Sinatra. On the dust covers of these albums were the lyrics to which I would follow along. I learned to read, sing, and appreciate beautiful music from these albums. A natural, untrained soprano, my mother would sing as she did chores around the house. Humming show tunes, belting out Broadway favorites, and prayerfully interpreting hymns were standard daily fare. Of course, her melodious voice would also sing me, my older brother, and younger sister to sleep. Music surrounded us. Little did I know that music would be the vehicle that would take me to places that I could never have imagined, even in my wildest dreams.

Formal piano lessons for me began at the age of 8. My first piano teacher, Evelyn Rice, was an exacting and demanding mentor whom I dreaded, especially if I had not put in sufficient practice hours.

By the time I had learned my first few pieces, I was hooked and deeply in love with the piano and the sound of the music that my own ten fingers could make. Practicing for hours every day was never a chore but a welcome treat and a delicious delight for my artistic soul.

My shy and quiet self could easily find herself immersed in exploring music, playing whatever pieces I could get my hands on.

By the time I was in 3rd grade, because of my father's job in the US Navy, we had already moved to four different cities in two other countries. I was always the new girl in class. Consequently, I had trouble making friends because it seemed like I was constantly being uprooted by moving to yet another new place.

When the neighbors' kids came over to the house wanting to play, my sister Amy who took her cues from me would hide in the closet with me, hoping no one would find us. No amount of coaxing by our mother or father could get us to come out of hiding. Eventually, the kids would turn away disappointed.

Throughout school, I remained timid and shy, never raising my hand to volunteer an answer even if I knew the correct response. Finally, when the teacher called my name, and it was my turn to read a paragraph out loud, I would get a painful knot in my stomach, bow my head, quietly mutter under my breath, or simply remain silent.

"Speak up. We can't hear you," my teacher would invariably say as she tried to coax me to read louder.

Red-faced from embarrassment, I would try to speak louder but to no avail. No matter how hard I tried to speak up, only a whisper would make its way out of my mouth. It always felt like the eyes of the entire class pierced my soul. I did not want to play with the other kids at recess for fear of being ridiculed. Instead, I hid my face behind a book and read. I always got picked last when choosing teams for dodgeball, softball, or football. No one wanted to choose me, mostly because I was not very good at sports either.

After I finished the sixth grade, it was time for my family to move once more. This time it was a more significant move as my father was retiring from the US Navy and wanted us to relocate back to the Philippines. Now being the new kid in high school felt even worse. I kept to myself even more, unable to comfortably speak the language in this new place and having no friends.

One thing that I learned from being alone so much was that I enjoyed writing. Letting my thoughts flow onto a piece of paper, journaling every day, writing stories, and creating poems was something else that I grew to love. One of my essays caught the eye of my freshman English teacher, Mrs. Gallego, and she ascertained that I possessed a knack for writing. That teacher asked if I would consider joining the writing staff for the school's newsletter and yearbook. Reluctantly, I found myself nodding my head in agreement.

Eventually, the music teacher, Ms. Diaz, discovered that I also played the piano. The high school choir needed an accompanist. She showed me some music, and it looked doable. I played it for her, and she smiled. *"You're the new accompanist!"* Thus began my love for accompanying choirs, instrumentalists, and vocalists.

Before I knew it, I was busy doing multiple extracurricular activities and slowly breaking out of that shell of shyness. Making friends became amazingly easy. My classmates and schoolmates on the newsletter and yearbook staff became my friends. The choir members and other music-minded individuals and groups were calling on me to accompany and perform with them. Writing and piano playing became a fun way to connect and socialize. Soon I was no longer that wilting violet who wanted to hide when faced with the prospect of meeting people.

BECOMING A MUSIC TEACHER

Starting college brought me to a crossroads as I faced the dilemma of determining which career path I would walk. The decision was not easy. I experienced the fulfillment of finding a voice through both my writing and my music,

I started my first year declaring English as my major with the hope of either using it as a pre-law degree or launching into broadcast journalism. However, throughout my first and second years, I did continue piano lessons and did take on requests to perform for weddings and church services. By the time I had reached my third year of college, my piano teacher, Mrs. Coo, started giving me the responsibility of teaching some of her students. In this way, I was able to gain valuable experience and satisfy some of the requirements of practicing teaching.

Still undecided about my career path, my major professors suggested that I consider working toward a double major: a bachelor's in music with an emphasis in Music Education and English with an emphasis in Journalism.

In the summer of 1985, after spending six years in college, I successfully completed both degrees. I had completed a wide array of courses in these two fields of study but stood again at a crossroads. Even before I had obtained these degrees, professors from both the music and English departments were ready to hire me in their departments as soon as I acquired a master's degree. But was I ready?

My parents suggested I return to the US to pursue master's studies before jumping into teaching at Philippine Union College, soon to be the Adventist

University of the Philippines. So back I flew to California with the plan to begin working on a master's degree.

Learning Organizational Skills as a Legal Secretary

To help fund graduate school, I needed a job. So off I went to the AppleOne Employment Services to see what kind of jobs might be available. I took all the clerical tests and passed with flying colors. They declared my job skills to be highly marketable. Immediately they sent me on two job interviews: one at a detective agency and the other at a law office. Both places were ready to hire me on the spot. Since I liked the atmosphere at the law office and thought of it as possibly a springboard into law school, I started my job as a legal secretary at the Law Offices of John P. Kightlinger in the summer of 1985.

It was a small but busy, well-established law practice with two attorneys, one office manager, and two legal secretaries. For a day job that I had initially thought would only be a short stint, I ended up staying at this particular position for eight long but fruitful years. Here I learned to communicate with delinquent employers, write demand letters, manage the court calendar, deal with clients and defendants, examine, analyze and interpret legal contracts and so much more. Little did I know then that God must have had a hand in putting me there so I could add these essential tools to my organizational skill set.

Honing my Musical Talents: The Colburn Years

Never leaving behind my love for music, I found myself at the prestigious Colburn School for Performing Arts. Unbeknownst to me at the time was the significance of this chapter in my life. To quote from the mission and history of Colburn:

Founded on the principle of access to excellence, the Colburn School has remained committed to providing the best possible performing arts education to dedicated students for nearly 70 years. Under the care and guidance of an exceptional faculty, generations of students have discovered and expressed their passion for music, dance, and the performing arts (colburnschool.edu).

Upon the recommendation of Ray Puen, one of my mentors and the organist at my church, I auditioned at Colburn. Auditioning for a panel of Colburn faculty which included keyboard chair Richard Chronister, I was accepted and assigned to Dr. Louise Lepley. Only years later would I realize that

God was leading me in this next step on the journey to excellence and directing me down the road that would be taking me closer to experiencing the joy of sharing music.

Concurrent with my eight years at the law office, working every weekday from 9:00 a.m. till 5:00 p.m., I devoted my afternoons to a few hours of music: practicing the piano or teaching a few piano students. Rarely would I be found out and about town or gallivanting with friends but instead, I spent my free time practicing and perfecting Bach, Chopin, Brahms, or Beethoven.

My teacher, the highly renowned Professor Louise Lepley, recognized as a Distinguished Teacher by the White House Commission on Presidential Scholars, eventually became the head of keyboard studies at Colburn. Throughout my studies with her, she prepared me for my masteral studies and became a beloved mentor and friend. Such a gracious woman, she was brilliant but unassuming, deeply knowledgeable, and possessed a wealth of information that she generously shared with her students. As a result, Dr. Lepley has greatly influenced much of my teaching style.

After still struggling with a difficult passage from a challenging Rachmaninoff Etude, I muttered "sorry" for the umpteenth time. Dr. Lepley gently put her hand on my shoulder and said, "Don't be sorry. Fix the mistake and don't apologize. Be absolutely sure about what you're doing, and you'll never have to apologize." One important lesson I learned from her has stuck with me.

Teaching Music

I have been teaching for as long as I can remember. It's difficult to pinpoint an exact date when I began the chapter in my life as a teacher. As a young child, I remember reading stories to my sister, Amy. Holding up the book and pointing to the illustrations, I told her to pretend that I was the teacher and she was a student in my class.

Teaching is in my blood. I am a third generation teacher stemming from my maternal grandmother, an elementary teacher who in the 1920's through the 1950's was an active and highly revered educator in her hometown of Mataas na Kahoy in the province of Batangas. My mother, my grandma's firstborn child, also followed in her footsteps and became a high school and science teacher. Later in life, as an immigrant to the US, even as a full-time homemaker, my mom would take on part-time employment as a substitute elementary teacher and teach children's Sabbath School at church every Saturday. As I was born surrounded by music, I can say that I was born into teaching.

My first forays into formal piano teaching were in required teaching courses at Philippine Union College, now Adventist University of the Philippines. Although I intended to meet the requirements, I knew from those early experiences with students of different ages that sharing music through teaching was something that brought me unparalleled joy.

Venturing into the Music Business

Setting up my private piano studio at home in 1985 allowed me to continue creating teaching moments with three or four students for a few hours each week. Even as I worked as a legal secretary during the day, the opportunity to teach these few precious youngsters was the foundation for what would soon become my bread and butter, the profession that I would choose.

In the summer of 1990, in a beautiful church ceremony, I married Don Ferrolino, the wonderful man who had pursued me for nearly 15 years. Classmates since our high school days, my confidante, my soulmate, and my best friend through thick and thin, his determination and perseverance had finally won my heart. By this book's publication, we will have celebrated our 32nd wedding anniversary.

With the fast-approaching arrival of our firstborn child, Emily, in the spring of 1993, I officially terminated my employment at the law office and became a full-time mother. Upon the encouragement and coaxing of my husband and the gift of a new Steinway baby grand piano, I threw all my energies into the Piano Studio of Arlene Ferrolino.

Having only minimal and rudimentary business experience, when it came to running my own business, I had no other choice but to learn by doing. By consulting with other music teacher friends and receiving business advice from family and friends, I quickly figured out policies and guidelines, and my piano teaching business began to flourish. To date, I can mark 41 years of actual teaching and 29 years as a successful small business owner.

Joining Professional Organizations

I immediately joined the Glendale Branch of the Music Teachers' Association of

California (MTAC) and the Glendale-Burbank center for the National Guild of Piano Teachers (NGPT). These two professional organizations provide programs and events for their members to enter their students.

The mission of MTAC is to pursue excellence in music education and advance the music teaching profession through innovative programs that foster artistic growth and achievement.

The Music Teachers' Association of California®, incorporated in 1897, is a professional organization dedicated to the pursuit of excellence in music education. With over 4,700 members, there are more than 63 self-governing, affiliated Branches throughout the State (MTAC.org).

I was invited to join the Board of Directors of the Glendale Branch of the MTAC and have now been an active member for nearly 30 years. It has been an honor to have been elected to three terms as this Branch's President of the Board of Directors (2003, 2007 and 2010). During the installation of officers during my first term, I made history by being the first Asian American and the first Filipina to lead the Glendale Branch. Each Branch within the State of California, though under the umbrella of the State Office is still run by a local board of directors. Each Branch upholds the State programs, mission, and vision but is also self-governing.

In 2003 during my first term as President, the Glendale Branch first stepped into the world of technology and officially began using email as our primary mode of communication. From the monthly newsletters to weekly updates and connecting with fellow teachers, I had to bring the Branch into the realm of the world wide web. Considered a huge leap into the unknown since a large portion of the membership were older, well-established teachers, set in their traditional ways, and unsure of how to navigate this new means of connecting. It took enormous amounts of perseverance, tact, diplomacy, and, indeed, a measure of bravery on my part to win over the skeptics and bring the Branch into 21st-century technology.

Working closely with this Board and the many exceptional music teachers around me, I have been afforded the opportunity for even more significant professional growth. It has become an annual practice of mine to attend the MTAC State Convention to avail of performances, lectures, workshops, recitals, and continuing education programs. Students under my tutelage had the distinct opportunity of being asked to perform at these conventions nearly every year. As a result, the students have received many honors and awards.

From 2011 to 2015, the State President of the MTAC State Office located in San Francisco appointed me to head the Media and Publication Awards Committee, formerly the Scrapbooks and Awards Committee. This special committee oversaw searching for and awarding music teachers for their creativity and innovation in design and artistry in the categories of website design, recital program design, newsletters and other printed, or digital media by individual teachers and by Branches.

For many years I was the assistant chair of the Glendale-Burbank Audition Center of the NGPT. In 2007, upon the retirement of Chair, Virginia Hummer, another of my mentors, I took on the responsibilities of organizing and scheduling evaluations for approximately 100-150 students from 10-12 studios each year.

Along with these duties, I also took on the responsibility of being an adjudicator and evaluator for both the MTAC and NGPT. And this has allowed me to judge students from not only my hometown in Glendale and its surrounding communities but also statewide and even internationally.

Recently I was honored to be selected as a recipient of the Steinway Top Teacher Award for the "commitment with which you approach your piano students. The young people who develop their craft under your guidance will be the artists who fill our future with music, and we are most grateful for this. Steinway & Sons is a name that is synonymous with artistry, quality, and exquisite musical expression. The Steinway Top Teacher Award demonstrates your commitment to the same ideas."

Performing to Share the Joy of Music

Vivid memories of my first public performance take me to my childhood at the Paradise Valley Seventh-Day Adventist Church in San Diego, California. I was nine years old when I played an arrangement of Mozart's Alleluia for the prelude. My teacher, Mrs. Evelyn Rice, who was also the church organist, informed me that I was making history as the youngest to ever play for a worship service.

The reverence and awe of that sanctuary, along with the feeling of fulfillment and satisfaction of performing well, have stayed with me. Over the past years, as a church musician, pianist, organist, and accompanist, I have performed with choirs, chorales, instrumentalists, and vocalists as they have sung and played music of the great masters in sanctuaries and cathedrals, chapels, and concert halls. I have played love songs and sacred hymns for weddings, funerals, baptisms, and graduations. To this day, as I slide onto the organ bench or sit at the piano to play a prelude, offertory, postlude, or be an accompanist, my heart and my soul know that performing as a church musician is one of the most gratifying, elevating, and inspirational experiences of which I can partake each week.

Giving back to School and Community

One of the activities near and dear to my heart is my alumni association, the Adventist University of the Philippines, Association of Western North America (AWESNA). Having attended this institution from high school through college had an enormous influence on my life. This school, its classes, the faculty who taught me, and the friends I made have all been instrumental in what I am today and how I live my life.

As a way of giving back and helping the university continue to grow, both my husband and I happily and readily volunteer through AWESNA and have served on the Board of Directors or led various committees.

Over the past several years, a stop at AUP is one of the most exciting and memorable segments of our trips to the homeland. I regularly teach either in the form of a master class, a lecture, a workshop, or a seminar at the Music Department. Popular topics for these classes will range from The Art of Accompanying, The Spiritual Influence of a Music Teacher, or An Intermediate Master Class.

Most recently, since the pandemic halted travel and I was unable to make it in person to the campus, I was asked to lead a webinar on "The Business Side of Teaching Music." As I was introduced to the students, I was surprised to be called a "knowledgeable entrepreneur and a highly successful businesswoman." Those are terms that I had never personally used to describe myself. I realized then that this is how my peers and fellow musicians looked upon me. What an ego-booster and another reminder of where music had brought this once quiet and timid child.

At the River Cree Casino and Resort in Edmonton, Alberta, Canada, at the AUP AWESNA annual convention, my alumni association honored me with the Most Outstanding Alumna Award of 2018 *"in recognition of her commendable accomplishments and unwavering commitment to AUP and AWESNA."* The following are some excerpts of the introduction with epic music playing in the background in true award show style as I was escorted to the stage to receive a commemorative plaque.

> *"Arlene became a member of the Glendale Chapter in 1985 and has faithfully served in various capacities in the local chapter ranging from PRO to secretary and social vice-president. She has also been associate secretary and secretary of AWESNA for eight years, accompanied AWESNA leaders to various parts of the AWESNA territory to assist in forming new chapters in the Pacific Northwest, and held rallies at existing chapters. In addition, Arlene has been involved regularly in the musical aspect of AWESNA conventions as an accompanist, pianist, or organist."*

In addition to my musical talents, I was being honored for my organizational skills and coordinating capabilities whenever choral groups were in town. I was recognized and appreciated for my service by:

- Glendale Filipino Adventist Church as church clerk, organist, and leader in children's division, and youth and adult Sabbath programs.
- Altadena United Methodist Church as organist/accompanist
- Glendale Chapter AWESNA for Community Service
- Adventist University of the Philippines Association of Western North America – Outstanding Alumna of the Year 2018.

Leading an Orchestra

A new chapter of my life would unfold in August of 2012, when I received an email from Cecilia Coo, a violinist friend and daughter of my former piano teacher, Corazon Coo.Cecile asked if I might be interested in helping with the Filipino American Symphony Orchestra (FASO) board of directors.

"The what?!" I asked.

Until that moment, I had only heard of FASO but had never encountered an opportunity to listen to FASO play. However, before I gave her my answer, I wanted to know more about what I might be getting myself into. So off I went to do some research on FASO.

The first FASO performance I attended was held at the Ford Amphitheater when they featured "Bach to Rock." My ever-supportive husband Don, whose background in music consists of listening to performances and working the sound system, turned to me numerous times during the concert and exclaimed, *"Dear, they're really good!"* Indeed, they were! From beginning to end, it was truly a feast for the ears.

I was hooked on FASO and knew from that moment that this was something I wanted to be a part of in a big way! The wheels started turning quickly, and in March of 2013, FASO's founding members assembled at my piano studio in Glendale: Claire Espina, John Mina, Ruben Nepales, Asuncion Ojeda, Louie Ramos, Robert Shroder and Titus Verzosa. In addition, I was elected as FASO's first President of the Board of Directors.

An article written by Ruben Nepales states that "as board president... Ferrolino has been successfully steering FASO as it grows, with the wholehearted support and approval of her leadership by the board."

Indeed FASO did an enormous amount of growing. At the time when I first stepped into the shoes of president, the orchestra had already been in existence for some four years, performing and concertizing for various events. With the founding of a Board of Directors, it became our first order of business to get the organization to become a nonprofit 501(c)3 status. Assembling, organizing, maintaining and leading a Board a Board of highly motivated, sharp, strong and committed directors required that I bring my A game. Under my direction and command, I had some of the best people in finance, marketing, law, education, advertising, and, yes, music. With the ultimate goal of bringing the orchestra to the pinnacle of success and sharing the gift of music, specifically Filipino music, we harmonized our individual strengths and expertise together to form a dream team for FASO. The FASO Board are fiercely driven by the desire to help FASO succeed to fulfill its vision and mission. That continues to resonate in all that we do. Seeing the joy on each face at every performance, watching each child as they grow musically at our workshops, and knowing we played a small role in this is satisfaction enough for me.

I shared my feelings in the book *10 Years of FASO – A Decade of Music, Harmony, and Community*, published in 2018 on the occasion of the celebration of FASO's 10-year anniversary. Here are a few excerpts.

"Had you asked my younger self if heading the Board of a symphony orchestra was one of my ambitions, I would have laughed and shook my head. Stepping into the role as the first president of FASO was not something that I had ever dreamed of doing. After giving it much thought and prayer, however, realizing who I was working with, knowing the musical caliber of FASO, and just imagining where this organization could go, I was up for the challenge." I am proud of my leadership at FASO.

I am proud of my leadership at FASO. Over the years, FASO continued to stage concerts, earning a reputation for presenting quality, entertaining productions. As a result, audiences have flocked to FASO's shows, which showcased music ranging from classical to spiritual songs, from *kundimans* to Broadway, in venues that are just as diverse—from the Pasadena Civic Auditorium and the Hilton Glendale ballroom to the Alex Theatre.

While FASO features established talents, the orchestra also makes it a point to spotlight promising vocalists and musicians. Some of these young talents are discovered in FASO's music education outreach programs to communities.

FASO has received recognition for:

1. Excellence in Business and Community Service for a Nonprofit Organization from the FACC-SLAA (Filipino American Chamber of Commerce-South Bay Los Angeles Area.)
2. Historical Heritage Excellence Award from the San Diego Filipino American Humanitarian Foundation, Inc.
3. Silayan Filipino Award from the Silayan Filipino National Organization.
4. Proclamation and Recognition for 10th Anniversary from the Los Angeles City Council.

The pandemic did not slow us down one bit. While concert halls were shutting down, FASO kept the music playing by producing videos so that we were able to continue performances and provide free virtual concerts. The videos expanded our audience to include our surrounding community and the entire globe. Our educational programs continued an extended program using the online platform. Videos made our presence possible in multiple venues at any given time, creating community partners for FASO locally and worldwide. FASO celebrates its 14th concert season this year, and its programs continue to grow and flourish. The past two years saw our organization expand to add a paid staff consisting of an Executive Director, Director of Media, and paid interns. Indeed, the possibilities are endless. Having ended nearly a decade as FASO's historic first president, I now serve on their Advisory Board.

To learn more about FASO, please visit our website: www.fasomusic.org

Coming Full Circle: The Joy of Sharing Music

From shy to self-confident, from embarrassed to empowered, this once shrinking violet has budded and bloomed. In so many ways, my life has come full circle. Music and the joy of sharing music truly changed the direction of my life.

I have two beautiful, talented, accomplished daughters, Emily and Roxanne. They likewise can confidently attest that music has made a tremendous impact on them and will always be a significant part of their lives.

One of the most comprehensive and best-written summaries of my life thus far can be found in this article penned by Mary Lou Cunanan of the *Philippine Daily Mirror* entitled "Arlene Ferrolino: Sharing the Joy of Music." *"Arlene has enjoyed the spotlight on countless stages. She has graced prestigious concert halls and performed with numerous internationally renowned vocalists, instrumentalists, and choral groups. However, her greatest passion in life remains to be the subtle art of teaching and cultivating a love for music among young people."*

That is true. Anything that has to do with music and children will grab my attention. Bringing the joy of music to children and giving them the gift of learning music has always been my passion. Giving them opportunities for creativity and avenues to share their talents is a priority and is what brings me the most happiness and fulfillment.

What inspires me is, first, seeing the accomplishments and achievements of people who have come before me. I truly believe that we stand on the shoulders of those who came before us, which sparks me to action. Second, I'm constantly inspired by the exuberance, enthusiasm, and endless creativity of young people. That motivates me daily in teaching my students and working with FASO.

A verse in the Bible found in Proverbs 3:5 has been my guiding star. *"Trust in the Lord with all your heart and lean not on your own understanding. In all of your ways acknowledge Him and He will direct your paths."* Every step of the way, every door that has been opened and, yes, even the obstacles that may have obscured the road, they have all been part of the Lord's plan. I acknowledge divine guidance and my leadership in fulfilling that plan.

LEADERSHIP TIPS

1. Know your strengths and your weaknesses. Mine was about making music, sharing music, and teaching music.

2. Hone your craft and be the best at what you do. I practiced, practiced, practiced. As my mentor said, *"Be absolutely sure about what you're doing."* As I grew in confidence, I never had to apologize for any mistakes as I gave the best in each of my performances and nurtured the best in my music students.

3. Grasp the opportunities that present themselves. Take every opportunity to learn about the amazing Filipino culture and explore how we fit in the community where we live and work. Who knew that the organizing skills I learned as a legal secretary would be beneficial in my role as FASO President

4. Be generous with your talents and be willing to share them with others. I would like to say that I was able to share the joy of music with the world. Whether at a private piano lesson, in the classroom, or on the concert stage. I hope I have been instrumental in bringing music to people, giving them a vehicle to channel their emotions and express their feelings. That, I think, is the greatest gift that I have given and continue to give.

DR. BERNADETTE MONDEJAR-SCHLUETER

Principal, Feltwell Elementary School, RAF Feltwell, England
GLOBAL FWN100™ 2016

Finding My Why

"*Dr. Schlueter, you are the best principal ever!*" wrote a student on a notecard that accompanied a gift left on my desk. The note struck a chord in me during a hectic day. As an elementary school administrator, I get cards and presents from students and parents on special occasions like Christmas and the last day of school. However, I especially cherish those handwritten notes and handmade cards, which have pride of place in my office. They help nourish my soul and reinforce my why in education.

I am an educator dedicated to making the world a better place, one student at a time. My 26 years in education have been a journey of self-discovery, purpose, and teamwork. I was a teacher and a school administrator in the Philippines, Japan, Korea, Guam, Belgium, and the United Kingdom. I hosted queens, generals, and ministers at my schools. I worked with award-winning teachers and won awards myself.

What mattered most was how proud I was when our elementary students passed the DELF Prim A2, just three years after establishing the French immersion program at our school. I shared the joy with teachers and parents when students exited the literacy support program and continued to make gains in reading. The sense of accomplishment was shared with the community when I opened the Sure Start program for our youngest learners.

An educator's why is to support and nurture the students' potential no matter what it takes. I never thought I would be an educator while growing up in Tacloban City, Philippines. I could not decide whether I wanted to become a lawyer, a nun, or a businesswoman. Being a teacher was not on my shortlist of occupations, although I knew I wanted to make a difference in people's lives.

My parents ran several businesses, and we, their offspring, spent our time after school and during summers helping them. It was vital for me to have a purpose and contribute to the family at a young age. We experienced the responsibilities of running a printing press, a security agency, a catering business, a dress shop, and a computer college. I was active in family businesses and loved interacting with customers and employees.

My parents passed on to us two values: responsibility and leadership in the family businesses. All of us siblings were trained to work and grow the business legacy of our family one day. I accepted typing jobs as a 10-year-old in the printing business. But, I hid when the customer picked up the typing outputs. I was afraid we would lose the customer if he discovered it was a child typing for him.

I loved the hands-on part of our training. I learned all printing business aspects: cost estimation to labor management and marketing to machine operations. While we had modern Solna offset machines, we also used the vintage letterpress machines for small orders. We have the Minerva letterpress equipment still fully operational to this day.

My parents assigned me to teach some courses and be the school administrator of our JE Mondejar Computer College in Tacloban City, Philippines. I saw how hard students studied to pass their exams. I talked to parents who had to sign promissory notes during examination because the typhoon damaged their copra or rice harvest, disabling them from paying the school dues on time. I convinced students to continue their studies as working students whenever their parents could no longer afford the tuition fees. I witnessed the pride in the eyes of the parents watching their children walk across the stage to receive their college diplomas. Then it hit me. I found my why. As an educator, I know I can do so much more to help improve the lives of students and their families. In the next few years, I went to create an impact on American and international students in five countries.

Adapt and Adjust: Philippines

1995. A career in education was the last thing I expected to pursue. I was teaching but did not consider myself an educator then. After all, my bachelor's degree was in business administration. While I was helping manage our JE Mondejar Computer School by day, I was studying law at night. I thought I was doing good, and on track to realize my goal of becoming a lawyer. Fate, however, has a way of making things happen as it is meant to be.

The Oklahoma Bombing and its perpetrators Timothy McVeigh and Terry Nichols dominated international headlines. Everyone's favorite Superman, Christopher Reeve, fell from his horse and became paralyzed from the neck down. Alanis Morrisette exploded onto the global stage with the release of her third album Jagged Little Pill.

On the local front, Divine Word University hit Tacloban City with the news of its shutdown due to worsening labor issues. The largest and only university in the region was the education hub of the city and the region. Various businesses prospered around the university community, from tricycle drivers to sidewalk vendors, from boarding houses to restaurants. The university threatened to close the year before, but no one believed it. Thus, it shocked all when the university made good of its threat. The closure displaced thousands of employees and students, shattering businesses and dashing hopes and dreams.

The university closure was a catastrophic event that derailed my plan. By then, I was already in my third year of law, counting down to the days when I would be taking the bar exams and dreaming of being called "Attorney Mondejar."

The closure affected me deeply on a personal level. I spent elementary and high school at this university, so I felt a deep loss. I was in limbo. I was not ready to transfer to another school, but I was not prepared to stop either. My parents stepped in and gave me more responsibilities at our computer school. Doing so, they unwittingly influenced my future decision to become an educator.

My father, Jose Rene Mondejar, saw the university closure as a business opportunity. He had the vision to convert our computer school into a private college and absorb some of the displaced students from the university. He guided me to take a break from my law studies to focus on our school as its administrator and make it grow. My mother was the quiet powerhouse, making me feel confident and up to the challenge.

My family's support was all I needed to adapt and adjust to the changes around me. My first order of business was to change the name to JE Mondejar

Computer College and turn it into a private corporation. That was the easy part. The hard part was getting our application for the degree programs approved. We were already offering short-term computer courses. It was a natural choice for a Bachelor of Science in Computer Science to be our flagship program. I also decided to add a Bachelor of Science in Business Administration as the second degree program. I compiled all the required voluminous application documents to submit to the Commission on Higher Education. I made numerous trips to the offices of the approving agencies in Palo, Leyte, and Metro Manila.

I made many revisions to our applications. The family made a substantial investment in the school facilities that sometimes I thought we would never get approved. Yet, we persevered and continued to comply with the new requirements. Finally, we got the approval to start offering the two-degree programs during the first semester of that school year.

It was a challenging but fulfilling first year. No one in our administrative team had the experience of running a school before, but we all had our hearts in the right place. We wanted the school to grow and worked to make our students thrive. However, we did not have a reputation to bank on as a brand-new school.

The task of building our brand began. We facilitated various events to develop a sense of community with our students. The college organized sports teams to compete in athletic meets. We hosted academic competitions to promote our name to our feeder high school population. We developed linkages with local businesses and the local affiliate of software giant Oracle. As a college representative, I took advantage of networking opportunities through involvement in organizations such as the Tacloban "Love" Jaycees and the Tacloban City Toastmasters Club.

Starting in February of every year, we embarked on a road trip around Leyte and Samar provinces to do a school-to-school campaign to promote our college. We traversed hanging bridges and crossed seas to reach as many teachers, students, and parents as possible. I listened to their hopes and dreams. I realized that to attract more students to our college, we had to add more to our current programs, hire the best instructors, and expand our facilities.

Our college continued to grow in the next few years. We faced challenges and overcame them. Our facilities improved, transferring locations as our student population grew and our course offerings expanded. I was promoted to become the Vice President for Administration of our college.

I earned my Master of Business Administration degree from the Philippine Women's University and, on the side, passed the test to become a sergeant of the Philippine Air Force Reserve Command.

I knew then that my calling was in education as a teacher and administrator. Initially, I thought my destiny was with our computer college. However, my future changed when I met Richard.

Bloom Where You are Planted: Japan

2003. Philippine President Gloria Macapagal Arroyo survived her first *coup d'etat.* Beyonce Knowles ruled the pop charts with her solo debut Dangerously in Love. The Human Genome Project was completed as a joint effort of scientists worldwide, leading to the discovery of DNA composition in humans. The space shuttle Columbia disintegrated upon re-entry, killing all seven astronauts on board. One of these astronauts was CDR William C. McCool. A few years later, I will be working at a Department of Defense Education Activity [DoDEA] school named in his honor in Guam.

I met my husband, Richard, while on vacation in Boracay. We connected the first time we met. After a whirlwind long-distance courtship, we got married, and I moved to Japan, eager to start our life together. I had never lived overseas and was excited to see what opportunities were in store for me. It must be fate that he was a high school principal at an American base in Japan.

A small part of me was sad that I was leaving JE Mondejar Computer College, a school I love and helped develop. I will always be a part of this school, a part of the Mondejar family's legacy to the people of Leyte and Samar. However, it was time to move on. I had my eyes set on the future with my new husband.

I did not work during my first year in Japan. I was glad to dedicate my time to being a good wife. We spent time together exploring the differences between the American and Japanese cultures. I attended all events at Richard's school, compared the American education system with the Philippine system, watched three sports seasons during the school year, and learned the military way of life. Outside the base, we explored the wonders of Tokyo and the beauty of the Japanese countryside, learned conversational Nihonggo, and went skiing at Shiga Kogen and Zao. After a year, the need to work came back with a vengeance.

I was often in my husband's school, but I missed being around students and a school I could call my own. So I started looking for jobs. I was open to all employment opportunities, but I found it hard to find a job I liked. So I became a part-time English tutor to Japanese students.

Then, I took a job in Tokyo, going from a vice president position at a private college in the Philippines to a kindergarten aide job at an international school run by Catholic nuns in Japan. It was a humbling experience but a learning opportunity, which I presumed I could use as a stepping stone to an international teaching career. I dedicated my time to learning as much as I could while there. I also decided to start my Master of Arts in Education, majoring in Elementary Teacher Education, at the University of Phoenix.

After a year and a half, I completed my second master's degree and became an American citizen. A couple of months later, I took a job as a fifth-grade teacher at Yokota East Elementary School on base. The school was an ideal place to work. The staff was diverse and supportive.

I began to explore and see what I could do to contribute to the welfare of the students. I accepted my students' proposal to sponsor the school's talent show. I opened it up to all grade levels, and the performance became a huge success. High on this success, I set my eyes next on creating a school-based news network with students from Grades 1-5 taking turns as the daily news anchor. I also took on designing the yearbook and organizing the robotics club.

The next few years were a blur of activity. I became active at church as a lector at the military chapel and volunteer baker for the church's feeding program. I joined the Association for Supervision and Curriculum Development (ASCD) and the international association for education, Phi Delta Kappa (PDK). I served as the president of PDK Tokyo for one year. Finally, I began my Doctor of Education program at The Philippine Women's University, majoring in Educational Management. I saw how the impact of my husband's work at his school, and I was inspired to follow him on this career path.

Dedicated to my work and my involvement in private organizations, I also wanted a way to maintain an excellent work-life balance. I recalled that in my growing up years in the Philippines, I was not athletic. I was asthmatic and hated sweating. Thus, my cardio was a 20-minute walk on the treadmill when I worked out at the gym. One day, I impulsively challenged myself to run 20 minutes on the treadmill without stopping.

That personal challenge soon bloomed into a lifelong love for running. I joined Yokota Striders, a local running club for runners of all speeds. Training for the spring 2009 Tokyo Marathon started in the winter of 2008. I was very proud to finish my first marathon with a time of 5 hours and 21 minutes. "Dig deep," "Get it done," and "Be comfortable in the uncomfortable" became the running mantras that I also adopted in my professional life as an educator.

After three years at Yokota East Elementary School, Richard received orders to be the high school principal at the American garrison in Seoul, Korea. It was time for another adventure.

Dare to Dream: Korea
2009. The H1N1 flu pandemic reached the shores of the Philippines. Michael Jackson's death shocked fans worldwide, and Barack Obama was inaugurated as the 44th president of the United States.

Korea was as enjoyable as Japan. We arrived in Seoul in the middle of summer. We found a beautiful apartment at the Trump Tower right by the winding Han River. While Richard settled into his new school, I started working at Seoul American Elementary School. With over a thousand students in grades K-5, it was one of the largest schools in the Department of Defense Education Activity (DoDEA).

DoDEA provided many professional development opportunities for its teachers and aspiring administrators. I attended summer workshops for teachers in Alabama and Iowa, meeting like-minded educators and sharing tips and experiences to improve our professional practices. I was fortunate to participate in a summer academy for aspiring administrators aboard the iconic Queen Mary ship hotel in Long Beach, California. Aside from my teaching responsibilities, I took on several after-school clubs. I ran the robotics club, running club, yearbook club, and the Dolphin News Network. In addition, I was the secretary for the School Advisory Committee.

During my time in Seoul, I received two awards: The General Walter L. Sharp Plaque of Appreciation in 2010 and Teacher of the Year for the Korea District in 2011. Moreover, I served as the president of PDK Seoul for one year, connecting with educators from DoDEA and international schools in Seoul.

I became a member of the Seoul Flyers; a running club made up of expatriates worldwide. The club had talented runners and made a strong presence in Korean races. Even though I was nowhere near as fast as our superstar members, I was happy to be connected to the club to learn from the seasoned runners. In Korea, I ran marathons more frequently and began dabbling in longer distances. I started with the 50K Korea Adventure Race and completed the Jeju 100K Asian Championships three times.

I continued studying to add more categories to my educator certificate. Things needed to change again. On a whim, I applied for the assistant principal position, and I got selected for the open position at CDR William C. McCool Elementary/Middle School in Guam. *Hafa dai*, Guam!

Rise to the Occasion: Guam

2011. The cultural phenomenon *Game of Thrones* premiered on HBO. Pope John Paul II was beatified after his death six years earlier. Suspected September 11 bombing mastermind Osama bin Laden was killed by U.S. Special Forces in Pakistan.

Richard was still working in Seoul. I was traveling to a new country to take on a new job. We talked about our plans for our future. We wanted to be together, but we knew I could not pass this promotion in Guam up. So we decided to live apart for a while and come together for the holidays.

Guam was the first time I was indeed on my own. It was a blessing that I came to this country to work for a principal who was married to another Filipina and knew Richard when they were administrators in Japan. I learned so much from the experiences he shared as a DoDEA teacher and administrator. Later, I would become an administrator at a DoDEA school in Belgium.

The responsibilities were different and more challenging. Instead of just dealing with my classroom parents, I was dealing with the parents of several hundred students. In Japan and Korea, we had the School Advisory Committees. Guam had the School Board that discussed policies and issues affecting all four DoDEA schools on the island. I developed an impervious attitude and did not let comments bother me when parents disagreed about my disciplinary approaches. I assured them I was fair and equitable in my interactions with students, staff members, and parents.

I loved living on my own, but I missed my husband. I returned to cycling again to help me feel connected to Richard, an avid cyclist. I joined the Guam Running Club and participated in their races. However, I was missing the marathon distances. Guam specialized in the shorter 5K and 10K races and only had two long-distance races: the 48.6 Mile Solo Run and the Guam Marathon. I flew to Saipan to do the 50K race at the Festival of Runs, finishing first in my age group.

Six months later, Richard submitted his retirement papers and joined me in Guam. It felt great to be a family again! However, the situation was now reversed: I supported him while we were in Japan, and now it was his turn to support me in Guam. With him by my side, I knew I could do more. My first principal retired, and the district office selected a new principal. In addition, it was our school accreditation year. I took the reins and led the school through accreditation, earning one of the highest reviews for DoDEA that year.

Three years on, we were ready for a change. I applied for principal positions in DoDEA. They offered me the principalship of Supreme Headquarters Allied Powers Europe (SHAPE) American Elementary School in Belgium. We were going to Europe, *oui!*

Whatever It Takes: Belgium

2014. Russia annexed Crimea and heightened tensions in neighboring Ukraine. Scotland voted to remain part of the United Kingdom. In the Philippines, the people were still reeling from the devastating damage of super typhoon Haiyan.

My hometown Tacloban City was ground zero of the devastation caused by the strongest typhoon ever to hit land in November 2013. Six months later, there was still no electricity and limited access to potable water. My sister and her husband organized a donation drive in Switzerland to benefit the students and staff of our JE Mondejar Computer College back home.

While doing everything we could to support my family and the school at home, we quietly moved halfway across the world. I would lead a school transitioning to a US$54-million facility, going through a major accreditation process, and receiving the Queen of Belgium all in the same year. I hit the ground running.

We opened the school to much fanfare with DoDEA Director Thomas Brady in attendance and the presence of more than 500 schoolchildren from 22 NATO countries and 12 Partnership for Peace Nations. We had one of the highest accreditation scores in the district.

Taking the Queen of Belgium around my school was a huge honor and one of the highlights of my career. Here I was, a Filipina educator in charge of the most prominent American school on a NATO base in Belgium and touring her Royal highness, Mathilde, Queen of the Belgians.

I opened the K–5th grade French immersion program in 2015, becoming the only school with this program in all of DoDEA. The students excelled in math and literacy. We followed the DoDEA College and Career Ready Standards (CCRS) on a European school calendar.

As one of 13 international schools on SHAPE, we worked with each other to provide our staff with professional learning opportunities during International Educators' Day. Students took study trips to Paris and Amsterdam. In addition, they participated in after-school clubs led by French, American, and Portuguese teachers.

Meanwhile, Richard and I drove all over Belgium, France, the Netherlands, and Germany to run marathons during the weekends. Because Belgium was in continental Europe, we had border-free access to other countries. We took the short flights to other European marathon destinations if we did not drive. I completed my 100th long-distance race with the 40e Schneider Electric Marathon de Paris in 2016 and my 200th with Zurich Marató Barcelona in 2019.

After five busy years in Belgium, it was time to move to another school again. I will be in a location where marathons and ultramarathons are as common as they come and in the same base where my husband was a music teacher 25 years prior. I was fortunate to receive orders for England where I finally shared the same country with a sibling after 20 years. RAF Feltwell, here we come!

Stay the Course: England

2019. The US House impeached President Donald Trump. Plastic-eating bacteria were discovered in Zambales, Philippines. Divisoria in Manila went through an extreme makeover, with its perpetually clogged streets now clear.

After a short summer break in the Philippines, Richard and I drove our cars from Mons in Belgium. Then, we took the Euro Tunnel from Calais in France to reach Dover in England. We found a house in Newmarket, a town famous for its million-pound racehorses, and settled into our local community. I became the president of FilAm UK, a local association for all nationalities with ties to or interests in the Philippines.

I started at my new school in August 2019, energized and ready to give it my all. However, we had to fly back home to Tacloban City less than two months later. My father was in a coma in the hospital and would pass away a week after we arrived. His death made me analyze my priorities in life. My mother was not getting any younger and now runs the college independently.

My mother has been the driving force behind JE Mondejar Computer College. I know she is waiting for one of her children to return and take the reins and grow this family legacy. We were all located in different parts of the world: my big sister and I in England, our brother in the Philippines, the younger brother in Australia, and the youngest sister in Switzerland. For me, I know that I will have to go back to the Philippines and help my mother one day soon.

I have continued my career as a school administrator of DoDEA, committed to doing whatever it takes to help our students succeed. I started the school breakfast program that January. When COVID-19 hit England two months later, schools shut down, and we went into remote learning. The school breakfast and lunch program continued to support our families. In 2020, we had COVID mitigation policies in place and welcomed most of our students back to brick-and-mortar learning, but a few families went with the virtual school. The following year, I opened the Sure Start program for our youngest learners.

The past two school years have been extremely challenging due to the COVID-19 pandemic. However, I am grateful that all stakeholders have worked together to make the learning environment stable and academically rigorous for all students.

The Way Forward

It is now 2022. Five years after Russia annexed Crimea, it invaded Ukraine and put the rest of the world on edge with the threat of a world war. Countries are learning to live with COVID-19 and its different mutations. The Philippines held the presidential elections in May with eight candidates vying for votes. In February, Filipino students returned to limited face-to-face classes in selected schools.

I lived in different countries and worked at many schools. This experience has taught me valuable lessons in life that can help anyone find their why in life, love, and work.

Learn things that make you happy and give you purpose. You are never too old to learn new things. I was already married when my husband taught me how to ride a bicycle and ski. I was 33 when I started as a teacher with DoDEA, 36 when I started running, and 37 when I received my doctorate degree. I became a level two French speaker to better understand the program I started at SHAPE as the principal. When you enjoy what you're learning, you feed your mind, nourish your soul, and nurture your future.

Becoming a principal is hard work with many rewards. Becoming a principal in an American school in a different country is even more challenging and more fulfilling. Be comfortable with being uncomfortable. Build relationships but have boundaries. Be ethical and driven by purpose. When you put student achievement as your goal, you will make the best-informed decisions for your school.

Maintain a work-life balance. Be guided by your vision and goals for your work but make time for family and self-care. Climbing the corporate ladder or prepping for the next promotion will be easier when you also take care of yourself. I took up running to relieve the stress of working on my dissertation. I returned to writing articles and stories again to cope with the restriction of movement due to COVID-19. I joined organizations to connect and learn from like-minded people in different professions and careers.

Let God guide you. Trust in your faith to help you achieve your dreams and goals in life but do your best to make things happen. I believe that God helps those who help themselves. On the other hand, expect detours in your life. You may face a lot of failures before you find success. You may have missed goals and opportunities.

Trust in your faith to get you through the rough patches. You ill sometimes question your purpose but trust in your strength. Give your best each time. Persevere. Show up to work every day. Learn. Observe the habits and behaviors of others who are successful. Work hard.

Most of all, do not lose sight of the goal. You will get there just as you planned, or how God intended it.

Disclaimer: The views presented in this article are those of the author and do not necessarily represent the views of the U.S. Department of Defense or its components.

CYNTHIA MANALO RAPAIDO, ED.D.

*Adjunct Faculty, Teacher Education Department at
California State University East Bay
High School Principal (Retired)
GLOBAL FWN100™ 2011*

From Military Brat to Educational Leader: A Filipina-American Journey

My Filipina Identity Development and Awareness

I am a second-generation Filipina American. My parents are of Filipino descent. They attended Cavite High School—my dad was class of 1953; my mom was class of 1955. After high school, my dad studied Nautical Studies, and in 1957, he joined the U.S. Navy in Sangley Point near Cavite City, Philippines. During that time, the United States still had military bases in the Philippines. In 1959, my mom graduated from the University of the East in Manila, Philippines, and married my dad in the same year.

I have three older sisters, a younger brother, and a younger sister. Because my dad was in the U.S. Navy, my family relocated to several different places; hence, my siblings and I were born in different locations. My oldest sister was born in the Philippines in 1959. Shortly after, my parents and one-year-old oldest sister immigrated to the United States. My second and third sisters were born in Stockton, California, (1961 and 1963 respectively); my younger brother and I were born in Long Beach, California (1967 and 1964 respectively); and my youngest sister was born in the Philippines in 1968.

When my dad was stationed for duty in Cavite City, Philippines (1968–1970), my siblings and I were fortunate to live near our extended family - my grandparents, aunties and uncles, and cousins. Therefore, when I reflect on my Filipino culture and values, I mainly learned them from my parents and being exposed to the culture and people when I lived in the Philippines. I have only been there three times in my lifetime:

- 1968–1970 (age 4–6, grades K and 1) when my dad was stationed there.
- 1974 (age 10, grade 6) when my dad retired from the U.S. We visited for one month.
- Summer of 1980 (age 16, grade 12): My maternal grandparents celebrated their 50th wedding anniversary, and I was there for two months

I attended five different elementary schools; three for first grade and two for 6th grade. In 1st grade, I was enrolled at John Paul Jones School, located in the U.S. Military Base in Sangley Point, Cavite City, Philippines. Classes were held in Quonset huts, and we were taught in English by White American teachers. After that, I attended Loma Verde Elementary School in San Diego, California, for one month; and then I completed my 1st grade at Mary Morrison Elementary School in Groton, Connecticut. Later, in the middle of the 6th grade school year, we moved again. I attended Jimel Academy in Caridad, Cavite City, Philippines for a month and then completed 6th grade at Finney Elementary School in San Diego, California.

Many of my classmates in Groton had fathers on the same submarine as my father. There was not much diversity at my elementary school. Nevertheless, we all got along as friends and classmates. There were not very many Filipinos; hence, my Filipino identity development was limited to my mom's cooking and some Filipino culture and traditions she instilled in my siblings and me. In Groton, there were no fences between the naval housing, so the children in the neighborhood shared common yards to play. It was a safe environment among Navy brats. Our yards were filled with huggable oak trees, roving grass hills, and big rocks that we could either lay on top of or climb. We could walk the rolling hills, slide down them on sleds during the winters, or make cardboard slides and slide down during the summers. As for neighbors, it was common for the fathers in the neighborhood to be out to sea for months at a time. I was used to adjusting, moving around, and making friends with new neighbors and classmates. This was the lifestyle I grew up with as a Navy brat.

In December 1974, my dad retired after serving in the U.S. Navy for 20 years. I was ten years old and in the middle of my 6th grade school year. My parents moved from Groton, and the family took a one-month vacation in the Philippines to visit family. I attended Jimel Academy, a private school in Caridad, Cavite City, Philippines. After vacationing, my family settled in San Diego. After my dad retired from the U.S. Navy, he started his second career in Civil Service. For the next 20 years, he worked on the military bases in San Diego as a purchasing agent for the naval ships.

Reflecting on my upbringing as a Navy brat, I had many positive lessons and experiences. I lived in and assimilated into the various micro and macro cultures of the Philippines, as well as the East and West Coast of the United States. I adapted, adjusted, and thrived. I met new people and made new friends of different backgrounds. Being raised amongst other Navy brats, I grew up appreciating and respecting the U.S. military and the people who sacrificed, protected, and served my country. I developed patriotism and a sense of pride. I was taught to value the country's commitment, honor, and respect. I sensed safety and community among military brats. I learned to be emotionally strong and to build positive relationships with family and friends. I understood hierarchy—as a Filipina daughter with older siblings and a daughter of a father who served in the U.S. Navy. The hierarchy system and respect for authority were a part of the lifestyle of the U.S. military. It was common to see others salute each other while on military bases. The only challenge for me as a military brat was that my dad would be away for long periods, and my siblings and I missed him. Nevertheless, his absence taught me to value the family as a unit.

When I look back at my formative years growing up as a 2nd generation Filipina- American, I had many positive and memorable experiences. I developed my own identity, academically, culturally, and socially. I was taught Filipino values to respect elders and respect people of authority. I was raised to respect my older sisters; my younger brother and sister were raised to respect me. I helped take care of my siblings. There was a pecking order and hierarchy system within my Filipino family upbringing. I understood accountability and responsibility. I understood family dependency and family reliance. I understood sacrifice. My parents moved thousands of miles away from their own families to make a better life for their children. My parents spoke to each other in Tagalog. They spoke to my siblings and me in English. My parents believed we would be better off speaking, reading, and writing in English. Therefore, I have very limited ability to speak, read, or write in the Tagalog language.

From 1975–78, I attended 7th – 9th grade at Montgomery Junior H.S. in San Diego. A diverse student population surrounded me. I was accustomed to adjusting as a part of my lifestyle growing up, but this felt more challenging because I was considered an "outsider." I was judged by how I dressed, how I danced, and the music I liked. To add to the challenges, it was also a period of peer pressure and "crab mentality." *Crab mentality* is a term used to describe people pulling down others, to prevent them from succeeding. The visual is of a large pot filled with live crabs that are trying to get out but are unable to get out because the other crabs below are pulling them down. I *looked* Filipina but did not act or talk like one. I had an East Coast accent. Unlike Filipino cultural norms, my communication style was frank and direct.

I enculturated to the dominant Filipino American microculture of San Diego. I adapted, adjusted, and thrived. I was actively involved in student government as the Publicity Commissioner. I listened less to Top 40 music and instead listened to soul music. I learned how to dance the cha-cha, which all Filipinos knew how to do. I learned to rephrase my comments to be more polite, not direct or offensive. I changed my clothing from bell bottom hip huggers to Levi's. My hippie-child mentality changed from "Flower Power '' and "Peace not War" to "Filipino Power" and "FLIP Power."

At the end of 9th grade, my parents bought a new house, and we moved again to a different neighborhood. A handful of my Filipino classmates with whom I was close also moved to the same area. We ended up at the same high school, which was predominantly White. But, again, I adapted, adjusted, and thrived.

From 1978–1981, I attended an affluent high school, Bonita Vista H.S., in Chula Vista. With the limited number of people of color students, I identified and socialized with them, very aware and proud to be a Person of Color. As for academics, I was invisible to the high school guidance counselor. Throughout my high school journey, I was never called in to speak to a counselor about post-high school plans. I thought going to college was automatic—like going from elementary to junior high or junior high to high school. I did not know I had to qualify with a decent GPA and SAT scores to get accepted into a 4-year college. I had no guidance as to which classes were required for college admission. One day, my cousin mentioned that I should apply through San Diego State University's Education Opportunity Program (EOP), a program for first-generation family members pursuing college in the U.S. Thank God I was admitted into SDSU via the EOP.

From 1981–1986, I went to SDSU and graduated with a B.S. degree in Biology and a minor in Spanish. During my junior year at SDSU, I was invited to and joined Andres Bonifacio Chapter (ABC) Samahan, a Filipino organization on campus. Initially, I did not want to be connected with them. My junior high school experience with Filipino Americans made me not want to associate with them and their crab mentality. Fortunately, through ABC Samahan, I had a positive experience and connected with other Filipino Americans. The Filipinos in this organization were supportive, friendly, and inclusive. As a result, I developed my Filipino identity. I held two officer positions: Cultural Coordinator and Academic Coordinator. During my undergrad, I worked part-time as Peer Advisor in the Student Outreach Services at SDSU. As a Peer Advisor, I provided academic guidance to targeted high school senior Students of Color and helped them navigate the education system for post-high school. It was the perfect position for me. The EOP program also invited me to be a mentor in their new program, Mentor-Mentee Program. I was matched up with two freshmen, Filipina students who were considering majoring in biology. I found my career passion—mentoring, teaching, and helping others navigate the school system. Once I graduated from SDSU, I decided to get a single-subject teaching credential in biology.

I adapted, adjusted, and thrived throughout my formative years from a teenager to a young adult. Although there were times I felt marginalized by other Filipinos—either I was too "white-washed" or too "into the Filipino-ness," I eventually developed a positive Filipino identity and embraced it. I stayed focused and determined and had my parents' and family's love and support.

Filipino Culture and Values: Barriers and Challenges as an Educator and Educational Leader

Some of the Filipino culture and values became barriers and challenges for me as a Filipina American woman educator and educational leader. For example, I had the following barriers and challenges:

1) In a hierarchical system, it was typical and expected of me to obey and listen to people of authority and not question authority. I did not try to reason or disagree. As a result, I had a hard time expressing myself. I lacked freedom of expression and critical thinking skills.

2) It was typical of me to rephrase what I wanted to say in a way that was not offensive or too direct. As a result, I became more polite and more non-direct. I became non-confrontational.

3) Growing up, at Filipino family gatherings, the adults sat at one table, and the younger ones sat at other tables away from the adults. Rarely did I have adult conversations, and if I did, I was always respectful by listening to them and answering their questions. It was not a two-way conversation. Being among other adults was a challenge to be visible or vocal as an adult.

4) Being a middle child, I was more collaborative and inclusive. I was a *Bayanihan* leader who led by uniting the whole team.

5) I have a growth mindset, but because of my cultural upbringing, I was also a pleaser—I wanted to make the other person happy or proud of me. I did not want to bring embarrassment or shame (*Hiya*) to myself or my family. Instead, I was humble (I was not *yabang*) and enjoyed the acknowledgment of being a good worker, "*Mabait*" or that I did a good job.

Awakening and Overcoming my Cultural Barriers and Mindsets

In 1987, I was 23 years old when I started my science teaching career. I taught for two years at Holtville H.S. (Imperial County), one year at James B. Flood Magnet School (San Mateo County), and six years at Leland H.S. (Santa Clara County). Although the student demographics at each of these schools were diverse, there were very few students of Filipino ancestry; I was the only Filipino American teacher at each site.

From 1995–1996, I pursued and earned a M.A. Degree in Organization and Leadership from University of San Francisco. In 1997, at 32, I accepted my only high school Assistant Principal (AP) position at San Mateo H.S. (San Mateo County). I oversaw many areas, including student services, student affairs (student government and athletics), attendance and discipline, campus safety and security, and statewide testing. Again, although the student demographics were diverse, I was the only Filipino American educational leader at my site and in the district throughout my 17 years (1997–2014).

From 2007–2011, I pursued and earned a Doctorate in Education in International and Multicultural Education from USF. In 2014, I became the lucky 13th principal and the first Filipina Principal of South San Francisco High School (San Mateo County), which had existed for over 100 years. For the first time, I saw other Filipino principals at the elementary and middle schools in the district! I served as principal for five years (2014–2019).

During my years as an A.P., I had three different principals I worked under. The first one, Mr. Charles Douglas, an African American male, was extremely patient with me. He took me under his wing, and walked me through my many responsibilities during my first three years as an A.P. The second one, Dr. Jacqueline (Jacquie) McEvoy, a White female, was confident, courageous, consistent, and fair. The third one, Ms. Yvonne Shiu, a Chinese American female, was inclusive, visible, and created a school community. All three were excellent mentors and role models with their unique leadership styles. In addition, they were knowledgeable and supportive leaders. Below are the big lessons I learned as I became an effective educational leader.

1) **Have patience when mentoring others. Teach them well.**

   Mr. Douglas (Charles) took the time to walk me through the many duties for which I was responsible. For example, he took me to various athletic events because I oversaw the athletic program. We sat in the bleachers and talked about far more than just athletics. He made sure I knew enough about each sport and the rules of the game, the athletic league, the training of coaches, sportsmanship, transportation, and security coverage at the athletic events. This information allowed me to make crucial decisions as I sat on the Board of Managers for the Athletic League, Athletic Boosters, Athletic Hall of Fame, and Grounds and Facilities meetings. As my role model, I emulated him and did the same for others.

2) **Temper the tendency to emphasize respect for elders or people older than myself.**

As a teacher, I did everything on my own—I wrote lesson plans, taught lessons, xeroxed worksheets, set up/breakdown labs, graded students' work, created tests, and entered their grades into the computer. I collaborated with my fellow teachers. When I transitioned from being a teacher to an A.P., I was not accustomed to having others do my work or delegating duties to others, especially adults older than me, or to do specific tasks for me that were also part of their job description. For example, it was uncomfortable to give my administrative assistant things to do for me, such as type up my memos, because she was older than me. In addition, it was awkward for me to ask the custodian, who was an older male, to set up the library for a meeting that evening. As a leader, it was important for me to overcome the Filipino overemphasis on respect for elders, especially in the workplace. It was more important to lead respectfully and to get the job done.

3) **Communicate directly. Use my voice to advocate for myself and state my thoughts or opinions.**

When Dr. McEvoy (Jacquie) was Principal, Rich and I had been working together as counterparts. I respected him because he was someone who trained me in the A.P. position; in fact, Charles and Rich were the ones who hired me initially. Rich had a reputation—he was known for his gruff, confrontational, and direct manner. Many staff members felt intimidated by him. One day, I went to my mailbox and saw a handwritten note from him in large writing. The note said, *"This is BULLSHIT! You need to communicate with me!"* I was offended and angry and I showed Jacquie the note. I told her I was upset about it. I thought reporting this to my boss was the right thing to do. I thought it was her responsibility to address my colleague.

On the contrary! She told me, *"Tell him how you feel about the note."* I felt the stress level rise inside my gut. I did not want to deal with him even though I wanted to tell him off. I rehearsed the conversation in my head over and over and knew I had to get the courage just to say what I had to say. He came looking for me in my office. He asked, *"Did you get my note??"* I responded, *"Yeah."* He said, *"Well?!"* I countered, *"I'm not going to respond to you when you use profanity like that. Talk to me if you want me to communicate!"* He remarked, *"I like it when you get angry! You need to do that more often!"* Basically, telling me to say what I need to say and be direct about it. Although I was nervous confronting him, I was able to address him—a tall, Italian male who admittedly loved confrontations. Jacquie empowered me to have a voice, and Rich reinforced me by giving me his respect and encouragement. That was a huge step to stand up for myself—from being a respectful, harmonious Filipina female to being a direct, courageous leader.

4) Overcome saving face. Say what I really want to say.

Jacquie taught me the phrase, *"We can agree to disagree."* That expression made sense whenever there was a disagreement or a difference of opinion or when someone wanted to persuade me to change a decision I had made, such as not suspending their child from school. With this phrase, I did not need to argue or debate.

5) Don't be intimidated by others, no matter their race, gender, size, or level of education.

I observed Jacquie when she dealt with difficult parents. She stood her ground, spoke confidently, and was fearless and brave. I admired that quality and learned from her leadership style. She was not worried when I told her an angry parent would appeal my suspension of their child. She responded, *"They can just take a number and get in line."* When I became principal, I remained calm and brave with confidence. I also used that exact phrase!

6) Be inclusive. Get to know the students, faculty, and staff. Build a school community.

During Mrs. Yvonne Shiu's first year as Principal, she would ask me the names of everyone. For example, she wanted to know the name of the parent walking down the hallway. Or the name of the student in student government or the students who hung out in the cafeteria. I remember I would respond, *"I don't know."* By the end of her first year, she had known many of the students! She made marginalized students feel welcomed and visible on campus. She created a school community by getting to know the students, faculty, and staff. She celebrated wins no matter how big or small they were.

As Principal, I did this, too. I knew all of my faculty and classified staff members by name- custodial and cafeteria crew, instructional aides, campus security - and many of my students and their parents. I attended many school events to watch the students perform in extra-curricular activities. I made an extra effort to connect with my school community, and by doing so, I fell in love with it, too.

7) **Build capacity. Allow the team to grow and not get pigeonholed.** When Yvonne reviewed the list of my duties, she asked me if there was anything on the list I wanted to trade or if there was another area I would like to do that was on the list of the A.P. of Curriculum and Instruction. One year, she assigned me to oversee the Statewide Standardized Testing. I did not have hands-on experience with Statewide Standardized Testing. That was a challenge and a huge learning curve for me. I had to learn the new computerized testing and other details such as creating a Bell schedule for the different grade levels, administering when and where the tests would be taken, and training teachers who would proctor the tests. Once I accomplished it, I greatly appreciated the process, from start to finish. Yvonne helped me grow by challenging me with the task and building capacity so that the leadership team fully understood the process. When I left my A.P. position and became a Principal, I worked with my new leadership team and built capacity by promoting their professional development and encouraging them to grow.

8) **Overcome placing too much emphasis on respect for people of higher positions. Overcome colonial mentality barriers.**
I noticed that my counterparts, my equals, stated or were outspoken in their thoughts and ideas. I was reluctant to speak up. I often was reticent

about sharing my thoughts and ideas. I would ask clarifying questions but rarely shared my ideas because I believed I was respectful to my superior by following orders, being compliant, and being harmonious. I would wait for my superior to ask me if I had anything to say or add. I was always the "respectful Filipina." I never disagreed or questioned their authority. I did this with my first and second bosses—Charles and Jacquie; However, once I started my doctoral studies and learned about colonization and the relationship between the colonizer and the colonized groups, I began to break down my cultural barriers. During my time with my third boss Yvonne, I stepped up and spoke up. I shared my ideas and broke down my colonial mentality barriers.

9) Overcome sexism barriers.

With Yvonne, there was a time the leadership team was an All-Women's team. People would make comments about the All-Women Leadership Team. They would question our abilities and make sexist remarks like, *"What are you going to do if there is a fight? Are you going to be able to break it up?"* Or, say inappropriate sexist comments such as, *"Here's Club Estrogen."* I first wondered about the dynamics of the All-Women Leadership Team. I asked myself, *"Are we going to be catty?"* *"Will we be able to run a school as an 'All Women's Team'?"* Yvonne brought out the best in all of us. She helped us empower ourselves. We were all smart, strong, confident, and competent. We were visible, consistent, and held ourselves and everyone else accountable. We were the only All-Women leadership team in the district, and our school became the school of choice for students to attend. She believed in all of us and our abilities to lead alongside her.

10) Stand up for what is right and just. No special privileges.

When I was Principal, a student came to my office to report that his teacher called him "an idiot" in front of the entire class. When I asked for the teacher to meet with me so I could hear her side of the story, she arrived with a CTA representative faculty member. During the meeting, she righteously admitted, *"The student was acting like an idiot, so I called him an idiot."* I responded, *"It is not appropriate to call any student any names—dumb, stupid, ugly, fat, ignorant...*" The CTA representative asked me, *"Could you write a list of names that teachers should not call students?"* I responded, *"Absolutely not! I will not create a list of words not to call students. You need to call the student by his name. That's it."* After that meeting, the teacher stopped calling students inappropriate names. I knew my purpose as the Principal: to serve the students. I stood my ground with confidence and with a moral compass. I quickly learned that to be a leader, I needed to be able to address the issues that came up, or no one else would. Otherwise, the staff would see this as either favoritism or lack of consistency.

RISING ABOVE AND TAKING OPPORTUNITIES AS AN EDUCATIONAL LEADER

During 2007–2011, I pursued a Doctor of Education degree with an emphasis in International and Multicultural Education. Throughout my dissertation journey, I had three incredible professors who were my mentors—Dr. Betty Taylor and Dr. Patricia Mitchell, both African American women; and Dr. Chris Thomas, a White male. Each one provided guidance, encouragement, support, and opportunities as I navigated higher education as a doctoral student, an educational leader, and later as a colleague. Below are lessons I learned as I navigated my way through leadership opportunities and into higher education.

1) **Be present and provide guidance and critical feedback.**

     Dr. Taylor, my advisor and dissertation Chairperson, advised many students. She was giving of her time, not just to me but to all of her doctoral students. She gave us her undivided attention, provided guidance and critical feedback, and showed interest and compassion. I, too, made sure I helped other doctoral students through their dissertation journey and was giving of my time.

2) **Be a Servant Leader—Offer opportunities and help others navigate and succeed.**

     Dr. Mitchell was the Department Chair of Organization and Leadership and a member of my dissertation committee. She was a servant leader and helped everyone along the way. She offered me many opportunities.

When I told her I aspired to teach classes at the university, she offered me opportunities to co-teach graduate and doctoral level courses with her during the summers. For many years in a row, we attended and presented scholarly work together at conferences. She invited me to write a chapter in her book, *"Lessons in Leadership: Tips for an Emerging P–20 Leader in the 21st Century."* My chapter is titled, "New and Aspiring Principal's To-Do List." Through her, I became aware of Servant Leadership. To pay it forward, I look for ways also to be a servant leader for others.

3) Network and be a leader of your professional organization.
While working full-time as an A.P. and a full-time doctoral student, I pushed myself to get involved and network with others. I joined the Graduate Student Association (GSA) to learn support systems through my academics. I became an officer (secretary, vice-president, and president). I networked with senior doctoral students and created network opportunities for other doctoral students.

Dr. Thomas, a professor of Educational Leadership Studies and the faculty advisor of the Graduate Student Association, provided me networking and leadership opportunities. He recommended that I get on the Board of the Association of California School Administrators (ACSA), Region 5, which served San Francisco and San Mateo Counties. Although I was a member of this association, it never crossed my mind to serve on the Board. Nevertheless, I followed his recommendation and became a Board member. Together, we served in different capacities on the Board. I learned a great deal about serving and representing educational leaders. I held many different leadership positions: Charter President, Members Services, President-Elect, President, Past-President, and President of the Secondary Education Council. Being on the Board gave me leadership responsibilities for other educational leaders in the region and in the State of California. My network went beyond my immediate district. I went to the State Capital during Legislative Action Days and spoke to State Assembly persons to advocate for public education policies and to discuss funding issues. I also served as State President of California of the National Association of Secondary School Principals (NASSP) and attended regional meetings to discuss education policies and best practices.

4) Give others visibility and voice.

Dr. Thomas taught me the phrase, *"It's not only important to have a place at the table but to have a voice at the table."* As a Principal, I valued the input of my leadership team. I gave each of them a place and a voice at the table. I valued them and their input. I wanted them to feel visible, recognized, and to lead alongside me. I did not want them just to observe and listen.

5) Surround myself with others I aspire to be like.

In 2013, I received the ACSA Secondary Co-Administrator of the Year Award from Region 5 and the State of California. In 2014, I received the Assistant Principal of the Year Award from NASSP. As the Assistant Principal of the Year, I went to Washington D.C. to represent California. I met and spoke with Senators Diane Feinstein, Barbara Boxer's staffer, and Congresswoman Jackie Speier. I advocated for public education. I was surrounded by the best of the best —the best Assistant Principals and Principals of the Year Awardees from their respective states. I met the Principal of Columbine H.S., the school in Colorado that had the mass shooting on campus by their own students. He shared how the traumatic incident affected his whole school community and shared the importance of community-building after such a traumatic incident. I met the Principal of a Mississippi high school that Hurricane Katrina had hit. It was his first year as a principal, and within weeks, his school was wiped out, students, families, staff, and teachers were displaced. He shared how he had difficulties trying to relocate his students and their families. He had demonstrated the perseverance to rebuild his school community.

In 2016, during my second year as a Principal, I was selected to represent the Principals from the State of California in Washington D.C. I met with the U.S. Department of Education Secretary John King to discuss education issues. Once again, I was among the best high school principals from their respective States. I wrote and submitted a White Paper titled, "Substitute Teacher Training, Recruitment, and Retention."

When I look back at the professional organizations in which I was involved, I took on many leadership positions. I surrounded myself with people smarter than me, where I brainstormed, networked, and learned from them. I championed students, advocated for public education, and voiced my concerns regarding education policies.

6) Break mental and cultural barriers.

During my dissertation journey, I became aware of the barriers and challenges of being a Filipina woman in educational leadership. I started to overcome these barriers that were placed upon me and what I placed on myself. I read books on leadership - how to be an effective principal, women in leadership, and women of color in leadership. It was important for me to develop my identity, skills, and strengths and to be the best I could be. I built capacity in my faculty, staff, and leadership team. I valued cultural synthesis. I had a growth mindset. I looked for ways to allow others to grow. I celebrated successes.

7) Embrace my identity as a Filipina woman educational leader.

I embraced my culture and my identity as a Filipina woman. I no longer have mixed feelings about my ethnic background or heritage. I value my Filipino values, and I lead with respect, integrity, inclusiveness, and collaboration. I am educated, culturally competent, and emotionally intelligent. I am a woman warrior and a "shero" for myself. I am proud of my identity—a Filipina woman, wife, daughter, sister, auntie, friend, and colleague who loves listening to music, dancing the cha cha, singing Karaoke, and playing the piano.

8) Broaden opportunities.

I continue to grow and broaden my opportunities. In 2019, at the age of 55, I retired from K–12 public education. However, my educational leadership journey continues with opportunities. I am currently an adjunct faculty member in the Teacher Education Department at CSU East Bay. I am a Field Supervisor and work with teacher candidates who are studying to obtain their teaching credentials. From 2020–2021, I was also a Dissertation Advisor at Edgewood College and advised my first doctoral student, a Filipina educational leader. Dr. Barb Buffington graduated Dec 2021. Her dissertation is titled, "Perceptions of Acculturation Among Filipino American Female Educational Leaders."

LEADING CHANGE:
ENTREPRENEUR

GEORGITTA "BENG" PIMENTEL PUYAT

Co-Founder & Chairman,
Philippine Orchard Corporation,
GLOBAL FWN100™ 2017

We Grow as We Sow

The story of our Puyat Farms in Tanay is almost as long as my fifty years of marriage, and like many good things, it began with an act of good faith and benevolence. My husband Alfonso "Jing" Puyat and I had just returned from our honeymoon, a wedding gift from Jing's parents, Senate President Gil J. Puyat and Eugenia Puyat, and Jing then just started his position at the Manila Bankers Life Insurance Corp. A few months into his job, Jing was approached by one of his employees, who was set to resign and emigrate to the United States. However, he was reluctant to leave without providing his daughters with financial security and the means to pay for their nursing school tuition. He approached Jing with a proposition to buy his land property, hoping that would be enough. Jing told him that he would help but he needed to talk to me first. After all, buying land is a big commitment, especially for a young couple about to become a family. We agreed that it would not hurt to buy the property, but we could not afford to give a lump sum. Eventually, we all decided that the 5.5 hectares of land in Tanay, Rizal would be sold to us sight unseen and to be paid in installments for five years. The employee agreed to the terms, content with the knowledge that his daughters were now provided for, and that he and his wife could migrate to the U.S.A. without too much worry.

Many would have questioned this decision, especially when you try to find the property's location before 2020 on any map. It was on forested, hilly ground with no access to proper roads. The only way to get there was a muddy track used by a farmer on the neighboring property. The price was not prohibitive because it was 1970, and the Philippine Peso was roughly equal to the U.S. Dollar in those days. Was it worth buying an inaccessible property on inconvenient terrain? Jing and I did not see it as a bad investment, but something to be set aside for a rainy day. We just never realized that rainy day would come how many decades later.

THERE'S NO BUSINESS LIKE THE AGRICULTURAL BUSINESS

In the intervening years leading up to the start of Puyat Farms, Jing and I each had our individual work focus, but we always banded together for any business that involved our family. They were forays into Banana Production (Tagum City, Davao), Mango Production (Cavite and South Cotabato), Rattan concessions for furniture-making, (Butuan City, Agusan del Norte), City Real Estate Development (Brentwood Realty and Development Corp), and the Puyat Fisheries, a Tilapia farming business based in Jala-Jala, Rizal. Throughout it all, we had our stalwart, the Philippine Orchard Corporation (Philor), the most enduring of the business endeavors that my husband and I worked on together. A family-owned company that we co-founded and established together in 1972, Philor's purpose was to create and to develop agricultural products and processes that aim to significantly increase productivity and yield, all the while being economical and straightforward in their instruction.

Why agriculture, you may ask? It seems so different from the volunteerism that I do and the insurance work of my husband. I spoke in the *Disrupt 3.0 Filipina Women: Rising Book* about my lifetime commitment to volunteerism and how my pioneer doctor father used to bring me along on his medical missions to the many corners of Cotabato, Mindanao, back in the 1950s when it was the biggest province in the Philippines. Together, we journeyed to the small townships and remote areas where the rural folks, the indigenous tribes, and the small farmers had settled and would need medical access. While my father would check them over their ailments, we would listen to them talk of their struggles and their daily practices, of how their fortunes would change depending on how good their crops were. Often, the medical services of my father were paid back with produce rather than money, and our dining table back at home would look like a feast of greens every time we came back from these missions. My knowledge of agriculture started from conversations with these farmers while Jing relied on his mother, Eugenia G. Puyat, one of the first CPAs in the Philippines and a farmer herself, to teach him early on in their property in Sta. Rosa.

Because of these regular medical missions, I decided that one of my earliest advocacies would support the empowerment of the agricultural sector and of the farmers, some of the poorest people in the Philippines. I believe that if we would provide the right tools and knowledge for our farmers, the Philippines can be sustainable and self-sufficient, not relying on importing our daily food staples from neighboring countries like Thailand, China, or Indonesia.

MAKING THE PARTNERSHIP WORK, HERE AND OVERSEAS

One of the reasons why Philippine Orchard Corporation works is because of our assigned roles in the company and that we do not limit ourselves, pursuing our interests in conjunction with the company. As the company President, Jing traveled all over the Philippines, and to some foreign countries, to visit farmers, see their own crops, and study their farm practices firsthand. In addition, he would use some of his time to experiment and create some of our products. I would run the day-to-day as Chairman and Treasurer, but I would also be the voice of reason, or of concern, depending on the situation. I took the reins of the business so that he could focus on the scientific side of Philor. I would occasionally join him on these visits to far-flung places all over the Philippines and the world. Trips like these are snippets of what the best Mother Nature can offer to the most industrious of people. I have seen many great world wonders in my time, but there is nothing like seeing all the greenery of the farms, forests, jungle, and the lush bounty of the earth in their natural setting. On one of these trips, I briefly got lost in the forest, admiring the flowers and the trees, while Jing talked to his partners in the Rattan Concessions. Our host found me quickly, but I will always be amazed at those wildflowers and their vibrant butterflies.

An excellent example of an agricultural farm visit overseas was when I accompanied Jing to an insurance conference in Tel Aviv, Israel in the early 1970s. Part of our travel itinerary to the Holy Land was an open invitation to visit a Kibbutz, a typically agricultural community that is found all over Israel. The Kibbutz was located in arid and sun-scorched area, with groves upon groves of orange trees growing from the rocky soil. Of course, you would wonder how hectares of trees would grow in such conditions, but we were shown how their state-of-the-art innovation, at that time, was being used to tend the oranges. Using a special system of pipes and computers, most of the irrigation and application of fertilizer were done through this automated system. It was a unique and eye-opening experience and it was easy to see why Israeli expertise was used to lay the irrigation system on our property in Sta. Rosa, Nueva Ecija.

STARTING OUR "FIRST" ORCHARD

People, typically new acquaintances, would ask me where our "Orchard" is. After all, it is in our company name. Essentially, it all began because of mangoes. Early in our careers, Jing and I joined a mango-producing business with rented property along Governor's Drive in Cavite. Visiting this place was wonderful to behold. Vast hectares of mango trees were neatly situated at measured distances from each other, so their branches barely touched. The hanging fruits were still green and abundant, and the air was a little hazy in the late afternoon. The workers picked the nearly ripe ones and placed them in baskets lined with newspaper. Each visit to Cavite was a chance at a family outing where our young boys would have the opportunity to run around. This place was the reason why we named our company Philippine Orchard Corporation, for the groves of mango trees- an orchard of fruit-bearing trees. It was a beautiful place but there was a problem needed to be addressed.

The Philippine Mango, or Carabao Mango, is a unique variety that requires external aid to induce the flowering of its own fruit. Traditionally, Philippine farmers would light fires and smoke the mango trees for 10–14 days and then wait for up to two weeks for the trees to flower and bear fruit. Seeing the process in action is very different from the hearsay of people. The smoke used on the trees was a health hazard for workers, and all that waiting around until afterwards was a waste of time. This was an in efficient and health-threatening process would take up to a month while the Indian and Thai varieties would flower naturally without help. This was why before the 1980s, the Philippines had no viable Mango Production Industry, despite the fruit being grown in many parts of the country, from Zambales down to Zamboanga.

My husband saw this as challenges to overcome and he set his knowledge to work. While he set about formulating the product that would put our company on the Philippine map, there would be a series of experiments which would be the method we would adhere to for our future manufactured goods. For some businesses to thrive, there should be a degree of experimentation to promote positive change. For us, it is indeed quite literal. Each of our agricultural products is thoroughly tested and tried, first on samples, and then out on the field in accredited testing areas with scientific observers and on volunteer farms that are asked to observe the same experiment parameters. Results that are found within the confines of a controlled environment could differ from actual results made by farmers. The experiments we made with the mango trees resulted in the creation of our original product Agri-Bloom (Now Miracle Bloom), an agricultural product that popularized a uniquely Philippine innovation- the chemical induction of the flowering of mangoes. All the time-consuming, hazardous work used in the traditional method was reduced to 15 mins of spraying onto the trees and waiting only a few days to see their flowering.

With our Agri-Bloom product as the catalyst, a new Philippine Agricultural Industry was created and steadily grew in strength, vastly increasing production volume by the 1990s. Today, the Philippine Mango is one of the country's biggest exports,with the Philippines ranked 7th in the world as of 2015, with Japan, Hong Kong, and the United States as our biggest trade partners. Despite growing international demands, most of our country's produce is sold locally, a testament to its popularity among Filipinos. The Carabao Mango may not be the biggest in size, but it is an exotic and sweet fruit that has been named 'The Sweetest Mango in the World' by the Guinness World Records in 1995. It has many edible uses, ranging from savory chutneys to delicious desserts. It is undisputedly our National Fruit. Without the innovation of Philor's first product, it would be difficult to imagine a scenario that does not recognize our mangoes as a world-class commodity.

Agri-Bloom was the cornerstone of Philippine Orchard Corporation; the one that started it all for us and the Philippine Mango Production Industry. However, our association with Mango Production did not last long. We had two seasons in Cavite and then three seasons in Gen. Santos City, South Cotabato before we decided to stop. In part it was because we lived in Manila and we had to rely on managers who worked for us. There were problems that we could not immediately address because of our lack of presence, like the uncontrollable stealing by the local populace and the unwelcomed advance of plant disease. Our involvement in Mango Production was at a loss, but the manufacturing of our agricultural goods gave us a way forward. We may not have those mango orchards anymore, but we placed it in our company's name as a reminder of how we started. Eventually, this would come back full circle.

LEARNING FROM OUR LOSSES

For Puyat Fisheries, we had an offshore bamboo stilt house in the middle of Laguna Lake from which we could watch over the fishnet pens and the blue waters. You could see the Sierra Madre Mountain Range spanning in the distance from the lake, which is significant for us in later years. Early hours in the lake house meant our workers lighting gas lanterns, going into the boats, and quickly hauling up the multitude of fish that will be brought to shore. By pre-dawn, the haul would have been sorted and sold to the fish sellers, then brought to various markets in and around Manila. Back then, the bank tellers would comment that the money we would deposit after such a harvest always smelled of fish and the wet market.

We often invited friends and relatives over for weekend day trips as it was such a unique experience that it was worth sharing, especially during those summer months when the wind and waters were calm, and meals was served with our freshly caught Tilapia and other local dishes. Among some of the great memories we experienced on the lake, the celebration of our 37th wedding anniversary with our closest friends and family. We had five wonderful years with Puyat Fisheries before we reluctantly had to close the business. The reasons were two-fold. The first was the sudden implementation of a law strictly regulating fishing within Laguna Lake. We tried to continue our operations after this, but the total devastation caused by two succeeding typhoons (Iliang and Loleng) that sealed the fate of Puyat Fisheries. The lake house and all the fishnet pens were totally swept away by the torrential rains and battering winds, leaving almost nothing but debris. To rebuild from scratch was daunting, and we agreed that it was best to take this loss and just move on.

This wonderful time period was immortalized in a poem by Luz Paredes Gaston, mother of noted UK-based portrait artist Rey Gaston, in her book *"In My Rocking Chair and Other Poems,"* reliving her experience visiting the lake house with Rey's family. A small snippet of the poem "A Fish Story" is as follows:

"On stilts relaxed the bamboo house
In the middle of a glassy lake
Fringed by the rolling hills around
Natural, permanent wind break.

Millions of aquatic vertebrates
Walled in by meshes white and blue,
Marauders, Human Sharks, KEEP OFF!
These pens do not belong to you.
Soft sheets of moonlight did I imagine,
That noon as we basked in the sun
Exquisite blue of the eastern sky
Yet pastel green the algae had done.

My memory dwells on things of joy,
In Jala-Jala I did enjoy,
When my soul's depth calls unto deep
And thus, I find myself asleep."

And then there was the outlier business that differed from our agricultural leanings, the Brentwood Realty and Development Corporation (Brentwood), another family-owned business. Through Brentwood, we developed one of the earliest condominium buildings to be built near the Ortigas Business Center back in the 1980s in an area now called Capital Commons. We built clinics and doctors' offices and bought properties for investment, some of which were sold to the government to relocate some of their executive offices. The best and the last of the properties we helped develop a small community of townhouses in Baguio City called Brentwood Village.

In my experience from those early years, farming for bananas, mangoes, and rattan were learning curve moments for us as optimistic expectations are often eclipsed by reality. From these early ventures, sometimes you must deem when it's time to move on and start something anew. Whether it be unmet expectations, an Act of God, or simply because it was not a good fit for you, your reasons must be valid through careful consideration and discussion if you are in a partnership. Whatever the case, the lessons you have learned are worth the experience and will eventually apply to any future endeavor.

INNOVATION MATTERS

Innovation matters in agriculture because there is a need to adapt to forces beyond the control of human beings, especially in these times of uncertainty. Overpopulation and Climate Change has forced us to seek new ways of farming to be futureproof and more sustainable. Aside from the extreme weather which the Philippines is unfortunate enough to regularly experience, there are other factors such as the soil losing its nutrients from overuse, the lack of available water, and the effect and solution versus sudden infestation. The truth is that the Philippines has the resources to be self-efficient and solve its problems. It would be easier if the government would actively pursue endeavors that promote and prioritize agriculture in the Philippines, much like how Thailand and Japan support their own programs. In time, I imagine that a future administration will be sympathetic toward the plight of our farmers and aim for modernization. Until then, it is up to the forward-thinking companies in the private sector like Philor to promote new technologies and innovations to ensure our country's future.

With Philor, we focused on manufacturing agricultural products and developed a series of products that would make us unique in the market. In the eighties, we have introduced our own line of fertilizers called Miracle Booster. In the 1990s, we introduced and reformulated a plant growth promoter called ANAA, which became the base of our more recent products. In the 2000s, the company shifted its focus towards rice production and created X-Rice, a silicon-based fertilizer enhancer used to increase the yield of rice. The results from experiments with X-rice proved the rice stalks to be stronger, weather-resilient, insect-proof, and produced more grains.

On April 13–14, 2005, Mr. Fernando Gabuyo, Jr., a prominent, multi-awarded farmer from Tondod, Nueva Ecija achieved a Philippine record yield of 332.5 cavans from one hectare of land. This yield was very close to the world record at the time in China, which was 17 tonnes per hectare. The Australian record was 16.8 tonnes or 336 cavans of rice. This record was done with a special hybrid rice variety and a collaboration with our company, using our scientifically tested protocols and applying our X-Rice product. The harvesting and threshing of the rice took two days and felt like a rice harvest festival. Witnessed by the locals and by agricultural VIPs, they applauded with amazement once all the rice was placed in 50 kg sacks as never in their life had they seen so much yield coming from one harvest. To this day, this monumental event is still a big source of pride for us, showing that our company's innovations and hard work have been recognized.

In recent years, Philor has specifically aimed to help farmers to greatly increase the productivity of their plants, such as rice, corn, sugarcane, cassava, mangoes, jackfruit, calamansi (Philippine Lime), dragon fruit, coffee, cacao, and tobacco. Farmers also use our products for flowering plants such as orchids, chrysanthemums; salad vegetables; fruiting vegetables, beans, etc. Our products reflect our willingness to address and solve the unique certain agricultural concerns. We made a product called XEMAS, a probiotic that creates on-site organic biologically friendly fertilizer out of last season's agricultural waste. This was our environmental and sustainable way of tackling the slash-and-burn practice in the Philippines and the rest of Southeast Asia. While the Clean Air Act deems open air burning of waste illegal, many farms still do this unsafe practice as they lack the knowledge to know otherwise. We also have two unique products that do not function as fertilizers but as catalysts and stimulants for plants to jumpstart their root absorption of the soil's nutrition, thereby increasing their growth and productivity. They are Power Grower Combo (a combination of ANAA and fertilizer 14-27-10), and Heavy Weight Tandem (a combination of ANAA and fertilizer 10-1-40), a product that increases the weight and sweetness of fruits and tubers. Lastly, we have Vibi Tall, a plant height enhancer that is very effective for Sugar Cane and other tall plants.

One of our biggest clients is a plantation in Bacolod that regularly uses our Vibi Tall product. Imagine our surprise when we visited one time near harvest time and saw the hectares upon hectares of sugar cane that are twice the height of the average Filipino. Much like the sensation of seeing the rice yield of Mr. Gabuyo, seeing the sugar cane soaring tall before us was immediately validating. On this trip we also visited another local farmer who used Power Grower Combo on his fruits and vegetables. The green vegetables were hearty-looking and the pumpkin gourds were unblemished and full of the brightest of orange flesh. However, it was the size of the bell peppers that amazed me as some were nearly the size of volleyballs.

Occasionally, we would receive an email or letter with an attached photo from some of our customers. The photos ranged from sky high sugar cane to abundant mangoes to large tobacco leaves hanging to dry. The most astonishing photo we've had seen to date is of a farmer and his wife, posing in front of a tree with over 50 huge jackfruits hanging off its branches. The photo, later featured in an agricultural magazine article, was noted have used our Heavy Weight Tandem product in its cultivation.

Like in many industries, women are rarely imagined as farmers and agricultural business owners. However, perhaps owing to forward-thinking or necessity, there are more Filipino Women than we think who are leading their own agribusiness, both small and large scale. An example would be the Cut Flower Orchid Farm of an old family friend, Edna Viterbo from Roxas City, Capiz, which she established out of her love of the beautiful Dendrobium Orchid. In 2014, Typhoon Yolanda rolled in and leveled her farm to the ground. What she could salvage of her precious orchids had a difficult time recovering using conventional cultivating means. Only though research did she discover what agricultural products we manufactured and promptly asked for our help. With a special protocol and the use of our Power Grower, her flowers rose from the devastation and bloomed again within 3 months.

FOCUS ON SUSTAINABILITY

In 2017 before flying to Toronto for the Filipina Leadership Global Summit, I was asked by Maria Beebe to talk about the SDG #12: Responsible Production and Consumption as she was heading a panel on the Sustainable Development

Goals. When I agreed to participate, I had to sit back and think about the topic. It was not as if I was unfamiliar with the SDGs, but I knew and focused more on SDG#5: Gender Equality because of my work with Zonta International. My research into SDG#12 was indeed aligned with the values of Philor and when I presented and showed how Philor and our products help contribute to SDG#12, I felt like more could have been said and discussed.

The Philippines is part of the globe where roughly half of the world's population lives within a 2,500 miles radius. Our location and the mounting population are only some of the reasons to why we have one of the biggest cultural diasporas now and why you can find a Filipino in every corner of the world. As such, we are all competing for resources that are rapidly depleting unless new alternatives are used.

Sustainability is more than a by-word in our modern dictionary. It is a real-life concern that even the highest levels of the world's governments are working to achieve. A simple reason why we must aim for sustainability is for our future, whether for our planet, our children, or our survival. By seeking out more sustainable, more environmentally friendly alternatives, we lessen the strain we put on the world. In Philor, part of our advocacy is to be part of the solution. By empowering those with the means to produce and manufacture resources that benefit humankind without harming the water we drink and swim in, the air we breathe, and the earth in which we grow and tend our animals, we change the cycle that binds us all. By supporting local, we support our own economy and become more discerning about what we consume, and waste much less in the process.

BEGINNING ANEW

When my lawyer son Noel resigned from his post with the government, it was at the request of my husband Jing because Philor was steadily expanding and we needed his expertise. For Noel, it was a relief because he no longer had the stressful, time-consuming working hours that took him away from his young family. While looking up at some of our paperwork, he was reminded of our two properties in Sta. Rosa, Nueva Ecija and in Tanay, Rizal. The first was a huge property on flat land that was sub-divided into leased plots and fishponds filled with tilapia. The latter was our hidden plot of land found on the foothills of the Sierra Madre Mountain Range.

The property in Sta. Rosa was not a mystery to us as we have been visiting it semi-regularly since Jing inherited it from his late mother. Sta. Rosa's first crops were rice, then had many decades of tilapia fish farming, until a change brought about by the pandemic that expanded its usage. Here, water management was never much of a concern because of the Israeli designed water system that continue to be used for irrigation despite being decades old by this point. Aside from our occasional use of a bit of hectarage for an experimental crop, the sub-divided plots were leased to other small farmers and tilapia fishermen.

Compared to Sta. Rosa, Tanay was unknown territory to all of us in the family. Tucked into the hills, the property was remote enough that we had no idea of the full topography or where were the physical boundaries or where the nearest water source was, despite knowing the boundaries on a map. In July 2019, Noel asked if he could have this property surveyed since it seemed that there was no lingering issue with the local government, despite us having not seen the property at all. This place would have remained nearly forgotten if it was not for us paying for the yearly real estate tax.

It was a series of good news and happy discoveries since then. We were told that the government planned to pave an access road towards the yet-to-be-built Kaliwa Dam, meaning the property could now be accessed more easily. Further exploration found the ground to be very fertile and there was an open water source as discovered by a waterfinder. The wild trees in the interior of the property had a decent variety from *guyabano* (soursop) to *chico* (naseberry or sapodilla). Because of the elevation, it was nice and breezy during most of the year. Furthermore, Tanay was starting to be a new day trip destination for the people of Manila, either to road trip with their families or to ride in groups with their motorcycles. This prompted the sudden building of new roadside restaurants and cafes that took advantage of the magnificent views of Laguna Lake and the Sierra Madre Mountains. Also, this was the place to try new outdoor activities such as nature trekking and glamping. It may have taken a few decades, but Tanay was now more than a rural retreat full of wilderness, but a small town on the cusp of nature tourism. There were long family discussions about what to do with the property and we decided that building a new farm would be the best decision. What was clear from the start was that we would only have one specialty crop, Dragon Fruit, owing to the terrain and the micro-climate of the area, and that other crops would be grown for seasonal and commercial purposes.

Once we had our groundbreaking with a Benedictine priest to bless the whole farm, it was full steam ahead in the construction. The main house and the first "storage" room was completed by Oct 2019. By this point, the most level part of the property was now tilled into rows and our dragon fruit seedlings were ready to be planted on the cleared-up hillside. The first of our greenhouses was erected as an incubation area for our seedlings and we terraced one area so we can farm using hydroponic methods. Finally, we were giving ourselves the room to experiment and grow.

PANDEMIC RESPONSE

Then on Thursday, March 12, 2020, the President of the Philippines announced that the country would close its territory and be placed in lockdown on March 15, 2020 because of the global onslaught of COVID-19. I remember this moment because our family was in Tanay for a long weekend, and we decided to return to Manila early the next day. We spent the next three days buying months' worth of groceries and other provisions because we had no idea at the time how long will all the restrictions last. One of the last people I met before the first day of lockdown was my FWN sister Benel Se Liban in the Makati Garden Club, when my eldest son called to tell me to go home.

During those first few months of the lockdown, it was next to impossible to go out of your home, especially as a Senior. We were lucky enough that Rizal Province was part of the Metro Manila restriction zone and we had access to regularly oversee the farm's limited construction being done by the hired on-site construction crew. At the same time, our Tanay workers tended to our very first crops of lettuce and *petchay* (Chinese cabbage). Eventually, in January 2021, our first harvest was ready for sale. Later on, we were offering a whole slew of crops like *kangkong* (water spinach), broccoli, cauliflower, red papaya, and herbs like tarragon, parsley, and peppermint. By the time my 52nd wedding anniversary came around, the travel restrictions around Manila were removed. We celebrated in Tanay with all of my family members, relishing our time together for the first since the lockdown was announced.

In the summer of 2021, we had our first crop of Dragon Fruit. Why Dragon Fruit? It is a high-worth cactus fruit with good nutritional value and can survive most conditions. Ours was unique as our scientific processes managed to easily attract the night pollinating bats and bees, and took to bloom half the time and bear fruit. We were pleasantly surprised that some of the Dragon Fruit harvested were larger than a baseball. The stakes on the hillside that support the climbing cactus of the Dragon Fruit may look strange from afar, but seeing the night-time harvest looked even stranger as our tireless workers picked them in the dark.

Because of the steady success of the Puyat Farms Tanay, we expanded a bit by planting rock melons, seminee variety watermelons, honeydew, and more papaya in Sta. Rosa in the vacated plots of our property. Soon we will be planting more fruit tree there, expanding our Orchard business.

We had an unconventional start to a produce-selling business. Our customers were people who lived within Makati, later expanding to further afield, who quarantined at home yet wanted available fresh fruits and vegetables. We communicated to them through a special Puyat Farms Community Viber Group that announced what would be offered on harvest day. It was farm-to-table, literally, as our truck would make the weekly trips to Tanay, and later to Sta. Rosa to pick up the week's yield. Word of mouth served us well as people would tell their friends, and our family friends soon wanted to try our produce, especially our fruits. It is difficult to see how business will be like when the world returns to some level of normal.

REFLECTIONS ON THE FUTURE

If there is a lesson I have learned during this pandemic, it is that we should never take anything for granted. You never know how life will be when a world-stopping event arrives. When a new opportunity comes to you, do not be afraid because you are not starting from scratch, you are beginning with a lifetime of experiences that will enhance your new venture. Our Puyat Farms is barely over two years in operation after a year of building, surprising to many of our more experienced friends with farms themselves. We may have been part of the few exceptions, but we still don't see ourselves as a success story yet. I am of the opinion that everything seems to go smoothly because of our previous experiences with mangoes, bananas, and other experimental crops that we have helped other farmers grow throughout the existence of our company Philor, as well as possessing the know-how from decades of scientific development.

The duality of my volunteerism and my family business of Philor co-exist peacefully within myself. Much like the crops of the farmers we help and support, you cultivate and give attention to your individual interests, so you will not suffer. However, the rewards you receive will not matter if you do not put in the work. In my volunteerism, it is to see firsthand the uplifting of women to be the best, empowered versions of themselves. In my work with Philor, it is to see poor farmers gain the financial and personal freedom that they earned with their hard work, given knowledge, and effective tools. Whatever the case, the main lesson we must learn is to be genuinely altruistic; by empowering others, you empower yourself.

Jing and I hope that the Puyat Farms and its foundation of agricultural innovation and sustainability will be the lasting legacy that we give to our children and the future generations. However, it is my personal hope that this will be a domino effect that will influence others to create a better collective future.

GINA MARIE GARCIA-ATIENZA

Chairman, SunStar Media Group
President, Java Pavilion
GLOBAL FWN100™ 2016

When the New Year Comes in October

Cebu City, Philippines, 31 December 2021.

It was nearing midnight when I finally woke up and looked out from the panoramic windows of our hilltop hotel accommodations overlooking the city of Cebu. It was New Year's Eve, a time for revelry, fireworks, and noise-making. A time for gratitude, hope, and welcoming 2022 as a new beginning.

Yet nothing but an ominous silence welcomed me that December night. I despaired over the deep darkness which blacked out my home city of 1 million inhabitants. I would have been partaking of a midnight meal with family by this time, I thought to myself. Enjoying a 180° view of glittering city lights and awed by the whimsical outlines of colorful exploding fireworks. It was New Year's Eve, after all.

Instead, two years of the unrelenting Corona Virus (COVID-19) pandemic and worldwide lockdowns left hundreds of thousands of Filipinos jobless and starving, only to be decimated by Super Typhoon Odette whose ferocity, the strongest ever to hit the Philippines, left them without a roof over their heads, homeless and starving.

As I continued to look out into the darkness from that tempered glass window, I felt bereft and incredibly sad. I could see the dying embers of a few sparklers lit by miscreants across the road, but other than that, it was simply the disquieting quiet and darkness that overshadowed me.

At that particular moment, a vivid memory of a distant past came back to mind, another New Year's Eve characterized by a deadly silence.

Jakarta, Indonesia, 31 December 1981.
The 1980s was a time of adventure and discovery for me. My husband and I were in our mid-twenties, and we found ourselves as first-time expatriates living on the exotic island of Java, Indonesia. He was on a diplomatic mission to the ASEAN Secretariat in the sleepy city of Jakarta. Yes, Jakarta was a sleepy city then, or a sleeping giant to be more precise.

On the eve of January 1, 1982, an expatriate friend who was single and alone in Singapore flew in to celebrate the New Year with us. Armed with party hats, blow horns, and other noise makers, we drove to the Jakarta Hilton, where we enjoyed a traditional Western buffet dinner, complete with balloons, hats, noise and all. By 11 pm, we slowly made our way out to make it to the house before midnight. An old Filipino tradition says a family must be together at home the second the clock strikes midnight so that you will be together as a family the rest of the year.

As we left the well-lighted major thoroughfare of Jalan Sudirman and turned into our residential village, I noticed the streets were dark and quiet. There was nary a squeak from the neighborhood cats, and all the house lights were off. Our neighbors were all asleep! But it's the New Year, I thought to myself.

My world turned upside down. It's THE New Year, I insisted inside my mind. How can they all be asleep? I clearly did not see nor understand what was going on. From infancy, I grew up knowing that December 31 is a day of celebration connected with a sense of gratitude and, always, with a sense of optimism and anticipation for a better year ahead. It was a given that the thunderous noise and blazing fireworks would drive out all evil spirits that could bring bad luck in the coming new year.

As bad luck would have it, we soon found out that my husband, he of the photographic memory, had forgotten and left the keys to our entrance doors inside the house! Almost midnight, it was too late to find a locksmith. So, there we were, three homesick souls from the Philippines, seated outside the main door, watching the minute hand of our wrist watches turn slowly towards the witching hour in a sea of silence. We looked at each other, and then, as the clock struck twelve, we defiantly, if a bit sheepishly, tooted a few play trumpets to drive 'them' bad luck spirits away. We found our way back inside the house but refrained from making any more noise. We were more afraid of waking up the spirits of our nearby neighbors, who could then report us to the Indonesian neighborhood police! A night spent in an Indonesian jail is definitely not on my list of good omens for any coming year.

I learned soon enough that Muslims follow a totally different calendar, known as the Hijri Islamic Calendar, for spiritual observances and Islamic religious celebrations. Muharram is the name of the first month in the Islamic calendar and Al-Hijra, or the Islamic New Year, starts on the first day of the month of Muharram. Since the calendar is based on the lunar cycle, the dates of the holy days are not fixed. It just so happened that going by the Christian Gregorian calendar of that year; the Islamic New Year fell on the 19 October 1982, A.D.

Unforgettable as being locked out of your own house on December 31, the impact of the unusual experience on me was more profound and personal. I saw that what I accepted as reality based on my experiences growing up was not necessarily the yardstick by which I could measure what is acceptable or unacceptable to others.

I was a global greenhorn in the 1980s, and I am glad that the experience happened when I was open enough to accept unfamiliar ways, unique and different from mine wholeheartedly. I learned to accept people having divergent perceptions of the same given situation. It is natural that people first read a situation based on their own experiences growing up, as I did when deciding when New Year's Eve should be. December 31, and it should be, well, raucous. But in a global world, a leader needs to see all sides of a given situation and accept that other sides are part and parcel of one and the same coin, diverse though the images may be. Accepting differing interpretations as valid is the first step toward creating global solutions.

Jakarta, 29 October 1984.

After that valuable lesson on adapting to a different culture, I moved on to enjoy life with friends in Jakarta. One of our favorite pastimes was strolling down a street called Jalan Surabaya, where several tradespeople sold antique wares at very reasonable prices. Here, I learned to appreciate works of art inspired by God-given creativity and fashioned by the work of human hands.

When I was in Jakarta for three years, I had a veritable collection of blue and white ceramics and antique teak furniture. My favorite was a large 19th-century opium bed with exquisite carvings and lacquered detailing that my husband and I found on the second floor of a dark antique shop.

The whole bed ate up more than half of our guest bedroom and was a good topic for conversation among our guests. Many would ask, "How are you taking this bed back to the Philippines with you?" The bed was enormous, and moving it around was no easy feat, a fact that finally came home to me on the evening of October 29, 1984.

Early evenings in South Jakarta, where many expatriates lived, were mainly tranquil and quiet. On a typical lazy late afternoon, I could hear the soft rustling of leaves from a large clove tree in front of our house. The balmy, languorous late afternoon atmosphere of sleepy Jakarta was perfect for a quick shut-eye before dinner.

This evening started as no different from others until we heard a deafening bang coming from outside, followed by high-pitched hissing and whistling sounds. We ran out to the front yard to check it out and saw missiles shooting up into the air and shrapnel raining down like fireworks. My husband immediately ran back into the house, while it took me some time to process what was happening. Were these fireworks gone awry, or was it something more sinister?

Within a few seconds, I saw in the distance what I thought was smoke coming up from the ground. The grey smoke went higher and higher, forming a giant mushroom cloud. I was too stunned to move from my position by the fence. The grey cloud expanded and changed to light orange. I looked around me and saw the darkening dusk turn into dawn. Everything was clear as day! A split second later, I heard a thunderous clap, and it was night again. What had just happened?

I ran back into the house, where my husband was already gathering essential items, passports, documents, car keys, and cash. "Gather what you need to bring," he said urgently. I understood immediately that we had to move away from this place where mushroom clouds thundered and hissing missiles rained down like innocuous raindrops.

I whipped through my closets; all I could take with me was a small collection of gold jewelry. Together with a few pieces of clothing, it went into one small hand-carry bag I could fit in the car. There was no time to assess what else we would bring: a fragile ceramic collection and an enormous century-old opium bed.

We decided to go to the Hilton Hotel in North Jakarta, where we had friends. As we drove out, we saw people running about in all directions, some with personal possessions wrapped in blankets balancing on top of their heads, others carrying bags of varying shapes and sizes. The area looked like a war zone, eerie in its similarity to photographs of the Vietnam war.

The lobby of the Jakarta Hilton looked no better. It was littered with small bags and hand luggage and packed with Ambassadors, Consuls, and all manner of expatriates, all asking each other what was going on. Was Jakarta under attack? By who? No one knew nor understood what was going on.

A long harrowing hour later, the government finally announced that the ammunition depot of an Indonesian military base in South Jakarta had blown up in a local fire. The raging fire reached the munitions arsenal of the military base, where hundreds of tons of bombs, grenades, mortar shells, and all types of explosives were stored. The ensuing explosions blew bombshells into random homes throughout the city and shattered glass windows in the South Jakarta neighborhood.

Much in the same way, I suppose, it blew into smithereens two large picture windows looking out into the garden from the living room of the house we lived in. Fortunately, nothing else was destroyed. The opium bed survived, as did the ceramic collection.

But that day in late October 1984 will forever stay fresh in my mind as the day I internalized the true meaning of the phrase "to let go." That was the day I realized that no matter how well laid out one's plans may be, they can all dematerialize in an instant. I now understand that "letting go" means giving up excessive attachment to material possessions, opium bed, and ceramics because they can be taken away at any time.

That day also taught me that "letting go" meant not only material attachments, but more importantly, I realized I also had to let go of disproportionate attachments to the pride of ownership and personal pride.

Letting go is particularly hard to do when it comes to giving up our home-grown biases and beliefs. It is even harder to let go of that feeling of personal entitlement to an achievement or a project carefully nurtured through the years. However, it is time to watch out when attachment to our personal biases and specific interests comes into play in our decision-making process. That is precisely when our projects and goals become blurred and our decisions compromised.

Another lesson the "ammunitions depot incident" taught me is that in life, one must make quick decisions under extraordinary circumstances. As a couple, my husband and I had to decide right then and there what to do when the bombs went off. Waiting for a diplomatic *Note Verbale* from the Ministry of Foreign Affairs announcing a Plan of Action would have been suicide.

There will always be instances in life where quick action and firm decisions are required of us, yet many of us loathe to do it. Many leadership decisions, especially in this fast-paced digital age, need quick thinking, a sense of urgency, and the stamina to follow through. The era of hemming and hawing and hoping that things will work themselves out is no longer an option. I tell my staff, *"When I say your assignment is short-term, I mean it is due this afternoon; when I say it's medium-term, it is due tomorrow, and when it is long-term, it means it's due next week."* Sometimes, they get a disbelieving, embarrassed laugh, but it gets my message across.

Faced with a potential "life or death" situation and making life-changing choices for a company, as many companies have had to do over the two years of the COVID-19 pandemic, require a sense of urgency, high standards of discipline, and a dogged persistence that will bring about the change that needs to be done.

A Lifetime of Change and New Beginnings.

Looking back at my life, I now see that Jakarta was just one in a series of moves in a lifetime of new beginnings.

I was born and lived the first 16 years of my life in the sunny, tropical island paradise of Cebu, Philippines. Then, in my 17th year, I was shipped off to the United States of America.

Don't get me wrong. It was with a heart brimming with excitement for new adventures that I flew off to the United States. I was enrolled in the 12th grade of Rancho Alamitos High School in Garden Grove, California, and lived with an American family through the American Field Service (AFS) Program.

For a Filipina teenager in the early 1970s, living in the United States with an American family was indeed a radical experience. I grew up in a small, conservative all-girls high school on a tiny island in the Pacific. I was thrown into a big American public high school in liberal, hippie, flower-power California where the in-house school druggie cum pusher, one in every high school, offered to sell me crystal meth. My American mother offered to give me birth control pills. Gasp!

But I was with a loving American family, and I cherish my memories of that gap year in California. California was where I learned to ride horses using a Western saddle, twirl on a balance beam in gym class, and chow down double cheese pizza with ice cold root beer in Shakey's. California will forever be in my mind as the place where my eyes first opened to a different culture and a world of change.

After finishing high school in California, my parents encouraged me to enroll at the Ateneo de Manila University in Loyola Heights. It was the first year the university turned co-educational, and they accepted a very limited number of women students. I was the only female accepted into the Economics Department. As a result, I would be the only girl seated in a room full of boys in most classes. It was quite a leap starting from an all-girls school to being the only girl in a classroom full of boys.

As it turned out, graduating from the Ateneo was simply another beginning of moving on and immersion in a new life experience.

By the late 1970s, I was in Europe on a scholarship at the International Institute of Social Studies (ISS) in Den Haag, The Netherlands. The Netherlands is well-known for its long tradition of liberalism, and it did not disappoint. Den Haag was where I got invited to attend my first Gay Wedding Recitation of Vows between a Dutch and a Filipino, although the vows were technically not legal then. They were both ecstatic and dapperly dressed in white suits, and we toasted them with lots of champagne, charcuterie, and cheese after the ceremony.

The women's liberation movement had gained momentum in the 70s, and ISS offered a course called "Women Studies" which perplexed me then. Why a special course on women? Discussions on colonialism, liberation movements, and the military-industrial complex were also common fodder in the lunch room.

I was exposed to a culture vastly different from North America in the Netherlands. A strong history of tradition and culture permeated every area of their lives. Yet, a certain grace and elegance emerged from their shared historical past. It was evident everywhere, whether in coffee shops or their homes. In their lifestyles. In their daily life.

Historical places and museums abound in Europe, and on long school holidays, my friends and I would take the train to visit other European cities. It was an education by itself.

But the most illuminating learning experience came from the international assemblage of students in ISS. I had classmates from Argentina, Burma, Colombia, Lebanon, Nigeria, Pakistan, Syria, and Canada. Talking and chatting with them daily was always interesting. Class discussions were sometimes fiery but always insightful. For example, I discussed the Middle East conflict with my Syrian classmate, who bristled angrily when talking about the war. My Lebanese classmate patiently explained Christian Orthodox beliefs to me. My Argentinian classmate would not stop talking about and extolling beef from Argentina. I asked him if his family owned a *"rancho de bovino"* in Argentina.

While in the United States, I learned to adjust to a new culture; in Europe, I learned to co-exist with people of vastly divergent beliefs, experiences, and personalities at odds with mine. Those were significant lessons that I learned by living them out daily.

Tokyo, Japan 1994.

I found myself once again at the cusp of another change in 1994. By this time, as you may recall, I was married, living in Jakarta, and raising two energetic young boys. My husband's tour of duty in Jakarta had ended, and he was assigned to the metropolitan city of Tokyo, Japan.

One of the biggest hurdles in moving from one country to another is the language problem. I am a naturally friendly person. I like chatting and getting to know people from all walks of life. But it is hard to make friends if one cannot communicate in the local language.

It was easy to learn the Indonesian language. I got myself an English to Indonesian Dictionary and spoke *Bahasa* Indonesia in no time. First, *Bahasa* Indonesia and Pilipino are both Malay languages, and there are many words with the same meaning, such as *payung, mahal, mura*. Secondly, both languages have similar sentence structures, and words are spelled out in the Roman alphabet, making them much easier to read and understand.

The Japanese language is a different matter. Because it is Japonic in origin, somewhere near the Korean peninsula, and has no Malay influence, it was impossible to study Japanese on my own. Moreover, one had to master three different types of script to read the written word: 1) *Kanji*, the logographic characters adopted from Chinese; 2) *Hiragana* is more syllabic, used for native words; and 3) *Katakana* used for foreign words.

And so, Japan is where I experienced being a true "illiterate" and learned a lot of humility. The very first time I entered a Japanese supermarket is a case in point. Initially, it was easy to choose from cuts of meat, bread, and rice, courtesy of see-through packaging, and pick up overpriced imported American food products labeled in English. However, when I got to the Laundry Section to look for liquid soap and fabric softener, it was all in Japanese. I could not distinguish one product from the other! I tried differentiating by looking at the pictures and illustrations, but they looked pretty much the same: depicting either a smiling lady or a stack of clean laundry! I went from aisle to aisle and realized I could not understand a thing if the items were in Japanese. Is this corn oil or olive oil? Mirin or sake? Sugar or salt? I left the supermarket frustrated with only half of the items on my list. It was a humbling experience.

I thought back to a housemaid we had in my youth whom we thoughtlessly labeled as "no read, no write". Well, I was that housemaid now. No read, no write. Talk about humbling experiences! I realized that I would have to learn to recognize some characters and memorize colors and pictographs like what an illiterate does.

I also committed to memory certain Japanese words and phrases, particularly those related to asking for directions. Eventually, I became a master at commuting on the railways and subways of Tokyo. I learned to drive and navigate through extremely narrow one-way back streets where one had to fold in the side mirrors to avoid hitting an electrical post or an oncoming car.

I learned to adjust to sudden earthquakes and live in a tiny house despite the office paying US$ 5,000 a month in rent. I had to adjust to paying US$25 for a small cup of cappuccino.

I even learned to love the sport and art of sumo wrestling. As a child, I watched several commercials making a parody of sumo wrestlers because of their humongous size and skimpy attire on the sumo stage. I found it hilarious!

While in Japan, I discovered that sumo wrestling, originally meant to entertain Shinto deities, is layered with ancient rituals, meanings, and traditions that are awesome to learn. The techniques of the sport require great strength and heft, yet at the same time call for agility and superior muscle control that could put a ballet danseur to shame. Becoming a *"rikishi"* or a certified sumo wrestler takes years of training and sacrifice. After watching and understanding sumo, I found a great respect for the sport and for the *"rikishis"* themselves. I am certainly not laughing now.

One cultural value I assimilated from Japan is the attitude of *"Ganbatte!"* It is a word of encouragement usually interpreted to mean "Good luck." But it has a more profound significance in Japanese, not easily translated into English. The words of encouragement carry with them the advice to "Stay strong. Don't give up. Put on a brave face. Persevere, even if it's tough."

When tough times come, I tell myself *"Ganbatte, Gina!"* Stay resilient and hang on despite the difficulty. Moving from one country to another may sound exciting, but it has its myriad challenges. Looking back, I now realize that living in a culture so different from mine engendered in me resiliency and toughness I did not know I had. Those characteristics helped me through challenging times. When the going gets tough, those are the times when it is good to bring out your strengths, to be resilient and not give up. As they say in Japan, *"Ganbatte kudasai!"*

In the end, I learned to love Tokyo, and, as many expatriates will tell you, it is a city that is so hard to say goodbye to. Tokyo is a city of contrasts that seamlessly blends the ancient and the modern. It is at once vibrant yet serene, cosmopolitan yet very Japanese. You have access to the latest, most sophisticated state-of-the-art technology and still find rest under 100-year-old gingko trees whose foliage turns gold in autumn and enjoy the splendor of pale pink cherry blossoms blanketing the city in spring.

Brunei Darussalam, 1998.

Having fallen in love with the sophisticated and effervescent city of Tokyo with its population of 7 million people in the 90s, imagine the shock adjustment I had to make when we moved to the mysterious Sultanate of Brunei Darussalam whose total population at that time was only 250,000 including non-residents staying on a working visa.

Eighty percent of the country is tropical rainforest, and a considerable percentage of its economic activity revolves around the oil and natural gas industry. Its capital, Bandar Seri Begawan (BSB), was rural compared to the cosmopolitan Tokyo I had come from. Retail and food outlets were limited. A handful of grocery stores and a couple of old-fashioned shopping bazaars reminiscent of the 1970s were popular with shoppers.

Language was not the problem this time since Malay and Bahasa Indonesia are very similar. The internal shock I had to contend with during this move was the complete change of pace. As a small country, BSB had a small expatriate community compared to larger metropolitan cities like Jakarta and Tokyo. It restricted the number of friends I could make and the social and civic activities I could participate in.

The slow pace was agonizing. I enjoyed the art exhibitions, museums, antique shops, and window shopping in Tokyo and Jakarta. They were a visual feast for my hungry eyes, and there was always something new to learn. There were none of those in Brunei Darussalam.

After I took my children to the International School in the morning, I had a whole day ahead of doing nothing much. So, I spent my mornings at the Royal Brunei Club, where I would swim a few laps, read a good book, and order samosas which I enjoyed for lunch. Then, a little past noon, I would pick up my children and still have nothing to do the rest of the day since we had a super-efficient Filipina *amah* who did the cooking and household chores. So, I would spend the rest of the afternoon in our study room putting together 1000–2000–piece jigsaw puzzles.

Technically there is nothing to complain about, given that lifestyle. I was exceptionally blessed by all standards. I am just stating it as it was and outlining the adjustments I needed to make due to loneliness and boredom. Again, resiliency and being able to accept things as they come became my saving grace.

And like in places past, I learned to love and appreciate the nuances of Bruneian culture and living in Brunei. I have wonderful memories of living "out of the box" in Brunei Darussalam. Attending Sultan Hassanal Bolkiah's Birthday Dinner at the Nurul Iman Palace, where the Dress Code was White. Luncheons and teas where the Dress Code was Black. White for nighttime, black for daytime. Driving down a two-lane highway ablaze with small fires and burning bushes along both sides of the road as a result of spontaneous combustion. This is forest country, after all. Wedding celebrations where my husband and I were ushered into separate reception rooms: one for men and one for women as per Islamic tradition. Late afternoons when we would see the Sultan driving himself past our house with no security cars ahead of him or behind him. He did have his personal bodyguard as his front seat passenger. Having picnic lunches underneath a thick canopy of green in cool rainforests where one must be sure to leave early so the daily downpour of afternoon rains will not drench you. It's called a rainforest because it rains practically every day.

These "out of the box" experiences can serve as dry runs for leaders who need to think out-of-the-box. Having lived through so many "out-of-the-box" experiences, I found it invaluable to my ability to judge and appreciate out-of-the box ideas that are much in demand in the digital era.

Coming Home, 2000.

The turn of the century marked my return from years of living abroad. Throughout those years, I also built a career of my own in corporate communications, working both in Jakarta and Tokyo. When I returned to Cebu, I helped out in the Sunstar Media Group, a family-owned news and content provider. My learnings and experiences abroad were crucial in the leadership roles I had to undertake back in the Philippines.

With other significant events in my life, I found that most, if not all, of the defining markers in my leadership journey were deeply connected to change and adaptation: whether abrupt or gradual, planned or unplanned, pleasant or unpleasant. I found that leadership is fraught with changes. People change. Situations change. Resiliency and the ability to face challenging work situations grew from simply being out in the field, taking on the challenges as they come, one by one, problem by problem, day by day, without losing heart or giving up.

The ability to think out of the box is a prerequisite. I am thankful for my relentless exposure to change and diversity in my younger days and that I embraced both with an open mind. Humility and the ability to recognize and let go of one's biases are invaluable when one has to make well-considered, fair, and sensible decisions.

My learning to adapt to change and new experiences involved immersion in different cultures in different countries. These were not simple summer vacations visiting Disneyland, 5-day familiarization tours, and rushing through European museums. Instead, I lived these experiences long-term.

These disruptions in life can rend and tear apart the very fabric of one's being, causing pain and insecurity that can sometimes make a woman question her abilities in a constantly changing world. Yet change and disruption are facts of life for Filipinas in the global diaspora. As more and more Filipina women leave the Philippines to live and work abroad, my experiences may strike a familiar or similar chord in their lives. They encounter ways and practices that may be alien to them and to their way of life. But these circumstances that DISRUPT the very fabric of a person's being are the same elements that can be transformed into qualities that can make one an outstanding Filipina in the worldwide diaspora. A woman with a global perspective. A woman who is analytical yet decisive. Who sees the necessity to be objective and embraces the importance of collaboration. A woman who is resilient and brave. A woman who has learned to be compassionate to people of different cultures and unconventional personalities. A woman who can accept that the New Year can indeed come in October for billions of other people in the world.

ILDEME "DEMEE" MAHINAY KOCH

CEO, DE MOI by DEMEE KOCH
Philanthropist
GLOBAL FWN100™ 2019

Beauty, Consciousness, and Leadership

When someone evolves and changes, others normally perceive some uncertainty, which usually results in criticism and disapproval. I compare my journey to a lotus that grows proud and luxuriant in the mud. Nothing affects it, and it does not let itself become dirty. The simplicity of the lotus leads us to a profound reflection: the difficulties it had going through the mud. However, create the suitable soil to blossom and live in its purest and most authentic manifestation. My evolution helped me to move forward at a steady speed with self-confidence, responsibility, and consciousness.

BEING A FILIPINA WOMAN LEADER

The paradigms of female leadership are affected by stereotypes, lights, and shadows, reconciling career and private life, prejudices, and unpleasant labels. It seems that the woman at the top is always an adjective—bossy, manipulator, decisive, bewitching, and crazy. The adjectives are seldom flattering. But the paradox is that there is a huge need for women's leadership at all levels, not just in the name of equity. Awareness is not enough to push for real change. Only when women stop being a minority can they influence the context. Women who changed the world never needed to show anything but their intelligence.

We need to reflect on the reasons things are done and on that sense of inadequacy, on how much money we spend, the people we work with and spend time with, the time we dedicate to our careers and families, and not because we like them but because they are an external diktat.

Reflecting on these things brings awareness. It is an empowerment discourse and gives a sense of personal power. The female presence makes the difference only when it is full-bodied. Because women can observe each other, reinforce each other, and act as models for each other. You empower yourself and start a movement of empowering women, initiating power and influence through talent and accomplishments, not just beauty and societal standards. We should eliminate judgment between women for us to tackle gender-based issues fully.

Some exceptional women make their way in masculine contexts, but we should not need exceptionality but normality. The idea that women must be perfect for filling roles of responsibility is not part of the solution but the problem. Women should not just be models of beauty and perfection. They do not need to be just flawless and unattainable but become game-changers capable of listening and enhancing the skills of others, accelerating leadership and empowerment of women.

The women of today carry power and great intelligence. They can forge and maintain relationships, have an awareness of their bodies, clearly know how to live in their bodies, and understand what is right and what is not right. They continue to flourish in their flowering path to self-care and self-love like flowers from the asphalt, spontaneous and rebellious.

This chapter discusses the challenges I had to overcome as a woman, a mother, and a serial entrepreneur. As a result, I have achieved success in business and personal growth in a society with a particular way of being a Filipina woman leader.

CHALLENGES AND SUCCESSES

Do You Think You Can Learn From Books?

We are most impressed by success stories in life. Why, on the other hand, is it necessary to discuss failures? Success and failure are relative concepts that do not always correspond with our judgments as outside observers. I mean, people try a hundred times before giving up, and I do not think they're failures. It is important to remember that there are life challenges, but not everyone accepts or is suited to high-level pressures. We often fail to consider the social, economic, and cultural contexts, as well as the contingencies that direct a career in one way or another. This context includes being in the right place at the right time, or vice versa, falling on the wrong path, or working with people who do not help us maximize our potential.

Because to get to the right place, to be heard or seen, one must first earn the right to be there and then have the authority to be heard. Success is earned through years of consistent hard work, vulnerability, failures, and seed planting. Staying true to oneself and having the courage to go against the grain is also essential. The ability to let go of one's ego and be sharp enough to listen to and learn from raw criticism from those who have earned their position.

Success stories are almost always focused on the individual. As if the person did everything by themselves, it's like a train that's moving too fast to see the scenery, whereas when you hear or read about less happy stories, you always end up pulling in what there is. In this sense, it is necessary to understand a story of failure, to break free from the tired rhetoric that we should go beyond our limits. My failures and slowdowns led to awareness. I could understand the reasons, and they became more helpful to my journey. It taught me to correct my mistakes, improve, and realize that my path was not a walk in the park.

A successful person's adversary is not their opponent but their personality. I do not want it to become a somewhat conservative message that one should not express one's personality or that there is a malaise within each of us that must be kept at bay. If someone has a problem with their life or work, I believe they have every right to express it and, more importantly, to act. Not to mention that many successful people, especially in the past, have had rebellious or even self-destructive personalities. I do not want the talent, the inspiration that a determined person can generate, the good they can do to people even by sharing their wisdom to be confused with the efficiency of those who always manage to achieve their goals through hard work.

I also had my fair share of many prejudices and rejections felt as an *"others are better than you," "you don't understand," "you don't belong here,"* and *"you stay behind"* as an immigrant woman from the Philippines. I wanted to change the beauty industry with the purest intentions and make people realize that brilliance has no race or gender.

We have to ask ourselves, what is the meaning of rejection? Let's all stop talking about rejection. We must give defeat a positive value, pause, and consider which decision is best for the future. We must stop instilling the myth of success in people. Above all, we must understand how to deal with failure because life will present us with setbacks and failures: you may lose your job, be abandoned by a loved one, or have your projects fail, but you must know how to move forward.

I have noticed that many people have a distorted view of success. This view does not surprise me because, even today, most schools and organizations reward those who do not make mistakes, instilling the notion that success is defined by avoiding mistakes. In life, success is measured by the "number of successful initiatives" rather than the "number of errors avoided." It's a tally that no one does. Suppose we grew up in environments that stigmatized and overemphasized error. In that case, we may believe those around us are intent on counting our mistakes and marking them in red or blue, depending on their severity. Few people keep track of it because it's complicated, exhausting, and uninteresting. To put it another way, no one cares about our failed attempts.

If you want to be successful, ask yourself, *"Have I had enough failures to be successful?"* In other words, be honest with yourself and ask if you've "experienced" the necessary failures or if you're just hoping you don't have to pay anything to succeed. If like many others, you are concerned when you encounter failures, I recommend changing your perspective. The failures you haven't had should concern you.

Feeling Powerless

There were many times I felt powerless. There was shame and anger over wrong decisions. I was disheartened by failure and paralyzed like a deer dazzled by the headlights. I had many of these episodes in my story that evolved, changed direction, and started over. I made attempts that did not go according to my hopes and forecasts. Sometimes I underestimated them and told myself, *"It wasn't my fault"* and *"Anyone would be wrong,"* or *"I did not think about them critically enough to draw the appropriate lessons."* Conversely, by dramatizing them, I ended up blaming myself and undermining my self-esteem without learning much. It is understandable to feel insecure after a failure. But understanding the fundamental role of my mistakes in my training helped me to acknowledge that if we do not accept failure, we end up creating an alternate world, suspended in time, in which failure has not yet manifested itself. We can still change the course of events. The limbo that is made of "ifs." *"If only I could make myself appreciated by other people;" "If I had managed to make myself more acceptable, more beautiful in front of others,"* etc. is as dangerous as quicksand: it sucks us in slowly and inexorably.

Sometimes, others "mark" us based on what they consider a failure: a failure in school, being unable to enter a particular university, not being chosen by a company, not having made a career, or being divorced. Those who do it may not realize that they can hurt us to the point of destroying our self-esteem. What we can do is defend ourselves by distancing ourselves from these people, arming ourselves with the right attitude, and remaining objective.

Before fear takes over, I try again and do something. Under no circumstances do I allow the fear of failure to stop me or to define my identity. I am so much more than my failures and successes, for that matter. I learned that failure is not only the price to pay but to learn and be successful. But also that success is built on failure that "opened my eyes" and, conversely, that failure, sometimes, comes from successes that, on the other hand, have blindfolded or blinded me.

Mistakes happen outside our comfort zone: if you have made a mistake, you have ventured or pushed yourself out. But, the exciting things and the real learning are there, so embrace them.

Or not, you've come to the right place. It meant having learned or, at least, understood something.

FLOWERS FROM THE ASPHALT

Flowers from the asphalt are spontaneous and rebellious. They flourish where they should not and sometimes falter, like us women in the company of fears, too many uncertainties, and everything unknown. Yet, step by step, we are flowers breaking the asphalt in defense of freedom, of peaceful rebellion in the name of ideals stronger than fear.

Becoming My Best Self

When I was still starting to reflect on how to evolve the best way, making an excellent personal development plan undoubtedly helped me express my potential and become the best possible version of myself. My goal was to push myself, not better than others, to the best version of myself according to my measure. I am convinced that women are how a new world can be built. A conscious woman can support her partner, children, and friends without getting caught up in the relationship or believing false security myths. When we are free of shame, judgment, and competition, we can shine without casting shadows on others and build a better world without relying on reflected light.

As human beings, we naturally tend to a kind of personal growth path; however, we often live in excess of fears, which slow us down and block our progress. This fear usually happens to us women because of a series of educational and social conditioning.

"What if we teach girls to be brave instead of perfect?" It is important to remember that women have been more penalized due to sociocultural factors in acquiring specific knowledge, such as those necessary for their essential inner well-being, developing their leadership, or managing their financial life.

Personal growth for me is discovering new territories and horizons and overcoming limits. I am not talking about trips around the world, but about journeys within ourselves. It is there that the most mysterious and vital "place" is found. That's where we have to go if we want to find happiness. Personal development is a topic that I am completely engrossed in. Developing our potential, and giving the best of ourselves, is our destiny, even if we get lost along the way in life's difficulties. Our purpose is tied to our dreams. Understanding who we are sometimes causes suffering, yet it is the best gift we can give ourselves. Because knowing how to accept the processes lead us to free ourselves from our conditioning, limitations, and fears.

I have often been plunged into many changes in a sometimes delicate way. In other cases, obligatory. From all these changes, I have learned that each time, I have been able to push myself beyond what I thought I could do, noting how much the limits of our minds can hinder our personal growth. To evolve, we have to get out of our comfort zone. Our comfort zone is our safe territory, where we are comfortable. Being in this area gives certain tranquility and even well-being at certain times. Now, with the passage of time and life, inevitable frustrations can arise, deriving from *"I regret not having done this"* or *"not having tried that."* We regret not having dared to risk more to get what we want and do not have in the present.

On the way to happiness, we are therefore destined to change certain aspects of our life from time to time: not necessarily make radical changes. But get out of that small comfort zone and allow ourselves to dare. If we always remain the same, we get stuck in the dark, but if we allow glimmers of change, light enters that will enable us to break the asphalt and grow.

Living in the Moment: Consciousness and Awareness

I would like to use the words of Eckhart Tolle, *"Working on one's state of consciousness is our primary responsibility."* Tolle's teachings are profound but straightforward to put into practice and have helped countless people worldwide find inner peace and greater satisfaction in their lives. An essential aspect of his theories is contained in the concept of transformation of consciousness, a spiritual awakening that forms the next step in human evolution. To achieve this transformation, it is necessary to transcend the state of awareness connected to our ego. Therefore, it is a prerequisite not only to attain personal happiness but also to end the violent endemic conflict afflicts our planet.

I always ask, is it necessary to wait for the answer by placing oneself in a condition of observation similar to that of a cat checking a mouse's den, waiting for its prey to come out? What happens is that, as long as we remain focused, no thought arises, giving a particular state of awareness that the background noise cancels the characteristic of the thoughts that crowds our minds. If applied daily by focusing on the present moment, this simple principle can wipe out many of the unnecessary thoughts and worries built by the oldest part of our potential mind, the one that has the task of protecting us from the dangers of the environment around us.

I have learned during my entrepreneurial journey not to resist life and to be in a state of grace, serenity, and lightness. This state no longer depends on whether things have to be in a certain way, positive or negative. At first, it seemed almost paradoxical to me. But when my inner dependence on form disappeared, the general conditions of my life, the outer forms, improved. The things, people, or situations I thought necessary for my happiness now come without struggle or effort, and I am free to enjoy and appreciate them as long as they last. Of course, they will all disappear; the cycles will come and go, but I started not to get addicted to them. As a result, I am no longer afraid of losing them. Even if sometimes I feel the weight on my shoulders and everything is about to collapse and shatter around me, I would continue to feel a deep inner core of peace. I may not be happy, but I am at peace.

Many people pursue happiness in the mistaken belief that once achieved, they will be delighted. But, surprisingly, once they have experienced a happy moment, they return in a relatively short period, feeling the need to seek out something new. As a result, without ever coming to an end, the dream of complete fulfillment perpetually moves into the future, never finding peace. Others, on the other hand, choose the path of serenity. A path is measured not by goals to be met but by an attitude that alters one's way of life and, at times, gives meaning to life. A serene person listens to, appreciates life's moments, whatever they may be, does not worry too much about the future, and lives in the present with gratitude.

Every aspect of our lives, like money, health, relationships, happiness, and every interaction with the world, helps us understand the hidden and yet untapped power within us, and this revelation will fill every area of our existence with happiness. First, we need to put aside our mind and the false self it created: our ego. Although the journey is full of challenges, we must make discoveries along the way, and that is to understand that we are not our minds. Most of the choices we make every day are not the result of conscious reflections but habits. And while they do not have much significance individually, habits greatly influence our health, work, economic situation, and happiness. Habits can be ignored, changed, replaced, or kept. Improving our life does not depend on our ability to face the difficulties we encounter with false positivity but on learning to recognize them. Once we embrace our fears, flaws, and uncertainties, we can begin to find the courage, responsibility, curiosity, and forgiveness we seek.

THE INVISIBLE POWER

Kindness, compassion, and love are words that sound very good but do not always have a good hold in a world where other qualities and values often prevail. In a society that encourages us to compete, to "climb the mountain of success," to accumulate goods, to the almost instantaneous consumption of every desire or appetite, to have and have more and more, there does not always seem to be room for these three qualities. It happens, however, when we reach these goals so much supported by our society, they turn out to be insufficient, which occurs when our eyes start looking for "something else." Indeed, beyond our insatiability and the consumption of all new products, there may be a more profound quest: to enjoy true happiness and alleviate our suffering and that of others.

Being Compassionate to Self and Others

The key, once again, is love. In this case, it is a specific type of love: that of compassion and self-compassion. Compassion prompts us to do something to contribute to the happiness of others. This is the true impulse, the invisible energy, and power that opens the door to states of greater tranquility, breadth, and depth of consciousness; that consciousness transcends the ego to reach a transpersonal state from which to establish an authentic empathy, from heart-to-heart.

How can we give others what we do not have or what is scarce in us? How can we be loving to others when we ignore love for ourselves? Undoubtedly, we must start "from within": our inner selves to investigate how much compassion or self-compassion we allow ourselves to express.

When faced with life challenges, I tend to be a little more strict or critical of myself. I examine my thoughts and behaviors in a way that can sometimes make me feel unworthy, ashamed, and frustrated. To move forward, I always tell myself, *"Demee, get over it."* For the intent to help me move forward in moments of emotional challenge. All the more, I realized that this mechanism could create an extraordinary amount of stress and become a hindrance to my ability to experience happiness.

Then I ask more questions and recalibrate. Do I allow myself to enjoy, rest, smile, and cry? Do I feel lucky for my body, family, and business? Do I feel worthy of what I have? Am I comfortable with myself? Fully recognizing myself helped me feel kindness and loving-kindness towards myself; this is who I am and what I am capable of giving, love. In general, I want little, very little. It is transmitted from generation to generation, from society to society. It is part of the great collective unconscious, perpetuating suffering over time.

If we want to alleviate our suffering, we should start investing in this little-frequented aspect: that of learning to love ourselves. This awareness helped me. By drawing attention to my true nature and recognizing it, I could discover all my potential, exercise compassion for myself in the first place, and expand it to my family, friends, and the rest of the world.

Loving acceptance of who we are and what we experience involves being kind to ourselves and understanding our emotions, feelings, and thoughts without losing the perspective of non-judgment and innocence. If we know and experience this reality in ourselves, it is easier to look at the other with empathy, as we are more similar than we think. When sustained attention and compassion are in tune, experiences of closeness and recognition of goodness arise in us and the other.

Strangers tease me and look at me with judgment. They insult me for no reason. They ask questions like, are those real? Do you have breast implants? These questions trigger pain. The emotional burden also became physical. It affected the way I dress up, the way I talk to people, and the way I look at myself. When I was in high school, I was bullied for my physical appearance, so much so that some days I preferred not to go to school. I used to hide from people, but I realized I am human, like everyone else. I was just blessed in a different way than other people. I was born with them. It is not my fault.

I have learned to accept it and developed a coping mechanism so that it would not affect me anymore. Acknowledging this does not mean being an inert observer. On the contrary, we can act motivated by the understanding that comes from careful observation. Acting can mean deciding and changing some aspects or not changing anything. In both, I took action. By looking at the problem in a particular way, I realized over time that it is not as immobile, rigid, or solid as it seemed.

Being Conscious

I noticed how I treated myself during those times, experiencing those negative emotions. I tried to rephrase my critical self-statements in a more positive and nurturing way. The new tone sounded more like a mentor or advocate than a critic or a judge. As I continued practicing methods of reframing critical thoughts into more nurturing self-talk, I discovered clues as to what I needed and wanted. Clarifying these needs helped me focus on where I want to go and what I am working toward. This attitude left me with a lot of strength, the power I can focus on to participate in all that life presents to me. I learned that I could emerge and take control of my existence. This invisible power allowed me to have a welcoming gaze toward everyday obstacles. These obstacles are converted by consciousness into a genuine source of growth and an opportunity for continuous improvement.

Consciousness allows us to be in situations and circumstances where we feel the pain brought on by experiences. In this sense, the intensity is subjective, but the experience is genuine. The practice of "letting go" of the mental elaborations that go with pain frees us from limiting the pollution caused by distorted thoughts, future predictions, and painful memories of experiences. Letting go does not mean we stop observing whether we can really do something about that pain and act accordingly, but evaluate and change the question. Why does it hurt me? What is the function of that pain? In this way, we observe an imbalance, a need that must be expressed; and we drag ourselves towards a resolution or equilibrium from a calmer, more serene, lucid, and compassionate accepting attitude.

Instead, we should ask what is causing the pain of this experience. What can I learn? What are the positive sides of this situation? It would be implausible to be able to live by reminding ourselves of everything that has to happen to us. Do not forget that we have free will and that everyone is free to do or not do what they planned before they were born. And if we do not, we will accomplish what is right for us elsewhere, in another way, while continuing to learn and evolve. Free will acts on space and time, on when and how, but it cannot prevent destiny from being changed. The power is ours.

SYNCHRONICITY: THINGS HAPPEN WHEN THEY MUST

Coincidence is a very personal experience. To live it fully and be able to appreciate its message, it would be better to keep it to yourself. But this, as we know, is very difficult. The human soul is led to confide, tell, and amaze. But be careful in choosing your people because envy and ignorance reign supreme in this world. People who listen to you seem amused and interested but could hide envy that leads them to gossip or laugh at you behind your back. When you are the main character of an unexpected synchronic event, thank the universe for the gift you received and make it intimately yours. Sometimes it can be so intimate that it takes on a mystical aspect.

I choose my people well. I cannot force the birth of a friendship simply because I feel alone and bewildered in a new city, nor look for it at all costs, thus risking coming into contact with people who are wrong and in whom I place, despite everything, false hopes. Changes often frighten and threaten our balance. A part of me remains fond of what I was before. When I moved to Switzerland, there were times when I wanted to bring into the present people and events from my past. Along the way, I realized that as people grow, they change, and situations also change simultaneously. Rather than "finding" myself, I tried to "find" that new part of me who knows to adapt to the times. Let me be clear: the past is part of us, and thanks to it, we have achieved specific goals. We cannot deny our past; we should keep its memories and teachings. However, the desire to relive past situations and emotions must be a choice and not a constraint dictated by laziness, and a routine one does not dare to abandon. Positive coincidences happen when we are truly ready for change and when, even without knowing it, we are moving in the right direction to build our future.

Positive Coincidences

There is a 50 percent chance that two people will celebrate their birthday on the same day. A very high percentage if we think about how rare it can be in life to meet a person with the exact birthdate as us, at least the day or month. I have met fantastic souls on my entrepreneurial journey who also happen to be my birthday twins. Talk about synchronicity and connections. But there is more to it than just the universe communicating with me, or is it the law of attraction telling me somehow that I can align with the universe and draw feedback from it? It has happened to all of us at least once in our lives to talk about a particular person, or simply think about it, and then meet them "by chance" shortly after. We live constantly surrounded by these synchronicities, but we only notice some of them because our subconscious makes a natural selection of what we think is relevant or not. These people have made a significant impact on my life. They are people who came to remind me of something important. They evoked inherent knowledge and helped me bring it to the surface. These people remain linked to me for eternity. But some people came to shake my reality. Even negativity has its purpose, making me grow. The universe knows what I can handle and what is best for me.

It is therefore vital to have a clear understanding of what we want, making light and order among the clouds of thoughts and thus remaining in resonance with what surrounds us, to manifest and recognize the relevant synchronicities to improve our life. Our reality is studded with "significant coincidences," and if we do not see or hear them, our world has conditioned us to such an extent that it has allowed our ego to dominate our lives. As Deepak Chopra would say, *"The more attention we give to coincidences, the more often they appear to us, and therefore the greater our ability to read the messages they send us about the direction to give to our earthly journey."* Discovering synchronicities in our lives surprises us, putting us in contact with another reality we are unaware of on ordinary days. Ethereal reality. The coincidences are signs that put us back on track to continue on the path of awareness and evolution.

My cosmeceutical business results from more than two decades of sweat, blood, and tears. What gave me the idea of creating something to change people's lives? I remember when I had to step in to help a cancer survivor who needed eyelash extensions because an employee called in sick. The client burst into tears after seeing her transformation. From then on, I became obsessed with finding a product that would address the risks, which included eye irritation and temporary lash loss. I saw the business potential of eyelash extensions and the potential stumbling blocks. This idea came after I operated a grooming salon which became a one-stop lounge offering high-level pampering services in Switzerland. Altogether, my businesses are the results of my experience in understanding clients. I take pride in what I have done and the people I have crossed paths with who have led me to where I am now.

A MOTHER'S PROWESS:
BETWEEN FAMILY AND BEING A CEO

Society, culture, and traditions dictate what a woman must do to be a good mother. Being the CEO of a global cosmeceutical company, I arrive at the office in the morning with great authority. The same is true in my family. I am a mother and manager of the house. I may never be the perfect mother I want to be, but I know I am precisely the mother my children need. In my heart, I know I am giving it my all. Still, other people think that the ideal mother is the one who keeps the house clean and tidy, cooks elaborate meals several times a day, educates children to obey, and teaches them good manners at all costs. An ideal mother takes care of all family members' physical, social, and emotional needs with a smile on her face and does it without complaining.

Being the Mother My Children Need

As mothers, we want everything to be perfect at all costs. But this inevitably leads to accumulating a series of frustrations. Moreover, we are so focused on this goal that we forget to be happy, the only thing that is important for the well-being of our children. Despite our superpowers as mothers, the model of a good wife and mother is now being increasingly questioned. We are reaching the unrealistic ideals imposed by society. We should not recognize ourselves in this stereotype and be allowed to be imperfect. We have the right to be tired and stressed from work, take some time off, and play down when possible to bring everything back to the proper perspective. Sometimes we need to focus only on ourselves, give ourselves small moments of relaxation, and realize that perfection is not the goal, but being happy is.

Many people ask me: *"You have your own company, you have employees, and you have two children, you travel a lot and take off other businesses, do philanthropic activities. How do you manage it all?"* It is impossible to manage everything! Without the help of so many people, my husband, my business partners, my employees, and my friends, it would not be entirely possible. I believe that any person who says otherwise is not telling the truth. It is a continuous juggling game, but there must not be a choice between my children and my career. I choose both.

I consider myself a domestic diva. When I was starting my cosmeceutical company, I had to breastfeed my youngest son and work till the wee hours of the morning just to get things done.

I also had to ensure that my other son was well cared for. I admit that I went through so much, but it made me even stronger as I know my sacrifices will pay off.

Being a Successful CEO

The concept of a career is very different from woman to woman, and for some, it can mean a leadership position within their organization. For others, it can be a middle management position or project responsibility. The important thing is not to give it up without fighting. If you have invested energy, resources, and time to make a professional dream come true, it does not have to end because you have to fulfill your role as a mother.

The word career gives the idea of the road, of a path to take. Who said it had to be linear and fast? Sometimes, the most beautiful itineraries are the panoramic ones: longer, occasionally dangerous, but without a doubt, they are the ones that give the most satisfaction. Nobody says it's easy, or you don't have to work hard, but why give up? Please do not wait for the time when you have to grit your teeth and regret it.

Being a mother of two amazing boys, I have become aware of many skills I have acquired through motherhood that I have applied to my business. These skills range from the ability to delegate, time optimization, managing conflicts, emotional intelligence, and understanding the people around me. As a mother, I always believe I can do many things simply by using my experience. As a woman and as a professional, in moments of exhaustion, I am also the person who tells herself, *"Demee, you can do it."* Being a mom isn't all I am. Pursuing my entrepreneurial dream does not mean I am being a bad mom. It just means I can add another feather to my cap: being a successful CEO and a great mother.

I would like to have more time to spend with my sons or dedicate myself, but having a demanding job leads me to value time more. It is acceptable that the house will be messy, the fridge empty, and that dinner will be burning while the phone rings and the children scream. When you have little time, deciding to make the most of every available minute is even more critical. Maybe I am wrong, but having little time helps to live the moment with greater intensity. Knowing how to bring conscious attention to the here and now. An empty glass cannot quench anyone's thirst. So we must do ourselves, our husbands, and kids a favor by taking some time for ourselves. We are not selfish. We are human, and we need to preserve our sanity.

MARIA FIDES BALITA

Financial Professional
GLOBAL FWN100™ 2019

Trust Your Inner GPS.

You are the driver of your own career. Know and plan your destination. But trust your inner GPS when it asks you for a re-route. Seventeen years ago, I was at an internal audit associate training in Chicago. Our trainer used the analogy that being an effective auditor is like being the driver: as you hold the steering wheel, you need four things: know the driving rules (audit procedures), know how to drive (audit skills), use the "Global Positioning System" (GPS) to navigate for directions (supervision), and you need to have a driver's license (relevant certification). This message made a significant impact on me, and had since taken that analogy to guide me as I tread my career with various certified public accounting (CPA) firms.

My New Beginnings.
My leadership journey has had several new beginnings. I started my career as a staff auditor at the largest CPA firm in the Philippines for six months and then worked for one of the largest banks for ten years. At that time, the Treasury Group – Operations Unit hired accounting staff with audit experience, and I

was hired for investment transactions. I also became part of a sub-unit where my audit experience became helpful. I had the privilege of working with high-level bank professionals, and that experience helped me learn to see things from a 30,000-foot level perspective. I then participated in the Branch Banking Management Training Program, which then allowed me to learn about retail banking. We were trained on every technical aspect of branch operations, such as cashiering, investments, loans, and customer service while simultaneously being trained on leadership. I worked my way up to the Branch Operations Officer position.

However, it was a whole new chapter of my life when I got married and went to Chicago. I remember we flew on December 28, 1999, so we could be in the United States before 1/1/00 (January 1, 2000) to avoid the "Y2K millennium bug" that the technology experts were configuring in preparation for Y2K (year 2000). It was overwhelming, from the hot Philippines climate to Chicago's cold weather with an average snowfall of 38 inches a year. I learned to adapt.

As I was starting my life in Chicago, I did not know my inner GPS would redirect me to my new destination as an auditor for the next 21 years. I was looking for job options and could not find one as a banker. By fate, my six months of audit experience at that large CPA firm in Manila helped me get a job as a Staff Auditor at a Filipino-owned CPA firm. I found it comforting that my co-workers were Filipinos, mostly CPAs with audit backgrounds. I have gained long-time friends, our second family away from home. I was grateful for the opportunity to have a place to start a professional career in the United States.

Since I had a very short audit experience in the Philippines, my career was back to square one. First, I reviewed and passed the CPA exam in the State of Illinois. Next, I had to equip myself with technical skills in audit and accounting standards. I had been blessed with peers, supervisors, and leaders who trained me to develop technical audit skills such as making tickmarks, organizing workpapers, learning Single Audit, compliance, getting appropriate certifications, preparing reports, and drafting audit findings. Through the years, I was blessed to have been involved in engagements across industries such as federal, state, and local governments, lottery, gaming, transportation, universities, not-for-profit, pension, and 401(k) plans. I worked for global accounting firms and Filipino-owned accounting firms in Chicago. I had been in various roles: staff auditor, senior, manager, and partner.

In my U.S. career, I worked for four different CPA firms. Each change in firm was always a BIG new beginning, and being BOLD and brave to the re-routing directed by my inner GPS. I have always looked far forward. As Steven Covey stated, *"begin with the end in mind."* My journey as an auditor has its ups and downs, too. Through the years, I have learned not to see setbacks as failures. Looking back, they were all just opportunities to take the next step toward the next ladder of accomplishment. I would, of course, give in sometimes to moments of sadness each time I have a setback, disappointment, or encounter negativity. And while I call these humility moments, I learned that no one would do it for you if you did not force yourself to rise back up. I learned to reach out, seek mentors, and refocus on my why and purpose. I push myself to find the motivation, courage, and inspiration to move on.

Taking the Leap.

Twelve years in my career as an auditor in the U.S., I joined a CPA firm three months after three Filipina siblings founded it. Two founders were my supervisors in my first job as an auditor in Chicago. At my interview, I expressed my intent to join not as an employee, but as a part-owner. I have learned to love what I do as an auditor; however, I needed the flexibility to handle only local clients until my three children were older. The three founding partners honored that request. I created a personal vision, business plan, and goals. Flexibility was enough for me to take the leap.

I brought to the table my experience and established the internal audit consulting services and employee benefit plan audit practice. And at the 2019 Chicago Institute of Internal Auditors Annual Conference, the firm was one of the gold sponsors, alongside large Internal Audit & Advisory Consulting firms. Being the only Filipino firm in the Conference Sponsors' Hall was indeed a proud moment.

Another meaningful part of my job was my involvement in hiring and recruitment. The firm hired U.S. and Philippines employees. The Philippines hiring process involved learning the immigration compliance requirements and working with immigration attorneys. It also involved handling the firm's employer accreditation with the Philippine Overseas Employment Administration (POEA), engaging a recruiting agency in the Philippines as required by the POEA, coordinating with the Embassy of the Philippines in the

United States for employer's paperwork, and handling the interview process. The firm receives many applications through the agency or referrals, and selecting the top applicants involves filtering resumes, reading their qualifications, and setting up interviews. But ultimately, from among those we filed for a petition, only the USCIS will determine who will get a working visa.

Although the hiring process was a long and challenging process, the times I welcomed an employee at the Chicago O'Hare Airport gave me goosebumps. At Terminal 5 (International Arrivals), I, and a few other staff, would stand right in front of Door B, and eagerly wait as international passengers come out. Each time the door opens, I would peek to see if the new employees were among the arriving passengers. And once I recognize them, my heart leaps with excitement. They are looking forward to a new life with their two suitcases, a carry-on, and a personal item. We will let them take a picture by the wall that says "Welcome to Chicago". Then, I would take a picture with the welcome group and update the other partners. I also let the Philippines recruiting agency know that the employees have safely arrived in Chicago. And then we would head to a restaurant for a welcome meal. I feel proud and humbled knowing that the firm has provided an opportunity to professionals whose accounting education and audit experience were their tickets to starting a new career in America.

Purpose is Front and Central in Business.

In mid-March of 2020, the Governor of the state of Illinois mandated a stay-at-home order due to the COVID-19 pandemic. The employees were informed to work remotely. Front and central to the firm's leaders was to take care of three things: our employees, customers, and vendors.

From a business standpoint, each partner had their respective ways of responding to the situation. I felt most of its impact on some of my consulting projects. We had to balance the commitment to serve the clients and on-site staffing for one of our year-round projects. In addition, knowing that my engagement revenues will be lower than in 2019, I did not wait for my inner GPS to make a re-route. I kept driving and ensured my inner GPS was set to focus on business development and client service. I also got invited to speak about how our firm is responding to the pandemic, including speaking at a virtual event hosted by the Embassy of the Philippines in Washington DC. The weeks went by, and most of the time, I was either putting together a proposal, preparing for oral presentations, or making a sales pitch as a vendor.

Lead. Mentor. Find Your Purpose. Make a Difference.

I am passionate about promoting mentoring, leadership, and networking as essential soft skills for tomorrow's leaders. Being a leader in the audit profession was an acquired skill for me. Most of my foundational leadership training was when I was in the internal audit services of a large firm. We were given training and mentoring on becoming technical auditors and developing leadership skills such as project management, communication, people skills, and networking.

A few months after I joined the Filipina women-owned firm, I was looking for an organization where I could network in the Filipino community with educational programs that would develop Filipino accountants. In July 2012, I got introduced to Benel Se-Liban, the founder of the International Society of Filipinos in Finance and Accounting (ISFFA). ISFFA is a Los Angeles-based organization formed in 2006 by young Filipino accountants. ISFFA, formerly known as The International Society of Young Filipino Accountants (ISYFA), is a California-based nonprofit public benefit corporation whose primary goal is to assist, educate, train, and mentor emerging professionals, domestically and globally.

On November 17, 2012, the weekend before Thanksgiving, I made a presentation about forming ISFFA Chicago to 12 other colleagues and friends. We then established the chapter, and I had the humble and precious privilege of leading the founding officers of the Chicago Chapter. First, I served as founding Chapter President, and then I got invited to be on the National Executive Board.

Filipinos are well-known to be technically competent, but most of the time, we need to supplement such technical expertise with soft skills to make us more competitive and move up to break the glass ceiling. While developing the chapter programs, I realized and experienced the impact that its programs could have on its members. As a result, my purpose changed from *"what's in it for me?"* to *"what can I give?"* I certainly am not a millionaire and do not have a lot of money to give as a philanthropist. However, as precious as money that I can give is my time.

When we formed the chapter, we were all excited to develop programs that will help train and empower emerging leaders who are fellow Filipinos in finance and accounting and non-Filipinos who support our mission. The Chicago theme was "Be a leader. Be a mentor. Make a difference". While organizing these events, I myself felt that I was evolving for the better. And some people shared positive feedback about their ISFFA experience and how it has influenced and developed them as leaders. After my term as Chapter President, my successors, Arvin Floresca (2015–2017), Andrew Guerrero (2017–2019), and Jan Paul Ferrer (2019–2021), continued the core programs. The ISFFA Chicago Chapter became a gift that kept on giving.

While I was at the National Executive Board, the Chicago Chapter hosted the 2018 ISFFA National Conference. It was a remarkable collaboration between Chapters and National Board. Through Arvin Floresca, a founding officer of ISFFA Chicago, we were able to invite his mentor, the Country Managing Partner of the largest CPA firm in the Philippines, to be our keynote speaker. We also organized an SGV Alumni Dinner attended by accomplished alumni and those in the Chicago area attending the conference.

The ISFFA Chicago Chapter is now in its 10th year. The legacy continues, and the chapter carries on to provide quarterly events to its membership. The members' events continue to cover its four core programs: mentoring, leadership, community service, and scholarship. While there were times with less than frequent activities, the chapter plans continue to be bigger, members-needs-focused, increase ISFFA awareness to the young professionals, and expand its membership to include finance, in addition to accounting professionals. The programs and activities implemented have impacted hundreds of finance and accounting professionals through the years. For example, in the past two years, ISFFA chapters and ISFFA National Board collaborated to coordinate relief goods for those affected by several typhoons. Such outreach helped thousands of families in the Philippines.

During my term as Chair of the National Executive Board, I had three goals: (a) re-establish the New York Chapter, (b) re-launch the San Francisco Chapter, and (c) recruit finance professionals to ISFFA. Through the proactive efforts and leadership of Daniel Galeon, the New York Chapter was re-established. He then connected ISFFA to other finance professionals and, despite the pandemic, Kristin Dandan and Kevin Suarez, who served as Chapter President and Executive Vice-President, respectively, led the successful re-launch of the San Francisco Chapter. Now all the chapters (Southern California, Chicago, New York, and San Francisco) are active. Key officers include finance professionals from prestigious firms in the financial sector. Finally, I had a fourth goal to start an international chapter, which was also a vision of my predecessors. This goal is yet to be realized, but we were able to expand our reach to global finance and accounting professionals through the ISFFA Global Speaker Series.

Through my efforts with founding ISFFA Chicago, serving as Chair of the National Executive Board, and my role during the foundational years of a Filipino women-owned firm, I had the honor of receiving the 2014 Chicago Philippine Reports TV Hall of Fame Award in Finance and Accounting. I received the 2019 Global Filipina Women's Network 100 Most Influential Filipina Women in the World Award™ in Paris.

Balancing Work and Life.

When I joined the firm, I had three children, all very young. An intern once interviewed me, and we talked about managing time, multi-tasking, and my definition of success. I shared with her how I organize my day. I maintain a small notebook where I line up my To-Do's. I keep my calendars up-to-date. I also maintain a paper family calendar that shows school activities and major travel for competitions or vacations. I shared with her how I allocate my time in three buckets.

My first bucket of time is allocated for work. I manage multiple engagements, at multiple locations, for multiple teams; some are seasonal, and some are year-round. I also have administrative work, business development, supervising the team, and after we have issued some reports, I would cook food for the team. Some of their favorites are peach cobbler cupcakes, espresso cupcakes, red velvet cupcakes, ozzo buco, pasta, baked salmon, and the most frequently requested is kare-kare. Preparing the meal was my very personal way of expressing my gratitude.

My second bucket of time is allocated for community service. While I am involved in several not-for-profit organizations, I channel a significant portion of my personal time to ISFFA due to my leadership responsibilities, especially at the National Executive Board. The leadership programs, mentoring programs, the people I meet, the people who have inspired me, the impactful activities, and the soft skills I learned have helped me improve myself further to who I am today. Another impactful activity I volunteer for is coordinating a scholarship program for accounting students in the Philippines.

My third bucket of time is allocated for family. Family time is all about my three children. I bring them to school, and my husband will pick them up. I drive my kids to practices, Filipino basketball league, year-round leagues, travel team, park district, school sports, school activities, music, and sports competitions. I check if they do their homework or if they need help with homework. And occasionally, I volunteer with the basketball moms or for the boy scouts to have fundraising events like selling chocolates, popcorn, pizza coupons, and even baked goods like ensaymada! A typical weekend is spent driving kids to their activities, running errands like groceries, or working while they are on practice or games. If there are games or practices during weeknights, dinner is either a meal already cooked in the morning, cooked the night before, or fast food.

My work-life for the past ten years has been characterized by balancing my time between work and professional goals and taking care of my children and community involvement. To answer the intern's interview question, it felt like I was at my peak and accomplishing a lot at that time. It felt like my life was running at 100 miles per hour. Sleep was just an average of 4-6 hours, and work and activities are seven days a week. There is little time for entertainment. I heard of K-drama, but have never seen one. There is no time to watch T.V. News and the weather are on my phone. That was my choice. Those are the sacrifices for the commitments I made. I knew what I had to give up.

That was all to change, of course, when the pandemic hit. So, the once *"lack of spare me-time"* changed to *"a lot of me-time."*

Being Brave. Third New Beginning.

In 2021, I transitioned to the financial services industry. My inner GPS showed this route to me in early 2018, but it was not the right time. Investments have always been an exciting topic for me, having worked at a bank for ten years in the Philippines and having audited 401(k) and pension plans in the U.S. Since 2018, I have taken two licenses—securities and life insurance. During the pandemic, as time was abundant, I went through self-reflection. After consideration of many factors, it was time to transition. In early 2021, I informed the partners of my plan to take early retirement from the firm to endeavor on financial literacy and retirement income planning. This plan was my third new beginning, first being a banker, then an auditor, and now a financial professional / registered representative.

I look forward to what the future holds. One year into this new career, the learnings were amazing! I am adjusting and remain optimistic. This year had been about building knowledge, learning about the system, attending conferences, meeting people, and letting friends, family, acquaintances, and connections know about my new endeavor. I stay positive and regularly self-reflect to understand what I need to give up and what to focus on.

While building a new business or career takes years, one thing I cannot rush is time. Growth needs to develop through a combination of hope (time and goal), love (dedication and hard work), and faith (praying for guidance always). I regularly assess my progress and carefully follow where my inner GPS is taking me this time. While my financial services endeavor is building, I will supplement it by opening my own CPA practice.

Closing:

Being a leader is a privilege. I am beyond grateful for the opportunities that were given to me and that I seized to serve in leadership roles, from when I was working at a bank to being an auditor and to my involvement in organizations.

While my leadership journey was not a straight-line single career, I learned that trusting your inner GPS when driving in unfamiliar areas and hoping to make it to your destination is the same gut feeling you get when you are trail-blazing into a new career and exploring new business horizons.

If you need guidance, never be afraid to seek mentorship and engage with people or communities who will stretch your vision and support you. Finally, if you encounter tough times, stay motivated and keep pushing forward and upward.

For the times that I felt like hitting rock bottom, for some reason, there would always be someone who would hold my hand and lift me up as well. A dear friend encouraged me and said: *"I look up to you. You have accomplished a lot. We all go through life's ups and downs. Be strong. Just focus, and you will soon rise back up. You got this, my friend."*

With that, I would like to share below the top 10 things I have learned and encouraged me in my leadership journey:

1. Know your why.
2. Have a vision. Create a business plan.
3. Build your skills: Technical. People. Communication. Project Management.
4. Surround yourself with the people who will stretch your vision and support your endeavors.
5. Always lift as you climb.
6. No, means just not the right time. Move on.

7. Be positive.
8. Know what you need to give up.
9. Focus on important things.
10. Be unstoppable.

You are the driver of your own career. Take the steering wheel. If you are ever at a crossroad, reflect and trust your inner GPS.

MARLA DE CASTRO RAUSCH

CEO, Animation Vertigo & Animation Vertigo Asia
Managing Partner, Kampilan Productions
GLOBAL FWN100™ 2021

The Strength of a Wallflower

My leadership journey is entirely unexpected. And the career I am in is definitely not an industry I ever imagined for myself. Coming from a very traditional Filipino family with conventional jobs, my career path was unusual. If anyone had asked me when I was young what I wanted to be when I grew up, the answer would not have been "the founder and CEO of a motion capture animation company and Managing Director of a production company." Not only did the technology and career not exist, but I certainly did not see myself as someone who could do it.

Growing up in the Philippines, my family heavily influenced a lot of how I see and do things.

My mother's side of the family was mostly doctors and teachers, and they were of a genteel family despite living in what is today the rougher and tougher side of Old Manila. I always thought it was such a contradiction. I remember our ancestral home looming over the other houses. In the summer, the breeze from the huge Spanish-style windows were cool and refreshing. One would not have thought this was Tondo. The house was built in 1902. Being one of the older families there, my maternal relatives witnessed the homes and people around them change as decades passed. As the community grew rougher, they took care of the people in the community. My grandfather would treat scrapes and wounds—often complete with some scolding. Many did not have much to pay and often gave what they could. From my grandparents, I imbibed the idea of serving one's community—of being a contributing part of your surroundings. Even at a young age, these ideals were expected of us. My Mommy-la and Daddy-lo passed away when I was very young, making all their siblings our *Lolas* and *Lolos*—who had the exact same expectations.

My paternal grandfather, on the other hand, was a military man. Most of his children followed in government service except for my father, who worked in the oil industry. I spent the most time with them growing up, as we lived in their house when I was young. As they were also a traditional Filipino family, my Papa, as we called our grandfather, was a strict disciplinarian, but Mama held court on the whole family. They, too, had high expectations from us kids. Coming from humble means, Papa always pushed my cousins and I to put in the hard work to our best. As many patriarchs are wont to do, he was stingy with praise but hearing about how proud he was of us from other people (who heard it from him) always surprised and pleased us.

Common to both families was the concept of doing your best in a field that will allow you to give back—medicine, education, government service, the law. They maintained that we should direct opportunities given to us in the service of others, our community, and our country.

I grew up following a path set for me. First, study at Maryknoll, an all-girl private school run by the Maryknoll sisters. And then college at the University of the Philippines. While no one explicitly said that this is what I had to do, the impetus of family ideals set the direction. Expectation, and its sibling, success, were built on both families' "investment" into our skills, talents, and intelligence.

It was impressed upon my cousins and I that our grandparents worked hard to ensure their families opportunities they did not have—and we were expected to not waste these opportunities. In today's world, that might have been taken as pressure and stress-inducing and, maybe it is, but for our generation who carried this teaching, it was just the way it was. And it really was not bad. I think expectations for your kids allow them to keep their eye on the goal, that there is a purpose beyond just themselves for all the work they do. I always take that to heart—that our path was beyond who we were. But it wasn't easy for me.

> *"Everything you want to be, you already are. You're simply on the path to discovering it."* – ALICIA KEYS, American singer, songwriter, actress.

When I think of leaders, I think of my Papa, Brigadier General Crispino M. de Castro, commanding his soldiers in Bukidnon during World War 2; or leading his police officers when he became the first Chairman of the National Police Commission. I think of the doctors in my Mom's family who were strict and gave directives to their staff and nurses—teaching their residents and medical students how to think. I think of my godmother, my Dad's eldest sister, Bernarditas de Castro-Muller, a diplomat and climate change negotiator, who was filled with so much conviction and fire that the Western negotiators called her the dragon lady.

When I thought of what made a leader then, it was one who was commanding, charismatic, and strong-willed. One had to be confident, determined, and not afraid to voice their dissent or opinions. Not afraid to speak. That wasn't me.

I was a quiet and painfully shy child. My Dad's favorite story was about how I would hide behind him and say, *"I'm shy!"* when they tried to coax me to talk to someone or do something alone. I remember my Mom would tell me to ask the server for water in a restaurant, and I wouldn't, preferring to remain thirsty rather than ask. Raising my hand during class was torture because I couldn't stand being looked at by my classmates. How could I ever be like my family?

> *"Shyness in the young may be charming to look at but is painful to the one who suffers it."* – DOROTHY WHIPPLE, "Because of The Lockwoods"

It was hard to reconcile these leadership models with the person I was. I was most comfortable with family. For me, being out and about in the world solo was terrifying. The thought of being seen or spoken to was equivalent to having a giant spotlight on me, everyone staring at me waiting for me to make a mistake. I was quite content to stay in the background; to be in a group just listening and laughing along; to participate in activities as one of the team, helping move it to success. Doing it all myself, I couldn't even imagine it!

But that Expectation, that path that my family set for me, was a driving force without me realizing it. Because, even though I was good at the supporting role, I still did try things so I could slowly break out of my shell. If I was going to be successful at something, the least I could do was be able to talk to people. Thus, without prodding from my parents, I worked on that—in High School, then University. Working towards being sociable required practice, I learned. I used my introversion and shyness to listen and observe, finding these as excellent ways to learn to communicate effectively. To this day, I still feel a bit of stage fright when I am called to speak in public or even participate in conventions and summits—but I have learned to manage that very familiar feeling of nerves and to keep walking forward.

During the pandemic, I was invited to be the speaker at Miriam College Middle School (my alma mater, Maryknoll's, new name) for their graduation. My topic was Empowerment. I found that ironic because I felt anything but in that same school where I spent my elementary and high school days. In grade school, my favorite place was the library. I could sit and read and not be with anyone because I was too shy to make friends. I could tell who were my grade school peers and my high school classmates by the name they called me. My full name is Maria Angela, but my family called me Marla, and I answered to Marla. Because I was so shy in grade school, I could not even correct teachers or classmates when they called me Angela.

In High School, I committed to being less shy and make more friends. My closest friends in High School were all transferees from other schools who were all looking for friends in the new school. And while it was not a new school for me, it was a new me. To them, I am Marla, which is what most people know me as today. It isn't a big thing today, but the idea of volunteering information such as my name was so scary. But I persevered and continued to do so—until the idea of talking about myself, my family, or anything became not so daunting.

> *"Shyness is the fear of social disapproval or humiliation, while introversion is a preference for environments that are not overstimulating. Shyness is inherently painful; introversion is not."* – SUSAN CAIN, author.

There was something I noticed once I got used to being around people, speaking, and gaining friends: because I was never too loud or talkative, people tended to listen when I spoke. Often it was because I spoke softly, so they had to force themselves to keep quiet to hear me. I also preferred the deep discussions in small groups to the big, loud social gatherings where people went around, met people, and 'networked.' So, in events like social gatherings for our school, I found my group and stayed with them. The more sociable ones met people and would bring them to our group to meet, which is how I made new connections. Still, I never sought those out. I was anxious of rejection or, at least, what I defined as rejection—which ranged from not responding to me when I spoke or asked a question to appearing disinterested or bored, to an inability to get a word in when everyone else was having a lively conversation. It was this that would discourage me from meeting people on my own.

As an introvert, I enjoyed the quiet and keeping to myself. I gravitated towards being part of a small group of writers and not being part of the popular crowd. I thought that popularity was just too much pressure. I was great at being a team player, but don't make me team leader. The dilemma was that, if I wanted to meet the expectations of my family, and be successful in my career as they were, I needed to take another step outside of my comfort zone. I needed to fully come out of my shell. So, building on the success I felt in high school, I took on a different tactic in college: talking the talk of being a social butterfly until you can finally walk it—or more appropriately, fly.

At some point in our journey, we go from looking inside to looking outside and figuring out where we are going. While my family expected me to go from Maryknoll to UP Diliman, what I would do there was all up to me. I enjoyed writing so I took up Journalism. There was comfort in that it was a career path that some of my aunts and uncles took, where they found fulfillment and contributed something to the world. It was a path I could follow and something I actually liked for myself. Two birds, one stone.

Writing was MY way of communication—one that worked more effectively for me than speaking. In a world where speaking up and fearing being ignored or questioned was a constant source of anxiety, pouring thought onto paper sounded safer and less confrontational.

After Journalism, I felt that the path to success would necessitate taking up Law. Of course, this was another acceptable career choice in my family, pioneered by my Papa De Castro. When my father proudly told my grandfather about my high grades in one of my classes junior year, my stern grandfather was heard to remark that perhaps there was person in the family who would indeed follow his path. That clinched it. I had to succeed at becoming a lawyer. Despite this, I could not escape my introversion. Law school's demands on reading and writing were the "easy" part. The talking, arguing, and persuading not so much.

That was until I talked my way into getting into the UP College of Law.

I initially made it into the Ateneo Law School right after college. In that first year of law school, Papa passed away, during my midterm exams, to be exact. His passing was particularly jarring because the inspiration why I wanted to get into Law was suddenly gone. I was confronted with the question: did I want to become a lawyer for me or was I doing it for him? Unfortunately, I didn't do well during my midterms, and the decision to stay in ALS or go was taken away from me when I failed to make it to the next term.

It was also a volatile time in my family. Papa's death was one thing, but at the same time, my parents were separating. When I failed Ateneo law school, it was triply devastating. The feeling of letting down my family, of not meeting expectation, took me to a low place. Failure consumed my every waking hour; the pain and humiliation I felt were overwhelming. It was an invitation from my godmother to spend the summer with her family in her home in Geneva, Switzerland that became a turning point.

> *"Alice came to a fork in the road. 'Which road do I take?'*
> *she asked. 'Where do you want to go?' responded the*
> *Cheshire Cat. 'I don't know.' Alice answered. 'Then,' said*
> *the Cat, 'it doesn't matter."* – LEWIS CARROLL, *Alice in*
> *Wonderland*

Despite how I felt about myself then, my family fully supported me, and I am grateful they did not lose their belief in me. But, being in another country gave me a different perspective. Spending time away from familiar, comfortable, and convenient things allowed me to see things in a new and different way. I realized I needed to see things for myself outside of the cocoon of familial ideals.

My godmother, and her daughter, my cousin, were catalysts to that new way of seeing. In our conversations, they did not delve too much into the why or the meaning of my failures. Instead, they were pragmatic and without judgment. They asked me the right questions. *"Do you still want to go into law?" "Is there something else you want to do?"* I went from dwelling feelings of failure and defeat to looking ahead and wondering: here's an unexpected fork in the road, where are you going?

That was a crucial lesson for me—to not dwell on failure on one hand and but also to embrace manifested emotions on the other. After that, make plan B, C, or, even, choose a whole new path. I also learned that I can will things to happen if I really want it—although we know that willing and wanting can be two different things.

I discovered things about myself that summer. One, that I even if I did not really care much about becoming a lawyer, I DID care about failing. I wanted to prove to my family and to myself that I was not a failure. An interesting twist was that instead of opting for another path, I applied to the UP College of Law and was waitlisted pending a panel interview. During the interview, the inevitable question was asked, why would they accept someone who was kicked out of Ateneo Law School?

I do not remember my exact words or how I even found the strength to answer the imposing Dean of Law and the law professors, but somehow, I convinced them to accept me. I took that to mean that I was still meant to be a lawyer; what I should have seen was that I had overcome a significant challenge in eventually becoming a leader—speaking up. Despite that, I imagine 20 something year old me still did not see herself as a leader, far from it, but perhaps I was progressing.

Sidenote on this story—eventually, I opted to leave Law School for good. Closing that chapter with a further step into taking control of my own path.

> *"None of us really changes over time, we only become more fully what we are."* – ANNE RICE, Author

I have always said that my husband is a breath of fresh air. He's spontaneous versus my being a planner. He's Mr. Gut-Feel to my rational analysis. And, he was "big ideas" to my logistical details. So different from me, so different from my family.

When Brian and I married and moved to the U.S. in 1999, I felt like I was back to being that shy girl in grade school. I left my family and friends and was starting a whole new life without anyone I knew. I did not know what I wanted to do yet but what I did know, and I really credit my family for that, was that I was going to find something and make something of my life.

I depended on my husband for much of my socialization then. When you move to a new country, you do not think about things you take for granted. Driving, grocery shopping, and taking care of a home. I had to learn how to do all that, and sometimes I had to figure it out on my own since Brian was working.

Making friends as a newcomer in the U.S. is also a different thing. All my friends in Manila were friends I had known since I was in school or at work. Finding these friends was hard enough as it is, how was I going to do all that again? No matter how confident one is, when you walk into a place where you don't know what you don't know, it takes a while to learn things. For a shy person, even harder.

Still, I took a deep breath, thought about all the things I have done and accomplished, and simply moved forward.

Moving to the U.S., setting new roots, and creating a new path. Did I question it? Did I think twice? Yes. I was familiar with a fork in the road, but this was not a fork; this was a freeway, something I had never been used to, being used to the highways of EDSA. Nevertheless, I decided to jump. As much as the planned family path was based on tradition, this one, I wanted to see where this would go.

Moving to America was never a dream of mine. I always thought that, if I lived anywhere outside of the Philippines, it would be Europe. What the U.S. did afford me was the freedom to become. Again, it wasn't easy. I was used to the comfort and privilege of Manila. I was pretty entrenched in the culture and practice of navigating through the business and 'how things work' in Manila. But my husband helped smoothen the transition. He helped me be comfortable with spontaneity; that, sometimes, it truly pays off. Trusting my gut was not something that came naturally, certainly not something I learned from my family, but Brian definitely gave me that ability to trust in my intuition, not just in the concreteness of our plans.

With Brian being that stable support who believed in me, I decided to do what I always did—one, learn interesting and enjoyable skills; two, find a career that passed the family's expectations test. As we began, as a couple, earning money and setting down roots, I felt it would be a good idea to learn about financial planning, so I became a financial advisor. I thought this would be it until something entirely out of the plan or any path my family laid out opened up something new. While pregnant with my little girl (and, of course, one doesn't question what pregnant women do when they are bored) I learned how to work on motion capture data, something my husband was doing.

Motion capture animation uses special optical cameras to translate what is seen in real life and convert it into a 3D space. Motion capture, or Mocap, is used in film, video games, and television to create realistic motion in characters, monsters, and animals so that what you see on the screen seems real and believable. Notable examples are how Mocap was used to create characters such as Gollum from the *Lord of the Rings*, the tribe of blue people from *Avatar*, and the Hulk from the *Avengers*, to mention a few.

I would assist at Sony Computer Entertainment America, my husband's studio, after the financial markets closed and I was done with work. During crunch time when the studio would need a lot of people to work, I would work as a contractor for him. I would do this when their team needed help because the turnover in temp work in the animation industry was quick. They would hire, train, and release people when the project ended but there was no guarantee that these people would be available when needed again. Thus, they would have to search, hire, and train new people over and over.

That was how the idea of Animation Vertigo started—to create a studio that was available to provide support for production companies that used motion capture anytime they needed it. Soon after my son was born, we started setting up in the Philippines, running it from the U.S., and periodically traveling back and forth to supervise and expand the business.

Still, it took me some time before I decided to completely pursue this new path. I straddled being a financial advisor, which I enjoyed, and being a business owner. My most considerable hesitation was that it was never in my plan. My path was not to be a CEO of a company. I was great at helping people reach their financial goals. I enjoyed being a part of a group of people working towards something. I was a team member who belonged; not a leader. Plus, the concept of selling was daunting—the idea of traveling by myself and meeting people to talk about my company made me a nervous wreck. And the fact that I was going to be responsible for the livelihood of so many people stressed me out.

But the truth is, when I look back at my journey, everything I had experienced gave me the skills to accomplish exactly that.

My journalism background ensured that I could effectively communicate through speaking or writing. My legal background gave me, not just the ability to read contracts and not be so uneasy with the legalities of business, but to be comfortable being at a negotiating table trying to get to a yes. The fact that I had grown up in Manila and was familiar with how things worked there made running a company in the Philippines almost second nature. Also, my financial planning experience allowed me to ask the right questions and find answers from people with much more business experience than I had. The only thing stopping me was fear. Would I really be able to do it? Can a shy introvert succeed as a leader in the business of motion capture animation, a highly competitive, fast-paced, and male-dominated industry?

Brian was the reason I decided to go from corporate work to the world of entrepreneurship. My traditional Filipino family had instilled in me the idea of fulfilling expectations and had not been remiss in providing the emotional foundations to do so. They were crucial to my concepts of failing up—picking yourself up when you fall and keeping on keeping on. Brian gave me the courage to try something no one I knew had done before: to forge an unknown path. He had absolute faith in me that I could do it and he could see I would succeed. For this, and more, I am grateful to him because it allowed me to envision it.

Apparently, being shy and introverted does not mean you cannot be a leader. This, I did not know earlier because I modeled my first idea of a leader from my family. I thought that our way was the only way. The problem with this is that I felt I needed to change who I was to do what was expected of me. I pushed myself to be louder, more aggressive, more confident, and I succeeded to some extent but it was exhausting. It was performative and required a lot of masking—until you could get home and be yourself again.

Recently, I came across a book entitled *Quiet: The Power of Introverts in a World That Can't Stop Talking* by Susan Cain. And a lot of what she wrote resonated with me.

"Introversion—along with its cousins, sensitivity, seriousness, and shyness— is now a second-class personality trait, somewhere between a disappointment and a pathology. Introverts living in the Extrovert Ideal are like women in a man's world, discounted because of a trait that goes to the core of who they are. Extroversion is

an enormously appealing personality style, but we've turned it into an oppressive standard to which most of us feel we must conform."

Leaders come in all shapes and sizes, and the true measure of a leader is their effectivity in moving a company or organization into the direction of their vision. I've met and learned about other entrepreneurs who were shy and introverted. I continue to discover that it isn't what we are but how we utilize the power of who we are that makes us succeed.

In the creative entertainment industry where I lead, I have learned how effective introverts are because it is a strength to take stock and listen in a non-stop, constantly changing, demanding, and loud world. Organizing, analyzing, and processing before succinctly and clearly communicating is a rarity that is appreciated and commended.

This realization does not stop me from being shy or unsure but, now, it makes me feel that it is an asset. And, I am grateful for my journey because I learned more about myself and the strength I had to bring into the business. I also appreciate the integration that I was able to navigate through as I processed my leadership journey because I found I could be my authentic self in this creative and technical industry. And I can also fulfill the path my family had set for me, to serve my community.

They showed me what being a Filipina leader is about: giving back to her community. To me, that is ensuring that more people, particularly women, create their own successful paths in industries that might not yet exist.

Even so, the journey is not yet over. I have been the founder and CEO of a motion capture animation studio for over 17 years. We have worked on Triple A games and blockbuster movies that I am amazed that we took part in creating. I am proud to have accomplished that and to celebrate my being chosen as a recipient of FWN's 2021 Most Influential Filipina Woman in the World Award. It is a heartwarming achievement as I was honored in the Founder & Pioneer category.

If there is anything I learned from my family, we keep going. That is what I am doing. There is yet another something I am doing that I have never done before—I am developing an animated feature, telling the story of a Filipino hero. My goal is to have it released and distributed in the Philippines and worldwide. I am energized to work hard at this, willing it to happen as much as I had willed myself to get into law school.

Working in this field has been a challenge. It is an industry where Filipinos are a minority. But that has emphasized to me how important it is for Filipino voices to emerge and be heard. That's why to give back to the community of Filipino creators, I have also been actively advocating for the development of original Filipino content in the Philippines. If I can help more Filipina women succeed in this, too, it will be a true achievement.

No one in my family has done this. I am paving a whole new path and I am proud that I can model these paths for my children and younger generation of cousins. It is a privilege to nurture a sense of confidence in them that anything is possible by being themselves, working hard, planning, and taking action.

Family members have asked me if I could speak to their students and companies about my experience. Friends have invited me to give talks to women and speak in various organizations in the U.S., the Philippines, and, even, Argentina! The most common question women ask me is about dealing with fear—fear of change, failure, or making a mistake. The second thing I am told is that they do not think they have it in them to be a leader. I honestly believe if we can empower women to see strength in who they are, put action into plans, and just take that first step despite the fear, we will find more women leaders in all industries.

If there is anything I learned from reliving this journey, we can make strengths out of things we thought were liabilities. For example, I initially thought being timid and shy was a disadvantage. However, I just needed maturity and to discover a different way of utilizing it. If we take the time, we can fulfill what we set our minds to do.

> *"The secret to life is to put yourself in the right lighting. For some, it's a Broadway spotlight; for others, a lamplit desk. Use your natural powers—of persistence, concentration, and insight—to do work you love and work that matters. Solve problems. make art, think deeply." – SUSAN CAIN, Quiet: The Power of Introverts in a World That Can't Stop Talking*

RHODA CASTRO-CALIWARA

Chairman & President, Executive Genesis Services, Inc.
National President, Philippine Association of
Legitimate Service Contractors (PALSCON)
GLOBAL FWN100™ 2021

Human Agency and the Divine:
My Leadership

This story is about a *probinsyana* [provincial girl] who dreamed of making it big in the concrete jungles of Manila. I left my hometown after college, full of hope and guided by a dream and the dawn of a new beginning. I did not know Manila—its terrains were new to me; its language was very different, and its lifestyle was a whirlwind. It was a different place, a new endeavor—a fresh start.

I waved my folks goodbye, boarded a bus, and went on that journey to Manila. I promised myself, *"One day, I will have my own car, and buy my own house."*

I reminisce about the memories I had with my family. My journey started when my father, who came from an affluent family, ended up as a *jeepney* driver with no regular income, was convicted, and sent to prison for a crime he did not commit. We were poor and barely had anything to eat. My mother worked multiple jobs just to make ends meet.

Eighteenth is the significant time when I lost my mom yet found a deeper purpose in my life. Resilience. It was one of the darkest parts of my life. My mother died of cancer at the age of 50. We were orphans at a young age, so we had no choice but to work even harder to be able to provide for our family. My older sister became our "mom." She cared for us, especially when my father was not there.

I needed to finish college, yet we had no other sources of income. A part of me wanted to give up, but giving up was not part of my option. When I started to acknowledge that grief is a part of who I can become, it made sense to give honor to someone I valued the most. I became more resilient. It was good grief. Looking at the big picture, I thought this situation was just for a season. It might overwhelm me for a moment, but I needed to focus on a greater purpose of a lifetime.

> *"Do not grieve, for the joy of the Lord is your strength."*
> (Nehemiah 8:10)

Behind this strong woman was a vulnerable person who relied on the strength of the Lord. I needed to go beyond my emotions. I needed to fight this personal battle. It was a call for me to go beyond my situation. It was not a battle between me against the world; it was between me against myself. That is when I decided that I needed to stand firm amid adversity.

I had a bigger vision of seeing everything from God's perspective. My purpose is more than my emotions. I must overcome myself to face the silent battle I need to move forward with life.

> Life is not over yet; it is just the beginning.
> It was a humble beginning.
> *Padayon,* to all the beginnings we have to endure.
> *Padayon,* to all the dreams we want to achieve.
> *Padayon,* to all the relationships we have to restore.
> Even in the most significant relationship, we need to locate our
> genuine connection to ourselves.

Pursuing Passion

My dream was to graduate from UP Broadcast Communication, but since we had no money, that was not an option. Many people would affirm that I had a natural gift for communication. I need to communicate who I am and what needs to be heard. I had a strong desire to pursue my passion.

My passion was broadcasting and journalism. My role model was Tina Monzon-Palma. I would always watch her and admire her. She became my inspiration, a great reminder of miracles and possibilities. She became my great encouragement to achieve my highest aspirations.

God knows the desires of my heart. So he opened an opportunity to sustain my passion. The same year, I worked as a disk jockey/announcer at DWON FM in Dagupan, which allowed me to finish college. It is a platform where I could develop my talent and pursue my passion, evidence that we could be good stewards of what God has entrusted us—our talent, time, and treasure.

Probinsyana in Manila

The wider the tent, the greater the transition. It all started when I did a voiceover for a radio commercial for Panasonic. The station's account executive submitted it and told me it was rejected. First, I found it hard to accept because I did my best. I worked hard for it. A part of me said I needed to take the extra mile for them to reconsider it. I had a firm conviction about my work.

Since I could not take no for an answer, I went to Panasonic to pitch the same idea and material, and it was approved. I convinced the area manager, who then asked me to try to apply for a sales position at the company because he saw that I had potential in Sales. Everything starts with potential. I learned to capitalize on my strength. It proved that excellence could open the door for another opportunity.

> *"I planted the seed, Apollos watered it, but it is God who will make it grow."* (1 Corinthians 3:6-9)

It was a great transition in my life. I learned to adapt and went beyond my comfort zone. I stayed at a relative's house. The first few months were hard. Since I was in Sales, I needed to leave the office to sell. I had no car, it was hard to commute, and I was unfamiliar with Manila. I wanted to quit, but I thought I would lose if I stopped and returned to Pangasinan. So I mustered up the courage and carried on.

Transformational Leadership: First Woman Area Sales Manager

When I was a coordinator, my boss introduced me to a client. The client rejected me, telling my boss to give him someone else to handle their account because I was a woman. That was my first rejection in Manila. I persevered. I knew it was a good account to have. Since I had an excellent work ethic that enabled me to get the trust and confidence of my boss, he told the client to give me a chance because he assured them that they would come to like me. After a few months, the dealer who initially rejected me told my boss, *"Don't let anyone else handle our account. I only want Rhoda."* Wise stewardship plays a significant part in handling everything accountable to us. He knew that I would take every responsibility with certainty. I was very intentional about the company's growth and development.

After being a coordinator, I was promoted to district sales manager. Being promoted is a fruit of what we have faithfully planted each day. All the coordinators I handled while being a district sales manager were men. Thankfully, they were respectful and cooperative.

I learned to collaborate and eventually built a strong team. I would always set the pace and make things work together. Our dynamic team eventually produced exceptional results. Because of my busy schedule, I really only got to spend time with my family on weekends. However, whenever we went to the mall, I still made it a point to visit dealers and stores to check on how my brand was doing. Work definitely did not stop for me. It became my rule to have the extra mile for work. It was natural for me. Soon enough, I became the Area Sales Manager of Northeast Luzon. First time in the history of Panasonic to have a female area sales manager. It was evident that nothing could stop a woman with an incredible drive to excel.

The main office was in Cabanatuan, but the entire office burned down, so I had to relocate to Isabela, a satellite office. My son was in Manila only with his nanny; my husband was in Cabanatuan. Our set-up was not ideal, but I had to do it because I had to work. My husband and I would visit our son on Saturdays and leave on Sundays. From Isabela, I would drive to Cabanatuan to pick up my husband and go to Manila together—that was our weekly routine. I made an extra effort to cater to the needs of my family. It was challenging to compartmentalize and excel in every role that needed to be filled. I am grateful to have a supportive and understanding husband. I was secure that I was meeting the needs of my son at the same time. He was in primary education, and I was at the peak of my career. I knew I did my best to be a loving wife and caring mom. When I started noticing that my son was beginning to have insecurities, developing separation anxiety and personal issues that resulted in him getting sent to the principal's office often, I decided to leave Panasonic and stay with him in Manila full time. Instead of working with Panasonic, I decided to focus on the company I put up while his dad, my husband migrated to the U.S.

God's Original Plan: Executive Genesis

1993 was a year of wonder, a year of taking chances and of blessings, most significantly—a time when courage stood pat over doubts and adversities, a time when taking the bet on what the good Lord is laying down for His servant to grow and cultivate, a time to start a faithful commitment.

While employed, I tried to get into several businesses like trading and retail. However, after working in a multinational firm for many years and dealing with promoters and dealers, I saw the potential in the service contracting business. It gave me a sense of purpose in helping the industry and the country's employment problem by offering business flexibility to enterprises to focus on their core competencies for better efficiency and productivity.

In 1993, I dreamed of starting a company with my husband Armando Caliwara and some friends. 1993 was when a group of people so driven by a vision to succeed came together to form this business establishment; some lowly dreamers were armed only with faith and a passion for excellence. And so Executive Genesis Manpower Services, Inc. (ExeGen) was born. The company will provide any service, directly or indirectly, for recruitment or supply of manpower to a specific company or industry.

We were confident then; we were courageous and so sure of ourselves. We were certain to succeed with one typewriter, room, desk, employee, and client— but we believed that we had One God to lead the way. That was all we needed.

We had a small office room on the first floor of the Diamond Finance Building, in Cubao. At least I remember that we started with one electric fan. The *aircon* came much later. I can still vividly picture how hard it was working during warm weather. I recall the legwork. We had to make do with so little with so many opportunities.

We knew that we had to compete to survive in the industry. But, as we recognized that we were at the bottom of the heap, we were constantly strengthened by a confident reminder that being at the bottom, there can never be anywhere else to go but up.

Lo and behold, we went up literally. We were given a more comfortable room on the third floor from a small office on the first floor. Climbing up to the third floor seems to have painted the future of ExeGen too. Because not only were we given an office on the higher level of the building, it was in that third-floor office where we started to grow our clientele, our manpower, and our resources.

Fast forward to 2013, ExeGen has come a long way from almost 30 years ago. Still dreaming big, still driven, still faithful to our promises of impeccable service, and still committed to excellence.

Gone is that lowly typewriter that may one day belong to a museum. Instead, a network of computers now graces its office with software systems that hasten its business operation. We have air-conditioned offices, conference areas, and training rooms. ExeGen now occupies almost the entire third floor of that building in Cubao—a far cry indeed from its small cramped office in 1993.

Twenty-eight years have gone by, and 28 more years will come; time may pass, and things may change, tides will turn, and age will show, but ExeGen will continue to be faithful to its commitment to service; the dream continues, the courageous quest for excellence goes on, the resilience to adversity will persist. ExeGen promises to forever stand up to the core values it planted almost 30 years ago.

For us, the possibilities of a much better tomorrow are endless.

And like that *probinsyana* dreamer who went to the big city in the quest for her dreams, ExeGen has dreamed, and it has delivered.

Intentional Parenthood

There was a season in my life when I earnestly asked God to give me the most valuable gift. I prayed for an opportunity to shape the next generation. My husband and I desired to receive our most treasured inheritance, and He gave us a son, "Ken," our *Unico Hijo.*

Indeed, it was a great call of motherhood.

And I was willing to answer that call.

It was a great privilege that I was entrusted with the role of being a mother. Except for the time I had to work from Isabela and commute to Manila weekly, I was a full-time mom. I was very intentional about it. I knew there was a part of me that I needed to honor God by serving my own family.

Indeed, during the first few years of every transition, it will always be a challenge to adapt and excel simultaneously. It was a season of pruning that enabled me to face the reality that my son needed more help and attention.

To acknowledge that you need help, in humility, is when the grace of God comes in that enables us to do immeasurably what we ask from Him. During his formative years, I focused on developing his character. I am blessed with my church community. I believe he needed to be surrounded by God-fearing people who modeled faith. He grew up in kids church. I sent him to Victory Christian School.

I prepared a buffet table so my son can discover his talents. I usually brought him to classes for him to develop his God-given gifts. I got him to dance classes, voice lessons, basketball clinics, and soccer training. I was always around to support, even abroad. He won a World Hip Hop Dance Championship in the U.S. He recorded commercials. He had opportunities to do Commercial Jingles. I would always pick him up from school and bring him to the studio. To date, we still travel to create memories. We discover great things together. It has been a joy for me to spend quality time with him. Time is our most valuable commodity. We can never bring back time. It is priceless.

God brings comfort through me when my son experiences defeat, failures, and frustrations. I make him understand that failures are opportunities for us to become better. It is a part of the whole success process. It is a significant part of how God develops our character. It is a room for God to move. It is the start of great miracles. Failures are God's way of pruning us to be more like Him daily. I always assure and encourage my son. I am here to boost his morale and uplift his spirit. As a mother, we are called to go beyond, always. It adds value to them. It adds more value to us. When love is shared, it multiplies joy. And it is something that can never be taken away. I remind him that his identity is not just about his skills, talents, and human agency. I always point him back to the cross, that our identity is linked to divine agency and how he uniquely created each one of us for His glory.

Wise Loves Discipline

Ken is not exempted from the rod of discipline. I talk to him privately, bring him to his room, explain to him why I did that—that I love him and that is why he needs to be disciplined. He needs to be corrected. As a parent, he respects my authority. I know in my heart that I make him understand the value of discipline. It is part of my core to hold on to this passage in Proverbs 22:6, *"Train up a child in the way he should go: and when he is old, he will not depart from it."*

Twenty-five years of being a parent have shown me that a child's character is very important. Excellent skills can bear opportunities but having a good character will sustain it. A great character can lead you to more extraordinary destinations.

We make millions of decisions in our lifetime. Every day, we make decisions. When we open our eyes in the morning, we decide what clothes to wear or what to eat. Big or small, it is important. Every accomplishment is the sum of your small wins. It is the foundation of having the right decisions.

Even if you excel academically, it will be hard for you to make decisions. We are always one decision away from a totally different life. I instilled with my son the conviction to make decisions anchored on Biblical principles. If you do not know the Word of God, it will be hard for you to make the right decisions. Always go back to the basics.

Being a parent, I consider it a milestone. So my confidence in parenthood is with God. We are with Him every step of the way. Apart from Him, we cannot do anything. We should always put God as a partner in raising a child. In that way, we are secure that our ultimate father leads our family in heaven—because He who started the smallest yet, most impactful unit in our society is faithful to guide us in having a great family life. Everything starts with God.

News I Never Wanted to Hear

My husband moved to the United States in 2004. This move was a huge change in our lives. I was reluctant because we have been separated before, and I know it is not a healthy family set-up. But he convinced me that it would improve our lives, and we would all migrate there and live better lives.

> *"Many are the plans in a man's heart, but it is the*
> *Lord's purpose that prevails."* (Proverbs 19:21)

It was hard on me because I had to raise our son single-handedly. Our child was a young boy, so it would have been a hundred times better if he had a father figure. On top of that, I was trying to build my company, so it was extra hard on me. In addition, I noticed that my son's relationship with his dad began to dwindle. He was starting to resent his dad for being away. But I had to continuously explain to him that his dad was doing this for our family and that he was sacrificing himself just to give us a better future. We were hopeful that we would get to follow him to the States and be reunited as one family unit again.

But, one night in 2010, my husband was rushed to the hospital because he was experiencing immense pain. He was later on diagnosed with terminal-stage cancer. He was given two weeks to a month left to live. But, he decided to go back home to spend time with us instead of staying in the States to get treated. I brought him to the best doctors, having him treated with radiation and all sorts of medication, but to no avail. It was hard to see my husband suffer, but I had faith that he would be healed, no matter what the doctors say. He also had the best support system. His family would always be in our home to spend time with him, eat with him, and take care of him.

Five months after his diagnosis, he was getting weaker and weaker. He was becoming unresponsive. I still had faith and prayed every chance, claiming he would be healed. A turning point in my life was when my son called me into his room. He was around 13. He told me something I thought I would never hear from a 13-year-old boy. He told me, *"I know it's hard for you mom, it's hard for me too. But we should know when to let go."* Seeing that his dad was suffering so much already, my boy, made me realize that I may be too selfish. Because of my fervent belief that he would be healed, I was depriving him of the eternal life he was bound to have with God. If my son uttered those words, I could lift everything to God and let Him do his work. Days later, my husband expired.

I became honest with my emotions; I was devastated. I was depressed. I locked myself in my room for a week. I cried every waking minute and often caught myself crying myself to sleep. I felt like I was going crazy. But I later decided not to let it get the best of me. I snapped out of it. I had a son who depended on me; and a growing business. I cannot continue sulking and letting depression eat me alive.

God knows me personally. He encountered me where I was. He picked me up when I found myself broken. Only by God's grace could I get back on track. I experienced that His mercies are new every morning. I held on to God's Promises in my life until it bore fruit in my heart, *"My grace is sufficient for you, my power is made perfect in weakness."* in 2 Corinthians 12:9. His healing is beyond physical. He healed every part of me that needed healing. God exposed the deepest wounds so I may experience His unconditional love—a love that redeems, rescues, and restores. It was Shalom—a supernatural state of wholeness and complete peace.

To let go is to have good courage. To fully let go is to trust God.

In my weakness, God sent people to comfort me. He gave me significant opportunities to realize that I have a greater calling. My purpose is greater than my emotion and situation. It was when I fully surrendered everything to Him—that beyond my roles in my life, there was a loving Father who would always encourage, inspire, and carry me all the days of my life. God filled the void in my heart; I am living a victorious life with Him.

NegoSHEnte—My 24/7 Tool

I started a YouTube channel called "NegoSHEnte by Rhoda Castro-Caliwara" that aims to empower women to pursue entrepreneurship. I share how one could become an entrepreneur and potentially make a difference in her community by providing for one's own family or generating opportunities for Filipino workers. In addition, I interview successful women entrepreneurs to get insights that could inspire other women. By highlighting women in business, I realize my dream of being an inspiration and hopefully a beacon to women of all walks of life. I realize my human agency.

An unwavering attitude toward learning is one core strength that I really valued. I learned through all my interviews that I should always have a hunger for learning, to never stop searching for stories to hear, experiences to live, and lessons to learn.

I prayed for a platform where I can establish an online community where people can grow and learn from each other. I intentionally created this medium and administered substantial influence with the use of technology. With the people God has entrusted me, I am grateful to share inspiring stories of grit and passion that can minister in every part of the world.

Success in being PALSCON President

I am the sitting President of the Philippine Association of Legitimate Service Contractors (PALSCON); I became the organization's first and (by far) the only multi-termed President.

Setting the pace and raising the bar for women leading the marketplace was an opportunity to have a platform where I can collaborate and set the vision for the people. I learned to compartmentalize, and it was also the reason why I stood firm with my core values.

A more significant wave came. It challenged me as a woman and as a leader. My leadership was tested by the struggles to quell the clamor for a total ban on all forms of contractualization or end of contract in the country. I became the voice of the entire industry.

It is in this struggle I was suddenly pushed to the frontlines of the employers versus labor sector tussle; making appearances on all fronts, including the Philippine Senate and the House of Representatives, the Department of Labor and Employment, the media, and even in labor consultations. I fought for the industry by bringing forward the truth about the indispensable role of the service contracting industry in the generation of employment, thereby playing its part in strengthening the national economy. Moreover, it opened the eyes of the people to the importance of the industry in helping make the country globally competitive; not only did the government understand, but my personal approach to the conflict has made even the hardened labor activists listen and take notice.

With these endeavors to save an entire industry, I successfully created a milestone of my vision of becoming a beacon of inspiration to all women everywhere, especially in business, that they can thrive in a predominantly male-dominated industry... and even lead the fight to save it.

I chose to deal with the contractualization issue, not with anger and pride but with humility and kindness. I learned through time that being a leader is much like being a mother. You have to be compassionate, fair, and forgiving.

MY LEADERSHIP TIPS

#1 Grit and Passion

Everything starts with a dream. God gives our natural strengths for a purpose. We need to cultivate the seeds with excellence. As we embrace the desires of our hearts, we take good courage to pursue our passion. He gives us clarity as we align ourselves in God's plans. We will be confident to have a clear direction. It's an excellent start to having a clear vision. In Hebrews 11:1, *"Faith is confidence in what we hope for and assurance about what we do not see."* Do not be afraid to dream even if you think it could not happen. Do not limit yourself. With God, all things are possible.

#2 Good Faith, Great Courage

Take risks. Move in faith. As we take calculated risks, God will send us people who will take good courage with us. As a community, you will move forward with great courage. You never know what good could happen. Nothing can stop what God has planned for your life. You need to be strong and courageous. *"Be strong and courageous."* (Joshua 1:9)

#3 Commitment to Being a Woman

A natural gift is given to only a few. We cultivate ideas. We incubate a child. We are given tasks that only a woman can accomplish. We should not compromise our standards. We need to fight like a woman. We need to raise the bar that only God has set before us. Woman, you are needed.

#4 Victory Starts in Surrender

We need how to let go and let God. You must trust the whole process even if you cannot see the big picture. You allow God to take over. If God calls us to move, we will move. When God calls us to be still, we need to be still. Only by God's grace can we come to God, carry the cross, and follow Him. It is the start of a victorious life.

#5 Start to Serve

Great businesses will always have the common denominator: Heart of Service. As we impart our ultimate goal to everyone who enters the room, we impart who we are. Entrepreneurship is a tool to generate jobs, and our greater goal is to empower them for a greater purpose. *"Whatever you do, work at it with all your heart, as working for the Lord, not for human masters, since you know that you will receive an inheritance from the Lord as a reward. It is the Lord Christ you are serving."* (Colossians 3:23-24) As we start to serve God, we finish strong.

After everything I experienced and went through, divine agency and human agency were the ones that helped me become the woman I am today and brought me to where I am now. We can achieve great things with hard work, dedication, and prayer. *"God revealed through human agency—Divine agency and embodied practices of faith, hope, and love."* (Henriksen 2016).

LEADING CHANGE: HEALTH

CARMINA MONTESA ALDANA

Founder and Executive Director,
The Neurosurgery Outreach Foundation, Inc.
GLOBAL FWN100™ 2019

Choosing, Being, Succeeding

I hear Shankar Vedantam's familiar voice announcing, "all of us make choices all the time, and we may think we're making those choices freely..." My left eyebrow raised; then, I made a choice with a chuckle. I opted to continue listening as I prepared dinner. And so, my education on choice architecture began.

The podcast made me think about the choices I've made in my life. Who was the architect behind my options when the environment I inhabited was dotted with disruptions? What outcome was expected of me? Am I supposed to be where I am now? Or had I been nudged too far off track? All I ever wanted was to help the disadvantaged of the world.

My diplomat father once declared that he envisioned me "jet-setting around the world" as a career woman. Indeed I was beginning at the toddler age of three! Disruption one, uprooting a child from her home country. This country-hopping occurred periodically throughout my life in intervals of 4–6 years. My stays were short enough that I grew accustomed to the culture but not long enough to feel that I belonged. Unlike immigrant families, our status as guests of the country inevitably brought a different layer of expectations—represent your country, your family name, and yourself—in that order. An international lifestyle did appear glamorous. But for us diplomat kids, it was a nuisance to constantly adapt and challenge, in my case, Filipino biases. It was frustrating when people associated you as a teen with a domestic or sex worker. Moving from country to country affected a few of my friend's mental health. I can empathize. What use was it to start anything worthwhile when we would be gone soon enough and leave it all behind?

As I matured, I realized my annoyance was not doing me any good. While it was irritating to start all over again, learning a new way of life and arriving in a yet-to-be-discovered place was liberating. It also helped advance my emotional intelligence. Moving also allowed me to leave any uglies behind and improve into a better me. Of course, I still had to overcome uncertainties, such as will I make lifelong friendships or would I ever plant roots. My youthful, inner arrogance believed that I would someday conquer those doubts. However, the constant change did teach me that I had control over how I would respond to, live with, and experience anything new. Indeed, the constant change was the only thing constant, just as Heraclitus philosophized and I learned. With that, I adjusted, reset, and continued to move on like water on a river—qualities that proved helpful later for me in my personal life and as a leader when the world went on lockdown.

However, conflicting choices continued to present themselves in my life. Although my career goals were not well defined in my youth, I gravitated to leadership positions. I was impressed by leaders' ability to make a difference in people's lives. Living in Europe as a child, I was particularly struck by Margaret Thatcher's strength as Great Britain's Prime Minister because she was a world leader, a woman, in a male-dominated environment. There were very few female leaders, let alone a Filipina woman leader, that I can recall. Nonetheless, I believed that Filipina leaders would emerge given time and opportunity. I even dared to dream it for myself. The plan was to get through school, graduate from a reputable college with a degree in economic development or something, pursue graduate school, enter the workforce, work hard and ascend as high as possible. Hopefully, along the way, find a great guy and have a happy family. Yet, despite my chances to study in the U.K. and against everyone's advice, I returned to the Philippines for my tertiary education. My reason was to understand myself as a Filipina and fully experience being a Filipina in the Philippines. Moving back home was a necessary choice to understand the Filipina part of me completely. Barely two years in, I met my great Cebuano guy, and he immigrated to the U.S. Suddenly, Carmina was left behind. It felt unfair.

In his effort to console me, my father presented a well-composed preposition: apply to the University of Toronto, Canada, his next post. Speaking as a seasoned diplomat, he argued, *"once you've applied, you will then have a choice; to remain here and complete college alone or to attend a university where you will be with your family and near your guy. The choice is yours."* Ugh. Up to this point, my mind had made up to stay put; I wanted to complete something I had started. I did not wish to move. Again. I, simply, wanted to start my path straight to my future.

Unbeknownst to me, my father engineered the situation and had already inquired with the University of Toronto. After I submitted my application, a placement offer arrived. As an independent young woman, I refused to think my acceptance would be due to my family or to be near my great guy. Being pragmatic, I chose to pursue my degree in Canada to increase my chances of success in finding positions to get me on track to "save the world." Five years later, with a degree and a non-profit founder under my name, I was in an intricately embroidered Renee Salud wedding gown, exchanging vows with my great Cebuano guy and not with a foreigner as most of my relatives anticipated. Why did I choose marriage over graduate school to follow him to America? Choosing a life partner and who that partner is are important career decisions as shared in *"Lean In"* (Sheryl Sandberg, 2013). I was honest enough to myself that I needed a true life partner if I were to achieve my goals. Like other women, it was typical to consider life-work balance early in a career. That included having a suitable partner on the same page as you about work and family life. Marrying my life partner was essential to me.

Married and transplanted to the U.S., it seemed that my career was on a path as crooked as San Francisco's Lombard Street. Disruptions continued, such as issues of immigration beyond my control; or when offered an upward career move that involved relocating out of state. In the latter, I had to pause, for as a married couple, we had to make a joint decision. Up to that point, I relied on my somewhat selfish decision-making to steer me toward a choice that would put me in a stronger position. Except it was no longer all about me. I also had to consider what was best for my husband; accommodating one another is part of a good marriage. If not considered carefully, this can lead to resentment. I rationalized my choice by pushing aside internal gender conflict or Filipina-wife submissiveness. It was choice architecture at play. My circumstances were more flexible than his. It was about being one with each other. My thinking forced me to have courage with my choice to not follow through with the upward career move. Sharpening my decision-making system was a constant exercise, but the critical part was trusting my system that it would not fail me.

For the next several years, I worked in the human resources industry, supporting my husband's medical career while keeping an eye on the elusive corner office.

Two cross-country moves later, the most profound thing happened to me. I became pregnant with twins. Within months, we relocated to Ohio with a gestational diabetes diagnosis. There I was again, in a new town with the closest relative one hour away, carrying a high-risk pregnancy and with no job prospects. With a belly stretched thin like an over-filled balloon, my sole responsibility, as instructed, was to carry my babies to term. In true character form, I took my responsibility seriously. I binge-watched Oprah like a walrus-size potato, on the couch, guilt-free.

BLESSED DISRUPTION

On one of my many visits to this exam room, a gray examining table lined with paper at one end, while the other had stirrups raised that screamed discomfort, my doctor announced smiling, *"let's have these babies tomorrow, Carmina!"* I had been waiting to hear those words and was thrilled that the day my husband and I prayed for was coming. Tomorrow. August 28, 2002. I hugged my doctor as she told me what to expect the following day. I could not wait to share the great news with everyone.

My parents, who flew in from Belgium two weeks prior, wanted to be with me before I gave birth so that they were sure to be present on the delivery day itself. They had been waiting for me and my husband to have children since we had been married for seven years. My father took three weeks off from work around my due date. Scheduled to return on September 4, he changed his departure to September 8. I argued, *"Dad, you could leave on the 4th now that we're certain these babies are coming tomorrow, August 28."* My father earnestly responded, *"that's OK. I'll keep my departure date for the 8th."* We did not know that God was already intervening and that September 8 was the better departure date.

Other signs indicated God was watching us, but we did not recognize them. Not until after the event. Two months before relocating to Ohio, I made phone calls to local Catholic Churches as I contemplated converting to Catholicism and potential OBGYN doctors as I entered my third trimester. I found a lovely church and spoke to Sister Angela. I also found an OBGYN practice that could see me in July. Unfortunately, the day the movers came and packed our furniture was when I discovered I had gestational diabetes. Four days later, we flew to Ohio. I rescheduled an earlier appointment because I needed to begin insulin treatment immediately because of gestational diabetes. Luckily for me, the practice was located only minutes from my new home. Because of the appointment change, I saw Dr. Wilkof, who was not my first choice but put me at ease. Dr. Wilkof was personable, respectful, caring, and a highly competent physician.

God's Intervention

On August 28, the hospital staff quickly brought me to a room and prepared me for my c-section scheduled for 12:30 in the afternoon. We listened to the babies' hearts as we waited. Meanwhile, my parents and my husband exchanged silly jokes and made nonsense conversations in the hope that time would move faster. As part of the routine preparation, a resident examined me and discovered that Baby B might be in a breech position! Baby B had not moved from her vertex position and was the reason that we opted for a c-section. To find she had changed her mind was a little surprise. The Aldana twins were not going to make it for their 12:30 birth. I was brought two floors down to the Fetal Maternity Medicine (FMM) where I saw my nurse pal, Linda. The first time I met Linda was in July, when I was about 29 weeks pregnant. She was responsible for strapping my tummy with color-coded belts for my non-stress test. For almost ten weeks, twice a week, I visited Linda and saw her colleagues; every week, they chanted aloud, *"You're still pregnant?"* Linda was sure that every time she saw me was when I would give birth. She said my belly felt very tight and did not appear it could stretch anymore. I got to know Linda, who got to know me and my babies. She knew that Baby B did not like to be bothered with her straps. And that Baby A was happy being snug under Baby B. Every week I told my babies to do well; that way, they would stay in my womb longer.

The longer they stay, the better I can nourish them, the favorable chances of carrying them to term and delivering healthy babies.

I entered week 38 on my delivery day. Around early evening, I was finally in the OR. My husband was by my side with a handheld video camera to record the event. I was calm and excited at the same time. First, the room filled with the sounds of *"uha, uha"* and I thought, *"wow, a baby's cry sounds exactly how it's spelled in the comic strips!"* And for the first time, I wholeheartedly understood the definition of joy. Next, I saw Carissa, and within a few minutes, I met her sister, Katrina, baby B. Then my eyes began to close, and things began to darken.

Like scenes from medical TV dramas, I was back in the OR.
Then my O.B. slammed on the OR table and yelled for more.
Then she harshly ordered someone to *"call my partner right now!"*.
Then she pleaded, *"I can't let this happen."*
More voices.
"I gave her more."
"Is she wearing contacts?"
"Oh my, there's just so much blood."
"Does anyone have a hair tie? Her hair..."

To which I calmly responded, but no one heard.
"Yes, I am wearing contacts."
"Shoot, I should have put my hair up."

Then someone whispered, *"you're going to die."*
To which I confidently responded, *"No."*

Maternal death happens 17.4 per 100,000 pregnancies. That is less than 0.01%. Postpartum hemorrhage (PPH) is the leading cause of maternal death. Among Asian-Americans, the risk of severe morbidity due to PPH is 21.4%.

Unbeknownst to me, my Jewish O.B. invited her Hindi anesthesiologist and her Presbyterian nurse to place their hands over me and join her in prayer. She asked that each pray to their creators, for she believed that they, as a team, had done everything within their powers to save me, a Protestant.

It was both a curse and a blessing that my physician husband understood what was going on. He, too, knew that all he had left was faith. So he knelt in prayer alone.

My Aglipay father and Methodist mother found themselves praying the Catholic rosary led by my brother-in-law's family.

My husband called in Sister Angela from Guardian Angel Catholic Church to give me the sacrament of anointing of the sick.

The CEO of the local Children's hospital, where my husband had just begun work, requested prayers from his church. And soon, it seemed a prayer chain had started for my life within our new hometown and with friends and strangers worldwide.

At the same time, two, healthy, beautiful, baby girls just entered this world.

To be honest, I do not know why strangers prayed for me. What I do know is never to underestimate the power of prayer. And never deny yourself a prayer. And to never decline an offertory prayer regardless of the person's belief. Prayers are an integral part of my life now.

When I opened my eyes, I saw Dr. Wilkof's gentle face first. At the foot of my bed, I smiled at Philipp. He looked awful. Behind him, in big red fonts, it read 30. Underneath, "August." On the third day, I woke up.

My teary-eyed husband hugged me. He whispered, *"I will always take care of you,"* and paused as if lost for words. I replied, *"no worries, I know, I can no longer have children."* How I knew, I do not know. I assured him I was fine, and he reassured me that he was fine.

The next few days my story began to unfold, including snippets of me assuring my startled family while being wheeled into the OR that I was fine with a thumbs up, lest they worry about me. It turned out I was brought to the OR three times, was sutured everywhere to stop the bleeding, and had blood transfusion three times my body's volume. I experienced uterine atony which occurs when the uterus fails to contract after the delivery of the baby and can lead to postpartum hemorrhage. Linda was right. My uterus was stretched to the point that it had lost its elasticity. Failing to spring back, it continued to supply blood, thinking it was sustaining my babies. As a last option, an emergency hysterectomy and removal of one of my ovaries were called. All the commotion over my life, I thought, while my two baby girls were at the nursery waiting for their mother's milk.

The colostrum is the first milk stage and lasts only a few days after a baby is born. This vitamin-, protein-, antibodies-rich liquid nourishes the baby. A baby's nursing will initiate the flow. However, I was in no shape. Philipp knew the importance of my colostrum for the babies and insisted that my breast be stimulated. My female O.B., respectful of my body, reluctantly agreed. My husband manually pumped my breast while I was out. Sadly, nothing came out.

He explained this to me and apologized. But I assured him that he had made the right decision. With nothing to lose, I gave my breast a go. My motherly body has to produce milk. Finally, slowly a thick yellow liquid began to flow! Philipp and I were both ecstatic and immediately placed both girls on me.

I didn't realize the amount of blood I had lost until my sister washed my hair a few days after my transfer from the ICU to the maternity ward. Bucket after bucket of merlot-colored water eventually turned clear made me feel uneasy. My sister turned wine into water. Meanwhile, my girls thrived as I mustered up all my strength to recover. Every movement was painful. Walking a few steps left me breathless. I willed myself to get better so I may bring my girls home.

The day I left the hospital, my O.B. confessed her fear of losing me and her joy in seeing me with my babies. So did my nurse. And so did everyone in the hospital. The message was clear: I was in bad shape. It was a miracle that I was discharged a week later, on September 4, a few days before my father's return to Belgium.

BEING

Unbelievably, I rocked my babies to comfort standing up when only the day before I did not have any strength at all. Caring for my girls required a lot from me physically, which was good as it kept me from getting into my head. I was grateful to have my mom, mother-in-law, and mid-western nanny to help me during the girls' first few weeks. The former two came with conventional Filipino expectations, though, while the latter came with her own biases on suburban American housewives.

> *"Don't let him do any baby duties. Kawawa naman.* [Pity him.] *He's had a busy day at the hospital."*
> *"I almost died delivering these TWO babies, remember?"*

"Let him sleep at night."
"Um, no, I am a bigger grouch without sleep."

"Ikaw ang babae. You're the wife. You should...."
"It's the 21st century, didn't you say you were a modern mom, mom?"

I was not having any of it. Fortunately, my husband and I were united as a team. We helped each other out, including letting our respective mothers know we shared duties. I have learned that setting boundaries early diminishes potential misunderstandings. It also promotes respect, something I learned by having a circle of friends as colorful as a Benetton ad through my travels. Perhaps it was unlikely for me, as a Filipina daughter, to set boundaries with my mom regarding raising my children. But this is not to say upon hearing their opinions that an internal struggle did not exist within me, especially with the option of staying home versus returning to work. Also, to what kind of work do I go back to now? Where am I in my career path? Can I enter the workforce and be the kind of mother I want to be? The answers I came up with all seemed trivial, meaningless, and unsatisfying. Drawing from my constant change experience, I zeroed in on adapting to the flow of things and kept the questions on the back burner. My lesson on resilience has taught me to trust in the process, for now.

I hoped that my Catholic conversion would enlighten me a bit. I began by meeting with Sister Angela weekly in the fall to keep me up with the RCIAA class. Sister Angela also tasked me to journal my spiritual journey. During our meetings, I shared my confusion about existence, fears for the future, and my wonder as a new mom coming out from the dead. After hearing my story unfold, I confessed that the thought of my children being raised without me terrified me; and the thought that our entity, our family, missing a mother, brought me to tears. I had genuine difficulty being referred to as "a miracle." Scoffing at the notion, I countered that I am no more special than the next person. Aren't we all children of God? Why save me? Am I supposed to start a foundation for maternal health? Be a patient advocate? Be a spokesperson for postpartum hemorrhage? Should I share my story? What about my career? My vision of reaching the C-suites was getting blurry. Has my purpose in life changed?

Answers to those backburner questions seemed insufficient. There were honest moments when I felt I failed the women before me who fought for equality, for I was leaning away from going back to work. Not many women had the option to stay at home, and fortunately for me, I did. I recognize the privilege but still felt inadequate. I thought I would fail as a mother to my twins if I returned to work. They almost lost me already. Could I not leave them at home to spend most of my days laboring at work for unequal pay? I also felt I failed. There must be a way that I could be all that and have a loving, balanced family, a successful, thriving career, and contented life.

At the same time, I believed in women supporting women. I ought to help other women who experienced the same. I cannot bear any more children. What does that mean as a woman? What does God want me to do with this experience? The more I explored my mind, the more questions emerged, and the more I felt uncertain about my existence in this world.

My emotional conversations with Sister Angela helped me be at peace with my choice. I was baptized as a Roman Catholic at Easter mass the following year. Sister Angela asked me to deliver the class message during mass. I barely remember what I said to the congregation. But I can't forget her words to me during our sessions.

"Accept that what happened to you was a miracle. Miracles happen beyond our human comprehension."
"You do not need to share your story. The time will come."
"The answer you seek may not be here yet."
"It is enough to be you." She uttered before it became a hashtag.

She also said I would be the most influential person to my girls because the world needs them. So the plan may just be that. I would retreat to these words during those ambiguous parenting years.

I believed that my experience was meant for something big. And I wanted to know so badly what it was. No answer was satisfying enough. Casting my impatience aside, I soaked up the joy my twins brought me. They gave me strength. Against my vision and plans, I chose to be a stay-at-home mom to my daughters. My energy had to focus on nursing them and me to health. It took over half a year before receiving a clean health bill. But the ripple effects of my trauma would linger longer.

In my heart, not going back to work was the best decision I made, even if it appeared that I was sacrificing everything I had wished for myself.

Disruptions are merely disruptions. They are not barriers. But this disruption appeared to be a barrier to what I had dreamed of. Yet, I needed to be thankful that I had a choice to stay home, that I was alive. And I was. I was grateful for my second life. I vowed to be patient and allow the world to reveal my future. The purpose I had envisioned for me has been altered. In time, I would bravely figure it out. These were my thoughts as I fed my babies football-style simultaneously.

SUCCEEDING

I enjoyed being a mom to my girls—teaching them, nurturing them, loving them. Our days were filled with play and lessons as I was determined to raise them to be strong, morally intelligent persons. It was never too early to teach them about kindness. Like most women who had careers before starting a family, I volunteered here and there. I was still restless. So to satisfy my urge, I began a small jewelry home business within two years of the birth of my babies. However, within two years, I had to end my side hustle. I was packing again, moving boxes for sunny Florida, a new land to conquer. At this point, I have lived in the Philippines for only seven years combined, on three continents and in over ten different cities. I have not realized my vision of reaching the C-suites; was I ever going to reach it? In a new town, with a husband with grueling work hours, staying home with the girls was the sensible parenting decision. It gave our girls the stability and assurance they needed. It mattered. I should know; I had been in their shoes many years ago. Indeed, the corner office was fading out of sight. I began to convince myself that it was OK. My purpose at that moment was to be a full-time mom. Meanwhile, my husband was doing very well at his work. I was happy for him, but I was also a bit envious. He expressed his appreciation for my support of his career regularly. Although my role as a parent was crucial to the quality of his patient care, he was aware that I could impact people's lives in a different capacity.

If you have seen the Broadway musical *Pippin*, you would agree that life as a stay-at-home mom drew similarities to the title's character. There were many moments when listening to the soundtrack, I quickly sprung into a dance number, singing out loud, *"..give me a chance, give me my wings... I'm extraordinary, I gotta do extraordinary things."* Pippin's signature song, *"..eagles belong where they can fly. I've got to be where my spirit can run free. Got to find my corner of the sky,"* resonated with me in those child-rearing years. Why did I have these continuing thoughts if I believed motherhood was the ultimate job? I had made my choice, or so it seemed. A small relentless voice inside me reasoned that the world had not revealed itself to me. Extraordinary accomplishments were waiting for me. My husband's unwavering belief in me and his encouragement prevented me from ignoring the voice.

On our drive back from Disney Orlando, while our two girls were fast asleep in the car, my husband and I had one of our deep conversations about life. We had promised early on in our marriage that giving back to the community would be central to our married life. It was about the act and not the amount of money we gave back that was important to us. For the past 14 years of our married life, we had sent used medical textbooks and supplies to a charity hospital in the Philippines. That was not enough. My husband commented that neurosurgery was all he knew to do. His surgical expertise saved many children's lives. I responded that I knew how to do operational matters. Neurosurgery plus operations, the lightbulb moment clicked. We could build our dream together, a non-profit that would advance neurosurgical care in places like the Philippines. We would have a structured way and multiplier effect to give back. We would do away with giving back passively. Instead, we would be proactive in answering the call of those in need. By the time we reached home, we had a plan for The Neurosurgery Outreach Foundation (NOF) to advance neurosurgery care in underserved communities through service, education, and support.

The world had finally revealed my future. It was not as far off as I had envisioned in my naive youth to help people live fulfilling, productive, happy lives. My earlier choices steered me here, after all.

The organization's set-up allowed me to be at home with the kids while utilizing my skills. It was ideal. But, behind the organization's success were countless hours of steady hard work, relationship building, sacrifices, and, more importantly, trust. Trust in me that I knew what I was doing. I had to draw from my trauma to endure the trial and error of building an organization. NOF celebrated its 10th year in 2019. NOF is in nine Southeast Asian countries. NOF has influenced the treatment of hydrocephalus, given over half a million dollars worth of gifts, and empowered young doctors-in-training. NOF is a player in balancing global neurosurgical inequity ahead of trends, such as the sustainable developmental goals set out by the U.N. We are making a difference in people's lives affected by brain diseases. Our work has disrupted the conventional medical mission model as NOF is grounded in the belief that a holistic, collaborative, education-based approach is more sustainable and impactful. Even more remarkable is that NOF inspires a new generation to follow our quest. Ruth Bader Ginsburg said it best, *"Fight for the things that you care about, but do it in a way that will lead others to join you."*

The lessons I learned throughout my crooked career path shaped the way I approach leadership challenges and formed my unique leadership identity. Let me explain.

The constant beat of change fostered resilience. According to the American Psychological Association, resilience is *"the process of adapting well in the face of adversity, trauma, tragedy, threats, or significant sources of stress."* Two major events characterized as traumatic, and stress-inducing are my home-hopping and the life-threatening birth of my children. The latter was particularly impactful as it took me a few years to acknowledge that the event was traumatic and realize that it impacted me in my daily activities. I learned the *"life is short"* lesson to mean things can go wrong at any time, even in the best circumstances. Hence, I worry a lot. But then I remind myself to have the courage to take the steps so things can go well. I have learned to be flexible towards changes but be prepared for surprises. Indeed a very delicate balancing act to achieve. I rely on having a good plan that includes contingency plans for projects and goal settings. As a leader, I provide the vision and direction. Laying out a well-thought-out strategy with my team eliminates unnecessary and costly mistakes and gives my team a high probability of success.

Resilience also means it is important to keep moving and adapting without losing one's essence. My choices, big and small, were guided by an underlying value characteristic of my essence. The basis of my value system is kindness to myself, the world, and the people with whom I share this world. I believe that I contribute to improving this world just as others have. My role perhaps is simply being a conduit to theirs. Adapting to environments and not losing my essence meant not compromising my choices. As leaders, tempting options appear well-intentioned but come with a cost. The cost may compromise the organization's future. To help minimize situations like this, I trust that my leadership would align with my values. Always.

My near-death postpartum underscored where I choose to put my time and energy. It has to be deeply meaningful for me. It is my life that I get to live. I apply this lesson in my personal life when confronted with projects, offers, requests, and anything else that will eat up into my family life. This lesson guided me when I matched individuals with employment opportunities and recruited talent for our non-profit. The work had to mean something to them. The key is to discover what was meaningful for them. And that requires intentional listening to their story, something I mastered, having met different people from different cultures through my travels. In addition, as a leader, the choices I make for the organization or my team has to pass a *"meaningful test"* to ensure that we remain true to our organizational mission. The other lesson I learned but sometimes struggled with is to have the courage to trust a favorable outcome when things go wrong, no matter how bad it looks. Beneficial outcomes are likely to occur when there are reliable systems in place and people who manage them.

Throughout women's history, having a choice was the central theme. We do not want choices to be made for us. We want to have the agency to choose; get an education, who to love, work, start a family, and over our bodies. Looking back, some of the choices presented to me were constrictive. However, I was adamant that I exercised my right to make my choices as freely as possible. It requires courage to make choices. Sadly, not all women have this privilege, even in this day and age. Exceptional leaders who inspire me are very aware of the constrictive choices they confront and are very adept at maneuvering their organizations through creative problem-solving. Plus, these leaders would go above and beyond to disrupt the status quo. These are qualities that I wish to nurture in myself and others.

My growth as a leader did not stem from a goal of simply wanting to be boss. I had to be in a leadership position to make a difference in this world on a macro level or disrupt the status quo. In middle school, I was teased for looking out to the horizon without looking at anything, a polite way of saying I was lazy. I was happy to watch others get things done until a need arose that brought out my leadership skills. First, I was rising to the need to represent the Filipino youth's collective thought on social issues or as a Filipina in a given situation from a woman's perspective. Ordinary me rose to emerge as a leader when given the opportunity. Secondly, getting a group in sync towards a common goal excited me. Combining these two aspects developed my ambition to reach a position of influence. However, having ambition was not enough. Ambition must be coupled with a purpose.

Filipina women worldwide have it in them to lead their organizations, cities, and ideas, but opportunities must be available. Exceptional leaders are made when given representation, mentorship, and opportunities to sharpen leadership qualities.

Although I did not fully believe it but have since accepted my postpartum recovery as a miracle, I believe I have a purpose in this world. Upon reflection, I have known I had a purpose but needed to go with the universe's flow to find it. My life path was not linear. It was as tangled as the flight map of Delta Airlines during the Thanksgiving holiday. Yet my globe-trotting life, marrying my life partner, staying at home after a traumatic pregnancy and birth delivery, and the disconnected choices I made paved the way for who I am now. Accepting the disruptions and their outcomes probably helped in keeping me grounded. It has also led me to my purpose: to be the best mom to my daughters and be the best person to lead NOF.

Undoubtedly, I was my choice architect. Choosing to return to the Philippines led me to my husband, marrying him secured a true life partner that helped me achieve my life goals. The agonizing choice to stay at home and pause my career ensured that I was involved in the lives of my two daughters. My job was to raise strong, well-adjusted, healthy girls to grow up as strong, well-adjusted, healthy women. My daughters are good-hearted individuals on track to contribute to society assertively. Seeing them now validates the right choice I made.

My leadership identity started as wanting to accomplish something and eventually realizing that I also have a responsibility to be a role model and inspire change. I have to make good choices that are rooted in kindness. I work on this by how I treat my team, inspire people to treat others with compassion, and help others re-think what it means to be a Filipina leader. When I turned half a century old and wiser, NOF reached a milestone. I received FWN's Global100 Most Influential Filipina Woman, and several doors of opportunities to further my position of influence opened up. From someone who viewed herself as ordinary, I am doing well in areas that matter to me. Instead of cashing in on a buyout, I am giving money away to get people the care they need. Founding a non-profit as a career was not one of my goals at all. But founding and running NOF makes perfect sense of who I am. NOF's work is global, helps people, and focuses on the Philippines and similarly overlooked places. I am doing this work with my life partner. Even our daughters partake in the cause. When presented with unsatisfactory choices, choosing "none of the above" is still a choice. I decided and created this reality for me. Perhaps Sister Angela was right that being me was enough. I need not have a grandiose response to my experience. It is in the everyday, modest things that I do in my life, my choices on how to treat a person, and where to put my energy; these ordinary things can make a difference in extraordinary ways to those around me. The view from my office is the corner street. The same sunny view for over nine years now. I found my corner of the sky.

FE ODSIGUE PUNZALAN, RNBC, MSN, PHN

Founder and CEO, Punzalan Homes
US FWN100™ 2009, GLOBAL FWN100™ 2019

Business *Not* as Usual

One morning in August of 1997, I was on my knees scrubbing the floor vigorously while my husband German (whom we all affectionately called "Nuno") was in another room setting up furniture. We spent sleepless nights preparing for our opening day while holding down full-time jobs at the hospital and post office. Reality was about to hit us that we really were business owners, and there was no turning back. Taking on the responsibility of operating an adult residential care home seemed enormous enough, but choosing to serve persons with intellectual disabilities seemed like a much higher mountain to surmount. In hindsight, despite the training Nuno and I received, and even with my 22 years in the nursing field, we had no idea of what we were getting ourselves into. The financial and sweat investments leading up to that moment were the less challenging part of the process compared to facing the severity of the conditions and behaviors of the residents who ended up in our care.

A Defining Moment

"Kon indi ka mabaton sa UP-PGH School of Nursing,
rudya na lang ikaw para magtanom kita ka tangkong."
— CRISPINA CORDERO ODSIGUE, my mother

I clearly remember when my *Nanay* reassured me in 1972 that if I did not get accepted to the University of the Philippines-Philippine General Hospital (UP-PGH) School of Nursing, I could stay home and plant *kangkong* or water spinach with her. My mother's words have fueled me ever since to give my best in everything I did. They still ring in my head to this day as I marvel over how my life has unfolded. I grew up as one of eleven children in a family in Sibalom, Antique, that had barely enough to eat. Now I am a mother of three and a businesswoman in California, where I can take my family and friends out to eat anytime I want.

People who are unfamiliar with my background and only see the current Fe—an entrepreneur, philanthropist, and board member—tend to think that I had an easy life and often tell me, *"Mabuti ka pa..."* Little do they know the countless times I went to bed hungry as a little girl, or when we did eat, it would usually be rice and salt or a little bit of *sapsap*, a type of dried fish. They do not know about my *Nanay* making *bandi*, or peanut brittle, that I would help sell for five centavos. They do not know about my going to college, having to make do with three textbooks, and the countless times I had to struggle to have basic items for daily life.

Few know that out of all the nice things I am fortunate to have now, my eight pillows are some of the most cherished items that I look forward to every night. They are a source of good rest and a constant reminder of how far I have come in life: from my family in Sibalom not having a permanent home growing up to having the resources I need to give my children a good education and help relatives in the Philippines attain financial security.

I love my *Nanay*, but I really did not want to plant *kangkong* as a career path, so I worked my tail off.

The Road to Entrepreneurship

How did I go from selling peanut brittle in the rural Philippines as a child to being the owner and administrator of Punzalan Homes (dba Flintcrest House I & II/Silver Star RCH/ICF/DD-N) in the Santa Clara County Area?

It was a long, arduous road, but the seed that led to opening a residential care home was planted in 1996 when I was an assistant department nurse manager at the Regional Medical Center of San Jose. A nurse colleague noticed how I successfully engaged with a belligerent patient when other care providers could not and suggested I help her at the community care facility she managed to serve adults with intellectual disabilities. I ended up volunteering for a year in addition to keeping my full-time job while also moonlighting in a psychiatric facility during weekends.

During this time, Nuno and I already had three children, with the eldest one about to start college, and we realized we wanted the financial freedom to give our daughters the best education we could. I also did not want to be confined to working 12–16 hour days, so Nuno and I took a leap of faith.

Opening a residential care facility took about eighteen months from start to finish. The two main components of it were first, to acquire the Community Care License by the Department of Social Services to be able to set up a residential care home, and second, to become an approved vendor for the San Andreas Regional Center, the state agency which would refer potential residents to the facility. Applicants needed to have a history of good credit reports and at least three months' worth of start-up funds. Per requirements to date, applicants need at least a year of formal experience taking care of persons with intellectual disabilities and not just in a volunteer capacity. I had to hire consultants to help navigate the application process.

After going through the process, purchasing a house and renovating it, then refinancing our own home to cover all the costs, Nuno and I had $200 left in the bank. That felt scary, and we were also intimidated by balancing full-time work and managing the business. Therefore, we focused on our North Star of how the investment will dramatically improve how we provide for our daughters and make a difference in the lives of the residents and their families.

In the beginning, Nuno and I were the only staff, and we started with one resident, but this person had to transition out after two months once his care team (which included his mother) determined that he was not ready to be in a less restrictive residence such as ours. He came from a locked facility, and his family hoped for him to receive less intense treatment and be in a less confined environment. Locked facilities generally are fully secure areas for individuals considered a danger to others or themselves and can only be accessed by registered primary caregivers. After this resident dismantled all six beds in a room, ripped signage, and left a pile of mattresses in the living room, there was no denying he still needed a higher level of support. Not long after he left, we found our next resident when a woman suddenly showed up at our door declaring she would be living at our facility. We learned immediately that she had set her previous care home on fire before coming to us! It was definitely an "Oh my God!" moment, but we let her stay anyway. We had four residents at the end of our first year in operation. We were able to finally hire staff and start building an interdisciplinary team that would eventually grow to include direct care providers, psychologists, behaviorists, recreational and occupational therapists, nutritionists, and special educators.

The People in Our Care

The American Psychiatric Association defines intellectual disability as challenges in people's mental abilities affecting two areas: intellectual functioning (e.g. learning, judgment) and adaptive functioning (e.g. daily life activities such as communication and independent living). Several mental health, neurodevelopmental, medical, and physical conditions like autism and epilepsy often co-occur in individuals with intellectual disabilities. Individuals with intellectual disabilities can have productive and meaningful roles in society given an accurate diagnosis and the proper support, not just by care providers and family members but by the broader community.

Punzalan Homes' philosophy is that all individuals deserve and have the right to respect and dignity and to experience typical daily activities to the fullest extent possible. We honor this by centering residents in our program design and providing them with meaningful activities, helping them to stay healthy, and supporting their community integration. Our residents participate, to the extent that they can, in developing individualized program plans based on their conditions and assessed needs. Our efforts aim to enhance residents' adaptive skills in personal management, such as self-care and independence and the ability for self-advocacy and leisure. Our behavioral services emphasize replacing maladaptive behaviors, including physical or verbal aggression, running away, negative reactions, and self-harm, with socially appropriate and safe behaviors.

Behaviors and deficits that residents at the Punzalan Homes display fall within a broad spectrum: we have a child with autism who is non-verbal and has mainly needed help with grooming, eating, and toileting; and then we had individuals who would topple down furniture, bang their heads on the floor, escape through windows and go missing, climb trees, or strike people. We also have residents with physical limitations who are wheelchair-bound, legally blind, or hearing impaired. Frequently, we are the last stop for persons with severe behavioral issues and co-occurrences as other facilities refuse to accept them.

The experience I gained over the years in various settings equipped me and gave me confidence in operating the care home. Opening a second facility was not part of the original plan. Still, a year after we opened Punzalan Homes, an opportunity to expand surfaced, and by 2007, we had a total of 24 residents and 25 staff members.

I continue to be amazed today by the positive momentum the business has had. Even though I became an entrepreneur in 1997, the moment that set me off on this trajectory was when I was eleven years old. I realized, while in bed hungry, that the first step for my family and me to get out of poverty was for me to become the sixth-grade valedictorian.

Overcoming Barriers One by One

While my family struggled when I was growing up from having very little means, this did not discourage me; and instead, it became my driving force to believe in greater possibilities. My mantra became "strive, survive, and thrive." I accomplished becoming a valedictorian in elementary, which enabled me to get a scholarship for high school. Money continued to be tight for the family, so I only had two sets of uniforms, but I did not complain. *Uba, laba, suksok mara.* As soon as I got home, I would take my uniform off, wash it and hang it to dry.

When I was accepted into the UP-PGH School of Nursing, it was another step toward breaking the cycle of poverty in my family, but a long road of studying and challenges still awaited me. In the end, I graduated Top 5 out of 75 in the nursing class of 1975.

When I moved to the U.S. in 1977, the striving and surviving continued. For one, I could not afford to take a review class for the Illinois Board of Nursing license exam, but I passed it anyway. Then, after six months of working at Provident Hospital, I was assigned to manage a unit providing acute care for adults despite having little training; it felt like being thrown into a lion's den. But I figured it out like I usually do.

Learning and Leading by Doing

My parents were my role models for authentic leadership and my inspiration on how to face challenges throughout my life. I always drew from their unwavering determination to make ends meet for our family.

My *Nanay* embodied resourcefulness and persistence. She always sold various things to put food on the table; she even had a small store and my older sister recalls *Nanay* wrapping me tightly in a *patadyong* fabric when I was a baby to keep me secure while I slept, so she could work. She was also a seamstress and often stayed up until 2 a.m. sewing to earn a few pesos to pay for the kids' tuition fees.

My *Tatay* emphasized the importance of education and showed me how to stand up for myself. I distinctly remember the time when I was unfairly given Third Honors only in high school in favor of two other students who had privileged connections to the school. My *Tatay*, having just suffered a stroke and feeling weak, went to meet with the school director to rectify the situation. Recognition with First Honors in the class meant I received a scholarship for the following school year. *Tatay* would say, *"Bisan pobre kita, kinahanglan mabato gid kita basta husto lang."* Ever since then, I never let being dirt poor get in the way of fighting for what is right.

My high school teacher, Mrs. Rabago, always told students that the key to success is to *"finish what you start."* Her voice never left my head, and to this day, when I am working late at night and feel sleepy, I would force myself to finish because she said that doing it the next day would take three times more of my time. As a result, whenever I fight the urge to procrastinate and choose to complete a task, I always feel relief.

Since I became affiliated with Filipina Women's Network (FWN) in 2009, I have started thinking more deeply about leadership. I was also inspired to explore how I showed leadership in various realms of my life. In addition, I have examined the intersecting roles of my identity as a woman, a Filipina immigrant, a mother, and a professional.

When I think of my leadership strengths, my tenacity comes to mind. I am the type who wants to find answers, and I cannot stop until I get them. I am also assertive and an independent thinker. I was timid growing up, and while that has changed, I am still usually the quiet one in the room, but I always speak up or take action once I think it is crucial. Listening more than talking allows me to assess a situation and make better decisions.

I also believe in having a generous spirit and helping others whenever possible. I benefited over my lifetime from the kindness of different people, and it has been a personal purpose of mine to keep paying it forward.

Looking at the Mirror

The invitation from FWN to reflect on my journey to being who I am now made me curious about how others see me and their overall experience of me. So I invited family members, friends, former classmates, and people from my professional network to complete a survey and share their thoughts on my leadership strengths, how I navigate adversities, and how I have impacted their lives. I felt honored to have everyone accommodate my request, and it was incredible how they vividly remembered details.

Reviewing the responses, I noticed alignment between my self-assessment and others' perceptions of me. I am pleased to learn they recognize that I give my best to live with integrity and also how motivated, persistent, hardworking, assertive, and approachable I am. It also makes me happy that people see my willingness to help and share resources and that they know how grateful I am when they are the ones who help me.

This experience of asking for feedback was very humbling and felt like a culmination of over fifty-six years of striving, surviving, and finally, thriving! It was touching to learn how some respondents consider me someone they look up to and try to emulate so they can succeed. I am thankful that sharing my simple life story has inspired them to pursue their destiny no matter how difficult the journey could be.

Business is Personal

I am often asked about the secret to my success, especially regarding my business. In return, I usually ask how success is defined because I do not subscribe to the traditional notion of success that is tied to power, wealth, and prestige.

I must say that while Punzalan Homes is a business that started with the hope of bringing financial stability to my family, it is not entirely profit-driven. I do not see residents as sources of revenue nor employees as subordinates.

Rather, I honor the inherent dignity and God-given talents each person possesses and do my best to bring in residents and staff whom I know the care home will be able to create a space to develop their potential.

One of the things that makes the organization unique is the culture we cultivate. As the primary administrator, it was important for me to establish from the very beginning a tone of professionalism, mutual respect, and a standard of excellence when it came to the service we provided and how we carried ourselves as human beings. I do not tolerate gossiping and instead promote a practice of healthy communication and an openness to improving, regardless of rank or tenure in the company. Even with residents with limited verbal ability, we find ways to ensure they can communicate with staff and feel safe and respected in our space.

Empowering others and creating a respectful environment conducive to collaborating are also important for me as a leader and how I run my business. I do my best to ensure that everyone's strengths are uplifted and there is room for everyone to participate in the planning and implementation of the work; this is true for staff, the residents, and their family members or guardians. I do not put a premium on hierarchy and titles, so I ensure everyone feels equal and that there is room to speak up to share ideas, concerns, and sometimes even disagreements.

Earning the trust and dedication of staff has been equally important to me therefore, the company offers them wages and bonuses above the industry average and various opportunities for professional development and advancement. These are all performance-based, and no one is exempt from improvement plans, including family members on staff. While I have hired relatives over the years, I maintain the same expectations from everyone regarding work. *Sa business wara ti pamilya pamilya.* People know I am very friendly but will not hesitate to make corrections or dismissals when needed. I have been fortunate to have capable team members who are trustworthy and make it easy for me to delegate responsibilities and develop a strong leadership bench.

I know the company has been on the right track because this is reflected in the level of motivation demonstrated by the staff and the low turnover we have. In addition, we get positive written evaluations from facility monitoring, surveys, and quality assurance reports from Community Care Licensing and San Andrea Regional Center (SARC) agencies. Other indications that our company has done a good job overall include: using as an example for others to follow a Home Based Community Services grant application I submitted in 2021, being awarded the Service Provider of the Year recognition by SARC in 2002, and receiving three grants from the same agency. Never in the history of SARC has this happened, let alone to an entity owned by a person from Antique! *Mabuhay ang mga taga Sibalom!*

Success is not only about how far I have come but what I do with that success. I had plenty of opportunities to open more care homes, and doing so would have been very lucrative, but I knew my limits and did not want to stretch myself thin. So, instead of expanding my company because the need for providers continues to be great, I taught other *kababayans* how to fish. From 2002 to 2005, I coached seven Filipino couples on becoming administrators and licensed care providers. I documented the detailed steps, gave tips, and even welcomed them to my facilities so they could shadow the daily operations. To this day, I make myself available to them if they have questions or need support. It has been very gratifying to see how these couples have established themselves as trusted and seasoned care providers and, as a result, improved their own families' financial situation and even created jobs for their local communities. The only payment I ever asked them is that they give the highest quality care to their residents.

I am grateful to feel like I am finally thriving. The challenges continue, but they look different for me now, and I have the privilege of bringing others along to thrive. My daughter once wrote me a letter quoting the rapper Frank Ocean that resonated with me: *"Work hard in silence. Let your success be your noise."* I do not usually say much, but if my success benefits others, then I do not mind making noise at all!

When the Impossible Becomes Possible

I am drawn to supporting individuals with intellectual disabilities because I can relate to them in some ways. So often, they are considered helpless, their condition hopeless, and there is no way they can live meaningful lives and contribute positively to society. I also feel an affinity with people, especially my fellow Filipinos, who struggle to make ends meet and likely see no relief.

As someone who grew up extremely poor, migrated to the United States with minimal English, and then dared to be a businesswoman, I have experienced being stigmatized and underestimated. Thankfully, I was determined not to have my circumstances define me, and a series of powerful transformations led to who I have become.

As an immigrant in America, I had moments of doubting my abilities and not feeling accepted, but these did not stop me from trying. In the end, the work ethic and respect instilled in me back in Antique worked to my advantage as this Filipina immigrant reached leadership positions. Often my promotions resulted from my managers advocating for me, which was a real validation of my exemplary performance. This diligence carried over to the business, which taught me that sometimes the best way to counter being treated negatively is to kill people with kindness and competence. These days nobody crosses me once they figure out I know what I am doing. Parents of residents in the care home have gone from questioning me to now saying, *"Do whatever you feel is right, Fe; you have my support,"* which is very empowering as it is a real privilege to be entrusted with the care of a loved one.

Working with people with intellectual disabilities has proved that no matter how seemingly hopeless someone's situation is, growth and progress are possible, even if they take a really long time. The residents in our facilities achieve a level of well-being almost unimaginable at the beginning of their placement when given the proper support and authentic belief in their potential. Hearing feedback from families and authorized representatives on how their loved ones made significant progress and are enjoying a better quality of life is the ultimate reward. For example, the autistic child who was previously unable to eat, shower, or toilet on her own can now do these things and even do exercises. Remember the resident who came to our facility after burning a care home? She left us two years later...to get married!

It is heartening that there are increased efforts to honor the dignity of the people we serve. Starting March 2023, the Department of Developmental Services is shifting the way it funds how community-based services are provided and will put a greater emphasis on person-centered approaches. The new Home and Community Based Setting Rule states that care settings will need to focus on the nature and quality of the experiences of people served, not only about the physical structure of where they are cared for, thus ensuring that people served play an active role in the development of their plan. This approach truly aligns with my philosophy and our facilities' current practices, and I am excited that it is being standardized.

Metamorphosis

Reflecting on my life journey, I feel like I shed a cocoon and turned into a beautiful butterfly. I went from being shy and naive to being self-directed and assertive out of fear of being unable to depend on others. All the striving and surviving made me a strong woman. Who I am today is a culmination of dedication, resilience, passion for my work, and empathy for people who need help. While I take pride in having made it this far due to my hard work and determination, some people paved the way for me, sustained me, and made all the effort worthwhile. Because of them, I am thriving and blessed to be able to enjoy the fruits of my labor with them.

My *Ate* Ray is the fifth child in the family and the reason the six of her younger siblings, including myself, were able to go to school. She was a teacher and my role model; without her encouragement and inspiration to pursue my studies, I would not be who I am today. She sacrificed a lot by giving her full pay to my *Nanay* to help buy food for the family. Even today, she selflessly provides for her family and continues to enrich my life with her company, skills, and wisdom.

The Lord blessed me with three daughters who have made my heart so full that sometimes I think it will burst. They all have become nurses and blessed me with six *apos* [grandkids], all girls too! Women and girls rule the world, at least in our family. Clarisse is my eldest daughter; she is very sweet, thoughtful, and mature. She is highly regarded by her friends and colleagues and very loving to her daughters. I am especially grateful for the help and understanding she extended to her Dad and me as we set up the business, and she would always take care of her younger sisters. Christina is my second daughter, who is very doting and curious. I was amazed when she would ask me questions, thinking I had all the answers. She is also very organized, driven, and supportive of her family, especially regarding their passions. Finally, Maureen is the youngest and the jolly one. She loves to dance to greet me, and I love it when she calls me, "My mommy sunshine." I am grateful for her recognizing the value of my work and encouraging me every step of the way.

My husband Nuno was my number one cheerleader and favorite dance partner of almost 40 years. He believed in me more than I did in myself and gave me unconditional support even when I chose to get my master's degree while holding a full-time job and taking care of three children. When I was unsure how to proceed with opening a care home, he told me, *"You're a nurse.*

You can do it." Unfortunately, he passed away too soon in 2018 from a cerebral aneurysm. This devastated me and led to an extended depression, but my daughters comforted me through this. While mourning a life partner never ceases, I have started taking care of myself again the way I know Nuno would want me to. Whenever I miss him, I would just remember the times he would always tell me, *"Ginahigugma ko ikaw tuod gid,"* to which I would answer back, *"I love you too, that's the truth."*

I feel very fulfilled at this point in my life and grateful for the rocky yet meaningful journey that got me here. Not a day passes when I do not think about my parents' struggles while growing up, but I will not exchange my childhood for anything. As poor as we were monetary, our family was extremely rich in love and support for one another.

Looking ahead, I want to enjoy the simple things in life, whether it is spending more quality time with my daughters, *apos*, and siblings or cultivating my newly found love for ballroom dancing. With work, I feel confident about my team at Punzalan Homes and the succession plan we set in place; while I am not stepping down anytime soon, I think it is important to be prepared for any scenario. Finally, I do not see myself ever stopping in advocating for our residents and, more broadly, for persons with intellectual disabilities and the field supporting them.

I also want to keep inspiring others to believe that nothing is impossible with hard work, self-confidence, and faith. If they do not believe me, I would tell them about the houses my nephews built near rice paddies in Antique with some financial help from me. I would also tell them that this area is where I would have spent my life planting *kangkong* with my *Nanay* had I not dared to believe in something more.

JOYCE RIVERA JAVIER MD, MPH, MS

Filipino Family Health Initiative
Associate Professor of Clinical Pediatrics,
Children's Hospital Los Angeles
USC Keck School of Medicine, Department of Pediatrics &
Department of Population & Public Health Sciences
GLOBAL FWN100™ 2018

For Us, By Us: From Listening to Leadership

For Us, By Us is a chapter about my experience being a second-generation Filipina American with multiple identities: daughter, sister, mother, wife, physician, researcher, educator, and community advocate. From discovering my Filipina identity during college to developing a statewide initiative to prevent teen suicide and depression among Filipino youth, I describe key moments in my life that have shaped me into the woman I am today and draw upon key lessons from the concepts of community-based participatory research and servant leadership. I describe key life lessons based on my favorite quotes and proverbs. I also share key leadership lessons in which I have applied the cultural values of *bayanihan, kapwa*, and awareness of self and others to my leadership journey. I share my unique experience as a Filipina physician-scientist who has dedicated her career to addressing behavioral health disparities among Filipino youth. By sharing how those before me helped pave the way for me and how I managed my personal life and career, I hope to inspire young Filipinas to pursue their true passions.

Shaping My Identity

I am a second-generation Filipina American born in an area of Los Angeles called Historic Filipinotown, quite fittingly the first geographical designation honoring Filipinos in the U.S. My parents immigrated here from the Philippines in the 1970s. I am the eldest of three daughters, and my parents and grandparents raised us to believe we could do anything if we set our mind to it.

Overall, my college experience shaped who I am today: a Filipina physician-scientist conducting community-based participatory research and an educator and advocate. I attended UCLA and before I arrived, Filipino alumni like the late Dawn Mabalon Ph.D. and Former Cerritos Mayor Mark Pulido were already paving the pathway to success for us. Because of their advocacy, Filipinos were identified as being at higher risk for college drop-out, and thus there were Filipino college organizations that were helping us thrive during college. For instance, Samahang Pilipino Education and Retention (SPEAR) was an organization that provided peer counseling and advising. SPEAR was actually founded by Dr. Dawn Mabalon, a previous FWN awardee and founder of Little Manila Rising in Stockton. I followed the advice of my SPEAR counselor, who recommended that I specialize (which is similar to a minor) in ethnic studies, specifically Asian American Studies. Since I liked science, I majored in Physiological Sciences. Although these two fields seemed unrelated initially, they proved synergistic in my education.

> I am the product of my ancestors and the Filipino community, who paved the way for me.

I did not always know I wanted to be a physician, and my family did not force medicine on me. I had never seen a Filipina female physician in my life until college, so I did not consider it a career. I still remember the first time I met a Filipina medical student who was also a mother. I was introduced to her at a pre-health conference organized by UC Irvine's Pilipinx Pre-Health Undergraduate Student Organization (PUSO) and UC Irvine's School of Medice's Filipino Americans in Medicine (FAIM) chapter. Filipino health professionals were sharing with undergrads about their perspective fields. Before meeting this Filipina, I had explored almost every other health career except medicine. After meeting her, I started believing that medicine was possible for me. I have told this story to my daughters many times, and they always share, *"I hardly see male doctors now, mom."* What a difference one generation can make!

Know History, Know Self

Two college courses I took also shaped my career choice. First, I took a Filipino American History course by the late "Uncle" Roy Morales. From him, I first learned about Filipino American History and the stories of our *"manongs"* and ancestors who faced racism and discrimination in the U.S. Second, I took a course called Asian American Health Disparities by Professor Marjorie Kagawa-Singer. In this course, I first learned about health disparities affecting Filipinos in the U.S., the importance of data disaggregation to paint an accurate picture of the health needs of Asian American, Native Hawaiian, and Pacific Islanders, and the dangers of the model minority myth. Overall, my college experience convinced me to pursue a medical and public health research career to give back to the Filipino community that raised me.

Falling in Love with Pediatrics

Medical school was a blur, but when I came out of it, I had fallen in love with pediatrics and my husband, a wonderful man who has always been supportive of my career. I was drawn to pediatrics because of the relationship we develop with families and children over time. As I reflect on my career choice, it is such an honor, privilege, and blessing to be a pediatrician. First Lady Dr. Jill Biden recently said in a speech addressing pediatricians, *"Pediatricians are so much more than doctors—you're healers, teachers, and counselors, you're lifelines for parents lost in worry and fear."* (Biden J, 2022)

After graduating from medical school, it was time to foster my interest in advocacy and public health. I was attracted to Stanford's pediatric residency program because it offered a community advocacy track. It was here that I started to learn about community-based participatory research, CBPR, a methodology that has become the backbone of my research team's initiatives. CBPR is epitomized by the saying, *"Nothing about us without us"* which was first coined by activists in the disability community who were proponents of involving individuals with a disability when determining policies that would affect them. CBPR involves listening to the community when addressing their needs and using their strengths to solve wicked problems they are facing collaboratively. It involves mutual respect and understanding and serving others with sustainability in mind, which are concepts and values that have shaped my approach to leadership. According to the WK Kellogg Foundation's Community Health Scholars Program, CBPR is defined as "a collaborative approach to research that equitably involves all partners in the research process and recognizes the unique strengths that each brings. CBPR begins with a research topic of importance to the community, has the aim of combining knowledge into action and achieving social change to improve health outcomes and eliminate health disparities. (WK Kellogg Foundation Community Health Scholars Program)."

I also wanted to go to Stanford because of the faculty member I interviewed with for my residency. I had an interview with Dr. Fernando Mendoza, a Latino pediatrician who was an expert in immigrant child health disparities and the Assistant Dean of Minority Advising and Programs. I still remember sitting in his office looking at the books on immigrant child health that he had written on his shelves. He shared his passion for bringing light to the importance of disaggregating Latino subgroups to understand health outcomes and inspired me to think I could do the same with Asian American, Native Hawaiian, and Pacific Islander populations. Dr. Mendoza eventually became my mentor during my postdoctoral fellowship and, to this day, still provides his guidance and support.

Finding my Passion: Make a Difference

Completing my pediatrics residency and a postdoctoral fellowship in general academic pediatrics at Stanford University were pivotal moments in my training to become a physician-scientist. My mentors and femtors during this time shaped me into the researcher I am today by teaching me how to achieve work-life balance in a career involving clinical care, advocacy, research, and teaching. My mentors made me believe in President John F Kennedy's saying, *"One person can make a difference, and everyone should try."* They also taught me to pursue my passion, and often the most challenging thing about research is choosing what you are not going to research since there are so many problems to solve in this world.

During my pediatrics residency, I started my first community-based project, which focused on teen pregnancy prevention in the Filipino community. I began by looking at the data, which there was not a lot of, and by meeting with the Filipino Youth Coalition, a community-based organization serving the Filipino community in Milpitas, CA. Leaders at the Filipino Youth Coalition confirmed that teen pregnancy was an issue they also wanted to address and agreed to partner with me (Javier et al, 2010). We obtained funding from the American Academy of Pediatrics Community Access to Child Health program and this was the first time I received a grant in my career. We developed a teen pregnancy prevention conference in partnership with clergy, community partners, and students and held it twice. At the end of the second conference, we presented a survey to attendees who were youth and learned that, in their opinion, the most dangerous thing that affected youth was mental/emotional health. This opened my eyes to the importance of listening first to the voices of whom we are trying to serve. In retrospect, it would have been ideal to ask the youth their perspective first so that we could have focused earlier on mental health. Nonetheless, I learned from these early career experiences and applied lessons learned in the next chapter of my career.

Another important issue I learned after listening to the community was that Filipino community-based organizations shared feedback that there are not enough data and research studies that highlight the needs of Filipino youth. This motivated me to pursue a Masters of Public Health during my fellowship focused on epidemiology. This training enabled me to conduct studies describing disparities among Filipino youth in the U.S. so those community organizations, policymakers, and future researchers could advocate for funding to develop programs to address these health inequities. My subsequent peer-reviewed publications that described these studies were more than research papers. They were labors of love and advocacy (Javier et al, 2007, Javier JR et al, 2010) and continue to validate the experiences of Filipino youth and families that are often overlooked and underrecognized.

Balancing Motherhood with Career Aspirations

I recently learned that the United States has the most extended medical education system in the developed world (Thompson D, 2022). For myself, I studied for an additional 14 years after graduating from high school before starting my first real job. During this long journey, I chose to wait until I neared the end of it before starting a family. When I became a mother, my world turned upside down as I struggled with wanting to be the best parent possible while also succeeding in a demanding yet rewarding profession. It was challenging to be ambitious while also balancing motherhood. I was often envious of both stay-at-home mothers and successful female and male colleagues who seemed to be advancing faster in their careers. However, one of my female mentors reminded me that there will always be someone at work to replace you, but at home, you are irreplaceable. This was an important realization as I let go of my envy and instead gave myself the grace to take my time during my career and prioritize what to say no to and what to say yes to so that I could be as present as possible for my two daughters. I have no regrets about my choices and treasure the many memories I have made with my daughters, from volunteering in their classrooms, or during field trips, to watching them perform as talented dancers and grow into confident young women. They both amaze me every day, and I am so proud to call them my daughters.

My children also inspire me to try to do my part in making the world a better place for them. I have also realized that making sure that the work I choose to do is meaningful has helped me deal with the working mom's guilt. I am very fortunate to be able to do work that I love. I thank my parents, grandparents, extended family, and ancestors who paved the way for me to have the luxury of being able to balance motherhood and work. And I have my mentors and femtors to thank for teaching me how to advocate for myself and pursue my passion.

I have also learned that research shows that if we do meaningful work, it can help prevent work-related stress and prevent a concept called moral injury. Moral injury is a concept that physicians may feel from working in a health care system that prevents them from providing the best care they can for their patients. I have had the opportunity to advocate for system changes in how we practice medicine by working with fellow pediatricians as a leader in pediatric professional societies, which is another rewarding aspect of my career (Dilley K, Javier JR, 2021).

As a faculty member, I listened to what the youth identified as a critical issue to address while I was a fellow: mental health. I quickly learned that in order to address the mental health of Filipino American youth, we needed to listen to their stories, break down silos, and partner across sectors. It helped me realize the meaning behind the African proverb, *"If you want to go fast, go alone, but if you want to go far, go together."* My first faculty research project involved asking youth, parents, grandparents, clergy, health and mental health professionals, educators, and government officials the following questions: What are the mental health needs of Filipino teens, and how can we prevent these issues? The community's collective answer was to offer parenting workshops during the school-age years (Javier et al, 2014). I did not come up with this solution; I just provided the support to harness our community's collective voice and create a shared solution (Javier et al, 2016, Javier et al, 2018). Also, when we faced barriers, we continued to engage community voices through a community advisory board that provided feedback. For instance, to increase enrollment in parenting workshops, our community advisory board and the first group of pioneer parents who completed the workshops recommended that we make a culturally tailored video (Javier et al, 2014). Many of the parents offered to be in the video to provide their testimonials (Flores et al, 2015). We conducted a randomized control trial to evaluate this video with the help of many Filipino student interns, providers, and community partners (Javier et al, 2018, Javier JR 2018, Javier et al 2019). Another example of "For Us, by Us." More than a decade later, our Filipino Family Health initiative continues offering evidence-based parenting workshops to Filipino families and has expanded beyond Los Angeles to other communities.

Another important part of my leadership journey is being accepted into the Robert Wood Johnson Foundation's Clinical Scholars Fellowship. This fellowship requires that mid-career health professionals apply together in teams. Our team was called Team *Kapwa*, which means shared identity in Tagalog. During the three-year fellowship, leading Team *Kapwa* helped me understand the power of authenticity, vulnerability, and collaboration. As a result, we expanded the Filipino Family Health Initiative's community partners, offered the first ever conference on Filipino Family Wellness focused on decreasing mental health stigma, conducted a study to create a shared definition of youth mental health for Filipino-Americans, obtained additional funding, and grew individually as leaders (Sepulveda A, et al, 2019; Sepulveda A et al, 2021).

Coping with the Impact of COVID-19 on the Filipino Family Health Initiative

By the time the COVID-19 pandemic hit the world, the Filipino Family Health Initiative had been offering the Incredible Years®, an evidence-based parenting program to Filipino families for ten years. We offered Incredible Years® in partnership with community-based organizations, school districts, churches (multiple denominations), and mental health and primary care clinics in person. The trust we built over this decade with families and community organizations enabled us to adapt to offering Incredible Years® online. Our community advisory board of parents, grandparents, and community partners agreed to pilot test an online version of the program before we provided it to families as part of an ongoing study. I am very grateful to our community advisory board members; their impact on our work is another example of how the Filipino Family Health Initiative is for us and by us. Also, when we work in teams together, we can achieve even more. In addition to moving the Incredible Years® online, we expanded beyond Los Angeles to the entire state of California. Through *kapwa* [shared identity], we identified additional Filipino community organizations and school districts in the Bay Area and Stockton to partner with.

Beyond mental health, we were also able to partner with our *kababayan*, who were addressing the health and economic impact of the pandemic on our community. It was inspiring and amazing to see how our Filipino/a/x brothers and sisters mobilized to ensure Filipinos were seen in this pandemic. The theme of working across sectors continued during the pandemic, and I am confident this will continue post-pandemic. For instance, I was asked to speak on topics such as combatting domestic violence, vaccine hesitancy, the impact of COVID on children, and the implications of Anti-Asian hate on youth. I was also invited for interviews by fellow *Pinays* and the mainstream press on television, the radio, and newspaper articles (See Footnotes 1-11). This ability to work together in the spirit of *bayanihan* [spirit of helping others without expecting anything in return] fueled me. It helped me from suffering racial battle fatigue and moral injury as a healthcare worker. It made me even more proud to be a *Pinay*, despite the darker moments of this pandemic, such as the disproportionate number of Filipino nurses who were dying of COVID-19 and the rise in hate crimes again Asian women, the elderly, youth, and adults. Being proud of my ethnic background is very important to me as this was modeled to me by my parents and is something I want to model to my daughters. Increasing cultural pride promotes positive mental health outcomes, academic achievement among our youth, and higher self-esteem.

Moreover, the sisterhood developed by FWN was also critical to my well-being. For instance, during one of our virtual water cooler sessions, I learned about the term racial battle fatigue from FWN sister Dr. Janet Stickmon. I was grateful to participate in a workshop she developed to promote self-care during the pandemic. She reminded me that rest is also a form of resistance and that it is important to have fun and enjoy life. Thanks to this realization, I have found joy in continuing old hobbies such as crocheting and trying new things such as hip-hop, ballet, and tap dancing.

Sharing Life Lessons

> *"Leaders must transition from being responsible for the job to being responsible for the people who are responsible for the job."* – SIMON SINEK

When reflecting on the different types of leadership philosophies, I feel that servant leadership resonates the most with me. The quote above describes servant leadership. It involves listening to those we lead so that they feel heard, appreciated, and respected. This approach transcends all aspects of my life: when I conduct community-based participatory research and listen to the voices of youth, parents, and community members; when I teach parents positive parenting principles that involve spending quality time with their children and actively listening to their children; and when I navigate parenting my children and relationships with family members.

> *"Each time a woman stands up for herself, without knowing it, possibly without reclaiming it, she stands up for all women."* – MAYA ANGELOU

The first time I experienced discrimination was around age 8, when a group of boys chased my sisters and me and yelled racial slurs. My mother, one of the strongest women I know, stood up for us and told them to stop. My mother was modeling to me at an early age to always stand up for what I believe in. In fact, both my mother and father taught me to serve others and stand up for those who might not be able to advocate for themselves. Their example explain why I gravitated towards pediatrics and community service.

"We cannot seek achievement for ourselves and forget about progress and prosperity for our community... Our ambitions must be broad enough to include the aspirations and needs of others, for their sakes and for our own." – CESAR CHAVEZ

This quote epitomizes the meaning of *kapwa*, which is shared identity. In other words, what happens to me, happens to you and what happens to them, happens to us. It means we are all connected to one another. We need to lift each other and not bring each other down. It also means femtoring the next generation so that they will do the same for future generations. As an educator, I have the privilege of teaching undergraduate and graduate students a course on addressing health inequities in the U.S. It is truly rewarding to share my story and knowledge through academia and encourage the next generation of public health, health, and mental health professionals to address racism and discrimination in their future work.

"Your legacy is like planting a garden with seeds that you will never get to see." – LIN MANUEL MIRANDA

This quote makes me think about my legacy and what I am going to leave behind. How will my relationships with my children affect my children's children? How will my work affect generations to come and honor the labor and sacrifices of my ancestors? Will there be more that look like me who become change leaders advocating for a system that truly celebrates gender and racial equity? I would say yes, the future looks bright. For when I leave this world, I will be proud of what I did to make it a brighter place.

MARIVIC LUALHATI, PH.D.

President and CEO, Beyond Medical Hub
Corporate Trainer, Inspire Leadership Consultancy Inc.
GLOBAL FWN100™ 2019

Leadership in Healthcare

The landscape of healthcare is intricate, dynamic, and volatile. Long before the concept of the VUCA world existed, the healthcare industry evolved in volatile, uncertain, complex, and ambiguous circumstances. The industry breathes unpredictably. Thus, leading a healthcare organization entails having a visionary, strategic and collaborative leader.

As visionary leaders, we know clearly where we are bringing the organization, what culture we are to develop, or, in some cases, redirect the culture to become patient-centric that operates in a most efficient process. Strategic leaders concretize the vision into chewable chunks of measurable terms like financial viability, learning and growth, sound internal business processes, and ingrained customer delighting culture. These organizational measures serve as the lighted pathways in leading healthcare institutions. Consequently, the healthcare team, from the glass wall of the executives to the administrative services, emergency room to busy patient floors, doctor's clinic to ancillary services, back of house support departments, among others—must clearly understand how those measures resonate with their departments.

Understanding and believing those organizational goals are essential for a patient-centric culture ignites a consuming passion that renders excellent quality service.

ORGANIZATIONAL MEASURES

Keeping the healthcare organization afloat is the first order of my leadership. As I would say, *"Let's stop the bleeding first."* Such entails a review of the budgetary performance with the Finance Managers and an Internal Audit. The priority is to look into the inventory levels, receivables, and purchase terms. Addressing those would create the "quick wins" that might put the organization in the black if it is in the red or an immediate impact on the net having posted a decrease in expenses or stopping procurement of certain medical supplies.

As President and CEO of one of the hospitals managed by Metro Pacific, I initially implemented the abovementioned strategy. When we leased the hospital from the religious congregation, it was financially bleeding and seemed on its way to closure. Metro Pacific came in and placed a new management team. One significant step we had to take was to focus on our inventory. To our surprise, most of the inventory was 120 days or more. The inventory would immediately contribute to the company's financial viability if converted to cash. We established inventory levels, and the benefits included quick financial wins and a more organized and spacious warehouse.

Alongside enforcing cost efficiency was putting procurement processes and negotiating for longer payment terms, requesting discounts for cash payments, and returns/exchange of some non-moving items. Supplier relationship management was vital. Recognized as one of the customer groups in healthcare, we, hospital leaders, build relationships with our suppliers and collaborate with them not only in terms of procurement but also in the field of education and research. As a personal choice, I do not usually meet with suppliers. I, however, invite all suppliers for a Thanksgiving Suppliers meeting at the beginning of the year. This event is where the suppliers meet with the Management team and key managers. While this is a party meant to be enjoyed, they bring home essential information about the significant capital expenditures the hospital would invest in. It is a win-win strategy for the hospital management team and the suppliers. From the hospital team, we can efficiently create the pricing database of the Capex and other inventories while allowing all accredited suppliers an equal chance of being part of the procurement process. This strategy has likewise shielded the team from some unproductive time of meeting and discussing procurement requirements and, yes, shielded from the ugly intrigues of favoring one supplier over the other.

When the Bleeding Stops...

While arresting the financial challenges that beset the organization, the healthcare team builds relationships with the other healthcare group segments. Doctors' and employees' involvement are done simultaneously with strategies for financial viability because the key to having patients recognize the healthcare organization is through doctors' referrals. Hence, it is a recognized fact that doctors are the driving force toward consensus building and diagnostic service utilization.

Meanwhile, departmental or cluster meetings follow town hall meetings. These became our data mining on how we can be better as a patient-centric organization. We can use these platforms to lay down the corporate vision and directions. Several times, some not-so-nice healthcare team members will challenge and take their frustrations with the previous owners to the newly assumed healthcare leadership team. As I weigh between forming relationships and dealing with those not-so-nice welcome, I usually stand on choosing my battles. I encountered many, and if they are worth my struggles, I humbly ask, which I did to some great performing doctors, *"Why do you hate my leadership?" "How can we develop a productive working relationship?"* These are tough questions to ask. However, as a significant healthcare team member, I knew I had to bite the bullet.

The idea of asking the doctors tough questions leads to meaningful insights as part of a more intimate SWOT analysis. In addition, feedback is always a piece of welcome information we can utilize to improve. Nonetheless, I was blessed to have developed meaningful collaborative relationships with most healthcare team members by God's grace.

Clarity of Values

The "Bite the Bullet" strategy is a prelude to informally letting our voices be heard. People expect their leaders to speak out on matters of values and conscience. We must know what matters to us and what we genuinely care about. Communicating our core values and beliefs can earn and sustain our credibility. It takes time to unearth those core values, but we need time to ponder them and craft strategies to translate them into action.

Henceforth, the clarity of our values acts as our moral compass. It shall determine our leadership decision-making pattern. Faced with challenging circumstances that can throw us off course, our team can see the landmarks of where we would lead the organization. It will strengthen the organization's core and give a sense of stability in our corporate direction.

Learning and Growth for Enhanced Customer Satisfaction

Increased productivity and achieving the desired service levels entail training. Therefore, the learning and growth of the healthcare team is a focal point of leadership. We intellectually stimulate the team at all levels and encourage them to think beyond the box. Nurturing talents through intentional coaching is a responsibility we face to such an extent that we do not paralyze the healthcare organizations. Otherwise, inexperienced service providers will cater to customers under our name.

In cooperation with training and development are other Human Relations disciplines for succession planning and establishing a career ladder for the employees. While we provide a high training and development culture, we give employees opportunities for personal improvement and have the foresight of their career growth within the organization. Appointing them to training programs also increases their reach and provides an opportunity to strengthen relationships across departments or divisions. That in itself is team building. As they enhance interdepartmental relationships, the ultimate beneficiary would still be the patient.

Learning and growth strategies are anchored on one goal—customer service. Therefore, the training framework covers what I fondly call the KASH—Knowledge, Attitude, Skills, and Heart. This is holistically designed to enhance what the employees possess and provide behavioral indicators for expressing service more favorably in any circumstance. Thus, we facilitate learning on critical thinking and empower them as self-effacing leaders.

Leadership Roles in Action

The interconnecting services of each department in the healthcare organization are like living organisms. Therefore, each department plays a vital role in patient management. The slightest mistake or inability to coordinate may be life-threatening. As leaders, we ensure that the processes and communication lines are in sync, understood, and primarily executed correctly.

Being in sync does not just happen. It is a deliberate effort that the leadership team should focus on. Regardless of whether the balanced scorecard and performance matrix is carefully crafted and communicated, the leadership challenge is how to have a team that is inspired, engaged, capable, and recognizes the team's critical role in managing each patient's care. We give directives. We also convince our team to buy into our visions and encourage them to work towards achieving corporate goals.

The healthcare organization is workforce intensive. Varied in disciplines and specialization, each team member requires dynamic and collaborative leadership. While the abovementioned skills are possibly woven into the Healthcare Executive's leadership persona, implementing those is a different story. The most challenging but which can be rewarding is collaborative management. Given the uniqueness and character priorities for both, bringing them to work together to meet the organizational goals involves having them believe in your vision, strategies, and integrity. As healthcare leaders, we must be the first to model collaborative behaviors, such as motivating and inspiring team members. When we agree with them, it's easy. But when we disagree on certain decisions, we face some painful realities. If relationships are well rooted, the team can agree to disagree, a characteristic highly dependent on the Emotional Quotient of the team members, which, in turn, is influenced by our ability to lead the team and manage those uncomfortable circumstances.

Leadership and Management Intertwined

Similarly, the leadership executive needs to master management skills in her daily grind as a President, Chief Executive Officer, or Chief Operating Officer. There will be intervening variables to becoming an effective leader and manager, but at the end of the day, those skill sets will either make or break the healthcare executive. While being a leader would involve crafting the mission and vision of the company, as a manager, the healthcare executive shall ensure that the mission and vision is concretized into attainable goals and performance measures aligned with corresponding work processes. Common to both and serving as "The GLUE" that will bond leadership and management skills shall and will always be "the PEOPLE."

Intellectual Quotient

Intellectual Quotient (IQ), as we know, enables us to have a job. We are gifted with a certain IQ, and we commonly perceive this as our ability to think critically and reason. As workers or leaders, we face interconnecting functions daily that require being a team player. It is always our call to make efficient decisions in disparate work contexts.

Hence, a leader's IQ is meager without the ability to interact with grace and respect towards each other. Knowledge of the patients' beneficence, non-maleficence, and prioritization of equal service amid dilemmas is essential. Nonetheless, navigating crucial choices requires empathy and assurance that our patients receive the highest regard, calling for an Emotional Quotient (EQ). One cannot be a healthcare provider without being socially attuned with the rest of the organization.

Emotional Quotient

Different folks, different strokes. We flex our leadership muscles to engage each one and make them feel valued. As leaders, we try to cultivate a high appreciation culture but integrity in giving feedback. It is being honest yet exemplifying grace in challenging times.

Opening channels of communication and practicing the art of listening sustains relationship building. As a leader, we agree to disagree. We ensure that the battles in the boardroom do not affect relationships. It's a "dictum," I tell my Management Team. It entails a strong trust relationship amongst peers to achieve that gut-level of communication. In as much as we encourage openness and honesty, we should never forget that there are specific means of conveying the message. We invoke graciousness in every sentence we speak. We do not forget that we are accountable for every word. We choose to be honest yet respectful as we argue with one another. And if we are the recipient of that brutal truth or opinion, we choose to think the best of the message's sender.

As a member of various BOD, ExCom, or ManCom, I do not want to downplay my ideas and even my passionate way of presenting my perspective.

But as I communicate my opinion or directives, I have discovered that those with whom I have a high level of trust relationships are the ones who can freely object or freely present a perspective I usually do not notice. Brainstorming in a non-judgmental arena has produced brilliant ideas and significant outputs.

A highly appreciative and transparent feedback system is part of the culture I try to develop with my Healthcare Team. The toxicity of being in healthcare, and having to face life and death situations, is emotionally draining. Therefore, affirming gestures that include smiling and verbally expressing gratitude induce happy hormones. These happy hormones can be contagious and conducive to high job satisfaction. As we know, happy employees will produce significant results. In healthcare, satisfied and happy employees are more caring and active contributors to a patient-centric culture.

Indeed, the climate of the organization begins with the healthcare leadership. Deliberate attempts to forge meaningful and trusting relationships contribute to every employee and doctor going beyond ensuring a patient-centric culture. Leaders must then be at the forefront, initiating the change and pointing the direction towards excellence.

Leadership Quotient

Drawn from the context clues mentioned above, Quotient refers to the level of quality or characteristic a subject portrays. Leadership Quotient (LQ) is a recent trend that assesses an individual's leadership ability. It is the price of competence, character, and capability. LQ's measure follows the same indicators as intellectual Quotient and Emotional Quotient; IQ + EQ + XQ = LQ. Others, however, claim that LQ is about the sum of morality and power. My stance on the concept of LQ complements this.

I believe that the effective execution of my role is measured by my reflection on my staff and the contribution of my influence to the team's overall success. Because of this, I mentor my staff to ensure they are equipped with the necessary SKILLS and VALUES they are likely to enact on unforeseen events. One of my objectives is to hone their potential and inspire them to become motivated supervisors and chiefs in the future.

Leaders like us opt to exhibit active listening and empathy, strategic planning, flexibility, and innovativeness. These develop trust, elucidate purpose, align systems and unleash talents. Assuring that disseminated ideas and messages, regardless of complexity, are clear and understandable is also part of my job. To make all of these possible, I needed to possess an evolving range of physical, mental, emotional, and spiritual factors as my cornerstones to a favorable Leadership Quotient.

Resilience Quotient

The VUCA world in healthcare is an everyday occurrence at work. The healthcare scenario changes every hour, every day. Nothing is predictable. As we face the daily grind, we face satisfied and dissatisfied doctors and patients, employees, and relatives of patients, among others. We make decisions that may or may not be favorable. High-strung demi-gods can tear the leadership team into pieces. There are employee unions and organizations which can impose unreasonable demands. Faced with those, we can either give a "fight or flight" response. As I would always say, we face challenging situations but select out battles.

The weighing between keeping the organization financially viable and maintaining an acceptable service level or astonishing the customer groups is a strategy that leaders work on with the team. Similar to most organizations, healthcare leaders need the team together. As dissatisfied team members disagree, we should stand firm in managing them. Flying ego and entitlement can be discouraging. But as we focus on our balanced scorecard, we pursue the path of objectivity, regardless of how it will impact the dissatisfied team members. Frequently, we as leaders are called to embrace the situational leadership approach.

Developing leadership resiliency entails a growth mindset. First, we choose to rise above the circumstances. Second, we decide to restart when we commit mistakes. Third, we choose to move on. Then, we move towards becoming the best version of who we are. That's resiliency!

Some partners in the industry do not always favor me. I am known to be very strict, very direct, and can be easily angered. It is not precisely the reputation I wanted. I have mellowed over the years. I have stopped flagellating myself, too, for having been that way. Resiliency is not only seeing the organization through difficult times. Resiliency is also seeing where we are at a certain point in leadership and acknowledging our weaknesses without self-flagellation. At some point, we need to forgive ourselves for moving on. We smartly strive and evolve to become better leaders. We survive our weaknesses. We become more resilient in the process.

Spiritual Quotient

A famous saying goes, *"When all things fail, we go to God."* On the contrary, I always believed I turned to God before things failed. Colossians 3:23-24 eloquently says, "Whatever you do, work heartily, as for the Lord and men, knowing that from the Lord you will receive the inheritance as your reward."

Acknowledging our human frailties, and yet, we aim to be the best we can be. We shift from being situational leaders to being transformational leaders. We wish to be the healthcare of choice. We wish to position our institution in healthcare's complex yet beautiful landscape. WE do what we can do. We do what is within our control. For those which we have no control or power over, we surrender it to God. Regardless of religion, our faith will direct us to the path of righteousness and carry us through the difficult times in our careers. Tapping on our faith, we work beyond the call of duty and ensure that we give the best we can to render the best possible care to our patients. We implore kindness to everyone. We turn our compassion to sound decision-making for the good of the patients. We excel in rendering service because we are privileged enough to be called to be of assistance in providing utmost care at a reasonable rate. We respond to calls for excellence as leaders and be good stewards of God-given talents.

MY LEADERSHIP STORY

Akin to a cliche story of every inspired leader, mine started with familiarity and admiration. As a child, the hospital was my playground. I used to be sickly, ergo, a frequent visitor to the hospital. As a result, I could not resist observing each health practitioner's roles and workspaces. I also learned the appeasing approaches that they do to customers and patients. To this date, I am very particular with service providers' manner of communication. I constantly nudge my team to display a smile, greet customers, and converse with them with basic courtesy since it used to impress me.

Eventually, I was galvanized by how hospitals construct and adhere to their principles which further caught my interest. The essence of establishing visible parameters that guide the organizational bodies was not reliant on profit earning alone. Instead, hospitals integrate how the patients would benefit from trusting them, achieving their fidelity, upholding patient and customers' security, and minimizing, if not eliminating, harm. At that point, I knew the healthcare system pivots to service toward the patients. However, I did not identify what makes an effective healthcare administration by being a patient alone.

Leadership as a Calling

My father, on the Board of Directors of two hospitals, used to tag me along to work. I would be excited to make rounds with him, which is when I told myself, *"I will not become a doctor, but I like 'going around' the hospital and talking to doctors, employees, and patients."* When I had the word for the job, I wished to become a "Hospital Administrator." That was the job I wanted. I am blessed to have found myself in the healthcare arena by God's grace and extraordinary design. I was in the right place at the right time. I am blessed to be on the healthcare C-level for over a decade. I started as HR Manager at the premier St Luke's Medical Center. It was supposed to be a post for a male, 30 years and above. I was curious about those two qualifications and thought about what a male HR aged 30 can do, which I can not do in the arena of HR. So I submitted my resume and got the job intended for a male HR Manager. That was the springboard of my healthcare leadership journey.

There were endless working hours and never-ending training, cross-functional meetings, and reporting, but those were all worth it. I had to be the best version that I could be. Our organizational culture does not accept mediocrity. We were laying the foundation for JCIA, with endless meetings between the mountainous policy-making and standards development. Those meetings were the foundation for the development of my EQ and AQ.

INFLUENCE Through Transparency and Accountability

The healthcare landscape has drastically changed with the evolution of the pandemic. As a result, the challenges that confront the Healthcare Executive multiplied exponentially. The scarcity of material and human resources threatened the very core of what healthcare is—to provide the community with an appropriate, efficient, equitable, and sustainable solution to the emerging life and death situations.

The "business as usual" leadership style evolved to critical management to ensure the highest safety protocols. Focusing on processes and business goals shifts the priorities from being healthcare-centered to profit-centered.

Critical to the leadership journey is being influential. The ability to influence the team entails integrity, charisma, and an emotional quotient. Just like the ICE that makes cold brewed iced tea taste superb, the ICE as a leader enables one to get each team member on board.

Integrity attracts the team to join in the project development. People claim that as leaders, we can be credited with having the best interest of EVERYONE in the organization. The complexity of healthcare is highly dependent on having the Board of Directors, Doctors, employees, patients, and their relatives, and the third-party payers that every project, every change in process, and every decision made will be for the greater good.

As the primary decision-makers in the organization, we are bound to give direction, comply with government regulatory requirements, achieve corporate goals, and make doctors and employees happy. Hence, we ensure that the highest service level is purposefully extended to the patients, the very reason for our existence. Therefore, everyone who is part of the healthcare organization needs to believe and respect that what we do as leaders is not just driven by financial targets but by a compelling desire to deliver the utmost care at a reasonable cost for the patients. If they see that passion for being of service to patients, doctors, and employees will work beyond, have manageable expectations, and work with the leadership, only then would the numbers make sense.

There will be a significant conscious effort from the doctors and employees to increase productivity and improve healthcare service delivery cost-efficiently. The teams are likely to perceive the cost efficiency measures as beneficial in rendering quality of care at a manageable cost for the patient. It will not be viewed as simply cost-cutting measures. They will find meaning in every cost-efficiency action we implement because they trust, respect, and perhaps acclaim the administrator's leadership style.

Unpopular Decisions

Faced with tough, unpopular decisions, it would be our integrity that will carry us through. The balancing act between reasonable purchases and pleasing the end-users is part of daily decision-making. One hospital we took over was due to bankruptcy. On the brink of closing down, it had a "family-oriented" process of approving requests in the hallways or over *merienda cena* [early evening meal]. The style of leadership was muddy and described as democratic. As to their management style, it was about pleasing the end-users without consideration of market needs and return on investment. With our company coming in, there was a shift from family matriarchal leadership style to corporate leadership and management. As a result, some doctors had temper tantrums, lessors solicited signatures for my removal, and the religious invoked religion.

How did I address the issues? I initially focused on financial viability through operational efficiency. Stop the bleeding! I could not be effective in fighting every word the opponents were saying. I had to do a job, and the first order was to complete my management team, glance at the organization with strategic eyes, and fix the stockroom. I converted the list of unnecessary stocks like toothpaste into cash. More so, the inventory level was reestablished to 30–45 days, a far cry from 90–120 days.

At the same time, placing corporate communication together was deemed crucial. The public thought that the hospital was closed. We had to communicate the message of continuity in service through reputable hospital managers. Rebranding the hospital included a facelift and changing the logo to communicate the change that was happening powerfully. This move had to guarantee that the modifications emphasized more exemplary service and facilities that appeal to the public and reassure customers.

Output more than effort

I cannot exactly say that I am consistently a gracious leader. Crunch time used to get the best of me. It was impossible to escape phases when my orchestration methods did not produce the most favorable results. There were also periods when we accomplished the best outcomes sluggishly, if not failing. These instances would trigger professional and personal emotions, including frustration and exhaustion. Nonetheless, I remained constantly humbled by God's grace to redefine my leadership style.

As my mouth traced the word "leadership" in conferences and training, among others, I had to recalibrate my leadership style and re-engineer the way I lead and manage to achieve a balanced scorecard. It was a journey of self-effacing and self-redirecting, putting a higher premium on inspiring team members, whether EXCOM, MAN-COM, or Department Heads, to be committed healthcare providers.

Therefore, I would consistently pick healthcare even if you fill my table with various seemingly irresistible career choices. Despite the intricate and delicate service delivery processes, the output of catering for therapeutic, curative, and preventive care is rewarding. Most of all, every decision I make as a CEO is a response to my calling for service. Such a gift of opportunity!

TERESITA BATAYOLA

President and CEO, International Community
Health Services (ICHS)
GLOBAL FWN100™ 2019

The Arc of Purposeful Leadership:
My Story

Fortune cookies are just that, cookies with fortunes inside. With inspirational morsels that affirm. *"Attitude is a little thing that makes a big difference." "You have an optimistic faith and confidence in life." "You have a natural grace and great consideration for others."* Taped at the top of my computer screen at the office, these slips of fortune papers give hope when the going is uncertain. And when there is certitude, a reminder that the best is yet to come.

Poised to retire from International Community Health Services (ICHS) in December 2022, I received an important announcement in February 2022. I will be among 25 leaders selected for the U.S. President's Advisory Commission on Asian Americans, Native Hawaiians, and Pacific Islanders. The Commission will help the executive branch with policies to prevent and document anti-Asian hate incidents and to improve health, economic and educational disparities among Asian American (AA) and Native Hawaiian and Pacific Islander (NHPI) communities.

SELF-MANAGEMENT:
BEGINNING WITH SELF

Born in Manila, my childhood centered on our street with outings to Luneta Park, visits to our relatives in Santa Mesa, and trips to Antipolo in May. Dusty Porvenir Street, Pasay City, teemed of the ordinary in the Philippines. Houses ranged from adobe-block enclosed compounds to gated wooden houses to make-shift homes built of advertising boards and signs. We lived in one of the wooden houses with a gate that kept my sister Maria Luisa, brother Louie, and me inside. We were not allowed to play with anyone. My parents made it clear that they worked hard to send us to Malate Catholic School, a parochial school run by Columban nuns from Ireland, and that our job was to study and do well. We did have advantages. We had a black and white TV, a new and rare thing in those days, and my parents would open the gate and let neighborhood kids watch shows from the stairwell. We had a big ole black 1950s Ford, which my Dad drove. It broke down regularly, and the windshield wipers did not work well. The side windows fell out if you slammed the door too hard. But we were among the few with a car.

Thriving as Second Best

During the 60s, I thrived at Malate's girls' school, joining as many activities as possible. Volleyball hits to my body outscored my returns. Principal Sister Pius chose me to be among a select few for training in speech and elocution. My Dad took on the trainer role, driving me to Luneta Park at five most mornings. I had to recite without shouting but speaking in a loud voice so that anyone in the last row of the Luneta Grandstand could hear me endlessly repeating, *"Thirty Thousand Thundering Thieves."* Succeeding with these exercises meant I could compete in oratory and storytelling for Malate. Skilled, but not the prettiest, and short meant I got supporting roles in play productions —the mole in *Thumbelina*, a goateed actor in *Hamlet*'s play within a play, and endless flippant best friends. I was among the school's leaders, though never the top one. I did well academically, graduating salutatorian at both elementary and high school. So I was gleeful when I found my name in the *Manila Times* issue that published the names of those accepted at the University of the Philippines, Diliman. I thought I had it made until that dirty phrase 'going to America' came up.

Immigrating to America

Our family was middle class. Until we weren't. My Dad came home one day and we learned that the Olivetti distributor, he worked for had closed down. He was employed erratically after that, but more often, he was unemployed. The car was gone, and soon the TV, the washing machine with the hand-cranked roller dryer, and some furniture. My siblings and I did not wear brand new sets of uniforms at the start of the school year. The carefree life became a careful one. Aside from our family, my Mom was helping her brother's widow with six kids. Her brother was a cop moonlighting at the Manila Bay Club when scions of wealth gunned him down, displeased that my uncle asked them to leave when they became too drunk, wild, and threatening. My parents had many late-night fights about money when they thought we were asleep. Increasingly, the subject of going to America recurred. Mom who rejected the idea for years was now on board.

In July 1969, Luis and Dolores Batayola immigrated to Seattle, Washington, with kids in tow, determined to keep our family intact. We left an increasingly unstable Philippines with a prolonged bad economy, widespread political wars and corruption, and spreading civil unrest. My parents, part of a good governance group, became increasingly concerned for their safety. My Mom took to carrying a small paring knife for protection. No one believed the paring knife would do her good, but it kept her feisty. Activists started to disappear, never to be seen again. Salvage became the dreaded term for these increasing disappearances.

The U.S. had passed the 1965 immigration and Nationality Act which abolished the national origins quota and replaced it with a system that admitted immigrants based on their relationship to a U.S. citizen, lawfully present permanent resident family member or U.S. employer. My father's oldest sister was a U.S. citizen. Boeing's newspaper ads trumpeted its desperate need for aerospace workers. My father held an aeronautical engineering degree. The decision to immigrate became pragmatically obvious but emotionally hard. As deeply patriotic and religious people, my parents were gravely worried about their country of birth. They grieved, leaving their family and friends.

That same month, Neil Armstrong walked on the moon, and Boeing lost the supersonic SST bidding wars to Airbus. Boeing's loss plunged Seattle, a one-company town, into the Boeing Bust, a 15-year recession, which produced the infamous billboard, "Will the last person leaving SEATTLE – Turn out the lights."

Struggling in America

Luis and Dolores spent all their resources to get to Seattle and, in their forties, had no option but to tough it up. We crammed into my aunt's small duplex until my parents could secure a house despite the collapsed economy. My father found a job picking up scrap iron at the shipyard; he eventually retrained through a public vocational program as a steamfitter and found employment at Harborview Hospital maintaining operating rooms. My mother found a secretarial job at United Good Neighbors. Then, she transferred to the University of Washington School of Forestry. Luis had no time to lament his professional loss of stature. He had a family to feed and felt pride in his work. Dolores found joy assisting foreign graduate students, bringing many lonely students home for holiday celebrations.

In Seattle, my sister Maria was held back two years in high school because she was too young to graduate. My brother Louie attended elementary school. Both were bullied, roughed up, and taunted because they were fresh off the boat. As for me, I refused to attend high school in Seattle since I had college admission to the University of the Philippines before immigrating. For months, I was isolated and confined to house chores because *wala naman akong ginagawa*. I had nothing else to do. I spiraled into deep distress until Seattle University admitted me on probationary status under its new Minority Affairs program.

Learning About Social Responsibility

Surly, sullen, and withdrawn, my world was as gray and rainy as Seattle before starting college in January 1970. My parents pressured me to volunteer with Sister Heidi Perreño, a young nun who was an early nurse practitioner. She was working with isolated and poor elderly Filipino men living in decrepit single-room occupancy (SRO) hotels in Seattle's Chinatown and Pioneer Square.

These older men were alone and frail after years of back-breaking migrant work in Eastern Washington farms or the salmon canneries of Alaska. A policy outcome when the Spanish American War ended in 1898, the Philippines became a U.S. colony and a ready source of cheap field and factory male workers but limited opportunities for women and families.

Sister Heidi spearheaded obtaining public funds for a nursing demonstration project for these sickly older men without families. Pressed to be one of her interviewers for the study, I reluctantly took on the assignment though I felt awkward as a young female talking to older men who were also strangers. These older men, *manongs*, were more eager to quiz me about my family and my studies instead of answering my questions. They treated me like a long-lost niece. Nevertheless, the experience, although uncomfortable, helped me learn about others' more challenging lives, giving me hope that my young life could become better.

Learning About Commitment to Community Engagement

Sister Heide's work helped fuel the fire of student and community activists who were outraged at the condition of the old Filipino and Chinese men living in deplorable SROs. Chinatown was physically halved when Interstate 5 was built, and a proposed new sports stadium would sever two historical areas; Pioneer Square divorced from Chinatown. The area was the epitome of urban blight in the sixties and seventies. Demonstrations occurred in Chinatown, demanding services for the elderly. Like many cities, Seattle erupted because of civil rights and anti-Vietnam war demonstrations. This movement did spawn a free clinic, a social services organization, and a drop-in center for the elderly, all serving Asian Americans. What forced Asians to live together in the extended Chinatown area was redlining, the banking practice of only lending mortgage loans in limited neighborhoods to persons of color. Redlining added a spark to create unity across racial groups.

The movement was significant because it forged a long-term advocacy relationship among the early Asian immigrant groups to the area—the Chinese, Japanese, and Filipinos. The blowback in Chinatown united community leaders with university students to focus their ire on King County, which eventually acceded to funding a small clinic. Officially incorporated in 1973, that clinic became the International District Clinic, popularly known as the ID Clinic, which evolved into today's International Community Health Services (ICHS), where, unbeknown to me, my arc of purposeful leadership will manifest. The ID Clinic served the elderly but quickly started serving Vietnamese and Southeast Asian refugees of all ages after Saigon fell in 1975 and the Vietnam War ended.

Seattle continues to have a solid Pan Asian character in its organizing and advocacy as it works across national origin, ethnic, and language lines, moving beyond the Asian Pacific Islander communities to bridge relationships with the African American, Native American, and Latino communities. For example,

Seattle's Chinatown was later formally renamed Chinatown International District (CID) to include Little Saigon and to recognize the other Asian ethnic groups that settled in the area.

SEEKING THE LIGHT TO BE
SOCIALLY RESPONSIBLE

The anguish of being an immigrant and a young adult seeded internal confusion, giving way to learning beyond my immigrant experience. Coming into the light of Sister Heidi and meeting others in worse circumstances made me realize that there were more significant needs. I met other leaders in the community who were fighting for human and civil rights. I realized that many were Filipino and Filipino American leaders that were amazing to my yet unformed being. Among them: Robert "Uncle Bob" Santos, a second-generation Filipino who fought for better living conditions in Seattle's Chinatown and coalesced with other leaders of color for a united front in fighting injustice. Second-generation Dolores Sibonga, the first Filipino lawyer in Washington State and the first Filipino elected as Seattle City Councilmember, was outspoken and consistently affirmed young people's place in the movement. First-generation Larry Itliong, a national organizer of the 70s grapes boycott for better living conditions and wages for Filipino and Mexican grape pickers in California, regularly traveled to Seattle to raise awareness and funds for the fight. These 3 Filipino Americans were among many Filipino leaders who dared to assert being Filipino and establish a Filipino American identity.

My parents were still looming in my life, and I was too intimidated to join the marches and protests. Instead, I found ways to volunteer at meetings and fundraisers to listen from the sidelines and be moved and inspired. The anti-Marcos movement was growing in the Philippines and spreading to the U.S., but that cause seemed remote to me. The issues I paid attention to were urgent and local. Chinatown International District became my touchstone. My time was filled with school and a part-time job at a department store. But what kept me wide-eyed were activities in the Asian American community and Asian American women's movement.

From these early years in the U.S., I pushed to go beyond myself, learn of other people's circumstances, discern injustice, and find the courage to be more visible. Volunteering inevitably led to organizing and leadership roles. Chairing an activity here and there eventually led to being the co-chair of the Asian Pacific Women's Caucus. Considered radical for its time, the Caucus dispelled the notion that Asian women are quiet with its very vocal advocacy. As a result, the disruption and displacement from the life I could have had in the Philippines receded in time and memory. The previously known path became an unknown forward march.

Zig-Zagging to My Purpose

My parents embodied faith, hope, and charity. Fierce believers and devoted Catholics, they taught us empathy, service, and sacrifice. They were generous with others but strict and controlling with their children. They were very Filipino, demanding filial devotion and staying in the same household. I gasped for air at home. I became more aware of discrimination and what I could expect as a minority, an Asian, and a woman in America. It was a time of return for Vietnam vets, and they either scorned or flirted with me for looking Vietnamese. Part-time jobs I pursued were lost before I even opened my mouth because of a presumed accent. Ignorant of wool clothing, my clothes were too thin for the weather; my perpetual goosebumps and blue fingernails made others wary that I may transmit disease. So many times, my true self wanted to be even more invisible than my American double. I did not know how to dress, speak, and carry my body in America. Eyes and body in subservience, I was *kime* [hesitant], I was content to be around community leaders, constantly listening, learning, and helping.

Distorting Affirmative Action

I graduated in 1973, shoe-horning in 3 years a Bachelor of Arts in Public Affairs degree from Seattle University. I quickly landed a paid internship with the Department of Licensing at the state capitol, Olympia. It was the early days of affirmative action, the government policy and practice of selecting excluded populations for opportunities, mostly in public education and employment. Every day, I came in early, eager to work, but there was nothing for me to do. Relegated to a chair, the small planning unit I worked for was totally white male with one white woman doing graphics. They were nice enough, but I had no assignments and was nothing more than a fixture to fulfill the entire organization's affirmative action slot of one. It was a grind-in, ground-out agency with the same routine. Little else changed, and there was no need for any planning. I was proudly introduced to the executive director as the affirmative action hire. When I left, their parting comment was that they might not do affirmative action again. I failed them in proving affirmative action worked. Seared in my brain, 'This is not the place for me.'

Being devalued at work, independent living during the week, and weekends in Seattle were a potent mix as I began to feel emotions repressed when we immigrated. Feeling marginalization while rapidly learning what work did not appeal to me stirred questions of identity.

Building My Competencies

Thanks to my cousin, I landed my first real job at the Tacoma Human Rights Commission in communications. For the first time at work, my identity was an asset. Every person at the Commission was unique in what could be considered stereotypical. My black smart *boujee* executive director in stylish clothes. The women's libber heading up women's rights. The assistant was a single mom working in clubs to make ends meet. A human rights investigator, another single mom, was a part-time UPS driver for that needed second income. The compliance officer had big jokes and an even bigger belly laugh that sharply slammed shut when a problem was brought to him. And there was me, on the road to self-awareness.

At home in Seattle, I was free to seek out community as long as I slept at my parents' home. Already I was feeling the me I would become. Breathing became easier, and the Pacific Northwest gray weather showed streaks of sun trying to break through for the first time in a long time.

If a journey describes an itinerary and destination, my career and development as a leader is a series of accidents of chance, opportunities, and relationships. From the Tacoma Human Relations Commission, I jumped to a series of jobs trying to satisfy restlessness and cope with a lack of known career trajectory. Next was a stint in community involvement with a regional Bilingual Education Technical Assistance Center assisting school districts with Southeast Asian refugees. Finally, in 1979, the restlessness eventually led me to apply successfully as a National Urban Fellow, pursuing a Master of Science in Urban Administration from Bucknell University, Pennsylvania. The

Fellowship included an assignment as a Fellow with the U.S. Office of Personnel Management's executive director.

Learning from the Master Networker

Back in Seattle after the Fellowship, I took an easy job with a national technical assistance non-profit for Asian American senior programs. I knew I would only be there a year while I wrestled internally, trying to figure out my career path. What made Seattle special this time was a chance to be closer to some community leaders. *"You'd be good at this,"* was a frequent comment from Ruth Woo, who became my mentor, surrogate Mom, and constant cheerleader. Ruth was unassuming and shunned attention, but she was astute and had friendly relationships with leaders around the state. Once an assistant to the governor, she knew how to wield the phone as her weapon, the rolodex her ammunition. She could call any official about any subject, including securing jobs for people. She was her own pressure group and affirmative action machine. But her biggest desire was to get men and women of color or their advocates to run for office. With elected office and different people in key positions in government came real power. She had a legion of believers, many young and eager to pursue equality and achievement. We had dinners at her house cooked by her husband Ben. We were her crew at political fundraisers. We learned grace, humor, and tenacity in going around naysayers and finding friends who would support or advocate for our cause. All the while, we all laughed and traded political gossip. Being warriors and co-conspirators was fun! Not just earnest.

Lightening up was a new experience. The seriousness of school while working a low-wage job to help the family, volunteering for different events, finding a good job after graduation, finding a better job, and trying to meet people all felt endless. However, being welcomed into Ruth's circle showed me that being a serious human being can be a sparkling experience.

Learning the 80/20 Rule

Ruth's connections landed me back in the state capital of Olympia, this time ironically as the director of communications at the Department of Licensing. The very same agency where I swore I would never return. The agency was in the public eye as the state attempted to raise taxes for drivers, vehicle, boats, and houseboat licenses. No longer an affirmative action intern, I faced my first difficult employee. Standing nearly 6 feet with broad shoulders, Dorothy came to my office slowly, stood at the door, and calmly informed me that she had been with the agency for 20 years, she does her job, and she was not going to change. She said she had seen people come and go in my position as a political appointee. She was a civil servant and was there to stay. I just as calmly told her that many projects were coming up, and I hoped she would find some of them interesting. She calmly responded no. This is how I eventually learned the 80/20 rule. If you spend 80% of the time on 20% of the people, you are not managing but being managed. We had many conversations where she just sat and looked at me until, one day, it came out that she loved photography. We talked about the possibility of her taking photos and maybe using her photos in our newsletters. Though she did not show enthusiasm initially, Dorothy and her camera became a familiar image around the agency. When a new governor came, and I was out of a job, she thanked me for making her work interesting.

Learning to Design Economic Development Programs

Ironically, this led to a much better job at another state agency, working economic development for a star, Merritt Long, executive director of the Commission for Vocational Education. He exuded enthusiasm for my abilities as he gave me wide latitude to establish small business incubators and design retraining programs in depressed communities. Again, the Ruth connection was working.

Sidestepping: Learning to Strategize

Seattle had seeped its way into my core. But much as I loved Seattle, part of me still felt untethered, subject to everyone else's desire for who I should be and what I should be doing. Many supported and cared for me, but their vision of who I was and my career direction was static electricity for my own vision of myself. Only my women's group was genuinely happy that I wanted to move away.

New York! New York! The bright lights of Broadway seduced me for years, and I succumbed to its call. I moved to New York under the guise of finishing my masters thesis for my parents' sake. Seattle was too distracting, I said, and I needed to be closer to my advisor at Bucknell University. The bigger distraction in Seattle was meeting my future husband and life partner, Dionnie Dionisio. Unsure about settling down versus pursuing the promising career climb was another reason to work and play in New York first before making a life commitment.

For three years, I was the director of communications for a large, century-old non-profit, the Community Service Society of New York. It was large-scale, unusual for a non-profit if it were in Seattle. Founded by old New York money to serve the Irish and Jews in the lower east side, the organization's focus evolved to serve and empower Blacks and Latinos, registering voters, educating them on ballot issues and candidates, and turning out the vote. In the 80s, the HIV epidemic raged, and CSS developed innovations to meet the needs of forgotten HIV victims like babies and children in minority communities. CSS organized volunteer grandmothers who would go into hospital wards and rock babies with HIV. Everything we did mattered. Their fundraisers attracted New York elites. Their events were graced with Black national leaders. Rosa Parks. Jesse Jackson. Al Sharpton. I had an article published in the New York Times about our work. We stayed late in the CEO's office talking about innovations in strategies and programs to serve the low income. Among my treasures is a photo I took of Rosa Parks surrounded by New York religious, union, and government leaders. Taken from the rafters of a Brooklyn church, I captured the congregation looking at Rosa Parks with suspended reverence. Those were heady days.

Those days were leavened by the increased closeness of my long-distance relationship with Dionnie. Telephone calls created large monthly bills in the hundreds of dollars, vastly different from today with cell phones and unlimited calling plans. The time came for me to return to Seattle.

Sidestepping, Strategizing, and Rising

After leading communications for a prominent non-profit in New York, I deliberately chose to become more technical and move away from leading soft services. Public utilities are notoriously impervious to outsiders. Breaking into this world was taking on a fortress. My network had limited impact, so I took a sidestep as an assistant to the top executive before I could rise up the ladder again. It turned out to be a strategic choice as I became a one-woman strike force for the Superintendent, addressing labor and tribal issues while being responsive to the Mayor and City Council. Hiring, training, and retaining women in non-traditional jobs like water pipe workers resulted in labor unrest and pushback from the men who traditionally held these positions. The Muckleshoot tribe asserted its traditional rights to access the watershed as its hunting, gathering, and worship grounds. In a seven-year period, I was promoted several times, directing programs that included 50-year strategic planning, rate setting, managing water dams, working with regulators, and managing complex community engagement on contentious issues. Getting agreements in these areas were nearly impossible until we adjusted our mindset to get to grudging yeses. We had to accept that there will always be fierce opponents to any utility issue because of rates and environmental impacts. Getting to a grudging yes meant enough people could support the benefits of any project or issue for us to get approval from the Mayor and City Council.

The utility years opened the opportunity to work with the World Bank. Seattle is a sister city to Surabaya, Indonesia. Surabaya received loans from the World Bank and the Asian Development Bank to expand potable water service to 80% of the population. A condition of the World Bank loan was to learn utility standards in an advanced country. I hosted the Surabaya delegation for a month to learn how Seattle provides water services.

Sidestepping in Indonesia: Achieving Strategic Focus

A year later, I was invited to be the strategic development adviser and serve as the liaison with the World Bank. The engagement moved my young family to Indonesia from 1995 to 1998. The project also hired Dionnie as an advisor, using his construction background for large project segments. I learned to be functional enough to do presentations in Bahasa Indonesia. Still, the true value was being able to succeed in a world that was more rigid in protocol with a highly centralized government. An ongoing challenge was striking a balance as a woman in an advisory role in the traditional field of water services with enough weight as the World Bank liaison to sway government leaders. Unfortunately, the downfall of the Suharto government abruptly cut the engagement. The United States, Canada, United Kingdom, Australia, Japan, and France evacuated all their citizens. Though we were invited back to the project, we decided to head back to Seattle because of our young kids and the ongoing instability in Indonesia.

Learning and Executing Alignment of Strengths and Resources

Culture shock hit my family when we returned to Seattle. From living in a city with millions of people to living in Seattle with hundreds of thousands of people, we adjusted back to fewer crowds and having more personal space. No more chauffeur and a privileged expat lifestyle.

My networks quickly came into play again, and I became the assistant director in charge of Seattle's comprehensive planning for growth management and neighborhood planning. The art of politics and Not In My Back Yard (NIMBY) roared hot and fast regarding where to place and where not to place growth. Property owners, renters, developers, businesses, churches, and random groups had special interests and competing visions for their neighborhoods and the entire city. It was head-spinning to move from the rigid processes in Indonesia to the come-one-come-all fracas of city planning. Mayor Paul Schell was visionary, and was destined for another term as mayor when the Battle of Seattle occurred. The World Trade Organization (WTO) Ministerial Conference was about to start new trade talks in 1999 when over 40,000 protesters converged from around the world. Days of fighting between protesters and police doomed Schell's political future.

A new mayor was elected. I loved government work. Unlike the stereotypes of bureaucrats obsessed with process at the sacrifice of being a good public servant, a good bureaucrat influenced or made meaningful changes, whether in education, economic development, or long-range planning. I believed I was the latter. But Seattle politics was mired in process and more process. The macabre joke was Seattle's biggest product is process. Strife and gridlock became the norm. Though the opportunity to lead another department became possible after serving two governors and four mayors, I left government to refresh, tend to my preteens, and care for my sick father.

MY ARC TO PURPOSEFUL LEADERSHIP

I gravitated to the Chinatown International District orbit back in Seattle. This time, while marching on Martin Luther King Day 2003, I was next to Sharon Maeda, founder of a small consulting firm, Spectra, which chose only projects that gave purpose and joy and lifted communities. I felt like it was the right fit to slow down as a principal but stay relevant.

ICHS Beckons

I did not recognize what it foreshadowed. The first contract won by Spectra was to conduct strategic planning for International Community Health Services (ICHS). After interviewing the board members and staff leaders, I informed the Board Chair that they needed a needs assessment and organizational capacity review before they could do strategic planning. I would be happy to facilitate a retreat but noted that I would not consider that strategic planning.

Yet, another detour beckoned; David Della, the second Filipino-American elected to the Seattle City Council, asked if I would serve as his Chief of Staff. Not wanting to be in the mix of brutal city politics again, I agreed to serve six months to set up his legislative agenda, organize his office, and find my replacement. The issues were exciting, and the insider game to fix problems in the neighborhoods was exhilarating, but I could feel the burnout of politics creeping back.

During my fifth month working with David, Dorothy Wong from ICHS asked if I would consider helping her to implement two big projects. These were to open ICHS' second clinic at Holly Park and go live with ICHS' first electronic health records system. Still unsure what I wanted to do next, I agreed to do six months. I felt I could easily do the projects with end dates since I had done significant capital projects and electronic records conversions,

Once onboard, I was asked to triage and address troubling issues with the dental practice, pharmacy, and the closure of defunded programs. The vacuum whoosh sucked me deep into operations beyond the initial engagement. I agreed to extend for another three months but clarified that I would not stay beyond that. I needed to pause and think about the direction for the rest of my career. However, Dorothy announced her resignation, indicating that she was burnt out and needed to take time for herself. Instead of leaving the organization, I was named acting Executive Director.

Making ICHS Home

In 2003, I became the strategic planning consultant for ICHS. I expected a small storefront clinic and was surprised to find a thriving clinic with 200 staff and two sites. The ID Clinic struggled financially to stay open for its first 20 years, chasing grants and dependent on donations.

In 2004, I became the project manager for the latest and bigger replacement clinic at Holly Park with medical, dental, laboratory, pharmacy, and community health services.

In 2005, ICHS implemented its first electronic health records and was considered an early adaptor.

In 2006, I was appointed Executive Director and immediately started visiting and talking with staff members. The clinic staff were proud of their work. Many were long-time employees, serving long-time patients. Friendships and close connections existed with patients and their families. I listened closely to the Medical Director, the Finance Director, and most readily to a couple of administrative support staff. Both had fulfilled different roles in the organization and knew everyone, what happened where, and who did what. It was refreshing to meet such a giving team of community servants.

The scene was different on the non-clinic side. Brush fires were the norm, anywhere from cleaning and garbage pick-up to resolution of salary demands. Finance did its job, with days receivable below average, bringing income efficiently. Health education programs were inconsistent, with some program staff still on the payroll for defunded programs. Other programs did not have verifiable results.

Leading Organizational Change

My early leadership years at ICHS focused on professionalizing the organization, developing policies and procedures, ensuring grants performance, working on consistent clinic quality, developing a comprehensive needs assessment followed by a strategic plan, and gaining malpractice coverage under the Federal Torts Claims Act instead of paying for commercial insurance. Once change started, we had to maintain momentum. Change begat more change. The Board of Directors learned of the Malcolm Baldrige National Quality Criteria. We hired a consultant to guide us towards becoming a high-performing organization.

Establishing Performance-Driven Change Management

Identifying the performance measures was a painful process. Staff gravitated towards process measures, not results. Some were puzzled why we needed measures when our patients loved us. After a couple of years of learning and revisiting, we eventually hit ICHSQ: Infrastructure, Customer Service,

Human Investment, Sustainability, Quality. For comparison, measurements considered the performance of other community health clinics and healthcare organizations. In time, we pursued 'national stamps of approval' by being fully accredited by the Accreditation Association for Ambulatory Health Care for our medical and dental clinics, including recognition as a Patient Centered Medical Home or Patient Centered Dental Home for most sites.

It is forever true that change is hard, and not all people want change. For example, some staff complained to the Board that I was too business-oriented and not community enough. When confronted by two board members with this complaint, I responded, *"You hired me to make improvements and turn this organization into a high performer. Do you want me to be popular? Or to make changes? I can do popular, but I will also be gone."* Thankfully, my bosses agreed that they did want the organization to change and become stronger.

By 2007, we launched a community needs assessment that had not been done in years. We went beyond demographics and decided to map out the transportation grids, identified the cities and neighborhoods where other low-income populations lived, and overlaid the location of other community health centers. Once we understood the gaps of service, we began to dream of growing to serve our target patients. We also launched the ICHS Foundation with its sole focus on raising funds for ICHS' mission.

The 2008 – 2010 recession hit ICHS hard. We had to slim down administration and conduct furloughs to preserve essential services. The administrative diet turned out to have benefits in shedding inefficiencies. However, the prolonged recession forced ICHS to go beyond administration and lose a dental team. The recession also produced an opportunity with the American Recovery and Reinvestment Act of 2019. ICHS received a major grant to modernize and expand its main medical and dental facility, consolidate its health workers and administrative staff into one location, and create learning, meeting, and community spaces in Chinatown International District.

Socially Responsible Management

To lift morale during this recession, we began imagining and planning for ICHS' future to take services outside Seattle, where Asian and Pacific Islander communities settled.

Betting that the Affordable Care Act would pass under Barack Obama, we dove into outreach and enrollment, succeeding in drawing more patients while driving down our uninsured rate from over 30% to a low of less than 8%.

We began to shift the paradigm of having patients come to us to opening clinics where our patients lived. We had to have clinics and services wherever our target communities dispersed in the county. Though we were targeting Asian Pacific Islanders, affordable housing lies outside Seattle in south King County and other surrounding areas where other immigrants and refugees of different origins live. Thus, we planned for the construction of 2 new clinics in Bellevue and Shoreline. In 2014, ICHS opened its first new site since the relocation of Holly Park in 2005. ICHS was serving a diverse clientele speaking 50 languages. While many of those languages were Asian, other languages were East African, Eastern European, and Spanish. Some community leaders and staff questioned why ICHS opened in Bellevue, a high-income city, home to Microsoft, Expedia, and other high-tech companies. However, the needs assessment showed that Crossroads in Bellevue had many low-income immigrants and refugees whose health needs went unrecognized. Shoreline was not questioned because it had a middle- and working-class profile. However, community leaders and staff wondered why ICHS did not choose south King County, the favored destination for affordable housing. The needs assessment showed that two community health centers had multiple sites in the area.

Once we grew confident that we could execute plans, ICHS grew services beyond the four "one-stop shop" clinics offering medical, dental, behavioral health, laboratory, pharmacy, health education, community health, WIC (Women, Infant and Children services), and other programs. ICHS pioneered a mobile dental clinic in an urban setting serving 13 schools, and non-profits during school vacations. We opened a primary care clinic in a mental health setting, 2 school-based health centers in a middle school and multilingual high school, and a vision clinic.

Twenty percent of ICHS patients are seniors who continue to get frailer as they age. The idea of keeping seniors who qualified for nursing home care but living in their home or community settings took root in 2011 when the Board decided that our care for seniors needed to extend beyond services within the clinic walls. Living at home or in community settings can only happen if seniors have comprehensive benefits that include preventive and specialty medical, dental, and behavioral therapies and services; socialization; home services as needed; and transportation to get to specialty and other services. Without a doubt, this project has been the most intense and prolonged for my leadership. Planning for and bringing to life a deeply regulated Program of All-Inclusive Care for the Elderly (PACE) serving nursing-home-qualified seniors who want to stay in the community has run into many stoppers. Yet ICHS is on the brink of groundbreaking for a second PACE site.

Along the way, a community development partner requested that ICHS take over its assisted living, adult day health, and congregate meal programs at Legacy House. The Seattle Chinatown International District Preservation and Development Authority conducted its strategic planning and consciously chose to focus on community development and affordable housing development and management peeling off the heath care services. Though unexpected, we decided to take those programs and envision a continuum of care as seniors age from independence to end of life. Starting with primary care at our clinics, seniors can choose to be in the congregate meal program for nutritional and socialization needs, join adult day health if they need more services, reside in assisted living if independent living becomes a challenge, and eventually be a PACE participant for comprehensive wrap-around services. ICHS named these senior services the Healthy Aging and Wellness Program. We added a small PACE component to Legacy House while waiting for the new, larger site. It was an opportunity to learn about the intricacies and challenges of a highly regulated program while caring for the frailest of seniors.

The Power of Teams: Creating a Pipeline for the Home Team

Without a committed and skilled workforce, no one can succeed as a healthcare and service organization. The U.S. faces a national crisis in the shortages of medical providers, nurses, and other healthcare staff. To meet ICHS' needs, we created our pipeline with family practice and nurse practitioner residencies, apprenticeships for medical and dental assistants, externships, internships, and training opportunities for career and leadership development. We also intentionally recruited and hired people with shared values, similar or shared experiences, and a passion for social justice.

SHOW UP, STAND UP, SPEAK OUT

One thing that distinguishes ICHS from other community health centers is our voice's strength and influence. Over the years, ICHS went from a quiet, do its job health center to one that fiercely promotes and defends affordable health care, access to health for all those who need care, especially people of color, and sustainable program funding. I am the primary spokesperson as the named leader, but our board members, staff, patients, their families, and community partners are advocates who can be easily activated. ICHS' advocacy sophistication and muscle were developed incrementally and bloomed during the development of the Affordable Care Act under Barack Obama. Our advocacy tested its fortitude under Donald Trump when the laws, programs, and funding to lift low-income people, including immigrants and refugees, came under attack. The Affordable Care Act, Medicaid, housing, nutrition, childcare, and many more programs addressing social determinants of health were reinterpreted with stricter criteria, defunded, or altogether eliminated. Virulent and vicious attacks were unleashed on the low-income, immigrants, people of color, gender and gender identity, religion, and other protected classes. Anti-Asian hate and the COVID pandemic led to blaming and victimizing of Asian and Pacific Islander community members.

Today, leadership in a community-based non-profit demands high-level executive organizational building, team inspiration, and community-wide influence and power. ICHS serves around 30,000 people a year for over 100,000 visits. Its 600 staff serve low-income patients, providing over $1 million in uncompensated care. Its team has won numerous awards for quality and outstanding care. ICHS' success is because of a passionate, committed, and skilled team who see ourselves as community members and as stewards for healthier people, thriving families, empowered communities, and a just society.

PURPOSEFUL LEADERSHIP

In the *Sunday in the Park with George* musical, Stephen Sondheim's song "Putting It Together" extols, *"Every moment makes a contribution." "Every detail plays a part."* I finally put it all together in my ultimate leadership at ICHS, greatness from small beginnings. Doubts and anxiety are long gone, ceding confidence and certainty that I am the right person for the right organization at the right time. Every lesson came together from my character-building days in the Philippines to my early awkward immigrant days, where I discovered my commitment, compassion, and core values for community and civil rights. Beginning with self, building confidence as I figured out who I am, to a series of professional, managerial, and executive jobs that built competencies for community development, economic development, and political savvy. Leadership experiences in team management, organizational management, and socially responsible management leavened with a determination to succeed in leading ICHS mattered. The vision mattered. The execution made the difference.

Of those fortunes taped to my work computer monitor, there are two that top the rest.

> *"You can't stop the waves, but you can learn to surf."*
> *"You have an iron will, which helps you succeed in everything."*

LEADING CHANGE:
LEGACY

Legacy

Aileen Cassinetto
San Mateo County Poet Laureate, 2019 – 2022

To tell her story, you must know when
to put courage in a matchbox and conceal

it in a loaf of bread. You must learn how
a message betokened deliverance

when courage is simply a word someone
wrote on a slip of paper and the sweet

scent of bread could no longer sustain you.
You must grasp your other hand with what

grit remains, growing and unyielding.
To tell her story, you must walk in her shoes.

If forced out of your leased farmland,
don't forget to bring rice if you can pack

only what you can carry. And if
your mother did not speak inside the bus

with the windows covered with brown paper
on the way to the barracks, it was only

because she was praying that you would not be
housed in the horse stall with the manure

whitewashed over. And if you were, she was
deciding what to do about the smell.

To tell her story, you must remember
the landscape from behind barbed

wire fences. You must gaze at your body
and know its history, look beneath

the tender, ridged scars and see the bone
protruding out of your right arm

and hole the size of a football
on your right thigh, wondering how

the lights never went out. You must
look at the image of your grandmother

with the weight of rammed earth against
what you survived. To tell her story,

you must say a prayer, not of sorrow,
but of grace. You must loosen the earth,

pick daffodils to the base of the stem,
remember your roots and ordinary days,

and the grit under your fingernails,
the way your grandmother taught you.

ATTY. LORNA PATAJO-KAPUNAN

Senior Partner, Kapunan & Castillo Law Offices
GLOBAL FWN100™ 2016

A Block Off the Old Chip

"It's a girl"! My father, expecting a son, not another daughter, thought it was an April Fool's joke of the nurse who pronounced my entry into this world on April Fools Day 1952. My being a girl did not stop me in my childhood days from playing rough with the boys in my neighborhood, climbing trees, competing in slingshot, *tex*, yoyo, *barilan, paramihan ng rubberbands, palayuan ng dura*. Although my lovely dolls and doll house were nicely kept clean in the *aparador*, all felt neglected. And "no ballet lessons for me, please!"

Being a girl did not stop me from speaking up, and sharing my opinions at the dining table with the adults. I happily did my share of household chores, but "don't make me cook in the kitchen, please!"

My being a girl did not prevent me from wanting to be always the best in class, the leader of almost all my school organizations, and competing against exclusive boy schools—whether it be oratorical contests, spelling bee, math, science, or English.

My being a girl did not deter me from entering what was then referred to as a communist university—the University of the Philippines (UP) by the Religious of the Virgin (RVM) nuns. They gave me my elementary and high school education. Nor did my being a girl prevent me from attending rallies, boycotts, and the Diliman Commune despite the danger of being locked up as a subversive for my progressive, anti-establishment, anti-martial law views.

My being a girl did not make me hesitate to take up law and fulfill my father's dream for his two sons to follow in his footsteps and honor the legacy of the lawyers, judges, and justices in our family tree. Unfortunately, my two brothers frustrated that dream by deciding to be a businessman and a doctor. My being a girl did not stop me from raising my 5 sons as a young widow and solo parent, attending father and son nights, going drinking and camping with the other fathers, and being the parent representative of my sons' classes at Ateneo and La Salle.

My being a girl at the UP College of Law, then a male dominated Law School, did not stop me from being amongst the top of my class. I was the best debater, the first female Captain of the Moot Court Team competing against other Law Schools abroad. I was a consistent member of the Purple Feather and Pi Gamma Mu Honor Societies and the Editorial Board.

My being a girl defined me and shaped my being. Now at 70 years of age, I am grateful that little girl grew up to be the woman I am now.

I have my parents to thank—the genes I inherited from them, reinforced by the core values of being truthful, honest, self-disciplined, compassionate, passionate, loving, and sincere, which they instilled in me and my siblings, a sister and two brothers. These core values were the tools I needed to achieve the level of success. Success I am blessed to have and enjoy.

Even as a young girl, I already wanted to be a lawyer as great as my father, Supreme Court Justice Lino Mejia Patajo. While my mother, Dean Cristeta Taaca Patajo was in her own right successful as a Dean of top nursing schools, Manila Doctors and Far Eastern University, I never aspired to be a nurse or educator. Instead, I romanticized being a slayer of demons, dragons, and bad guys, wielding the mighty sword of justice, truth, and punishment of evil and evil-doers.

The path to success was not easy.

In my second year of law school, I got pregnant and then married, in that order, to a classmate, Eduardo Roden Kapunan. He later was appointed Judge of the Regional Trial Courts of Pampanga and then Manila. Being a mother while studying complex subjects was a balancing act. Also, my pedigree created expectations on the part of my teachers. I was always asked if I was the daughter of my famous father. At that time, he was Commissioner of the Commission on Elections. A tough act to follow! My reputation always preceded me, hence the added burden of living up to expectations. But this emboldened me to rise to the challenge and not disappoint. I wanted to be a "CHIP OFF THE OLD BLOCK!" My exceptional record in Law School earned me an invitation to join after graduation, one of the most prestigiouslaw firms then—ACCRALAW. When there were over 100 lawyers, most of them male, senior to me in years and experience, I had to be better and the best amongst my batchmates in the office. The long hours, diligence in preparation, hard work, empathy with clients, and my love for the law made me stand out amongst my peers.

I knew even then that I could do more. And the opportunity did come post-EDSA People Power. One of the Partners, Senator Raul S. Roco, invited me to break away from the establishment and pro-administration ACCRALAW and form our own law firm, which I happily joined. Years later, with that law firm's dissolution upon its founding partner's demise, I created my own law firm. And, as the cliché goes, the rest is history.

But my life is not a cliché, far from it. This was not the end of a chapter but just the beginning of one-- more challenging, exciting, and definitely more disruptive.

I. LOOKING BACK

By the time this book goes into print, I will have turned 70 years old. My only concession to hitting 70 is to give up a quarter of my "bucket list;" "can not scale the 29, 029 feet Mount Everest; can not walk the Camino de Santiago 500-mile pilgrimage across Spain nor attempt the hike-only Appalachian Trail. But I have not given up on Chichen Itza, Machu Picchu, Petra, the Pyramids, Pompeii, Christ the Redeemer, the Great Barrier Reef, and many other Wonders of the World."

Looking back, I have not done too bad with places to visit. I have seen the Taj Mahal, the Colosseum, Eiffel Tower, Grand Canyon, the Great Wall of China, Angkor Wat, and Niagara Falls. As my sons were growing up, I have been to all the Disneylands in HongKong, Tokyo, Los Angeles, Florida, and Paris. With my family, I have toured great cities, museums, and parks across Europe, Asia, and the USA.

WHY? BECAUSE I COULD!

As a child, my parents told me to dream BIG dreams. I dreamt of one day having enough money to travel to places and conquer the world. I did earn money and fulfilled my dream to travel.

But do not get me wrong. Money, to me, was not and is not the motivator. Instead, it's what money represents; the luxury of having options, and the wherewithal to make choices.

Through the years, I have known successful women who are driven more by what they hope to achieve rather than what they aspire to earn. Each woman has her definition of what money symbolizes and what achievement means. Successful women have a vision of their lives based on cherished values like recognition, security, challenge, or independence. These intangible goals, more than hard cash, fueled their financial success. Money became the by-product of their value-based ambition and simultaneously gave them more opportunities to live out their authentic values.

My ambition was chiseled in a wall at Malcolm Hall at the University of the Philippines College of Law. Justice Oliver Wendell Holmes reminded us daily as we entered our classrooms *"that the business of a law school is not sufficiently described when you merely say that it is to teach law, or to make lawyers. It is to teach law in a grand manner and to make great lawyers."* My ambition then, as it still is now, is to be a GREAT LAWYER!

The path ahead of me then as a young lawyer in the early eighties was not easy, although I must admit that my pedigree and genes made it easier for me than most female lawyers then. Those were the bad days of blatant sexism, conservatism, male-only golf/tennis/executive dining rooms, old boys' networks, and men-only toilets in courtrooms and board rooms. The worst was being nudged out of promotion to make room for some idiot male.

These did not hinder my ambition of wanting to be a great lawyer. *"You have to believe in yourself, that you can do anything you set your mind to."* That catchphrase from my father, *"I CAN DO ANYTHING"* emerged as a recurring mantra for me. I loved what I was doing. I loved the law. Lawyering made me happy; it was my passion. And I think passion is important in whatever anyone sets out to do. So I believed, no matter how impossible it seemed, that no one can stand in your way once you decide to do what you love and be excellent at it.

MY RULE NO. 1: Do What You Love and Be Passionate About It!

But belief in yourself does not necessarily mean the absence of self-doubt. I admit to grappling with feelings of inadequacy, incompetence, and fear. Fear of failure, fear of rejection, and fear of criticism lay like fault lines just beneath my seemingly confident exterior. But one of the secrets I have learned is to look and act confident even when you do not feel it. It is like being a duck, calm and unruffled on the surface but paddling like hell underneath!!!

There were times I have sat in board of directors meetings looking as if I was reading a complicated report or dissecting financial statements, and yet I did not know what the hell I was reviewing. Or, at times, I stared at a judge in court pretending to know the case or the cited statute or arguing with an opposing counsel with the calmest tone whilst seething with anger underneath for not reading that one cited case that I had not read. But I would put on a good show and invariably pull it off. But these *faux pas*, gratefully, were few and far between and reinforced the importance of always being prepared. A reminder I tell all my lawyers in my firm to this day. There is no substitute for being prepared for anything, whether in the boardroom or the court's *sala* or meeting with clients.

Many of us women, not only lawyers, have wrestled with what therapists refer to as the "Imposter Syndrome." Beneath our confident exteriors lurk layers of insecurity. We wrestle with the thought that people will see that we are not that smart, that our bravado is fake, so it's better not to talk lest they discover how dumb we are once we open our mouths. But my advice to myself and you women out there is:

MY RULE NO. 2: Feel the Fear, Have the Doubts, and Go For It Anyway!

And if this fails, go back to Rule No. 1—Do what you love and be passionate about it. Easier said than done, of course, especially for women who have to balance career and family, which I went through.

The struggle for balance is even more pronounced in the life of a single mom. Few people know that I am a single mom. I lost my husband to Colon cancer in 2001. I thought this was the end of the world until, in 2003, I lost "King," the youngest of my five sons who was eight years old, to leukemia. That really was the end of the world for me, and I cursed my God, *"Nag quota na ako Lord, why me?"* [I met my quota, Lord. Why me?] But I had to bounce back. I had four sons to take care of, my law firm, and a hard-earned reputation of being a FIGHTER. So I fought hard to keep body and soul together. A cheering team of my parents, extended family, loyal friends, supporters, and believers made me hurdle my loss and come back tougher.

I formed the King Kapunan Leukemia Foundation for Children in honor of my son and to help other mothers losing their children to cancer deal with their grief. I joined INA Foundation (*Mga Inang Naulila Sa Anak*) to give grief counseling. After oceans of tears shed over my double loss of husband and son, I steeled myself and bounced back.

I learned from experience that being a single working mom is always a balancing act. You are never at work enough and never with kids enough. So you have got to make hard choices about your time. Sometimes you have to skip being home because you have to be at a business event or be out of town for a conference. And then you'll feel terrible that you are not with your kids. It is a constant choice; you never know if you are making the right ones. But, you have choices. Mothering while working is still a herculean task, even with a husband at your side.

The work/family dilemma is an intricate web of complex issues, issues of identity, autonomy, and a maternal instinct that exerts a fiercer pull than the force of gravity. Yet, to be successful, we must settle on a workable equilibrium. Through trial and error, I have learned that there are viable solutions for preserving mental health while managing multiple roles. These solutions can come from taking a hard look at our personal priorities, knowing what we cherish most in life, and discerning between what we think we should do and how we want to live our lives.

MY RULE NO. 3: Think in Terms of Trade-Offs, Not Sacrifices to Find a Workable Equilibrium
For me, it was clear that I wanted to succeed in my career for my FAMILY. What

use was success if I had no family to share it with? So, the family came first. I had to learn not to work absurdly long hours, that the critical factor is not the number of hours one works as much as the intensity of focus. Know where the work stopped, and the personal life began. I stopped being the superwoman on steroids who had no clue how many hours I worked but felt how few hours I slept. I learned from stories of many successful women who once loved their jobs, but their passion had turned to obsession, their work had become an addiction, their long hours felt more like hard labor, and their generous salaries were but golden shackles.

Ambition or money is not the only reason successful women have lopsided lives. Overwork has become an occupational hazard for ambitious women trying to make it in a man's world. Women have to make a disproportionate sacrifice to compete equally in the work world. Women have to work twice as hard as men to keep up.

It is an easy, perhaps inevitable trap to fall into, and I told myself I would get out of this trap before it was too late. I have learned that over-work is a self-inflicted punishment. Working hard does not mean working all the time. I have learned to work smart, putting in productive, not long, hours and giving myself "ME" time. "ME" time is being alone with myself, or just to relax, be with family and a short list of authentic friends, paint, read a book, watch Korean telenovelas while gulping *soju*, going shopping and buying yet again bags, shoes, or jewelry I absolutely do not need. But these delightful, simple little pleasures in life are necessary distractions from the drudgery of a heavy workload. It means a "time-out" to smell the flowers and watch the grass grow.

MY RULE NO. 4: Say No to Discrimination

Another battle that may be even more painful than juggling too many hats or getting over-invested in work is contending with gender bias and sexual harassment. Of course, not all women have to confront these problems. However, it can be the most frustrating and distressing challenge for those who do. Discrimination has always been a workplace threat for aspiring women, and these days, the higher a woman climbs, the more acute this problem seems to become. Corporate women complain of being excluded from social occasions, passed over for promotions, or ignored for challenging assignments. Entrepreneurs resent not receiving the same referrals, networking opportunities, or start-up capitals as their male colleagues.

"I wish we were all treated equally, but it just is not the case" "The guys will get asked by the people that run the firm to go golfing, but they would not ask me because I'm a woman. So my peers hang out with the decision makers on weekends, and I am not invited." How often do we hear these laments from women executives?

That was the norm when I started my law career in a big, male-dominated law firm. My solution: RECOGNITION, NOT RESIGNATION! I had to work hard and exceptionally well to be recognized. I did not resent that I was not invited to play golf. I considered it a stupid game to chase a small ball for two hours. I wanted to be recognized for the excellence of my work, not by hanging around with the big bosses or the high-paying clients. There was no big or small client for me, no simple or difficult task. I took everything that came my way. I chose not to blame the system nor to become a victim. I dealt with gender bias and other injustices in the workplace my way. Guided by my Rule No.1—"Do what you love and be passionate about it."

My love for my work and my passion for doing it made me recognized for being ME.

MY RULE NO. 5: Be Grateful / 20 Hugs a Day

Whatever one's definition of success is and there is no 'one size fits all' definition, there are people we attribute our success to in our lives. No one achieves success does so without the help of others, and we must acknowledge this help with gratitude.

I have a 'gratitude list' of the people in my life who have helped make me who I am. My husband, my children, my siblings, teachers, mentors, partners, co-workers, friends, and even my enemies who made me tough. They know who they are, and I shall be forever grateful to them.

But one person needs to be mentioned, my mom, Cristeta (Titay) Taaca Patajo. While my father was my anchor and inspiration, my Mommy Titay was the iconic presence in my life. I can never say thank you enough.

Mommy Titay succeeded in everything from the mundane to the sublime. The daily grind of raising us four children, managing our household and farms, taking care of my dad, tending to the needs of relatives, growing our garden, and lovingly spoiling her *apos*, albeit ordinary tasks, were done with extraordinary compassion and joy. She did these mundane tasks while also "saving the world." She supported the schooling of our relatives with no financial means, started a review school for nurses so they could go to greener pastures abroad, and improved the curriculum as Dean of Far Eastern University and Manila Doctors. She championed the rights of students and workers as Vice President for Academic Affairs of United Doctor's Medical College. She authored the Nursing Code to improve the plight of nurses and health workers, gently pressuring Congress, which enacted it into law. She organized our Homeowners Association in our village and pioneered the Supreme Court Ladies Circle, among many others.

Mommy Titay was my "Exhibit "A" for the perfect balance of family and career. Because she could do it, I knew I could do it too. She inspired me to dream and, through my life's journey, helped me achieve those dreams. So, for all that I am or still hope to be, my gratitude goes to you, Mom.

Be grateful to the Mommy Titay's in your lives who have made you who you are!

Likewise, to the people who have made your life at home or in the workplace more comfortable, organized, less complex, orderly, and bearable, I advise you to follow my "20 Hugs A Day" Quota. A simple thank you, a smile, a pat on the back, a genuine handshake, kind words, and a softer tone of voice to our household, *kasambahays*, drivers, secretaries, office staff, and subordinates, these are my 20 hugs a day. Giving "20 hugs a day" will lighten not only their burden but yours as well!

II. THE PRESENT

The lessons I learned from the challenges in my early legal years have made me a better lawyer and a better person.

When I founded my current law firm, Kapunan & Castillo Law Offices, after several years of working for others, I, along with my other Founding Partners, envisioned a law firm grounded on three C's: COMPETENCE, CHARACTER, and COURAGE. We would seek out the best and the brightest young practitioners to join our firm. We vowed to be faithful to our lawyer's oath: *"to do no falsehood, nor consent to the doing of any in court; not wittingly nor unwillingly promote or sue any groundless, false or unlawful suit, or give aid or consent to the same; delay no man for money or malice and conduct ourselves as lawyers according to the best of our knowledge and discretion."*

As important as featly to our lawyer's oath, I have impressed upon our lawyers in our law firm that we must have the COURAGE to do what is right to win our cases on the merits, not to corrupt the justice system. We had the courage to be the first law firm to hire a Mangyan lawyer and also be among the first to employ an openly LGBT lawyer, breaking the bias and barriers for them. My law firm now has an almost all female save for one male legal staff, not because of affirmative action but because we recognize talent and genius where we see it, regardless of gender. We pride ourselves in being an equal opportunity workplace!

Our firm's mission is to shine in the practice of law because of WHAT you know, not WHO you know! I am proud that our law firm has the unique distinction of being the only law firm in the country that the Bishops Businessmen's Conference has awarded SPIRITUALITY AT THE WORKPLACE for our high standard of ethics and excellence in the practice of law.

Another strength of our law firm is the TEAM SYSTEM. Every client, every case has a team assigned to ensure the efficiency and quality of work. I may have earned recognition and received many awards as an outstanding lawyer, litigator, and corporate practitioner, and likewise acknowledged for my many socio-civic engagements and advocacies, but I AM NOT A SOLO PERFORMER, nor have I ever wanted to be a solo performer.

I stand on the shoulders of the brilliant and dedicated team of lawyers I have in my law firm. And needless to say, "the lessons I learned in kindergarten," the authentic values ingrained in me by my parents, and the inspiration and guidance given me by my mentors and role models, women and men alike, through the years are the anchor of my BEING!!!

My Partners and I have always felt blessed not by the figures below the bottom line indicating profit but by the many big and small clients we have served who appreciate the zeal, dedication, diligence, and loyalty we give them. That is what we consider OUR ABUNDANCE—WE ARE BLESSED BECAUSE WE GIVE BLESSINGS TO OTHERS!!!.

Because there are legions out there needing legal advice and assistance, especially the marginalized, I wanted to expand my reach. I decided to write a weekly column for *Business Mirror* entitled "Legally Speaking" to expound on current legal issues so that the public could understand the intricacies of the law and new legislation. I also currently host a weekly Saturday program,

"Laban Para Sa Karapatan" [Fight for Rights], with a nationwide audience and reaching our diaspora and global Filipinos. Through this medium, I have been able to give legal advice on protecting and asserting one's legal rights. To be able to do so, with the help of friends and sponsors, is a blessing. My way of paying back and paying forward.

III. THE FUTURE

We have five generations of lawyers in the family, from my grandfather, Don Domingo Patajo, who served as Assemblyman in the Spanish times, to my grandson Kyle Linus who just passed the bar with exemplary performance during this historic pandemic. However, my life's dream was for my father, the best lawyer I know and admire, to recognize me as "A CHIP OFF THE OLD BLOCK." After years of practice, the highlight of which was arguing my first case in the Supreme Court and appearing before the EnBanc with my father, Justice Lino M. Patajo, amongst the esteemed sitting Justices, I got the biggest compliment of my life.

After our oral arguments in the EnBanc hearing that day, my father said to me, "YOU ARE NOT A CHIP OFF THE OLD BLOCK—YOU ARE NOW A BLOCK OF THE OLD CHIP."

I dream of the day I can say that to my children and grandchildren. When that day comes, I shall happily retire and see the other Wonders of the World... and write "FINIS" to my bucket list!!!

MARIA BEEBE, PH.D.

President, Kaisipan Inc.
Consultant, USAID Indo-Pacific Opportunity Project,
Asia Open RAN Academy
US FWN100™ 2011
GLOBAL FWN100™ 2012
CONTINUING GLOBAL FWN100™ 2019

Engendering Leadership

Four women leaders. Four women leaders exercised their power for peace. Dr. Anne Itto in the Sudan. President Corazon Aquino in the Philippines. President Ellen Sirleaf Johnson in Liberia. Graça Machel in Mozambique and South Africa.

Crucible: Tested and Better for It

Socio-economic-political forces shaped the political leadership of these four women. Their crucible was borne out of civil strife caused by authoritarian leaders. Such was the case of Jaafar Nimieri in the Sudan, who held onto power for 40 years; Ferdinand Marcos in the Philippines for 20 years; and Samuel Doe in Liberia for ten years. These autocratic leaders might have started with good intentions to make a difference, then became despots in their quest for power, embodying man's inhumanity. For Graça Machel, her first crucible was Mozambique's fight for independence and then South Africa's transformation from apartheid.

The leadership of these four women resonates with me because I lived and worked in their home countries and with the people who heeded their call to action for peace. In the Sudan, from 1979 to 1983. In the Philippines, from 1983 to 1987. In Liberia, from 1986 to 1990. In South Africa, from 1994 to 1996. Except for President Cory Aquino, I did not overlap with them. Historical influences beyond our control were at play as my husband James heeded his foreign service postings. As the accompanying spouse, I had two concerns: raising our children, David and Ligaya, as foreign service kids while finding a career niche. At each posting, I applied for and was hired for positions that allowed me to work on meaningful activities that would contribute to human well-being.

All four women leaders believed in a culture of peace as *"a set of values, attitudes, modes of behavior and ways of life that reject violence and prevent conflicts by tackling their root causes to solve problems through dialogue and negotiation among individuals, groups, and nations."* (U.N. Resolution A/RES/52/13). They walked the talk in engendering leadership and en-GENDER-ing leadership in their words and actions. Anne Itto (2006) contends that *"Women were not passive victims of war"* and *"… as combatants, supporters of fighting forces and peacemakers qualify them to sit at the negotiating table and to assume an active role in implementation."* For Corazon Aquino (1986), her choice was not to be *"consigned to the bedroom of history."* Corazon Aquino (2000) believes *"there is much that women can bring into politics that would make our world a kinder, gentler place for humanity to thrive in."* *"Seeing gender as integral to the economy brings the true value of women into the conversation,"* according to Ellen Sirleaf Johnson (2019) who adds, *"We ask justice, we ask equality, we ask that all the civil and political rights that belong to all citizens, be guaranteed to us and our daughters."* On women and leadership, Ellen Sirleaf Johnson (2020) asserts, *"Once the glass ceiling has been broken, it can never be put back together, however one would try to do that."* Graça Machel (2020) is emphatic that *"Women must redesign the table, and not just expect to be at the table."* Machel and Johnson continue redesigning the table with The Global Elders, a group of world leaders of a certain age, to continue contributing their wisdom, leadership, and integrity to tackle some of the world's most challenging problems.

This chapter reflects on how and why these four women leaders influenced my leadership repertoire in international development. First, I summarize the social-political-cultural context, highlight a few vignettes about living and working during those times, and reflect on what I learned from the Sudanese, Filipinos, Liberians, and South Africans. Then, I explain the leadership lessons I learned from the four women leaders – Anne Itto, Corazon Aquino, Ellen Sirleaf Jones, and Graça Machal that continue to guide my advocacies and my recent giving back initiative, Kaisipan.

Being an Expatriate in the Sudan – Cross-Cultural First

Our time in the Sudan (1979–1983) was during a relatively peaceful time, after the first civil war and before the second civil war. The first civil war resulted from the southern Sudan's demand for representation and regional autonomy. This war lasted from 1955 to 1972 and ended with the Addis Ababa Agreement for the Southern Sudan Autonomous Region. A decade of relative peace followed; however, when the military regime tried to impose sharia law as part of its overall policy to "Islamicize" all of Sudan in 1983, the Sudan People's Liberation Army (SPLA) led insurrections in the south, a region dominated by Animists and Christians.

Living and working in Khartoum, Sudan, required cross-cultural adjustments with no significant cultural shocks. We lived outside the U.S. Embassy compound in a residential area where upper-middle-class Sudanese and other expatriates lived. Our son David went to a Montessori School run by an Indian whose husband worked for Total, a French company. David learned Arabic script at the same time he was learning his ABCs. David's nursery school friends were a veritable United Nations with whose parents we socialized and worked. In addition to Sudanese and American, there were Chinese, Filipinos, German, Israeli, Lebanese, and Palestinian kids who played soccer, swam at the American Club, and celebrated their birthdays with Star Wars and Disney themes.

In May 1982, I was medically evacuated to California to give birth to Ligaya, and six weeks later, we received our clearance to travel back to the Sudan. I decided to go back to work and negotiated half-time work, two hours in the morning, back home for an hour to nurse the baby, then return for another two hours. The initial answer was "no." However, since I had proved my worth, my supervisor eventually agreed. As we were getting ready for our foreign service re-assignment to the Philippines in June 1983, Ligaya had her first birthday in Khartoum. I thought it strange that a colleague brought uninvited guests from southern Sudan. They wanted to talk to James about seeking help for their cause. Instead, James gave them the name of another officer. It was then that we sensed that the talk about unhappiness resulting from the mandate to "Islamicize" all of Sudan was about to turn from talk to insurrection.

"Guests at the Negotiating Table?"
— DR. ANNE ITTO (2006)

In 1983, Dr. Anne Itto finished her Ph.D. at Kansas State University. She could have decided to stay in the U.S., yet she chose to return to the Sudan. She was voted the Sudan People's Liberation Movement (SPLM) Deputy Secretary-General for Southern Sudan. Her efforts included adopting the policy of 25 percent representation for women in all SPLA branches. As a result, the party's executive branch has women in 40 percent of its core leadership positions and 25 percent women in all governmental departments. Despite these gains, Anne Itto and other women negotiators felt disappointed about the lack of gender-sensitive provisions and being underestimated or ignored during negotiations. Anne explained that women were treated as guests at the negotiating table despite women's roles *"as combatants, supporters of fighting forces, and peacemakers qualify them to sit at the negotiating table and assume an active role in implementation." "Women were not passive victims of war."* Yet, she suggested that new democratic spaces have opened, especially in the south, notwithstanding the lack of a level playing field for women. She urged women to mobilize effectively and seize the opportunity for more political participation. She voiced her *"fears that political progress is at risk of being undermined by conflict"* and *"we could lose all our gains."*

From Anne Itto, I learned these Leadership Lessons:
"Women need to lead the change we want to see" (2011). What change do I want to see? More quality education for girls. Research has shown that better-educated women tend to have better information about nutrition and healthcare, have fewer children, and get married at a later age. When they choose to become mothers, their children are usually healthier. I advocate for girls' education, but I also plan initiatives, such as coding for girls, digital growth mindset for

girls, and leadership for girls that advance their digital capabilities. When I hire, all competencies being equal, I hire women.

"Women must make sure they create ladders for women to climb" (2011). Upon reflection on my leadership journey, there was not one point when I declared, *"I am a leader."* My leadership is a journey of an accumulation of experience and a growing realization of my ability to influence others. Being recognized as bright, elected to the student council, and tapped for student plays were all positive influences that built self-confidence. Being the only woman and being the only Filipina at the negotiating table gave me a reason to celebrate; however, I recognized that it was not sustainable to have only me. Thus, the need for a counter-narrative to the crab mentality of pulling others down, but instead to create ladders for women and to have more women in leadership positions. That is my motivation for femtoring and continuing to volunteer to edit the *DISRUPT* leadership books.

"Don't sleep. Keep monitoring and continue to demand" (nd). I am not done yet. There is work to be done in equity for all. That is why I maintain my Association of American University Women (AAUW) membership. AAUW is at the forefront of advocating for gender equality in education, economic security, and leadership.

From the Sudanese, I first learned to appreciate Islam and, later on, the ISLAM model of leadership where the leader: Inspires the Vision, Strengthens the Heart, Leads the way, Assesses their actions, and Mobilizes the Community.

Back to the Philippines as an Expatriate

Being in the Philippines from 1983 to 1987 was the best time for me to witness People Power and work with not-for-profit organizations to implement USAID projects. The Beebe family arrived shortly after the assassination of Senator Ninoy Aquino upon his return from exile in the U.S. to the Philippines in 1983. Senator Aquino was the most vocal of the opposition to the Marcos regime.

Cory Aquino could have chosen to be remembered as the "wife," yet she became the reluctant leader of the opposition. Cory proved to be a charismatic leader, inspiring orator, and skilled campaigner. When President Marcos called for snap elections in 1985, Cory won, but Marcos was declared the winner. Cory called for a series of civil disobedience marches, now known as the People Power Revolution, that led to the ouster of Marcos. President Corazon Aquino served as President of the Philippines from 1986 to 1992. Despite nine coup attempts, Cory brought back democracy, restored investor confidence in the economy, and enacted legal and constitutional reforms. She died in August 2009.

Cory is quick to acknowledge that she owed her presidency to People Power. *"I resolved during my presidency that I would, in turn, empower the people"* (1996). She was vocal about what *"women can bring into politics that would make our world a kinder, gentler place for humanity to thrive in"* (2000).

I worked as a USAID Private Voluntary Organization (PVO) consultant, the best of times for a Filipina, working as an American in grassroots projects. I always chose marine-based projects, oyster and pearl farming, aquarium fishing, and mangrove reforestation until that day when a storm chased us from one of the 75 small islands to Tagbilaran, Bohol. The local boatman told us to hurry as he could smell a storm brewing. Noting that it was a sunny day, we took our time, as we wanted to enjoy the island breezes. When the boatman finally got us on the motorized *banca* [outrigger canoe], he made us face away from the sea and battened us down. We complied to humor him until we got to the open sea and the ten-foot waves started slamming on us. And we understood why our backs were against the sea and why we were battened down the hatches. That was a lesson of the need to listen to the locals. They know best about local conditions.

A Cory memory happened when I was doing a workshop on the baseline, monitoring, and evaluation of Private Voluntary Organizations (PVO) projects at a hotel in Cebu on February 25, 1986. I heard my name being paged because of an urgent phone call. My supervisor told me to get on the next plane to Manila. I pushed back, *"But we have just started. Are the kids fine?"* He hemmed and hawed and finally blurted out, *"Woman, when your man tells you to come home, you better come home."* So I flew back, livid, and let my husband have it. Until we heard the unsecured emergency band radio, *"The guests are on their way."* So that was it; my husband and supervisor worried there would be trouble because of a huge pro-Cory rally. Instead, the Marcoses decided to take the offer of a helicopter ride out of Malacañang and fly out of the Philippines to Hawaii.

"It is not I who have been consigned to the bedroom of history." – PRESIDENT CORAZON AQUINO (1986)

Like Cory, I had choices. I choose not to be consigned to being only a "foreign service spouse." But instead, I decided to build on elements of my life that contributed to my readiness for global engagement.

- Growing up in the Philippines immersed me in the Filipino social value of *kapwa* [shared humanity]. One explanation of *kapwa* is together with the person where together comes first before you break it into separate selves. Therefore, when someone says *pakkikipagkapwa*, the meaning is accepting and dealing with the other person as an equal in a continuous manner. Thus, building and maintaining relationships was a competency I brought to my work in international development.

- Like most Filipinas, I grew up multilingual (*Chabakano*, *Kapampangan*, *Ilokano*, *Tagalog*, English), an often-overlooked advantage for leadership across cultures. Growing up multilingual appears to "facilitate the development of perspective-taking tools that are critical for effective communication" (Fan, Liberman, Keysar, & Kinzler, 2015, p. 1).

- My grandmother, Candida Turla dela Rosa often reminded me that in addition to being intelligent, I had the blood of a *katipunero*! As a young boy, my grandfather, Juan dela Rosa, was a runner for the *Katipunan* during the late 1890s. He memorized the messages and ran for his life to deliver the messages. I imagine this took courage.

- As it turns out, my grandmother, too, showed courage as she sat at the table, not as a guest but as an equal with the *Hukbong Bayan Laban* sa *Hapon (hukbalahap)* [People's Army Against the Japaneses]. She joined the movement in the fight against the Japanese. She even had a *nom de guerre*, Kumander Dayang-dayang. My grandmother shared this untold story with James because he reminded her of William Pomery, an American who joined the *hukbalahap* movement.

- I remember my grandmother saying, *"Matas ka api."* [literally high fire]. I imagine *katipunero* blood on fire explains why the courage to fight for social justice became a guiding force in my leadership.

Two Leadership Lessons from Corazon Aquino:

"It's not just in politics that you can be a servant of the people, you can do it in so many ways" (2005). Since running for elective office is not for me, I have served by heeding the call as in my work in Afghanistan from 2005 to 2008 and by

giving back by starting Kaisipan in 2020 to advance the digital capabilities of Filipino educators.

"I've reached a point in my life where it's no longer necessary to impress. If they like me the way, I am, that's good. If they don't, that's too bad" (1987). In Passion, Risk, and Adventure, I highlight the leadership actions in three projects I helped design and implement after turning 50 during my third chapter in life. The common elements in these projects were policies related to access and use of information and communication technologies (ICTs) and leadership by cooperative efforts, the bayanihan spirit. As I transition to the fourth quarter of my life, like Cory, what matters is not to impress, but to carry on with passion, risk, and adventure.

From the Filipinas who participated in the people power rallies, I learned the power of collective action and the courageous solidarities against a twenty-year authoritarian regime. However, I also learned that while people power brought a sense of limitless hope and possibility, the hoped-for agricultural and economic reforms require a more sustained effort.

From One U.S. Colony to Another U.S. Colony

From the Philippines, the Beebe family assignment was to Monrovia, Liberia, in 1987. Liberia was a project of the American Colonization Society (ACS), which believed black people would face better chances for freedom and prosperity in Africa than in the United States. From 1822 to 1861, the ACS relocated more than 15,000 freed and free-born black people who faced social and legal oppression in the U.S. to Liberia. These settlers developed an Americo-Liberian identity forming a small elite with disproportionate political power. The Americo-Liberians did not relate well to the indigenous Africans, who were excluded from birthright citizenship in their land until 1904. These ethnic tensions erupted in a 1980 coup led by Samuel Doe, who subsequently won the 1985 election. While we lived and worked in Liberia during relative calm, we were evacuated in May 1990 when Charles Taylor started an insurrection in December 1989.

I had a job lined up before we arrived in Monrovia. The USAID mission director, who was the Deputy Mission Director in the Philippines, noted that if we were to move to Monrovia, there was a possible opening for a PVO Consultant. It would be a step up from what I was doing in the Philippines. My work made it possible to visit project sites outside Monrovia, including Nimba County, where the 1989 insurrection started. It was December 1989, and our son David had gone on a school trip to Sapo National Park, the country's largest designated rainforest. David, his schoolmates, and chaperones had just entered the park when Charles Taylor and his rebels cut off transportation on the main road that led to the park. With the activation of the emergency network, a missionary near the park chartered a helicopter to get the kids out, who wondered why all the brouhaha. While in the forest, they played mind games, having read Joseph Conrad's *Heart of Darkness*. *"What if everyone we know is gone when we emerge from the forest?"* Their mind games were prescient. Despite the uncertain outcome of the insurrection, most of the USAID staff and families, myself included, decided to stay because of our work commitments until the Ambassador declared that all non-essential personnel would go on mandatory evacuation in May 1990. The intersection of the public-private sphere was unavoidable while on a foreign service assignment.

> *"To girls and women everywhere, I issue a simple invitation. My sisters, my daughters, my friends; find your voice."*
> — PRESIDENT ELLEN SIRLEAF JOHNSON (2011)

President Ellen Sirleaf Johnson is a Nobel Peace Laureate: a leading promoter of peace, justice, and democratic rule, a voice for freedom, and an advocate for health for all. She served as Assistant Minister of Finance but resigned after a disagreement about spending. She then became Minister of Finance from 1979 to 1980. In April 1980, Master Sergeant Samuel Doe seized power in a military coup wherein President Tolbert was assassinated. A purge followed; Sirleaf escaped and went to exile in Kenya, where she served as Vice President of the Africa Regional Bank of Citibank. After lifting the ban on political parties, she returned to Liberia where she was placed under house arrest. Allowed to go into exile, she went to Washington, DC, where she served as Vice President of the Equator Bank and the Synergos Institute board member. In 1992, she joined the UNDP as Assistant Administrator and Director, Regional Bureau of Africa. Back in Liberia in 1997, she ran against Charles Taylor as President and won second. From 2004 to 2005, she chaired the Governance Reform Commission. Finally, in the 2006 election, she became the 24th President of Liberia.

President Ellen Sirleaf Johnson documented her leadership journey in *This Child Will Be Great: Memoir of a Remarkable Life by Africa's First Woman President.* For Sirleaf, *"Leadership is never given on a silver platter, one has to earn it."* She advocates enabling women, demanding *"more rights for women because I know what women can do."* Sirleaf believes a woman has specific attributes *"that give her some advantages over a man."* Sirleaf adds, *"Women are usually more honest, more sensitive to issues, and bring a stronger sense of commitment and dedication to their work. Maybe because they were mothers, and being a mother, you have that special attention for the family, for the young, for children."*

From Sirleaf, I Learned the Following Leadership Lessons:

"There will always be those who will tear us down and tear us apart because they want the status quo to remain. But together, we can break down the barriers that have kept women from achieving the equity they rightfully deserve" (2020). Articulating the how and why of disrupting the status quo is one of the critical leadership principles espoused by the Filipina Women's Network (FWN). As an FWN member, awardee, and board member, I subscribe to the vision and mission of FWN. I believe that each Filipina woman leader honored by FWN has demonstrated an impact on advancing women's equity. Together, the Filipina women leaders can harness collective impact.

"The size of your dreams must always exceed your current capacity to achieve them. If your dreams do not scare you, they are not big enough" (2011). When I choose to do something new, I scare myself with "what ifs." Then, I take a deep breath, and somehow, regardless of the situation, what gets me going is Shakespeare's:

> All the world's a stage,
> And all the men and women merely players;
> They have their exits and their entrances;
> And one man in his time plays many parts...

Recently, I was asked if I would do a short-term consultancy to design a curriculum for Open Radio Access Network (RAN). My first thought was that knowledge about Open RAN is outside my comfort zone; however, I have developed expertise in curriculum design for hyflex learning, and I have excellent research skills. It was a fifty-fifty risky, scary decision. I went for it.

From the Liberians, I re-learned the complexity and extremes of ethnic tensions that have led to civil wars. True in the Sudan with the intersection of ethnicity, race, and religion. True in the Philippines with the intersection of ethnicity, class, and political ideology. True in South Africa with the intersection of race and government policy.

Up Close and Personal with Apartheid

James' assignment to South Africa came in January 1994, and Nelson Mandela's election in May 1994. When we arrived, South Africans were looking to transition away from apartheid by tackling institutionalized racism and fostering racial reconciliation. Once again, I had to forge a career path. Eventually, I was hired as a Social Scientist, Gender, and Monitoring and Evaluation Specialist. My discourse analysis became useful when I argued that the USAID development mission should not be a transition, which meant moving from A to B. What was needed was a transformation similar from a chrysalis to a butterfly.

The challenges posed by the intersections of being a woman, a Filipina, and an American became more pronounced in South Africa.

- As a woman, I could not open a bank account unless a male guardian or spouse endorsed it. Therefore, I valued having my own money, bank account, credit card, and financial independence, which my husband and I agreed on early as part of our marriage equality.
- As a Filipina holding hands with my husband, who is white, I angered an Afrikaner who cupped my crotch from behind and ran off laughing with his friends.
- As a foreign service spouse, I should have been happy consigned to the bedroom, yet there I was, occupying a workspace and being good at it.

Yet there were some surprising intersections. I met a woman who named her daughter, born in 1986, Corazon after Cory Aquino. I asked her why. She said, *"Some of us black South Africans fighting for our civil rights learned from*

Cory Aquino and people power." I explained to her that Corazon also translated to "heart." She was doubly pleased with her decision, *"Heart. For civil rights."*

It was in South Africa when I saw my first website. The possibilities of using websites for learning and teaching, not just communicating or sending information, seemed limitless. So I decided to learn how to do a website, including learning to code. As a result, I built the first website for the USAID mission in South Africa. To this day, I continue to be amazed at the digital opportunities that could be made available for all. Moreover, while most are happy to include girls and women as participants in the digital revolution, I always say *"not just participants but also leaders."*

> **"Women must redesign the table, and not just expect to be at the table."** – GRAÇA MACHEL (2020)

Ms. Graça Machel is a women's and children's rights advocate, former freedom fighter, and first Education Minister of Mozambique; co-founder of The Elders. Ms. Graça Machel was the first lady of Mozambique (1975-1986) and South Africa (1998–2000). In 1973, Ms. Machel joined the Mozambican Liberation Front (FRELIMO) and became a schoolteacher. In 1975, following the independence of Mozambique, she was appointed Minister for Education and Culture and married President Zamora Machel, who died in a plane accident in 1986. After that, in 1998, she married Nelson Mandela, the first black South African President.

Machel produced a ground-breaking United Nations Children's Fund (UNICEF) report, *The Impact of Armed Conflict on Children,* which changed how the United Nations and member states respond in conflict zones. Since then, she has worked tirelessly to support global health, child welfare, and women's rights and empowerment.

She founded and served as president of the Foundation for Community Development, the Zizile Institute for Child Development, and the Graça Machel Trust. She has focused on advocating for women's economic and financial empowerment, food security and nutrition, education for all, and good governance.

With Nelson Mandela, Graça formed The Elders, an independent group of global leaders working together for peace, justice, and human rights. The

Elders work both publicly and through private diplomacy. Per their website, the mission of the Elders is to engage with global leaders and civil society at all levels to resolve conflict and address its root causes, challenge injustice, and promote ethical leadership and good governance. The Elders' vision "is of a world where people live in peace, conscious of their common humanity and their shared responsibilities for each other, for the planet, and for future generations." Ellen Johnson Sirleaf is also a member of the Elders.

From Graça Machel, I Learned these Leadership Lessons:

"To be a powerful woman means to have the possibility, the right & responsibility to make choices that better oneself & better one's community" (2020). I continue to heed this call for the "right and responsibility" to better one's community in creating Kaisipan as a giving back project in the Philippines, which I explain in the last section as a passion project in my advocacy for women in technology.

"Power is making a conscious effort in both your private & public spaces to tear down the walls of disrespect, discrimination, and disenfranchisement wherever you meet it" (2020). Of course, my power differs from that of Anne Itto, Corazon Aquino, Ellen Sirleaf Johnson, or Graça Machal. Still, I dare say as impactful as theirs, given the socio-historical-political context where I found myself and what was within my sphere of influence.

Using your influence to create impact and better the lives of others—is what being a powerful woman means to me. Having been honored as one of the FWN's influential women in the U.S. and the world, and as a continuing influential, my choice is to use my influence to create impact and to better the lives of others, especially women through the use of information and communication technologies.

I learned about *ubuntu* from the South Africans and the extraordinary power of truth and reconciliation. This court-like restorative justice is crucial to the transition to full and free democracy in South Africa. When asked to participate in the Liberation in Practice workshops which explored racism, model minority myth, relational social power, and the history of Asian Pacific Islanders (API) in Oregon, I discussed Revolutions and Revelations: What is racial healing? How can we engage in racial healing within ourselves, our communities, and society? I shared one of the critical revelations I learned from the South Africans. In the decade after Mandela's release, the question often asked was how, after whites had systematically pillaged and tortured his country and sent him to prison for nearly three decades, he could be free of hatred. The answer Mandela always gave was *"ubuntu."* *Ubuntu* is the belief in a universal bond of sharing that connects all humanity. Mark Mathabane (2028) shares the lessons of *ubuntu* and its application for racial healing in the U.S. The book chapters correlate to *ubuntu* principles. The principles of *ubuntu* apply to leadership that is rooted in *kapwa*.

>> Empathy: Listening Instead of Labeling
>> Compromise: Talking to the Enemy
>> Learning: the Power of Education
>> Nonviolence: The Key to Social Change
>> Change: Even Racists can be Transformed
>> Forgiveness: The Pathway to Healing
>> Restorative Justice: Saving the Future
>> Love: Healing through Agape (love for humanity)
>> Spirituality: The Instrument of Our Common Humanity
>> Hope: Rebirth of the American Dream

The Third Chapter: Passion, Risk, and Adventure in the 25 Years After 50

Soon after saying goodbye to South Africans, I began what Sara Lawrence-Lightfoot called *The Third Chapter: Passion, Risk, and Adventure in the 25 Years After 50*. I continued to work in international development. First, I traveled back to South Africa to develop partnerships between the U.S. and South African universities in Knowledge Exchanges and Learning Partnerships (KELP). Second, I led the development of a Network for Capacity Building in Telecommunications Policy and Regulation between African and American partners. I wrote about this in "Developing a Leadership Repertoire" in *DISRUPT 2.0*. Finally, I led the Afghan Equality Alliances from 2005 to 2009, which I wrote about in *DISRUPT. Filipina Women. Proud. Loud. Leading without a Doubt.*

Almost the Fourth Chapter: Advancing Digital Capabilities

In June 2020, I launched Kaisipan as a giving back project in response to learning that the Philippines was number 79 out of 79 countries in reading and number 78 in science and math. A group of us academics decided to advance digital capabilities among educators in the Philippines. By digital capabilities, we at Kaisipan mean a set of cognitive, technical, and humanizing competencies to use information and communication technologies to transform learning and teaching. Cognitive means mental competencies to acquire, interpret, and extrapolate knowledge, thoughts, and social-emotional experience. By technical, we go beyond office productivity to digital competencies required of teachers, including synchronous and asynchronous tools for learning and teaching. Thus, we promote open solutions, open education resources, and leveraged technology. Humanizing competencies include social-emotional learning (managing emotions, working with others, and achieving goals), developing a digital growth mindset, and integrating values in ICT education. Our desired end is that digital capabilities will enhance the 21st-century 4Cs skills: critical thinking, creativity, collaboration, and communication, improving Programme for International Student Assessment PISA scores. As critical thinkers, we problem solve. Where there is no connectivity, we look for solutions. We communicate about those solutions and strategies. We collaborate with partners. And each other. Our founding board of directors, Dr. Emmanuel Lallana, Dr. Lilia Juele, Ms. Antonette Torres, Dr. Maria Victoria Lualhati, Ms. Audrey Codera-Mills, and Ms. Belen Sevilla Castillo, our teaching fellows, and partners think together and act together. We create. We co-create. To advance digital capabilities. To transform learning and teaching. iLEARN. iCREATE. iSHARE.

The digital literacy programs/activities align with the Philippine Department of Education's Most Essential Learning Competencies (MELC) in Empowerment Technologies and Personal Development. Our vision and mission will contribute to DepEd's quality of learning outcomes and to sustainable development Goal 4: To ensure inclusive and equitable quality education and promote lifelong learning opportunities for all by 2030.

Coda

As political leaders, Dr. Anne Itto, President Corazon Aquino, President Ellen Sirleaf Johnson, and Graça Machal prioritized society's needs, development, and interests and future generations over their own. Moreover, they demonstrated that political leaders could be authentic leaders who know how to negotiate, facilitate positions, transmit positivity, and sacrifice their interests and desires if that is good for the country.

May what I have learned from these four women leaders resonate with you. May we be guided by sound moral convictions and act following deeply held values, even under pressure. May we be aware of our views, strengths, and weakness. Finally, may we strive to understand how our leadership impacts others.

In walking the long road to making choices that better one's local or global community, by engendering leadership and enGENDERing leadership, I live by Mandela's words (1995):

> *"I have tried not to falter; I have made missteps along the way. But I have discovered the secret that after climbing a great hill, one only finds that there are many more hills to climb. I have taken a moment here to rest, to steal a view of the glorious vista that surrounds me, to look back on the distance I have come. But I can only rest for a moment, for with freedom come responsibilities, and I dare not linger, for my long walk is not ended."*

MARIA RHODORA P.I. PALOMAR-FRESNEDI

President, Center for Growing and Giving Foundation, Inc.
Founder, Sunshine Farm Philippines
GLOBAL FWN100™ 2019

Planting Seeds of Hope and Happiness

"*How long have you been doing diversity?" "All my life!*" I did not know my answer to the question until I was asked. I am looking at the blue, cloudless sky outside my window. The fog is not here today, allowing me to get a picture-perfect view of the row of houses climbing up the hill across Highway 101 and the tower atop Twin Peaks. If I had climbed up our rooftop, the Bay Bridge and the Golden Gate bridges would have been in clear view. I enjoy a daily view now. It is a far cry from the windowless in-law apartment my cousins and I rented at 46th Avenue more than three decades ago or the much better accommodation we could afford a few years later at 12th Avenue. I used to walk to Golden Gate Park, soaking in perspective at eye level. If I wanted a more expansive view today, I could climb up to Bayview Park just behind us and see where vehicles come from and where they are going via the freeway. I could also sit there, enjoy the cool breeze on my face, and look inside me to see where I came from and where I am going.

My physical spaces could not have been better metaphors for my journey.

Leading, Learning
San Francisco, 1984

I arrived in San Francisco hopeful, excited, and open to a different future. By that time, I had been a teacher for four years. I came from a family of teachers. I played "school" as a child, commandeering younger cousins to sit through my class, passing on whatever I have learned, aided by my chalk and blackboard. I told my mother that I wanted to pursue a degree in education right after high school. She was quick to discourage me. She said, *"you could do better than me."* She wanted to be a lawyer but ended up teaching because it was an acceptable profession for women.

I took the next course that appealed to me: Mass Communications, a relatively new degree in the 80s and a risky profession in the era of the Marcos dictatorship and martial law in the Philippines. I did well, graduating magna cum laude and among the top five outstanding students in the country. But I still wanted to teach.

So, I did.

For four years in exclusive schools, I was addressed as Miss Palomar, an honorific I carried with pride. I was a Ma'am. Treated with respect. My work mattered. I mattered. I had the dignity that my profession accorded everyone.

That was my background when I arrived in San Francisco, looking for a path to higher education, following family members who had migrated to the U.S.

It took only a matter of days for me to feel the loss of identity. I was in a strange land, and I was a nobody. I was no longer Miss Palomar, not a Ma'am. I was not addressed with a *"po"* or *"opo,"* the Tagalog words that signal respect and reverence for someone older or in a position of authority. Soon, I had to find a way to feed myself. Higher education had to wait.

I knew someone who was working as a receptionist. She also told me a support organization, Broadcast Skills Bank, helped mass media graduates land a job. I mentioned I was willing to start at whatever position I could, maybe a receptionist in San Francisco like her.

The answer was immediate, honest, piercing, and a bitter dose of reality. *"You would not be hired as a receptionist because you have an accent."*

My thoughts went wild. I felt my entire set of capabilities was attacked. I could not even start at the front desk of a corporation because I have an accent?! Never mind that I speak and write grammatically perfect English. It did not matter. What mattered was how I sounded.

I thought I could not win the accent game. I would not be able to get rid of 23 years of tongue formation in days. I decided to draw from my learning ability and study any kind of work in any business. Just give me a chance. I found my chance as an administrative assistant in a ship chandler across the Bay Bridge. I took and processed orders from ship supply officers, from a tiny box of nuts and bolts to a truckload of breakfast cereal. It was a job where my Filipino accent helped. A lot of navy supply officers were Filipinos. As I did with any job I took, I learned as much as I could about my work environment, the business, and the nature of work in the U.S. I interacted with Hispanics in the warehouse, the white founder of the business, the senior WASP ladies in accounting and finance, and my boss from Guam. I spent a year in that job in Oakland, then took a couple of months off and returned to the Philippines. I was a U.S. immigrant, but I felt the need to ground myself again. I had to be clear about who I was becoming and who I would like to be. What better way than to go back and feel my roots again.

When I returned to the U.S. in August 1985, I had a new vision for myself.

Leaving behind my path as a teacher, I started over. I looked for jobs in the city. While my headhunter looked for appropriate matches for me, I took a temp job at Bank of America, sorting out bonds in the backroom. It was a painstakingly tedious job that gave me a glimpse of financial institutions. I felt I was losing my essence. Soon after, I felt saved by the offer from a property management firm to be an accounts payable assistant.

There I was, re-starting literally on higher ground. I was in one of the tallest buildings in the financial district, the 33rd floor of 50 California. On a clear day, I could see both the Golden Gate Bridge and the Bay Bridge. I could also see where I had been the year before. I was shuffling invoices, but it did not matter. I was not a receptionist, and I did not have to be afraid of not being understood because of my accent.

I buried myself in work and learned everything I could. I worked overtime without pay, bargained for comp time instead, and delivered beyond what was required. Soon I was asked to help with payroll. I moved up quickly and supported myself with other accounting and finance knowledge by enrolling at Golden Gate University, a short walk from our office. Again, I studied hard, worked hard, and delivered more. I soon found myself steadily rising professionally, transforming from an English teacher in an exclusive school for girls in Manila to a financial controller in San Francisco. I used to manage classes of 40 young ladies. I ended up managing a portfolio of 100M USD across the country. I was only 26.

My new corporate vantage point revealed to me diversity and inclusion and the dynamics and relationships in the workplace. Our business was founded and led by a group of well-educated white men, supported by very competent white women in the middle and Asians in key roles. The Head of I.T. and the Head of Accounting were American-born Chinese. Then there was me, Financial Controller, a Filipino immigrant. There was one African American, our messenger.

My new city, San Francisco, introduced me to equality through the lens of sexual orientation, gender identity, and gender expression. I carried with me the framework of simple gender demarcation lines when I moved to the United States, with predetermined gender roles and expectations. My early life in San Francisco introduced me to the more complex world of LGBTQIA. I took to heart the lessons in the phrase that San Francisco is a city where "the women are strong, and the men are beautiful." It was a period of developing skills to unlearn stereotypes and drop labels.

I was leading myself. I was learning how to lead and leading how to learn.

Leading, Loving
Manila, 1994

"It is easier to find a good job than it is to find a good husband." That was my answer to the question of why I went back to the Philippines.

I was rising in corporate America when a dilemma arose. Should I go back to the Philippines and support my husband's career, or should I pursue Ayn Rand's path, following the virtue of selfishness? It was not difficult to find the answer. I followed my heart.

I married the person who was my best friend from college, the one who made me feel heard, acknowledged, and celebrated every day. He was the one who wrote me letters that made me more knowledgeable and more engaged in what was going on in the world. He read me poetry and made me feel simply, deeply loved. Every day. I wanted to be with him.

I left my San Francisco career. I supported my husband's blossoming career as the youngest vice president in the biggest company in the Philippines back then. I took a break from work and decided to complete my masters at the Asian Institute of Management. We had a one-year-old baby.

We were 39 in a class of experienced, mostly male senior managers en route to higher levels of responsibilities. Most of my classmates were sponsored by their companies for the intensive program that tackled three Harvard cases a day, group work, a management research report, and a walk-about. I became the leader of my study group and vice president of my class. Our class president was a senior military man, a would-be general in the Philippine armed forces. I have often been elected leader in my classes. That time, however, was special. I headed a diverse team of senior men who permitted me to lead them through group presentations, class projects, and competitions.

It was an exhilarating period marked by quotable quotes from my classmates. My group mate and friend from Somalia who worked in Saudi Arabia commended me for my leadership, saying, *"I salute you. In our country, even women with Ph.D.s stay at home."* My Chinese friend Lin told me he felt energized by me and worked hard to keep up with my spirit and determination to excel. We did great work together. An executive from Taiwan, David, always addressed me as "Boss," eagerly asking for the next contribution he could make. He became an ardent follower. He named his baby girl after me. He jokingly told me he did it to get back at me. As the father, he could actually *"order Rhodora around."* It was a supreme honor Asians understand deeply.

I graduated with distinction and delivered the address on behalf of my class. Three months after graduation, I gave birth to our second daughter. There I was, jobless, with two babies, only two years apart, my husband rapidly climbing the corporate ladder. I was learning how to lead in a different way. I was learning to lead my family with my husband. I was learning to lead with love, in love. Navigating a dual career was not easy. Top that with the attention that two young children need. To manage that, I took a step back. My leadership skills were needed most in our home, in our young married life.

After a year of getting myself grounded with my new reality, I took a role in Unilever Philippines. While in business school, I became firmer in believing that people could be THE competitive advantage of corporations. I came from accounting and finance and was part of corporate America of the 80s, the period when money made the world go round. Then there I was, in the early 90s looking at people as the most powerful resources of a company. I was looking for a company willing to bet on someone like me who worked in finance and accounting in San Francisco to start in Human Resources in the Philippines. Well, it turned out, that Unilever Philippines was looking for someone who could change the face of H.R.

It is worth noting that my male classmates in graduate school made my job search one of the most extensive I had done without ever leaving my home. When they found out I was staying home with the kids, one of them blurted out that it was too expensive to keep me at home. He distributed my resume to their family businesses and other contacts. Other classmates did the same. My reputation at school helped me find jobs. That was how I found myself joining Unilever in June 1994, leading a human resources team.

As I took on the Unilever Philippines job, I realized I could not take any leadership position without regard for the other roles that I play in my life. To be an effective leader, I needed to bring my whole life into perspective. It was an early experience in work-life integration. In my twenties, I learned how to lead myself: how to take charge of my own learning, my own career. In my thirties, with a young family, I was learning how to lead a family together and navigate dual careers with someone I love. We took turns being the lead career. Whoever had the more significant opportunity became the lead career, but we made sure that no one traveled too far ahead that it made it difficult for the other to follow. Growing together apace meant staying together.

Leading, Leveraging
London, 2004

"You can accomplish a lot if you don't care about the credit,"
– NIALL FITZGERALD, former Chairman, Unilever

Niall's words still echo. I worked directly with him and his Co-Chairman, Antony Burgmans, on diversity and inclusion, first in Unilever and then later in Reuters, when he became Chairman of the same.

After three years in the Corporate Centre, I was finally making my most significant contribution. I was sent to London on expatriation in 2000. Back then, it meant preparing for more prominent roles. The senior people have spotted me and marked me as a high potential. In my first few days in the Center, I was called to the office of the Executive Committee member heading what was then called Personnel. He was at the top of my function. He saw me in one of the development programs for high-potential talents and ensured he welcomed me properly to the head office. He also made sure that I remembered his message well, something about not losing my uniqueness in the historic building. *"Do not become too Unilever."* I still hear his voice. Wise words. If I were to bring change, I could not allow myself to be fully absorbed in the very culture that I was meant to influence differently.

I did feel I was unique. I was one of the few senior women around the world who sat on country Boards. I was the first Filipina on the Board of Unilever Philippines in 70 years and the only one not grown from within. I was a mid-career recruit. In the head office, my brown skin, dark hair, Asian looks stood out in a sea of white European men. I was also small, by European standards. While I would tower over a group of Asian counterparts, I was constantly dwarfed in the company of our Dutch colleagues, coming from a country where the average height is six feet! The physical size of my colleagues, the volume of their voices, and the inborn assertiveness could be intimidating.

The top 100 in Unilever then had only five women. The next level, where I was, had only ten percent women. We used to have an annual gathering of senior leaders for a kind of state-of-the-business performance review and direction setting for the coming year. The lack of gender diversity became starkly evident in those gatherings.

When I came to the head office, gender diversity was a controversial topic. Nobody handled it long enough to make a significant difference. There have been many attempts to address the systemic loss of women in management at higher levels. Management Trainees were hired generally at 50-50 gender balance across the 150 countries, but women comprise only five percent at the top and ten percent at the level below. Research showed this decades ago, but actions failed to change the management mix. The pressure to address gender imbalance from socially responsible investors was increasing. Every stockholder meeting had shareholders raising the need for more women in management and greater diversity at senior levels.

In that context, I became Global V.P. for Diversity in Unilever. Some people thought that it was a high-stake career gamble. Many attempts failed before, the position did not exist before, and it was a highly visible role accountable to the Executive Committee. The high risk of failure based on previous results equates to a high probability of being fired.

I thought I did not have much to lose and a lot to gain. The truth was, I was not afraid of being fired. It would just mean I would be sent back to the Philippines where, I felt confident I could find another job. I was more afraid of doing meaningless work. I relished the challenge of crafting the agenda, shaping the role, and holding myself accountable for the results. I have broken the proverbial glass ceiling a few times, not just for women but also for non-white men. I was often the first or the only one. As I do now, I believe that being the first or the only one is an empty achievement if others cannot follow. And so, I took on the challenge of diversity in Unilever. I wanted to create a system that allowed for sustained efforts to build a more diverse leadership team and a more inclusive Unilever.

I succeeded well enough to see women leaders move up, and to see a Unilever that became more diverse in its 100-year history and continued to develop long after I left. Well enough to see local leaders from Asia to Africa, Indonesia to Ghana, get appointed as heads of Unilever businesses in their own countries. Well enough to get invitations from different companies to help them with their efforts. Well enough to be nominated as one of the Asian Women of Achievement in Business in the U.K. in 2005 and awarded as an Outstanding Filipino in Singapore in 2009. I also helped countries in any way I could. I sat on the advisory board of Singapore's Ministry of Manpower, delivered a paper on gender diversity for Korea's Ministry of Labor, and worked with a Japanese team to address women in leadership issues. I was an adviser to Asia Society's Women Leaders in the New Asia.

When asked about what I consider key success factors for my contribution to Unilever, I often said that I started not with 337,000 Unilever employees across 150 countries. Instead, I worked with the seven Executive Committee Members. Quietly, of course, I also worked on myself, developing the skills to work at a higher level of challenge with higher-level leaders. I believe I succeeded because I learned how to leverage who I was, and who I was becoming fully. To drive the diversity agenda, I drew from my own experience and focused on leveraging what I knew in my heart, validating them with what my research data said.

From the heart, I spoke truth to power, telling the Executive Committee the change they needed to make themselves and their teams if we were to drive the agenda forward. I had to learn to use various tools from my communications toolbox to be heard and to be effective. I learned when to put to good use, as my British boss told me, my Asian deference or my American assertiveness. There is a perfect situation for either. I applied what I learned as I coached more executives and more teams. I often said, *"If you do not know what someone from the west is thinking, you are not listening. If you do not know what someone from the east is thinking, you are not asking."*

I brought everything I was, my whole self, to my work. In doing so, I learned how to lead an Executive Committee toward specific results from where I was, two levels below. Influence without authority.

Leading, Leaving a Legacy
Philippines, 2014

By the time 2014 rolled in, I had lived my hyphenated name. I have worked and traveled to seven continents, lived in three, changed careers, and led teams of different sizes, functions, and contributions. I was back in the Philippines with my husband, in our words, to pay it forward. We were motivated by two things: first, the opportunity to give back, and second, the opportunity to develop Asian leaders. In our work across the globe, we saw the same patterns of modern colonization: the education, the development of leaders through western models, and the retelling of western leadership stories. In our little way, we said that we needed to change the global narrative of the Asian leader. We had to tell our own stories. We could help amplify the voices of the east in the west, enabling a more inclusive, more authentic dialogue on international matters.

I came back to the Philippines in 2011, eager to create something from the ground, Unilab Foundation, and build on the steps of Filipino entrepreneurs that enabled the quiet expansion of a Filipino multinational in Asia. Unilab International gave me the drive to grow a Philippine business beyond the shores of 7,100 islands. There was pride in being a Filipina business leader doing what I considered nationalistic work. I led businesses in Vietnam, Myanmar, Cambodia, Singapore, and Malaysia. I showed the men reporting to me that I was keen to focus on their development and invested accordingly. I was thrilled. I had the opportunity to grow an Asian business and develop Asian leaders! Grow the people. Grow the business.

But pride also came in creating a community for persons with disability (PWD). One of the flagship projects I built under the Unilab Foundation was Project Inclusion. This initiative worked on the sustainable employment of PWDs, beginning with persons with an intellectual and developmental disability (PWID) like Autism and Down Syndrome. I have always believed that tackling the challenges of other dimensions becomes more manageable if one starts with the more difficult dimension of diversity. Moreover, the process of learning the more difficult task enables the development of competencies necessary to handle similar challenges.

Three years into my role and my advocacy back in the Philippines, I received a note from someone I have mentored through the years. She told me that she applauded what I was doing for the PWDs and would like to remind me that she was my first PWD. She would also like to ask if I could keynote an event she was launching, awarding a select group of people who lived with epilepsy and managed to be exemplars in their chosen field.

"But of course, she was my first PWD case!" The images came back vividly. I was her class adviser in high school, just before senior year. A bright young lady who had polio as a child. As a result, she ambled through three flights of stairs daily, her metal braces announcing her arrival at every step. The contraption did not keep her from playing softball, running across bases, her one leg struggling to keep pace with the other. She was a lively teenager, confident on the outside, but keeping her desire to be a doctor tightly held a secret. But I knew. I also knew that her chances of getting accepted into a good school in preparation for a medical degree depended on getting to the honors class. So, I guided her through it. She got into the honors class in her senior year, did relatively well, and got into the first stage of her dream. She wrote to me when she had difficulties in college, and I wrote back, cheering her on.

We lost track of each other when I migrated to the U.S. She found me again when she was on a fellowship in Canada for child neurology. She became a doctor! And she was on her way to being one of a handful of child neurologists in the Philippines. She worked through the self-inflicted doubts and those who doubted her capability because of her physical limitations. She vanquished them all.

In 2014, as our worlds reconnected, we worked together on our shared advocacy of inclusion. By that time, hers was a significant voice in medical society.

She eventually became the President of the Child Neurology Society of the Philippines (CNSP) and a Philippine League Against Epilepsy board member. (PLAE). The young lady with the metal braces has gone very far in creating a path for herself, and, thereafter, a path for others to make a difference. She was planting many seeds for many like her.

Lin Manuel Miranda in *"Hamilton"* asked and answered what a legacy is. He rapped, *"Legacy is planting seeds in a garden you wouldn't see."*

I suppose I was very fortunate to see the garden from seeds I planted 40 years ago.

Leading, Living a Life of Purpose

> *"If you are free, you need to free somebody else. If you have some power, then your job is to empower somebody else."* – TONI MORRISON

I left my last corporate role in 2017 and founded the Center for Growing and Giving Foundation, Inc. The name was drawn from what my husband, best friend, and business partner, considered a default expression for someone who cannot yet articulate a life purpose. Grow and Give. We learned the same from one of our life's mentors, Richard Leider. After masticating different versions, I have arrived at my own purpose. I expressed my purpose as: *"To give light and color to dark and gloomy places."* I saw the consistency of what I do wherever I am. I found what fulfilled me. Light and color are in my wardrobe, home, and objective when I write. Light and color find their way into my work. I feel joy when I glimpse a glow in the face of someone I am coaching; the glow that shows something finally makes sense, and there is a way to make informed decisions. I am elated when I see people develop to be the best they could be and make a contribution at a level they never thought possible.

Grow and Give. We grow in our gifts, talents, and capabilities, and we grow in giving those gifts in the service of others. That, to me, spells meaning and purpose.

One of our key projects is an extension of Project Inclusion. I wanted to explore other means to provide jobs to persons with disability. One of those unexplored industries is farming. The other is agri-tourism.

I wanted to grow in my giving. I also wanted to find the combination of what I love to do and what I love to give. From that vantage point, Sunshine Farm Philippines was born. It is a sunflower farm built to provide jobs for persons with disability (PWDs). It combines what I enjoy doing—growing flowers and my advocacy, PWD employment. I created a pilot for others to follow. I believed I could build on many employment and livelihood generation models. I made it happen.

I have been given many opportunities to become who I need to be to make a difference in people's lives to the fullest extent possible.

Building Sunshine Farm Philippines required a different kind of leadership. I knew my purpose and could lead myself through its every expression. But I needed to help others lead themselves to a life of meaning and purpose. Sunshine Farm Philippines became the platform for PWDs to learn and live three tenets:

1. *May kakayanan ang may kapansanan.* [Persons with Disabilities have abilities.]
2. *Nagbibigay, hindi lang binibigyan.* [PWDs have something to give. They are not only recipients of the kindness of others.]
3. *Inspirasyon, hindi lang obligasyon.* 'PWDs are our inspiration, not just our obligation.]

We are now in our fifth year of operation. We sustained the model through two years of the pandemic. We now have a group of PWDs who know they are free to dream, to pursue those dreams, and to enable the dreams of others. One of the mothers in the farm was afflicted with polio as a child, and has limped her way through different jobs that did not last long. She has been employed on the farm since 2018. Through the years, she has sent her two daughters to school. Her husband died during the pandemic, but her steady employment kept her strong through the struggle. Another farm employee has been sending his brother to school, a capability he did not have before Sunshine Farm Philippines. He had muscular dystrophy and was never employed. At the farm, he manages the operations and works at the front desk.

Two of our employees fell in love and had a wedding reception at the farm. A married life for one who uses a wheelchair from her teenage years, and the other who limps through his life after a motorcycle accident. Unimaginable before Sunshine Farm Philippines.

These stories express our mission: planting seeds of hope and happiness. For PWDs, hope is a job.

We rise by uplifting others. It is heartwarming to see possibilities created for the marginalized and see them, in turn, create possibilities for others in their families and community.

I found myself leading so others could lead forward.

There and Back Again with a Beginner's Mind
San Francisco, March 2022

How long have I been doing diversity? Indeed, all my life.

I consider myself now synergized. I am the product of all my experiences, everyone I met, every place I have been, every job I held, every leadership position I occupied, and every service I delivered.

I was interviewed for the Most Influential Filipina in the World (Global FWN) award in 2019. The thorough process, akin to the rigors of a top-level screening for senior government jobs, had me think through my life patterns. I realized that throughout my life, I had been building on my leadership through the lens of diversity and inclusion.

I had to start with leading myself, taking charge of my learning and development, and my career. I made difficult choices, supported by the clarity of what fulfills me and where I find meaning, wherever it was and whatever I had to leave behind.

I built on my experience as an outsider in different forms: an immigrant with an accent, a mid-career recruit in a multinational, an Asian woman in the corporate center with a predominantly white male population, a Filipina business leader standing before men who are not used to be led by a woman. Finally, I drew from the same experience to craft diversity and inclusion strategies built on empathy, compassion, and business understanding.

I developed a deeper understanding of the challenges and issues surrounding different dimensions of diversity: gender, nationality, style, religion, race, class, sexual orientation, disability, and other forms of uniqueness.

My experience in San Francisco allowed me to help an LGBTQIA Chamber of Commerce create a manifesto and direction for greater inclusion in the workplace. My experience as a woman leading in a multinational corporation who faced challenges of family and kids became a foundation for crafting work-life integration programs, flexible working arrangements, managing dual careers, and other issues of women in management. Working on the barriers to the advancement of African and Asian talents in corporations broadened my understanding of the issues of race, class, and inclusion. Finally, my experience helping one PWD in the 80s informed my work on employing a greater number of PWDs.

I have learned to lead, learn, love, leverage, and live with purpose.

I have chosen to keep growing in my capability to lead and advocate for diversity and inclusion. Grow and Give.

I am back in San Francisco, feeling viscerally what T. S. Eliot meant when he said that we will arrive at the end of our exploration, where we began, *"and know the place for the first time."*

I am knowing this place differently. My sentiment is about starting over. Begin again. Not from a perspective of action, but from a mindset perspective.

My leadership journey has led me to be an advocate for diversity and inclusion. I have defined the measure of my success as expressed in every person, no matter what race, gender, creed, religion, sexual orientation, identity, ability or disability, or any other form of uniqueness will be able to say, *"I am valued. I belong. I make a difference."*

The sunset on the horizon signals another end of the day. The city's two iconic bridges glow with golden light. We are getting closer to the end of winter. The bulbs I have planted have started to bloom. The swaying daffodils greet me each day. I reflect on the seasons my own leadership story has gone through. I look at my diversity and inclusion work, the bridges I have crossed, and the bridges I have built. For every stage of my career, I make progress when I begin with what Yo-Yo Ma calls the beginner's mind. My life's work is about upholding the dignity of every person and the necessity of fighting for our shared humanity.

I echo Yo-Yo Ma.

"Common humanity has become a necessity. It's calling us to reclaim a beginner's mind, to peel away the layers of preconceived difference and constructed identity, and remember that before we had nations and religions, we are just human and still are." – YO-YO MA, *Beginner's Mind*

MILDRED CHRISTINE "MITZI" FLORES PIAD, PH.D.

President and Chairman of the Board,
F. F. Flores Enterprises, Inc.,
President and Owner, St. Ferdinand Memorial Park, Inc.
President and Owner, St. Ferdinand Crematory
and Memorial Homes
CEO, LF Builders Construction and Project Development.
Federation Director, Soroptimist International
of the Americas Philippines Region
Director, International Board of Soroptimist International
of the Americas
GLOBAL FWN100™ 2018

The Fruit-Bearing Tree

The symbiotic relationship between a mother-daughter is like a fruit-bearing tree. The tree provides nourishment and care, protection, and warmth. Standing strong and tall, the tree nourishes its fruit through every situation that Mother Nature presents to her. And each hardship helped produce a succulent, beautifully textured fruit with the sweetest taste.

My mother was my fruit-bearing tree and I was her favorite fruit. We shared secrets and magic whispers, thoughts, and ideals. We lived in our dream world, complete with a house made of wishes. We romped through our fairyland, a paradise with the tree untainted by the curse of a wicked witch.

A SPECIAL KINSHIP

Every daughter dotes on her mother, and I am no exception. My relationship with my mother had a heavenly flavor, and because she is my friend, soulmate, inspiration, and lifeline, there is an extraordinary alliance between our souls.

My friend often said that no one ever cut the umbilical cord connecting me to my mother. We were a twosome—a duo. God blessed our relationship. We endured the travails and joy, the pain and pleasure, the ills and good health that visited our lives every day from the time the sun rose on the horizon to the time of its setting.

Our unique connection extended to my six children. Nobody could have raised my children better than my mother. She was the force and that sustained the core of my family. She always strove to bring harmony and unity. Furthermore, she spent hours in front of the altar, praying for all of us. My mother was my partner in guiding and disciplining my children. They are all that they are today because of her. My mother and I have raised two lawyers, one CPA, a lawyer, two doctors, a pilot, and a very successful entrepreneur.

Mommy and I traveled the world together, attended conventions, and visited family and friends. She preferred to travel with the "Family *Barangay*." My husband, children, and our close relatives. How can my children not remember those memories?

MY MOTHER'S LEGACY

Mommy believed the tragedy of aging is that the elderly, who have gone through so much in life, end up feeble, fragile, and floundering. While the younger ones are brimming with energy and enthusiasm, full of bravado and ego, yet sadly wanting in experience.

Throughout her life, my mother always gave of herself. Her calling card was the grace of surviving through determination under pressure and coolness under fire. She showed me how to cope with life's unexpected twists and turns with fortitude, tolerance, resourcefulness, generosity, selflessness, and kindness.

My mother was an ideologist who habitually listened to her inner voice and acted on her judgment. She was very spiritual, enabling her to transcend the hurts and ills, the darts and arrows that flew her way. She often exhibited what I called her 'martyr's complex. When confronted, she retreated in silence and abeyance.

When asked, she described herself as frail, diabetic, arthritic, and rheumatic, while everybody saw her as a vibrant, alive, and quite animated woman. My mother had the sagacity of someone who experienced countless challenges, has known pain and joy, and shed a bucket of tears.

My mother's intelligence, decisiveness, and leadership greatly influenced my life. Her ability to get along with people intensely rubbed off on me. She taught me how to comport with the high and mighty and not forget to manifest the common touch. She showed me that empathy and sensitivity to the needs and feelings of others endeared her to the people she helped. She was also a civic leader known for her honesty and commitment to the people she served.

I learned that the fundamental law of human happiness is when we serve others. We achieve accomplishment and fulfillment when we work together to alleviate suffering, misery, and poverty. I will never forget that the noblest life is the life that gives and loses itself in sharing and providing.

My mandate is to continue my mother's legacy, blending the older, wiser generation with the younger, bold, more youthful generation and bringing out the best from both ages for the good of my family and society.

EVERYTHING WILL COME TO PASS

My mother used to say, *"todo llegara a pasar."* We all have our crosses to bear, and everything will come to pass. I transformed adversarial forces, such as the tyranny of deadlines and lengthy reports, into positive points of commitment. I battled the temptation to succumb to indifference, passivity, and laxity that every volunteer experiences. Instead, I channeled my resources, dynamism, and enormous potential to tackle the challenges I faced. Finally, I crushed self-serving, self-glorifying attitudes and worked with passion, empathy, and the idealism of an authentic leader. My mother taught me all these.

To give life to the vision of using my resources to help others, I knew I had to attain the experience and qualifications to reach positions where I could most benefit.

I received my first Doctorate of Philosophy degree in Organization Development from the prestigious South East Asia Interdisciplinary Institute (SAIDI. My second Ph.D. is in Public Administration, majoring in Good Governance and Social Responsibility, *Honoris Causa.*

I used the skills. I learned to assist people in attaining a better life. Unlike my mother, I am no martyr. I learned to carve a whole new world for myself. I ignored malicious gossip and left friends who maligned me. Instead, I relied on those who loved and supported me. And fortunately, just as a battered tree brings forth fresh leaves and twigs after every storm, each challenge in my life gave way to blossoms and fruits. Disappointments littered my path, yet I do not regret any of them. I simply pray I can overcome them. Happily, I think of my many friends and forget the snakes in the grass who tried to bring me down, as I always hear my mother's voice saying, *"todo llegara a pasar."*

WORKING TOWARDS HELPING OTHERS

My mother strove to improve the quality of life of the poor, particularly the sick, poor, and rural women. She exemplified female leadership in local, civic, and religious movements and raised awareness to alleviate the plight of abandoned, malnourished street children and the out-of-school youth.

I am who I am because of my mother. I dedicated a significant slice of my life to reaching out to others with a sincere disregard for self-emulation or building my image. My indomitable spirit manifests in the success of the organizations I have led. I strove to overcome the trials in the formidable programs I faced and succeeded.

I was a Mary Rogers Scholar at Maryknoll College, where I was actively involved in school events and organizations. The college recognized my contributions and received the honor of being the sole recipient of the Maryknoll Award, the highest coveted award for exemplary leadership, honesty, Christian values, and academic honors from the College. On September 10, 2022, I was awarded by my alma mater, Maryknoll/Meriam College, the Triple A "Alumni Amazing Achiever" Award during our Grand Alumni Homecoming and Golden Jubilee Celebration.

Soon after acquiring a degree AB Economics at Maryknoll College, I became a professor of economics and statistics. Also, I helped run my family's subdivisions, construction business, and memorial park. During this time, I received the Most Influential Filipina Woman in the World award in 2018 in London U.K., for the founder and pioneer award category.

Oh yes, I mentioned a memorial park, didn't I? Our family built the first memorial park in the Philippines.

I inherited the role of chairman for the memorial park and subdivision development when my father passed away. As chairman, I partnered with the government to provide socialized mass housing for the urban poor. The project established 12 homeowners associations which benefitted 1,343 resident families under the Community Mortgage Program of the Social Housing Finance Corp (SHFC). In addition, I received the "1992 Top Real Estate Developer" award from Pag-Ibig's Home Development Mutual Fund for that work.

In 1998, I was appointed a member of the provincial Board of the 2nd District of Quezon Province 1998 and was the Ex Officio Co-Chairman of the Poverty Alleviation Committee (*Kapasiyahan* Blg 276–98). I authored and campaigned for Solutions for Agenda of Change during that time. My principles in the Agenda For Change were threefold: a) to provide a favorable climate for existing economic ventures to thrive and entice investors to do business in Quezon Province, b) to provide food on every table, and c) to bring credit facilities to the countryside and even to the depressed areas.

Fully aware that we create the world we live in, I felt I had to contribute what I could to improve it. For example, I authored a book entitled "Vanguards of Youth Against Illegal Drug Abuse." The book enumerated the different interventions, strategies, and action programs against potential illegal drug abuse. I probed the youth's awareness of the misuse and abuse of illicit drugs and explored possibilities to initiate change through organizational development interventions. The next goal is to institutionalize programs to empower the youth to be vanguards against illegal drug abuse. Having written this book, I felt the future generation could forgive us for allowing the country to become the number two producer of marijuana plants and allowing 15% of the population to become drug addicts. This publication will show our attempts to stop its use.

SHARED LEADERSHIP, SHARED GOALS

My mother and I had the same value system. We both believed in giving back to the community, elevating the underprivileged, and supporting equality for women. We spearheaded countless fund drives to support worthy causes.

Mommy was the paragon of integrity and truth and would always advocate peace. I always partnered with her when she was the Lucena Community Council of Elders chairman. One of the main projects she led was the biennial search for five outstanding police officers from the Philippine National Police (PNP). My mother wanted to bridge the widening gap of trust and confidence between the citizenry and the PNP, so I organized the search, which later grew from five to "Ten Outstanding Policemen of Quezon Province." We provided incentives and inspiration as encouragement for them to fulfill the duties and responsibilities of a member of the PNP. The organization is now called Lucena Council of Advisers, where I am currently its acting chairman.

Besides mommy's support of civic causes, she was selflessly committed to rendering invaluable service to the scouting movement. In mommy's heart, her love for the Girl Scouts of the Philippines (GSP) transcended the limitations of time and space. Mommy was a life member and served GSP devoutly at the council, regional and national levels. At the same time I was the president of the GSP Quezon Council for three successive trienniums. In addition, I received numerous citations and awards for spearheading the construction of a three-story building that housed 2,000 girls. I called this building *Ating Tahanan Sa Quezon.*

Working with mommy as a Girl Scout enabled me to see the true meaning of the scouting movement. I took to heart the Girl Scout Promise to serve God and my country, to help people at all times, and to live by the Girl Scout Laws.

Girl Scout Laws
I will do my best to be
honest and fair,
friendly and helpful
considerate and caring,
courageous and strong
and responsible for what I say and do
and to respect myself and others
respect authority,
use resources wisely,
make the world a better place,
and be a sister to every Girl Scout.

In all my projects, and leadership roles, I embodied behaving and acting as a true Girl Scout.

THE SOROPTOMIST INFLUENCE

As governor of the Soroptimist International of the Philippines Region (SIAPR), my mother spearheaded the *"Adopt a Barangay"* project which resulted in over 100 Soroptimist clubs all over the country adopting depressed *barangays*. Mommy received the Best EcoSoc Project award at the 1990 Kyoto Convention for that project. Mommy also authored PNP Women's Desk to protect and rescue women from all forms of abuse and exploitation. By 1996, every police precinct was required to have a "Women and Children's Desk." Mommy was an unwavering force for women's rights and equality.

And she did not stop there. *"Paglingap sa Kababaihan"* was a radio program mommy hosted and broadcast in Lucena City and neighboring towns. Mommy used it as a vehicle to promote and enhance her gender-responsive efforts advocating human rights and gender equality.

My mother, with her bosom friends, Attorney Antonio Pastor and the late Don Ado Escudero, were not only sensitive to the concerns of the marginalized and the disadvantaged. They also established the Southern Luzon Association of Museums (SLAM), one of the National Commission for Culture and the Arts (NCCA) regional museum associations. I joined initiative and was appointed as a consultant in the Arts & Culture Department for the Province of Quezon and headed the Provincial Commission on Culture & Arts (PCCA). I was also their Execon Member of the National Commission for Culture & Arts as board representative of Southern Luzon.

When I was the chairman of the Education Committee of the Society for Cultural Enrichment, Inc., Mommy would support me in my projects. She was with me when we brought hundreds of Calabarzon public school teachers on a museum tour of the Yuchengco and National Museums. Their mandate was to share their experience with their students.

My mother performed unique and creative roles in the parish as a former regional officer of the Mother Butler Guild. She joined me for the original Ugat Lucena, Inc. (TOULAI) and developed and pursued relationships that allowed sharing, mutual help, and reaching out to others.

We worked together for the Women's Rights of the Philippines (WRMP), where I regularly conducted seminars and forums on women's rights. Mommy also joined th Catholic Women's Club (CWC) and enjoyed our annual tea and CWC Annual Ball.

As educators, mommy and I deeply understood the issues of the present generation, especially the youth, the marginalized, women, and our girls. We loved working together, partnering in community projects, and contributing to the community through our volunteer efforts.

There was a time when we wrote separate columns for a weekly provincial newspaper. I wrote "Quezon Chroniclings" for the *Millennium Times*, emphasizing love, sincerity, friendship, peace, integrity, generosity, understanding, hope, courage, reaching out, and prayer.

Meanwhile, mommy also had a regular column called "Wings of Dove" for the Hospice for Wingless Angels. Writing about cancer patients made her realize that our years on earth seem to have flown swiftly. While we are on this earth, we spend our time manifesting that selfless work of service to uplift one's spirit like a dove, pure and luminous, enabling the days and years to fly without the dimension of time.

GREAT INFLUENCE, GREAT REWARDS

I will never be able to condense the many memories to reflect mommy's humility, simplicity, and strength. In my numerous roles, lessons my mother taught me about the need for sensitivity and compassion for others drove me to be a good leader.

Her selflessness and tireless work for women's equality inspired me to serve with Zonta. Zonta stands for women's rights and advocates for equality, education, and an end to child marriage and gender-based violence. (Zonta International, 2022).

I served as district chairman in all the working committees of the district including the Area 5 chairmanship, handling 18 clubs, all working for the advancement of the status of women. I was the Zonta International Foundation Ambassador and raised $40,000. for the foundation through selling the coffee table book *"The Legacy Zonta International,"* which I authored and published. The book portrayed the philosophy and goals of Zonta International. I am happy to say that the book inspired Zontians to advance the status of women worldwide through service and advocacy.

I received the national award for the "Most Outstanding Woman in Public Service" bestowed by President Fidel Ramos in Malacañang Palace. I was the recipient of the National KKK Award for "Most Outstanding Civic Club" for my drug project.

Hand in hand with my involvement with Zonta my mother advised me to be more active in Soroptimist International, "a volunteer organization providing women and girls with access to the education and training they needed to achieve economic empowerment" (Soroptomist.org, 2022). Her advice led me to receive the recognition of "Most Outstanding President" from the organization. In line with my work to advance women's rights, I also received the 2018 Most Outstanding Alumna Awardee for Gender Equality and Women Empowerment during the 80th Maryknoll/Maryhill Grand Alumni Homecoming. And September 2022, I was the recipient of Triple A Award from Maryknoll/Meriam College for my civic and social achievements.

TO ETERNITY

Pancreatitis took mommy away from me. The day she left felt like a flash of cold winter in the fury of a hot day. She did not suffer much except for the stomachache she complained about the morning of her passing. I was clueless and did not realize that she would not last for 24 hours. Her death was swift and sudden. We were all devastated. My children tried to hide their pain from me, yet I knew they suffered as much as I did. I felt blank and stagnant. It felt like I was stretching drearily towards some cosmic blankness. Farewell, mommy, and I weep with the rain. I was in a deathless space, a dream without a dream. Our dream ended.

Life was hollow without my mother. She was my mentor-tormentor, my inspiration. She was as solid as the Rock of Gibraltar, my strength. Without her, I felt rudderless. With so much to do, so much to learn, and so much to experience. I felt adrift. Every day without mommy will be a red headline across the emptiness of time. Sixty-six enchanting years with my mother were fleeting. The knot that bound us dissolved into that space with no time or horizon. Mommy is now with my daddy Kits and siste Sylvia while I am left alone.

I advise all daughters who still have their mothers to hug them and tell them, *"Mommy dearest, I love you so much. How can I reach the top without you? You are the best mother in the world. You're irreplaceable. You're the best. You're the most. You are me all over again."* Give your mother a tight and big hug and follow it with a warm kiss before it's too late.

Mommy Siony left us a legacy of service and love. She taught us to serve others, give gratitude, share blessings, and live in humility and grace, taking us closer to the ultimate gift of being together in heaven. She left lessons to ensure we leave an indelible mark in this world. I accept these lessons because of her unforgettable impact on the world.

NOW ALONE

Mommy passed on March 16, 2018 It has been four years, and I still endure the gray sunset that quietly envelops me. I take gratitude in knowing that mommy is rejoicing in heaven's sunrise.

2022. The unthinkable happens. A global pandemic and a worldwide lockdown forced us to re-evaluate our priorities. As head of my family's organizations, as head of my family, how do I illuminate the gray areas and the dark alleys that COVID-19 brought upon us? I am president and chairman of the Board of F. F. Flores Enterprises, Inc. the umbrella company of St. Ferdinand Memorial Park, Inc., and Flores Aqua Farms engaged in fishpond operations and crab fattening farms. I am also the CEO of LF Builders Construction and Project Development. I am responsible for over a hundred employees and their families. I could not find it in my heart to lay anyone off. But, as a singer once said you're dancing on this earth for a little while found myself dancing in ways that would help sustain the people I was responsible for.

Observing COVID-19 IATF guidelines, I ordered the cleaning of four existing warehouses in our family for over 50 years. Then, I decided to demolish and construct a satellite Medical Center complete with nine doctors' clinics, x-ray and ultrasound rooms, a dialysis area, a laboratory, and a pharmacy. In addition, I finished an events place that would accommodate 350 guests, repaired the drainages and roads of St. Ferdinand Memorial Park, added five memorial chapels and a mortuary, improved the existing columbaria. Finally, I installed a high-tech, state-of-the-art modern crematorium. St. Ferdinand

Crematory and Memorial Homes can now proudly proclaim, "Honoring our dearly departed has been deeply ingrained in our culture. We are a family business that wishes to alleviate people's grief of losing their dearly departed. We aim to provide the best services and comfort to our patrons." All these projects kept my people employed through the pandemic.

Leadership requires selflessness and an honest desire to help. I am motivated by this yearning to reach out and enable women and girls to reach their full potential and fulfill their dreams. And yes, even after the loss of my mother, her influence, deeply ingrained in me, makes me move forward and reach for the stars. She will forever be my inspiration to create windows and open doors to help our less fortunate brothers and sisters.

MY SOROPTIMIST WORLD

I now bury myself in my mother's Soroptimist world and devote most of my time to Soroptimist International of the Americas, Philippines Region (SIAPR).

Soroptimist International of the Americas (SIA) is a worldwide service organization composed of business and professional women who use their collective power to provide resources and opportunities for women and girls. Today, there are 30,000 members and supporters in countries across North America, Latin America, and the Pacific Rim.

My purpose in joining this organization is to improve the lives of our less fortunate sisters. I just finished my role as Public Awareness Pillar for two biennia and now the Federation Director for two regions, SIA Northern Philippines Region and SIA Philippines Region, with 93 clubs. My goal is to fulfill the vision of providing women and girls the resources to reach their full potential and live their dreams.

My responsibility is to provide them with access to the education and training they need to achieve economic empowerment and to work in coalition with Soroptimist International and other Soroptimist federations.

What would my mother, past governor of this prestigious organization, have done if she was in my place? Soroptimist wants to help the population of women and girls who have the greatest need. Women and girls who have faced obstacles such as poverty, violence, and teen pregnancy often lack support to reach their full potential. I am part of the Pillar for Public Awareness, and my mandate is to inform the world about our work.

Inspired by my mother's precious memories, I visited all the SIAPR clubs and suggested marketing strategies for effective public awareness. All clubs had Public Awareness Club Committee chairs, and I saw that they knew their responsibilities and duties and how they fit in with the organization's goals. In addition, we created action plans and objectives, including gainful access to e-mail or cell phones to utilize these platforms to spread the word: traditional media, online, social media, website development, and management.

I encouraged tapping into traditional media to broadcast our message on radio and television. Likewise, we campaigned for advertisements in print media—newspapers, magazines, journals, newsletters, and flyers. We utilized billboards, and banners. You may notice club markers stating that Soroptimist is the "Best of Women for other Women" situated strategically along major thoroughfares and national highways. I encouraged some clubs to put up a LED and video wall displays flashing the organization's activities in strategic locations, for example, in front of Camp Crame and along EDSA. Finally, I campaigned for merchandise such as fans, umbrellas, wearables with the Soroptimist brand which we used as club giveaways and souvenir items. Finally, I encouraged each Soroptimist to post a sign by their door stating "A Soroptimist Lives Here" or "Soroptimist Investing in Dreams."

We went full bore with our marketing campaign. All club chairs identified opportunities for other region pillar programs, membership, and fundraising opportunities, with established timelines for every activity. Calendars were distributed with ample time to get the word out. We implemented performance measurements through regular monitoring, constant follow up, and reminders. The club's evaluation through the Governor's Annual Club Awards Points System was the most significant incentive.

Citing the importance of having an online presence to serve as the club's professional representation, I campaigned for the 100% Club Website (www.soroptimistinternationalph.org) project during the 2018–2022 biennium. Each club paid P5K and submitted the content requirements, a list of members and officers, pictures, programs, and activities. In addition, the website would serve as an information hub for prospective members, a platform to educate and inform the public of the clubs' projects and a fundraising arm for benefactors, sponsors, and donors.

All that work paid off. During the 2018–2022 Soroptimist International Convention in Montreal, Canada, SIAPR received an award for my 100% Club

Website project. In the annals of the organization, this was the first time any region developed and implemented a public awareness project.

In the following Biennium 2020–2022 SIA appointed me for another term as Pillar for Public Awareness. I was elected as a federation director by both SIAPR and Soroptimist International of the Americas Northern Philippines Region (SIANPR. I now sit on the International Board as director with 14 other regions in Japan, Brazil, Taiwan, South Korea, Canada, and the United States.

The COVID-19 pandemic has wrecked unprecedented damage to the world economy. Undeterred, I continued to move the Soroptimist mission forward amid this epic pandemic, where disadvantaged women and girls are most vulnerable and need our help, now more than ever. A daunting task, yet I am determined to perform well in the three international positions as expected.

As a re-appointed public awareness pillar and now the federation director, how can I continue creating energy and excitement over my strategy and plans? How can I share updates on collective progress with all the club members and region leaders when everybody is locked down? How can I achieve a more significant societal impact, economically empower women and girls, and continue to provide a sustainable impact through our dream programs. Again, how when everybody is locked down?

As the world adapted, we, too, had to adapt. Adapt and adopt. We utilized what technology had to offer. For example, Zoom, Facebook, Twitter, YouTube Channel, Instagram, Screen Sharing, and Video Conferencing were a few of the platforms we tapped to spread the word of our mission. We all had steep learning curves to hurdle as we familiarized ourselves with virtual communications in real time. Clubs started hiring technical assistance and conducted regular webinars and Zoom meetings. In addition, several clubs joined the frontliners and distributed Personal Protection Equipment (PPEs), medical/face masks, face shields, and food.

As the federation director for two Philippine Regions, my meetings are held monthly at the International Soroptimist House in Philadelphia , which means waking up at 5:00 a.m. to prepare for 6:30 a.m. meetings.

Soroptimist is now celebrating its 100 years as a global voice for women and girls. As part of this milestone, the organization launched its Dream Big Campaign. This capital campaign aims to raise $15M to reach their Big Goal of investing in the dreams of a half million women and girls through access to education by 2031. My challenge is crafting the organization's strategic direction, and how would they ensure resources to scale impact? How can I guide the organization's brand-strengthening campaign and efforts to engage more people in the Soroptimist mission and help in the Dream Big Campaign?

The Board members of Soroptimist International of the Americas are the ambassadors and relied upon to carry the torch. So how can I light the torches to give the flame needed for Soroptimist International's 2021–2031 Big Goal of raising $15 million for the education and training of 500,000 women and girls?

SIA Philippines Region has 93 clubs. I gathered all 93 clubs and held several Zoom meetings, communicating with club presidents and their district directors. I dream of inspiring them to conduct fundraising events to raise a minimum contribution of $1000 for each club. The funds would go towards the Big Goal Campaign. Despite constraints and seemingly unsurmountable obstacles, I tried to convince them to forge a partnership, teamwork, and linkages based on a covenant relationship to engage even non-member donors. Finally, I gave incentives to source for donors who could provide a significant gift of $5,000 or greater to the Federation. The Federation, in return, will donate 20% to their club for their projects and activities.

I tried to build the capacity and capabilities of each club by sending them solicitation letters explaining the Dream Big Campaign, seeking support in investing in access to education and training needed to achieve economic empowerment for women and girls. This time, I aimed for a 100% Club Donation and a target of $90,000 from the clubs within the year.

When we fully embrace a mission and unite locally, we can lift half a million women and girls out of poverty through access to education. There is power in investing in a woman's education. With education, our women and girls will find their true path, confidence, autonomy, and inner strength. They can fight to lift their family out of economic poverty and set them on a course that will provide future success.

TO LIVE AND PAY ITS PRICE

By focusing my work on women's empowerment through education, I can drive the impact needed to grow as a successful, life-changing, well-recognized Soroptimist organization. I understand fully well that uniting efforts may not always be easy. But when I ask for my mother's intercession for divine guidance and see the resilience of the women and girls that we can help, I can do it.

I miss my mother and wish she was still here, working side by side with me. Yet, I know that I am channeling her energy and drive. I can prove I am worthy of donning her mantle. I can be the catalyst she was. And if I continue to reach out to people the way I do and bind myself into the fabric of serving and changing lives, my life without my mother would have attained its meaning.

TO MY MOTHER

My life's meaning is to see things in a positive light. My attitude and commitment are to unshackle my negative emotions. How can I distill my mother's ability to perceive nuances in human relations, her pureness of heart, and her positive intent in everything she was involved in? She never had a bad thought nor an ill word for anybody. There is a saying that all good things come to an end. She never lost the desire for growth, development, and passion for serving others. But, above all, the unwavering faith and affirmation, the blessings and guidance of our loving God, whose divine mercy lights our path and directs all our undertakings.

To my mother, this chapter is a tribute to your unwavering and unconditional love and support. You never failed to lift me when I faltered or trod the valley of despair. Instead, you taught, guided, and showed me how to navigate the mysteries of life. You knew the sweetness of life's success and the bitterness of life's humiliation, taking both with unruffled composure and coming out a winner.

You will always be my pillar of strength, of hope with ever unfailing compassion and perseverance. Furthermore, you have proven that kindness and humility manifest empowerment and leadership. That one does not have to shout to be heard. You have shown the refreshing reassurance that God listens to all my prayers.

Every day brings an endless tomorrow. Death is the last sleep and though unseen and unheard, the last and final awakening till we meet again. I love you, Mommy, and I miss you so much.

SONIA T. DELEN

Senior Vice President, Bank of America Gloal Leasing
US FWN100™ 2007
GLOBAL FWN100™ 2013

Power of Connection

As I drive through the snarled traffic of the San Francisco Bay Area and make my way to another Board meeting at the peak of the weeknight commute, I ask myself—What am I doing? I am tired, cranky, and starving. I could be at home resting or enjoying dinner with friends instead of navigating the congestion of San Francisco traffic. So why am I pushing myself so hard?

While discussing the plight of survivors of domestic violence and child human trafficking or relief efforts to support those affected by natural disasters such as typhoons or volcanic eruptions, I realized why I am doing this. I give voice to the underrepresented and promote underappreciated Filipino arts, culture, and cuisine.

The answer to the question "why?" is that the work fulfills me.

I am privileged to be involved in organizations and partner with others who selflessly pursue common causes. We brainstorm, debate, and connect as we work towards lifting the lives of people who need assistance and support. As part of a collaborative partnership with people dedicated to doing good for the community, I can give back to the country and our people.

The operative words are connecting and relationship building. The power of building a coalition, leveraging human resources, and developing and mentoring new leaders and programs are all multipliers to change.

It was daunting when I first came to the United States in the 1980s as a single parent of a disabled child with no immediate family. I had to find a job and childcare for my son. That was when I realized early on the value of networking, reaching out, building relationships, and being involved in the community to help each other. Without finding a support system and community organizations to lean on, I would not be where I am now. The work of these organizations made me realize the importance of giving back. That began my involvement as a board member, fostering alliances with policymaking bodies and networking with medical and educational institutions.

Fast forward to the 2000s. Today, I am Senior Vice President with Bank of America Global Leasing, a division of Bank of America, the Fortune 500 multinational investment bank and financial services company. In 2020, I received one of the Outstanding Filipinos in America Award. In 2022, I shared the honor of being one of the Top 50 Women Leaders of San Francisco by Women we Admire. Inconceivable upon my arrival here.

My chapter will show the value and impact of networking, my passion for connecting people, building coalitions for common goals, being a mentor to many women and girls, and the strengths and challenges of maintaining meaningful and sustainable relationships.

WHAT WOULD THE BEST OF SONIA DO?

In the small barrio of Conde Labak, Batangas City, public school teachers Aquilino and the late Consuelo raised three daughters, Ester, Delza, and me. We lived simple lives. Our barrio was a unique paradise for me, a natural playground surrounded by fields and trees. Yet, despite the lack of electric power or running water, it was a place that served as a landscape full of meaningful childhood memories. It was home.

Living the *Bayanihan* Way

My first encounter with selfless giving was as a young child. During the heavy rainy season, the streams at Conde Labak would turn quickly into an impassable river and getting to school was almost impossible. Then, the *bayanihan* spirit kicked in. Brave young men hoisted my sisters and me onto their broad shoulders, and they waded across the surging waters to a bus waiting on the other side. That experience taught me a valuable lesson. At that young age, I realized I needed to be brave and strong to face life's adversities, a learning I hold close to my heart to this day.

Our home was like a community center whose doors were open to everyone. My father welcomed and assisted the barrio's farmers with legal documents, free of charge. Our living room became a makeshift office. With the aid of a hurricane lamp, my father would work on real estate documents and have them notarized and registered with the city's assessor's office.

I could see that my father had a big heart for this cause, and I became curious. At nine years old, I offered to be his assistant. As I listened to the personal stories of our neighbors, my world widened with a deep appreciation that life was not perfect. Their powerful narratives opened my understanding that independence, maturity, and discipline were essential, and above all, a great and big heart for our fellow man. That's when my passion and vision to serve crystallized.

While in high school at St. Bridget College, I became interested in leading various community projects and joining the school's outreach. I led the Young Christian Life Community and helped open the apostolic social center with the St. Bridget religious sisters. In addition, we organized various disaster relief initiatives to bring food, clothes, and supplies to the flood-ravaged towns of Quezon and Laguna. It was here that the seeds of leadership were sowed.

Martial Law was in full effect when I attended the University of the Philippines, where I was the first chairperson of the Consultative Committee on Student Affairs (CONCOMSA). Being vocal in dissent and having a high profile in student affairs was, to a high degree, dangerous. My gamble paid off as I gained the trust of students and the community. However, my efforts caught the attention of the Marcos administration.

My parents feared for my safety and appealed for me to step down. I remember receiving kidnapping threats during the national plebiscites, which replaced national elections at that time; we had to endure the challenge of being safe and secure.

I shared a house with some professors when we awoke to a loud banging on the front door. A half-dozen soldiers converged upon us and searched the house for documents or papers deemed anti-government. Huddled together, we were fearful for our lives and safety, but our strong moral compass and sense of right and wrong kept us strong. We persisted in our dissent.

Surviving and Contributing as an Immigrant

I immigrated to the U.S. in the eighties as a single mother with a young son, David, who was born blind and deaf and had special needs. I immediately began advocating for the rights and welfare of the disadvantaged and differently-abled.

Navigating the health care and community support systems for disabled individuals made me realize I could contribute to improving services and access to government and private resources to help ease lives. For example, I served on the boards of Support for Families of Children with Disabilities and the Blind Babies Foundation. In addition, I advocated for children's individualized education programs and legislative policies affecting disadvantaged children and their families.

My passion for helping my fellow Filipinos continued while living in the U.S. In 1986, the peaceful Epifanio de los Santos Avenue (EDSA) People Power Revolution ended Martial Law. The post-Martial Law era clean-up started. In my previous work with the U.P. community and other organizations, I was recognized by community leaders who invited me to be the office coordinator of the Presidential Commission on Good Government (PCGG) in San Francisco, California. Then President Corazón Aquino created PCGG to recover the Philippines' stolen assets and investigate Marcos' ill-gotten wealth and other graft and corruption during the Marcos era.

I continued volunteering for the local San Francisco community, helping survivors of the civil unrest in Central America. I attended festivals and retreats and worked as a coordinator for the Young Adult Ministry of the Archdiocese of San Francisco (YAM). I honed my skills by organizing seminars and festivals for groups of 300 or more, securing resources, and bringing in motivational speakers. My confidence in leading and empowering much larger groups began to expand.

In March 1986, one of the significant connection points happened in my life. The Archdiocese hired a lay director, Christopher Fitzsimmons, a solid person of impeccable character; he inspired me with his strong core values. Then, as it turns out, we built the ultimate relationship. Thirty-three years late—we continue to nurture our lives with our children, David, Justin, and Matthew Fitzsimmons.

In 2003, I joined the Filipina Women's Network (FWN), a global organization of women for women based in San Francisco. FWN's mission is to empower and elevate Filipino women in every aspect of their corporate, civic, and professional lives. As a former board director for FWN, I am proud to be part of an organization that developed a robust platform to enable connections among the most remarkable, influential women in the U.S. and worldwide.

THE POWER OF NETWORKING

I have been blessed and privileged to complete several community-based projects. Anything that I have accomplished, I owe to the power of networking. Just as words matter, relationships matter.

As an empowered Filipina Asian American, I strive to elevate, lift, and encourage other Filipino women, leveraging my networking skills. As a connector of people, I recognize the importance of promoting and looking out for others.

Especially in times of adversity, we find new hopes and new dreams and aspire to see each one of us see our goals and dreams to fruition.

In 2010, I became a co-investor in a high-end Filipino restaurant in the San Francisco Bay Area. I quickly became aware of the not-so-kind environment when businesses were siloed and held up by one-upmanship and crab mentality.

As I saw it, we needed to unite and show cohesiveness to thrive as a small, minority-owned business in the food service industry. We needed to elevate Filipino cuisine and culture and celebrate talented chefs of Filipino descent.

Several things occurred to help with this transformation. Ultimately, the legacy I am most proud of—**Kulinarya Showdown**—was born.

Connecting. Forging. Nurturing.

First, FWN launched a dinner series called **"Salo-Salo"** [sharing-meals] for members who attended various workshops. Each workshop featured a Filipino dish, partnered with a discussion on the history of the food. In addition, members met Pinay/Pinoy restaurateurs and talented FilAm chefs, creating an environment to form camaraderie and dispelling the crab-mentality attitude.

Second, in 2010, as part of the San Francisco Philippine Consulate commemoration of the Philippine Independence Day in June, then Philippine Consul General Marciano (Jun) Paynor Jr. created a month-long event to promote Filipino cuisine and restaurants. As part of the planning committee, I forged deep and lasting relationships with chefs such as Cocoy Ventura, Nicole Fonseca, Francis Ang, and Claude Tayag, to name a few. In addition, a significant relationship with PJ Quesada of Ramar Foods was forged, which subsequently led to the co-founding of the **Filipino Food Movement**.

Third, after meeting all the talented chefs, we realized we needed a platform to celebrate and showcase their unique culinary talents. With the help of Department of Tourism Director Rene de los Santos and chief of staff Debbie Galliano, we created a competition among professional and amateur chefs to rousing success. Thus, the **Kulinarya Chefs Competition** was born. The Kulinarya Competition organized cooking contests in San Francisco with the participation of chefs from Los Angeles, Hawaii, and New York. We also secured engagement from food suppliers, Filipino food bloggers, and the Department of Trade & Investments representatives promoting and introducing new products from the Philippines, such as pili nuts.

A few years later, in 2014, with our shared passion for elevating Filipino cuisine, PJ Quesada, along with Susie Quesada, Al Perez, Joann Boston, Pearl Parmelee, Pauline Vera, and myself, founded the Filipino Food Movement® (FFM), a 501(c)3 non-profit organization with the mission to promote, preserve, and progress Filipino cuisine in the mainstream U.S., education of Filipino cuisine, and community building. FFM brought together the Filipino community through food-centered events, mainstream media advocacy, and social media platforms. FFM proudly brought Filipino American chefs to showcase Filipino cuisine at the prestigious James Beard House Foundation for the very first time in the history of the James Beard House. With that milestone, we can proudly say that Filipino cuisine has arrived and is here to stay.

During the pandemic, leveraging the connections I had made, and with the support of the board members of FFM, the organization established a weekly live stream called **Kulinarya Live!** showcasing Filipino small businesses centered around food. We featured 100+ chefs from the Philippines, Australia, France,

Switzerland, UAE, UK, and the U.S. To complement this effort, we created a global directory of businesses that offered take-out and delivery services to help with their marketing efforts.

Through my connection with another power Pinay, Demee Koch, I met Jovy Tuano and Janet Tuano of **FilFood Trade** based in the UAE. Through them, I expanded my network of talented and prominent chefs in the Middle East. With our common goal, we forged a collaboration to promote Filipino cuisine and chefs in the Middle East and Europe.

When I look back to when I joined FWN and met PJ Quesada, I could not have foreseen how these connections would lead to such a global phenomenon and success in Filipino cuisine.

Serving the Citizens and Government of the State of California.
The Filipina Women's Network has a rich base of successful, powerful Filipinas worldwide. Through FWN, I met one of the most influential Filipinas in the state of California, Mona Pasquil Rogers, the first Filipina-American lieutenant governor of California. Much later, she held the office of the Appointments Secretary of Governor Jerry Brown. I reached out to her and expressed my desire to serve on commissions in the state of California.

In 2015, I received a call from the office of the Governor of California, inquiring if I would be interested in serving as a Trustee of the Health Professions Education Foundation (HPEF). I have never heard of HPEF and immediately 'googled' it. I was pleased to learn that HPEF is the only state foundation established in 1986 that provides scholarships and loan repayment to health professionals pledging to work (upon graduation) or already working in underserved areas in the state. I immediately accepted the appointment. I saw this as an opportunity to be a voice for the many Filipino Americans and Asians who comprise a large percentage of health professionals. According to the 2016 Survey of California Registered Nurses, Filipinos make up the second-largest group of the state's active R.N. workforce, nearly 18 percent. They are even more predominant, with Filipino nurses representing almost a quarter of nurses between 35 to 44 years old and more than one-fifth of RNs 45 to 54 years old. (DeSha, 2019)

Midway through my 3-year term, I received another call from the office of the Governor. They offered me the opportunity to serve as a non-lawyer public member of the Board of Trustees for the State Bar of California.

The State Bar is an agency of the Supreme Court which administers admissions, regulations, and discipline of the lawyers in the state. The Board of Trustees under the State Bar of California is mandated to protect the public's interest. They are in charge of all the accredited and unaccredited law schools and can vote to penalize or close a school. Upon recommendation of the staff or committees, trustees can bring suit against impostors misrepresenting themselves as part of the legal and justice system. In addition, trustees approve the staff and committees reviewing regulations of the legislature and oversee the Office of the Chief Trial Counsel (OCTC), tasked with reviewing complaints and disciplining attorneys.

Learning about legislation and judicial statutes and pouring through reports, policies, and regulations is challenging for a non-legal person, so I am on a continuous learning path. As a non-lawyer member of the Board of Trustees, I offer a layperson's view of the legal profession as an engine for a just society. I represent consumers, the public in general, and the under-represented, which adds to the diversity of law professionals, and levels the playing field for legal representation of all citizens.

I am the first Filipino American member to serve on the Board of Trustees—lawyer or public member—and I am honored to be of service. A service I could not have been privileged to provide without the support and recommendation of Mona Pasquil Rogers.

Giving Back to the University of the Philippines

My roots with the University of the Philippines run deep. And connections with fellow alumni bring great gratitude and the ability to serve and give back.

A great example of the power of networking and leveraging relationships is what we accomplished with the UP Alumni Grand Reunion and Convention, held in San Francisco in August 2019. Through friends and connections, I invited the best of the best in various fields and industries, including Dr. Jacquiline Romero Amor, named as one of the most promising women scientists of the L'Oréal-UNESCO For Women in Science (FWIS) International Rising Talents. She is also the resident Quantum Physicist for the University of Queensland, Queensland, Australia. The alumni's enthusiastic participation invigorated the organization through inspiring talks, thought-provoking conversations, exchange of ideas on mentoring young people, and using the power of collaboration to create unique opportunities for our community.

Making a Difference During the Worldwide Pandemic

One of the advantages of being a connector is that people recognize what you can contribute, which opens many more opportunities. Throughout the pandemic, we reached out to the health professional front liners, essential workers, and innovators. Such was the case with Yobie Benjamin, a UP alumnus with access to a substantial quantity of COVID-19 testing kits. Yobie donated close to 300,000 COVID-19 saliva collection testing kits worth $2,850,000.00 to the Apl.de.ap Foundation International (ADAFI). Yobie, aware of my roles as chairperson of ADAFI and board member of the UP Alumni Association of San Francisco (UPAASF), knew I could leverage my relationship with the University of the Philippines president, Atty. Danilo L. Concepción and Dr. Gerardo Legaspi, director of the national hospital, UP Philippine General Hospital, and arranged for a direct donation to the hospital. Yobi's generosity and ADAFI's network benefitted thousands of students who began in-person instructions at the University in Diliman and accessed testing for free (Nucum, 2021).

Preventing Blindness

Networking and collaboration extended beyond the San Francisco Bay Area. For example, Ted Benito, a close friend based in Los Angeles, California, invited me to chair the 'Campaign for Filipino Children, a healthcare initiative of the Apl.de.ap Foundation International, to combat preventable blindness.

Retinopathy of Prematurity (ROP) is a potentially blinding disease caused by the abnormal development of retinal blood vessels in premature babies if not treated within 48 hours of birth. Addressing the lack of access to diagnostic equipment in the Philippines is a cause near and dear to Apl.de.ap's heart. As a baby, Apl.de.ap did not have access to early diagnosis and care.

Today, thousands of premature newborn babies are affected by ROP in the Philippines and become permanently blind, exacerbating their families' socio-economic status.

Through the director of the Vision Center of the Children's Hospital Los Angeles, Dr. Thomas Lee, ADAFI was fortunate to work with the Academy of Ophthalmology (Academy) in the Philippines, led by Dr. Pearl Tamesis-Villalon.

The Academy and its ROP working committee identified regional hospitals where ADAFI could donate retinal imaging systems to diagnose ROP and laser equipment to treat the disease.

For all of this work to be possible, sponsorships are critical; fundraising is the lifeline, and this is where relationships are meaningful. Through the many contacts and associations, we were able to fund access to this equipment and establish a sustainable program for the patients in Davao and Pampanga (*Inquirer.net* US Bureau, 2019). We are confident that we will continue the success of financing the third leg of the program to bring retinal imaging equipment and medical training to the Visayas region in 2023.

Building a Coalition for Climate Change

We recognize that relief efforts stemming from the massive devastation of natural disasters are no longer the ultimate solution to help the affected population. Teaching resilience and combating climate change is the more urgent need to reach the climate change survivors. I partnered with fellow FWN100 awardee Paula Rosales, a staunch climate defender. Together we formed One Ocean Coalition. Organizations including the Ocean Defenders, Apl.de.ap Foundation International, the UP Alumni Association of San Francisco, and the San Francisco Filipino Cultural Center will focus on making a maximum positive effort for our community to provide fast response and sensible solutions. We also collaborated with grassroots organizations such as Waves for Water Philippines to deploy water filtration systems to the typhoon-stricken areas in the Visayas, providing access to clean water and preventing the spread of waterborne disease life-threatening dehydration. Climate change is a never-ending challenge for the coalition.

WHAT WOULD THE BEST OF YOU DO?

Giving and Sharing

I believe that we should GIVE more, SHARE more. There are myriad avenues for a person to be involved in something. So here are some suggestions to be a networker for good.

1. Provide financial support to Asian-American social entrepreneurs. Provide finance support when you can. Use your buying power to

influence decisions to support the causes you believe in. Be a sponsor.

2. Give back to your educational institutions and the community. The nuns at St. Bridget molded my character and instilled the values of integrity, dignity, kindness, and truthfulness. The professors and liberal thinkers at the University of the Philippines forged the ideals of service to the people, truth, and justice. I am what I am because of them. Being of service to others brings fulfillment and honor.

3. Mentor others by giving them the gift of time and attention. Our life experiences can serve as a guide to those who are just starting in the world. We have gained life experience that can translate to being a mentor to young professionals, high schoolers looking for direction, or those looking for a path to a future.

4. Use your voice. Share advocacy on social media. Share your story. Be vulnerable. Our stories impact and empower people, changing minds, inspiring dreams, and making a difference in the world.

5. Be a bridge. Be a connector. Connect people and serve as a conduit to others. That's what I am passionate about, the unrelenting promotion of people and passions. Lift women with us instead of putting them down.

Building your Network

To network for good, you must learn to build, maintain, and sustain your various networks. Networking is about relationship building.

1. Widen your reach, look around. Be interested in meeting people, knowing them genuinely. Listen to what they say; wait for them to finish before speaking, and be mindful and purposeful.

2. Volunteer for a community event. Seek out networking opportunities. Working with organizations, and connecting with people with the same passion as you, are prime opportunities. Support grassroots campaigns.

3. Join associations compatible with your principles and interests. Together you can promote, empower, amplify, and uplift.

4. Find a sponsor or a mentor. An influential person (not necessarily your manager, co-worker, or same company) who would be your advocate and promote you for opportunities not readily available. Such a person will think of you and say – "I have exactly the right person for the job."

5. Thank people. Show gratitude. Always.

As women and Asian Americans, we bear the brunt of discrimination in all its forms. Let us practice self-awareness to ensure we do not contribute to this form of hate or bigotry. Let us use our voice and networks for the good of Filipina women, our Asian American wider community, and humanity.

Connect with me. I am happy to listen to views on diversity and inclusion, generate ideas to make the legal system more accessible to the people, and be an instrument of the community for our voices. Let's talk.

The Importance of Family

With all the connections I have made, nothing trumps the relationships I have with my family. Without their support, I would not be able to do what I love to do—serve our community.

My late mother, Consuelo and sister, Delza, from whom I learned to be strong and kind, continue to be my role models.

My dad, Aquilino Delen, my early idol who first instilled the purpose of serving, continues to root for my success. My beloved sister Ester Delen and cousin Nancy Liu always cheer me on. Surrounded by our nieces and nephews, we share our philosophies and values with them and celebrate their talents and successes.

Christopher Fitzsimmons, my husband of thirty-three years, provides guidance, advice, and encouragement to pursue my passions.

Chris and I are proud of our three sons. David reminds us daily of the challenges of people with disabilities and the need to be his voice and advocate. Justin is a licensed attorney in California, trained to be a public defender and to serve those who cannot afford legal representation. Matthew is an officer of the United States Army, serving with valor and integrity and giving back to his country. Chris and I see ourselves in our sons' idealism by working with those needing help.

During my son Justin's commencement exercises at Santa Clara University in 2012, the Reverend James Martin, S.J., said that in any situation requiring our thoughts and action, we must contemplate and ask, *"What would the best of Jesus do?"* What he said resonated with me and led me to ask, *"What would the best of Sonia do?"*

This question continues to be a powerful and impactful tool for me, with integrity know I will achieve optimum results in building relationships and collaboration.

What would the best of you do?

SYNTHESIS

Maria Beebe, Ph.D.

*D*ISRUPT 4.0. *Filipina Women: Being* highlights the leadership themes of being Filipina, being Filipina women, and being Filipina women leaders punctuated by the time of COVID-19. Each influential Filipina woman leader shares her reservoir of psychological capital of optimism, resilience, hope, self-efficacy; key life experiences; and perspective-taking that help her realize her authentic leadership. Self-development, enhanced performance, and the development of others are closely linked to her advocacies for social and economic change and her arc to purposeful leadership within an intercultural milieu and its implications for diversity, equity, and inclusion (DEI).

LIBERATION

The right to live our lives as we want

Liberation is the state of being free. Free to choose how we live. Free to choose how we lead. Liberation is when we refuse to accept our fate. Instead, we chose to triumph over it.

The liberation themes of the Filipina women leaders demonstrate their refusal to accept fate as an inevitable and often adverse outcome, condition, or end. Instead, they chose faith, a strong belief, and trust to triumph over it. Below are vignettes from their stories.

When **Anna Sobrepeña** joined the publishing industry as editor-in-chief of the longest-running glossy magazine in the Philippines, the reaction was to dismiss her *"as a housewife wannabe and a socialite looking to keep herself busy."* Instead, she channeled her energies into creating content, expanding the magazine's reach, getting to know the stakeholders, and earning accolades for the magazine.

Laarni San Juan improved her *"younger self from the 1970s with crooked teeth, thick glasses, and an awkward frown"* by opening windows so the fresh breeze could push her to where she wanted to go. Mentors and support systems were the wind that helped her overcome being sad, stressed, overwhelmed, and burned out.

Despite her hearing disability, **Maria Santos Greaves** heard the call to the hearing industry, first in the Philippines and later when she immigrated to Canada. Maria became an audiometrist, a hearing instrument practitioner, and an owner of five clinics. Again, she found ability in disability.

Cora dela Cruz's fear of the unknown made her question her plan to go to Canada. She could have listened to the friends who discouraged her, telling her that she would be living with the brutal, harsh winter cold weather with salmons and sardines to pack as her form of employment in Canada. But, instead, she thought about the endless possibilities and boundless opportunities to fulfill her dream.

"Verlaengerung ausgeschlossen," visibly stamped on page six of **Marizel Rojas's** first Philippine passport, were the first words she learned in German. It meant finding an employer who could sponsor her stay in Austria. Twenty-two years later, Marizel still works at the Comprehensive Nuclear-Test-Ban Treaty Organization (CTBTO) in the United Nations headquarters in Vienna.

Joanne Rico did not have a formal education in Marketing or Business Management. However, she *"took that as a challenge rather than an obstacle. Right from the first day, I studied the business model and landscape."*

The supervisor wrote: *"Lucy has adjusted slowly in ICU but is now ready to take charge."* **Lucia Reyes's** retort: *"How could my adjustment to Canadian nursing be termed as slow when at three months I was already taking charge?"*

Part of **Pamela Gotangco's** *"being artistic comes with an abundance of blind and burning emotions."* *"I was in a hurry to feel romance, to be in a love story, and to be in my ever after. But as we all know, not every story has a happy ending. I became a single mother at the age of 19."* Despite her family's loving and financial support, Pamela wanted to give her daughter the best. So she became an Overseas Filipino Worker (OFW) in Kuwait at the age of twenty.

The world almost crumbled when a developmental doctor finally delivered the findings. **Rosario Chavez's** second son had "Autism Spectrum Disorder." This diagnosis meant that he would be non-verbal for life and not capable of emotions. Rosario decided to lay low and focus on her particular son's therapy. A decade of hard work, dedication, and close coordination with developmental doctors, special education teachers, and therapists of Anton finally paid off! Aside from becoming self-reliant, Anton could talk and, most importantly, able to express his basic needs.

Annabelle Morgan's defining moment was *"When I was told they had to remove 40 percent of my child's brain at just five weeks old—and how that would significantly inhibit Macario's developmental processes both physically and mentally."* Annabelle sprung to action not only as a terrified mother but as a trained scientist. In her words, *"I instantly took Macario off all medications and administered CBD through his GI tube. The miraculous effects were almost immediate and thus began Macario's remarkable, triumphant road back to normalcy."*

Isabelita Manalastas-Watanabe wrote her first business plan at ten. In high school, Lita fell in love, married secretly, suffered betrayal, and decided to have a child through artificial insemination. Decades later, finding her Ima's letter gave her *"the courage to impart the lesson that, no matter the gravity of missteps, no matter how many times a person stumbles, one can, with determination, hard work, and focus, rise again."*

TRANSFORMATION

An internal shift that brings us in alignment with our highest potential... (Cooks-Campbell)

Human transformation can happen instantly or through many transformative experiences to live up to our full potential to live with greater purpose, clarity, and passion. Therefore, the transformation themes of the Filipina women leaders included being intentional about developing their physical well-being, mental fitness, emotional health, and cognitive agility.

Alicia del Prado turned *"her personal history with fractured family relationships, mental health, and ethnic identity"* into important pieces leading up to her career path. As a psychologist, Alicia now helps others with their anxiety and other psychological and health concerns.

In *Becoming Ruth*, **Angelica Urra Berrie** transformed from the convent girl she was to later convert to Judaism, take Ruth as her Hebrew name, and embrace Israel as her spiritual home. While this transformation was gradual, it fast-tracked when one morning in 2002, she woke up and knew nothing in her life would ever be the same again. *"Overnight, I was a widow, CEO and Vice-Chair of a public company on the New York Stock Exchange, and President of The Russell Berrie Foundation."*

Kristine Custodio Suero went from fears to fierce. Kristine shares how she shifted from the heavy burden of paralyzing fear and grief in losing both of her parents within a year and a half to finding the fearless, fierce Kristine Custodio Suero.

Reflecting on her leadership, **Marietta Evelyn P. Revilla** danced her way to opportunities in Europe. Evelyn teaches Philippine folk dances *"to promote social integration, including solidarity, social assistance, protection of civil rights, and social-cultural promotion among Filipinos."* As a Corporate Relations Consultant, Evelyn's professional life centers around the Italtrans Moto2 Racing team.

Sugarcane Princess **Patricia "Denise" Lopez** transformed into steely sampaguita by rebelling against being labeled *"pretty face"* and by honing her reading, writing, and mathematics skills. To shift from privilege to purpose and authenticity, Denise worked harder than most to prove her worth through her accomplishments. She made herself smarter.

As demonstrated by the Filipina women leaders, human transformation is based on being self-aware, open-minded, adaptable, innovative, and proactive. Transforming the self leads to becoming a transformational leader who considers each individual, inspires and motivates, models ethical behaviors, and stimulates thinking. The Filipina women leaders show us how to be more aligned with the Filipina woman leader we want to become!

CHANGE

Experiencing new and exciting things that affect how we see and relate to the world and understanding our place in it

Liberation and human transformation lead to changes within us which propel us to be a force for social change. Strip to its basics; leadership is a simple process of thinking well or thinking clearly about people and their conditions and acting. A sampling of conditions faced by Filipina women leaders includes education, entrepreneurship, finance, health, and law. Filipina women leaders in these sectors are agents of change in an inclusive world as they ensure their legacies for the next generation.

EDUCATION

Bernadette Mondejar-Schlueter writes, *"I am an educator dedicated to making the world a better place, one student at a time. My 26 years in education have been a journey of self-discovery, purpose, and teamwork."* Bernadette was a teacher and a school administrator in the Philippines, Japan, Korea, Guam, Belgium, and the United Kingdom, where she hosted queens, generals, and ministers at her schools. Bernadette worked with award-winning teachers and won awards herself.

Arlene Tordecilla Ferrolino's greatest passion in life remains to be the subtle art of teaching and cultivating a love for music among young people. *"Anything that has to do with music and children will grab my attention. Bringing the joy of music to children, giving them the gift of learning music, and providing opportunities for creativity and avenues to share their talents brings me the most happiness and fulfillment."*

Cynthia writes about her journey from a military brat to an educational leader: *"I embrace my culture and identity as a Filipina woman. I no longer have mixed feelings about my ethnic background or heritage. I value my Filipino values, and I lead with respect, integrity, inclusiveness, and collaboration. I am educated, culturally competent, and emotionally intelligent. I am a woman warrior and a "shero" for myself. I am proud of my identity—a Filipina woman, wife, daughter, sister, auntie, friend, and colleague who loves listening to music, dancing the cha-cha, singing Karaoke, and playing the piano."*

ENTREPRENEURSHIP

There are Filipina women leaders who are also entrepreneurs. The common denominator about being both a leader and an entrepreneur is their ability to influence others, with or without authority.

Beng Puyat is Chair and Treasurer of the Philippine Orchard Corporation (Philor), which promotes new technologies and innovations to ensure our country's future. *"By seeking out more sustainable, more environmentally friendly alternatives, we lessen the strain we put on the world."* Philor's advocacy is to be part of the solution. Produce and manufacture resources that benefit humankind without harming the water we drink and swim in, the air we breathe, and the earth where we grow and tend our animals.

When tough times come, **Gina Atienza** tells herself, *"Ganbatte, Gina!"* *"Stay resilient and hang on despite the difficulty. Moving from one country to another may sound exciting, but it has myriad challenges."* Living in a culture different from the Philippines engendered Gina's resiliency and toughness as a leader. She also built a career in corporate communications, working both in Jakarta and Tokyo. When she returned to Cebu, she helped in the Sunstar Media Group, a family-owned news and content provider.

Ildeme "Demee" Mahinay Koch discusses the challenges she had to overcome as a woman, a mother, and a serial entrepreneur. As a result, she has succeeded in the cosmeceutical business to change people's lives. From helping a cancer survivor with eyelash extensions, Demee writes: *"I became obsessed with finding a product that would address the risks, which included eye irritation and temporary lash loss. I saw the business potential of eyelash extensions and the potential stumbling blocks. I take pride in what I have done and the people I have crossed paths with who have led me to where I am now."*

Being an effective auditor is like being the driver. This lesson has guided **Maria Fides Balita** in her career as a certified public accountant. As she tells it, *"you hold the steering wheel, you need four things: know the driving rules (audit procedures), know how to drive (audit skills), use the "Global Positioning System" (GPS) to navigate for directions (supervision), and you need to have a driver's license (relevant certification)."* You learn to trust your inner GPS.

Marla D. Rausch, while pregnant, learned how to work on motion capture data, something her husband was doing. Motion capture animation uses special optical cameras to translate what is seen in real life and convert it into a 3D space. Motion capture, or Mocap, is used in the film, video games, and television to create realistic motion in characters, monsters, and animals so that what you see on the screen seems real and believable. From working as a contractor, the idea of Animation Vertigo started —to create a studio available to support production companies that used motion capture anytime they needed it.

Rhoda Caliwara saw the potential in the service contracting business. It gave her a sense of purpose in helping the industry and the country's employment problem by offering business flexibility to enterprises to focus on their core competencies for better efficiency and productivity. Rhoda credits divine and human agency in becoming the woman leader she is today. Human agency embodies practices of faith, hope, and love. Through the human agency, we can achieve great things with hard work, dedication, and prayer.

HEALTH

Leadership in the healthcare industry evolved in volatile, uncertain, complex, and ambiguous (VUCA) circumstances. **Marivic Lualhati** notes that the industry breathes unpredictably, thus entailing a visionary, strategic and collaborative leader. With strategies for financial viability, Doctors' and employees' involvement is done simultaneously because the key to having patients recognize the healthcare organization is doctors' referrals. Marivic explains that *"Leadership Quotient (LQ) is a recent trend that assesses an individual's leadership ability. It is the price of competence, character, and capability."*

Carmina Montesa Aldana recounts that for 14 years of their married life, she and her husband sent used medical textbooks and supplies to a charity hospital in the Philippines. Finally, they agreed that was not enough. Her husband commented that neurosurgery was all he knew to do. His surgical expertise saved many children's lives. Carmina responded, *"I know how to do operational matters."* Neurosurgery plus operations, the lightbulb moment clicked. The Neurosurgery Outreach Foundation (NOF) will advance neurosurgery care in underserved communities through service, education, and support. It would be a structured way with a multiplier effect to give back.

Fe Odsigue Punzalan reflects on how far she has come from selling peanut brittle in the rural Philippines as a child to being the owner and administrator of Punzalan Homes in the Santa Clara County Area. The people in her care have intellectual disabilities, defined as challenges in people's mental abilities affecting intellectual functioning (e.g., learning, judgment) and adaptive functioning (e.g., daily life activities such as communication and independent living).

For Us, By Us is a chapter about **Joyce Javier's** experience being a second-generation Filipina American with multiple identities: mother, wife, physician, researcher, educator, and community advocate. From discovering her Filipina identity during college to developing a statewide initiative to prevent teen suicide and depression among Filipino youth, Joyce describes key moments in her life that have shaped her into the Filipina woman leader she is today. Joyce draws on lessons from the concepts of community-based participatory research and servant leadership.

Poised to retire from International Community Health Services (ICHS) in December 2022, **Teresita Batayola** received an important announcement in February 2022. She will be among 25 leaders selected for the U.S. President's Advisory Commission on Asian Americans, Native Hawaiians, and Pacific Islanders. The Commission will help the executive branch with policies to prevent and document anti-Asian hate incidents and to improve health, economic and educational disparities among Asian American (AA) and Native Hawaiian and Pacific Islander (NHPI) communities. In her Ark of Purposeful Leadership, her selection as a Commission member forms part of Teresita's reflection on building character, competence, commitment, and compassion on the road to social responsibility.

LEGACY BUILDING

According to her father, **Lorna Patajo-Kapunan** is a Block Off the Old Chip. *"Even as a young girl,"* Lorna intimates, *"I already wanted to be a lawyer as great as my father, Supreme Court Justice Lino Mejia Patajo."* *"I romanticized being a slayer of demons, dragons, and bad guys, wielding the mighty sword of justice, truth, and punishment of evil and evil-doers."* So, when she founded her current law firm, Kapunan & Castillo Law Office, after several years of working for others, she, along with her other founding partners, envisioned a law firm grounded on three C's: competence, character, and courage.

Maria Beebe writes about the legacy of four women leaders who exercised their power for peace. Dr. Anne Itto in the Sudan. President Corazon Aquino in the Philippines. President Ellen Sirleaf Johnson in Liberia. Graça Machel in Mozambique and South Africa. All four women leaders believed in a culture of peace as *"a set of values, attitudes, modes of behavior and ways of life that reject violence and prevent conflicts by tackling their root causes to solve problems through dialogue and negotiation among individuals, groups, and nations."* They walked the talk in engendering leadership and en-GENDER-ing leadership in their words and actions.

By 2014, **Rhodora Palomar-Fresnedi** had lived her hyphenated name, worked, traveled to seven continents, lived in three, changed careers, and led teams of different sizes, functions, and contributions. Rhodora writes: *"I was back in the Philippines with my husband, to pay it forward."* They were motivated by two things: first, the opportunity to give back, and second, the opportunity to develop Asian leaders. In their work across the globe, they saw the same patterns of modern colonization: education, the development of leaders through western models, and the retelling of western leadership stories. Rhodora writes about the need to change the global narrative of the Asian leader. *"We had to tell our own stories. We could help amplify the voices of the east in the west, enabling a more inclusive, more authentic dialogue on international matters."*

"The symbiotic relationship between a mother-daughter is like a fruit-bearing tree," says **Mitzi Flores Piad.** *"The tree provides nourishment and care, protection, and warmth. Standing strong and tall, the tree nourishes its fruit through every situation that Mother Nature presents to her. And each hardship helped produce a succulent, beautifully textured fruit with the sweetest taste. My mother was my fruit-bearing tree, and I was her favorite fruit. We shared secrets and magic whispers, thoughts, and ideals. We lived in our dream world, complete with a house made of wishes. We romped through our fairyland, a paradise with the tree untainted by a wicked witch's curse."*

Sonia Delen writes, *"I am privileged to be involved in organizations and partner with others who selflessly pursue common causes. We brainstorm, debate, and connect as we work towards lifting the lives of people who need assistance and support."* Sonia continues, *"As part of a collaborative partnership with people dedicated to doing good for the community, I can give back to the country and our people. The operative words are to connect and build relationships. The power of building a coalition, leveraging human resources, and developing and mentoring new leaders and programs are all multipliers to change."*

Being a **Filipina** shows the multiple forms of Filipino-ness, with evolving, varied, and fluid Filipina identities, Filipina diasporic identities, and global citizen identity. Being a Filipina **woman** shines a light on the paradox posed by gender, from positive stereotypes of being matriarchal to opposing views of being submissive. Being a Filipina women **leader** in any sector, such as education, entrepreneurship, health, finance, law, and philanthropy, affirms her as an authentic agent of change in an intercultural milieu. **Filipina women leaders** ensure their liberation, transformation, and personal change are for purposeful leadership embracing diversity, equity, and inclusion as they assure their legacies for the next generation.

ACKNOWLEDGEMENTS

This book required a *bayanihan,* collaborative effort made possible by the following:

- Marily Mondejar, Founder, and CEO of the Foundation of Filipina Women's Network, provided executive oversight.

- Thirty–six contributing authors shared their leadership reflections, narratives, vignettes, setbacks, outcomes, global competencies, and success stories; whether en route to Austria, Canada, Cebu, Dubai, Feltwell, Florida, Manila, Italy, San Diego, San Francisco, Switzerland, Turkey, or elsewhere in the world.

- Aileen Cassinetto, Academy of American Poets Laureate Fellow and San Mateo County Commissioner on the Status of Women, for giving us permission use her poems.

- For book cover design, Lucille Lozada Tenazas, Global FWN100™ 2013 and Henry Wolf Professor of Communication Design & Associate Dean of Art, Media and Technology, Parsons The New School for Design.

- Al S. Perez (Creative i Studio) served as our layout designer and provided an extra set of critical eyes. Al is President, FAAE / Pistahan Parade and Festival; Commissioner, San Francisco Entertainment Commission; Board Member, Grand National Rodeo Cow Palace Fair; Board Member, Filipino Food Movement; Board Member, SF Hep B Free; Board Member, SF Community Police Advisory Board.

- Franklin M. Ricarte (Draft Orange), Social Media and Tech Guru, updated the Filipina Leadership website http://www.filipinaleadership.org/ and provided various media communications support.

- Edwin Lozada, President of the Pilipino American Writers and Artists (PAWA), Inc., whose work in *DISRUPT 1.0* and *DISRUPT2.0* provided a template for *DISRUPT 3.0* and *DISRUPT 4.0*.
- Georgitta "Beng" Puyat for underwriting the printing of the unlimited edition. Carol Enriquez, MD, for printing the magazine. Accessprint Corporation for accommodating our tight schedule.

- Our FWN and external peer reviewers who did a blind review and provided comments, recommendations for improvement, and suggestions for edits – Barbara Barry, Christina Calaguian, Editha Tijamo-Winterhalter, Elena Mangahas, Geri Alumit Zeldes, Juslyn Manalo, Leah Laxamana, Leonor Vintervoll, Ligaya Beebe, Lily Samoranos, Maria Hizon, Melissa Orquiza, Rowena Romulo, Susie Quesada, Teresa Frediani, Wennie Conedy, and Wilma Eisma.

- Alain McLaughlin Photography, Megan di Piero Photography, Melissa de Mata Photographer, and Splento Photography for the photographs of the FWN Board members.

- Marizel Secuya-De Castro, CPA and Jesus Coronel, Accountant.

- FWN Fellows, Eljean Chan, Isabelle Santiago, and Michaella Mae Galoy.

- Mari Reyes, VJ7 Printing and Packaging, Inc.

- Fatima Wang, Gani M. Ricarte, and Gary Cruz for help with the magazine.

- Ramar Foods International and Wells Fargo for their unwavering support.

- FWN Ambassadors for Global Award Selection: Carmina Montesa Aldana, Global FWN100™ 2019 (Florida), Cora dela Cruz, Global FWN100™ 2017 (Canada), Cristina Calaguian, Global FWN100™ 2017 (Dubai), Edith Winterhalter, Global FWN100™ 2017 (California), Maria Fides Balita, Global FWN100™ 2019 (Chicago), Pam Gotangco, Global FWN100™ 2018 (Switzerland), Rhodora Palomar-Fresnedi, Global FWN100™ 2019 (California and Philippines), Rosary Escaño, Global FWN100™ 2017 (Canada), Rox Magbanua, Global FWN100™ 2018 (Dubai), Teresita Batayola, Global FWN100™ 2019 (Washington).

- FWN Ambassadors for Awardee Countries: Benel Se Liban, US FWN100™ 2011 (California) and Marla Rausch, Global FWN100™ 2019 (Utah) are the Co-VPs for Membership.

- FWN Ambassadors for Public Affairs: Lorna Kapunan, Global FWN100™ 2016 (Philippines) and Juslyn Manalo, Global FWN100™ 2015, Continuing Influential 2018 (San Francisco) are the Co-VPs for Public Affairs with Bambi Lorica, US FWN™ 2007, Global FWN100™ 2013 (Washington DC)

- FWN Ambassadors for Communications: Gina Atienza, Global FWN100™ 2016, VP for Communications (Cebu) with Co-Chairs Roxie Magbanua, Global FWN100™ 2017 (Dubai) and Ann Michelle Mondragon, Global FWN100™ 2018 (Switzerland).

- FWN Ambassadors for Finance: Fe Punzalan, US FWN100™ 2009, Global FWN100™ 2019 (California) and Mica Tan, Global FWN100™ 2019 (Philippines) are the Co-VPs for Finance and Fundraising.

- FWN Ambassador for Professional Development: Carol Enriquez, Global FWN100™ 2016 (Philippines) is the VP for Professional Development.

- FWN Ambassadors for Leadership: Maria Beebe, US FWN100™ 2011, Global FWN100™ 2013, Continuing Influential 2019 (Florida) is the Editor of the *DISRUPT* Leadership Book Series and Georgitta Puyat chairs the *DISRUPT* Leadership Book Series Funding.

- FWN Ambassador for Filipiina Leadership Global Summit: Marily Mondejar and Leonor Vintervoll Co-Chair this committee.

- Interested in being the FWN Ambassador for Femfor Match? Marily Mondejar will train the Ambassador.

Other *kapwa* global Filipinas are too numerous to mention here who gave us support in spirit and cheer us on.

Maraming salamat!

APPENDICES

APPENDIX A

Select References

Abouelsoud, N. (2010, June 18). Herbal medicine in ancient Egypt. Journal of Medicinal Plants Research, 4(2), 82-86. 10.5897/JMPR09.013

Achor Hayes, T. (1988) "Dressing to Win." *Dallas Morning News.*

AGD Impact (1988). The Newsmagazine of the Academy of General Dentistry, Volume 16 Number 7.

Aguila, A. N. (2015). The Filipino, Diaspora, and Continuing Quest for Identity, Social Science Diliman, 11:2, 56-89.

Allure Magazine (1991). "The Image Police."

Asis, M. M.B. (2007, February 02). Living with Migration: Experiences of left-behind children in the Philippines. Taylor and Francis Online, 2(1), 45-67. https://doi.org/10.1080/17441730600700556

Asis, M. M. (2017, July 12). The Philippines: Beyond Labor Migration. Migration Policy Institute. https://www.migrationpolicy.org/article/philippines-beyond-labor-migration-toward-development-and-possibly-return

Aquino, C. (1986, November 30). Speech of President Corazon Aquino before the ADB Women's Club. Official Gazette. https://www.officialgazette.gov.ph/1986/11/30/speech-of-president-corazon-aquino-before-the-adb-womens-club/

Assad, C.D. (1995). "Improve Your Communication: Seven Aspects of Image for Influencing Results." *Cintermex Magazine,* November/December, Volume 3, Number 17, Monterrey, Mexico

Barr, J. (2014, July). Vascular medicine and surgery in ancient Egypt. Science Direct, 60(1), 260-263. https://doi.org/10.1016/j.jvs.2014.04.056

Batha, E. (2011, June 20). Q+A with Anne Itto: Is women's position in South Sudan... Thomson Reuters Foundation News. https://news.trust.org/item/20110620192300-v1ycg/

Beebe, M. A. (Ed.). (2015). *DISRUPT: Filipina Women: Proud. Loud. Leading without a Doubt.* Filipina Women's Network.

Beebe, M. A. (Ed.). (2016). *DISRUPT 2.0: Filipina Women: Daring to Lead.* Filipina Women's Network.

Beebe, M. A. (2017). The leadership repertoire of select Filipina women in the Diaspora and implications for theorizing leadership. In J. Storberg-Walker, & P. Haber-Curran (Eds.). *Theorizing women & leadership: New insights & contributions from multiple perspectives.* Information Age Publishing.

Beebe, M. A., & Escudero, M. O. (Eds.). (2015). *DISRUPT 1.0. Filipina Women: Proud. Loud. Leading Without a Doubt.* Filipina Women's Network.

CIA World Factbook. (2022, September 22). Exploring All Countries–Philippines. CIA. https://www.cia.gov/the-world-factbook/countries/philippines/#people-and-society

Cohn, A. (2017, September 11). Marshall Goldsmith Pays It Forward With The Marshall Goldsmith 100 Coaches Project. *Forbes.* https://www.forbes.com/sites/alisacohn/2017/09/11/marshall-goldsmith-pays-it-forward-with-the-marshall-goldsmith-100-coaches-project/?sh=40debbba764b

Colossians 3:23-24. *Holy Bible New International Version.* (2011). Biblica Inc

Commission on Filipinos Overseas. (2013). Stock estimate of overseas Filipinos as of December 2013. http://www.cfo.gov.ph/images/stories/pdf/Stock Estimate2013.pdf

Commission on Filipinos Overseas. (2013). Philippine Migration at a Glance. https://cfo.gov.ph/statistics-2/

Commission on Filipinos Overseas. (2017). 2015 CFO statistics on Philippine international migration. https://www.cfo.gov.ph/images/pdf/2017/2015 compendiumstats-inside pages-2017-06-29.pdf

Cooks, A. (2022, January 20). What is human transformation? What it means to become more you. BetterUp. https://www.betterup.com/blog/human-transformation

Corinthians 3:6-9. *Holy Bible New International Version.* (2011). Biblica Inc.

Corinthians 12:9. *Holy Bible New International Version.* (2011). Biblica Inc.

DeSha, A. D. (2019). Why are there so many Filipino nurses in California?. *GV Wire.* https://gvwire.com/2019/10/04/why-are-there-so-many-filipino-nurses-in-california/

Dominguez, G. B., & Hall, B. J. (2022, August 12). The health status and related interventions for children left behind due to parental migration in the Philippines: A scoping review. Elsevier, 28. https://doi.org/10.1016/j.lanwpc.2022.100566

Dooley, J. L. (2019). *Own Your Everyday: Overcome the Pressure to Prove and Show Up for What You Were Made to Do.* Crown Publishing Group.

Dudman, J. (2014, July 2). Women want to be decision-makers about peace, not passive victims of war. *The Guardian.* https://www.theguardian.com/public-leaders-network/2014/jul/02/woman-government-rwanda-genocide-peace

Dweck, C. S. (2007). *Mindset: The New Psychology of Success.* Random House Publishing Group.

Ellen Johnson Sirleaf. (2020, July 21). Ellen Johnson Sirleaf's TED Talk: How women will lead us to freedom, justice and peace. EJS Center. https://www.ejscenter.org/news/ellen-johnson-sirleafs-ted-talk-how-women-will-lead-us-to-freedom-justice-and-peace/

Forbes Africa. (2020, March). Africa's 50 Most Powerful Women. *Forbes Africa.* https://cms.forbesafrica.com/wp-content/uploads/woocommerce_uploads/2020/03/FA-MAR-2020-Digital-1.pdf

Forbes Africa. (2020, March 6). Celebrating powerful women: there is enough on the table for all of us. Graca Machel Trust. https://gracamacheltrust.org/2020/03/06/celebrating-powerful-women-there-is-enough-on-the-table-for-all-of-us/

George, B. (2004). *Authentic Leadership: Rediscovering the Secrets to Creating Lasting Value.* Jossey-Bass.

Gladwell, M. (2005). "Intuitive Repulsion." In *Blink. The Power of Thinking Without Thinking.* Little, Brown.

Gladwell, M. (2005). "Snap Judgments." *In Blink. The Power of Thinking Without Thinking.* Little, Brown. Retrieved from https://www.bookpage.com/interviews/8284-malcolm-gladwell-arts-culture/

Global Forum of Women Political Leaders. (2000, January 17). Women Leaders Can Make A Difference. Cory Aquino. https://www.coryaquino.ph/index.php/works/article/9ef489aa-f38b-11df-b3cf-001617d76479

Global Gender Gap Report 2022. (2022, July 13). World Economic Forum. https://www.weforum.org/reports/global-gender-gap-report-2022/

Graham, E., & Jordan, L. (2022, August). Migrant Parents and the Psychological Well-Being of Left-Behind Children in Southeast Asia. National Library of Medicine, 73(4), 763-787. https://doi.org/10.1111%2Fj.1741-3737.2011.00844

Green, A. (n.d.). The Fragrance Foundation. Retrieved from https://fragrance.org

Harrison, C. (2022, January). Turning Milestones into Stepping Stones. Craig Harrison. https://www.expressionsofexcellence.com/ARTICLES/milestones.htm

Heath, J. L. (1981). CEO and co-founder of BeautiControl Inc.

Hebrews 11:1. *Holy Bible New International Version.* (2011). Biblica Inc.

Hewitt, D. (2017). How the Kennedy-Nixon debate changed the world of politics. Retrieved from https://constitutioncenter.org/blog/the-debate-that-changed-the-world-of-politics

Hunter, C. K., & Hunter, W. D. (2018). Global Competence Model. Global Competence Associates. https://globallycompetent.com/global-competence-model/

Inquirer. (2019, February 12). Apl.de.ap donates another retinal imaging system to PH. *Inquirer USA.* https://usa.inquirer.net/21160/apl-de-ap-donates-another-retinal-imaging-system-to-ph

Itto, A. (2006, December 18). Guests at the table? The role of women in peace processes. Conciliation Resources. https://www.c-r.org/accord/sudan/guests-table-role-women-peace-processes

Iyer, P. (1987, January 5). Woman of the Year: Corazon Cory Aquino, *TIME*. Videos Index on TIME.com. https://content.time.com/time/subscriber/article/0,33009,963185-11,00.html

Jackson, C. (1981). *Color me Beautiful.* Ballantine Books.

Johnson Sirleaf, E. (2009). *This Child Will Be Great: Memoir of a Remarkable Life by Africa's First Woman President.* HarperCollins.

Johnson Sirleaf, E. (2011, May 26). Text of Ellen Johnson Sirleaf's speech. *Harvard Gazette.* https://news.harvard.edu/gazette/story/2011/05/text-of-ellen-johnson- sirleafs-speech/

Johnson Sirleaf, E. (2011, December 10). Ellen Johnson Sirleaf—Nobel Lecture—NobelPrize.org. Nobel Prize. https://www.nobelprize.org/prizes/peace/2011/johnson_sirleaf/lecture/

Johnson Sirleaf, E. (2020, June 26). How women will lead us to freedom, justice and peace. TED. https://www.ted.com/talks/h_e_ellen_johnson_sirleaf_how_women_will_lead_us_to_freedom_justice_and_peace/transcript

Joshua 1:9. *Holy Bible New International Version.* (2011). Biblica Inc.

Jouzaitis, C. (1990). "Firms Help Clients Put Best Forward." Chicago Tribune.

Khalil, R. B., & Richa, S. (2014, March 1). *When Affective Disorders Were Considered to Emanate From the Heart: The Ebers Papyrus,* 171(3), 275. https://doi.org/10.1176/appi.ajp.2013.13070860

Kron, J. (1991). "The Image Police." *Allure Magazine*

Lawrence-Lightfoot, S. (2009). The third chapter: passion, risk, and adventure in the twenty-five years after fifty. Farrar, Straus and Giroux.

Levitt, M. (1983). *Executive Look How to Get It How to Keep It.* Atheneum Books

Levitt, M. (1984). *Class, What It is and How to Acquire It (A guide to Living Well).* Atheneum Books

Lopez, D., & Hilliard, P. (2019). *Lead, Motivate, Engage: How to INSPIRE Your Team to Win at Work.* Amazon Digital Services LLC – KDP Print US

Lurie, A. (1981) *The Language of Clothes.* Random House.

Manalo-Morgan, A (2023). *Mighty Flower: How Cannabis Saved My Son.* New York: Forbesbooks.

Mandela, N., & Van Wyk, C. (2010). *Long Walk to Freedom.* Macmillan Children's Books.

Mangahas, R. (2008). Cora dela Cruz accepts appointment. *Philippine Times Canada,* Vol.3(8)

Mathabane, M. (2018). *The Lessons of Ubuntu: How an African Philosophy Can Inspire Racial Healing in America.* Skyhorse Publishing.

McLeod, S. (2018). Erik Erikson's 8 Stages of Psychosocial Development. Simply Psychology. https://www.simplypsychology.org/Erik-Erikson.html

Molloy, John (1975). *Dress for Success.* Warner Books. Retrieved from https://en.wikipedia.org/wiki/Dress_for_Success_(book)   https://www.bostonglobe.com/magazine/2018/09/19/forty-years-later-advice-dress-for-success-old-hat/qPAJ8hKAXvDE55b7XBcqLO/story.html

Mondejar, M. (1984). "Dressing to Influence: Oliver North." In *The Image Report.* Mondejar and Associates.

Morin, T. (2009). Asian of the Year Award 2009. *Asia Network Magazine.*

Morton, R. (2021, November 9). Filipino American caregivers reflect on trauma and healing on COVID-19's Frontlines. NPR. https://www.npr.org/sections/health-shots/2021/11/09/1052062334/covid-filipino-american-health-workers-burnout

Moyela, C. (2018, November 16). Women Must Redesign the table, and not just expect to be at the table, says Graça Machel. African Development Bank. https://www.afdb.org/en/news-and-events/women-must-redesign-the-table-and-not-just-expect-to-be-at-the-table-says-graca-machel-18710

Munsell Color Science Laboratory. Retrieved from https://www.rit.edu/science/munsell-color-lab

Nehemiah 8:10. *Holy Bible New International Version.* (2011). Biblica Inc.

Nucum, J. (2021, December 23). UP alums, friends in San Francisco donate Covid test kits worth $3M to PGH. Inquirer USA. https://usa.inquirer.net/90024/up-alums-friends-in-san-francisco-donate-covid-test-kits-worth-3m-to-pgh

OECD Development Pathways. (2017, May 30). Interrelations between Public Policies, Migration and Development in the Philippines. https://www.oecd.org/countries/philippines/interrelations-between-public-policies-migration-and-development-in-the-philippines-9789264272286-en.htm

Orme, G. (2021, August 21). Women Leaders Have Shone During The Pandemic: Men, Take Note. Forbes. https://www.forbes.com/sites/gregorme/2021/08/04/women-leaders-have-shone-during-the-pandemicambitious-men-should-take-note/?sh=30e9d9e751c6

Pantone Color Institute. Retrieved from https://www.pantone.com/color-consulting/about-pantone-color-institute

Pimentel, B. (1996, February 18). SUNDAY INTERVIEW – CORAZON AQUINO / The former president of the Philippines reflects on losing a husband to the cause they believed in, the revolution that later swept her to power and the difficulties of ruling in a democracy. *SFGATE.* https://www.sfgate.com/news/article/SUNDAY-INTERVIEW-CORAZON-AQUINO-The-former-2993014.php

Philippines: Deployed OFWs 2021. (2022, September 7). Statista. https://www.statista.com/statistics/1243681/philippines-deployed-overseas-workers/

Philippines: OFW cash remittances 2021. (2022, June 8). Statista. https://www.statista.com/statistics/1242750/remittance-overseas-filipino-workers-to-philippines/

Pinoy Eh Community News. 2009 Asia Network Asian of the Year Award included another Filipina. Ottawa, Canada. Vol. 8(3) June 2009

Proverbs 19:21. *Holy Bible New International Version.* (2011). Biblica Inc.

Proverbs 22:6. *King James Bible Text.* (2012). INT Bible

Pussy Bow. Retrieved from https://en.wikipedia.org/wiki/Pussy_bow

Rayray, M. P. (2019, March 15). Filipina physicist receives international rising talent award. ABS-CBN News. https://news.abs-cbn.com/overseas/03/15/19/filipina-physicist-receives-international-rising-talent-award?fbclid=IwAR08IzC_EsTynCY4zlYSXlvBjeNMC8OAnOBceFIBiC5AXN4f3tR3g_5z1mU

Roces, M. (2021). *The Filipino migration experience: Global agents of change.* Cornell University Press.

Sergent, K., & Stajkovic, A. D. (2020). Women's leadership is associated with fewer deaths during the COVID-19 crisis: Quantitative and qualitative analyses of United States governors. Journal of Applied Psychology, 105(8), 771–783. https://doi.org/10.1037/apl0000577

Sins of Omission: How government failures to track COVID-19 data have led to more than 3,200 health care worker deaths and jeopardize public health. (2021, March 2). National Nurses United. https://www.nationalnursesunited.org/sites/default/files/nnu/documents/0321_Covid19_SinsOfOmission_Data_Report.pdf

Solomon, M. R. (1985). *The Psychology of Fashion.* Lexington Books.

The Elders. (2007). The Elders: Independent global leaders | Ethical Leadership. https://theelders.org/

Then & Now: Corazon Aquino – Sep 19, 2005. (2005, September 19). CNN. https://www.cnn.com/2005/US/09/19/cnn25.aquino.tan/

The Philippine Reporter. (2004, April 1). Dela Cruz honored Woman Entrepreneur. *The Philippine Reporter.* https://philippinereporter.com/index.php/2004/04/01/dela-cruz-honored-woman-entrepreneur/

United Nations Digital Library. (1998). Culture of peace. United Nations Digital Library System. https://digitallibrary.un.org/record/249723?ln=en#record-files- collapse-header

UN Women Philippines. (2020, June). Gendered Dimensions of COVID-19 in the Philippines. UN Women Asia and the Pacific | UN Women – Asia-Pacific. https://asiapacific.unwomen.org/sites/default/files/Field%20Office%20ESEAsia/Docs/Publications/2020/06/FINAL-Gender%20Snapshot%202-PHL.pdf

Virgin, N. (1977). Founder and President, Beauty for All Seasons, Inc.

Wagner, C. and Wagner Institute for Color Research (1988). Color Communications.

Walch, M. (2004). "Guest Room With Color Expert Margaret Walch." Color Association of the U.S." Retrieved from https://www.specialevents.com/decor/guest-room-color-expert-margaret-walch

Walumbwa, F. O., Avolio, B., Gardner, W., & Wernsing, T. (2008, March). Authentic Leadership: Development and Validation of a Theory-Based Measure. Research Gate, 34(1), 89-126. http://dx.doi.org/10.1177/0149206307308913

Westside Toastmasters. Involve and Inspire Your Audience. Retrieved from https://westsidetoastmasters.com/resources/powerspeak/toc.html

APPENDIX B

Additional Web-Based Resources

Filipina Women's Network. 2007–2022. Interviews with FWN100™ awardees. The Filipina Women's Network interviews its Top 100 Most Influential Filipina Women awardees as part of its time capsule project intending to document the contributions of Filipina women to society to inspire future generations. https://filipinawomensnetwork.org/

Filipina Women's Network. 2007–2022. FWN Global 100: The 100 Most Influential Filipina Women in the World. Filipina Women's Network has published the Filipina Leadership Summit magazine from 2005–present. The magazine serves as a program and resource for attendees. The 2013-2018 issues showcase the Global FWN100™ Most Influential Women in the World. https://filipinawomensnetwork.org/

AAUW. Barriers and Bias: The Status of Women in Leadership. This report examines the causes of women's underrepresentation in leadership roles in business, politics, and education and suggests what we can do to change the status quo. Retrieved from https://www.aauw.org/research/barriers-and-bias/

Comprehensive Assessment of Leadership for Learning (CALL) Assessment. CALL measures key practices across the district that impact school leadership. Download various papers that CALL researchers have written. Retrieved from https://www.leadershipforlearning.org/research.

Hart Leadership Assessment. This is a short questionnaire created to measure where your leadership strengths lie and where there is room for improvement. Retrieved from https://www.smu.edu/Lyle/Centers-and-Institutes/Hart/Leadership-Development/ Hart-Leadership-Assessment

Institute for Intercultural Communication. 2014. Provides a list of selected intercultural training and assessment tool. Retrieved from https://intercultural.org/intercultural-training-and-assessment-tools/

Kozai Group. The global competencies inventory (GCI). Global Competencies Inventory measures three facets of intercultural adaptability in identifying personal characteristics related to successful performance in contexts where cultural norms and behaviors vary from one's own. This tool is generally used for professional development, team building, and succession planning. Retrieved from http://www.kozaigroup.com/global-competencies-inventory-gci/

Leadership Assessment Tool Inventory – Assess Your Skills. These exercises assess ability to apply critical management skills to identify and solve key organizational problems. Retrieved from http://www.kellogg.northwestern.edu/faculty/uzzi/htm/teaching-leadership.htm

Leadership and Management Development Strategy. Developed to endorse learning and development opportunities to strengthen the leadership and management capacity of the Newfoundland and Labrador Public Service. Retrieved from http://www.exec.gov.nl.ca/exec/hrs/forms/Peer_Assessment_Form2_Forms_and_Applications.pdf

Najafi Global Mindset Institute. Global mindset inventory's three capitals. The Global Mindset Inventory is an assessment tool for identifying one's capacity to lead and influence individuals and companies in a global context, particularly those who are from a different culture. Retrieved from https://thunderbird.asu.edu/faculty-and-research/global-mindset-inventory

Northouse Authentic Leadership Self-Assessment Questionnaire. This questionnaire contains items about different dimensions of authentic leadership. Retrieved from http://people.uncw.edu/nottinghamj/documents/slides6/Northouse6e%20Ch11% 20Authentic%20Survey.pdf

Office of Personnel Management Assessment & Evaluation LEADERSHIP ASSESSMENTS. A suite of leadership tools enhances self-awareness by measuring leadership effectiveness from multiple approaches. Retrieved from https://www.opm.gov/services-for-agencies/assessment-evaluation/leadership-assessments/

Pew Research Center, 2015. Women and Leadership: Public Says Women are Equally Qualified, but Barriers Persist. Retrieved from http://www.pewsocialtrends.org/2015/01/14/women-and-leadership/

Via Institute on Character. Do you know your 24 character strengths? The VIA survey was created to help individuals identify the make-up of their character strengths that are classified under six virtue categories. The survey can be taken online and is free of charge. Retrieved from http://www.viacharacter.org/www/the-survey

Vincent on Leadership: Leadership Assessments. The Vincentian Leadership Assessment (VLA) offers participants the opportunity to evaluate and grow in their leadership competencies in relation to the five orientations of the Vincentian Leadership Model 2.0. Retrieved from https://resources.depaul.edu/vincent-on-leadership/training/Pages/assessments.aspx

APPENDIX C

Suggestions for Workshop Activities to Enrich the Book Reading Experience as Stand-Alone Activities or as Part of a Leadership Course

Target Audience: Corporate Employee Resource Groups, Human Resources Professionals including DEI (Diversity, Equity, and Inclusion), Staffing, and HR Business Partners (HRBPs).

1. Activity: FWN Disrupt Leadership Workshop

Objectives: To stimulate ideas to complement or enhance DEI initiatives in your organization. To raise awareness around hiring, recruiting, and developing diverse leaders through stories of Filipina women. To bring back new insights to your organization. To discuss what it means to belong in addition to being in a diverse, equitable, and inclusive environment.

Activity Description: Two-hour workshop to help HR and DEI professionals learn more about hiring, recruiting, retaining, and developing people of color, specifically Filipina women, using stories of their leadership journeys as data.

The book series project aims to fill the gap in the leadership literature that highlights the unique qualities of Filipina women whose culture, values, and faith make them influential leaders and managers. The leadership book series chronicles Filipina women's leadership skill sets and how Filipina women contribute as active participants in the global workplace.

2. Activity: Leaders You Admire.

Objective: To seek leadership characteristics through personal experience Activity Description: Divide the group into small groups. Ask participants to share a story about the best or most influential leader they have read about in the book. After each story, identify leadership characteristics by asking the question: "What was it that made this person such an effective leader?" Then as a group, identify the traits that all the leaders seemed to share.

Check out: http://www.workshopexercises.com

3. Activity: Stand by Your Quote.

Objective: To introduce leadership discussion and awareness

Activity Description: Place thoughtful leadership quotes from the women authors on the walls, making sure the print is readable. Ask the participants to walk around the room reading each of the quotes. Then have them stand by one quote that resonates well with their personal views on what makes a good leader (there can be more than one person standing by a quote). When all participants have selected a quote, have each explain to the group why her chosen quote is important to them—share a leadership insight.

Check out: http://www.workshopexercises.com

4. Activity: Character Strengths.

Objective: To learn your character strengths

Activity Description: Great leaders have identified and clarified their core working values. They understand how each of their core values translates into leadership behavior. Take the VIA survey to know your character strengths. Which character strengths do you share with any of the 3 or 4 women leaders? Are these character strengths unique to Filipino culture? Or to American culture?

Check out: https://www.viacharacter.org/survey/account/register

5. Activity: Leadership Tips.

Objective: To find ways to strengthen leadership ability

Activity Description: Choose 2–3 chapters from the book. Compare and contrast the leadership story and the leadership tips and their implications for your own leadership experience. Make a list of intentional simple, on-the-job self-improvement strategies. For example, list ways of building meaningful work relationships. List ways of motivating others.

6. Activity: This I Believe Essay.

Objective: To describe the core values that guide your daily lives.

Activity Description: Follow the instructions for submitting an essay to "This I Believe." Write and submit your own statement of personal belief. Reflect how you approach new challenges through your interpretation of the individual chapter readings.

Check out: http://thisibelieve.org/guidelines/.

Variation: Choose one of the women leaders and write a "This I Believe" essay from the woman's perspective—pretend you are that woman writing the essay. You may interview the author if possible.

7. Activity: Leadership Theory and Practice.

Objective: To define your own leadership theory and practice

Activity Description: From two or more of the chapters, share which leadership theory or practice you found most valid to your work-life and explain why. If none of the theories or explanations spoke to your personal experience, feel free to challenge the theory and propose your own explanation.

8. Activity: Reflected Best Self.

Objective: To compose a portrait of you when you are at your best.

Activity Description:
1. Solicit feedback about your best-self from others—classmates, work or community service colleagues, clients, personal friends, mentors, family members. Give them at least 2 weeks to respond.
2. While waiting for their responses, you should engage in a deep personal reflection about the times when you were at your best, write three short stories that stand out as times when you were at your best, then identify patterns or commonalities that arise across those stories.
3. Review your best-self feedback from others and look for themes.
4. Revise the portrait of who you are at your best, incorporating feedback from others with your own reflections. Your revised portrait should be a written description of the essence of your best-self. What are your key insights? What are the action implications for you, as you think about (a) being at your best more often, and (b) making your best-self even better? Which of the women authors is most like your best self?

Checkout: http://positiveorgs.bus.umich.edu/?s=reflected+best+self or http://faculty.som.yale.edu/amywrzesniewski/documents/Reflected BestSelfExercise Introduction2014Careers_000.pdf

APPENDIX D

Most Influential Filipina Woman in the World Award Categories

BUILDER

Builders have demonstrated exceptional organizational impact in a large workplace environment, displaying a deep passion for a cause through collaborative initiatives or alliances with institutions, corporations, or nonprofit organizations on behalf of her own company. Builders demonstrate high potential and skill with measurable results at government agencies, higher education institutions, nonprofits, or corporations in the public and private sectors. "Buildership" is about developing better organizations, leading broken organizations to adjust, repair, and re-align, including journalistic views redefining traditional methods.

EMERGING LEADER *(BELOW AGE 35)*

This award category recognizes Filipina women below age 35 who are making their mark in a leadership role and are on the pathway to principalship and building capacity across an organizational system. Emerging Leaders have powerful mindsets and skill sets that help drive performance for their organizations. Emerging Leaders may be renominated after three years to another award category when the EMERGING LEADER is over 35 years old and continues to be influential.

INNOVATOR & THOUGHT LEADER

This award recognizes Filipina women who have broken new ground in the global workplace and delivered unique applications of emerging technology. Women who have influenced how people think in business, education, sports, literature, journalism, the arts, and pop culture, improving the lives of others by developing a product or service in the fields of finance, science, engineering, fashion, publishing, cuisine, architecture, film, and entertainment. This award category is also for someone who has launched a new enterprise, a learning function, or completely overhauled an existing way of doing things, resulting in a new development or community initiative.

FOUNDER & PIONEER

This award honors Filipina women as the chief executive, president, executive director, or founder of a company, community organization, non-profit, or business venture that they helped start, build or significantly grow. This award category is for the trailblazers who have marshaled resources and applied innovative practices, processes, and/or technologies in a new and groundbreaking way to address a significant business or organizational opportunity.

NICOLE

This award honors a Filipina woman whose words, actions, and activism, inspire others to act and revolutionize society's way of understanding traditional beliefs and customs, thus leaving behind a Filipino global imprint. "Nicole" is named after the young woman identified as "Nicole," who sparked an international dialogue about women's rights, national sovereignty, and international law as she steadfastly pursued justice against her four rapists, inspiring this category.

POLICYMAKER & VISIONARY

This award recognizes Filipina women leaders who have demonstrated exceptional business acumen combined with a forward-looking vision in the development or influencing of policies, campaigns, or laws that impact business, industry, and society; leaders who enrich the lives, careers, and businesses of others by sharing the benefits of their wealth, experience, and knowledge; actions that significantly change how we think and live.

KEEPER OF THE FLAME

Sustaining Global Pinay Power is quite daunting. As the excitement dies down and the reality of executing FWN's Vision sets in, many drop out, and others pick up the torch. The Keepers of the Flame are the caretakers that ensure the FWN Vision is kept alive.

BEHIND THE SCENES
(Please note that this category was retired in 2019)

This award category recognizes Filipina women who may not have a big title or corner office. Still, she is a driving force behind the success of a social cause or life issue, a community organization's project or initiative, or her employer's organizational business unit or department. Someone who has gone beyond the call of duty to devote time, energy, and resources to advocate for those who need a voice or support the organization she represents or works for.

CONTINUING INFLUENTIAL GLOBAL FWN100™ AWARD

The "Continuing Influential FWN100™ Award" is for a remarkable woman selected for the second time for continuing to be influential in her field, workplace, and community.

ALWAYS INFLUENTIAL GLOBAL FWN100™ AWARD

A Global FWN100™ Awardee selected for the third time as she continues to inspire and influence her Filipina women constituency, global workplace, profession, industry, and community will be inducted into the FWN "Hall of Fame."

APPENDIX E

List of FWN Awardees
2007 – 2022

Most Influential Filipina Women in the U.S.
US FWN100™ 2007 – 2012

Most Influential Filipina Women in the World
Global FWN100™ 2013 – 2022

BEHIND THE SCENES LEADERS

2007

Asia Yulo-Blume
Aurora Cavosora Daly
Cheely Ann Sy
Cora Basa Cortez Tomalinas
Denielle Palomares
Edna Austria Rodis
Evangeline Buell
Flor Alcantara-Reyes
Kai Delen-Briones
Laarni San Juan
Lolita Kintanar
Lorna Lardizabal Dietz
Maria Jocelyn Bernal
Perla Gange Ibarrientos
Rosalinda Medina Rupel
Susie Quesada

2009

Aileen Suzara
Belle Santos
Cherie Querol Moreno
Daisy Magalit Rodriguez
Dolly Pangan-Specht
Elsie Rose
Helen Marte Bautista
Jian Zapata
Kathleen Davenport
Lorrie V. Reynoso
Lottie T. Buhain
Lovette Rosales Llantos
Lydia Castillo Fontan
Lyna Larcia-Calvario
Mady Rivera
Maria Concepcion Banatao

2009 *(cont.)*

Naomi Tacuyan Underwood
Nerissa M. Fernandez
Nida L. Recabo
Priscilla Magante Quinn
Roselyn Estepa Ibañez
Shirley Orille Brazis
Sunny Dykwel
Tess Ricafort Alarcon

2011

Bennie Lou Quevedo
Cherina Viloria Tinio
Evelyn Javier-Centeno
Evelyn Luluquisen
Francine Villarmia-Kahawai
Gloria Ramil Omania
Gretheline Bolandrina
Henni Espinosa
Julieta Zarate Hudson

2011 *(cont.)*

Mary Ann C. Ubaldo
Pearl Parmelee
Rosario "Puchi" Carrion
  Di Ricco

2012

Angie Louie
Edcelyn Pujol
JoAnn Fields
Marian Catedral-King
Maritessa Bravo Ares
Pureza Belza
Theresa Noriega-Lum
Yong Chavez

BUILERS AND EMERGING LEADERS

2007

Arlene Marie A. "Bambi" Lorica
Bettina Santos Yap
Claire Oliveros
Edna M.Casteel
Genevieve Jopanda
Jennifer Briones Tjiong
Laura Izon Powell
Laureen Dumadag Laglagaron
Lorna Mae DeVera
Lyna Larcia-Calvario
May Nazareno
Melinda Poliarco
Milagros "Mitos" G. Santisteban
Nieves Cortez
Paz Gomez
Polly Cortez
Rachel Buenviaje
Rebecca Samson
Regina "Ging" E. Reyes
Rose-Ann K. Ubarra
Shirley Raguindin
Sonia T. Delen Fitzsimmons
Susan Afan
Sylvia Lichauco
Thelma Boac
Theresa Tantay Wilson
Zenei T. Cortez

2009

Ana Julaton
Cielo Martinez
Cynthia Aloot
Denise Castañeda Miles
Gel Santos Relos
Isabelita M. Abele
Jannah Arivan Manansala
Jennifer Ong
Katherine Abriam-Yago
Katrina R. Abarcar
Maria (Mimi) Amutan
Mivic Hirose
Raquel Cruz Bono
Raquel R. Redondiez
Rebecca Delgado Rottman
Rowena Verdau-Beduya
Stephanie Ong-Stillman
Valerie Pozon-de Leon

2011

Cynthia Rapaido
Diana Reyes
Estela Matriano
Esther Misa Chavez
Genevieve Herreria
Gloria B. Gil

2011 *(cont.)*

Kathleen Quinn DuBois
Keesa Ocampo
Leah Beth O. Naholowaa
Leia Lorica
Maria Africa Beebe
Melanie A. Caoile
Mila M. Josue
Odette Alcazaren Keeley
Selenna Franco-Cefre

2012

Belinda Muñoz
Cora Aragon Soriano
Cynthia A. Bonta
Eleanore Fernandez
Esther Lee
Jacqueline Dumlao Yu
Lili Tarachand
Nadia Catarata Jurani
Natalie C. Aliga
Olivia Finina De Jesus
Prosy Abarquez-Delacruz
Rita Dela Cruz
Rocio Nuyda
Sheryll Casuga
Stefanie Medious
Theresa Chua

FOUNDERS & PIONEERS

2007

Celia Ruiz-Tomlinson
Connie S. Uy
Cora Alisuag
Ellen M. Abellera
Erlinda Sayson Limcaco
Gina Lopez Alexander
Gloria T. Caoile
Joy Bruce
Linda Maria Nietes-Little
Loida Nicolas Lewis
Ludy Payumo Corrales
Luzviminda Sapin Micabalo
Marietta Aster Nagrampa Almazan
Mary Carmen Madrid-Crost
Nimfa Yamsuan Gamez
Patricia Aldaba Lim-Yusah

2007 *(cont.)*

Rozita Villanueva Lee
Sony Robles Florendo
Tessie Guillermo
Virna S. Tintiangco

2009

Alice Bulos
Adelamar Alcantara
Analisa Balares
Carina Castañeda
Cora Oriel
Delle Sering Fojas
Ethel Luzario
Evelyn Silangcruz Bunoan
Fe Martinez

2009 *(cont.)*

Fe Punzalan
Fely Guzman
Imelda Ortega Anderson
Judy Arteche-Carr
Maria Maryles Casto
Mivic Hirose
Mona Lisa Yuchengco
Nanette D. Alcaro
Nelsie Parrado
Nini RB Bautista de Garcia
Norma Calderon-Panahon
Patricia Espiritu Halagao
Rosie Abriam
Ruthe Catolico Ashley
Sherri Burke
Zenaida Cunanan

FOUNDERS & PIONEERS

2011

Alma Onrubia
Chateau Gardecki
Christina Rodriguez
  Laskowski
Dellie Punla
Geri Ferrer-Chan
Herna Cruz-Louie
Janelle So
Josefina R. Enriquez
Jossie Alegre

2011

Joy Dalauidao-Hermsen
Lillian Pardo
Maria Benel Se-Liban
Marjan Philhour
Perla Paredes Daly
Rhoda Yabes Alvarez
Soledad Manaay
Tess Mauricio
Vellie Sandalo Dietrich-Hall

2012

Betty O. Buccat
Conchita Bathan
Constance Valencia
  Santos
Elaine R. Serina
Josie Jones
Kristine Custodio
Victoria J. Santos

INNOVATORS & THOUGHT LEADERS

2007

Angelita Castro-Kelly
Carissa Villacorta
Charmaine Clamor
Connie Mari
Diana J. Galindo
Edith Mijares Ardiente
Elena Mangahas
Elenita Fe Mendoza Strobel
Gemma Nemenzo
Jane Hofileña
Leila Benitez-McCollum
Lilia Villanueva
Malu Rivera-Peoples
Marisa Marquez
Mutya San Agustin

2009

Brenda Buenviaje
Cora Manese Tellez
Esminia "Mia" Luluquisen
Hazel Sanchez
Jei Africa
Lenore RS Lim
Marlina Feleo Gonzales
Marissa Aroy
Nana Luz Khilnani
Norma P. Edar
Ma Rowena Verdan-Beduya
Robyn Rodriguez Canham
Sokie Paulin

2011

Angel Velasco Shaw
Celia Pangilinan-Donahue
Christina Dunham
Evelyn Dilsaver
France Viana
Gemma Bulos
Minerva Malabrigo
  Tantoco

2012

A. Fajilan
Cris Comerford
Janet Nepales
Maricel Quiroz
Penélope V. Flores
Vivian Zalvidea Araullo

NICOLE

2007

M. Evelina Galang

2009

Jessica Cox

2012

Nilda Guanzon Valmores
Paulita Lasola Malay

2013

Annalisa Enrile

POLICYMAKERS AND VISIONARIES

2007

Christina Arvin Baal
Eleonor G. Castillo
Grace Walker
Gwen de Vera
Irene Bueno
Kris Valderrama
Kymberly Marcos Pine

2007 *(cont.)*

Lillian Galedo
Lourdes Tancinco
Marissa Castro-Salvati
Miriam B. Redmiller
Mona Pasquil
Norma Doctor Sparks
Rida T. R. Cabanilla

2007 *(cont.)*

Ruth Asmundson Uy
Sonia Aranza
Tani Gorre Cantil-
  Sakauye
Vanessa Barcelona
Velma Veloria
Vida Benavides

POLICYMAKERS AND VISIONARIES

2009

Carmelyn Malalis
Carmen Lagdameo Stull
Faith Bautista
Hydra B. Mendoza
Gertrude Quiroz Gregorio
Joanne F. del Rosario
Joselyn Geaga-Rosenthal
Lorraine RoderO-Inouye
Lynn Finnegan
Marissa Garcia Bailey
Myrna L. De Vera

2009

Noella Tabladillo
Rose Zimmerman
Dr. Rozzana Verder-Aliga
Stephanie Ong Stillman

2011

Agnes Briones Ubalde
Amy Agbayani
Arlie Ricasa
Cheryl Nora Moss
Katherine M. Eldemar

2011 *(cont.)*

Mae Cendana Torlakson
Melissa Roxas
Monique Lhuillier
Pat Gacoscos
Rosa Mena Moran

2012

Alicia Fortaleza
Rosita Galang
Zenda Garcia-Lat

KEEPERS OF THE FLAME

2007

Al Perez
Arlene Marie "Bambi" Lorica
Elena Mangahas
Franklin M. Ricarte
Genevieve Herreria
Maria Roseni "Nini" M. Alvero
Marily Mondejar
Maya Ong Escudero
Nida Recabo
Rowena Mendoza Sanchez
Sonia T. Delen Fitzsimmons
Thelma Boac

2009

Al Perez
Arlene Marie "Bambi" Lorica
Elena Mangahas
Ellen Abellera
Franklin M. Ricarte
Gloria T. Caoile
Jocelyn Bernal
Josephine "Jopin" Romero
Lilia V. Villanueva
Marily Mondejar
Mutya San Agustin Shaw
Shirley S. Raguindin
Sonia T. Delen Fitzsimmons
Thelma Boac

2011

Al Perez
Arlene Marie "Bambi" Lorica
Franklin M. Ricarte

2011 *(cont.)*

Gloria T. Caoile
Josephine "Jopin" Romero
Lilia V. Villanueva
Mutya San Agustin Shaw
Shirley S. Raguindin
Susie Quesada
Thelma Boac

2012

Al Perez
Arlene Marie "Bambi" Lorica
Cherina Tinio
Cynthia Rapaido
Elena Mangahas
Esther Chavez
Franklin M. Ricarte
Gloria T. Caoile
Josephine "Jopin" T. Romero
Judy Arteche-Carr
Lilia V. Villanueva
Mutya San Agustin Shaw
Shirley S. Raguindin
Sonia T. Delen Fitzsimmons
Susie Quesada
Thelma Boac

2013

Al Perez
Arlene Marie "Bambi" Lorica
Alicia Fortaleza
Cynthia Rapaido
Edcelyn Pujol
Elena Mangahas

2013 *(cont.)*

Franklin M. Ricarte
Gloria T. Caoile
Marily Mondejar
Maria Roseni "Nini"
  M. Alvero
Maya Ong Escudero
Mutya San Agustin Shaw
Shirley S. Raguindin
Sonia T. Delen
  Fitzsimmons
Susie Quesada
Thelma Boac

2014

Arlene Marie "Bambi"
  Lorica
Alicia Fortaleza
Delle Sering Fojas
Edcelyn Pujol
Elena Mangahas
Franklin M. Ricarte
Gizelle Covarrubias
  Robinson
Gloria T. Caoile
Marily Mondejar
Maria Roseni "Nini"
  M. Alvero
Maria A. Beebe, Ph.D.
Maya Ong Escudero
Mutya San Agustin Shaw
Shirley S. Raguindin
Sonia T. Delen Fitzsimmons
Susie Quesada
Thelma Boac

2013 Awards – 100 Most Influential Filipina Women in the World (Global FWN100™)

BEHIND THE SCENES LEADERS

Bessie Badilla
Elizabeth Ann Quirino
Emma Cuenca

Genevieve Jopanda
Loisa Cabuhat

Maria Beebe
Regina Manzana-Sawhney

BUILDERS

Carmela Clendening
Imelda M. Nicolas

Jocelyn Ding
Nina D. Aguas

Rebecca Delgado Rottman

EMERGING LEADERS

Ariel Batungbacal
Christina Luna

Meriam Reynosa
Michele Bumgarner

Patricia Gallardo-Dwyer

FOUNDERS & PIONEERS

Allyson Tintiangco-Cubales
Bella Aurora Padua-Belmonte
Dawn Bohulano Mabalon
Delle Sering-Fojas
Ernestina de los Santos-Mac
Evelia V. Religioso
Isabelita Manalastas-Watanabe

Joselyn Geaga-Rosenthal
Julieta Gabiola
Librada C. Yamat
Loida Nicolas Lewis
Lydia Cruz
Maria Almia de los Santos

Mariedel Leviste
Marife Zamora
Norma Fulinara Placido
Patricia Zamora Riingen
Rosemer Enverga
Tess Mauricio

INNOVATORS AND THOUGHT LEADERS

Amelia Duran-Stanton
Annette M. David
Carmencita David-Padilla
Janet C. Mendoza Stickmon

Janet Susan R. Nepales
Lirio Sobreviñas Covey
Lucille Lozada Tenazas
Mary Ann Lucille L. Sering

Mary Jane Alvero-Al Mahdi
Mira Soriano Gillet
Rozita Villanueva Lee
Suzie Moya Benitez

POLICYMAKERS & VISIONARIES

Astrid S. Tuminez
Cora Manese Tellez
Eleanor Valentin

Hydra Mendoza-McDonnell
Imelda Cuyugan
Gloria T. Caoile

Kris Valderrama
Margaret Lapiz
Patricia V. Paez

2014 Awards –100 Most Influential Filipina Women in the World (Global FWN100™)

BEHIND THE SCENES LEADERS

Consuelo "Chit" Lijauco
Elvie Abordo
Fritzie Igno
M. Evelina Galang

BUILDERS

Aida Garcia, Esq.
Carmen Lamagna Ph.D.
Filomenita Mongaya-Hoegsholm
Ivic Mueco
Judy Arteche-Carr
Ma. Rhodora "Ayhee" L. Campos
Marianne Hontiveros
Marie Claire Lim Moore
Wafa 'Marilyn' R. Qasimieh, Ph.D.
Mary Ann Covarrubias Ph.D.
Milagros Sering
Myrna Obligacion Carreon
Nora Kakilala-Terrado
Olivia Valera Palala
Sarah Songalia
Zenei Triunfo-Cortez RN

EMERGING LEADERS

Janice Lao-Noche
Melissa Ramoso

FOUNDERS & PIONEERS

Analisa Balares
Angelica Berrie
Catherine Feliciano-Chon
Conchita "Chit" Bathan
Darlene Marie Berberabe
Delia Domingo-Albert
Edith Villanueva
Karen Batungbacal
Ma. Victoria Añonuevo

INNOVATORS AND THOUGHT LEADERS

Boots Anson Roa-Rodrigo
Cris Comerford
Grace Princesa
Ida Ramos-Henares
Jennifer Lopez Fernan
Josefina "Chef Jessie" Sincioco
Maria Lourdes (Marides) Fernando, MPS
Maria Ressa
Patricia Espiritu-Halagao
Teresita Pullin

NICOLE

Monique Wilson

POLICYMAKERS & VISIONARIES

Delia Rodriguez-Amaya, Ph.D.
Maria Castañeda
Maria Teresa Bonifacio Cenzon
Rida Cabanilla
Ruth Uy Asmundson, Ph.D.
Thetis Mangahas

2015 Awards –100 Most Influential Filipina Women in the World (Global FWN100™)

BEHIND THE SCENES LEADERS

Agnes Joyce Garlit Bailen
Angelica Ligas
Cheryl Sevegan
Em Angeles
Hazel Dolio Tag'at

Leonor S. Vintervoll
Leslie Y. Tabor
Lisa Suguitan Melnick
Maria Cecilia "Cecile" Gregorio Ascalon
Susan Bautista Afan

BUILDERS

Aimee Alado
Annabelle Misa Hefti
Aurora Abella Austriaco
Catherine Campbell
Cathy Salceda Ileto
Elizabeth J. Bautista
Grace Trinidad Vergara
Imelda "Emmie" Collado Ortega Anderson

Leticia "Letty" Quizon
Pet Hartman
Salve Vargas Edelman
Sonia Lugmao Aranza,
Stephanie Lomibao
Tess Martillano-Manjares
Tiffany Bohee
Trina Villanueva

EMERGING LEADERS

Francine Maigue
Juslyn C. Manalo
Kharissa Fernando

Michelle Joyce Florendo
Noelani Sallings
Patricia Quema La Chica

FOUNDERS & PIONEERS

Ace T. Itchon
Hedy Marie Leuterio Thomas, PE
Irene Sun-Kaneko
Juanita Nimfa Yamsuan Gamez

Maria Nieves Santos-Greaves
Myrna Tang Yao
Tessa Yutadco

INNOVATORS AND THOUGHT LEADERS

Glenda Tibe Bonifacio
Melissa Orquiza

Ramona Diaz
Vina Lustado

POLICYMAKERS & VISIONARIES

Lorna G. Schofield

Luisa Vicerra-Blue

KEEPERS OF THE FLAME

Amar Bornkamp
Alicia Fortaleza
Bambi Lorica, MD, FAAP
Edcelyn Pujol, CFP
Elena Mangahas

Gloria T. Caoile
Maria Beebe, Ph.D.
Maria Roseni "Nini" M. Alvero
Marily Mondejar
Colonel Shirley S. Raguindin

Sonia T. Delen
Susie Quesada
Thelma Boac

2016 Awards –100 Most Influential Filipina Women in the World (Global FWN100™)

BEHIND THE SCENES LEADERS

Ana Bel Mayo
Belen M. Saramosing- Ramirez
Carlota Hufana Ader
Carmen Garcia
Elena "Jingjing" Villanueva Romero
Imelda Martin Hum

Maria Victoria Jose Cuisia
Melanie C. Ng
Rachel U. Salinel
Rocio Nuyda
Sandy Sanchez Montano
Theresita "Tita" Q. Dumagsa

BUILDERS

Arlene Abe Pulido
Bernadette M. Schlueter
Cristina "Bea" Teh-Tan
Charina Mundo Vergara
Eloiza T.B. Domingo-Snyder
Irene Corpuz
Lorna Patajo-Kapunan
Magnolia Misolas Uy

Maria Cristina "Ginbee" Layug Go
Maria Socorro "Cory" Valenzuela Vidanes
Marites T. Dagdag
Milalin Sarenas-Javellana
Mona Lisa Bautista Dela Cruz
Patricia "Pixie" Javier- Gutierrez
Rosario Cajucom-Bradbury
Stella Solero Bernabe

EMERGING LEADERS

Anne Quintos
Eva Marie Wang
Mary Lou Flores Cunanan

FOUNDERS & PIONEERS

Agnes A. Gervacio
Amparito Llamas Lhuillier
Christine Amour-Levar
Cynthia Romero Mamon
Gina Garcia Atienza
Glenda Barretto
Janette Nellie Go-Chiu
Karen Graciles Libarios Remo

Maria Rosa 'Bing' Nieva Carrion, Ph.D.
Malou N. Santos
Marylou Ty Garcia
Nancy Reyes Lumen
Ophelia Mananquil-Bakker
Paulette Deduque-Liu
Raquel Toquero-Choa
Rosalind L. Wee

INNOVATORS AND THOUGHT LEADERS

Caroline Marian Santos-Enriquez
Cynthia Carrion, President
Edita A. De Leon
Mylene Romualdez Abiva

Karen Ida Alparce-Villanueva
Marina Durano
Olivia Limpe Aw

NICOLE

Leni Robredo

POLICYMAKERS & VISIONARIES

Maria Milagros Fernan Cayosa

CONTINUING INFLUENCERS

Ace Itchon

Annabelle Misa Hefti

Chit Lijauco

Emma Imperial

Josefina "Chef Jessie" Sincioco

Karen Batungbacal

Maan Hontiveros

Myrna Tang Yao

Nora Kakilala Terrado

Pet R. Hartman

KEEPERS OF THE FLAME

Amar Bornkamp

Bambi Lorica

Delle Sering

Elena Mangahas

Gloria T. Caoile

Josephine Romero

Maria Beebe, Ph.D.

Maria Roseni "Nini" M. Alvero

Marily Mondejar

Colonel Shirley S. Raguindin

Sonia T. Delen

Susie Quesada

Thelma Boac

2017 Awards –100 Most Influential Filipina Women in the World (Global FWN100™)

BEHIND THE SCENES LEADERS

Ann Mariza Nepomuceno Sanchez-Bensurto
Editha Tijamo Winterhalter, Ed.D.
Cristina Calaguian

Engr. Lilian Maria Soriano Bautista
Rosary Escaño

BUILDERS

Isabelita "Lita" M. Abele
Jacqueline D. Yu, Esq.
Leah L. Laxamana
Lou Olvido Parroco
Mary Ann Gamboa

Myrna P. Young, MSN, RN, CNOR
Rebecca Murry
Rowena Romulo
Roxane Martin Negrillo
Wilma 'Amy' Eisma

EMERGING LEADERS

Claire Aquino Quito
Joanne Michelle Fernandez Ocampo
Kristina Laranjo Alabado

FOUNDERS & PIONEERS

Cherry Pua Africa
Claire Navarro Espina, Esq.
Cora dela Cruz
Dina Dela Paz Stalder
Edna Consing Concepcion

Joji Ilagan Bian
Kalika Nacion Yap
Mercedes Muldong Calderon
Nikki Tang

INNOVATORS AND THOUGHT LEADERS

Anna-Karina Tabuñar
Catherine Teh, M.D.
Fidelina "Faye" Adan Corcuera
Georgitta 'Beng' Pimentel Puyat

Geri Alumit Zeldes, Ph.D.
Gizelle Covarrubias Robinson
Jennifer Marie B. José, M.D.

POLICYMAKERS & VISIONARIES

Hon. Cynthia Alcantara Barker
Jerrilyn Malana, Esq.
HE Junever Melchor Mahilum-West
Lily Torres-Samoranos

Ma. Nieves R. Confesor
Mila Eustaquio-Syme
HE Petronila P. Garcia
Hon. Rosalinda V. Canlas

CONTINUING INFLUENTIAL

Mary Jane Alvero-Al Mahdi

KEEPERS OF THE FLAME

Amar Bornkamp
Bambi Lorica, M.D., FAAP
Elizabeth Bautista
Gloria T. Caoile
Leonor Vintervoll
Maria Beebe, Ph.D.
Maria Roseni "Nini" M. Alvero
Maria Santos Greaves
Marily Mondejar
Rosario Cajucom-Bradbury
Colonel Shirley S. Raguindin
Susie Quesada
Hon. Thelma Boac

2018 Awards –100 Most Influential Filipina Women in the World (Global FWN100™)

BEHIND THE SCENES LEADERS

Lolita Johansson
Maria Trinidad Manalo Maramba

Marietta Palacio Revilla
Novabel Teves Fossgard

BUILDERS

Cristina Manahan Llamzon, Ph.D.
Elena Francisco Samson
Joy Murao
Joyce Rivera Javier

Maria Victoria M. Acosta
Mary Cheryl Bravo Gloner, MPH
Consuelo "Chit" Lijauco
Ruby Canteras Pacis

EMERGING LEADERS

Ann Michelle Bagayna Mondragon
Christen-Leonor Santos Montero
Trish Marie Edar Marco

FOUNDERS & PIONEERS

Angela Katrina Adams
Conchita Labao Manabat, Ph.D.

Crystal Dias LLB
Mildred Christine Flores Piad, Ph.D.

INNOVATORS & THOUGHT LEADERS

Alexandra Noelle Cuerdo
Angie Go Flaminiano
Marissa Estiva Magsino, MD, ARFM

Pamela Gotangco
Hon. Susan Pineda Mercado, MD, MPH

NICOLE

Hon. Gwendolyn Fiel Garcia

POLICYMAKERS & VISIONARIES

Hon. Rachelle Sumagaysay Pastor Arizmendi
Hon. Wendy Lee Ho

CONTINUING INFLUENTIAL

Hon. Juslyn Cabrera Manalo

KEEPERS OF THE FLAME

Amar Bornkamp
Dr. Caroline Marian Enriquez
Georgitta "Beng" Pimentel Puyat
Leonor Vintervoll
Maria Beebe, Ph.D.
Maria Roseni "Nini" M. Alvero
Maria Santos Greaves
HON Marily Mondejar
Susie Quesada
HON Thelma Boac

2019 Awards –100 Most Influential Filipina Women in the World (Global FWN100™)

BEHIND THE SCENES LEADERS

Cristina Manahan Llamzon, Ph.D.
Corazon Sobrevega Laraya-Coutts
Gemalin Batino Diaz
Lorena Domanog Clerc
Maria Consolacion P. Geroche

Maria Paz Rosales Alberto
Maria Zelda Magistrado Rojas
Pauline Plata Bondad
Dr. Yasmin Balajadia Cortes
Zarah Jane D Juan

BUILDERS

Dr. Aileen Mariategue Villanueva
Ana Margarita Navarro Hontiveros
Erlinda Lacson Olalia-Carin
Madelene Eloisa Labandilo Ortega
Atty. Margarita Navarro Gutierrez

Maria Amparo Victoria Trinidad Yee
Maria Fides Lagamon Balita
Maria Jacinta Victoria Torino Lualhati Ph.D.
Teresita Ignacio Batayola

EMERGING LEADER

Nicola Louise Negapatan Paclibar

FOUNDERS & PIONEERS

Dr. Bernadette Jardiolin Madrid
Carmina Montesa Aldana
Charina Palomares Garcia
Ellen Ferrer Samson
Fe Odsigue Punzalan

Mildred Vande Vusse Vitangcol
Dr. Ninez Ponce Dr. Ninez Ponce
Nora G Galleros-Tinio
Rhodora Perpetua Palomar-Fresnedi
Atty. Rosario Calixto Chavez

INNOVATORS & THOUGHT LEADERS

Anna Isabel Crisostomo Sobrepeña
Arlene Oliveros
Charlene Consolacion
Ildeme Mahinay Koch
Kristen Nicole Brillantes
Maria Ester Follosco Bautista

Maria Francesca Dela Fuente Tan
Ma. Kristina Grace Penalosa Carpio
Maria Victoria B Garcia
Nerissa Mendoza Gerial
Rose Anne de Pampelonne

POLICYMAKER & VISIONARY

Clarissa Eleanor Bravo

CONTINUING INFLUENTIAL: INNOVATOR & THOUGHT LEADER

Maria Beebe, Ph.D.

KEEPERS OF THE FLAME

Amar Bornkamp
Caroline Marian Enriquez, MD
Georgitta "Beng" Pimentel Puyat
Leonor Vintervoll
Maria Roseni "Nini" M. Alvero
Maria Santos Greaves
Marily Mondejar
Susie Quesada
Hon. Thelma Boac

2021 Awards –100 Most Influential Filipina Women in the World (Global FWN100™)

BUILDERS

Alicia del Prado, Ph.D.
Arlene Tordecilla Ferrolino
Charity Nicolas
Cynthia CK Suero-Gabler

Holly Vocal
Joanne De Guzman Rico
Kathy V. Lai
Melissa Sanvictores

EMERGING LEADERS

Carla Laurel
Korina Alvarez Mercado

FOUNDERS & PIONEERS

Grace Reyes
Marla D. Rausch
Dr. Mary Joy Canon Abaquin
Rhoda Castro Caliwara

INNOVATORS & THOUGHT LEADERS

Annabelle Manalo-Morgan, Ph.D.
Denise Lopez, Ph.D.
Giovannie Espiritu

Jaclyn Tolentino, Ph.D.
Lucia Olalia Reyes
Paula Rosales

KEEPERS OF THE FLAME

Benel Se Liban
Carol Enriquez, MD
Charina Garcia, Esq.
Fe Punzalan
Genevieve Jopanda
Georgitta "Beng" Pimentel Puyat
Gi na Atienza
Juslyn Manalo

Leonor Vintervoll
Lorna Kapunan, Esq.
Maria Beebe, Ph.D.
Marily Mondejar
Marla D. Rausch
Mica Tan
Susie Quesada

2022 Awards –100 Most Influential Filipina Women in the World (Global FWN100™)

BUILDERS

Catalina Manarin Bagsic
Dr. Eileen P. de Villa
Gwendolyn T. Pang
Jane Po Panganiban
Judis Guintu Santo

Kristine Custodio Suero
Malve Peralta Ildefonso
Patricia Kaye Yeh Choa
Patricia Quebada Clerkin

FOUNDERS & PIONEERS

Annaflor Feliprada-Patrizio
Cymbeline Tancongco Culiat, Ph.D.
Elena Cacho Tesoro, Ph.D.
Ma. Cristine Caringal Melad

Maria Regina A. Alfonso
Ma. Teresa Beltran Chan
Melesa Dy Chua
Myra Colis

INNOVATORS & THOUGHT LEADERS

Grace Gorospe-Jamon, Ph.D.
Jenette E. C. Ramos
Dr. Jennifer Camota Luebke

Joycelyn David
Judy Anne Santos-Sierszula
Regina Pascua Berba

POLICYMAKERS & VISIONARIES

Mayor Maria Sheilah Honrado Lacuna-Pangan
Deputy Mayor Myla Arceno
MP Rechie Valdez
Mayor Sofia Asuncion Anis Aragon

KEEPERS OF THE FLAME

Benel Se Liban
Carol Enriquez
Fe Punzalan
Georgitta Pimentel Puyat
Gina Atienza
Juslyn Manalo

Leonor Vintervoll
Lorna Kapunan
Maria Beebe, Ph.D.
Marily Mondejar
Mica Tan
Susie Quesada

BIOGRAPHIES

MARIA A. BEEBE, PH.D.
Editor
Introduction
Engendering Leadership
Synthesis

Global ❧ Educator ❧ Katipunera

Maria Beebe has expertise in engendering women's leadership in international development, discourse analysis, and digital technologies for improving quality education. She has a masters in Anthropology and a Ph.D. in Education from Stanford University. For over 25 years, Maria has successfully developed large multistakeholder programs that bring together academics, industry practitioners, and policymakers in Africa, Afghanistan, and the Philippines. She led Knowledge Exchanges & Learning Partnerships (KELP) in South Africa (1995), Nettel@Africa in Africa (1996-2005), and Afghan eQuality Alliances in Afghanistan (2006-2009). Maria has shared her global experience through international conferences, such as the International Leadership Association annual conference, the Internet Governance Forum, and the FWN leadership summit. Maria is on the Fulbright Specialist Program roster and a Department of Anthropology affiliate at Portland State University. Maria co-edited AfricaDotEdu and edited three books about the leadership of global Filipina women: *DISRUPT 1, 2 and 3. Filipina Women: Rising* (2018). Maria is a consultant to develop the Asia Open RAN Academy based in the Philippines with an Indo-Pacific focus. Her latest pro-bono initiative is Kaisipan, launched at the time of COVID-19. Kaisipan aims to improve digital capabilities for all educators and learners in the Philippines to contribute to Sustainable development goal 4. Inclusive and equitable quality education and promote lifelong learning opportunities for all.

SUSAN CELIA SWAN
Preface

Visionary Activist ❧ Movement Architect ❧ Dynamic Leader

Susan Celia Swan is an activist, organizer, and producer whose work has centered on the role of art in culture and system change. Instrumental in creating RAINN, Feminist.com, and V-Day, she serves as the Executive Director of V-Day, the global activist movement to end violence against all women, girls, gender expansive people, and the planet, and sits on the boards of V-Day and Feminist.com.

Susan's efforts have been integral to developing the V-Day movement, which grew from a one-night benefit to a wide-ranging global non-profit with a presence in over 200 countries and territories. V-Day campaigns have educated communities, changed laws to protect women and girls, and raised well over $120 million in urgently needed funds for groups working to end violence and serve survivors and their families.

Susan oversees all aspects of V-Day, including One Billion Rising and City of Joy, creating and developing campaigns, producing award-winning films and videos, staging artistic events, and managing finance, development, and communications. V-Day has taken Susan across the United States and the world addressing the issue of violence against all women and girls, including the Philippines, Haiti, Kenya, Europe, India, Egypt, and the Democratic Republic of Congo, where V-Day opened and supported the City of Joy. In this transformational leadership center, survivors of gender violence turn their pain into power.

MARILY MONDEJAR

Foreword
Becoming Influential to be Influential

Fearless Leader ❧ Grassroots Organizer ❧ Community Advocate

Marily Mondejar has parlayed her success as a business leader and image consultant into founding the successful non-profit, non-partisan advocacy organization, the Filipina Women's Network (FWN). FWN has members in 28 countries and seeks to increase the influence of Filipina women as leaders and policymakers in the private and public sectors. Mondejar has steered the organization to a leading position in the Filipina women community worldwide. Ms. Mondejar's campaign to re-shape the Filipina image grew out her necessity to elevate the status of Filipina women. In 2001, an internet search for the word Filipina returned millions of hits, including "mail-order brides, sluts, exotic, sexy and submissive wives." Her plan was to highlight the leadership roles and economic contributions of Filipina women in corporate America, small business, public service, and the government.

As an executive coach and management consultant, she has provided counsel to the senior leadership of prestigious organizations. Ms. Mondejar is recognized for the Image 360®-degree assessment questionnaire,

a method for measuring executive image performance and corporate reputation. She has delivered business, career, and image presentations in a variety of formats and has reached over 10,000 participants internationally. A select list of international and trade publications that have quoted Mondejar include The Chicago Tribune, Dallas Morning News, AdWeek, Self, Allure, Working Woman, Black Enterprise, Academy of General Dentistry's AGD Impact, El Norte (Mexico), Cintermex Magazine (Mexico), Momentum (magazine for Mercedes Benz owners), and various TV, radio and publications in the US, Philippines, Canada, and the UK.

Ms. Mondejar balances her professional life with advocating for other women in the business arena and serves on multiple boards engaged in public service, community, philanthropic, and professional development. She has been appointed to commissions and task forces by San Francisco Mayors Willie Brown, Gavin Newsom, and Edwin Lee.

A resident of San Francisco, she has raised two wonderful sons as a single mother and is a proud grandmother of three boys and adores her new great-granddaughter.

CARMINA MONTESA ALDANA
Choosing. Being. Succeeding.

Loving ✐ Thoughtful ✐ Principled

Born into a diplomat family, Carmina has an international view of social issues and had early exposure to the hardship minorities endure. Her experiences inspired her to improve people's lives.

Mother, wife, philanthropist, and 2019 FWN Global 100™ Awardee, Carmina is co-founder and executive director of The Neurosurgery Outreach Foundation (NOF). NOF is a U.S.-based non-profit organization that advances neurosurgical care globally in underserved communities through service, education, and support. Its education-focused programs impact the lives of patients, providers, students, and health systems in Southeast Asia.

As a University of Toronto student, she founded the Kabataan Theatre Group, which produced original plays. Professionally, she began in Human Resources, which included work in a Fortune 500 company. Later, she launched a jewelry business and was involved in the Junior League of Akron. In 2021, Carmina successfully became a member of Leadership Jacksonville. Recently, she commissioned the first Filipino Heritage Mural in the city in partnership with the Cultural Council of Greater Jacksonville and The Jessie.

Carmina continues collaborating with individuals and organizations on children's wellbeing, Philippine culture, Jacksonville's cultural arts, and women's causes. She enjoys relaxing with family and friends, traveling, reading, walking, and dogs for recreation.

GINA GARCIA ATIENZA
When New Year Comes in October

Friendly ✐ Caring ✐ Hardworking

Gina Garcia Atienza is an FWN 100 Most Influential Filipinas in the World Awardee 2016. She grew up in the island paradise of Cebu and finished her fourth year in high school at St. Theresa's College, Cebu, but graduated from the Rancho Alamitos High School, Garden Grove, California. She obtained her Bachelor of Arts Degree in Economics from the Ateneo de Manila University, Quezon City. In addition, she earned a post-graduate Diploma in International Relations and Development from the International Institute of Social Studies, Den Haag, The Netherlands. Gina worked in Corporate Communications in both Jakarta, Indonesia and Tokyo, Japan. She returned to Cebu in 2000 and produced the first annual *Cebu Yearbook* for the SunStar Media Group. She later became President of SunStar Management Inc., which manages the Group's affiliate network. Gina retired in 2020 but has remained as Acting Chairman of the Board of SunStar and President of SunStar Davao. She now runs Java Pavilion, an online boutique and shop selling curated Asian furniture and antiques, including petrified wood and obsidian crystals from Indonesia.

MARIA FIDES BALITA
Trust Your Inner GPS

Charismatic ❧ Entrepreneurial ❧ Driven

Maria Fides Balita is a Certified Public Accountant and a financial professional. Maria recently retired as a partner at a woman and minority-owned Certified Public Accounting Firm in Chicago, Illinois. She provided audit and consulting services to clients in the government, lottery, gaming, transit, housing authority, university, 401k/403b, pensions, and not-for-profit industries. Maria served as Chair of the National Executive Board of the International Society of Filipinos in Finance and Accounting (2018–2021) and now serves on the Advisory Board. In her new endeavor as a financial professional and registered representative of a broker/dealer, she aims to pursue another passion: to guide and educate families and individuals about financial independence, particularly in helping prepare for retirement and protecting their assets.

TERESITA BATAYOLA
The Ark of Purposeful Leadership. My Story

Visionary ❧ Tenacious ❧ Communicator

Teresita Batayola is a first-generation Filipino American. Immigrating to the U.S. in 1969, her family encountered the prolonged Boeing Bust economic recession. Like many immigrants, Luis and Dolores Batayola struggled to make a better life for the family, succeeding in having their children Teresita, Maria, and Louie educated and distinguishing themselves with public service careers. Teresita is the President and Chief Executive Officer of International Community Health Services (ICHS) in King County, Washington. ICHS is Washington state's largest Asian and Pacific Islander non-profit health center providing comprehensive health care to all who need affordable care in 70 languages, especially immigrants and refugees. She grew ICHS from 2 sites to 11 sites. Over 75% of the patients are low-income, with ICHS providing over $1 million in uncompensated care. Under her leadership, ICHS has received numerous state and national awards for high-quality care. In 2022, Teresita was appointed by U.S. President Joseph Biden to the President's Advisory Commission on Asian Americans, Native Hawaiians, and Pacific Islanders. In addition, Teresita serves on the Seattle Community Colleges' Board of Trustees and community health care boards. She is a tenacious advocate for health equity, access, and quality. She draws her balance and core from her loving husband Dionnie Dionisio, and her daughters, Gabriela and Ariana Dionisio, who are making their own impact on humanity.

ANGELICA URRA BERRIE

Becoming Ruth: A Transformational Journey

Passion ❧ Purpose ❧ Philanthropy

Angelica Urra Berrie is President of The Russell Berrie Foundation, a philanthropic leader known for transformational gifts to the Naomi Berrie Diabetes Center at Columbia University in New York, the Russ Berrie Nanotechnology Institute at the Technion in Israel, and The Pope John Paul Il Center for Inter-Religious Studies at St. Thomas Aquinas University of the Angelicum in Rome. A widow leader, Angelica took the helm as Vice-Chair and CEO of Russ Berrie & Co., a global gift company, after the loss of her husband, New Jersey sales entrepreneur Russell Berrie. Angelica was Board Chair of the Center for Inter-Religious Understanding and Co-Chair of the Jewish Funders Network. In addition, Angelica is Chair of the Shalom Hartman Institute, a center for pluralistic Jewish learning in Jerusalem. Angelica is Co-President of the American Friends of Ofanim, a nonprofit organization in Israel whose mission is to deliver high-quality supplemental education to children in the periphery using mobile classrooms. Angelica is the Co-Founder of Global Nomad, an experiential travel company established by Lorenzo Urra in Hong Kong. She co-authored a book on philanthropy: *A Passion for Giving: Tools and Inspiration for Creating a Charitable Foundation*, with wealth adviser Peter Klein.

RHODA CALIWARA

Divine and Human Agency in My Leadership

Clarity ❧ Consistency ❧ Compassion.

Consistency is what makes an average transform into excellence. As a woman who mustered up grit and courage, Rhoda will let you rediscover the power of being a woman with a strength that comes from God. She will highlight the celebration of her small wins. Her inner drive to set clear goals and communicate effectively to her people set her apart. Yet, her being is shaped by what she consistently does each day. She will let you experience a one-of-a-kind journey of self-compassion that helped her to move forward gracefully as she allows herself to cope and have a safe space to grow and build again. Rhoda will remind you that you are not your crisis. You are not your mistake. It is inevitable. Let it not overwhelm you. As you keep your eyes on your purpose, you can have a better perspective on things that enables you to maintain your identity. Focus is more valuable than intelligence.

Rhoda is Future Focus. It is beyond the ability of your foresight. It is your ability to focus on solutions for positive change that encompasses adversity. As you actively listen to current challenges, it enables you to find long-term solutions for potential challenges. She will emphasize that building genuine connections, and finding and becoming a mentor empowers us a life beyond our personal interests. It's adding value to people, respecting differences, and building a community where we can capitalize on our strength—our natural being.

ATTY. ROSARIO CALIXTO "CHITO" CHAVEZ
Creating Destiny

Steadfast Leader ❧ High Achiever ❧ Compassionate

"Chito" as she is fondly called, received the "Most Influential Filipina Woman in the World AwardTM (Global FWN100TM)" in 2019, and now advocates for increasing the power and influence of Filipina women worldwide as a member of the FWN. A consistent achiever in college, Chito earned the distinction of representing the Philippines in the Asia Pacific Project of the U.S. Department of State in the USA, besting all student leaders in the Philippines. She was also Captain Ball of the Volleyball Varsity team, bringing the first WNCAA championship to PWU. After retiring from HSBC where she spent 35 years, Chito reinvented her career as a one-stop shop for estate settlement as a lawyer, financial and investment specialist, and real estate broker. She also became active in the academe as a law professor and ex-officio member of the PWU Board of Trustees, a position she concurrently held as President of the PWU Alumni Association from 2019–2022. Notable accomplishments included: Charter President of the first all-woman club in the world of the Kiwanis International; DCC for Service Projects and Editor of the Governor's Monthly Letter in Rotary. As Zontian, she advocated projects closest to her heart—"No to Violence against Women;" as an environmentalist, she introduced solid waste management in Tahanan Village, paving the way for her being selected in a conservation expedition in Tasmania, Australia by HSBC London.

ALICIA DEL PRADO, PH.D.
Follow Your Heart

Kind ❧ Strong ❧ Persevering

Alicia del Prado, Ph.D. is a licensed psychologist, consultant, author, and tenured faculty member at the Wright Institute. Dr. del Prado earned her Ph.D. in counseling psychology from Washington State University, specializes in diversity, equity, and inclusion work, and provides therapy to clients in her private practice. She created the first enculturation scale for Filipino Americans and has co-authored numerous publications on cross-cultural studies of personality. In addition, Dr. del Prado wrote *Proud of my Mommy* and *It's Time to Talk (and Listen): How to Have Constructive Conversations About Race, Class, Sexuality, Ability & Gender in a Polarized World* She is a past-chair of the Asian American Psychology Association's (AAPA) Division on Filipinx Americans, chaired the first national Filipino American Psychology Conference, and co-editor of the first Special Issue on Filipino American Psychology. Moreover, Dr. del Prado founded the AAPA's Division on Multiracial and Adopted Asian Americans. Dr. del Prado values making psychological literature accessible to the public and writes a Psychology Today blog, "Speaking from the Heart." Nationally recognized for her leadership, service, and scholarship, Dr. del Prado received awards from the National Council of Schools and Programs in Professional Psychology, AAPA, and the California Psychological Association.

CORA DELA CRUZ-TORRES
Leading My Life

Confident ❧ Compassionate ❧ Committed

Cora has been President of Trade Alliances Canada Inc. since 2018. She has over 20 years of experience working with entrepreneurs, small and medium-sized companies, and government organizations and establishing connections between Canada and the Philippines. Until she retired from the Ontario provincial government in 2001, she held a wide range of executive positions in the Ministry of Consumer and Commercial Relations, Business Practices Division. Roles included those in the real estate sector, tourism and travel sector, bereavement sector, ICT sector, and legislation for business regulation and consumer protection. She then moved and lived in the Philippines from 2012 to 2018 to serve as National Executive Director for the Canadian Chamber of Commerce. In Canada, Cora served as President of the National Alliance of Philippine Business Trade and Tourism from 2009 to 2012, President of the Philippine Chamber of Commerce from 2005 to 2007, President of the Canadian Association of Philippine Travel Agents from 2001 to 2005, and Regional Vice President of the National Council of Filipino-Canadians from 1992 to 1998. Her awards include One of the Most Outstanding Filipino-Canadians; One of the Most Outstanding President of Philippine Associations in Canada; 1999 Asian of the Year in Business and Public Service category; 2004 Entrepreneur of the Year at the International Women's Day, and One of the Global FWN100. Cora was born and raised in Tarlac City, Philippines. Cora and her husband have lived in Canada for over 50 years. They have six children and eight grandchildren who live in the U.S., Canada, New Zealand, and the Philippines.

SONIA DELEN
Power of Connection

Community ❧ Compassion ❧ Stewardship

Sonia Delen is Senior Vice President at Bank of America-Global Leasing, a division of Bank of America. Sonia serves on the Board of the Bank's Leadership, Education, Advocacy and Development (LEAD) for Women. Appointed by Governor Jerry Brown in 2018, Sonia is a non-lawyer and public member of the Board of Trustees of the State Bar of California, the regulatory, admissions, and disciplinary agency of the Supreme Court of California, the first Filipina American to serve as trustee. Before the State Bar, Sonia was a Health Professions Education Foundation Trustee. Sonia is president of the Filipino Food Movement, aimed to preserve, promote and progress Filipino cuisine in the mainstream globally. She is a film executive producer and author (chapter in *DISRUPT. Filipina Women: Proud. Loud. Leading Without A Doubt*). Her awards include the Top 50 Women Leaders of San Francisco 2022 by Women We Admire publication; FilAms Among the Remarkable and Famous 2021 series of Positively Filipino; and Founders Award from the San Diego Filipino Cinema. In 2021, Sonia received the TOPHATS Gibbey Award (Top Outstanding Professionals and High Achieving Teams); and in 2020, 100 Most Influential Filipinos in America by The Outstanding Filipino American (TOFA) Awards. In addition, the Filipina Women's Network (FWN) honored Sonia as one of the 100 Most Influential Filipina Women in the World, 2013; and FWN100 Most Influential Filipina Women in the U.S., 2007. Sonia graduated from the University of the Philippines. Sonia lives in San Francisco with her spouse, Christopher Fitzsimmons, and their children: David, Justin, and Matthew.

ARLENE TORDECILLA FERROLINO
The Joy of Sharing Music

Pianist ❧ Music Educator ❧ Advocate

Arlene's background combines bachelor's degrees in Music Education and English from the Adventist University of the Philippines (AUP) with post-graduate work in piano performance and collaborative piano at The Colburn School of Performing Arts and the University of Southern California (USC). She is a professional pianist, organist, accompanist, classroom teacher and church musician, a nationally renowned piano adjudicator, clinician, and lecturer. As the first Asian president of the Board of Directors for the Glendale Branch of the Music Teachers' Association of California, she served three terms. In addition, she is the historic first president of the Board of Directors of the Filipino American Symphony Orchestra (FASO), the first and only Filipino symphony orchestra outside the Philippines. In 2018 she was awarded outstanding alumna by the AUP AWESNA (AUP alumni of North America). She recently received the Filipina Women's Network award as one of the 100 Most Influential Filipinas in the World 2021. Also, she received the Outstanding Teacher Award 2021 from Steinway and Sons. As a music educator and advocate, she enjoys sharing the joy of music with her students and the community locally and globally.

PAMELA GOTANGCO
Heart Full of Passion

Creative ❧ Resilient ❧ Kind

Pamela Gotangco is a visual artist, wearable art designer, and entrepreneur living in Switzerland. Recently she received the 2021 Pamana ng Pilipino Presidential award. This award is conferred on overseas Filipino individuals who have brought the country honor and recognition through excellence and distinction in the pursuit of their work or profession. Her art is heavily anchored in advocating for the empowerment of all women and girls, promoting the Filipino culture and artisans in the global arena, and uniting the Filipino migrants abroad by highlighting the beauty of our culture and heritage. On the same note, she aims to inspire and encourage Filipinos worldwide to showcase their talent and shine in the global arena.

In response to the pandemic, Pamela co-founded PamPinay clothing line. PamPinay is a fashion-forward brand born at the height of the global pandemic as a social project with a mission to provide income opportunities for women in the Philippines who were affected by the pandemic. In addition, PamPinay showcases one hundred percent Filipino-made crafts aimed to promote social entrepreneurship, sustainability, and responsible branding through the playful illustration of funny Filipino habits and traits.

Pamela received her Bachelor of Arts in Communication from Miriam College, Philippines.

JOYCE JAVIER MD, MPH, MS
For Us, By Us

Mother ✎ Pediatrician ✎ Scientist

Joyce Javier MD, MPH, MS, is an Associate Professor of Clinical Pediatrics at Children's Hospital Los Angeles and the Keck School of Medicine at the University of Southern California in the Departments of Pediatrics and Population and Public Health Sciences. She completed pediatrics residency training and a postdoctoral fellowship in general academic pediatrics at Stanford University. She is a pediatrician scientist whose research has focused on promoting the well-being of Filipino youth and families by using community-based participatory research to implement and evaluate evidence-based parenting interventions. She leads the Filipino Family Health Initiative, funded by the National Institutes of Health, the American Academy of Pediatrics (AAP), and the Robert Wood Johnson Foundation (RWJF) Clinical Scholars Program. She serves as an Executive Committee Member on the American Academy of Pediatrics (AAP) Council on Community Pediatrics, Co-chair of the Society for Pediatric Research Advocacy Committee, and a member of the Pediatric Policy Council. She also teaches trainees as a pediatrician at AltaMed Health Services and as an instructor in the USC MPH program. Dr. Javier has received several awards for her work, including the AAP Local Hero Award and the 2021 RWJF Award for Health Equity. She is the proud mother of two daughters.

Website:filipinofamilyhealth.com

ILDEME "DEMEE" MAHINAY KOCH
Beauty, Consciousness, and Leadership

Multipreneur ✎ Investor ✎ Forbes Influencer

Ildeme "Demee" Mahinay Koch a fearless woman, mother of two, multipreneur, and advocate of many causes, like many women – decided to change her destiny with her own strength and embarked on a journey to get to where she is right now.

As a sought-after speaker, guest author, and commentator on the subject of conscious beauty and entrepreneurship, she strongly advocates healthy beauty, inclusivity, empowerment, and social impact. Recognized and honored with awards as one of the most influential Filipinas in the world by Global FWN and as Ambassador of Peace by Universal Peace Federation UK, an NGO with general consultative status with the Economic and Social Council of the United Nations, Demee uses her influence to give back. In addition, she shares her expertise in business and conscious entrepreneurship as a Forbes Business Council influencer through her articles.

Demee is a Corporate Advisor of the revolutionary boxing brand SPARBAR. She is also a board member and shareholder of Luxvivendi GmbH, a company celebrating the finest in luxury products, services, food, and experiences. She supports various charity organizations like the Voice of the Free, a hybrid organization that combines social care, social entrepreneurship, and mobilizing social movements to achieve lasting social change. The Breaking Silence Movement (BSM), a private, non-profit organization that fights gender-based violence, recently welcomed Demee as a board member. She also established the DE MOI fund to benefit all the non-profit organizations DE MOI collaborates with, including BSM and Voice of the Free.

PATRICIA "DENISE" LOPEZ, PH.D.
Sugarcane Pricess. Steel Sampaguita

Inspiring ❧ Insightful ❧ Supportive

Dr. Patricia "Denise" Lopez is a Full Professor of Organizational Psychology at Alliant International University. She teaches and researches leadership, work motivation and productivity, team effectiveness, and organizational change management. She was born and raised in the Philippines and moved to the United States to complete her Ph.D. in Organizational Psychology from Columbia University, New York City.

Over the last 25 years, Denise has taught, trained, coached, and consulted with diverse managers, teams, and organizations in the United States and Asia-Pacific. She has authored several publications on leadership, employee engagement, and diversity and globalization issues. In addition to the bestseller book, *Lead, Motivate, Engage: How to INSPIRE your team to win at work*, Denise has written book chapters and journal articles on employee engagement; diversity, equity, and inclusion; retention and career development of women and minorities in science and technology; developing culturally competent employees; authentic leadership; power and influence; change management and innovation. She also serves as a board director of Leadership Education for Asia-Pacifics (LEAP). Based in Southern California, Denise enjoys music, art, dancing, traveling, hiking, watersports, and simply hanging out with family and friends.

MARIA VICTORIA LUALHATI, PH.D.
Leadership in Healthcare

Elan ❧ Empowered ❧ Purposeful

Dr. Maria Victoria Lualhati is the president and CEO of Beyond Medical Hub, a corporate trainer under Inspire Leadership Consultancy Inc., and one of the awardees of the Most Influential Filipina in the World from the Filipina Women's Network (FWN). In every affiliation, she ensures to leave her mark. She enters the door, strengthens institutional management, and exits with good-running administration. She is easily remembered as someone embraced by enthusiastic-colored blazers, painted lips, and persuading words. Behind her smiles are words that actuate people to navigate their limits and perform at their best. Dr. Lualhati is the epitome of a woman—an empowered and purposeful leader who transforms her vision to life.

Isabelita "Lita" T. Manalastas-Watanabe

Just me, Lita's Mom

Very Independent ❧ Generous ❧ Warrior

Isabelita "Lita" T. Manalastas-Watanabe was an economist, diplomat, and banker before she became a businesswoman. Her professional career outside the Philippines started when she became an Ambassador of Goodwill for Japan and the ASEAN Countries. Lita graduated from the University of the Philippines (UP) in Diliman with a B.S. degree in Business Economics, received her diploma in Japanese language from Osaka University of Foreign Studies and an M.A. in Economics from the University of Tsukuba, on full scholarship from the Japanese government. In addition, she completed an Executive Program for Leaders in Development at Harvard University's Institute for International Development. Having achieved financial comfort and success, Lita plans to devote more time to being a social entrepreneur launching in Sept. 2022 the Ecumenical and Innovative Women and Children Dialogue in Digital World. Lita has assisted overseas Filipino workers in Japan through her *Dear Tita Lits* advice column in *Jeepney Press*. Lita assisted Filipina caregivers and nurses in Japan, whose maximum tenure as trainees or professionals is almost up, to deploy to other countries and give them a chance at a better quality of life and career advancement. Lita set up an educational foundation to formalize her years of commitment to sending poor but deserving students to college. Lita plans to spend her retirement on a learning l farm that is also a place for a silent retreat. Lita has been chosen for UP's Outstanding Alumni Award, 2022, by the UP Sigma Alpha Sorority.

Annabelle Manalo-Morgan, Ph.D.

Macario's Oil

Courageous ❧ Happy ❧ Powerful

A native of Canada, Annabelle Manalo-Morgan, Ph.D. balances life as a scientist, educator, author, wife, and mother of five. Dr. Annabelle has completed an NIH clinical trial certification and began her graduate work at Georgetown University in Neuroscience. Dr. Annabelle has a doctorate in Cell and Development Biology from Vanderbilt University and focuses on genetic mutations that mimic the offset effects of chemotherapy on heart disease. She has presented and published on the resulting cardiotoxicity of these pathways and the developing cardiac mesothelium. In 2016, Dr. Annabelle saved her son's life using a cannabis formulation that she created and now pursues the possibility of implementing cannabis and/or plant compounds into modern medicine. She served as Tikun Olam USA's Chief Scientific Officer and started her own company, Masaya Medical Inc., in 2019. She now serves as the Chief Scientific Officer of Nasdaq company Flora Growth Corporation which has recently acquired Masaya. With her new team, Dr. Annabelle consults on legislation and leads multiple clinical trials around the globe while advocating as an international speaker for medical cannabis backed by scientific rigor. This year, she will release her book Mighty Flower with ForbesBooks.

BERNADETTE MONDEJAR-SCHLUETER, PH.D.
Finding My Why

Resourceful ❧ Persistent ❧ Flexible

Dr. Bernadette Mondejar-Schlueter is an educator and school administrator who has worked in the Philippines, Japan, Korea, Guam, Belgium, and the United Kingdom. She is currently the principal of Feltwell Elementary School on the Royal Air Force Feltwell base in Norfolk, England. She received the 2010 Scroll of Appreciation from US Forces Korea General Walter L. Sharp for her dedication to the education of US military children. In addition, she was the 2012 Teacher of the Year for the Korea District and was one of the Filipina Women's Network Most Influential Filipina Women of the World in 2016. Dr. Mondejar-Schlueter writes for Educator's High, a regular column published in the Philippines. She was selected as the Best Newspaper Columnist of the Year in 2021 at the Eastern Visayas Media Awards. She wrote two children's books, *Maya and Her Loyal Friends* and *Adventures of Maya: The Lost Fields of Palale*, translated into Tagalog, Waray, German, and Italian. Her coloring book, Pinoy Life, showcases Filipino customs and traditions. She loves running and traveling with her husband, Richard. She has completed 438 marathons and ultramarathons in 47 countries on six continents.

MARIA RHODORA P. I. PALOMAR-FRESNEDI
My Leadership Journey

Passion ❧ Purpose ❧ Possibility.

Rhodora is an internationally awarded advocate for diversity and inclusion, a global business leader, international speaker, and executive coach. Rhodora considers herself a hyphenated person. She has lived and worked in the U.S., Europe, and Asia. She has been a teacher, financial controller, HR professional, general manager, consultant, and author. She has held senior global executive roles, led global teams, built NGOs, and has been an adviser to Fortune 500 and FTSE 100 CEOs and businesses in global leadership, business strategy, corporate social responsibility, large-scale organization transformation, and innovative interventions. Rhodora is the Founding President and CEO of the Center for Growing and Giving Foundation, Inc. This non-profit organization created Sunshine Farm Philippines, a sunflower destination farm built to employ persons with disability. Her professional and personal achievements are noteworthy, but her passion remains deeply rooted in changing the world from wherever she is. She would like to help build a world where every person, no matter what gender, race, creed, religion, sexual orientation, ability, disability, or any other uniqueness, will be able to say: *"I am valued. I belong. I make a difference."*

ATTY. LORNA PATAJO-KAPUNAN
A Block Off the Old Chip

Courage ❧ Competence ❧ Integrity

Atty. Lorna Patajo-Kapunan graduated from the University of the Philippines AB Political Science (1973) and LLB (Law) 1978 and had seminar courses in Japan Institute of Invention and Innovation (JIII) Tokyo (1997); World Intellectual Property Office (WIPO) Asian Region, Taejon Republic of Korea, (November 1998); National Institute of Humanitarian Law, San Remo Italy (September 2005); Summer Course International Humanitarian Law, Magdalene College, Cambridge University, London UK (July 2010). Atty. Lorna Patajo Kapunan, founding Partner of Kapunan & Castillo Law Offices, has been a practicing lawyer for 40 years. She has been recognized among the Top 100 Lawyers of the Country for three consecutive years (2019–2021) and was recently awarded the global "Women In Law Awards" for Corporate Law-Philippines. Although known as a leading litigator because of her high-profile cases, her legal expertise is extensive. It includes intellectual property, corporate and commercial, international humanitarian, family, estate, and succession laws. Atty. Kapunan is an awardee of the prestigious TOWNS Awards in Corporate Law (1995) and was Bar Examiner in 1988 in this field of law. She was a recipient in 1998 of The Outstanding Women of the UP Awards and an awardee in 2016 of the FWN, composed of acclaimed Filipina women leaders worldwide. Atty. Kapunan has a weekly column in Business Mirror, "Legally Speaking" and a regular Saturday tele-radio program, *"Laban Para Sa Karapatan"* (Fight for your Rights), from 11–12 at DWIZ 882 AM radio. She is a Governor of the Philippine Red Cross (PRC), Vice Chairman and Trustee of Cultural Center of the Philippines.

MILDRED CHRISTINE "MITZI" FLORES PIAD, PH.D.
The Fruit-Bearing Tree

Devoted ❧ Compassionate ❧ Empowered

Mildred Christine "Mitzi" Flores Piad, Ph.D. completed AB Economics at Maryknoll College and her Doctorate in Organization Development at the South East Asia Interdisciplinary Institute. She was conferred her second Ph.D. in Public Administration major in Good Governance and Social Responsibility Honoris Causa. She was awarded "1992 Top Real Estate Developer of the Year" by Pag-Ibig's Home Development Mutual Fund for providing Socialized Mass Housing for the Urban Poor. She authored and published a book on *Vanguards of Youth Against Illegal Drug Abuse* and a CTB on *The Legacy of Zonta International*. Mitzi was President of GSP, Quezon Council for three trienniums, where she constructed "Ating Tahanan Sa Quezon" for 2000 Girl Scouts of Quezon Province. She established 13 Homeowners Association benefiting 1,343 families under the Community Mortgage Program of Social Housing Finance Corp. Mitzi was Centennial Provincial Board Member, 2nd District of Quezon Province, and became its Ex Officio Co-Chair on Poverty Alleviation. She received the Triple A Amazing Alumni Achiever in Maryknoll College in its 2022 Golden Jubilee Celebration. She is currently the elected Federation Director of Soroptimist International of the Americas Philippines Region and Board Director Soroptimist International of the Americas Northern Philippines Region. Trustee and Past President of Women's Business Council (WBC), Board of Adviser of World Wildlife Fund (WWF), among others.

Fe Odsigue Punzalan
Business Not as Usual

Diligent ❧ Insightful ❧ Tenacious

Fe Odsigue Punzalan was born in Antique, Panay Island. From an early age, she was motivated to excel in her education to improve her family's economic situation. She graduated from UP Philippine General Hospital School of Nursing and migrated to the United States in 1977, becoming a Registered Nurse in Chicago. After that, Fe moved to the Bay Area, where she worked at various healthcare institutions, including Kaiser Permanente and the Regional Medical Center of San Jose. In 1997, she opened Silver Punzalan, Inc., a group of residential care facilities serving people with special needs and intellectual disabilities. Fe's leadership and community service have been recognized over the years, most recently in 2020 as Outstanding Alumna for Community Services by the Philippine General Hospital School of Nursing Alumni Association. In 2019, Fe was named one of Filipina Women's Network's 100 Most Influential Filipina Women in the World. Fe finds joy in dancing and spending time with her daughters and grandchildren when not working.

Georgitta "Beng" Pimentel Puyat
We Grow as We Sow

Inspirational ❧ Altruistic ❧ Passionate

Georgitta "Beng" Puyat is the Co-founder and Chair of the Philippine Orchard Corporation. Its mission is to help marginalized farmers improve their economic status by introducing innovative products that promote quality and sustainability. She joined the Filipina Women's Network Board in 2018, became FWN Global President (2019–2022), and is currently the FWN Global Chairman. She graduated from the University of the Philippines Diliman with a degree in AB Political Science and a Masters in Sociology. A lifelong Volunteer, she is an inspirational, result-oriented leader whose experiences shaped and committed her to be a "Volunteer" for Women's Issues through Service and Advocacy. As a member of the Zonta Club of Makati and Environs for 36 years, she has initiated and nurtured projects that have affected and empowered generations of women and young girls. She managed the East Rembo Livelihood and Skills Training Center and co-founded the ZCME Psychological Center for Sexually Abused Children (ages 3–17). She was elected Zonta International District 17 Governor (2010–2012). She was President/Chairman of the UNIFEM (now UN Women) Philippine National Committee for four biennia, a Trustee of the Philippine Philharmonic Orchestra Society, and the Chairman/ President of the Sigma Delta Phi Alumnae Association.

Cynthia Manalo Rapaido, EdD
From Military Brat to Educational Leader: a Filipina-American Journey
Mentor ❧ Leader ❧ Teacher

Cynthia Rapaido received her Ed.D. with an emphasis in International and Multicultural Education and her M.A. in Educational Administration with an emphasis in Organization and Leadership from USF. She earned her B.S. in Biology from SDSU. Her dissertation was titled "Filipino American Educational Leaders in Northern California K–12 Public Schools: Challenges and Opportunities." Her 31 years of educational leadership and teaching experience include: 5 years as a principal, 17 years as an assistant principal, and 9 years science teacher, all at the high school level. In addition, her experience in higher education includes being an adjunct faculty member as a lecturer, doctoral advisor, and field supervisor for teacher candidates. In 2011, FWN honored her as one of the 100 Most Influential Filipinas in the United States in the category "Builders and Emerging Leaders." In 2013, the Association of California School Administrators (ACSA) honored her for exemplary performance in promoting the success of all students and was given the State award, "Secondary Co-Administrator of the Year." In 2014, the National Association of Secondary School Principals (NASSP) honored her for outstanding, active, and front-line leadership. She received the national award "Assistant Principal of the Year State Finalist" for the State of California.

Marla D. Rausch
The Secret of a Wallflower
Creative ❧ Pioneering ❧ Driven

Marla D. Rausch has been a trailblazer as the founder of Animation Vertigo for almost two decades. She has set the standard in motion capture external development with a roster of titles in leading video games franchises. This roster includes *Activision's Call of Duty*, *NetherRealm's Mortal Kombat*, critically acclaimed *Hitman by IO Interactive*, and Triple A sports titles like *NBA2k*, *FIFA*, and *Madden*, to mention a few. Not a small feat for a woman in a highly competitive, fast-paced, male-driven game and 3D animation industry.

Beyond outsourcing, Marla has ventured into developing her own IP—an animated feature that her company, Kampilan Productions, is currently producing. In addition, Marla dreams of bringing Philippine stories to the world by sharing a Filipino hero's tale.

As passionate about growing businesses and helping organizations thrive, Marla is also a mentor, sharing her lessons and experiences through talks and panels. Her goal is to inspire, encourage and motivate women to enter or start a business.

Today, she continues to expand her role as a leader by starting new ventures focusing on capability growth and more opportunities in her home country—the Philippines.

MARIETTA EVELYN P. REVILLA
Reflection on My Leadership

Compassionate ❧ loyal ❧ religious

Marietta was born in Cebu City and her family migrated to Manila when she was only 6 years old. She's known as Evy, Beng or Evelyn. A dedicated mom of two Italian-Filipino daughters Stephanie and Sheela, a family oriented person and grandma to Andrea Clara, Asia, Cecilia Giovanna and Orlando Leone. As Corporate Relations Consultant, she travels frequently all year round to support and keep track of the family's team – Italtrans Racing team Moto2 Grand Prix for Motorbikes. She used to work in the family owned business company "Ortobell" in the cultivation and distribution sector of ready to eat pack salad. She owned by concession and managed Prenatal Shop Curno and Italpoint Viaggi in Milan. Evelyn is a golden hearted person with a clear vision that motivates, inspires and leads people to achieve their goals. She's one of the founders and President of Sodalis Association in Milan, which envisions and elevates the Filipino migrant workers and quality of life. She's in close cooperation with the Philippine Consulate, supports different Associations in Milan and widely acclaimed Grand Sinulog Festival In Europe. She received a Special award as "Woman of the Year 2016" by Federfil Europe. Being a woman leader, she exemplifies the common traits or nature of a woman in leading the organization like team approach, clear vision, believing oneself or self confidence and willingness to help. She participated on one of the most important conventions in Europe: Women's Federation for World Peace, Annual European Women Leadership Conference in Lisbon. In 2018 she was awarded as 100 Most Influential Award for her successful leadership and dedication to the community.

LUCIA "LUCY" OLALIA REYES
Living the American Dream

Creative ❧ Honest ❧ Achiever

Lucy has contributed more than four decades of progressive and diverse experience in the care of people with complex medical needs, outpatient settings as a frontline clinical manager, health informatics specialist, and project management leader to several organizational initiatives such as the planning and implementation of the Electronic Health Record at four acute care hospitals in Calgary in 2006, the development and launching of the first Health Informatics credit course at the University of Calgary in anticipation of the Electronic Health Record readiness for frontline leaders within the Calgary area after Y2K, and the amalgamation and transformation of the four Hospital based Ethics Committee into one Regional Ethics team. In addition, extending her Ethics expertise, she was a volunteer instructor in her faith community focused on Ethics and Caring in Pastoral Care for four years. More recently, she was instrumental as project Clinical Engagement lead and project manager in connecting patients living with Cardiac Electrical Implantable Devices (CIED) remotely from their homes to their clinics throughout Alberta. Thus reducing their travels to the clinics, especially during the winter, yet having the option of being assessed by their clinicians remotely and reducing emergency admissions. This project received the 2020 Health Quality Council of Alberta Patient Experience Award and the 2022 Canadian Council of Cardiovascular Nurses Health Promotion and Advocacy Award. In addition, Lucy was one of the 2021 Awardees for the Filipino Women's Network Global Award in the Innovation and Thought Leader Category held in San Francisco.

JOANNE RICO
Gusto

Purpose ❧ Grit ❧ Resilience.

Joanne Rico is an empowered Filipina who has risen above adversity. From humble beginnings in Manila, she has gone a long way from her first job to now being a genuinely inspiring global woman. A consistent A-student, Joanne believes a solid academic foundation will serve as a springboard to success. Armed with resilience, grit, and ambition, she did not let poverty define her future, so she studied hard to earn scholarships. Joanne graduated Valedictorian in high school and Magna Cum Laude with a Bachelor of Arts, Major in Philosophy at the College of Social Sciences and Philosophy at the University of the Philippines, Diliman. Joanne has 17 solid years of work experience in Marketing and Brand Management. She has managed brands in local and international markets, including Qatar, UAE, Oman, and the Philippines. She is currently the Head of Marketing in a government healthcare facility in Abu Dhabi, the first Filipina to take a senior leadership role in the public sector in the UAE. Joanne has received numerous recognitions for her accomplishments: Marketing and Advertising Professional of the Year by The Filipino Times in 2017; a nominee for Huwarang OFW by GMA 7's 700 Club Asia in 2018; one of the Thought-Leaders in Illustrado's 300 Most Influential Filipinos in the Gulf in 2020; and one of the Most Influential Filipina Women in the World by the Foundation for Filipina Women's Network in 2021. Joanne is a genuine advocate of paying it forward. She has been a sponsor of World Vision Philippines for over 15 years. She has been supporting needy children together with their families and their communities in depressed areas of the Philippines.

MARIA ZELDA "MARIZEL" AQUINO MAGISTRADO ROJAS
#Serial Organizer

Passionate ❧ Infectious ❧ Resilient

Currently working at the Preparatory Commission for the Comprehensive Nuclear-Test-Ban Treaty Organization (CTBTO) at the United Nations Headquarters in Vienna, Austria, since 1998. Marizel finds great fulfillment in working for an organization that bans nuclear explosions by everyone, everywhere: on the Earth's surface, in the atmosphere, underwater and underground. Marizel received a Bachelor of Science in Physics for Teachers (BSPT) degree from the Philippine Normal University – De la Salle University consortium through a National Science Development Board (NSDB)-National Science and Technology Authority (NSTA) scholarship. She taught at the Camarines Sur National School for four years. In 1991, she migrated to Austria. Since 2012, Marizel has been actively involved as a leader of various organizations in Filipino and international communities. She received the 2019 Most Influential Filipina Women in the World™ (Global FWN100™) "Behind the Scenes" award. The values inculcated by her parents, coupled with the education she received from Colegio de Sta. Isabel, during her formative years in high school and elementary, as well as her experiences in the Filipino diaspora, laid the foundation for her being the kind of leader she chose to be.

Kahlil Gibran says: *"You give but little when you give of your possessions. It is when you give of yourself that you truly give."*

LAARNI SAN JUAN
Opening Windows

Curious ❧ Determined ❧ Changemaker

Laarni San Juan is a nurse, bestselling author, community champion, and thought leader. She received her Bachelor of Science in Nursing at San Francisco State University and a Masters in Public Health at UCLA. She openly shares the many awkward experiences in her childhood that have taught her the true value of resilience and the will to win. Laarni embraces the five pillars of family, education, community, career, and health that continuously guide her to revisit at each life milestone as a woman, wife, mother, daughter, and friend. With over 29 years of experience as a healthcare professional, Laarni deeply understands the unique journey that each human possesses and encourages all she meets to share their story. Her own journey filled with loss, grief, and disappointment has challenged her to rise and discover her true potential. She believes anything in life is possible with the right mindset, support system, and staying true to oneself.

MARIA SANTOS-GREAVES
Find Ability in Disability

Resilient ❧ Strong-Willed ❧ Visionary

Maria Santos-Greaves is a hearing health professional who has been in the industry for over 30 years. She began her career at the pioneer hearing clinic in the Philippines after graduating from Centro Escolar University. After that, she received additional education and training in Canada from reputable institutions such as the MacEwan University and the British Columbia Institute of Technology. Having hearing loss herself, she has made it her life's work to help the hard-of-hearing, especially the elderly, in various communities. A firm believer in the importance of good hearing in relationships, her clinic, Surrey Hearing Care, Inc., provides affordable hearing services through its five locations in the Lower Mainland. Throughout her career, Maria has received various recognitions such as the Rotary Foundation Paul Harris Fellow, Top 25 Immigrants Across Canada, and recently, the Surrey Women in Business Awards—the first Filipina to earn the title.

ANNA ISABEL C. SOBREPEÑA
Independent Consultant

Tenacious ❧ Multi-faceted ❧ Enigmatic

The first published work of Anna Isabel C. Sobrepeña was an obituary. The award-winning writer and editor was a high school student who channeled the pain of loss into a unique tribute to a beloved grandparent. A magazine editor and family friend read the announcement and invited her to become a contributing writer in a nationally circulated Sunday journal. The satisfaction of creative writing took a backseat to the greater joys of marriage and motherhood. Happenstance took the journey from contributing writer to the editor in chief (EIC) of the largest circulating glossy when most people were already considering retirement. Unperturbed at being dismissed as a housewife wannabe, she went on to win awards in her first year as EIC. She translated the magazine's tagline of "living at its finest" to mean more than visible wealth, defining luxury as a generosity of spirit that separated the rich from the truly rich. Magazine content subscribed to highest order values with stories and features that provided a trajectory towards meaningful lives. She disengaged from the magazine after 11 years, capping that chapter with an award as Editor of the Year given by the Asia Leaders Award. She is currently doing consultancies, contributing to media platforms, working on commissioned book projects, and being involved in civic and social work.

KRISTINE CUSTODIO SUERO, ACP
From Fears to Fierce

Coach ❧ Educator ❧ Change Agent

Kristine Custodio Suero is an award-winning legal professional and a highly sought-after speaker in her profession, inspiring legal professionals to achieve authentic, purpose-driven careers and lives. A true servant leader, she has led the San Diego Paralegal Association (SDPA) and California Alliance of Paralegal Associations (CAPA) as President. Kristine is a member of the University of San Diego School of Law Paralegal Program's Advisory Board and is also Adjunct Faculty. She serves as the Chair of the National Association of Legal Assistants' Paralegals Diversity, Equity & Inclusion Committee. In 2020, Kristine was selected as the California Paralegal of the Year. In October 2021, Kristine was appointed to the Center for Judicial Education and Research Advisory Committee by California Supreme Court Chief Justice Tani Cantil-Sakauye. She is a Commissioner and served as the past Chair of the City of San Diego Citizens' Equal Opportunity Commission, advocating for supplier diversity. She is currently a Senior Paralegal/Business Development Director for Butterfield Schechter LLP, specializing in ERISA/ESOPs/employee benefits law, business law, and civil litigation. Kristine may be reached at kristine.custodio@gmail.com. https://linktr.ee/kristinecustodio

FILIPINA·WOMEN'S·NETWORK

SIGNIFICANT MILESTONES

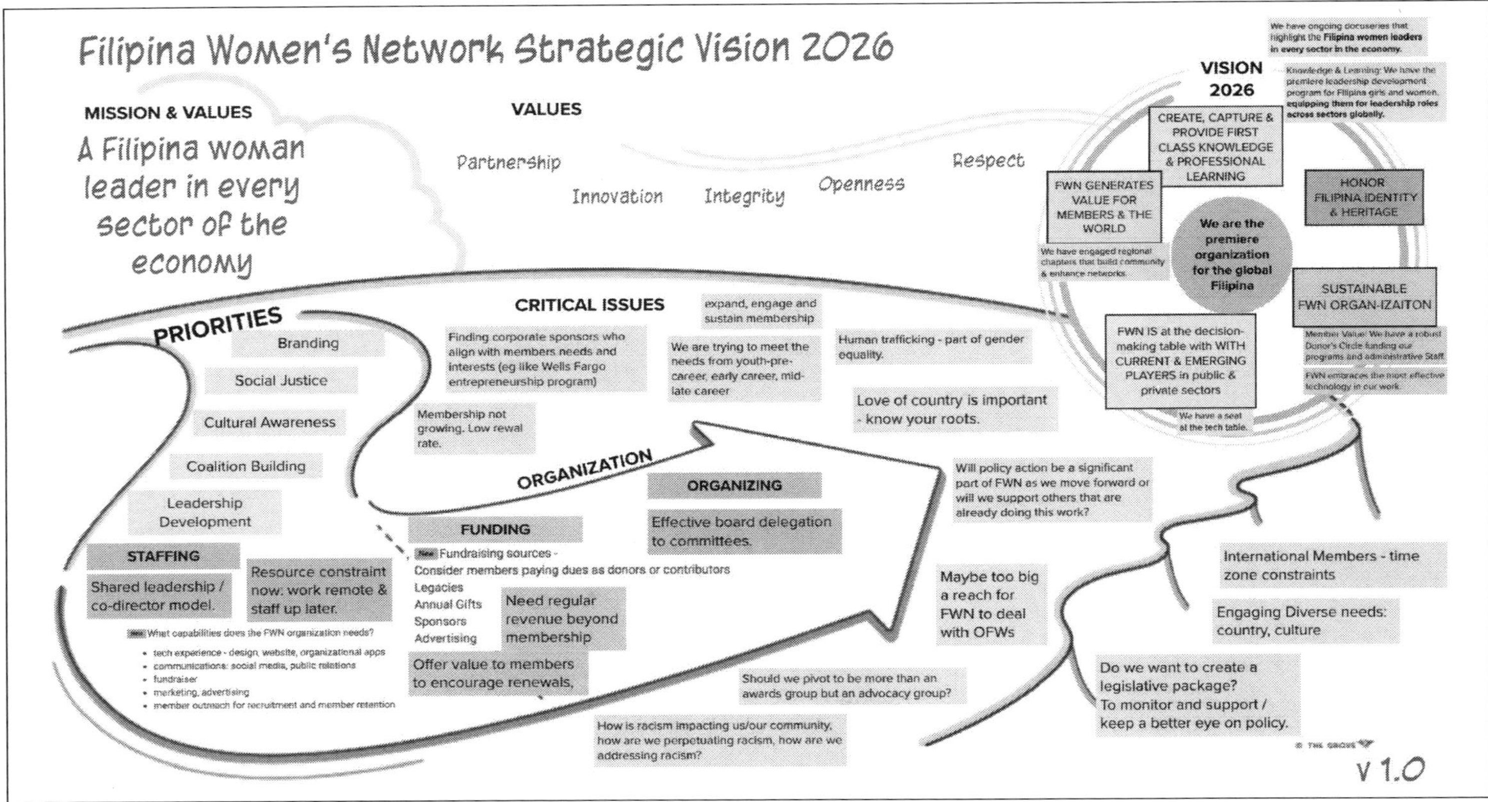

FWN Board Retreat: Strategic Planning for Vision 2026.

Here we are – going for FWN's North Star.

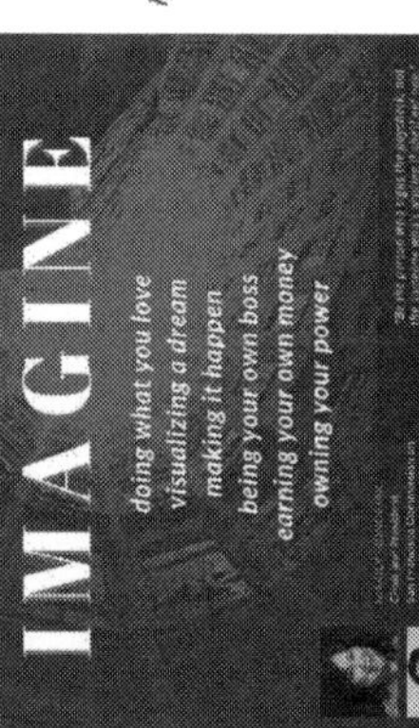

Clockwise from top left:

Global FWN100™ Awardees at the Filipina Summit 2017 in Toronto, Canada.

FemtorMatch Femtees with their Femtors at Filipina Summit 2014 Manila, Philippines.

Pinay Entrepreneurship Speaker Panel sponsored by Wells Fargo and MegaWorld.

The prestigious and coveted Most Influential Filipina Women in the World Awards.

The Comfort Women Memorial in San Francisco capturing the tender ages of young women conscripted by the Japanese Imperial Army during WWII.

Chief Justice Tani Gorre Cantil-Sakauye is the 28th chief justice of the State of California. She was sworn into office on January 3, 2011, and is the first Asian-Filipina American and the second woman to serve as the state's chief justice. Appointed and sworn in by Governor Arnold Schwarzenegger. Her term ends January 1, 2023.

Far left: Celebrating Filipino Americans elected to public office in the San Francisco Bay Area in 2018.

Left: Faces of Global Pinay Power leading International Women's Day, March 8, 2022.

Rowena Romulo selected Face of Global Pinay Power 2017 in Canada.

Francine Maigue selected Face of Global Pinay Power 2015 in San Francisco.

Joyce R. Javier MD, MPH, MS
Physician Scientist
Filipino Family Health Initiative

Kathy Lai CPA
Partner
Crowe LLP

Alicia del Prado PhD
Psychologist and Author
del Prado Counseling & Consulting

Giovannie Espiritu
Actor, Filmmaker, Owner
Hollywood Actor's Workshop

Natalie Garcia Lashinsky
Attorney
Husch Blackwell LLP

Ninez Ponce MPP, PhD
Director
UCLA Center for Health Policy Research

Jessica Caloza
Commissioner
Board of Public Works
City of Los Angeles

Joanne Rico
Senior Manager
Bareen International Hospital
Abu Dhabi

Top: Filipina Summit 2015 candidates for Face of Global Pinay Power pose to memorialize their participation. **Above:** At the Filipina Summit 2017, Pinay Sheroes join forces in Toronto to fight the good fight.

Clockwise from left:

Faces of Global Pinay Power leading International Women's Day on March 8, 2022.

FWN Sheroes and Legends Tribute to Vangie Buell, Award-winning author, FWN's Vagina Warrior 2004 and 100 Most Influential Filipina Women in the U.S. 2007 Awardee, on February 23, 2019.

FWN Giving Circle "Fab 4" – Lorna Kapunan, Mica Tan, Marily Mondejar and Marylou Garcia.

From left:

2013 Global FWN100™ San Francisco

2015 Global FWN100™ San Francisco

2017 Global FWN100™ Toronto

2016 Global FWN100™ Cebuu

Clockwise from left: 2019 Global FWN100™ Paris, 2021nPinay Rising Leadership Salon, The very last issue of the V-Diaries 2022

Above from left:

DISRUPT 2.0 leadership book authors in Washington, D.C.

DISRUPT 3.0 book launch at the House of Lords in the U.K.

Book covers of the 4 *DISRUPT* leadership book series.

2017 – Cynthia Barker

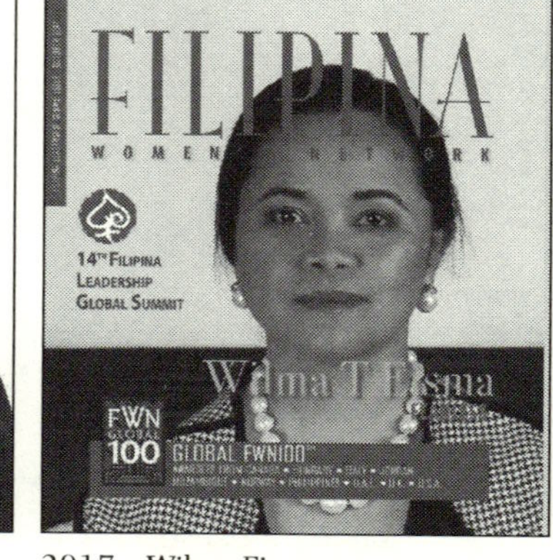

2017 – Wilma Eisma

2018 – Juslyn C. Manalo

2018 – Leonor Vintervoll

2019 – Susie Quesada

2019 – Thelma Boac

2021 –Fe Punzalan

2021 – FWN Awardees

Made in the USA
Middletown, DE
08 January 2023

20480962R10385